DATE DUE

Contemporary Marriage

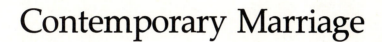

Contemporary Marriage

F. PHILIP RICE

University of Maine

Allyn and Bacon, Inc.

Boston · London · Sydney · Toronto

Copyright © 1983 by Allyn and Bacon, Inc., 7 Wells Avenue, Newton, Massachusetts, 02159. All rights reserved. No part of the material protected by this copyright notice may be reproduced or utilized in any form or by any means, electronic or mechanical, including photocopying, recording, or by any information storage and retrieval system, without written permission from the copyright owner.

A previous edition was published under the title *Marriage and Parenthood*, Copyright © 1979 by Allyn and Bacon, Inc.

Library of Congress Cataloging in Publication Data

Rice, F. Philip.
    Contemporary marriage.

    Rev. ed. of: Marriage and parenthood. c1979.
    Bibliography: p.
    Includes indexes.
    1. Family life education. 2. Marriage. I. Title.
HQ10.R48   1983   306.8′1   82-16413
ISBN 0-205-07890-7

Printed in the United States of America

10 9 8 7 6 5 4 3 2 1   87 86 85 84 83

To Irma Ann Rice

Contents

Preface   xi

PART I   CONTEMPORARY MARRIAGE   1

1   Marriage Today   2

Marriage Success   3
Marriage Rates   5
Marriage, Careers, and
    Children   6
The Need for Intimacy   6
New Marriage versus Traditional
    Marriage   7
Conclusions   12

PART II   PREMARITAL INTERACTION AND MATE SELECTION   13

2   Dating and Premarital Sexual Behavior   14

Dating as a Sociological
    Phenomenon   15
The Reasons for Dating   18
Dating Partners versus Marriage
    Partners   20
Adolescents' Sexual Attitudes
    and Behavior   21

College Students' Sexual
    Attitudes and Behavior   23
Sexual Standards   23
Influences and Correlations   25
Use of Contraceptives   27
Conclusions   29

3   Nonmarital Cohabitation   32

Definitions   33
Incidences of Cohabitation   34
Persons Who Cohabit   36
Description of Experiences   39
The Nature of the
    Relationships   42
Other Problems   44
Effects and Implications   45
Conclusions   48
Dialogue   49

4   Maturity and Marital Readiness   52

Age and Time Factors   53
Social Experience   56
A Mature Concept of Love   57
Motivation and Maturity   65
Vocational and Educational
    Readiness   67
Parental Readiness   68
Marriage While in College   68

Conclusions   73
Dialogue   74

5   Marital Compatibility   78

Compatibility through
   Homogamy and
   Endogamy   79
Compatible Needs   80
Compatible Personalities   81
Compatible Backgrounds   82
Compatible Attitudes and
   Values   89
Compatible Role Concepts   90
Compatible Interests, Activities,
   and Friends   90
Compatible Habit Systems   91
Conclusions   92
Dialogue   93

**PART III   MALE AND FEMALE
         ROLES   97**

**6   Changing Concepts of
     Masculinity and Femininity   98**

Genetic Bases of Gender   99
Hormones and Sex Identity   100
Theories of Sex Role
   Development   102
Masculine-Feminine
   Concepts   106
Homosexuality   109
Conclusions   113
Dialogue   115

7   Women's Rights and Roles   118

The Women's Movement   119
Chauvinism and Sexism   121
Legal Equality   122
Sex Role Differentiation and
   Discrimination   123
Women's Sexuality   124
Employment and Income   124
Education   126

Marriage Roles and
   Housework   128
Child Rearing   129
Reproduction   131
Conclusions   132

8   Men's Conflicting Roles   134

The Husband's Changing
   Role   135
The Effect of the Male's Role on
   Himself   136
Occupational Roles and
   Marriage   139
Housekeeping and Parental
   Roles   143
Companionship Role   144
Roles of the Low Socioeconomic
   Status Husband   145
Conclusions   147
Dialogue   148

9   Dual-Career Marriage   150

The Husbands and Wives   151
Benefits of a Dual-Career
   Marriage   155
Job Establishment   156
Childcare   158
Effects on Children   159
Strains   161
Conclusions   162
Dialogue   164

**PART IV   MARITAL
         RELATIONSHIPS   167**

**10   The Intimate Life: Its
      Satisfactions and
      Adjustments   168**

Marital Satisfaction over the
   Family Life Cycle   169
Correlations with Marital
   Satisfaction   172

Marital Adjustment   172
Early Adjustments   173
Adjustments during
    Parenthood   176
Adjustments during the
    Postparental Years   178
Adjustments after
    Retirement   180
Adjustments by Widows and
    Widowers   183
Conclusions   187
Dialogue   188

**11 Power, Decision Making, and
    Communication   192**

Marital Power Patterns   193
Power in Decision Making   194
Sources of Power   196
Communication in
    Marriage   200
Barriers to Communication   203
Improving Communication
    Skills   204
Conclusions   206

12 Marital Conflict   208

Some Sources of Conflict   209
The Focuses of Conflict   212
Cause and Effect   212
Some Positive and Negative
    Values of Conflict   213
Methods of Dealing with
    Conflict   217
Family Violence   222
Conclusions   225

**13 Money and Its
    Management   226**

Money and Marriage   227
Why People Go into Debt   231
Money Management   233
Housing   235
Consumer Economics   238

Conclusions: Getting the Most
    for Your Money   239
Dialogue   241

**14 Couple, In-Law, and Kinsfolk
    Relationships   244**

In-law Adjustment and Marital
    Happiness   245
The Kind of In-laws People
    Like   245
In-laws People Dislike   246
The Roots of Conflict   247
When Parents and Married
    Children Live Together   250
The Extended Family
    Network   250
Conclusions   254
Dialogue   255

**15 Sexual Adjustments and
    Difficulties   258**

The Functions of Sexual
    Intercourse   259
Sex and Happy Marriage   260
Sexual Anatomy and
    Physiology   261
Male-Female Differences and
    Similarities   265
Sexual Adjustments   267
Sexual Dysfunction   270
Causes of Sexual
    Dysfunction   274
Conclusions: Getting Help   278
Dialogue   279

16 Divorce and Remarriage   282

Facts and Figures on
    Divorce   283
Divorce and the Law   286
The High Cost of Divorce   289
Children and Divorce   290
Adult Adjustments after
    Divorce   293

Remarriage 296
Conclusions 299
Dialogue 300

PART V   PARENTHOOD 303

17 Family Planning, Pregnancy, Prenatal Care, and Childbirth 304

The Importance of Family
  Planning 305
Hormonal Control: The Pill 306
Chemicals and Spermicides 309
Mechanical Devices 309
Sterilization 311
Attempts at Birth Control
  Without Devices 313
Which Method? 315
Successful Family Planning 317
Birth Defects 317
Pregnancy 320
Prenatal Care 321
Preparation for Parenthood 323
The Hospital, Labor,
  Delivery 326
After Childbirth 327
Conclusions 329

18 Infertility, Adoption, Unwed Pregnancy, and Abortion 330

Infertility 331
Adoption 333
Unwed Pregnancy 337
Abortion 340
Conclusions 344
Dialogue 346

19 Parenthood 348

Philosophies of Child
  Rearing 349

Parental Roles 350
Meeting Emotional Needs 352
Fostering Cognitive and
  Intellectual Growth 356
Socialization and Discipline 357
One-Parent Families 359
Conclusions: No-Parent Families
  or Both-Parent Families? 364

PART VI   NONTRADITIONAL MARRIAGES 367

20 Variant Marital Forms 368

Marriage as a Personal
  Contract 369
Marriage as a Renewable
  Contract 373
Marriage as a Contract by
  Stages 373
Extramarital and Comarital
  Sex 375
Swinging 377
Intimate Friendships 379
Group Marriage 381
Communes 384
Voluntary Childlessness 390
Attitudes of College
  Students 394
Conclusions 394
Dialogue 395

Epilogue: The Future 397

Bibliography 401

Glossary 445

Author Index 451

Subject Index 459

Preface

This book is offered as a comprehensive text-book for students in marriage courses at the college level. The book is written with six major needs of students in mind.

First, students need to understand social change. Contemporary marital forms and functions are undergoing rapid and significant change. Sometimes students have been so used to these changes that they don't stop and realize how profoundly social conditions have influenced the way they think, feel, and act. One of the major purposes of this book is to describe and analyze marital changes from a sociological perspective and to show their significance in our lives.

Second, students need knowledge and information, which are basic to all human understanding and to intelligent living. This book seeks to share the vast amount of factual data that has been made available through empirical research. More than twelve hundred and sixty different references—most of them research studies from the 1970s and the 1980s—have been used in presenting the material.

Third, students need to be flexible and tolerant—they must be able to appreciate various points of view. Certainly, successful marriage requires flexibility and the ability to be adaptable. Students who admire their own

parents tend to feel that the way they were reared is the "right way" and that their parents' marriages are "ideal." Even those who disapprove of the example set by their own parents find themselves adopting parental habits and relationships that they hoped to avoid. One task of this book is to present the pros and cons of important issues and to discuss even controversial subjects from a variety of perspectives.

Fourth, students need to clarify their own goals, attitudes, and values. It is not enough to discover what others think and feel and do. One must analyze one's own thoughts, feelings, and philosophies. This book attempts to stimulate personal growth, the development of individual identity, and the realization of self-actualization and personal fulfillment.

Fifth, students need to be able to solve their own personal problems and make decisions with which they can live. This book assumes that the majority of students have a personal, as well as an academic, interest in marriage and parenthood and that they are concerned with present and future involvements, relationships, and decisions.

Sixth, students need professional preparation. Many students are preparing to work with families or are already engaged in such work as teachers, social workers, psychologists, counselors, personnel managers, religious workers, or other professionals. Much of the subject matter of this book should be of professional, as well as personal, interest to such persons.

I would like to acknowledge the special help of the following professors who have offered valuable guidance and suggestions during the tedious process of writing this book:

Kathleen G. Auerbach, University of Nebraska at Omaha; Jeanne M. Gilley, Louisiana Tech University; Sylvia Clavan, St. Joseph's University; Nila S. Magdanz, University of Nebraska at Omaha; Brent C. Miller, Utah State University; Kay Pasley, Washington State University; Carolyn Rutledge, Louisiana State University; Rita Phylliss Sakitt, Suffolk County Community College; W. Frederick Stultz, California Polytechnic State University—San Luis Obispo; Charles Varni, Allan Hancock College; Elizabeth Winstead, Jacksonville University; Maxine Baca Zinn, University of Michigan—Flint.

Special thanks go also to the editorial staff of Allyn and Bacon—Rowena Dores, Alan Levitt, and Wendy Ritger—and to the designer, Nancy McJennett, for diligent assistance in the preparation of this text for publication.

Contemporary Marriage

CHAPTER
1

Marriage Today

CHAPTER OUTLINE

Marriage Success

Marriage Rates

Marriage, Careers, and Children

The Need for Intimacy

New Marriage Versus
Traditional Marriage

Conclusions

Modern marriage as it exists in the Western world is an experiment. It is an experiment to link institutional needs and personal, romantic needs into one relationship. The basic question is: Can it work? Can married mates be working partners and romantic lovers at the same time? Can they provide physical needs and services and satisfy emotional needs for love and companionship? Can authority be shared equally without destructive conflict? Can tasks be performed without a fixed division of labor? Can a marriage relationship be permanent if it is easy to escape? Can marriage succeed if its criteria for success is personal fulfillment and happiness (Roleder, 1979)?

Answers to these questions are still being formed. On the negative side, skeptics point to rising divorce rates, an increase in the number of unmarried persons, widespread family violence, extramarital sex, and neglected children. All of these conditions are emphasized to show that modern marriage is dysfunctional.

On the positive side, others point to continuing high rates of marriage and remarriage and to the fact that a majority of persons stay married for a lifetime. The majority of children grow up to be normal and happy. Only a minority are abused or delinquent. These arguments are offered as clear indications that contemporary marriage is functional and viable.

Part of the lack of unanimity of opinion about modern marriage is due to the fact that it is undergoing drastic change. Marital forms, structures, and functions today are very different from those of yesterday. The important task of this chapter is to discuss the changes that are taking place and to show how marriage is evolving to keep pace with current needs and expectations.

Marriage Success

Skepticism

I recently asked a woman in college: "What do you think of when you think of marriage?" Her reply was: "Divorce." This remark reflects widespread skepticism over whether modern marriage can really succeed today. Increasingly, one hears: "How many married people do you know who are really happy?" People are aware that increasing numbers of marriages are failing. Seeing how unhappy parents or friends have been, and how often marriages break up, people have become skeptical, concerned, and convinced they don't want to duplicate these tragedies in their own lives. Their reaction sometimes is: "I wouldn't think of getting married without living with a person first." At other times, the reaction is one of "I'm not sure I want to marry," or "I want to wait."

Divorce Rate

One indication of failure is the divorce rate, which continued its historic rise until it reached a peak of 5.2 per 1,000 population in 1979 (Glick, 1979). As can be seen in figure 1-1, however, the divorce rate has begun to level off.

Number of divorces

Divorce rate

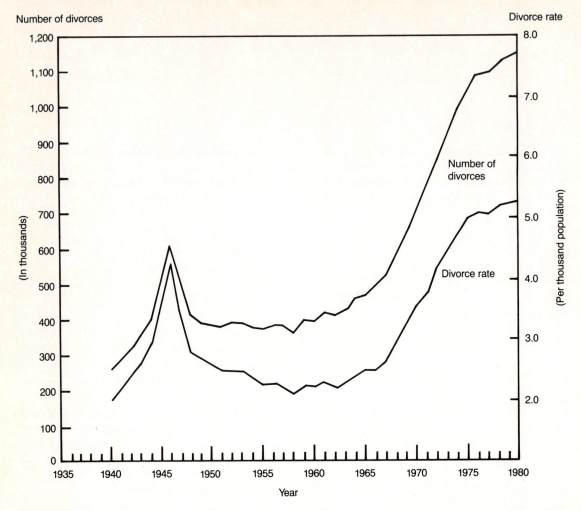

FIGURE 1-1. *Number of divorces and divorce rate: United States, 1940 to 1980   (Source: U.S. Department of Commerce, Bureau of the Census. "Divorce, Child Custody, and Child Support." Current Population Reports, Series P–23, no. 84, June 1979, p 2; and U.S. Department of Health and Human Services, "Births, Marriages, Divorces, and Deaths for May 1980," Monthly Vital Statistics Report, DHHS Publication no. [PHS] 80–1120, Vol. 29, no. 5, August 7, 1980, p. 1.)*

Whether the rate will continue to stabilize remains to be seen. If the current level of divorce continues, the proportion of marriages ending in divorce will be close to 40 percent (U.S. Department of Commerce, June 1979).

One of the reasons for the high divorce rate is that increasing numbers of couples are unwilling to stay in marriages that they find unfulfilling. They don't want to settle for mediocrity in their relationships. When trouble arises, many seek the help of marriage counselors to try to solve their problems and to develop the kind of meaningful relationships they want. Many succeed. If they don't, large numbers divorce.

Success Ratios

In spite of the high rate of failure, however, the fact is that *two out of three persons who marry remain in the same relationship for a lifetime.* Among those who remain married, there doesn't seem to be any decline in the percentage of persons who say they have a happy marriage. In one nationwide survey, two-thirds of married adults reported being "very happy" (U.S. Department of Commerce, May 1980). Most of the remaining one-third said they were "pretty happy." Only about 3 percent reported they were "not too happy." Apparently, those who were unhappily married had already divorced.

Marriage Rates

Trends

Some of the attacks on modern marriage are made by the disillusioned, by those who have tried marriage and found that it did not work for them. Other attacks come from the unorthodox who live only on the fringes of conventional society and who look with disdain upon those who are "straight." In spite of these attacks, *the percentage of those entering marriage has varied little over the past decade.* Glick indicates that the marriage rate increased until it reached a peak of 11 per 1000 population in 1972. It declined from that level to 10 in 1975 and has increased slightly since then, as shown in figure 1-2.

Glick expects that the marriage rate will remain fairly stable over the next few years with a slight rise as those who have postponed marriage decide to marry.

There has been an increase in the number of never-married persons in the United States. This, however, is due to the delay of marriage rather than to remaining permanently single. Only 8 percent of the people in the United States have not married by thirty to thirty-four years of age (U.S. Department of Commerce, April 1979). This is a relatively small proportion of the population.

Most people do marry eventually, even though the urge to marry early in life is not as strong as in the past. Women are placing more importance than formerly on getting an education, establishing a career, and becoming economically independent before marriage (U.S. Department of Commerce, February 1980). Even with the delay of marriage

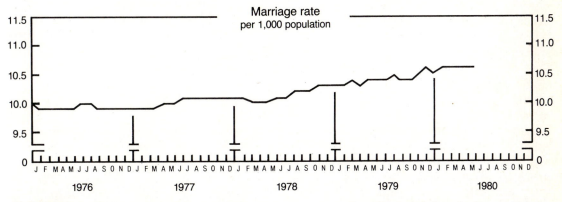

FIGURE 1-2. *Trend: Rates for successive 12-month periods ending with each month indicated* (*Source: U.S. Department of Health and Human Services, "Births, Marriages, Divorces, and Deaths for May 1980," Monthly Vital Statistics Report, DHHS Publication no. [PHS] 80–1120, Vol. 29, no. 5, August 7, 1980, p. 2.)*

and the rising divorce rates, three out of four people in the United States live at any one time in husband-wife households (Glick, 1979).

There has also been a dramatic rise in the number of unmarried men and women living together, but the numbers still amount to only 2 percent of the population (U.S. Department of Commerce, April 1979). Among the divorced, more than 80 percent eventually remarry. Apparently, first failures have not dissuaded them from trying again. And the majority of these second marriages are successful. Modern adults still believe in marriage.

Marriage, Careers, and Children

Marriage is immensely more popular than nonmarriage, but, at the same time, it is not the only goal in life for the majority of men and women. A Roper organization survey in 1974 showed that 52 percent of all women in the United States wanted marriage, children, and a career. Only a little over a third were willing to settle for marriage and children without a career, and only 2 percent would accept a career only.

One survey of male and female readers of *Psychology Today* showed that marriage was a major source of happiness for these persons (Shaver and Freedman, 1976). This same study, however, revealed a paradox in the lives of married women. More married than single women said they were happy, but among unemployed housewives, particularly, many were also more likely to report stress, anxiety, loneliness, and worthlessness. How could these housewives say they were happy and also report psychological symptoms of disturbance? The answer to their happiness lay partly in the fact that they felt they had achieved the American dream—a husband, children, and a comfortable home. The chief source of their stress lay in the fact that they

felt relatively isolated from adult contacts, or they felt they were not fulfilling themselves like their unmarried friends. One wife said she wanted to change lives with her single girlfriend who had a good job.

Her time is her own. She can travel and go places whenever she wants to. When you're married and have children your life is never your own (Shaver and Freedman, 1976, p. 29).

The happiest women were those who were married and employed outside the home (three out of four wives). They were happier than single women and had fewer psychological problems than housewives. These and other findings indicate that modern women want the best of all possible worlds—marriage, career, and children, and are happiest if they succeed at all three.

The Need for Intimacy

The most important reason why people in our culture get married is to love and be loved (Landis and Landis, 1973). Ask them, "Why do you want to get married?" They will invariably reply, "Because we love one another." The idea of love that is implied is often a highly romantic concept, supercharged with intense feelings (Martinson, 1972). For most couples, however, these highly emotional feelings give way to more permanent understanding and emotions. These are just as real as romantic love feelings and are more lasting and satisfying (Coutts, 1973).

Human beings above all seek to love and to be loved. There is a universal and primitive longing to be attached, to relate, to belong, to be needed, and to care (Neubeck, 1979). Men and women can have companionship outside of marriage with their own sex and with large numbers of persons with whom they share common interests and whose company they enjoy. Such companionship fills real needs. But most humans have an even more personal need: the need for intimacy, what Kennedy (1972) calls "the profoundly reaffirming experience of genuine intimacy." Erikson (1959) says that the achievement of intimacy is one of the major goals during the period of young adulthood. In a highly impersonal society, where emotional isolation is frequent, developing a close relationship with an individual is vital to one's identity and real security (Fullerton, 1972). Bach and Deutsch (1973) write:

What men and women seek from love today is no longer a romantic luxury; it is an essential of emotional survival. . . . For in today's world, when men and women are made to feel as faceless as numbers on a list, they want intimate love to provide the feelings of worth and identity that preserve sanity and meaning. They hunger for one pair of eyes to give them true recognition and acceptance, for one heart that understands and can be understood. Only genuine intimacy satisfies these hungers (p. 157).

The more society tends to alienate and isolate individuals, the more they become aware of a great need for one person who is committed on more than a temporary basis to travel the same road in life (Allen and Martin, 1974). This commitment to share the future together is the basis of marriage. In-so-far as marriage meets the important needs of married people, especially emotional needs, it remains viable and functional, and it is not, as some radical literature would claim, an obsolescent institution (Glenn and Weaver, 1979).

New Marriage versus Traditional Marriage

A Comparison

It seems evident that modern couples want love, companionship, and self-fulfillment and that they want to combine marriage, parenthood, and a career in achieving these. But the kind of marriage that allows personal and vocational fulfillment is radically different from traditional marriage concepts. One way to understand the differences is to set up a hypothetical contrast between one contemporary marital form, which will be labeled here as *new marriage* (Hunt, 1974; Otto, 1974; Otto, 1973), and another form referred to here as *traditional marriage* (Burgess et al., 1971; Myers, 1973; Rogers, 1972a). Neither exists in "pure" form. The descriptions as given are hypothetical constructs only. For this reason one cannot say that today's marriages are "new" and those of previous generations "traditional." Elements of new marriage existed in previous generations just as elements of traditional marriage exist today, especially in the more conservative cultures. Most marriages are a blend of the two extremes: some marriages are "newer," some are more "traditional," but the trend is toward the new.

The contrast between new marriage and traditional marriage is summarized in the following outline and is offered as one way of assisting students in discovering where their ideas of marriage fit along the continuum of contrasting forms.

New Marriage	Traditional Marriage
Marriage for love, companionship, and satisfaction of emotional needs. Intrinsic marriage.	Marriage for utilitarian reasons, such as providing for physical needs, services.
Marriage is personal. Places greatest value on individual.	Marriage is institutional. Places greatest value on family group.
Marriage allows personal freedom, self-fulfillment, self-actualization. Seeks individual growth, development of personhood. Enhances, clarifies identity.	Marriage requires self-denial. Holds back personal growth, since emphasis is on group development and maintenance rather than individual.

New Marriage	Traditional Marriage
Democratic power structure. Husband, wife are equals.	Authoritarian power structure. Wife subjugated by husband.
Involves maximum emotional, personal involvement. Open communication.	Limited personal, emotional involvement. Little personal communication.
Flexible sex roles. Evolving, developing relationship.	Rigid sex roles. Static relationship.
Sex is for love, pleasure, with procreation secondary. Emphasizes mutual sexual satisfaction of husband and wife. Emphasizes family planning, use of contraceptives.	Sex is for procreation. Sex is a man's pleasure and a wife's duty. Wives not expected to enjoy sex. Acceptance of number of children born.
Small family size. Nuclear family.	Large family size. Extended family network emphasized.
A voluntary relationship with couple choosing one another. Couple stay together because they want to.	Sometimes an involuntary relationship with others actively involved in mate selection. Couple stay together because it is expected and there are few viable alternatives.
Strives for permanence through marital integration. Divorce is a viable alternative to an unsuccessful marriage.	Permanence required by social sanction. Divorce is unacceptable for most.
Expectations of what marriage should be are high, increasing the possiblity of failure and disappointment.	Little expected of marriage itself, with possibility of failure and disappointment minimized.

New Marriage	Traditional Marriage
Criterion of success is marital integration, personal fulfillment, and happiness.	Criterion of success: couple has lived up to society's expectations, faithfully performed roles and duties, regardless of personal consequences.
Monogamy, legal marriage, nuclear family, sexual fidelity are considered ideal by majority. Alternative lifestyles allowed, adopted for periods of time by minority of persons.	Monogamy, legal marriage, sexual fidelity required. Alternative lifestyles infrequent.

These aspects of marriage deserve a closer examination.

Intrinsic versus Utilitarian

One of the major differences between new marriage and traditional marriage is in the purposes of marriage. Traditionally, people were married for economic security, physical protection, to provide goods and services for one another, to raise children; or to gain social status and prestige. This type of marriage was **utilitarian:** a means to an end. New marriage is more **intrinsic:** that is, its value is not as a means to an end but an end in itself (Saxton, 1972). And this end is love, companionship, and the satisfaction of emotional needs (Bell, 1971). New marriage is closest to what others refer to as companionship marriage (Mace and Mace, 1974). Mace (1972b) writes:

The change of goal [of marriage] actually corresponds with the change of environment. In the old rural-agricultural society, the major business of life was economic survival and physical safety, and marriage had to conform to these requirements. But in an affluent society, economic survival is taken for granted.... Now our deepest need is for *emotional security.* . . . By shifting its focus, marriage has now become the primary means by which the individual need for comfort and support and love and understanding can be met (p. 5).

Personal versus Institutional

New marriage places a great deal of emphasis on the worth and value of the individual. The marriage itself is considered important only because of what it will and can do for the individuals involved. The individual's well-being and happiness are of primary importance (Udry, 1974). As Martinson (1972) says: "The American family aims to serve persons within the family." This emphasis stands in contrast to traditional marriage, where the value of the institution of marriage was considered more important than the individuals in it. As a result, the goal was to preserve the institution, even if individual members suffered as a result. Figure 1-3 shows the contrast between new marriage and traditional marriage. As can be seen, in new marriage, the purpose of the marriage is to serve the needs of the husband and wife. In traditional marriage, the purpose of the husband and wife is to serve the marriage.

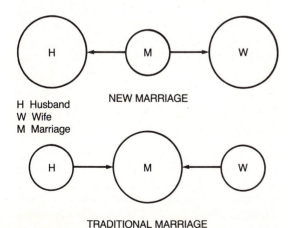

H Husband
W Wife
M Marriage

NEW MARRIAGE

TRADITIONAL MARRIAGE

FIGURE 1-3. *New marriage and traditional marriage*

Self-actualization versus Self-denial

New marriage facilitates self-fulfillment and self-actualization. It enables persons to continue to grow as individuals, it fosters the development of personhood and the clarification of identity. Just because people get married does not mean they must give up discovering and expressing their true selves. True, they make a commitment, "forsaking all others," to be loving and faithful to one another. But this does not mean they must give up their uniqueness or opportunities for fulfillment. Freedom, however, doesn't imply directionless or solitary wandering through life. It allows persons the opportunity to find emotional fulfillment and love through voluntary commitment and involvement (Olim, 1972). As they find love, they find meaning. This means that new marriage involves a close, loving, supportive relationship in which each person accepts and loves the other person as the other is. This acceptance is the most growth-promoting type of love possible, because the person is prized for what he or she is and may become (Rogers, 1972b).

Traditional marriage may require self-denial and the submersion of personal identity, since marital roles are fixed. Individuals are expected to conform to them; thus the possiblity of free expression is minimized. Certainly, the husband's subjugation of the wife, which leads to her submergence of self, is detrimental to any kind of real partnership (Rogers, 1972a).

Equality versus Subjugation

In new marriage, the husband and wife are much more nearly equal, with both enjoying similar rights, so that decision-making procedures are more likely to be democratic. In traditional marriage, the wife is subservient to the husband and decision making is more likely to be autocratic (Glen, 1972).

Maximum versus Limited Involvement

Because the emphasis in new marriage is on intimacy, personal contact, and emotional fulfillment, open communication is a necessity to release tension and avoid misunderstanding. This relationship is in contrast to traditional marriage, where less attention is given to whether the couple have a personal relationship or not. The man performs the general duties of husband and father; the wife is expected to be sexually available, to run the home, cook, and raise the children. Beyond these functions, both are free to pursue their own interests and cultivate their own friendships. It may be more difficult for the husband and wife to communicate, since they aren't

New marriage involves interchangeable sex roles.

necessarily friends and companions (Mace, 1972c). In a survey of what university youths felt was wrong with parental marriages, a large number said there was too little communication (Whitehurst, 1973).

Flexible versus Rigid Sex Roles

In new marriage, sex roles are quite flexible, allowing the husband and wife to provide mutual help and assistance in performing the total tasks inside or outside the home. There is no sharp distinction of "man's work" or "woman's work," but only "our work." This enables the wife to share in income earning and the husband to participate in child rearing and homemaking. This arrangement takes some pressure off the husband to produce all of the income and some pressure off the wife to rear the children and care for the house by herself. This arrangement is in contrast to that in traditional marriage where sex roles are more rigid and static and the couple has less choice in the matter.

Loving versus Dutiful Sex

In new marriage, the philosophy and use of sex is different. Sex is for love and pleasure, with sex for procreation accorded a secondary role. Also, it is assumed that the wife will respond sexually along with her husband, with both the husband and wife finding mutual satisfaction. Furthermore, couples try to have their children by choice, not by chance, and contraceptives are used to limit and plan the birth of children, who are usually few in number.

In traditional marriage, the primary use of sex is for procreation. Only the husband is considered to need sexual release, so the wife is not expected to enjoy it, even though she is expected to cooperate. In fact, little thought is given to the wife's satisfaction, since she is thought incapable of responding with orgasm and pleasure in intercourse. Since the use of contraceptives is inefficient or is sometimes forbidden, the wife develops a fatalistic acceptance of childbirth and of the large numbers of children born.

Nuclear versus Extended Family

Another difference between new marriage and traditional marriage is in the relationship of the married couple to relatives. In new marriage, the family is more **nuclear,** with the essential core or nucleus being the couple and their children. This does not mean the couple shut themselves off from their parents and relatives, since visitation may be frequent, but it does mean they live in a separate household where feasible and remain as financially and physically independent as practical. Traditionally, couples were an addition to the **extended family** network, involving several generations and including unmarried family members, oldsters, and children. The young husband was subservient to his own father, often assisting him on the farm or with his trade, while his wife was expected to assist her mother-in-law.

Voluntary versus Involuntary Relationship

Another emphasis in new marriage is on the voluntary nature of the relationship. The couple freely choose each other. They get married because they want to, at a time chosen by them, without pressure and coercion from family, friends, or circumstances. Furthermore, if they stay together it is because they want to.

Traditional marriage is sometimes the result of social pressure or coercion. In some countries, the partners are chosen by parents or marriage brokers. The marriage might even

be arranged without the couples' consent. In the U.S. parents may limit possible suitors and the conditions under which marriage might take place. If premarital pregnancy is involved, the couple get married.

Permanence Through Integration versus Permanence Through Social Sanction

In new marriage, the couple strive for permanence in the relationship. But the permanence depends on the extent to which marital integration (the satisfaction of mutual needs) and personal happiness and fulfillment are achieved. Divorce is allowed if the goals of marriage are not achieved for any reason and marriage becomes a source of frustration and unhappiness. Marriage is for life in a large number of instances (Landis 1970), but it is not a prerequisite of a marital arrangement. In traditional marriage, the couple are bound together for life by social sanction, with divorce unacceptable for most persons.

Maximum versus Minimum Expectations

The expectations for new marriage are hard to fulfill. People marry for love and companionship and expect that marriage will fulfill their deepest emotional and social needs. Furthermore, when individuals choose their own mates, they expect that they will make a superior choice. A survey of 300 university students revealed that 96 percent felt that they were capable of developing a successful marriage even though the majority found fault with their parents' marriages (Whitehurst, 1973). With such high expectations, if love does not endure, if sex does not measure up to expectations, if disagreements interfere with good compansionship, the couple tend to become disillusioned and disappointed.

This is in contrast to traditional marriage in which expectations are more easily fulfilled, so that disappointment is less frequent.

Satisfaction versus Obligation

The criterion of success in new marriage is obviously different than in traditional marriage. In new marriage, success is measured by the extent of marital integration, which may be defined as "the extent to which each marital partner receives from the other partner the attitudes, services, and goods needed" (Eshleman, 1965). It is also measured by the degree of satisfaction, happiness, and the extent to which the couple feel fulfilled. Crosby (1973) writes:

Young people frequently (if not always) maintain that their chief goal or desire in married life is happiness. Happiness is the great "goal" of married life. "We want happiness together more than anything else" (p. 22).

Under these circumstances, regardless of the judgment of friends and society, the marriage has failed in the minds of the couple to the degree that they feel that marriage has not given them happiness or satisfaction.

A traditional marriage is considered successful if it fulfills its utilitarian functions: raising healthy children, providing adequate income, keeping a respectable house, and providing for the physical needs of the family. The marriage is a failure only if the wife cannot bear children, or doesn't know how to bring them up properly, or is an inadequate homemaker, or if the husband is irresponsible or an inadequate provider.

Alternatives Allowed versus Alternatives Forbidden

One other word needs to be said about the relationship of new marriage and traditional concepts to various alternative lifestyles. The majority of youth desires a legal, monogamous marriage with children, and with sexual fidelity as a central ideal (Humphrey, 1977; White and Wells, 1973; Yankelovich, 1974). Since the tenets of new marriage imply individual freedom, growth, openness, and flexibility, however, various alternative lifestyles are tried by a minority of persons, usually for relatively short periods of time. Some of these persons are honestly searching for viable improvements to the marriages they see around them. No one has a monopoly on truth, and modern research is throwing some valuable light on different lifestyles. Traditional marriage insists upon legal, monogamous marriage, and sexual fidelity as the only form, so alternative lifestyles occur infrequently.

Conclusions

Marriage is in a state of flux, but the changes that are occurring ought to make it more viable and meaningful than ever. Human beings seek love, companionship, and intimacy, so they are striving to revitalize monogamy, realizing its intrinsic worth in fulfilling personal human needs.

Premarital Interaction and Mate Selection

CHAPTER
2

Dating and Premarital Sexual Behavior

CHAPTER OUTLINE

Dating as a Sociological Phenomenon

The Reasons for Dating

Dating Partners versus
Marriage Partners

Adolescents' Sexual Attitudes
and Behavior

College Students' Sexual Attitudes
and Behavior

Sexual Standards

Influences and Correlations

Use of Contraceptives

Conclusions

Dating patterns have changed considerably over the years. Dating systems did not emerge in the United States until the years after World War I. In the early 1900s, if a man desired the company of a woman, he had to meet her family, be formally introduced, and obtain permission to court her as well as gain her permission to be courted before they could go out together. Over the years, this pattern became less structured and more informal, until today people no longer "date" in the formal sense, but rather "go together" or "go out." In spite of its informality, contemporary **dating** still occupies a central place in the lives of individuals, and is still the ordinary prelude to mate selection and marriage.

Up until a few years ago, most experts had been insisting that any revolution that had taken place in premarital sexual attitudes and behavior occurred in the 1920s, not in recent years. There was substantial evidence to support this view. The incidence of premarital sexual intercourse had remained fairly stable. Then in the late 1960s and early 1970s, researchers began to reveal a rapid rise in the percentages—particularly in various forms of premarital sexual experiences (Walters and Walters, 1980). The revolution seemed to start on college campuses and filter down to include young adolescents. This chapter discusses some of the changes in sexual attitudes and behavior among youths, the influences that affect these attitudes, and the consequences that result.

Dating as a Sociological Phenomenon

The Emergence of Dating

The emergence of dating was a consequence of several developments. Urbanization, the rise of secondary education, and increasing geographic mobility brought large numbers of young people into association with one another, increasing the possiblity of informal contacts and associations.

The free, public, coeducational high school was not a widespread development until after 1872 when the Michigan Supreme Court declared it lawful to use public money for secondary education (Good, 1947). After this decision, other states followed with similar declarations, so by the beginning of the twentieth century more pupils were enrolled in public high schools than in private academies. The fact that large numbers of physically mature youths were now brought together for coeducational education (many academies had segregated the sexes) encouraged the development of subcultural heterosexual activities of youths who banded together for emotional support, status, companionship, and social activities, one of which was dating (Rice, 1981).

Increased affluence and leisure time enabled youths to devote more time to their own pursuits and social life. With youths having money, and the leisure time in which to spend it, having a date became a pleasant way of spending an evening.

Decreasing parental supervision and liberalized standards of social behavior gave youths the opportunity to get together at earlier ages without incurring the wrath of adults. As soon as U.S. parents found it more difficult to enforce segregation, and gradually stopped trying to do so because of more liberal standards of social behavior, adolescents became free to make heterosexual contacts at younger and younger ages.

The 1920s represented an early surge of the feminine equality movement (Freeman, 1973). The women's movement encouraged women's rights politically, socially, and sexually and made it possible for young women to participate on a more equal basis with young men in the total life of the community. Liberated women with their bobbed hair and flapper dresses were now free to take a ride in their boyfriend's jalopy, and to engage in a little petting on the sly without being under the watchful eye of chaperones. As a result, dating emerged as an important part of the life of American youths, replacing the previous system of formalized courtship.

Dating and Courtship in the 1940s to 1960s

The most important dating pattern to develop just prior to World War II was that of steady dating (Moss et al., 1971). This pattern developed as an outgrowth of heterosexual contacts at younger ages and was an outgrowth of the practice of group and random dating that developed in junior high school and the early years of high school. Steady dating was an intermediate form between casual dating and engagement, since it involves a transition between the no commitment of casual dating and the very high commitment of engagement. Such an intermediate stage was neces-

sary for individuals who were allowed the personal responsiblity for the selection of their own mate. It gave them the chance to sort out compatible mates and to try out their own roles.

Dating also became a means for attaining adult social status during high school. With the growing emphasis upon romantic marriage in American culture, youths turned to steady dating as a means of imitating monogamous adult romantic associations and, in so doing, found some semblance of security and adult status (Reiss, 1971). In his 1949 report, *Elmtown's Youth*, Hollingshead (1949) found a lack of widespread "going steady" in the midwestern high school he studied, and considerable criticism of the practice. Poffenberger (1964), however, in his 1964 study of eleventh and twelfth grade high school students in eight California schools, found that only 25 percent of the females and 42 percent of the males had never gone steady and that less than 10 percent of the students disapproved of steady dating. Going steady had gained acceptance.

One of the best descriptions of the dating and courtship system of the 1950s was given by LeMasters in his book, *Modern Courtship and Marriage*. LeMasters identified six stages in the system as shown in table 2-1. These stages represented an orderly progression from the first date in the junior high school years until marriage in the late teens or early twenties. An adolescent girl usually had her first serious crush in junior high school; boys reached this stage one or two years later. At each stage, the relationship of the boy and girl was super-romantic, with all other considerations subordinated to the fact that the two were madly in love. Also, each successive stage involved a progressively deeper commitment. "Steadies" frequently broke up and realigned themselves with others, but broken engagements were serious matters.

There was sense and logic to the system, except when youths moved too rapidly from

TABLE 2-1.   *Stages in dating and courtship in the 1950s*

Ages or Grades	Stage
7th, 8th grades	Group dating
9th, 10th grades	Random dating between "steadies"
11th, 12th grades	Steady dating
College years (earlier for women, later for men)	Pinning
College years, or post-high school years	Engagement
Ages 19 to 21 for women, 20 to 24 for men	Marriage

Source: Adapted from E. E. LeMasters, *Modern Courtship and Marriage* (New York: Macmillan, 1957). Copyright © 1957 by Macmillan Publishing Co., Inc. Used with permission.

the earliest stages to marriage. Speeding up the courtship process was more common among lower socioeconomic status youths than among the middle class—resulting in an increasing number of marriages at younger ages—until the trend began to be reversed in the early 1960s (Bartz and Nye, 1970; Rice, 1981).

Dating and Courtship Today

There are a number of differences between dating and courtship today and that of previous generations. While these patterns vary somewhat, there are some recognizable changes that have taken place. *One major change is the increased opportunities for informal heterosexual contacts.* High schools and colleges that used to be exclusively for men or women are now coeducational. Some college dormitories have become coed. Academic programs that used to attract only one sex or the other now enroll both men and women. Men and women share apartments. Some fraternities, at Stanford University and other schools, are now coeducational. These changes represent a drastic departure from the days when college men and women ate and slept on dif-

ferent parts of the campus. With such segregation, it was more difficult to get together, often requiring a formal phone call to arrange a meeting or a date. Today, group or paired social activities develop as a natural result of daily informal contacts in residences, classrooms, and social centers.

Another major change is in the lack of any set pattern of progression of intimacy and commitment from initial meeting to marriage. Previously, couples followed a fairly consistent pattern: casual dating, steadily dating, going steady, an understanding (engaged to be engaged), engagement, and marriage. Today patterns vary. Some couples follow closely the traditional pattern already described. Other couples decide to date one another exclusively and, after a period of time, decide to live together before getting married. There is no formal engagement, but marriage develops out of the cohabitation experience. In other words, not all couples become formally engaged and follow the traditional pattern. Patterns of dating and courtship vary among different couples.

Dating today is also much less formal than in previous generations. It is not necessary for the man to make a formal request in order to arrange a date. This sometimes happens, but a date may be arranged by mutual consent as a

Dating has become much less formal than in previous generations.

result of conversation about the evening activities. Also, more and more women are taking the initiative in arranging a get-together. Dress is certainly more casual, and the activities are often less formal or more casually planned. Many times, a social evening could not really be called a date. The couple just go out together for an informal evening.

One of the most significant changes in dating patterns is in the reasons for dating. These changes are discussed in detail in the following section.

The Reasons for Dating

Dating fulfills a number of important functions in the lives of today's youths.

Dating is recreation. One of the reasons couples go out is simply to relax, enjoy themselves, and have fun. It is a form of entertainment and thereby an end in itself (Husbands, 1970; Moss et al., 1971).

Dating is for companionship, friendship, and personal intimacy. One of the problems of modern youths in an impersonal society is the problem of loneliness. Dating is one way to escape loneliness. It expresses the human need for compansionship and friendship. Komarovsky writes:

The desire to escape loneliness, to find support, reassurance, appreciation, perhaps absolution—all generate the need to share feelings and thoughts with others (Komarovsky, 1974, p. 679).

One recent study found that those couples who were able to share their most important thoughts and feelings in an egalitarian relationship were those most likely to be compatible and in love (Rubin, 1980).

Dating is a means of gaining status and recognition. This is particularly true if the individual is in a group, such as a fraternity or sorority, that places a great deal of emphasis on social position and status ranking among its members (Scott, 1979). One study at the University of Iowa revealed that fraternity and sorority members dated those in Greek societies with prestige ratings similar to their own (Krain et al., 1977).

Dating is a means of socialization. Dating helps the individual learn social skills, gain confidence and poise, and begin to master the arts of conversation, cooperation, and consideration for others. The following example illustrates the need of one college male for help with his social relationships.

Bert was a college sophomore who considered himself a social misfit. He was a social isolate in the dorm and his only contact with the fellows was when he bore the brunt of their jokes. Mostly he tried to stay by himself. He had never had a date in high school or college, and would get very red-faced in the presence of girls. He tried to bury himself in his books as a compensation but became more and more miserable and lonely. Finally, he approached the teacher of the marriage and family class and wanted to know how he could learn to make friends.

Dating is a means of personality development. One way individuals have of finding their own personal identity is in relationship to other persons. Students who feel important in the eyes of other persons find self-esteem, ego-fulfillment, security, and identity. Since individuals mature as persons primarily through successful experiences with others, and since an adequate self-concept is partly a result of successful human associations, an important part of all individuals' personality

development is that they have successful dating experiences. One of the reasons that students go steady is precisely because such associations give them security and feelings of individual worth. High self-esteem college women do not as often feel the need to go steady as do low self-esteem women, even though the high self-esteem women date more frequently (Klemer, 1971).

Dating provides an opportunity for trying out sex roles (Davis, 1978). What is a man, and what is a woman, and how are they supposed to act and behave in relation to one another? Sex roles must be worked out in actual situations with the opposite sex partner. Many women today find that they cannot accept a traditionally passive role. Dating helps them to discover this and to learn what kind of a role they find fulfilling in a close relationship.

Dating is a means of fulfilling the need for love and affection. No matter how many casual friends students have, they fulfill their deepest emotional needs for love and affection in close relationships with individuals. Those who are not very close to their parents have a special need for affection from their dates. This need for affection is one of the major motives for dating.

Dating provides an opportunity for sexual experimentation and satisfaction (Sorensen, 1972; Vener and Stewart, 1974). Dating has become more sex oriented, with increasing percentages of students engaging in sexual intercourse. Most students who desire sexual intercourse want intercourse with affection (Mirande and Hammer, 1974).

Dating is a means of mate sorting and selection. Dating is the method in our culture of sorting out compatible pairs (Murstein, 1972). The process is one of filtering out, gradually narrowing the field of eligibles from a pool of several to a specific few and eventually to one individual. Couples tend to idealize one another less as serious romantic involvement and engagement develop, indicating that given sufficient involvement, couples are more likely to see one another as they really are. While not unexpected, these findings substantiate the fact that there is a correlation between the closeness of a relationship and the knowledge of self and of another person that an individual develops.

Dating is a means of preparation for marriage. Not only can dating result in the sorting of compatible pairs, but it can become a means of socialization for marriage itself (Avery, 1979). Through dating, couples develop a better understanding of the behavior and attitudes of the opposite sex; they learn how to get along with another person and how to discuss and solve problems. All of these are vitally necessary as preparation for marriage. The longer the dating period before marriage, the more dating fulfills this function of "anticipatory socialization" for marriage.

Of all of the reasons for dating just discussed, which ones seem uppermost as actual motivations of modern students? An important study of male students at Harvard University showed that students were most interested in dating as a form of companionship and as a means of finding sexual intimacy (Vreeland, 1972). Vreeland (1972) writes:

For today's student, the most important dating motive is *finding a friend who is female.* The most essential characteristic in a good date is her ability to make conversation and the primary dating activity is sitting around the room talking. At the same time, the sexual component of dating should not be ignored. Sex was one of the most important dating activities (p. 68).

Dating Partners versus Marriage Partners

In spite of its benefits, not all dating is helpful in mate selection or marital preparation. It can be counterproductive if it emphasizes personal qualities that are not always important in marriage. In a study at the College of San Mateo in California, 350 randomly selected males and 350 randomly selected females were asked to write down the three qualities most valued in a date and the three qualities most valued in a spouse (Saxton, 1977). The results are shown in table 2-2.

For both men and women, *looks* and *personality* in a date ranked first and second in importance. In addition to the qualities desired in a date, both men and women mentioned *love, being compatible,* and *being understanding* as important qualities in a spouse. Women also desired a husband who was *loyal and faithful,* and *responsible.* The point is, if dating is the primary means of mate sorting, but different qualities are desired in dates than are expected in marriage, how can suitable mates be discovered through the dating experience? It becomes more difficult.

Physical Attractiveness

Throughout this study and in others (Feinman and Gill, 1978; Miller and Ruvenback, 1970) physical attractiveness shows up repeatedly as one of the most important considerations in date selection. In a cleverly designed study, Walster (1966) and her colleagues found that physical attractiveness was the only important determinant of whether or not college students wanted to see each other again after a first date. This was true of women as well as men. The more attractive a man was, the more his partner liked him and the more she wanted to date him again. Other personality or social measures such as social skills, acceptable manners, courtesy, masculinity-femininity, or extroversion were found to be inadequate predictors of liking and of whether or not two individuals wanted to date one another again or not. It must be said, however, that the subjects saw one another for only two-and-a-half hours at a dance. This made it harder to really get to know one an-

TABLE 2-2. *Qualities most valued in a date and in a spouse*

Qualities Men Valued Most in a Date	Qualities Men Valued Most in a Spouse	Qualities Women Valued Most in a Date	Qualities Women Valued Most in a Spouse
Looks	Looks	Looks	Love
Personality	Love	Personality	Honesty
Sex appeal	Compatibility	Thoughtfulness, consideration	Compatibility
Intelligence	Sex appeal	Sense of humor	Understanding
Fun, good companionship	Personality	Honesty	Loyalty, faithfulness
Sense of humor	Understanding	Respect	Intelligence
Good conversation	Intelligence	Good conversation	Sense of humor
Honesty	Honesty	Intelligence	Responsibility

Source: Adapted from *The Individual, Marriage, and the Family.* Third Edition, p. 196 by Lloyd Saxton, © 1977 by Wadsworth Publishing Company, Inc., Belmont, California 94002. Reprinted with permission of the publisher.

other. It is quite likely that in a more intensely personal situation, such as spending an evening together in private, other considerations would also appear.

Complementarity or Similarity in Partners

Some efforts have also been made to determine the combinations of partners or personality types that make the most compatible dating partners. In a study of date selection by computer, several researchers found that randomly selected dating partners were not ranked nearly as "good" a date, as those selected either for similarity of social and personal characteristics, attitudes, tastes, and values, or for **complementarity** of needs (Strong et al., 1969). In another study, individuals who dated those with similar value orientations were more satisfied with their partners than individuals dating persons with dissimilar values. Also, the greater the satisfaction and value consensus the greater was the ease

of communication between the two people. Not only was interpersonal attraction enhanced by value consensus but so was communication ease, especially when the individual perceived that he or she was liked by the other person (Coombs, 1966).

Adolescents' Sexual Attitudes and Behavior

Premarital Intercourse Among Females

Three professors from Johns Hopkins University studied, in 1971 (Zelnik and Kantner, 1972) and again in 1976 (Zelnik and Kantner, 1978; Zelnik et al., 1979), the premarital intercourse behavior of national probability samples of fifteen- to nineteen-year-old never married females. The researchers found that the percentages of those who had experienced premarital **coitus** increased from 27 percent in 1971 to 36 percent in 1976. Figure 2-1 shows the comparisons.

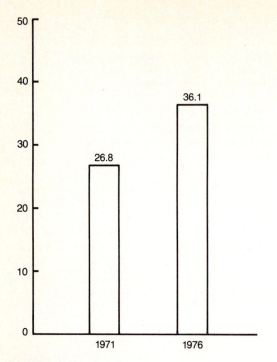

FIGURE 2-1. *Percentage of never-married women, aged fifteen to nineteen at interview who had ever experienced premarital intercourse, United States, 1976 and 1971 (Adapted from M. Zelnik and J. F. Kantner, "First Pregnancies to Women Aged 15–19: 1976 and 1971." Reprinted with permission from* Family Planning Perspectives, *Volume 10, Number 1, 1978.)*

There was an increase in the prevalence of premarital coitus at each age between fifteen and nineteen years (Clayton and Bokenmeier, 1980). By age sixteen, one out of five females had had premarital coitus, but by age nineteen, more than half had experienced it (Zelnik et al., 1979). Figure 2-2 shows the trends.

Premarital Intercourse Among Males

Cross-sectional surveys of thirteen- to seventeen-year-old students in a Michigan community in 1970 and again in 1973 showed that greater percentages of males than females, ages thirteen to sixteen, had had premarital

sexual intercourse (Vener and Stewart, 1974). The older the students, however, the less the difference between males and females. By age seventeen, the differences were eliminated with about one out of three males and females having premarital coitus. Another 1972 study in Colorado showed that the farther along in high school, the more likely that greater percentages of females than males had experienced premarital coitus. Among twelfth graders, 33 percent of the males and 55 percent of the females had had premarital intercourse. The researchers suggested that earlier sexual

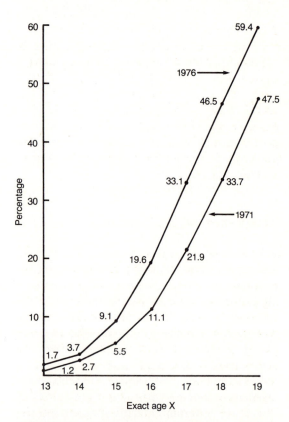

FIGURE 2-2. *Cumulative percentage of women who had ever had premarital intercourse by exact age X, United States, in 1976 and in 1971 (Adapted from M. Zelnik, Y. J. Kim, and J. F. Kantner, "Probabilities of Intercourse and Conception Among U.S. Teenage Women, 1971 and 1976." Reprinted with permission from* Family Planning Perspectives, *Volume 11, Number 3, 1979.)*

sophistication among females from dating college males might have been a factor in this community (Jessor and Jessor, 1975). Certainly, the evidence points to the fact that traditional male-female asymmetry in rates of premarital sexual activity among high school students seems to be disappearing.

College Students' Sexual Attitudes and Behavior

Changing Attutides

A number of studies have been conducted in recent years to determine if college students' attitudes toward various degrees of premarital sexual permissiveness have changed (Calderone, 1974; Croak and Barbara, 1973; Hampe and Ruppel, 1974; Herold and Foster, 1975; King et al., 1977; Singh, 1980). *The evidence shows overwhelmingly that modern college students have become more permissive in their attitudes.*

Sexual Behavior

Behavioral changes seem to have kept pace with liberalized attitudes. A study of college women repeated in 1958, 1968, and 1978 showed a significant increase in premarital coitus over the twenty years. In 1978, one-half had premarital coitus while dating, two-thirds while going steady, and three-fourths while engaged (Bell and Coughey, 1980). A random sample of male and female students, ages eighteen to twenty-three at the University of Wisconsin revealed that 75 percent of the males and 60 percent of the females had ever experienced premarital coitus. Sixty percent of the males and 56 percent of the females had ever experienced **oral-genital sex.** More than half of those currently going with a heterosexual partner were having intercourse with

that person, with intercourse taking place about one out of every three times they were together (Delamater and MacCorquodale, 1979).

Sexual Standards

The fact still remains, however, that not *all* college students are having intercourse. Certainly, one cannot say that *one* standard of behavior pervades the college campuses. Actually, there are still four different standards which are prevalent to a greater or lesser degree, depending upon many factors. The four standards are: *abstinence, double standard, coitus with emotional intimacy,* and *coitus without emotional intimacy* (Reiss, 1971). These four standards are represented in a sampling of 231 sophomore and junior dating couples attending four colleges in the Boston area (Peplau et al., 1977). An examination of the attitudes and behavior of the students in each of these four groups should provide some insights into their personal feelings and behavioral motivations.

Abstinence

Eighteeen percent of the couples in the sample had abstained from coitus in their present relationship. Students gave four possible reasons for not having intercourse. Those reasons were:

"My partner does not wish to have sexual intercourse at the present time."

"It is against my moral or religious convictions."

"It is too early in our relationship."

"I am concerned about the possibility of pregnancy."

Typically, the majority of men indicated that their girlfriend's decision not to have intercourse was a major reason for abstinence. Only 11 percent of the women indicated their boyfriend's reluctance to have sex played a role. Women were more likely than men to say sex violated their ethical standards or to say that it was too early in the relationship. Nearly half the men and women listed fear of pregnancy as a reason for abstention. The abstaining couples were generally more conservative in their attitudes about sex than other students.

Double Standard

Most studies indicate that the double standard, permissiveness for men and abstinence for women, is disappearing (Berger and Wanger, 1973; Ferrell et al., 1977). Ninety-five percent of the men and women in the Boston area study advocated identical standards for men and women in love relationships (Peplau, 1977). The women were less favorable toward casual sex than were the men, however, and, overall, the men appeared to emphasize sex more and to have a greater interest in intercourse than did the women. Men rated "sexual activity" more important as a dating goal than did women. Couples often reported both partners were equally interested in sex, but when their interest was unequal, it was most often the man who had greater interest than the woman. Apparently, traditional sexual role playing was common, with the men encouraging intercourse and the women limiting sexual intimacy. The women held negative control, rejecting the man's advances or slowing the pace of increasing intimacy. This finding was in keeping with those of other studies which show that a minority of students have stereotyped concepts: that having sex is a male goal and avoiding sex is a female goal (McCormick 1979). This does not mean that women are always passive. In the Boston study, a number of women had a part in initiating sex. The women might communicate, often subtly,

that they were interested and willing (Peplau et al., 1977).

Coitus with Emotional Intimacy

The majority of college couples believe in coitus with emotional intimacy, or "permissiveness with affection" (Walster and Walster, 1978). Sex is permissible if a man and woman love one another, even though a long-term commitment is not necessary. Sex, in this context, is an expression of emotional closeness. Since it takes time for love to grow, couples move only gradually toward sexual intimacy. In the Boston area study, couples with this orientation reported having intercourse an average of six months after they started going together (Peplau et al., 1977). After coitus, an equal number of men and women repeated that the reason for their actions was that they were in love.

Coitus without Emotional Intimacy

Couples in this category believe that sex without affection is acceptable, so they enjoy casual or "recreational" sex, even though they are also capable of intercourse as an expression of emotional sharing. These couples are more interested in eroticism without necessarily requiring love. In the Boston area study, these couples reported a high frequency of intercourse (four to five times per week versus two to three times per week for other couples), and intercourse came *before* the couples decided to go together (Peplau et al., 1977). Despite their sexual permissiveness, the students were, for the most part, not promiscuous. Only about one in seven reported having coitus with someone else during the previous two months.

It is quite evident that not all college students are alike in relation to their sexual attitudes and behavior any more than they are identical in other respects. Overall, students today are certainly far more liberal than were others only ten years ago. Greater percentages of men and women have premarital coitus with more different partners, earlier in their relationship, with less guilt or anxiety, and with less frequent commitments to marry. This has led to the depersonalization of sex to some extent (Frankl, 1979). But the greatest numbers still felt that sex ought to be an intimate expression of closeness and love.

Influences and Correlations

Researchers have sought, also, to discover those factors that influence and/or correlate with sexual attitudes and behavior (Bayer, 1977; Davidson and Leslie, 1977). *Age* has already been mentioned as an important factor (Laner and Housker, 1980). Other factors may be listed: *race, religiosity, parent-peer influences, personal factors, prior sexual experience,* and *exposure to sexual information and stimuli.*

Race

An analysis of a number of studies that correlate race with premarital sexual attitudes and behavior reveals that *blacks are more permissive than whites* (Christensen and Johnson, 1978; Inazu and Fox, 1980; Staples, 1978). When socioeconomic class differences are controlled statistically so as to eliminate any black-white differences, the differences in the levels of premarital sexual permissiveness remain (Mardnell et al., 1970; Middendorp et al., 1970). There is, however, a range of permissiveness within different social classes of each race, with both conservative and liberal positions represented (Mahoney, 1978).

Religiosity

One important fact that is correlated significantly and negatively with the degree of premarital sexual permissiveness is religiosity.

The more religious the person the less he or she is inclined to be sexually permissive (Clayton, 1972; Libby et al., 1978; Middendorp, 1970). In most studies, religiosity is measured by the frequency of church attendance (Hornick, 1978; Inazu and Fox, 1980; Libby et al., 1978). One study found that a strong interest in religion and frequent church attendance stimulates sexual guilt, which in turn was the major predictor of sexual attitudes held and sexual behavior expressed. This supports the findings of other researchers that sexual guilt was a better predictor of behavior than just church attendance alone. After all, other influences such as parental teachings and early sex education contribute to sexual guilt and sexual behavior (Gunderson and McCary, 1980).

Parent-Peer Influences

To what extent do reference groups such as close friends, peers, fraternity or sorority associates, or parents have an influence on premarital sexual permissiveness? Apparently, they all have considerable influence, but *the influence of peers appears to be greater than that of parents* (Davis, 1974; Jorgensen, 1980; Kaats and Davis, 1970; Maddock, 1973; Mirande and Hammer, 1974).

Teevan (1972) found that if a college student perceived friends or age mates as sexually permissive, he or she tended to be permissive. Three times as many students who believed their friends had "lots of sex," reported some coitus, than did students who perceived their friends as sexually conservative. Teeven also found that if a student perceived friends or age mates as sexually conservative, he or she tended to be conservative. A student who perceived friends as having little sex experience was much more likely to remain a virgin. These relationships held true both for present coital behavior and for attitudes toward future coitus, so that having permissive friends was not only associated with a high incidence of past coitus but with a high probability of future coitus. Thus, students' perceptions of their friends' sexual behavior has a very strong influence on what they do.

Students are also affected by the kind of relationship they enjoy with their parents. One researcher found that the closer daughters were to their mothers, the less likely the daughters were of having premarital sexual intercourse (Inazu and Fox, 1980). Teevan (1972) also found some negative relationship between the degree of parent orientation and permissiveness. Students who were more parent oriented engaged less often in coitus, were less permissive in their attitudes toward coitus, and said they were less likely to engage in coitus in the future. Conversely, those most estranged from parents said they were more likely to engage more frequently in coitus now and in the future. Other studies suggest that students who perceive their parents as sexually liberal are more likely to be permissive themselves (Libby et al., 1978).

Personal Factors

At least two different personal factors have been correlated with premarital sexual permissieveness: *physical attractiveness* and *self-esteem*. Kaats and Davis (1970) found that physically attractive college women differed little from less attractive women in sexual attitudes and values, but, nevertheless, a greater percentage of the attractive women were nonvirgins.

The most physically attractive females had a more favorable self-image, had more friends of the opposite sex, believed that more of their friends had had intercourse, dated more frequently, had been in love more often, and had had more petting experience. The fact that these women were more popular and dated more frequently greatly increased their opportunities and the pressures for premarital coitus. Another study found that sexually active women with high self-esteem had more positive attitudes about using birth control pills, were less embarrassed about obtaining contraception, and were more effective contraceptive users than were low self-esteem women (Herold et al., 1979). Another study emphasized that college men who felt they were most attractive socially were also more permissive (MacCorquodale and DeLamater, 1979).

Whether or not high self-esteem students are generally more permissive sexually than are those of low self-esteem will depend upon the prevailing sexual standards of the group. An investigation of the relationship between self-esteem and sexual permissiveness of Canadian students showed some slight negative correlation. Those of high self-esteem showed a tendency toward lower permissiveness (Perlman, 1974). This is because Canadian society as a whole is quite conservative. In such a society, to be permissive is to be deviant, which is less likely to happen with high self-esteem individuals.

Prior Sexual Experience

Sex is pleasurable to most people, so sexual activity tends to be self-reenforcing and to stimulate further activity (Kelley, 1978). Thus, whether or not students have had intercourse has considerable influence on whether they are sexually permissive or not. This is especially true of females. In her study of college dating couples, Peplau (1977) found that when both partners began a relationship as virgins, only half of them subsequently had intercourse, but when both partners were sexually experienced, almost all couples had intercourse. When a virgin male dated a sexually experienced female, all had coitus, but when a virgin female dated a sexually experienced male, a third of the couples abstained.

Thus, *the previous sexual experience of the woman is a better predictor of whether or not a couple will have coitus than the experience of the man.*

Exposure to Sexual Information and Stimuli

One of the most interesting questions is the extent to which sexual knowledge influences behavior. This question has important implications for sex education (Spanier, 1975). Will education about sex influence what people do? The answer is yes, but this must be explained (Gunderson and McCary, 1980). Providing factual information, as such, gives people more knowledge and understanding to use in ways they choose. It has been shown, for example, that providing contraceptive knowledge to teenagers can reduce unwanted pregnancies considerably (Hansson et al., 1979; Zelnik, 1979). But it does not necessarily change their sexual behavior (DeLamater and MacCorquodale, 1978; Weichmann and Ellis, 1969). Many teens want to know out of curiosity, or in case they need the information at some future date. Those actually wanting contraceptives have already decided to have sexual intercourse, so providing medical help has not changed their behavior.

Similarly, knowledge of the parts of the reproductive system, of how sexual stimulation takes place, or of the stages of sexual response can help people in their lovemaking, but it does not—in and of itself—determine whether or not they have intercourse. If they do have intercourse, they can use their knowledge to enhance their experience. Or, an exploitative person, could use this knowledge to try to break down the resistance of an unwilling person through application of sexual stimuli. But possession of knowledge is not moral or immoral—it is amoral, and can be used to help or to hurt.

Sex education that includes discussion of moral principles, or discussion of how to evaluate rightness or wrongness in making judgments, *can* influence moral behavior by providing the tools for making decisions. Even then, there is no guarantee that knowing what is right or being able to make moral judgments will assure that right decisions will be made. *Moral knowledge does not guarantee moral behavior, but at least it makes it possible.*

The churches have been using moral education and indoctrination for years and have had a significant influence on moral behavior, as we've seen. But here, also, not everything that is taught is accepted and put into practice, even though the facts are understood. To influence behavior, knowledge must be internalized, accepted as truth for oneself.

We do know that sexual stimuli can influence sexual actions. *There seems to be an especially close relationship between sex and aggression.* In one study, male and female subjects exposed to an erotic film showed various degrees of sexual arousal, but those most sexually aroused showed the most aggressive behavior subsequently in mock battles with accomplices (Feshbach and Malamuth, 1978). Male subjects exposed to sadomasochistic material expressed fewer inhibitions against raping a woman themselves than when not exposed to such material. These findings indicate that *combining sex with violence, such as happens in many movies and television shows, does condition violent responses to erotic stimuli.* The message that pain and humiliation can be "fun" encourages relaxation of inhibitions against sexual violence including rape.

Use of Contraceptives

Adolescents

With more than one-third of fifteen- to nineteen-year-old adolescents having premarital coitus, the question arises about what percentages of these young people are using some form of protection against pregnancy. Results from the Zelnik and Kantner (1978a) study already cited show that 31 percent of sexually active fifteen- to nineteen-year-old unmarried girls or their partners never used any method of contraception. Forty-two percent said they sometimes used **contraceptives.** Only 27 percent always used some method of contraception whenever they had intercourse. These figures are in general agreement with other national studies (U.S. Department of Health, Education, and Welfare, May 1972; March 1974).

Unfortunately, *the contraceptive methods which adolescents use are not always the most efficient.* Zelnik and Kantner (1978a; 1979) found that of those young women who used contraception at first intercourse, only 25 percent used a medical method: the **birth control pill, IUD,** or **diaphragm.** The other 75 percent of the young women used nonmedical methods such as the **condom, chemicals, withdrawal, douche,** or **rhythm.** Of these methods, only the condom is very efficient in preventing conception. Some nonmedical users subsequently switched over to more efficient methods, but of those who continued and always used nonmedical methods, 17 percent became pregnant. Of those who never used any contracpetion, 58 percent became pregnant.

College Students

How do college students feel about contraception? Theoretically, they accept it. Ninety-six percent of undergraduate students in a study at Earlham College indicated they believed in limiting family size; more than 90 percent said they were concerned about the population crisis (Scarlett, 1972). Only 2 percent of undergraduate students in three coeducational institutions in the Boston area said that

they believed "it is wrong for a couple to use contraception" (Corman and Schaefer, 1973). But these comments were made in the context of marriage. Students believed in using contraceptives, if married. But judging by actual behavior, not nearly as many believed in using contraceptives, if unmarried.

Table 2-3 shows the results of a 1970–1971 study among 582 undergraduates in health science classes at California State University in San Diego (Bender, 1973). Even though these students said that the male and female have equal responsibility for contraception, 45 percent of the males and 21 percent of the females expect their date to come equipped. If the man has not taken precautions, only 7 percent of them will ask their partner if she has. If neither person has taken precautions, 60 percent of the males and 34 percent of the females will have intercourse with no protection. The figures indicate that men still put the burden of responsiblity upon the women and that one-third of the females are still willing to have intercourse without using any effective method of birth control.

One study of 823 never-married white undergraduates at Michigan State University indicated that contraceptives were readily available to them in the areas immediately adjacent to the campus (Gunderson and McCary, 1980). Certainly, lack of availability in this area—and in most areas near college campuses cannot be used as an excuse for not using contraception. Some students have psychological barriers to the use of contraception (Perlman, 1980). They cannot admit to themselves that they are going to have coitus, or are already sexually active. Some females need to feel that they are in love and committed to their partner before they can use contraceptives on a regular basis (Nornick et al., 1979). Others feel that contraception interferes with the spontaneity of sex; others feel it is unnecessary, or immoral; still others are dissuaded by their partners or by fear of their parents; others are misinformed (Ambrose,

TABLE 2-3. *Attitudes of undergraduate college students toward intercourse and contraception*

Response	Percent Giving Affirmative Response	
	Male	Female
Want first sex to be spontaneous and extemporaneous in nature	78	72
Will possibly engage in premarital sex	86	84
Male and female have equal responsibility for contraception	80	83
Expect date to come equipped	45	21
If haven't taken precautions, will ask date if he or she has	7	96
If neither person has taken contraceptive precautions, will use withdrawal, rhythm method, or just go ahead and hope for the best	60	34

Source: Adapted from S. J. Bender, "Sex and the College Student," *Journal of School Health* 43 (May 1973): 278–280. Used with permission of the publisher and Stephen J. Bender, HSD, Professor of Health Science, Department of Health Science, San Diego State University, San Diego, CA 92182.

1978), irresponsible, or just plain foolish (Thompson and Spanier, 1978; Torres, 1978; Zelnik and Kantner, 1979). Many feel: "It won't happen to me" or "I don't have sex often enough to get pregnant." Actually, pregnancy can occur with only one sex act if the woman is ovulating and the man is fertile. One study found that half of first premarital pregnancies to teens occurred in the first six months of sexual activity (Zabin et al., 1979).

Conclusions

The changes that are taking place in dating patterns are very much in keeping with the changing functions of marriage. Youths today marry for love, companionship, intimacy, and sexual fulfillment. Dating patterns seem to be evolving in the same direction. There is less emphasis on dating just for recreation and fun, and more emphasis on companionship,

friendship, intimacy, and emotional and sexual fulfillment. While fewer young people say that they date to find a mate, the fact remains that the type of personal and intimate dating experiences they are seeking are those that will better prepare them for intimacy and companionship in marriage. Less rigid sex roles in dating and greater equality between the sexes are also preparing young people for more democratic, egalitarian marriages.

There are aspects of contemporary dating patterns, however, that are detrimental to wise mate selection and to happy, successful marriage. Most of the negative aspects relate to the type of dating partners students select. The emphasis is still on physical attractiveness as the most important requirement in a date, even though this quality is only minimally related to marital success and happiness. In the study at San Mateo, students desired spouses whom they loved, who were understanding, and with whom they were compatible but they largely overlooked these qualities in a date. Instead, they listed such characteristics as looks, having sex appeal, a good sense of humor, and being fun. Dating could fulfill better the important function of mate sorting and selection if students were motivated to seek a person for dates who had the same characteristics they desire in a mate.

The changes that have taken place in premarital sexual attitudes and behavior have resulted in both desirable and undesirable consequences. Healthier and more matter-of-fact attitudes towards sex are contributing in a positive way to fewer sexual hang-ups, and thus resulting in a more satisfying sexual expression in marriage. The sexual openness and honesty of many youths is refreshing, and should help them in mature marital relationships.

The fact that greater numbers of youths are having premarital intercourse, more frequently, at younger ages than ever before, and often without protection from pregnancy, is creating some real problems. More than a million teenagers a year are becoming premaritally pregnant. These pregnancies result in thousands of hasty and often short-lived marriages. They also result in more than two hundred thousand illegitimate babies born each year to girls fifteen- to nineteen-years-old, and in more than three hundred thousand abortions each year among this age group (Byrne, 1977; Forrest, 1978; Rice, 1980). Venereal diseases have reached epidemic proportions, with the VD rate in the sixteen to twenty age group triple that of the rest of the population (Yarber, 1978).

Certainly, the present situation is untenable. Those teenagers who are sexually active need complete knowledge and help in obtaining the best contraceptives available. Most of all, youths need more sex education, including education in moral decision making, to enable them to make more thoughtful, knowledgeable, and responsible decisions in relation to their sexuality (Juhasz, 1975).

CHAPTER 3

Nonmarital Cohabitation

CHAPTER OUTLINE

Definitions

Incidences of Cohabitation

Persons Who Cohabit

Description of Experiences

The Nature of the Relationships

Other Problems

Effects and Implications

Conclusions

Dialogue

In 1968, Linda LeClair, a sophomore at Barnard College, became a national celebrity after the public revelation that she was unmarried and living off-campus with a Columbia University dropout. Linda made the front page of *The New York Times. Time* magazine did a feature story on "Linda the Light Housekeeper" (Macklin, 1974). But in her testimony before the college Judicial Council, Linda was unrepentent and placed the blame on university rules: "I have disregarded a regulation which I believe to be unjust" (McWhirter, 1973). Apparently, the Council agreed with her. Her punishment was suspension from the Barnard snack bar.

Nonmarital cohabitation has become a widespread phenomenon across the nation. This means that increasing numbers of cohabitors are faced with the problems and adjustments of living together. It means that thousands of others are trying to decide whether or not they want to cohabit outside the bonds of marriage. In the meantime, others have not seriously considered such a relationship but are nevertheless curious to learn more about it, while others have definitely decided against it for themselves. It means also that many parents, and other adults working with youths, are raising some serious questions about the effects of such relationships on individuals, on marriage, and on society.

The information presented in this chapter is based on research findings and on information the author has obtained in direct contact with students. One purpose in presenting the information is to offer a sociological analysis that should enable others to make more knowledgeable and wiser decisions about cohabitation. Another purpose is to assist adults in developing greater understanding of the phenomenon so that they can relate to students in more objective and helpful ways. The really important question each person might ask after reading the chapter is: What do I think about cohabitation?

Definitions

One of the problems in defining "cohabitation" is that professional researchers have not yet developed a universally accepted definition (Danziger, 1978). The words "nonmarital cohabitation" as used in this chapter refer to *the practice of two unrelated persons of the opposite sex living together under marriage-like conditions without being legally married to one another* (Macklin, 1972a; Randall, 1979). In an effort to further define the relationship, researchers at California State add the phrase "living together *in a relatively permanent manner*" (Macklin, 1974). Macklin (1972b) of Cornell University defines cohabitation as "having shared a bedroom and/or bed with someone of the opposite sex (to whom one was not married) for four or more nights a week for three or more consecutive months." The intent of both the California and Cornell definitions is to exclude those instances where couples live together only for brief periods of time: over a series of weekends, during a semester break, or while traveling to Florida. Certainly, such temporary instances do not really constitute marriage-like conditions.

There is some difficulty, however, in setting time limitations. What constitutes a "relatively permanent manner" such as implied in the California State definition? Research at different colleges shows that large numbers of couples cohabit for periods of less than three months, then break up (Kahn et al., 1972; Peterman et al., 1974). Yet, including information from their experiences might be highly significant, especially in discussing reasons why couples separate. Therefore, the discussion in this chapter is not limited only to those who have cohabited for longer than three months. Rather, the focus is on understanding various types of cohabiting relationships, each with their different meanings and sometimes different problems. Time periods are mentioned insofar as they are important in understanding the total relationships discussed.

Incidences of Cohabitation

Percentage

What percentage of unmarried college students have cohabited? One study of students at fourteen state universities estimated that one-quarter had at some time cohabited (Bower and Christopherson, 1977; Macklin, 1978). The rates vary from 9 percent to at least 36 percent, depending upon the type of school, housing and parietal policies, the sex composition and ratio of the student body, as well as the researcher's sample and definition of cohabitation (Henze and Hudson 1974). Certainly, the total number and percentages have increased greatly over the past ten years ("Dramatic Rise . . .," 1980; Glick and Spanier, 1980; United States Department of Commerce, February 1980a). Of course, there is a difference between those who have *ever* cohabitated and those who are at any one time. The percentage who are cohabiting at any one

time is about 15 percent according to one national sampling (Clayton and Voss, 1977).

Reasons for the Increase

Why this rapid increase in the numbers of students involved? *One of the most important reasons has been the liberalization of university regulations and attitudes in relation to housing.* It is significant that schools with the highest rates of cohabitation, such as Cornell (31 percent), Pennsylvania State (33 percent), and the University of Texas (36 percent), all allow living off campus as well as twenty-four-hour-a-day heterosexual visits in the dorms. This is in contrast to a small liberal arts college in the Midwest that has no off-campus housing and where only seniors in one dorm are allowed overnight visits. In the latter, only 9 percent of the sample indicated they had ever cohabited (Macklin, 1978).

Of course, changing housing policies are a reflection of more basic philosophical and ethical changes. These include *the gradual elimination of double standards for women and changing standards of premarital sexual behavior.* For years, coeds chaffed under rules that required dorm residence, dormitory doors locked after set hours, and allowed only a certain number of "late dates" per week while male students were free to come and go as they pleased. Women are now insisting on equal rights, and they have largely won the battle as far as university housing policies are concerned.

Along with an improvement in the status of women has come a gradual liberalization of standards of premarital sexual behavior for everyone, but especially for females (Perlman, 1973). Permissiveness with affection has replaced a double standard that required female abstinence as the acceptable sexual ethic of college students.

Certainly cohabitation enjoys wide peer group acceptance. Practically all surveys show that the great majority of students feel it is all right for their friends to live together without marriage. The standard has become widely accepted on college campuses. In fact, there often is considerable peer group pressure to cohabit (Jacques and Chason, 1978).

Along with changing sexual standards has come *increased availability of contraceptives and abortions.* Actually, fairly adequate contraceptives have been available for years, yet unmarried students weren't living together so contraceptives alone cannot account for the increase in cohabitation (Rosenfeld, 1973). Many students still worry about possible pregnancy, but availability of abortion as a back up measure, as well as improved methods of contraception—especially the pill— have taken part of the worry out.

Some students who cohabit have become disenchanted with traditional courtship and the superficiality of the dating game. Fewer and fewer students want to go through the usual steps of casual dating, steady dating, engagement, and marriage. Instead *they are searching for more intimate, meaningful relationships with a high degree of emotional involvement* (O'Neill and O'Neill, 1972). The human need for love and affection and the need to belong to someone who cares is an especially powerful need within the shadow of a large, impersonal university.

There are some students who have become doubtful or even cynical about traditional marriage. The majority still approve of marriage and want to be married, but increasing divorce rates and the unhappiness of many of their parents' marriages have made them more cautious about entering such relationships unprepared and uninformed (Peterman et al., 1974). Many desire to experiment with living with someone before making more permanent commitments. Others feel that cohabitation offers the best means of personal preparation and growth; still others want to test their compatiblity with a particular person. Some feel that nonmarried cohabitation is far

more enjoyable and meaningful than steady dating and is less risky than marriage (Lyness et al., 1975, Shuttlesworth and Thorman, 1975). Others look upon it as a permanent substitute for legal marriage.

Breaking up can be painful and traumatic, but it is less devastating than legal divorce. For the short term at least, cohabitation appears to be quite attractive to a good many students and carries a minimum of risk and responsiblity (Eshleman, 1974; Johnson, 1973).

Student Attitudes

It is also clear that more students would like to cohabit than do. The percentages of those who aren't cohabiting but would like to range from a low of 43 to 57 percent of females to a high of 63 to 71 percent of the males (Henze and Hudson, 1974). Fifty-six percent of all students surveyed at Florida State University indicated that, given the right conditions, they thought they would sometime (either during college or after) be living with a person of the opposite sex without being married (Kieffer, 1972).

Why Some Do Not

The most common reasons students give for not cohabiting are the following:

- They have not yet found the right person.
- Their partner is unwilling.
- They are separated geographically from their partner.
- They feel it would be unwise at this stage of their relationship.
- It is not possible from a practical point of view (lack of money, housing, and so forth).
- They fear what their parents would say or do if they found out.
- They feel too immature to enter into such a relationship.

- They are afraid of pregnancy.
- They feel it would be morally wrong to do so.

At Illinois State, females more often than males agreed "that possible reasons for not entering cohabitation are parental disapproval, societal disapproval, fear of pregnancy, a matter of conscience, morality, legal issues, and religious beliefs." Male students more often said that the reason they did not participate in cohabitation was due to the unwillingness of their lover (Huang, 1975).

Tenure

When students start cohabiting, how long do the relationships last? Studies at American University showed that only a third of the relationships had endured six months or longer. A little more than a third lasted less than one month (Kahn et al., 1972). At Pennsylvania State, one-fourth of the females—but only 18 percent of the males—reported their longest cohabiting experience was longer than six months. Half of the men and almost one-third of the women said their longest experience had been less than a month (Peterman et al., 1974). Studies at the University of Texas, however, showed that, for the most part, couples had continued the cohabitation for more than six months. In a few instances, couples had been living together for two years or longer (Shuttlesworth and Thorman, 1975). These figures and those from other studies show that *couples are staying together for fairly short periods of time.*

Persons Who Cohabit

Class Standing

The findings are consistent in showing that *the older the students and the farther along they*

are in school, the more likely they will cohabit (Macklin, 1973b). Figure 3-1 shows the incidence of cohabitation among students at Pennsylvania State by sex and class standing (Peterman et al., 1974). These figures indicate that the onset of cohabitation appears to be a gradual one, with the cohabiting rate increasing 10 percent a year each year between the sophomore and senior years. This indicates that it takes considerable time for students to find suitable partners and for relationships to grow. It may also be that their attitudes toward cohabiting change during these years.

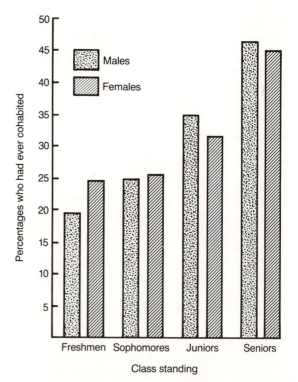

FIGURE 3-1. *Incidence of cohabitation among students at Pennsylvania State University by sex and class standing (Source: Adapted from D. J. Peterman; C. A. Ridley; and S. M. Anderson, "A Comparison of Cohabiting and Noncohabiting College Students,"* Journal of Marriage and the Family *36 [May 1974]: 347. Copyright 1974 by the National Council on Family Relations. Reprinted by permission.)*

Emotional and Social Adjustments

Some efforts have been made to discover if there are any significant differences in the emotional and social adjustments of persons who cohabit versus those who do not. The results of research are variable. Studies at Pennsylvania State University indicated that cohabitants felt they had reached a somewhat higher level of personal adjustment than had noncohabitants, and that a greater percentage of male cohabiters than noncohabiters reported the largest number of friends and acquaintants. The authors concluded: "There are no immediately obvious negative effects of cohabitation, at least in terms of self-described personal adjustment.... If anything, cohabitation is associated with more positive self-attitudes and heterosexual rating" (Peterman et al., 1974, p. 354). In this study, cohabitants appeared to be interpersonally oriented, at least according to their own evaluations, and cohabitation was a natural addition to their wide interpersonal base.

There is some indication that some persons enter into cohabitation as a means of solving difficulties with heterosexual adjustment or as a means of finding identity. In her studies at Illinois State University, Huang (1975) discovered that cohabiting couples had not been dating early in their teens, nor had they dated frequently. In fact, quite a few male students admitted they had not been very comfortable with girls and had not dated until they were eighteen or nineteen years of age. For these students, cohabitation became a substitute for steady dating but, because of their lack of skill in dating, their cohabitation experiences were short and frequent. Some of them were on their third or fourth experience.

Research at the University of Colorado revealed some tendency for women who cohabited before marriage to have a greater sense of nonidentity than women who did not cohabit (Lyness, 1975). Furthermore, they scored lower on the sense of self variable than

did other groups. Two explanations are possible. Either they actually had greater problems with their own identity than did noncohabitants, or they perceived their spouse and/or their cohabitation experience as threats to their identity. It is difficult to sort out cause and effect. Did those with poor identity cohabit as a means of finding themselves, or was it that the experience of living closely with another person had limited the development of their identity? The answer seems to be that *some used cohabitation to find identity, others discovered that cohabition limited their identity, while the identity of others was unaffected by the experience.*

There is some indication of a higher frequency of drug usage among cohabiting than among noncohabiting students. Data from Arizona State University indicated that students with cohabitation experience were more inclined to smoke pot and use hard drugs than were noncohabitants. But the researchers attribute this to an overall more liberal and nonconforming lifestyle rather than to personality or social maladjustments (Henze and Hudson, 1974).

Parental Marriages and Relationships

What about family background? Do parents of those who cohabit have happier or less successful marriages than the parents of those who do not cohabit? *Generally speaking, parental separations appear more frequently in the backgrounds of those who cohabit* (Henze and Hudson, 1974; Peterman et al., 1974).

The reasons that cohabiters more often come from separated families than do noncohabiters can only be partially surmised on the basis of limited evidence. Do the students seek intimate cohabiting relationships as an emotional and social substitute for their own disrupted family experiences? Are these students more estranged from both parents than are those from intact families and so more able to do as they desire? Are the sons and daughters of separated parents more liberal in their philosophies than those from intact families? Or are they trying out a type of relationship to insure that their marriages would last longer than those of their parents? Probably all of these reasons are valid.

Generally speaking, cohabitants report less satisfactory relationships with parents while growing up than do noncohabitants (Lautenschlager, 1972; Yost and Adamek, 1974). This point of view is expressed by psychiatrist Murray Bowen:

It is my hypothesis that college students who live together do so as an escape from, or a compensation for, an unsatisfying emotional relationship with their own parents. . . . As a consequence, the present generation distance themselves from *their* parents and escape into other relationships. In contrast to others who are more goal oriented, they are more relationship oriented. They are more sensitized to rejection and hurt, and they spend more time thinking about, and working on, their relationship with others. . . . These are all relationship-oriented students, with some degree of emotional cutoff from their own families, who act out the same relationship orientation in "living together" (or later in marriage) without achieving goal-oriented lives (Bowen, 1973, p. 3).

Socioeconomic Status

There does not seem to be any consistent relationship between the socioeconomic status of parents (as measured by educational level, occupation, and family income) and the tendency to cohabit (Macklin, 1974; Trost, 1974). Some of the couples come from low socioeconomic status families, some from middle, and some from high status families. Certainly, cohabitation is not limited to students and intellectuals from upper-middle-class families. The poor have cohabited outside of marriage for generations before the practice became common among middle-class people.

Demographic Considerations

There does not seem to be any consistent relationship between the size of the community from which students come and their tendency to cohabit. Neither is geographical region alone a consistent determinant of the tendency to cohabit (Edward and Stinnett, 1974; "Family Life," 1975).

Scholastic Variables

Most studies show that *cohabiting students are more likely to be majoring in the social sciences and humanities than in other disciplines.* Cohabiting males are less likely to be enrolled in the physical sciences than are noncohabiters. Cohabiting females are less likely to be in education than are noncohabitors. However, *there does not seem to be any significant difference in academic performance between cohabitants and noncohabitants* (Kieffer, 1972; Peterman et al., 1974). Their grade point averages are similar.

Religion and Values

Religion does seem to be an influential factor. *Cohabiters are less likely to attend church and are less likely to indicate any current religious preference as compared to noncohabiters* (Arafat and Yorburg, 1973; Cannon and Long, 1971; Driscoll et al., 1972; Peterman, 1974). Most of the students who cohabit at college are no longer active in the church. *Jewish students have a higher rate of cohabitation than do either Catholic or Protestant, but the highest percentage of cohabitation is among those with no religious preference at all.*

Those who cohabit may be described as more liberal in their lifestyle and values than those who do not. There is a strong emphasis on personal relationships and humanism and a firm rejection of the old "thou shalts" and "thou shalt nots" (Macklin, 1974; Trost, 1975c; Ward, 1975).

Description of Experiences

Beginnings

Quite typically, couples who cohabit drift into the situation without ever making a conscious decision to do so (Montgomery, 1975). One Columbia coed describes the beginning of her cohabitation experience in this way:

We began studying together . . . then I made his dinner before we started. Then we came back and I made him coffee. At first, I let him out. Then he let himself out, then he stayed and I made him coffee in the morning. Then he went shopping for groceries and in a week he was here all the time (McWhirter, 1973, p. 207).

The unplanned, almost unintentional way in which couples start cohabiting led one coed to remark: "People fall into it" (McWhirter, 1973). If and when any conscious decision is made, it is precipitated by an external force such as graduation, a room change (a roommate moves out), or an unexpected pregnancy (Macklin, 1972b).

Living Arrangements

A large number of students who cohabit also maintain their own separate rooms in a dorm, a fraternity or sorority, or in an apartment with others. This is done for several reasons: to keep parents from finding out about the cohabiting arrangement, to serve as a place to live if the relationship doesn't work out, to allow the person to see friends, or to have a place to study or to store belongings. Most go back to their rooms once a day to pick up messages, mail, belongings, or to visit or study (Macklin, 1972b).

Many cohabiting couples share their living quarters with other persons or another couple (Olson, 1972b). Because of joint living quarters, about a fourth of cohabiting couples at the University of Texas reported that lack of privacy and lack of space was a matter of concern for them (Shuttlesworth and Thorman, 1975).

Some students report difficulty in finding quarters, but rarely do they encounter landlords who refuse to rent because they are living together unmarried. In other localities, more often in smaller, more conservative communities, landlords hesitate to rent to unmarried couples. Some landlords try to enforce conventional morality. Others won't rent to any unmarried students because the students often don't stay very long. For this reason, students do not always tell their landlord who is sharing an apartment and who isn't. Because of frequent comings and goings, landlords are hard put to find out.

The most common pattern at Cornell was for the woman to move into the man's room in an apartment or house which the male was also sharing with other men or another couple. Less often, the man moved into the woman's living quarters. Either way expenses were shared by several persons. Usually, each heterosexual couple had their own bedroom. Living arrangements were usually not jointly arranged until the couple had been cohabiting for over one school year. Even then, couples hesitated to arrange a single joint living space. Usually, the man arranged to have other apartment mates who were willing to have a girl move in (Macklin, 1972b).

The older they were, the more likely were Cornell couples to be living alone in an apartment or house. Freshmen couples were likely to share a dorm room in a coed building, since they were required to live on campus the first year. Men and women were placed in segregated floors, wings, or suites, with some living in

*"Well, so long, Jeff, and give my regards to
the little woman you're living with."*

Drawing by Mankoff; © 1980 The New Yorker Magazine,
Inc.

the same corridors. But since students could
entertain someone of the opposite sex in their
rooms, this policy made almost continuous
cohabitation possible (Macklin, 1972b).

Finances

*In most situations, the total pooling of finances
does not occur.* As a matter of principle and because of economic necessity, the female usually pays her share of the expenses and maintains her own separate finances (Kahn et al.,
1972). Most couples maintain a high degree of
flexibility in the handling of money and in
deciding who is responsible for what expenses. In a study at the University of Texas,
cohabiting couples, without exception, held
part-time jobs. Most students received money
from parents in addition to earnings, and part
of their contributions generally were used to
defray joint expenses. A third of the couples
reported that insufficient money was a problem. Disagreement over money management,

however, was not frequently mentioned
(Shuttlesworth and Thorman, 1975).

Sex Roles

To what extent is there sex-role equality and
flexibility of roles among cohabiting couples?
When cohabitation involves persons who
consciously reject standard sex roles and concepts, it is quite possible to break down old
double-standard sexist habits. Certainly, "cohabitation often creates an awareness of a liberating potential for females" (Whitehurst,
1974b, p. 3). Most cohabiting women maintain jobs and some degree of financial autonomy. Some have their own cars, separate
friends, and the rights to a private life. But
commonly, *couples tend to slip into conventional
modes of behavior* (Stafford et al., 1977). A study
at American University in Washington, D.C.
revealed that the women were primarily responsible for most household duties. *A comparison of the cohabiting couples with married couples, however, revealed some trend for cohabiting
couples to divide more evenly the responsibility for
household tasks and to be more satisfied with this
divison of labor* (Kahn et al., 1972). Other research indicates that couples usually do many
chores such as the laundry or shopping together, but there is still a tendency for the
woman to assume the responsibility for
household chores (Stafford et al., 1977).

In some situations, there is as much or
more male dominance, exploitation of the female, and segregated sex roles as in some marriages. One student reported to the author
that she had moved out of her boyfriend's
apartment because he expected her to cook
and clean for him and his two male companions. She complained bitterly that after supper, which she cooked, he and his two friends
would move into the living room to watch
TV, leaving her to do all the dishes. The men
never picked up after themselves, made their

Most cohabiting couples divide expenses and responsibilities.

own beds, or assisted in any of the household chores. In a study at Illinois State University, several female students complained that one of the reasons they discontinued their cohabiting experience was that it was too much like a monogamous marriage, with the responsibilities for cooking, washing, and cleaning house and typing papers for the male partners (Huang, 1975). One woman stated that her man left her daily for hours to play basketball or to ride motorcycles with other men, and when he came back to the apartment, he was ready for dinner and sex. In this instance, the woman also paid for rent and groceries and supported the man when he was broke. In other cases, three females were pregnant and decided to keep their babies, but only one male took care of the hospital bills. The other two men felt it was the

female who should take birth control precautions.

It is evident that *living in an unmarried state does not insure complete sex role equality*. In some respects, the female is even more at a disadvantage than in marriage. Because of the tenuous relationship, she may feel she has no right to make demands. Whitehurst describes the dilemma of women in double-standard relationships:

Females entrapped into a double-standard relationship in cohabitation are at a double disadvantage; on the one hand, they are powerless at the hands of the male, who tends to define the nature of the relationship and lay out rules unilaterally. On the other hand, a woman in such a relationship [allows] . . . her life to be defined by men and is not likely to demand much. Evidence of the inability to demand things may be seen in the inability to get a man to marry . . . Power, in these relationships runs rampant in favor of the male. . . . It is, at any rate, hardly equality. Cohabitation can as well be an expression of the worst form of sexism in which nearly complete denial of personhood and rights of one person by another occurs (Whitehurst, 1974, pp. 1, 2).

Of course, whether or not exploitation occurs will depend upon the persons involved. Two people who consider themselves equal partners in all ways have the potential of creating a flexible relationship where neither is burdened by the demands of living or by the expectations of the other.

Sexual Relationships

The sexual relationships of cohabiting couples do not seem to be too different from those of married couples. One report indicated that cohabiting couples had intercourse on the average of four times or more per week as compared to three times or less per week for married couples (Kahn et al., 1972). But greater frequency is also quite common for newly married couples, so it is doubtful if this finding is significant. There is a high incidence of **fellatio** and **cunnilingus,** but these forms of sexual stimulation are also on the increase in marriage (Kieffer, 1972). Practically all couples use some form of contraception, with the majority using the pill.

A few couples do not have any sexual intercourse at all during their first weeks or months together (Simmons and Winograd, 1972). Macklin (1974) found that nearly 10 percent did not have intercourse for the first three months. In these instances, certainly sex could not be said to be *the* focus and reason for the relationship. A few couples were not really very well acquainted before they started living together under the same roof. Others needed time for the relationship to grow and mature before sex became a part.

Most couples desire sexual exclusiveness, so that sexual monogamy is the rule rather than the exception (Kahn, 1972). A few couples even *demand* sexual exclusivity as a condition for the continuation of the relationship, and they feel that going outside the dyad is sufficient grounds for dissolution of the arrangement. There are also a few persons who demand complete sexual freedom to have intercourse with others as a condition of living together. One author reports considerable upset, crying, and tears when such an arrangement was forced on the woman by a dominant male (Huang, 1975). More often, couples claim that extracohabitant sexual activity should be allowed, but in actual practice, they restrict themselves so that sexual exclusivity is maintained (Montgomery, 1975).

It must be emphasized that, in most cases, sex is but a part of the total involvement of the couple who seek complete intimacy. As one young man insisted: "We are not [just] sleeping together, we are *living* together." In most instances, of course, sex is a very important and satisfying part of the total intimate experience. Sixty to 90 percent of cohabiting couples (the percent-

age varies with the study) report that their sex life is satisfying (Kahn, 1972; Macklin, 1974).

The Nature of the Relationships

Patterns of Relationships

One of the most important considerations is what the relationships mean to the couples involved. Actually, there is no single pattern, no set meaning which can be applied to all cohabiters. Any one relationship may fall along a continuum from friendship to substitute marriage. For purposes of analysis, the relationships may be grouped into five basic types (Storm, 1973).

The convenient, temporary, transient relationship without commitment is found in only a small minority of situations (Ridley et al., 1978). In this arrangement the couple may be living together for practical reasons: to save money, because each needs someone with whom to share an apartment, or for more personal reasons; i.e., in order to have a friend to live with, to have sex with no strings attached, or because it is exciting or fun. Where sex is involved, it may not be exclusive. Each person feels free to go out with others. The arrangement is considered temporary: for the remainder of the semester or until one person decides to leave. When members of a couple are asked what their relationship means, they reply: "We're good friends" or "we're just roommates."

The second type of relationship may be classified as *an intimate involvement with emotional commitment.* The majority of cohabiting college couples, especially the younger students, place themselves in this category. Couples describe themselves as having a strong, affectionate relationship (Macklin, 1973a). The majority consider dating others as "out of bounds," so consider themselves as "going steady." While there is a strong commitment to one another, there are no permanent, long-range plans for the future or for marriage. Couples consider their relationship to be satisfactory for the present and intend it to go on, but when asked if they have any plans for marriage, they usually reply, "Heavens, no!" They are content to maintain a "wait and see" attitude about the future, and the majority do not consider themselves married in any sense of the word (Macklin, 1974).

The third type of relationship is one as *a testing ground for marriage, or as a* **trial marriage** (Berger, 1971). In this type of relationship, the couple are highly committed to one another and are consciously testing themselves and their relationship to determine the advisability of marriage. Sometimes they want to find out how they like living together with someone over a long period of time or to determine their individual aptitudes for marriage. At other times they want to test their compatibility as a couple to see if they are suited to one another. Usually couples whose relationships have grown to this point are older, or in their last year or so of college, and are more ready and *willing to think about a more permanent* future. Studies at the University of Georgia showed that a fourth to a third of cohabiting couples considered their relationship a testing ground for marriage (Storm, 1973).

The fourth type of relationship is one that couples consider *a logical step before marriage.* In this arrangement, the couples are completely committed to one another and to marriage and are living together in the interim. They see no reason to wait to cohabit but consider their situation only an interlude until they are able to take the last step.

The fifth type of relationship is *cohabitation as a nonlegal, voluntary substitute for marriage* (Trost, 1975b). Such relationships involve only a minority of couples. A few older cohabiting couples are already married to someone else, and separated but not divorced. Others have been married—unhappily so—and have become very skeptical about the viability of legal marriage. Others have seen

their own parents' marriages end unhappily. Others simply feel that legal marriage is too drastic a step to take, that it is unnecessary, or that it is destructive to real love and intimacy. Such couples can offer numerous and strong legal or ideological arguments as to why they do not believe in marriage: it's no longer valid; it's too hard to get divorced; it forces people to stay married after love is gone; it forces them into established patterns and sex roles; it destroys freedom and individualism; if marriage is not strong enough to keep people together without legal ties, it's no real marriage anyhow, and other arguments (Greenwald, 1970).

Male-Female Differences

One of the problems of cohabitation is that men and women may look upon the relationship differently (Kieren et al., 1975). The relationship is very often male initiated, yet undergraduate males more often than females see it as a transient relationship without commitment or, if an intimate involvement, as a means of sexual gratification but with no commitment to marry. Undergraduate females more often than undergraduate males consider cohabitation the equivalent of an engagement for marriage and an interlude marriage with marriage as their goal (Jedlicka, 1975; Newcomb, 1979).

Studies at the University of Colorado showed that females who had the unhappiest adolescence and a high need for their partners were those most likely to report a greater commitment to marriage. Often, the male partners completely rejected this need of their partners and showed little respect for them—a situation that would make one have serious doubts about the future stability of these living-together relationships. The authors conclude:

Not only did living-together couples disagree as to what the relationship meant to them, they came to it for differing reasons. . . . If the females' commitment to marriage resulted in pressure on the male, he might respond to it by finding a new mate for the living-together arrangement. Of course, pressure might lead to marriage; but if no changes occurred in the strengths of positive feelings and the degree of reciprocity of feelings, the chances for a happy and lasting marraige would be low (Lyness et al., 1972, p. 311).

In actual practice, collegiate males cohabit for shorter periods of time and with more partners than collegiate females, indicating that these young males are interested in avoiding long-term liaisons. Research at the University of Hawaii indicates that one of the reasons is that *males and females progress to higher levels of commitment at different rates*. It's not that males are less interested in commitment that might lead to marriage; they are as interested, but at older ages than are females. Older males are more willing to consider cohabitation as marital commitment than are younger males (Jedlicka, 1975).

Other Problems

Cohabiting couples soon discover that they cannot escape problems by avoiding legal ties. If the members of a couple are at all committed to one another, problems arise that are strikingly similar to those of young marrieds. Other problems arise out of the peculiar set of conditions under which the couple live (Croake et al., 1974).

Parents

The number one problem of undergraduate cohabiting couples is parents. The majority of undergraduate couples do not tell their parents that they are cohabiting, primarily because they feel that parents will object. Couples don't want to hurt parents. Also, they are afraid parents will try to break up the arrangement, or that they will apply pressure by withdrawing support, or through rejection. As a result,

such couples live in fear that their parents will find out, they feel guilty that they are deceiving parents, or they have real regrets that they are not able to talk about their experiences with their parents. As a result, some couples develop elaborate schemes to prevent discovery. As time goes on, however, the necessity for this is becoming less and less, since more parents are accepting the fact that their offspring are cohabiting (Hudson and Henze, 1973).

At the present time, parents who find out and object don't want to be in the position of sanctioning behavior of which they disapprove, so they may either try to break up the relationship or pressure the couple to get married. At other times, parents have a strong dislike for the particular cohabiting partner. Sometimes the more the parents object, the more the romantic love of the couple is intensified, so that they turn to one another for support in striving to stay together: a phenomenon that has been called the "Romeo and Juliet effect." Those parents who share their children's confidence are usually just resigned to the arrangement. Some are understanding and helpful, offering wise counsel and guidance. Others are more concerned about appearances. One parent even offered to pay for a second apartment to maintain appearances (Macklin, 1972b; McWhirter, 1973).

Emotional

Another major category of problems relates to the emotional involvement and feelings of individuals concerned. *A minority of individuals complain about overinvolvement and a consequent overdependency, a feeling of being trapped, a loss of identity, the overpossessiveness of their partner, or a lack of opportunity to participate in other activities or with other friends.* Without their realizing it in the beginning, these persons found themselves deeply enmeshed in relationships for which they were not emotionally prepared or which were not emotionally satisfying and fulfilling. Once involved, many felt trapped and did not know how to escape, especially if they were concerned about going back on commitments already made or about hurting the other person (Shuttlesworth and Thorman, 1975).

In a few instances, individuals have the feeling that they are being used or exploited by the other. In other cases, individuals are jealous of their partners involvement in other activities or relationships. In still other instances, one of the major worries is concern about the future and the uncertainty of not knowing what to expect. Sometimes the strain of uncertainty builds up to the point of pushing couples into marriage before they had intended. In other cases, the strain is relieved by breaking off the arrangement (Beck, 1972).

It should be emphasized, however, that while a few individuals indicate that these problems cause them a great deal of trouble, *the majority indicate few or no emotional problems.* (Macklin, 1972b).

Sexual

The great majority of cohabiting couples report that their sex life is satisfying. When there are problems, they are similar to those married couples report: different degrees or periods of sexual interest, orgasm dysfunction, fear of pregnancy, vaginal irritations or discharge after intercourse, discomfort during intercourse, or impotency. (Macklin, 1974). (See chapter 15 for a full discussion of these sexual problems.)

Effects and Implications

Beneficial Effects

One of the concerns of students and professionals alike is the effect of cohabitation on those involved. Is cohabitation helpful or harmful? What are the consequences? *Surveys of those who are cohabiting, or who have cohabited, indicate an affirmation of the experience.* More than half of Macklin's (1972b) initial sample at Cornell rated their relationship as "very successful." Only 4 percent indicated they regretted being involved in cohabitation. Students at the University of Texas often mention companionship, sexual gratification, and economic gain as the three most important positive consequences (Newcomb, 1979).

In explaining why they felt cohabitation was a wise thing for them, *numerous students mentioned that it fostered their personal growth and maturity* (Wells and Christie, 1970). Students reported that they had achieved a deeper understanding of themselves and of their needs and inadequacies, an increased knowledge of what is involved in a relationship, clarification of what they wanted in marriage, and increased emotional maturity and self-confidence. One said," I learned not to commit myself too soon. " Another remarked, "Because we have coped with problems and come out top side, I have more faith that we will be able to do so again" (Macklin, 1974). Throughout these student evaluations is the feeling that cohabitation has fostered growth and maturity. One student writes:

Love is defined in terms of the notion of shared growth. . . . Mutual growth should be an ultimate goal in any union. Nonmarriage unions are made by individuals who want to grow together.

Negative Effects

In spite of the fact that a majority of cohabiters felt that the experience had been beneficial, *there were a minority who very much regretted the experience.* Some began cohabiting without really knowing the other person very well at all. A number said: "If I had known that, or if I had really known him (or her), I certainly wouldn't have wanted to live together."

There are some students who have been deeply

hurt or even emotionally devastated by cohabiting. These minorities show up in student counseling centers or in the offices of family relations experts. In some cohabiters, there's a gradual buildup of fear and insecurity arising out of the fact that their companion could leave tomorrow, leaving them rejected and depressed. One woman explained:

At first I agreed to live together because I thought we would grow closer together and would be married. It didn't work out that way. He never mentioned marriage and got angry when I brought it up. His indifference finally got to me so I moved out. I feel guilty and sorry about the whole thing. Living together is not for me (Knox, 1975, p. 74).

Dr. James Rue of the American Institute of Family Relations feels that the female is especially vulnerable because of a double standard. If the relationship does not succeed, some women feel used and compromised. Or they develop a reputation among men: "If they know you sleep with somebody, they think you'll sleep with everybody." And of course there is the obvious anxiety about pregnancy, in spite of contraception (Likkick, 1971).

Even though there has been a steady decline in guilt among both males and females who engage in premarital sexual intercourse, *there are still some cohabiters who can't avoid the feeling that they are "living in sin"* (Whitehurst, 1974a). Many develop anxiety because of the attitudes of parents or of society. Many students hate to deceive parents but feel they must, so they live in fear that parents will find out. Sometimes the fear arises in relation to professional goals. Some employers take a dim view of hiring cohabiting, unmarried persons. One senior woman who was negotiating with a local school board for a position was fearful that the board would not hire her if they found out that she was living with a man to whom she was not married. The collegiate environment is generally supportive of cohabitation, but once students graduate, some discover that a particular group may not be so tolerant. It takes very strong-willed people to buck the mores of a group. As a result, some couples who don't want to marry end up pretending to others that they are married.

There is real concern among family life experts that cohabitation will prove to be counterproductive for those who aren't ready for the experience. *One fear is that some persons will be pushed into marriages for which they are not ready.* Some students will feel obliged to marry because they have lived together. Sometimes it is parents who force the decision once they find out what has been going on (Rice, 1981).

Another fear is that those who go from one short experience to the other will find only superficial relationships that are disappointing. Will these persons become cynical and despair of developing really lasting and permanent relationships? This is happening to some students.

One question being asked relates to the growth of the individual. *To what extent will cohabitation limit individual growth and the development of identity?* Do youths need to become persons in their own right before they develop identity as couples? Insecure, unsure persons who enter into cohabitation out of emotional need may develop further dependency rather than autonomy. Will the process of social maturation be impeded by cohabitation so that marital success becomes less likely? While individuals are learning to get along in a family setting, some will miss the opportunity to get to know many persons of the opposite sex and to develop the capability of picking and choosing a mate from many eligibles.

Effect on Marriage

At the present time, however, there is no conclusive evidence to show that nonmarital cohabitation will lead to healthier, happier marriages or that it will result in worse marriages (Jacques and Chason, 1979; Ridley et al., 1978). One writer predicts that those who cohabit will have more unstable marriages than those who do not (Boren, 1973). Whether this prediction will turn out to be true or not still remains to be seen. *If cohabitation pushes some persons into marriage prematurely, or if it pushes them into marriage with an unsuitable person, these marriages will be less happy.* When asked what they would do if the woman became pregnant, a number of cohabiting couples indicated they would want the female to have an abortion: others said they would get married. Yet marriage because of pregnancy has a very poor prognosis of success (Reiner and Edwards, 1974). If the research of Lyness (1972) and colleagues turns out to be generally true—that the more insecure, unhappy cohabiters are the ones who are most likely to marry early—this fact in itself would result in less stable marriages.

There is no evidence that the majority of cohabiters generally do not desire to marry at some time or that cohabitation will replace marriage for most (Edward, 1972; Hassett, 1977). Most cohabiters still want to marry, but not yet. If the example of Sweden is any indication of what is to come, one effect of cohabitation is to delay marriage (Cherlin, 1979; Trost, 1975a; Trost, 1978). If this happens, the median age of first marriage should rise, a fact in itself that should contribute to marital success.

There are numerous examples, of course, of individuals who have been prevented from marrying an unsuitable person by living together first. In such instances, cohabitation has served a useful purpose in mate sorting. But *living together before marriage is no guarantee that subsequent marriage will be successful* (Rosenblatt and Budd, 1975). One couple lived together two years and were then married; six months later they were divorced. Another couple had regular and satisfying sex relations for almost a year before marriage, only to discover after marriage that the male developed impotency. The point is: cohabitation

is no guarantee against marital failures. If problems arise in the relationship, it is easy for the couple to separate, so they may not develop problem-solving skills at all.

A number of questions remain unanswered. *All that can be said with certainty now is that cohabitation has been helpful to some and hurtful to others.* It hasn't solved all the problems in marital preparation or mate selection but than neither has marital education or traditional dating and courtship. Since the numbers cohabiting before marriage are growing, the phenomenon seems here to stay, so that much more research needs to be done before the results can be analyzed completely.

Legal Implications

Whenever cohabitation becomes a more permanent way of life for some, numerous legal complications arise. Since common law marriages have been abolished in approximately two-thirds of the states, *most state laws do not contain adequate methods for dealing with nonmarital cohabitation.* For example, it is not possible to claim the other as a dependent on one's income tax; health insurance policies taken out by one will not cover the other; only a legal wife can get maternity benefits through most hospitalization policies; there are no marital deductions for gift and estate tax purposes, and no consistent and well-defined legal rights of children to child support or inheritance (Newcomb, 1979; Randall, 1979).

Since the case of Marvin v. Marvin in 1979 in California the courts have begun to recognize that persons can be unmarried and still have legal rights (Myricks, 1980). For example, the courts can infer a contract from the fact that two people lived together, even if there is no marital certificate or verbal agreement. This means a court may compensate a person for the value of services rendered in a "living together" relationship. A cohabitant may be entitled to one-half of the accumulated property, and "palimony" may be awarded for rehabilitation purposes (Kay and Amyk, 1977; Myricks, 1980).

Conclusions

At the present time, only a minority of students are cohabiting outside of marriage. Others would like to but haven't yet. The following questions should be helpful in examining attitudes and feelings concerning cohabitation (Jackson and Jackson, 1973).

First, and most important, what is the meaning attached to the relationship? Is it to be a temporary relationship for convenience? Is it to be considered a deep emotional involvement with commitment? If the latter, what type and extent of commitment has been made? Is it a testing for marriage, an arrangement while waiting to marry, or is it to be a more permanent substitute for marriage?

Second, what living arrangements will be made? Will either person maintain his or her own living quarters in addition to the joint quarters? Will arrangements include other persons sharing the same quarters? What arrangements can be made to insure privacy? Will rental units be in one name or in two or more names? If leases are required, in whose name(s) are they to be drawn? What provisions are made if someone moves out? Will the remaining persons be expected to assume the entire financial burden? What furniture and equipment are needed? To whom will they belong and what will be done with them if the couple separate? Is a joint automobile needed or desirable? To whom will it belong? Who will pay for it, register it, insure it, or buy gasoline?

Third, what are the financial arrangements? Who will pay for what? Are all expenses to be shared or only part? Where will the money come from? Will everyone be expected to work, to ask parents for money, and to contribute financially? How will the money be handled? What accounts will be set up and in whose names? Who decides on joint expenditures and by what process?

Fourth, what roles will each person perform, especially in relationship to household maintenance and chores? Who will do repairs, clean, cook, mow lawns, do laundry, do shopping, or pay the bills?

Fifth, what is the understanding with regard to sexual relations? Will the arrangement include sharing the same bed and having sexual intercourse? If so, what method(s) of birth control will be used and by whom? Does the arrangement include sexual exclusiveness, or the freedom to have intercourse outside the relationship? What are the couple's feelings, needs, and desires with regard to the method, frequency, and type of sexual expression? Are there any problems that need to be revealed? If pregnancy should occur, how will it be handled?

Sixth, will parents be told about the arrangement? What are their feelings; what will be their reactions if they are told or find out? What are the pros and cons of being completely honest and above board with parents?

Seventh, what understandings are developed with respect to friends and social life? Will the two people seek social life as a couple, as separate individuals, or both? Will dates be allowed with others of the opposite sex, or does the relationship exclude all dating with others? If they split temporarily for vacations or in the summer, will they go out with others while not at school?

Eight, if one or the other want to break off the arrangement, what provisions are made for doing so? (This is especially troublesome with regard to any belongings jointly owned or any expenses that might continue, such as rent on a leased apartment.)

As can be seen, cohabitation raises a number of questions and issues. If couples are able to work these out ahead of time, the possibilities of misunderstandings, conflicts, and unnecessary difficulties can be reduced.

A problem recently developed in the hitherto untroubled relationship between the young, unmarried couple, George Tucker and Jenny Abrams. The couple had been living together for more than a year in secrecy from their parents. A short while ago Jenny's father Harry found out. The revelation created almost unbearable tensions among the three. Harry had been subsidizing Jenny's apartment and living expenses. The fact that he might also be helping to support George clearly exacerbated his feelings—confused and troubled—about their living together. After a few angry discussions Jenny persuaded George and her father to participate in an encounter discussion group at a neighborhood church. The subject, of course, was nonmarital cohabitation. Two professional psychologists in attendance introduced the group and invited the participants (ten) to offer their opinions. The following dialogue excerpted from the discussion gives the trio's differing points of view. Drs. A and B follow with two separate analyses.

George is a young man in his early twenties. Earlier in the discussion he had said that a sexual relationship was a private affair. "Sex is not all there is to living together," he added. "My relationship with Jenny is not just a sexual thing. By living with her I've learned about her, about myself, and what it's like to be intimate with someone in a close relationship. I don't think that sex ought to be a marriage trap. Why can't we just enjoy one another's company without worrying about the future? Jenny and I care about one another and that's good enough for me."

Jenny is tall, well-dressed, about twenty-two. She teaches at a local high school. "I love George very much," she began, "but I've had a very moralistic upbringing as far as sexual intimacy is concerned. I've kept myself aloof from the 'in' thing for a long time. Yet I'm human; I want what other women want. I want someday to marry George. My father thinks that I'm naive for living with him, but I want our marriage to be a success. If we can't make it as unmarrieds, then we won't be able to make a marriage."

Harry is a very successful real estate manager. He considers himself a liberal, yet he is troubled. "Look, I feel as if I'm trespassing, but I'm worried," he said. "I've always been close to my children. Until recently I've felt that my daughter and I had a close relationship. I'm really upset that my daughter wouldn't confide in me. To me that's a sign that she knew something might be wrong with her experiment."

Jenny: I don't think that I did anything so wrong. Some things are personal, even between father and daughter.

Harry: Why did *I* have to discover everything, that you were living with George? If nothing is wrong with the relationship why hide it from me?

Jenny: Because I knew when you found out that you would lay a guilt trip on me. My relationship with George is personal. I'm not naive about what I'm doing.

Harry: Well, it seems to me that you and George are not very sure about whether or not you want to be married. I realize that the times have changed and so has morality. But part of growing up is learning to be responsible and to make commitments.

George: We're not engaged. Jenny and I. We're living together because we love one another. It may not last, I don't know. If not, then we'll split.

Harry: I still say that a parent's job is to know what's happening to their children. I'm responsible for you and I don't want you to be hurt.

ANALYSIS

Dr. A: The romantic feelings that Jenny feels for George are understandable. Romance is Jenny's motive for living with George. She also considers living together a test to see if they would be happy in marriage. I'm not certain, but George's relationship with Jenny may well be as Harry implies, just a fortuitous opportunity. George had said that he just wanted to enjoy the relationship without commitment. She, on the other hand, had expressed an interest in eventual marriage.

Cohabitation presents a problem of motives. Love and sexual need may conceal a power game—or hidden motives. They also sometimes mask the real problems of living together in marriage. Harry's concern—aside from the moral issue—is that his daughter not be hurt. He wants some evidence of marital commitment. He is concerned about Jenny's risk and seems to be asking why take that risk. He is also understandably hurt that his daughter was not able to confide in him.

Dr. B: It seems to me that the crucial issue is the difference in motives between George and Jenny and the possible superficiality of the relationship. George appears to have consciously planned the relationship around avoiding a commitment. Jenny seems to accept his feelings, but she hopes for marriage. Neither mentions anything about the practical problems which arise in living together such as housekeeping roles, finances, and other things. Jenny accepts her father's financial support, but resents his intrusion into her life. The real question is: What is the meaning of this relationship to the persons involved?

QUESTIONS

1. Why do couples say they live together?

2. Discuss George's and Jenny's motives for living together. What are some possible outcomes because of differences in their motives?

3. Why are some persons not willing to make commitments even while living together? Is noncommitment indicative of personality faults and personal hangups?

4. Can you be in love without commitment? Can a relationship last without commitment? Discuss.

5. Is nonmarital cohabitation just another form of male exploitation and chauvinism? Why or why not?

6. How do you react to Harry's point of view and concerns? Are his fears justified. Why or why not?

7. Discuss how you feel about students not telling their parents that they are cohabiting.

CHAPTER

4

Maturity and Marital Readiness

CHAPTER OUTLINE

Age and Time Factors

Social Experience

A Mature Concept of Love

Motivation and Maturity

Vocational and Educational Readiness

Parental Readiness

Marriage While in College

Conclusions

Dialogue

Based on the research findings we have, we believe there are a number of factors that are important in determining whether or not individuals are ready for marriage: age, how long two people have known one another, the amount of dating and social experience, their concept of love, their motivation for marriage, their readiness and willingness as to assume the responsibilities of marriage, their readiness for sexual exclusiveness, their emotional independence from parents, their level of educational and vocational aspirations and the degree of their fulfillment, and the readiness and willingness of their parents for them to marry.

The subject of collegiate marriage is also an important one. How many students in different types of colleges are married and going to school? How do the majority of students feel about collegiate marriage? What are the disadvantages and advantages of campus marriage? How does marriage affect one's grade point average? How is marriage affected if both partners are going to school? What are the common problems and adjustments that married students face? How many parents contribute financially to their married children's expenses? Should married people accept financial help from their parents? What are some of the important factors to consider in dealing with the problems of pressure and lack of time? How are masculine-feminine roles affected by collegiate marriage? What about having children while going to school? These are some of the questions relating to collegiate marriage with which this chapter is concerned.

Age and Time Factors

Age and Marriage Stability

One important consideration in evaluating marital readiness is age. Those who marry young have more marital tensions and less satisfaction than those who marry when they are older (Lee, 1977). The younger the couple at marriage, the greater the likelihood the marriage will end in divorce. The divorce rate of those who marry in their teens, for example, is two to three-and-one-half times the rates of those who marry in their twenties (Bumpass and Sweet, 1972; U.S. Department of Commerce, October 1971). There are a number of reasons: the older couple are usually more emotionally mature, have more social experience, have better jobs and income, and in many other ways evidence greater readiness for marriage. This direct correlation between age and marital stability, however levels off for men at about age twenty-seven, at which time the decline in divorce rate slows down considerably. For women, the divorce rate declines with each year they wait to marry until a gradual leveling off occurs at about age twenty-five (U.S. Department of Commerce, July 1970). *Therefore, strictly from the standpoint of marital stability, men who wait to marry until at least twenty-seven years of age, and women who wait until about twenty-five, have waited as long as practical to maximize their chances of success* (Barry, 1970; Lasswell, 1974; Miller and Siegel, 1972; Nye and Berardo, 1973; U.S. Department of Commerce, October 1971).

Age at the time of marriage is one of the most important factors in marital success.

Median Ages

How do these figures compare with the ages at which couples marry? In 1978, the median ages for first marriages were twenty-three for males and twenty-one for females (U.S. Department of Commerce, Stat. Abstract, 1980). From the standpoint of minimizing the chance of divorce, however, the ages are still about four years too young. An encouraging sign is that the median ages have been increasing. Figure 4-1 shows the trend (U.S. Department of Commerce, Stat. Abstract, 1980). In 1975, 47 percent of males and 35 percent of females who were between eighteen and thirty-four years of age were still single (U.S. Department of Commerce, Stat. Abstract, 1980). But the percentage remaining unmarried beyond the age of thirty-five had declined during the previous several years, indicating that more and more couples were marrying later in life.

Age Differentials

What effects do age differences between the husband and wife have on marital stability? Age differentials seem to have a negligible effect, even though there may be a problem created late in life. Statistically, a wife much younger than her husband is more likely to be widowed for a longer period than a wife who is closer to her husband's age or a little older. Also, one might expect more problems in sexual adjustment and in finding satisfactory companionship, but whatever problems are created by age differentials, these do not

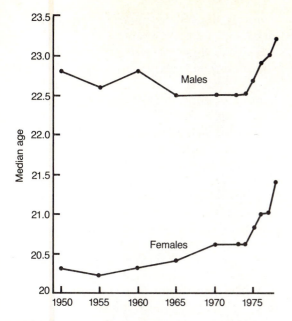

FIGURE 4-1. *Median age at first marriage in the United States   (Source: Adapted from U.S. Department of Commerce, Bureau of the Census,* Statistical Abstract of the United States, 1980 [*Washington, D.C.: U.S. Government Printing Office, 1980*], p. 83).

to really know one another before marriage (Hicks, 1970). Of course, the actual time required will vary with circumstances. Some couples have known one another from childhood before they start dating; they've grown up together and know one another's families and friends. Such couples do not require as much time between beginning dating and marriage as those who meet for the first time as complete strangers, who know absolutely nothing about one another or their families, and who have to get acquainted "from scratch." If two people come from different backgrounds and see one another only occasionally, it may take years before they are really acquainted. Certainly, it takes less time to know a person whom one is seeing everyday or with whom one lives prior to marriage than an individual whom one dates only sev-

seem to affect substantially the stability of these marriages (Bumpass and Sweet, 1972). Figure 4-2 shows the age differentials between husbands and wives in March 1977 (U.S. Department of Commerce, Stat. Abstract, 1979). As can be seen, the trend seems to be for women to marry men slightly older than themselves (U.S. Department of Commerce, February 1971). It is still true, however, that the age difference between spouses is inversely related to the age of the bride. The younger the bride, the greater the age difference between her and the groom (Rice, 1981).

Length of Acquaintance and Engagement

Another important factor in marital stability is that couples give themselves sufficient time

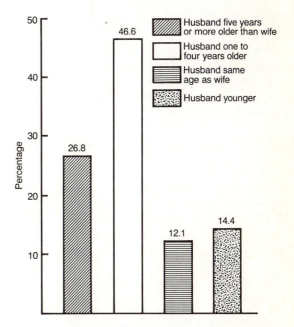

FIGURE 4-2. *Differences between ages of husband and wife in the United States, March 1979 (Source: Adapted from U.S. Bureau of the Census. Department of Commerce Statistical Abstract of the United States, 1979 [Washington, D.C.: Government Printing Office, 1979]).*

eral times a month. Extensive periods of separation also interfere with two person's getting to know one another and adjusting to one another. Ordinarily, couples who are older and more mature when they start going together will require less time to make decisions and adjustments before marriage than will couples who are quite young when they first meet. Also, previous dating experience helps in mate selection and in the adjustment process.

Landis and Landis (1973) made a study of 122 student couples who were engaged and found that the average time from first date to marriage was approximately three years. This period of time was broken down into divisions as shown in table 4-1.

As can be seen, the average length of engagement was thirteen-and-one-half months from the beginning of formal engagement until marriage. Paul Landis (1970) reports that his students favored engagements of not more than four to six months. Most experts feel that the longer the period of dating and engagement, within reason, the better the chances of marital success (Saxton, 1972). The significant factors, however, are the age and maturity of the person, the total period one has dated, the length of time one has gone with the particular person, and the intensity of the relationship, not just the length of engagement as such. Certainly, there is ample evidence to show that those who shorten the total dating and courtship process have less chance of marital success than those who give themselves ample time (Saxton, 1972). So couples who run into serious difficulties or questions about their relationship can partially answer the questions by giving themselves additional time.

If couples don't know one another very well, they may appear on the surface to be getting along fine. Schulman (1974) found that couples who overidealize one another seldom have any conflicts. Their relationship is too superficial for them to know whether or not there might later be any problems. Either extreme—many problems or no problems—is an indication to the couples that they need more time in order to become better acquainted.

Social Experience

Number of Friends

Generally speaking, the more friends of both sexes one has before marriage, the better the chances of successful marriage (Burgess et al.,

TABLE 4-1. *Average length of time from first date until marriage for 122 engaged couples*

Stage of Courtship	Period of Time in Months
Casual dating	5
Dating steadily	8
Had an understanding	8
Had been formally engaged for this many months at time of study	6
Average time yet to go until the wedding	7½
TOTAL	34½

Source: Judson T. Landis and Mary T. Landis, *Building a Successful Marriage,* 6th ed., © 1973. Adapted by permission of Prentice-Hall, Inc., Englewood Cliffs, N.J.

1971). Those who have few intimate associates or who are social isolates are less likely to marry happily. The suggestion is that those who are unable to establish and maintain satisfactory social relations before marriage, and outside the marriage, are less likely to be able to get along in marriage (Renne, 1970). It is obvious also that the fewer acquaintances, the narrower is the field of potential mates.

Length of Dating Experience

It is particularly disadvantageous for a person to start dating one person exclusively soon after dating begins. Among youth of lower socioeconomic status, the earlier a girl or boy begins to go steady, and the more steadies they have had, the more likely is early marriage and the less likely the marriage will succeed (Call and Otto, 1977). It is important to emphasize that early dating as such is not a disadvantage. Higher socioeconomic status youths start dating earlier than lower socioeconomic status youths, yet the former marry later. The reason is that higher socioeconomic status youths proceed at a slower pace from dating to marriage, whereas the lower socioeconomic status youths proceed quickly from beginning dating to marriage. Therefore, the crucial factor is not on the age when dating begins but on how rapidly the young person advances to serious dating, to going steady, to engagement, and to marriage (Bartz and Nye, 1970). Thus, it is the length of the dating experience prior to marriage which may have a crucial impact on subsequent outcome.

One other important aspect needs to be recognized. It is helpful if the individual feels that he or she has had enough dating and social life before assuming the responsibilities of marriage. Most adolescents want a period of carefree fun after emancipation from parents: a chance to come and go as they please, to go to new and different places, to make new friends or enjoy themselves with their present ones. If they marry before they have

a chance to do these things, some regret it afterwards and wish they had waited. Later in marriage some of these individuals seek to "have the fling" they feel they were deprived of earlier.

Social Participation

There is an advantage also in participating in a variety of social organizations. Those who participate in a number of activities and groups generally have happier marital adjustments than those who do not (Burgess et al., 1971). Participation helps one to meet new people and to develop social skills, poise, and the ability to get along with others: all traits that are needed in happy marriage.

A Mature Concept of Love

Five Elements of Married (Conjugal) Love

While love is considered the most common basis for marriage in U.S. culture, it is seldom understood. Yet most individuals contemplating marriage are very concerned about love. They want to know what is "true love," because they consider this sufficient justification for marriage.

This acceptance of being in love as an important criterion of whether two people get married or not places a great burden on the couple to gain considerable knowledge of the nature of love. This section seeks to help the reader gain this clearer understanding by discussing five different elements of **conjugal (married) love: romantic love, dependent love, erotic love, friendship love,** and **altruistic love.**

Romantic Love

Romantic love has been described as "a profoundly tender or passionate affection for a person of the

Mature married love includes romance, sex, friendship, need, and care.

opposite sex" (Stein, 1973). It is marked by *intensity of feelings:* so much so that a glance, a smile, a brushing of the hand of one's beloved may arouse strong feelings of warmth and affection. In such a heightened emotional state, it is common for the individual to find *renewed emotional sensitivity* to other things or persons. The individual may be more sensitive to the beauties of nature; the glories of a small flower, the song of a distant bird, the hush of night. Other persons may notice a more kindly attitude and tone. Individuals report that they "become alive again," and have started "to really feel for the first time in years." If the love is mutual and fulfilling, there is a great *sense of joy, ecstasy, exhilaration, and well being* (Critelli, 1977). Along with ecstasy and joy is the feeling that *love alone*

makes life worthwhile and nothing else matters. As expressed by Robert Browning (1895):

All the breath and the bloom of the year in the bag of one bee:
All the wonder and wealth of the mine in the heart of one gem:
In the core of one pearl all the shade and the shine of the sea . . .
In the kiss of one girl.

Because of these feelings, there is a *desire to be together* so that one can continue to enjoy the pleasure of love. When apart, lovers almost become possessed by thoughts of one another. As one man reported: "When Julie and I are separated on weekends, I can't think of anything else. All I do is think of her: what she looks like, the things we've talked about, the good times we've had, and the love we've shared together." It is common also for romantic love to result in *physiological changes and manifestations*: palpitations of the heart, a quickening pulse, breathlessness, trembling, a tightness in the chest, or halting speech. Loss of love can cause physical upset so that the person can't eat or sleep. The literary portrayal of unrequited or of lost love is one of a debilitated and unhappy person. There is more truth than fiction in this portrayal.

There is also a strong feeling of *sexual attraction* in romantic love, and the desire for physical contact. In such a state of passion, it is probably inevitable that romantic love is accompanied by much *idealization and adoration*. Romantic love exalts feminine beauty and virtue and manly strength, virility, and chivalry. One's love becomes the incarnation of all of those physical traits and qualities of character that are one's ideal of womanhood or manhood. Theodore Reik (1944; 1957) theorized that when individuals fall in love they do so with persons who manifest the characteristics of their ego ideal. They project these characteristics onto the other person with whom they identify (Williamson, 1972). This type of love is narcissistic, since it is really love of self, as represented in the other person.

But romantic love can also result in much *altruism and unselfishness*. It results in feelings of generosity and in wanting to shower the other person with gifts. The sense of devotion and willingness to serve and to sacrifice is often astounding. Along with this desire to give up much for the sake of love comes a *renewed feeling of self-confidence* that one is beautiful and capable and that one *can* do the impossible. Each person is thus able to feel that he or she has become a new person, handsome, or beautiful, gay, and exciting, and developing attributes that one has longed to possess. The symptoms and characteristics just described are fairly typical examples of what

happens to persons in various stages of romantic love.

According to popular tradition, women are considered to be more romantic than men. Investigation reveals, however, that men are faster to romanticize than are women (Baum, 1972; Kanin et al., 1970; Kephart, 1973). Males are much more easily attracted to the opposite sex than are females to males. They more often show a romantic interest in their partner after a first date (Lowen, 1972); they consistently develop love feelings earlier in a relationship; fewer males than females report they would marry someone they didn't love. The girl "chooses and commits herself more slowly than the male, but, once in love, she engages more extravagantly in the euphoric and idealization dimensions of loving" (Kanin et al., 1970). Thus, once a relationship develops, females more often idealize than do males. Women become more seriously involved as the relationship moves toward marriage (Bell, 1971).

For all persons, love changes over a period of time. Generally speaking, single students have more romantic concepts of love than do married students (Lowen, 1972). Nonengaged are more romantic than engaged (Spanier, 1972). High school students are more romantic than those married less than five years (Knox, 1970). Younger college students are more romantic in their concepts than older college students. In other words, concepts and ideas of love change at different stages of courtship. Love become more rational and less romantic over a period of time.

Once married, however, there is evidence that in good marriages in which love is nourished, it continues to grow. A study of couples married on the average of five years showed that one-third of the wives felt their husbands were more romantic now than when first married. Two-thirds also said they now loved their husbands more, and felt their husbands now loved them more. Ninety percent of the wives felt no decrease in love either by their husbands or themselves (Bell, 1971). It is evident, however, that couples' ideas of love changed over the years, with fewer components of superromanticism and more components of friendship, trust, cooperation, dependability, and acceptance (Driscoll et al., 1972).

The crucial question regarding romantic love is this: Is it a sound basis for marriage (Lee and Stone, 1980)? One study of married couples in a college community who had been married on the average of about two and a half years showed no statistically significant relationship between romanticism and marital adjustment. Romanticism was not generally excessive, and even in those cases where there was unusually high romanticism, marital adjustment was not lower. Rather, a slight positive correlation was found (Spanier, 1972).

Of course, the study did not measure romanticism *before* marriage. Romanticism plays a significant role in whether or not couples marry. One researcher found that a high score in romanticism was correlated with a couple saying they were in love and that their chances of marrying were good; a low score correlated with a couple saying they were not in love and that they would probably not marry (Rubin, 1970). Therefore, notions about love and romance are important factors in the development of a relationship. Romanticism brings individuals into serious male-female associations that may eventually lead to marriage. In this sense, romantic love is very functional. To eliminate romanticism before marriage would make mate selection either arranged or computerized. *"What is dysfunctional is the inability of some individuals to separate the romantic from the realistic as necessary in a real life marriage relationship"* (Mukhopadhyay, 1979; Spanier 1972, p. 486). As long as romance is also based upon real life, couples can be as romantic as they please. In fact, it adds spice to any marriage.

Some efforts have been made also to discover if there are any significant correlations between personality factors and romanticism. Are romantic persons less emotionally mature than those who are not as romantic? No, according to research by Dean (1961), but he did find that women of lower social status showed more romanticism than women of higher social status. Another researcher found that girls who feel in love with younger boys showed some evidence of maladjustment: poorer college grades and poorer scores on the Bell Personality Inventory. Overall, however, romantic love is a normal experience of normal people, not just something that the maladjusted and immature fall into as an escape from life (Kephart, 1973; 1970).

Several of the most interesting research studies on romantic love show its association with intense emotional stimulation (Brehm, 1970; Jacobs et al., 1971). Schachter's (1964) two-component theory of human emotional response says that for a person to experience true emotion two factors must coexist: (1) The individual must be physiologically aroused, and (2) it must be reasonable to interpret his stirred-up state in emotional terms. In applying this theory to romantic love, Walster writes:

We would suggest that perhaps it does not really matter how one produces an agitated state in an individual. Stimuli that usually produce sexual arousal, gratitude, anxiety, guilt, loneliness, hatred, jealousy or confusion may all increase one's physiological arousal, and thus increase the intensity of his emotional experience. As long as one attributes his agitated state to passion, he should experience true passionate love. As soon as he ceases to attribute his tumultuous feelings to passion, love should die (Walster, 1971).

There is some research evidence to support Walster's contention. Brehm et al. (1970) found that when male subjects were frightened by the threat of an electric shock and then introduced to a young coed, the threatened men experienced more attraction to the girl than subjects who were not previously frightened.

This experiment showed that emotional arousal, even from a frightening source, facilitated attraction. Perhaps this is why lovers who meet under dangerous conditions or with the threat of discovery experience greater excitement and passion than under more secure conditions. Perhaps this is why the forbidden or secret love is the more intense love.

In another experiment, male college students who were given very critical personality reports of themselves, and who were then immediately introduced to a young female college student who was warm, affectionate, and accepting, were far more attracted to her than were subjects who had been given flattering personality reports just prior to the introduction (Jacobs et al., 1971). The experimenters concluded that the upsetting reports stimulated the emotions of the males, so they responded more readily to the female student's positive feelings. When the female acted cold and rejecting, however, a dramatic reversal occurred. The students who were upset by critical personality reports disliked the female far more than did those who had received flattering reports. Apparently, the individuals' upsets were easily transformed into dislike.

It is not just negative emotions that influence romantic love, it is positive ones as well. Sexual arousal produces intense physiological changes in the body, which facilitate attraction (Walster, 1971). Valeris (1966) found that males labeled as most attractive the photographs of those seminude girls which had aroused them sexually. If there were no arousal, the pictures were rejected as less attractive.

These studies emphasize the importance of emotional excitement as an important component of attraction, and of romantic love.

The more positive excitement a relationship generates, the more likely the participants are to report that they are in love. Since intense emotional arousal and excitement cannot be constantly sustained, however, if love is to endure over years of marraige it must include components other than just emotional excitement.

Dependent Love

One of the components of a durable love is dependency (Maslow, 1962). *Dependent love is that which develops when one's needs are fulfilled by another person.* In its simplest form it works like this: "I have important needs. You fulfill those needs, therefore I love you." This is the type of love the dependent child feels for his mother who feeds, clothes, and cares for him: "You give me my bottle, you keep me warm, you hold me, cuddle me, and talk to me. That's why I love you."

But is is also the kind of love that develops when intense psychological needs of adults, which have been denied in the past, are now fulfilled by a lover (Viorst, 1979). An adolescent boy who is coddled and babied at home and who finds a girl who acknowledges his masculinity, may be overcome with love for her. The good, reliable, hard-working man may be captivated by an alert woman who recognizes his potential to be a playful and reckless lover. "To the person who has been deprived of such rewards, an intelligent, artistic, witty, beautiful, athletic, or playful companion may prove a passionate and absorbing joy" (Walster, 1971). This is why men or women frequently fall in love with those who meet important needs that have not been met by others.

Erotic Love

Erotic love is sexual love (Koller, 1974). This type of love is aroused when one is attracted sexually to a member of the opposite sex. It is the biological, sensual component of love relationships.

According to Freud (1953a), love and sex are really one and the same thing. Freud defined love as "aim inhibited sex," as a yearning for a "love object"—for another person who could meet one's sexual needs. Love, to Frued, was narcissistic in that it was measured by the extent to which the love object could satisfy one's sexual aim.

Freud emphasized two important elements of the sexual aim of adults. One element is physical and sensual. In men, this aim consists of the desire to produce sexual products, accompanied by physical pleasure: in other words, the desire for ejaculation and orgasm. In women, the desire is for physical satisfaction and the release of sexual tension (orgasm) but without the discharge of physical products (Freud, 1953b).

The second element of the sexual aim in adults is psychical; it is the affectionate component. It is the desire for emotional satisfaction as well as for physical release. Freud emphasized that a normal sexual life is assured when there is a convergence of the affectionate current and the sensual current, both being directed toward the sexual object and sexual aim. The desire for true affection and for the release of sexual tension combined are the underlying normal needs that motivate the individual to seek a love object. Freud (1953b) also felt that once an appropriate love object was found that this diminished sexual strivings, so that—ordinarily—diminished yearnings resulted in seeking only one love object at a time.

While Freud emphasized that love and sex are the *same thing*, other writers would say that love and sex are two *separate entities*, that they are not identical, and that a definite distinction must be made between them (O'Neill and O'Neill, 1972). This was the view of Theodor Reik (1944; 1957), who said that love and sex are different in origin and nature. Sex,

according to Reik, is a biological function whose aim is the release of physical tension. Love stems from psychic needs and seeks affection and emotional satisfaction.

There are those today who feel that romantic love arises when sexual expression is denied (Wilkinson, 1978). This "sexual blockage" emphasizes that romantic love is most felt toward those who play "hard to get" and that once sexual involvement happens, romantic love declines. This view is similar to that in romantic stories of the troubadours who distinquished between love and sex. Love was a yearning for psychic gratification that only the beloved could give; sex was an impersonal desire that anybody of the opposite sex could gratify by physical actions. The troubadours fretted lest sex abate love's fervor. The Romans sometimes wondered if love would not blunt their sexual pleasures. The Victorian ethic implied that sex was unworthy of those who were truly in love. One consequence was that those who truly loved one another did not feel it proper to have passionate sex.

In modern western society, there has been considerable fusion between love and sex. In his book, *Love and Orgasm*, Lowen points out that love increases the pleasure of sex:

Sex and love are not distinct and unrelated feelings. Sex is an expression of love. . . . When the feeling of love is reduced to a minimum, the erotic desire is superficial and mostly confined to the genital organs. In this circumstance the pleasure of discharge is low and neither satisfying nor fulfilling (Lowen, 1972, p. 18).

Fromm writes:

If the desire for physical union is not stimulated by love, . . . it never leads to union in more than an orgiastic, transitory sense. Sexual attraction creates, for the moment, the illusion of union, yet without love this "union" leaves strangers as far apart as they were before . . . (Fromm, 1956, p. 46).

Other writers emphasize that sex is important as a mutual confirmation of the love relationship in marriage (Rice, 1978a). It says to the other person, "I love you." In this view, sex can be a physical expression of the deepest feeling. Whichever view the individual holds, the majority of youths today want sex with affection, not without it, and insist that love and sex should go together.

Friendship Love

Another important element of love is friendship. This implies a type of *love between those with common bonds of friendship or concern.* This type of love may exist between those who are good companions because of similar interests; it may arise out of respect for the personality or character of the other (Rubin, 1973); it may include a profound element of care for one another (Winthrop, 1972); or it may exist because of kinship ties (Swensen, 1972). In other words, close friendship and companionship are certainly not limited to relationships with a lover, since they are common between those of the same sex. But research has shown that the most comprehensive and profound friendships are between two lovers whose relationship includes a friendship type of love. While romance may exist without friendship, love in marriage becomes more complete and enduring with it (Miller and Siegel, 1972; Rosenbaum, 1979).

There is some evidence to show that loving and liking are separate phenomena and may be measured separately (Rubin, 1970). But this research defines love only in romantic terms. Other research emphasizes that as marital love matures over the years it contains more and more elements of friendship (Driscoll, 1972).

In other words, it is helpful if a couple not only love one another but also like one another. In fact, liking has been called the key to loving. Liking in a relationship brings re-laxation in the presence of the beloved. It is a stimulus for two people to want to be with one another. It is friendship in the simplest, most direct terms.

Saxton writes: "The companionship component of love, although the least dramatic, is probably the most commonly and frequently experienced (and thus, in a sense, the most important) aspect of married love, despite mass media emphasis on romance and sexuality" (Saxton, 1972, p. 35).

Recent investigation has also shown that *trust* is an important element of intimate relationships and is vitally necessary to the maintenance of love (Larzelere and Huston, 1980). Couples most able to trust one another are those who show a high level of self-disclosure and commitment to one another. They know they can believe one another, can depend upon one another, and are loyally committed to one another.

Altruistic Love

Altruistic love is unselfish concern for the well-being of another. It means to invest one's psychic energies and abilities in caring for another individual and in seeking what is best for the other person (Coutts, 1973). By nurturing someone else and doing all one can to make the other person happy, the individual finds meaning and satisfaction in his or her own life. This is the type of love that parents show for their infant when they assume the responsibility for the care, and growth of their child (Fromm, 1956). This is the love of the New Testament in which the love of God is bestowed on creatures unconditionally, not because they deserve it. This is love "in spite of" rather than "because of." In marriage, altruistic love includes acceptance of one's mate as a fallible human being without conditions or demands to change or conform to the other's image (Crosby, 1973). Its chief components are care, concern, and self-giving.

One of the chief exponents of altruistic love is Erich Fromm (1956). To Fromm, love is an activity, not a passive affection; it is a "standing in," not a "falling for." In the most general way, the active character of love can be described by stating that love is primarily *giving* not receiving (Lester, 1979). To Fromm, giving is not "giving up" something, being deprived of, sacrificing. It is giving of oneself: of that which is alive in one, of one's joy, interest, understanding, knowledge, humor, even sadness. Thus, in giving of one's life, the other person is enriched.

In addition to the element of giving, Fromm emphasizes four basic components of love. These are *care, responsibility, respect,* and *knowledge.* Fromm uses the illustration of a woman who says she loves flowers, but forgets to water them. It would be difficult to believe she really loves her flowers. *"Love is the active concern for the life and growth of that which we love"* (Fromm, 1956, p. 22). Where concern is lacking, there is no love. Care and concern also imply *responsibility,* not as a duty imposed from the outside but as a voluntary act in which one responds to the need (primarily psychic) of the other person. Love also depends upon *respect,* which is not fear and awe but awareness of the unique individuality of the other and concern that the other person should grow and unfold as he or she is. Respect is possible only where freedom and independence are granted. It is the opposite of domination. And finally, love also requires *knowledge* of the other person, in order to see his or her reality and overcome any irrationally distorted picture.

Complete Conjugal Love

The most complete conjugal love (love between two married persons) includes elements of all of the types of love already described. Western culture emphasizes *romantic love* as *the* basis for mate selection. Because it is so highly regarded, and operates functionally in this respect, its importance cannot be minimized. When based upon reality, romantic love is *not* dysfunctional as a basis for marriage.

Dependent love is valuable as a basis for marriage when it involves the mutual dependency of two emotionally mature adults. Marital integration takes place to the extent that each person meets the needs of the other. Unless people need one another, and fulfill one another's needs, why get married? The difficulty arises when the needs of one person are excessive, so that neurotic, possessive dependency becomes the basis for the relationship. In such a situation, one person does most of the giving, the other most of the receiving. Most persons need to receive as well as give if they are to remain emotionally healthy. Those who enjoy giving without receiving become either martyrs or masochists, with neurotic needs to assume either role.

Erotic love is an important part of conjugal love. Certainly, sexual attraction is an important beginning, and sexual satisfaction strengthens the marriage bond. If there is repeated sexual frustration, love can be replaced by anger and hostility. Ordinarily, therefore, love and sex in marriage are interdependent. A loving relationship becomes a firm foundation for a happy sex life. A fulfilling sexual relationship builds the total love of the couple for one another.

Friendship love or love based upon companionship is an enduring bond between two people who truly like one another and enjoy one another's company. It can endure over all the years of a long marriage. Alone, it is not enough reason for marriage for most people, but, for most, it is an important ingredient of a comprehensive love.

Altruistic love adds genuine concern and care to the total relationship. It is more of a way of behaving than a way of feeling and is the active means by which the individual shows he or she truly cares (Swenson, 1972). It allows the person expressing it to gain satisfaction through serving another, and it allows the person receiving it to be cared for and loved for his or her own sake.

A mature concept of love includes all five of these elements.

Motivation and Maturity

Motives

The motives for marriage are extremely important in marital success or failure. Some people get married for the wrong reasons. The number one reason for marriage while still in high school is *pregnancy* (DeLissovoy, 1973). It is hard, however, to make a success of marriage forced by pregnancy (Reiner and Edwards, 1974). The couple has to deal with a "triple crises"—adolescence, early marriage, and parenthood (LaBarre and LaBarre, 1968). As a result, about half of adolescents who marry because of pregnancy are divorced within five years.

Other people marry to try *to escape*—an unhappy home, school failure, personal insecurity, or an unhappy social adjustment with peers (Rice, 1981). But people take their unhappiness and problems with them into marriage, so escape is futile. Sometimes people marry *to try to hurt others*—parents, an ex-boyfriend or girlfriend, or even themselves. One way people have of showing contempt for themselves is to marry a completely unsuitable partner.

Other individuals want *to prove their worth or attractiveness.* Sue grew up under the constant criticism of her older sisters. They made her feel that she was homely, that no man would ever look at her, that she would never marry, and that it was her responsibility to stay home to look after their sick mother. But Sue was determined to prove her sisters wrong, so when she was twenty she married a man seventeen years her senior, not because she loved him, but to prove to herself that some man did want her and that she didn't have to remain single. Such situations are not unusual. Some men marry to prove their manhood, to prove that some woman wants them, or to show that they are not homosexuals.

It is not unusual for people to believe they are in love with those who have helped them. Clients often "fall in love" with their counselors, patients with their doctors, parishioners with their clergy, or students with their teachers. Such persons mistake *gratitude* for love.

Similarly, very paternal or maternal type people are attracted to those for whom *they feel sorry.* Men marry women who seem defenseless, alone, in trouble, or who need a strong shoulder on which to lean. Such marriages build the egos of the men involved. Or, some women are invariably attracted to men who are maladjusted and problems to themselves and others. One woman married an alcoholic because she thought he needed her and she wanted to take care of him.

In a society that overromanticizes marriage, and overcriticizes staying single, it's hard to resist the temptation to get married simply *as a means of avoiding condemnation* (Bell, 1971). When her friends are announcing their engagements and getting married, the individual woman feels left out if she doesn't do likewise. She begins to feel something is wrong with her, and to prove there isn't she gets married. Or well-meaning friends and relatives ask the eligible bachelor: "When are you going to get married? Why don't you find yourself a nice wife and settle down?" To marry because *other* people think one should, because other people are, or because one is talked into it or is *pressured into it*, makes success more difficult (Koller, 1974). Sometimes people never really make a conscious decision about marrying; they just drift into it and marry because it's expected.

Willingness to Assume Responsibility

Many young marriages fail because the couple is not yet able or willing to assume responsibility. The couple who is suddenly faced with the financial responsibility of supporting an infant child as well as itself has to be quite ready to assume this responsibility at the time of marriage or it may grow to regret the marriage and resent the child. Many young marriages could work if the couple didn't have children right away. Unfortunately, the younger the people are when married, the sooner they have children (U.S. Department of Commerce, July 1978a).

Lack of responsibility is evidenced in other ways. Typically, "young married wives . . . complained that their husbands had 'not settled down' and 'were running around too much'" (DeLissovoy, 1973, p. 248). "One man who had seven jobs in less than a year was accused by his wife of neglecting her for his boyfriends and of having an affair with her best friend" (Reiner and Edwards, 1974, p. 386). One researcher wrote:

Essentially it was clear that the husbands remained "boys" in a number of ways. They went "out" with former "buddies," stayed after school to play basketball and other sports. They were active in part-time work and socialized beyond working time. The realization that a married status required a different orientation to life came slowly (DeLissovoy, 1973, p. 248).

As far as young wives are concerned, many feel that they are "too tied down" or "too busy with the baby," that they are "taken for granted," "left out," and "lonely." Wives who are not employed are often marooned during the day in unfamiliar neighborhoods. Some young mothers seem to resent their children as evidenced by the fact that they are "impatient and intolerant" of them. Other wives show their immaturity in their uncertainty about what to expect in their marriage.

Two researchers wrote: "One wife asked if she could change her husband; another wanted to know if the husband would "settle down" as her sister's husband did; and a third wondered, "Should I expect my husband to love our child" (Reiner and Edwards, 1974)? It is evident from these comments that marriage and parenthood require a great deal of maturity and that many young couples have difficulties only because they haven't yet grown up enough to assume the responsibilities required.

Readiness for Sexual Exclusiveness

Ordinarily, monogamous marriage in our society means that husbands and wives desire sexual exclusiveness (Duvall, 1971). While many youths are quite tolerant of premarital sexual intercourse, most are insistent upon the marital fidelity of their mate. Marital readiness for the majority of couples requires an attitude of sexual exclusiveness.

Emotional Independence

Another indication of marital readiness and maturity is emotional emancipation from parents. Individuals who still seek emotional fulfillment primarily from their parents are not yet ready to give their chief loyalty and affection to their spouse, which is necessary for a successful marriage. No wife or husband wants to play "second fiddle" to an in-law or to compete with the in-law for the affection of their child. (See chapter 14 for additional information on in-law relationships.) Of course, sometimes a young husband or wife is so emotionally insecure that *any* affection the spouse gives to parents is resented. In such cases, the problem is not caused by the spouse's immaturity but by personal insecurity or feelings of inadequacy.

Vocational and Educational Readiness

Aspiration Levels and Marriage

There are some significant relationships among socioeconomic status, educational-vocational aspirations, and the age at marriage. The following correlations are especially important.

The lower the educational and vocational aspirations of youths, the more likely early marriage will occur (Bartz and Nye, 1970). Those adolescents who have no post-high school educational plans are likely to feel that since they have completed their education, marriage is the next possibility (Duvall, 1973). A study of graduate students in engineering and science showed that the higher their educational level, the longer after college graduation before they married. Once married, the higher their educational level, the longer after college graduation they began their families (Perrucci, 1968). One study of women in their twenties showed that those who had career aspirations married later in life than those who planned to be housewives (Cherlin, 1980).

The lower the socioeconomic status of individuals the more likely early marriage will occur (Carlson, 1979). This is due to lower educational and vocational aspirations, to high rates of premarital pregnancy, and fewer sanctions against marriage at young ages (Moerk and Becker, 1971). In some rural areas, for example, or in some ethnic groups, marriage at early ages is expected (Hogan, 1978; Woodrow et al., 1978).

Marriage and School Dropout

Not only are low aspiration levels associated with earlier marriage, but some reverse correlations are also true. *Those who marry young are more likely to drop out of school than those who marry later, so that the younger the age at first marriage, the fewer the number of years of schooling completed* (Carter and Glick, 1970; Marini, 1978).

While the dropout rates of married college students are not as high as those of high school students, marriage adds to pressures to drop out of school, especially for wives (American Council on Education, 1972; Feldman, 1973; Waite and Moore, 1978; Watley, 1971; Watley and Kaplan, 1971; Wegner and Sewell, 1970). Of course, increasing numbers of college women are determined to stay in school even if married, pregnant, or a mother. Divorced women are also strongly motivated to remain in or go back to school (Feldman, 1973).

Males who marry while in high school are less likely to go on to college than single men (Kerckhoff and Parrow, 1979). Those who get married while already in college, however, are determined to stay in school, even if only part-time. Their motivation increases because they become more interested in getting an education to support their family (Bowman, 1974).

Effects of School Dropout

The results of dropping out of school to marry or because of marriage are most often negative. The husband or wife who drops out is seriously limiting his or her earning ability and income, which, in turn, creates marital problems and instability. If the wife drops out of school to put her husband through college, as some women do, there is a possibility that her husband will "grow away from her" and that an intellectual gap will be created between them. Even more important, as the years pass, the wife may resent more and more the fact that she gave up her education for marriage. She may need to work for financial reasons, or because of a need for personal fulfillment, yet she is limited in what she can do because of an inadequate education.

Personal Mobility

One of the unfortunate results of premature marriage is its interference with personal mobility. When persons are relatively free of responsibilities, they have the option of changing major fields of study if in school or of changing jobs if working. If they're married and supporting a family, by the time they discover who they are and what they want to become, they are already "locked in" doing a job just because it's a way of making money.

Parental Readiness

Not only is it helpful if the couple are completely ready for marriage, but it is of benefit if the couple's parents are also willing for the marriage to take place. Parental approval has been found to correlate with marital happiness and success, whereas disapproval is related to marital failure. While parental approval does not insure marital success, it helps.

Sometimes parents object to the person their son or daughter is marrying. At other times they object to the timing of the marriage and would prefer that the couple wait. At other times, the parents' only objection is that they don't really know the other person. Whatever the reason for the objection, parents can create ill feelings or real difficulties for the couple. It is wise, therefore, for the couple to try to get their parents' cooperation and blessing. If they cannot, and if they decide to marry against their parents' wishes, they need good reasons for taking a step that may so

drastically affect their relationship with their families (Bowman, 1974).

If the parents do not object to the individual but only to the rushed marriage, or to the particular timing of the wedding, it is helpful if the couple will give themselves and their parents more time to work things out. One way to do this is to take their parents into their confidence almost from the beginning of the courtship, then when the plans to marry are announced, the news comes as no great surprise. If the couple go together for some time without parental knowledge, then suddenly spring a wedding announcement, the parents are caught off guard and are more likely to raise objections.

Marriage While in College

Incidence

In 1980 there were 11,631,000 students enrolled in institutions of higher education (U.S. Department of Commerce, 1980). This did not count military service personnel or others in institutions who were not enrolled as college students. Of the total enrollment in 1978, ages eighteen to twenty-four, 9 percent were married. The percentage of college students, who are married has decreased considerably over the past 10 years, (U.S. Department of Commerce, October 1979).

Figure 4-3 reveals some interesting trends (U.S. Department of Commerce, 1979; U.S. Department of Commerce, 1973). Far greater percentages of part-time students were married than full-time students, indicating that married students had considerably more difficulty in being able to attend full time. Fewer married females attended college than did married males (American Council on Education, 1972; Watley, 1971; Waltey and Kaplan, 1971).

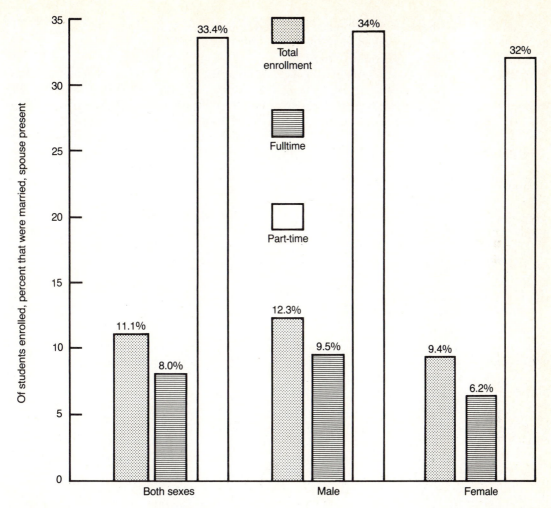

FIGURE 4-3. *Percentage of undergraduate students 14 to 24 years of age who were married, by type of enrollment, October 1972 (Source: Adapted from U.S. Bureau of the Census, Department of Commerce.* Current Population Reports, Series P-20, no. 257, November 1973, p. 18.)

Student Attitudes Toward Collegiate Marriage

Actually, the majority of young college students do not want to be married while in college. Even in 1965, only a minority of University of Minnesota freshmen thought that college women *should* marry while in college.

These results were somewhat at variance, however, with those obtained when more than three thousand students in eighteen colleges were asked: "If you found the one you hoped to marry eventually, would you marry while an undergraduate" (Landis and Landis, 1973)? Half of both the men and women said they would marry if they were undergraduates. Apparently, there is a difference between the *preferred time*, as asked of the University of Minnesota freshmen, and an *acceptable time*, as asked of students of all college classes. Generally speaking, however, students today are not as anxious to marry while in college, as were those in the 1960s.

Satisfactions

Campus marriages like any others have the possibility of contributing to the welfare and happiness of couples or of making them miserable. Happy collegiate marriages offer the same satisfactions as any marriage: love, companionship, sexual fulfillment, emotional security, acceptance, increased status, and the sharing of responsibilities.

Already married students were asked: "Knowing what you now know, would you marry before finishing college if you were unmarried?" Three-fourths of the couples said they would marry in college if they had it to do over again (Landis and Landis, 1973). The remainder said they would not or were uncertain. A majority of the students at Syracuse University who were married did not regret their marriages (Chilman and Meyer, 1966). Only one in eight students at a Kansas university regretted being married (Bergen and Gergen, 1978).

There is some evidence that marriage stimulates increased maturity and a sense of responsibility (Kelley, 1974). Most couples who marry young indicate that marriage forces them to grow up much faster. Many admit that they were immature and irresponsible when first married but that marriage has helped them to become more adult. Of course, if a couple is too immature, marriage will only add to their difficulties, not solve them. Therefore, it is probably wise to say that *marriage will contribute to personal and social maturity, but a couple has to be responsible and old enough to start with or marriage may also destroy their relationship.*

Achievement and Grade Point Averages

One of the arguments that is sometimes used in favor of collegiate marriages is that married students get better grades than do single students. To what extent is this true? Before a categorical answer is given, the following facts need to be considered (Bayer, 1972):

1. Students who come from lower socioeconomic status families are more likely to marry early than those from higher status homes.
2. The more academically able the student, the less likely he or she is of marrying early.
3. Students whose aspirations are to earn an associate degree are more likely to marry early than those who aspire to get a four-year bachelor's degree.

With these considerations in mind, it would seem probable that since those who marry in college are more likely to be of lower socioeconomic status, academically less able, and have lower aspirations, that they would earn poorer grades than would single students. One research study of married male students seemed to bear this out (Hepker and Cloyd, 1974). It was also evident, however, that males made better grades after marriage than they did before, even though their overall grade point averages never came up to those of single students. The married students, age twenty-four and older, showed the greatest improvement in grades, followed by the single students, age twenty-four and older, indicating that there was an association between age and academic performance. Also, husbands did better academically if their wives were sympathetic and supportive of their roles as students.

There are no up-to-date and reliable studies at the present time that measure the effect of marriage on the grade point averages of college women. It is certain, however, that one result of marriage is that a large number of them drop out of college, either to work to put their husbands through or to bring up a child. From this point of view marriage has been a handicap to the academic and vocational progress of these women.

Marriage itself does not guarantee better academic performance. One must go beyond the fact of the marriage and examine the husband-wife relationship and the manner in which the couple have been able to integrate the roles of student and spouse. The more successful the marriage, the more positive the effect upon grade performance. No doubt, the results of any study are somewhat biased because some of the married students drop out of college along the way, leaving those who would tend to have more successful marriages and would be better students.

One Student Versus Both Students

Is it "easier and better" if both the husband and wife are going to school or if only one is attending? A study of couples at a midwestern university showed the pressures of both marriage and undergraduate enrollment led to lower quality marriages. The marriages were of higher quality if the husbands were not enrolled in school. Similarly, the marriages were of higher quality if the wives were not enrolled in school. If one or the other was already enrolled, however, the quality of marriages were significantly higher if the other also enrolled. The lowest quality marriages were those in which the wife only was enrolled either part or full time. Those marriages in which the husband only was enrolled were of average quality (Bergen and Gergen, 1978).

Common Problems and Adjustments

What problems and adjustments do married students most often experience? Chilman and Meyer (1966) studied the satisfactions and dissatisfactions of married male and female un-

dergraduates at Syracuse University. Married students were concerned about shortages of time, energy, and money and about their studies. More of the married women than men indicated problems in sex adjustment and "other" problems. Overall, however, greater percentages of married women than men indicated no *serious* problems. The married women had greater numbers of problems than married men, but evidently the women felt their problems were not as serious.

Money

Money was a serious problem to almost a third of the married males in the study just cited (Chilman and Meyer, 1966). The problem was not so much in the handling and allocation of money, as in the lack of money. Lack of money is the number one problem as revealed in most studies. Typically, the largest source of income is the employment of the husband and wife. Other sources include contributions from families, veteran's benefits, savings, scholarships, and student loans. Couples report more tension and quarreling in their relationship when loans are a major source of income than if they are not a source (Bergen and Gergen, 1978).

One of the biggest questions arises over the issue of parental support. Some parents will not give any support. They feel that once their children are married—whether students or not—they are on their own. Seventy-five percent of the married students in one study reported that their parents were not a source of income (Bergen and Gergen, 1978). In other instances, parents contribute less support after marriage than they did before. The reasoning seems to be that since the children have assumed a more adult status, they should be assuming a greater burden of the financial responsibility. Still other parents loan money to their children for college, whether the children are married or not. Only a small percentage of married students live wih their parents and receive help in this way (U.S. Department of Commerce, November 1979).

Similarly, the attitudes of student couples about accepting financial help from parents will vary. Some couples want to be on their own and will not accept parental assistance even if offered. Other student couples expect as much or more help than before. Actually, whether accepting a subsidy is desirable or undesirable will depend upon the total situation. Can the parents really afford it? Does accepting financial assistance mean losing some autonomy and the right to make one's own decisions and to run one's own married life? Will one or the other of the husband or wife have to drop out of school if assistance is not forthcoming, or are other sources of help available? Are the couple doing all they can— consistent with the task of being students—to support themselves? Will added employment damage their grades or their health? Does accepting a subsidy mean the couple will be hindered from growing up and accepting their own responsibility, i.e., will they grow too dependent upon parental help? It is helpful if couples discuss financial needs and resources *before* collegiate marriage takes place, both with each other and with parents. If financial resources aren't adequate, this may become one of the most important reasons why marriage while in school should be postponed.

Pressure and Lack of Time

Married students are under considerable pressure from conflicting sources. In addition to the usual pressures upon married couples to give sufficient time and energy to 1) earning a living, 2) performing the homemaking tasks, 3) maintaining the marriage, and 4) raising children (if such are present), they have the added burden of academic work. Not only is going to school a full-time job in itself, but the lack of flexibility in course registration means that everything else has to be arranged around the class schedule. It is often difficult to fit gainful employment into the class schedule and still have sufficient time to do the chores around the house, in addition to having some social life as a couple. Typically, the average married couple do not participate as much in the extracurricular activities of college as do single students.

Role Reversal and Flexibility

It is easier to work things out if both the husband and wife are completely flexible in their roles. Traditional roles with the husband as breadwinner and the wife as homemaker and baby tender do not always work out in campus marriages. Sometimes traditional roles must be reversed. The wife may be the full-time breadwinner, and the student husband the primary housekeeper and baby tender. Studies of wives who returned to school while the husbands worked showed the majority of husbands were willing to give verbal and moral support to their wives but were not willing to give direct help with household responsibilities. Some husbands would not help at all with any chore and saw their wives schooling as a threat to the marital relationship (Berkove, 1979; Hooper, 1979). A few more husbands were willing to help with the children than were willing to do housework. If either the husband or wife rebels against assuming part of the other's traditional role, this places a double load on the other person, which is understandably resented.

The Question of Children

Most college couples do not want children before graduation. Children add that extra burden of responsibility that makes an otherwise plausible marriage quite difficult. Not only do children make early marital adjustment itself more difficult, but, more than any other factor, they prevent the couple from completing their education. Most frequently, it is the wife's education that suffers, although many husbands too have to drop out of school after a child is born because of the added financial requirements of the family. Even if the wife has completed her education and is a full-time working mother, she is faced wtih the necessity of leaving her infant child during the day so that she can work. For these reasons, most college couples give careful attention to family planning and to contraception.

Conclusions

One of the functions of research on marriage is to discover what people ideally might do to maximize their chances of marital success. An examination of research findings relating to marital readiness shows the following factors

to be important to marital success (additional ones are discussed throughout this book):

- Being old enough
- Going together long enough to really know one another well before marriage
- Having considerable social experience before marriage (as measured by the number of friends, the total length and amount of dating experience, and participation in social groups)
- Having a mature concept of love
- Getting married for valid reasons and not because of pregnancy, as a means of escape, to try to hurt someone, to get even, to prove one's own worth, or because of social pressure
- Willingness to assume the responsibilities of marriage
- Readiness for sexual exclusiveness
- Being emotionally independent of parents so that one can look to one's mate for emotional fulfillment and can put loyalty to him or her before loyalty to parents
- Being educationally and vocationally ready for marriage
- Parental readiness and willingness for one to get married at this particular time

What people expect from marriage and what they find may be two conflicting things as shown in these autobiographical statements from an unhappy couple explaining why they think their marriage failed.

Peter, son of an Arabian mother who married an American salesman, grew up in Norfolk, Virginia. His father and mother were divorced when he was seven, and he rarely saw his father afterward. His mother kept up her nursing career to support Peter and a younger brother and sister. Though the younger children were successful in school, Peter was not especially hard-working and barely managed to graduate from high school.

Peter: Next birthday I shall be thirty-one. It seems that growing up has been a long and painful process, and even now I'm not sure I could describe myself as a mature person. I still remember my feelings of rage—at about age five— when I discovered that most people regarded me as some sort of gypsy foreigner in a white man's country. I think I have never gotten over that feeling.

My marriage to Felicia seemed like a good thing at first, but it only lasted about four years. Although we did in fact have a physical relationship, it was not enough. After leaving accounting school, I took a clerical job while Felicia graduated from the university with a major in chemistry. I was not especially interested in studies, and I couldn't remotely think of anything at all that I really wanted to do. I had my high school certificate and some accounting training and that's all.

What went wrong between Felicia and me was my feeling that she lacked real sympathy for what I as a "third-world" outcast was up against in a white and hostile society. Her parents didn't object to our marriage in any open way, but they weren't enthusiastic about it either. I could never develop a relationship with them. Most of her friends in our neighborhood were upper-class Anglo types. She didn't really like my friends either; she thought they were vulgar.

After we had our child, she quit work for awhile and I had to hold down two jobs to make ends meet. Life was hard. I didn't feel appreciated. We argued over money a lot. I always had to remind her that I couldn't earn as much as she. In the end I walked out of the house after a big fight. We didn't speak for one week. Then she said that she was determined to get a divorce. I apologized but it was no use. We'd reconcile, fight again; reconcile, fight again. I wanted to keep the relationship but she said that she had had enough. She wanted a better life than I was able to provide her. That night I moved out.

Felicia was the daughter of a wealthy international lawyer from a distinguished family. Her mother was prominent in civic and social life. She often felt lonesome and upset by her husband's long and frequent business trips.

Felicia described her adolescence as full of turmoil, with herself the center of tension between her generous and overindulgent but sometimes aloof father and her insecure mother. Soon after Felicia's break with Peter she married a lawyer whom her family had known and had a second child.

Felicia: I was young and idealistic when I married Peter. I liked the way he laughed. He was very handsome and sexy. We had a passionate relationship and were very jealous of one another. But people stared at us a lot in public. In those days, no one could believe a girl like me would be going with an Arab. We had trouble finding places to meet. If we went to a restaurant, we felt uncomfortable even holding hands.

Of course I wanted to introduce Peter to my family. I didn't think they would exactly throw an engagement party for me, but I did hope they would like him, although I was afraid the fact the he wasn't going to college would be held against him. But the night he was supposed to come around my mother said she didn't feel well and didn't want to see him. I was hurt and somewhat bitter. My father accused me of trying to make life difficult for them and of ruining the family name. My mother asked me to tell her where she had gone wrong in my upbringing. Only my older sister was sympathetic.

Far from making me want to leave Peter, my family's general reaction only made me more serious about marrying him. I was very naive. I can see now that he was not going to satisfy me for very long. He wasn't headed for a profession, he never did well in school, and he resented my complaints that he wouldn't take responsibility. For some reason I had to do everything at home. He was always saying that I had no idea of the amount of work involved in his jobs, that he had to fight with social prejudice. As if I didn't know that. But I had to live. Our little boy had to live. Peter was overdependent and undisciplined. He hated to work and worked only sporadically, when things were really desperate. I had few friends because of him. He was always running around. So finally I rebelled. I had a college degree and could get a good job. So we got a divorce. We were just too different. It could never have worked out.

QUESTIONS

1. In what ways did Peter show that he was immature and not ready for marriage?

2. How did Peter's negative self-concept influence his relationship with Felicia? Is there any way she could have helped him?

3. Should a man and woman complete their education and be established in a vocation before they get married? What are the advantages and disadvantages of marrying before becoming settled in a vocation?

4. Why do you suppose Felicia married Peter? In what ways did she show that she was immature and not ready for marriage?

5. What factors in her family background contributed to her marital problems?

6. Would the marriage have been any different if Felicia had not had a baby? Explain.

7. What should parents do if they discover their daughter is going with someone of another race or nationality or a man whom they don't like?

8. What would you do if your parent objected to the person you were thinking of marrying?

9. What would you do if your mate insisted on running around after marriage with his or her old friends whom you did not like?

10. What could a wife do if she found that her young husband was lazy and irresponsible?

CHAPTER 5

Marital Compatibility

CHAPTER OUTLINE

Compatibility through
Homogamy and Endogamy

Compatible Needs

Compatible Personalities

Compatible Backgrounds

Compatible Attitudes and Values

Compatible Role Concepts

Compatible Interests, Activities,
and Friends

Compatible Habit Systems

Conclusions

Dialogue

Compabitility refers to the capability of living together in harmony. This chapter begins with a discussion of the meaning of **homogamy, heterogamy, endogamy,** and **exogamy** as these relate to the process of choosing a compatible mate. Are couples more compatible if individuals choose others like themselves, or is it wiser to choose a mate who is just the opposite of oneself? How do needs influence compatibility, and what combinations assure the greatest marital harmony? What personality combinations are most likely to result in a compatible marriage? How do different background factors such as socioeconomic class, race, religion, education, and intelligence influence compatibility? How do different attitudes, values, role concepts, and interests affect marital compatibility? How do habit systems influence compatibility? These are some of the questions with which this chapter is concerned.

Compatibility Through Homogamy and Endogamy

Homogamy or Heterogamy

There is an old saying that opposites attract. This is sometimes true, but does this mean that opposites make more compatible couples in marriage? No, according to the research. In fact, just the reverse is true: Two people who have similar backgrounds, needs, attitudes, values, and role concepts or who perceive their personality characteristics as similar are more likely to be compatible in marriage than are those who are dissimilar (Burgess 1971; Pickford et al., 1966; Spuhler, 1968). The tendency of individuals to choose others similar to themselves is known as *homogamy*. Those factors that couples have in common are known as homogamous factors (Eckland, 1974; Karp, 1970; Kerchkoff, 1972; Saxton, 1972).

Just the opposite of homogamy is *heterogamy*, which means the tendency to be attracted to and to marry someone different from oneself. While there may be some heterogamy of factors in actual mate selection, such as age, education, or religion, the overall tendency is towards homogamous unions and away from heterogamy in both first marriages and remarriages. Furthermore, homogamous marriages tend to be more compatible than heterogamous marriages. This fact will be explored in greater detail in the remainder of this chapter (Dean and Gurak, 1978; Dressel, 1980).

Endogamy or Exogamy

Endogamy means the practice of marrying within one's own group: religion, race, ethnicity, or social class (Cavan, 1971a; Cavan and Cavan, 1971b; Greeley, 1970; McDowell, 1971). *Exogamy* means marrying across social lines, outside one's social group (Christensen, 1971). There are strong pressures to marry within one's group, but there are also pressures to prevent endogamous marriages which are seen as too close. Thus, incestuous marriages or those involving various degrees of **consanguinity** are forbidden (Leslie, 1973). Generally speaking, endogamous marriages tend to be more compatible than exogamous ones, although there may be significant exceptions to this generality (Jaco and Shephard, 1975; Monahan, 1970). This fact will also be examined in greater detail in the succeeding discussion.

Compatible Needs

Need Fulfillment and Compatibility

One of the most important reasons people marry is to find fulfillment of needs. When needs are mutually fulfilled, dependency develops, marriage becomes more integrated, and couples experience more satisfaction with the relationship (Ammons and Stinnett, 1980; Klimek, 1979). One way, therefore, of ascertaining compatibility is to discover whether or not two people are able to meet one another's needs (Coutts, 1973).

Parallel Needs

Sometimes the needs of two people are similar. Both the husband and wife may have a high sex drive and desire frequent sex relations. Or, they may be quite affectionate and need a lot of physical contact. Two other people may have a great need for status fulfillment, self-esteem, and recognition. The type and extent of needs vary from couple to couple, but individuals tend to select mates whom they perceive to have needs parallel (similar) to their own (Burgess et al., 1971; Murstein, 1970). Sometimes, of course, their perceptions are wrong; they discover at some time after marriage that their needs aren't

alike. But if the needs of a couple are parallel, this contributes to their compatibility.

Complementary Needs

A number of years ago Robert Winch (1967) theorized that individuals tend to select mates whose needs are opposite but complementary to their own. According to this theory, the **nurturant** person who likes to care for others would seek out a mate who was **succorant**: who liked to be cared for. The *dominant* person would select *a submissive* person. In more recent years, Winch added a third aspect of complementariness: *achievement-vicariousness.* The person whose need is to achieve tends to select a person whose need is to find recognition through vicarious attainment of his or her spouse.

Winch recognized that mate selection in the United States is largely homogamous with respect to social factors such as age, race, religion, social class, education, location of previous residence, and previous marital status. These variables, however, only define for each individual a field of eligible spouse-candidates. There remains for the person to select a mate within the field of eligibles. Winch says the individual does so by seeking out a person who gives the greatest promise of providing him or her with the maximum need gratification. This person, he says, is the one whose needs are complementary.

Since Winch's original formulation, subsequent research has shown either no support (Murstein, 1972a) *or only partial support of his theory.* In many cases, similarity of need may be more compatible or functional than complementarity. Some of the newest research emphasizes that if husbands and wives fulfill their marital roles according to their expectations, this is a better predictor of marital stability than is either homogamy of needs or complementarity of needs (Karp et al., 1970).

Compatible Personalities

Homogamy of Personality

Another way of evaluating compatibility is by comparing combinations of personality traits of well-adjusted couples and of unhappy couples to try to discover what personality combinations are most compatible. Are those with homogamous traits more compatible than those with heterogamous traits? Yes, according to some research findings (Farley and Davis, 1980). One study showed that happily married couples were significantly similar to one another in such traits as general activity (drive, energy, enthusiasm), restraint (self-control, serious-mindedness, deliberateness), friendliness and personal relations. Unhappily married couples were statistically dissimilar in emotional stability and in objectivity. The dissimilarity in objectivity indicated that the mating of a hypersensitive, egotistic, and suspicious individual with a "thick-skinned," coldly objective individual caused trouble in marital relations (Pickford et al., 1966).

A study of the relationship of personality patterns of marital partners to emotional disorder indicated that when both marital partners were similar in personality patterns, they had far lower incidences of emotional disorders (Boxer, 1970). These findings suggest that divergent personality patterns can be highly destructive emotionally. A case in point is that of a dependent, submissive husband married to an aggressive, dominating woman. If the husband can't accept his dependency needs, the relationship usually develops emotional conflict and the husband-wife interaction is harmful to them both (Heer, 1974).

Another research study indicated that couples whose marriages were stable had substantially greater number of correlations of personality traits between the husband and wife than did couples whose marriages were unstable (Catell and Nesselroad, 1967). Other research found that the adjustment of married couples—as well as dating couples—was greater when they possessed the same degree of mental health (Murstein, 1971a). Other findings suggest that individuals tend to choose partners whose levels of self-esteem and self-acceptance are similar to their own. Another research study using a computer analysis of couples who had married versus couples who had not married indicated that the married couples showed significant homogamy of personality factors such as pessimism-optimism, feelings of adequacy, carefreeness-seriousness, concrete-abstract thinking, emotional stability, submissiveness-dominance, tough mindedness versus tender mindedness, trusting versus suspicious nature, confident versus apprehensive, undisciplined versus controlled, or relaxed versus tense (Sindberg et al., 1972).

The available research studies are not extensive enough to match large numbers of personality traits to show their influence on compatibility, but on the basis of available evidence, *those with homogamous personalities are more likely to marry one another than are those with dissimilar personalities, and, once married, there is some tendency for homogamous traits to contribute to compatibility and stability in marriage.*

Physical Characteristics

Numerous studies show the similarities of spouses with respect to many physical characteristics such as weight, stature, hair color, health, physical attractiveness, and other factors (Murstein, 1972c). Spuhler (1968) lists hundreds of research studies comparing the physical characteristics of couples. These studies examine more than one hundred different physical characteristics. It is evident that *individuals tend to select mates who exhibit homogamous physical traits.* But the precise effect of this homogamy on marital compatibility is not known. The fact that individuals want to marry others similar in physical attractiveness, stature, and so on is an indication that they believe that such homogamy is desirable. Also, since the physical attractiveness of others is a strong determinant of whether individuals desire to continue dating them or not, it operates as a very influential factor in the mate selection process even though it may not have any influence on compatibility after marriage.

Compatible Backgrounds

As used here, the term *background* refers to such social characteristics as social and economic class and status, race, religion, intelligence, and education. Are couples more compatible if they come from similar backgrounds? As a general answer, yes. Furthermore, individuals tend to select mates with homogamous backgrounds. Since there are exceptions to these statements, however, they need to be examined in more detail.

Social-Economic Class, Status

There is a definite and marked tendency for individuals to marry within their own socioeconomic strata. This tendency has its beginnings during dating and courtship since young people associate mostly with others of their own class (Rice, 1981). Under these circumstances it is inevitable that marriage also tends to be ho-

Couples tend to be more compatible if their backgrounds are homogamous.

mogamous with respect to socioeconomic level (Blumberg and Paul, 1975; Eckland, 1974).

In recent years, however, there has been a slight alteration in this pattern. Since World War II, college students have been less inclined to marry someone *far* removed from their own social class but have not hesitated to marry when there is only a *minor* difference in class. *While heterogamous unions with respect to class are found among the happily married, heterogamous marriages contribute more than their proportionate share of divorces, so homogamous marriages are more compatible.* One study showed that wives appear to be more affected by social class heterogamy than do husbands (Jorgensen, 1977). The status seeking wife who marries down and then discovers she would like to move up the social ladder is especially unhappy in such a marital relationship.

Race

Marriages tend to be even more homogamous with respect to race than with respect to class. Despite

a continuing increase in **interracial marriage,** it is still a rare occurence. The 421,000 interracial couples in 1977 accounted for barely 1 percent of all 48 million couples in the United States (Rawlings, 1978). Figure 5-1 shows that 30 percent of the 421,000 interracial couples were black-white marriages. Three-fourths of the black-white couples in 1977 had a black husband and a white wife.

What about the stability of black-white marriages? Figure 5-2 shows the proportions of marriages still intact after ten years. Clearly, *black-white marriages were less stable than racially homogamous marriages* (Heer, 1974).

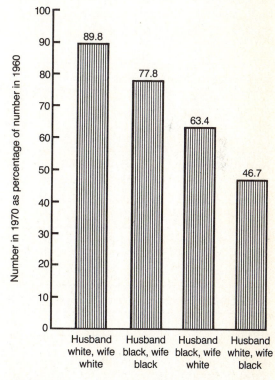

FIGURE 5-2. *Proportion of marriages still intact after ten years, by race, both spouses married only once (Source: Adapted from D. M. Heer, "The Prevalence of Black-White Marriage in the United States, 1960 and 1970,"* Journal of Marriage and the Family 36 [May 1974]: 250. Copyrighted 1974 by the National Council on Family Relations. Reprinted by permission.)*

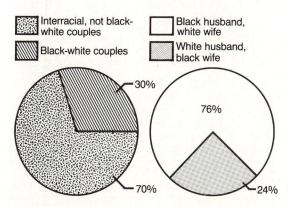

Interracial, not black-white couples
Black-white couples
Black husband, white wife
White husband, black wife

30%
76%
70%
24%

421,000 interracial couples   125,000 black-white couples

FIGURE 5-1. *Interracial (black/white) couples 1977 (Source: Adapted from S. Rawlings, "Perspectives on American Husbands and Wives,"* Current Population Reports, *Series P-23, no. 77 [Washington, D.C.: U.S. Government Printing Office, December 1978], pp. 7, 8.)*

Racial endogamy is not quite as frequent among Asians as among whites and blacks. Table 5-1 shows the percentages of Asian husbands marrying wives of other races (U.S. Department of Commerce, 1972). Table 5-2 shows the percentages of Asian wives marrying husbands of other races (U.S. Department of Commerce, 1972). The large numbers of Japanese females married to white males reflect the importation of Japanese war brides to the United States after World War II. The large numbers of American Indian females and males marrying whites suggests that there will not be many persons with 100 percent Indian heredity after several generations if the trend continues. Filipinos also seem to have a high rate of intermarriage with those of other races, particularly with whites.

Marriages of Caucasians with Asians are usually less stable than are marriages within the races. This is not universally true, however (Monahan, 1970). The state of Hawaii has the largest rates of Asian-Caucasian marriages in the United States, and little prejudice is shown against such unions (Schmitt, 1971). Caucasian males show the *lowest* divorce rates when they marry Chinese women (Vitousek, 1979). Caucasian females show the *lowest* divorce rates if they marry Japanese men. Caucasian men and women show the *highest* divorce rates when they marry Filipinos. Overall, however, interethnic marriages in Hawaii more often end in divorce than intraethnic marriages. Figure 5-3 shows the divorce rates in Hawaii for various combinations of ethnic and racial groups (Vitousek, 1979).

TABLE 5-1.   *Percentages of husbands marrying wives of other races: United States, 1970*

Race of Husband	Race of Wife						
	White	Negro	American Indian	Japanese	Chinese	Filipino	Other
American Indian	33.4	1.3	64.2	0.2	0.1	0.2	0.7
Japanese	8.3	0.1	0.1	88.6	1.1	0.5	1.3
Chinese	8.3	0.4	0.1	2.8	86.5	0.6	1.4
Filipino	24.4	1.1	0.7	3.1	0.8	66.5	3.4

Source: Adapted from U.S. Bureau of the Census, *1970 Census of Population: Marital Status,* Final Report PC(2)-4C. Table 12 (Washington, D.C.: U.S. Government Printing Office, 1972, p. 262.

TABLE 5-2.   *Percentages of wives marrying husbands of other races, United States, 1970*

Race of Wife	Race of Husband						
	White	Negro	American Indian	Japanese	Chinese	Filipino	Other
American Indian	35.6	2.3	61.0	0.1	—	0.4	0.6
Japanese	28.0	1.1	0.1	66.8	1.5	1.3	1.1
Chinese	8.1	0.4	0.1	1.5	87.8	0.6	1.4
Filipino	20.9	2.0	0.4	1.0	0.9	72.8	2.0

Source: Adapted from U.S. Bureau of the Census, *1970 Census of Population: Marital Status,* Final Report PC(2)-4C, Table 12 (Washington, D.C.: U.S. Government Printing Office, 1972), p. 262.

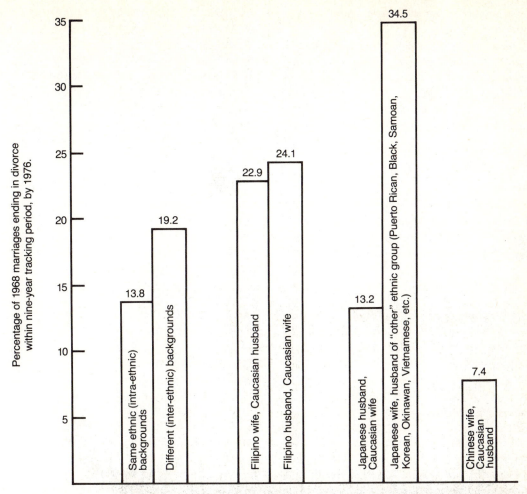

FIGURE 5-3. *Divorce In Hawaii (Source: Adapted from B. M. Vitousek, "Mixed Marriages Are a Mixed Bag." Reprinted with permission from* Family Advocate, *vol. 1, no. 3, published by the Family Law Section of the American Bar Association copyright 1979, American Bar Association.)*

Religion

Most studies of **interfaith marriages** in the United States divide religious groups into three broad categories: Catholic, Protestant, and Jewish. Interfaith in this context refers to marriage of a member of one of these groups to a member of another group. When so divided, a statistical analysis of interfaith marriage rates in the United States indicates that the rates have been increasing among all three major religious groups. *In spite of increases, however, only 6.4 percent of all intact marriages in the United States are interfaith* (Carter and Glick, 1970). One reason these figures are so low is that they measure current religious preference, not preference at the time of marriage. The majority of couples who plan to marry and who are of different faiths become homogamous through conversion of one of the spouses before or after marriage.

The rates of interfaith marriages depend

upon a large number of factors. Among them are the following.

Other things being equal, the smaller the proportion of members of a religion in a particular community, the more likely interfaith marriages will take place. The reason is that young people of the minority religion are more likely to have contact with others outside the faith, so the probability of interfaith marriage is greater.

When persons of different faiths come from similar ethnic backgrounds or socioeconomic classes, the rates of interfaith marriages tend to be higher than when differing ethnic backgrounds or socioeconomic classes are represented. The reason is that interfaith marriage is more likely when it does not also involve crossing the ethnic barriers or status lines.

The rates of interfaith marriages are higher among persons of low socioeconomic status and among the very young. Low socioeconomic status persons are less likely to be active and participating members of their church so are less likely to be influenced by pressures against interfaith marriages. Also, they tend to reject middle-class values and to be nonconformists in comparison to middle-class society. The very young also tend to be rebellious and nonconformists, and they more often reject denominational prejudices against selecting a mate outside one's own faith.

The rates of interfaith marriage among remarried divorced persons are considerably higher than among those married for the first time. Rosenthal concludes: "Divorce must be considered a major contributing factor in the formation of religious intermarriages" (Rosenthal, 1970, p. 440).

The rates of interfaith marriages are higher among those: whose parents are less religious, whose ties with parents were tenuous when they were young, or who are more emancipated from parental influence at the time of marriage.

The rates of interfaith marriages vary inversely with the cohesiveness and exclusiveness of the religious group. Some groups, such as the

Orthodox Jews or strict Protestant groups like the Mormons, are more opposed to interfaith marriages than are other groups and are able to exert greater control over their young people to prevent marriages outside the faith.

The majority of persons in the United States approve of interfaith marriages (Gallup, 1979). Among the three major religious groups, Catholics are most willing to marry outside the faith and Jews are least willing.

What about the survival rates and compatibility of interfaith marriages versus religiously monogamous marriages? When just survival rates are considered, the results indicate that *religiously homogamous marriages are more stable than are religiously heterogamous marriages.* This does not apply, however, when talking about denominationally homogamous Protestant marriages versus denominationally mixed Protestant marriages. The results of one study indicate that mixed Presbyterian, Lutheran, and Methodist marriages had higher survival rates than did homogamous Methodist, Presbyterian or Baptist. In interpreting the data, the authors emphasized that other important factors influenced the data besides religion. Survival rates varied tremendously with status levels and with age at marriage. "In all religious affiliation types (1) survival rates were greater among the marriages involving the older as compared to younger brides; and (2) survival rates increased directly with the occupational status levels" (Boxer, 1963, p. 357). One must be careful, therefore, in interpreting survival statistics to sort out different variables so that true causal factors are determined. For example, Rosenthal (1970) found that instead of interfaith marriage causing divorce, previous divorce led to interfaith marriage.

Another difficulty lies in equating survival with compatibility. Some churches have strong prohibitions against divorce, so fewer members get divorces. But does this mean that these couples who stay together are happier? Not necessarily, of course. Overall, *there seems*

to be more negative effects of interfaith marriage on Catholics and Jewish groups (especially Orthodox) than on Protestants (Eshleman, 1974).

Education and Intelligence

There is a definite tendency for couples to enter into homogamous marriages with respect to education (U.S. Department of Commerce, 1972). Figure 5-4 shows the percentages of females with some college education who married men with similar or different levels of education (Rawlings, 1978). These figures indicate that females with four years of college

either married men who were also four-year college graduates or those who had more education than they did. Of those females who had four years of college, only 18 percent married men with an elementary or high school education.

The tendency toward educational homogamy among males applies most to those with a high school education. Figure 5-5 shows that slightly more than half of males with some elementary education were married to women with more education than themselves. It also shows that among husbands with four years of college, a majority married women with

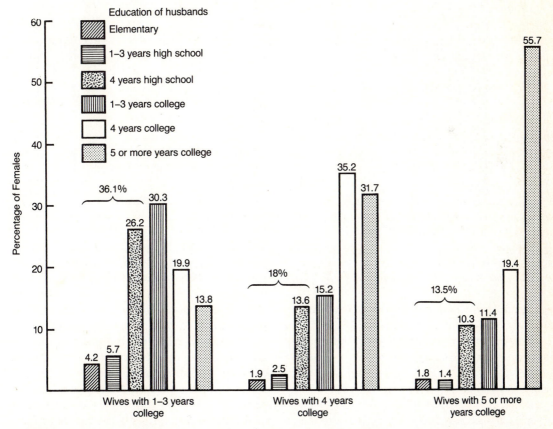

FIGURE 5-4. *Percentages of college-educated females who were married to men with various degrees of education: March 1977 (Source: Adapted from S. Rawlings, "Perspectives on American Husbands and Wives,"* Current Population Reports, *Series P-23, no. 77 [Washington, D.C.: U.S. Government Printing Office, December 1978], p. 13.)*

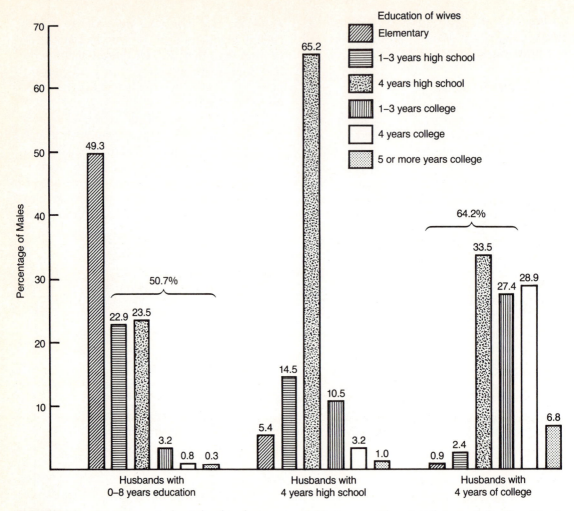

FIGURE 5-5. *Percentages of educated males who were married to women with various degrees of education: March 1977. (Source: Adapted from S. Rawlings, "Perspectives on American Husbands and Wives." Current Population Reports, Series P-23, no. 77 [Washington, D.C.: U.S. Government Printing Office, December 1978], p. 13.)*

less education than themselves (Rawlings, 1978).

What about the compatibility of marriages that are mixed with respect to education? *As a general principle, educationally homogamous marriages tend to be slightly more compatible then educationally heterogamous marriages* (Jaco and Shephard, 1975). If there is a marked difference in education, it is better if the wife marries upward. *The hypergamous unions (wife marries upward) have lower divorce rates than hypogamous unions (wife marries downward).*

Obviously, however, educational attainment is not the only important factor. People who lack the advantages of a formal education but who are quite intelligent may be very happily married to those who are well educated. Education and brilliance are not necessarily synonymous. *When couples are matched according to intelligence levels, however, their marriages tend to be more compatible than when* couples have dissimilar intelligence (Bowman, 1974). This is fortunate, since in actual practice individuals tend to select mates with intelligence similar to their own.

Compatible Attitudes and Values

Consensus

Compatibility may also be determined by the degree of consensus in marriage and the similarity of attitudes and values of the husband and wife. In general *the greater the degree of consensus and the more similar the attitudes and values of the husband and wife, the more compatible they are in marriage.* From this point of view, compatibility may be described partly as the extent of agreement or disagreement between the husband and wife in such areas as the following (Booth and Welch, 1978; Mace, 1972c):

- *Employment.* Type, place, hours of employment of the husband and wife
- *Residence.* Geographical area, specific community, character of neighborhood, type of housing
- *Money matters.* Amount needed, how earned, how managed.
- *Parents, families.* Relationships with parents and in-laws
- *Social life.* Extent, type, leisure-time activities
- *Friends.* Selection, relationships with men and women friends
- *Religion.* Ideas, beliefs, personal faith, church affiliations, participation in religious activities
- *Values, philosophy of life.* Individual ethics, morals, life goals, what individual wants out of life
- *Sex, demonstration of affection.* Type, amount, frequency
- *Matters of conventionality.* Manners, mores, living habits (i.e. table manners, dress, drinking, smoking, attitudes toward drug use or abuse, cleanliness, etc.)
- *Children.* Number wanted, disciplining, caring for and educating them
- *Roles.* Of husband and wife in and outside home

Obviously, husbands and wives can never agree on everything, but the greater their consensus the easier it is to adjust to one another in marriage. Couples who are considering marriage would do well, therefore, to explore their attitudes and values in order to prevent misunderstandings and problems that might damage their marraige (Kieren et al., 1975).

Development of Consensus

One of the things that research shows, however, is that *consensus develops slowly in a relationship* (Murstein, 1971a). A dating couple may not even get around to talking about important values until after they have gone together for some time. Dating couples show less consensus than couples who are going steady, and these show less consensus than engaged couples or happily married couples. The more intimate dating couples become, the more likely they express agreement in a number of important areas. There may be two reasons for this: (1) being together may create greater understanding and agreement, and (2) those who have disagreed too much may not have progressed to the next stage of intimacy (Udry, 1974). Whichever reason is more valid, *value consensus of a couple is related to satisfaction and to progress toward permanence in a relationship.*

There seems to be a point in courtship, however, at which consensus is not as important as other factors such as role compatibility. Several researchers found that high consensus couples made superior courtship progress during the first eighteen months of their relationship, but after that, fewer differences were found between high and low consensus couples, probably because they had learned to adjust to their different ideas (Levinger et al., 1970). These findings would indicate that the degree of consensus cannot be used alone as the measure of courtship compatibility, particularly for couples who go together for a long period of time. Other criteria of compatibility also need to be taken into account. In marriage too, consensus helps couples to make a satisfactory adjustment, but other criteria also need to be considered.

Compatible Role Concepts

Another measure of compatibility in marriage is to compare husband and wife role expectations with role performances (Araji, 1977). Every man has certain concepts of the kind of husband he is and wants to be, and certain expectations of what roles a wife should perform. Every woman has certain concepts of the kind of wife she is and wants to be, and certain expectations of what roles a husband should perform. What the two people expect and what they find, however, may be different. The following examples illustrate instances where role expectations were never realized in marriage:

A young husband: "I always wanted a wife who was interested in a home and family. My wife doesn't even want children."

A new bride: "In my family, my father always used to help my mother. My husband never lifts a finger to help me."

In each of these examples, either the husband or wife is dissatisfied with the role that the other is assuming in the family. *Role concepts may be said to be compatible if husband and wife role expectations are in agreement with role performances or—if there are differences—these are worked out to the satisfaction of both.*

Suppose, for example, the particular job a husband holds is as prestigious and supplies as much income and security as his wife expects. One could say that the husband's occupational role performance and his wife's expectations are compatible. But if the husband's job is not the kind that can provide either the prestige or the lifestyle desired by

the wife, his role performance is inconsistent with her role expectations of him. One researcher found that some husbands underperform and others overperform in relation to their wives' expectations of them as providers. One author concludes:

Where there is high consensus *(about occupational achievement and family life style),* the probability is greater that the marriage will remain intact as a social system; where there is divergence and conflict, the probability is greater that the marriage will not remain intact and may become dissolved (Scanzoni, 1968, p. 454).

The same principle holds true with respect to other aspects of role performance and role expectations: There needs to be a high degree of consensus and marital role satisfaction, otherwise major problems develop (McNamara, 1980).

Compatible Interests, Activities, and Friends

Most dating couples tend to look for similar interests to enjoy and activities they can do together as one important measure fo compatibility. So the question naturally arises: How important is this as a criteria of marital satisfaction? Actually, the answer depends mostly on the type of interests and activities one is talking about. Research emphasizes that couples who have mutual interests in their home, children, romantic love, sex, and so forth have more successful marriages than those whose mutual interests are in going out a lot to have a good time, in commercial entertainment, or in companionship with others to avoid loneliness (Saxton, 1972). Some people who have very poor marriages go out with others a lot or entertain frequently as a means of avoiding one another. So even though such activities seem to be shared, they may be indicative of marital maladjustment, or may even contribute to further alienation themselves.

It should also be pointed out that it is not the *amount* of time couples spend together that is the criteria of marital satisfaction but the quality of the relationship they enjoy when together. Having mutual friends is also a positive factor in harmonious marital relationships (Osmond and Martin, 1978).

Compatible Habit Systems

The columns, "Ann Landers" and "Dear Abby," are filled with letters from husbands and wives who are complaining about the annoying habits of their mates. Their spouses have terrible table manners, are careless about personal cleanliness, smoke or drink too much, crack their knuckles, snore too loudly, go to bed too late, won't get up in the morning, leave dirty clothes scattered all over the house, never replace the cap on the toothpaste, or have other habits their partners find irritating. The writers have either tried to get their mates to change or tried to learn to accept the habit, often without success. Over the years, some of the habits become serious obstacles to marital harmony. One letter is a typical example:*

Dear Ann Landers:

I wonder how many wives among your readers have my problem. I am accused by my husband of

*Ann Landers column, *Portland* (Maine) *Press Herald*, May 24, 1975. Copyright © 1975 by Field Newspaper Syndicate. Reprinted by permission.

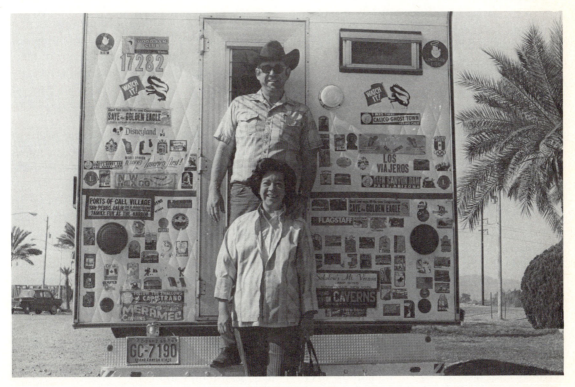

Couples with mutual interests as a couple have more successful marriages than those whose interests are outside their family.

being frigid, cold, and unresponsive. Why don't he take inventory and ask himself such questions as these. "When did I last shower, use a deodorant or brush my teeth? Am I sober? Does my breath reek of beer or booze?"

I'm basically an affectionate person. When we married, nearly 20 years ago, we were very much in love. Shorty after our honeymoon I became disenchanted. My husband's lack of personal hygiene was something I couldn't deal with. I hinted at first. Nothing changed. Then I came right out and told him. Still nothing changed.

This man is a college graduate. He holds an executive position with a well-known firm, is considered charming and intelligent—until he drinks too much, which is becoming more frequent. Our sex life is almost nil because of his lack of body cleanliness and excessive drinking.

Please print this letter. It's too late to help our marriage, but perhaps it will help someone else's
—Just Sad

Such situations as the above are quite common. In a recent study involving problem-solving situations for married couples, 32 percent of the 195 spouses reported disagreement over irritating personal habits of their mate (Henton, 1970). Most problems that are annoying before marriage become even more intensified in the closer and more continuous shared life of marriage.

Conclusions

Presentation of the material of this chapter to students in a classroom evoked this question from one student: "Since we live in a democracy where we believe that all people are created equal, isn't it undemocratic and unpatriotic to emphasize that marriages within one's own class, race, religion, and so forth are more compatible? How can we ever achieve true brotherhood and equality if everyone does this?" What this student said, in

essence, was that she thought it was showing prejudice to point out that homogamous and endogamous marriages were more compatible.

One can sympathize with her feelings. If prejudice is the motivation against heterogamous or exogamous marriages, then this student's feelings would be justified. It is not the intent of this chapter to champion homogamous or endogamous marriages because of social prejudice. What this chapter does intend is to present these truths (subject to limitations that have been discussed): that one's chances of marital harmony and success are greater if (1) one marries an individual whose needs are similar to one's own, (2) one marries another who has similar personality traits especially as related to mental health, (3) one's mate is of similar socioeconomic class, race, religion, education, and intelligence and has similar attitudes, values, goals, and role concepts. Furthermore, this chapter suggests that those who show interest in doing things together at home have a greater chance of marital satisfaction than those whose interests lie outside the home and family. Also, marital harmony is easier if the habit systems of two people are compatible.

It must be emphasized that these findings apply only to the present and in the context of the United States culture. Obviously there are many exceptions, such as the high rate of success of interracial marriages in Hawaii.

What about the person who is thinking of making a heterogamous or exogamous choice? Because the statistical probability of failure is greater, this means that greater caution is in order. Perhaps additional time, discussion, and examination of issues and relationships will reveal there is little to worry about, or will resolve differences or clarify future problems. If, after observing these cautions, the individual still finds serious problems that might destroy a relationship, he or she may decide the choice is a poor one.

After eight years of marriage, Toni and Joseph Maier had a violent quarrel over an affair that Toni had been having with a neighbor. The couple sought counseling about three months later. Altogether, they participated in eight joint sessions and three individual sessions each. Since then they have divorced on grounds of incompatibility. They present their separate accounts of what went wrong below.

Toni: I first met Joseph at a Fourth of July parade when I was nineteen and he was twenty. He was drinking a Coke and had a Doberman on a leash. He said hello to me; I patted his dog, and that's how we met and began going together. We were still living at home, but the following summer he dropped out of college and moved into an apartment. After two months, we started living together. He found a job as a lawyer's assistant, and two months later we decided to get married. He was the handsomest man I had ever known. He really seemed to love me. I would have died if he hadn't wanted to marry me.

He went back to college and worked part-time. But before the year was up I knew something was wrong. He never told me what he was thinking. He began to ignore me more and more. He seldom talked to me, paid attention to me, or expressed affection even in the simplest ways. If I got mad at him, he would get upset and just leave the apartment. He was never willing to talk about things. He spent more and more time with his friends, leaving me alone. Eventually, he finished law school. We moved to the suburbs, and I started teaching school. But nothing changed. We went our separate ways more and more. I didn't really want to. I needed companionship and affection, but Joe never gave it to me. In my family, all of us were very, very close, but Joe was not brought up that way. His folks are very cold people. I admit that I was lonesome and unhappy.

Then one day, just after Joe had to go out of town on a case, the bachelor who lives just down the block came over to borrow a wrench. I gave him coffee, we talked, and that started the whole thing. He was warm and friendly—all the things that Joe wasn't. Then one of the days Joe was away I invited him to sleep over. That did it, I never wanted Joe again. I saw this man as often after that as I could. It was inevitable that Joe find out. We had a terrible quarrel, and he left. We tried counseling but it really didn't help. I admit that I didn't want to save my marriage. So we gave up and got a divorce a short time after that.

Joseph: I realize that Toni and I never knew one another very well before we got married. How can you possibly know one another after four months, even though you live together for part of the time? After we were married, Toni acted as though she owned me. She wanted to go everywhere with me. She resented it if I wanted to go out and see my friends. She complained that I left her all alone, that I didn't pay enough attention to her. I tried, but all she did was complain. She's a very possessive person and I hate to be smothered. After I got married, it was as though I didn't have any more life of my own, that I had lost all of my freedom.

Another thing, Toni liked to talk about things. She would spend hours and hours just talking. But sometimes when I did try to talk to her, it would end up in an argument over my neglecting her. Toni only listened to what she wanted to hear. She never really tried to understand me and what I felt. So why talk, it didn't do any good.

We were so different in many ways. I'm outgoing and like people. Toni was quiet and more introverted. She never wanted to go out or to meet my friends. She was also very gushy; she would embarrass me the way she hung all over me in front of people. She would also ask me over and over if I loved her. I used to, but not after I found out that she was sleeping with that guy down the block. When I asked her about it, we had a terrible argument. I accused her of being a slut and other hateful things. I never felt the same toward her after that.

Dr. Carroll: During the short period that I saw this couple they were quite congenial, but they never explored any important strain in their relationship. I didn't think they really cared what the other one felt. The tension between them was there. Neither one met the desires and expectations of the other. Neither one was able to communicate, but they didn't seem to want to straighten things out.

I felt that they were roommates rather than a married couple. They seemed eager to be through with each session and I doubt whether there was any serious discussion of what was said when they went home. In my opinion, Toni's affair was a pseudo issue. The deeper problem lay in Toni's dependency and unsatisfied emotional needs and in Joseph's unwillingness or inability to fulfill his wife's emotional expectations and needs. Joseph apparently didn't want a close, emotional involvement while his wife did. That is why they were so incompatible. Also, Joseph still sought companionship primarily with his old friends rather than from Toni. He never really developed any real companionship with her, and he never really learned how to talk about his feelings in an understanding and intimate way while growing up. His family background did not provide opportunities to learn the real meaning of emotional intimacy. As a result, he was not able to relate to Toni as she desired, so he and Toni became more and more estranged. Toni's affair was only the symptom of her needs and the indication that her marriage with Joseph was not what she wanted and needed.

QUESTIONS

1. In what ways was Toni realistic and reasonable in what she expected of Joe, and in what ways were her expectations unrealistic and unreasonable?

2. What kind of a wife did Joseph want? How would you like to be married to him? Comment in relation to your own marital expectations.

3. When one did not fulfill the other's expectations, how did they each react? What could they have done?

4. Would it ever have been possible for Joseph and Toni to remain happily married? How?

5. When a couple find areas of incompatibility, what can they do?

6. How did family background influence role expectations and fulfillment? Is it possible to change one's role expectations and role fulfillment?

Male and Female Roles

CHAPTER
6

Changing Concepts of Masculinity and Femininity

CHAPTER OUTLINE

Genetic Bases of Gender

Hormones and Sexual Identity

Theories of Sex Role Development

Masculine-Feminine Concepts

Homosexuality

Conclusions

Dialogue

In recent years, social science has directed its attention to the changing concepts of **masculinity** and **femininity** and to the changing sex roles of men and women in our culture. Sex roles that were once rigidly determined are in a state of flux and what was once considered masculine or feminine is no longer necessarily so. In American society today, as well as in foreign societies, a movement has arisen that advocates **unisex** roles for men and women. This movement would eliminate masculine-feminine differences in dress, social treatment, behavior, and socialization. Closely allied to this point of view is the feminist protest against the discrimination of women and urging complete equality of the sexes and a reexamination of traditional sex roles and concepts.

The focus of this chapter is on changing concepts of masculinity and femininity and how these concepts develop. What is the role of heredity in shaping behavior and sex attitudes? Does heredity determine the degree of masculinity or femininity in personal behavior as well as physical sex differences? What are the influences of sex hormones on physical growth and development? On sex-typed behavior? What are the major social influences, and how do these influences contribute to the development of masculinity or femininity? How do modern concepts of sexuality compare with masculine-feminine stereotypes in our culture, and how do these new ideas fit in with changing ideas of marriage? Finally, the chapter raises the issue of male homosexuality and lesbianism with special emphasis on their implications for marriage.

Genetic Bases of Gender

To be masculine means to exhibit "maleness," to have "manlike" attributes. Similarly, to be feminine means to exhibit "femaleness," to have "womanlike" qualities. In both definitions there is implied the idea that there are varying degrees of "maleness" and "femaleness," so that no characteristic is bestowed exclusively either to all men or all women at birth. Actually, these traits are both physically and culturally determined. The physical basis of gender includes the genetic determination of sex, the influence of the sex hormones, and the action of the hypothalamus of the brain (Goleman, 1978). These physical bases will be discussed first and the cultural influences will be treated in a subsequent section.

Genetic Foundations

The genetic foundations of gender are familiarly known. Whether a baby is genetically male or female is determined at the moment of conception by whether or not the egg cell is fertilized by a sperm carrying a Y chromosome or an X chromosome. If fertilized by an X-carrying sperm, a female results; if fertilized by a Y-carrying sperm, a male results. Because Y chromosomes are much smaller than X chromosomes, the head of a Y-carrying sperm is considerably lighter and smaller; in addition, the tail of the Y-carrying sperm is longer, thus allowing it to swim faster and to have a greater chance of reaching the egg cell first and of fertilizing it. For this reason, an average of 160 males are conceived to every 100 females. Because of the greater vulnerability of the fetal male to prenatal conditions, however the ratio is reduced to 120 males to 100 females at the time of implantation in the uterus, and by full term the ratio is reduced to 110 males to 100 females (Potts, 1970). In terms of live births, the ratio is 105 to 100 (McCary, 1973). This means that the majority of spontaneous abortions or miscarriages are of male fetuses (Hutt, 1972). Throughout life, the human male remains more vulnerable to a variety of nongenetically based disorders, so that his life expectancy is seven and one-half years less than that of the female (U.S. Department of Commerce, *Statistical Abstracts*, 1980).

Following conception, it is the presence or absence of a Y chromosome that determines the organization of gender differentiation according to a particular pattern. In the absence of a Y chromosome, female development always takes place. If a Y chromosome is present, the inner portion of the embryonic gonad (sex organ) begins to differentiate into testes. This happens during the seventh week after conception. If a Y chromosome is absent, the differentiation of the testes fails to occur in the seventh week so that the outer part of the gonad differentiates into an ovary. Thus, it is the Y chromosome that plays the active role in initiating and guiding the formation of the male gonads.

Chromosomal Anomalies

Sometimes nature makes a mistake. The male may get one or more extra Y chromosomes. These males are labeled XYY, XYYY, or XYYYY. Studies of men with XYY chromosomes show them to be of tall stature, subnormal intelligence, and with severe acne. A higher than normal percentage have homosexual associations (Money, 1971). In addi-

tion, there are a significantly higher proportion of XYY males in prison populations than in the general population (Polani, 1970). In fact, there have been a number of legal cases involving murderers with the XYY chromosomal syndrome, including the murderer of eight young nurses in Chicago (Money, 1968).

Sometimes the male receives an extra X (female) chromosome (labeled XXY, *Klinefelter's syndrome*), producing a "man" with distinctly feminine appearance, small testicles incapable of producing sperm, low sex drive, decreased body hair, prominent breasts, and a tendency toward mental impairment (Money, 1968). Many times this abnormality is not detected until puberty (Hutt, 1972).

Sexual anomalies also occur in females, the most common of which is the absence of one X chromosome (labeled XO, *Turner's syndrome*). Females with this abnormality lack functioning ovaries. They have female internal and external sex organs, but the organs are small and incompletely developed. The newborn infant may appear normal, but by six or seven years of age other abnormalities may be evident: webbed neck, loose skin, nipples that are widely spaced on the chest, or short stature. Any tentative diagnosis at this age is confirmed at puberty when the girl fails to menstruate. Deafness and mental deficiency are also common (Money, 1968). Girls with this abnormality may be "ultra feminine" in some aspects of their behavior.

Hormones and Sexual Identity

Hormone Influences on Physical Development

It is evident that "maleness" or "femaleness" has a hereditary foundation. Strictly speaking, however, the genetic determination of sex goes only as far as the formation of the male or female gonads: the testes or ovaries (Hutt, 1972). The continuation of the process of sex differentiation is under the control of the sex **hormones**: those having a masculinizing action, known collectively as the **androgens,** and those having a feminizing action, known collectively as the **estrogens.** In every person, male and female, there are both androgens and estrogens bathing every cell of the body to exert their influence (Greene, 1970). Actually, it is partly the relative proportion of each of these groups of hormones in the body which influences the development of predominantly male or female physical characteristics.

In the male, both androgens and estrogens are secreted prenatally, but at puberty the maturing testes greatly increase their production of the most important of the androgens, **testosterone,** which results in the development of typical male physiology: broad shoulders and muscular body, body and facial hair, and a deep voice. Testosterone is also responsible for the development of the primary male sex organs: the penis and testes.

Both androgens and estrogens are also secreted in the female, but at puberty the maturing ovaries greatly increase their production of estrogenic hormones on a cyclical basis, with the amount of secretion depending upon the stage of the menstrual cycle. It is these estrogens which are responsible for the development of female secondary sexual characteristics: rounded hips and body contours, enlarged breasts, pubic and auxillary hair, and for the development of the primary sex organs: the vagina, uterus, clitoris, and labia.

The important point is that both male and female hormones may be found in the bloodstream of men and women, and it is the ratio of the level of the male to female hormones that is partly responsible for the development of male or female physical traits. Female homosexuals have been found to have higher levels of testosterone in the blood than do heterosexual women, leading some researchers to suggest a partial biological basis for this phenomenon ("Homosexual . . . ", 1978). A female with an excess of androgens may grow a mustache and body hair, develop masculine musculature and strength, or evidence an enlarged clitoris resembling a penis. Female track stars sometime take male hormones to increase their strength and endurance. A male with an excess of estrogens may evidence decreased potency and sex drive and an enlargement of the breasts (Rice, 1981).

Hormone Influences on Experimental Animals

It is quite obvious that hormones influence physical growth and development, but do they influence sex-typed behavior? A number of studies support the conclusion that they do (Parlee, 1978). This statement must be explained carefully, however. The lower the form of animal, the more its sex-typed behavior is instinctual and unlearned, depending more upon the chemistry of the body. Thus, castration of male rats or cats at birth does change their behavior. If male monkeys are castrated at birth, however, they continue to evidence some of the aggressive behavior of normal males—even though they become disinterested in sexual intercourse itself. Prenatal hormonal changes exert far greater influence on behavior than those taking place later in development. In monkeys, if female fetuses are androgenized before birth, they later show more threat, attack, chasing, and rough-and-tumble play than normal females (Hutt, 1972). If, however, the males are castrated at birth, they show no appreciable decrement in these behavior patterns, since sex differentiation of the brain has already partly taken place (Linton, 1970; Rose et al., 1971).

Hormone Influences on Humans

The same principle holds true for human beings. If human females are exposed to excessive androgenic influences prior to birth, they become more tomboyish, more physically vigorous, and more assertive than normal females. If testosterone is administered to adult females, their physical appearance changes, but their behavior is affected very little. In fact, in some adult females, testosterone inhibits aggression and causes hyperfeminization (Neuman et al., 1970). What the studies suggest is that changes in prenatal hormone levels in humans may have marked effects on sex-typed behavior; after birth, however, hormonal changes usually only accentuate or minimize certain masculine-feminine characteristics already in evidence.

Recent studies have shown a direct relationship between the rate of production of testosterone and amount of aggression and hostility among normal adult males (Persky et al., 1971). (See figure 6-1.) Interestingly enough, this relationship did not hold true for men over thirty years of age. This means that some of the variance in adolescent behavior and some of the turbulence of this period may be accounted for by the effect of the rapid increase in the secretion of testosterone at puberty. In older adult males, however, changes in hormonal levels do not have a marked effect on behavior.

Adult female behavior is often influenced by the cyclical changes in hormone levels during various periods of the menstrual cycle. The levels of estrogen are at a peak midway in the menstrual cycle and at their lowest point before, during, and after menstruation. Early adolescent girls experience increased irritability, depression, and emotional upset when estrogen is at an ebb (Kopell et al., 1969; Moss et al., 1969; Reynolds, 1969). Researchers have shown an increase in psychiatric hospital admissions, suicide attempts, crimes of vi-

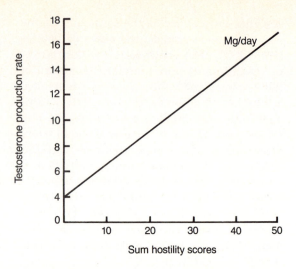

FIGURE 6-1. *The relationship between the rate of production of testosterone and hostility scores in 18 men between seventeen and twenty-eight years of age. (Source: Adapted from H. Persky; K. D. Smith; and G. K. Basu, "Relation of Psychologic Measures of Aggression and Hostility to Testostere Production in Man,"* Psychosomatic Medicine 33 [1971]: 265–277.)

olence, and accidents just prior to and during menstruation, indicating some relationship between emotionality and the levels of hormones. Hormones do not change the basic sex-typed behavior of a person, however. And since there are still many factors which cannot be explained either by genetic or hormonal influences, one must conclude that a major part of sex role behavior is learned.

Theories of Sex Role Development

There are three major theories that explain sex role behavior as learned (Hochschild, 1973a):

1. Cognitive development theory
2. Social learning theory
3. Parental identification theory

Cognitive Development Theory

The cognitive developmental theory suggests that sex role identity has its beginning in the gender that is cognitively assigned to the child at birth and that is subsequently accepted by him or her while growing up. At the time of birth, gender assignment is made largely on the basis of **genital** examination. The child from that point on is considered a "boy" or a "girl." If genital abnormalities are present, this gender assignment may later prove to be in error if it is not in agreement with the sex chromosomes and gonads that are present. Even if the assignment is in error, however, Money and Ehrhardt (1972) have pointed out that sex identification usually follows the sex that has been assigned and in which the child is reared. This is true despite ambiguities in physical sex characteristics.

It is important, however, that gender identity be consistent and unambiguous. Money (1972) reports an example of a **hermaphrodite** child—first registered as a boy—whose name was later changed to a girl without the name change recorded on the birth certificate and without masculinized external genitalia being surgically corrected. Consequently, the parents were indicating that they had no real conviction that their child was a daughter instead of a son, and they were transmitting their ambiguous gender expectancies to their child. Under such circumstances, it was inevitable that the child grew up ambiguous as to gender. If the parents had been unequivocal in their rearing of their child as a girl, the chances would be high that the child would have differentiated a girl's identity.

The cognitive assignment of gender influences everything that happens from that point on (Marcus and Overton, 1978). Kohlberg (1966) the chief exponent of this view, emphasized that the child's self-categorization (as a boy or girl) is the basic organizer of

the sex role attitudes that develop. The child who recognizes that he is a male begins to value maleness and to act consistently with gender expectations. He begins to actively structure his own experience according to his accepted gender and to act out appropriate sex roles (Skolnick, 1973). He acknowledges social role differences in fantasizing himself as a daddy with wife and children. A little girl will pretend that she is a grown-up married woman with a baby. Sex differentiation takes place gradually as children learn to be male or female according to social role expectations and the child's interpretation of them.

According to this theory, girls do not become girls because they identify with or model after their mothers; they model after their mothers because they have realized that they are girls. They preferentially value their own sex and are motivated to appropriate sex role behavior. A girl will say: "I am a girl, therefore, I want to do girl things" (Flake-Hobson, 1980). The truth of this was shown by one study in which boys performed significantly more poorly on tasks which were indicated as ones on which girls did better (Gold and Beger, 1978).

Social Learning Theory

The social learning theorists such as Mischel (1970) and Bandura and Walters (1969) reason differently. They say that a child learns sex-typed behavior the same way he or she learns any other type of behavior, through a combination of reward and punishment, indoctrination, observation of others, and through **modeling**. But from the very beginning boys and girls are socialized differently (Joffee, 1971). Boys are expected to be more active, hostile, and aggressive (Brindley et al., 1972; Shortrell and Biller, 1970). They are expected to fight when teased and to stand up to bullies. When they act according to expectations, they are praised; when they refuse to fight, they are criticized for being "sissies." Girls are taught to be more timid, passive, and dependent, and less aggressive physically and to use more subtle forms of assertiveness such as coaxing or crying. As a consequence, boys and girls grow up manifesting different behavior.

Traditional sex roles and concepts are taught both informally at home and more formally in school as the child grows up (Rosen and Aneshensel, 1978). Giving children gender specific toys may have considerable influence on vocational choices. Such toys influence boys to be scientists, astronauts, or football players, and girls to be nurses, teachers, or stewardesses (Kacerguis and Adams, 1979). A study of sex role socialization in nursery schools showed that even those schools

Many women are rejecting the traditional sex roles.

that tried to minimize differential sex role socialization of boys and girls still exerted subtle influence on sex role expectations (Joffee, 1971). For example, the girls received more compliments on wearing dresses than on wearing pants. The storybooks read to the children, the songs they learned, the games they played, all contained elements of traditional sex role attitudes. In one song concerning a child who made noise on a bus, the words went: "And the daddy went spank-spank and the mommy went 'shh-shh'." One of the greatest influences on sex roles was the fact that all of the nursery school teachers were females. This fact alone would make it more difficult for children to understand that fathers too can share in childcare responsibilities.

In recent years, a great deal of effort has gone into eliminating the sex role stereotypes reflected in many textbooks (Martin, 1971; U'Ren, 1971). One study focused on an annotated catalogue of children's books, distributed by the National Council of Teachers of English to thousands of teachers and used for ordering books with federal funds. It showed that titles were listed under headings: "Especially for Girls" and "Especially for Boys." It was found that boys "decipher and discover," "earn and train" or "foil someone." Girls "struggle," "overcome difficulties," "feel lost," "help solve," or "help out." One boy's story moves from "truancy to triumph." A girl "learns to face the real world" and to make "a difficult adjustment" (Howe, 1971). Such sex stereotypes are gradually being eliminated in a complete overhaul of children's textbooks.

Much has been done also to change school courses and programs promoting sex-typed roles. Traditionally, physical education courses for boys emphasized contact sports and competition; those for girls promoted grace, agility, and poise. Home economics was offered for girls, shop and auto mechanics for boys. Guidance counselors urged girls to become secretaries and nurses, boys to become business managers and doctors (Naffziger and Naffziger, 1974). Females were prepared for marriage and parenthood, boys for a vocation (Steinman and Zurich, 1975). Gradually, these emphases because of sex are being eliminated, so that both males and females are freer to choose the programs they want.

Sex role learning would emphasize, therefore, that boys develop "maleness" and girls develop "femaleness" by being exposed to scores of influences: parents, peers, school, the mass media, and others that teach and indoctrinate them in what it means to be a man or a woman in the culture in which they are brought up (Aneshensel and Rosen, 1980; Goffman, 1977; Long and Simon, 1974; Miller and Reeves, 1976; Peevers, 1979; Verna, 1975). They are further encouraged to accept the "proper" sex identity by being rewarded for sex-appropriate behavior and by being punished for sex-inappropriate behavior. According to this theory, a boy says: "I want rewards; I am rewarded for doing boy things, therefore I want to be a boy" (Flake-Hobson, 1980). Those who live up to societal expectations are accepted as normal; those who do not conform are criticized and pressured to comply.

Parental Identification Theory

Another influential view, which is built upon social learning theory, emphasizes how children find appropriate sex roles through a process of **identification,** especially with parents. *Parental identification is that process by which the child adopts and internalizes parental values, attitudes, behavioral traits, and personality characteristics.* When applied to sex role development, parental identification theory suggests that children develop sex role concepts, attitudes, values, characteristics, and behavior by identifying with their parents, especially with the parent of the same sex. Identification begins after birth because of children's early dependency upon their parents. This dependency,

in turn, normally leads to a close emotional attachment. Sex role learning takes place almost unconsciously and indirectly in this close parent-child relationship. The child may learn that some mothers are soft, warm, and gentle, that they are affectionate, nurturing, and sensitive. Others are rough, loud, and rejecting. Not only does each child receive different care from each parent but he or she listens and observes that each parent behaves, speaks, dresses, and acts differently in relation to the other parent, to other children, or to persons outside the family. Thus, the child learns what is a mother, a wife, a father, a husband, a woman, or a man through the example set and through daily contacts and associations.

Of course, the extent to which identification takes place depends upon the amount of time parents spend with their child and the intimacy and intensity of the contact (McIntire et al., 1972). Usually young boys and girls both identify more closely with the mother than with the father, primarily because they are more often with their mothers (McIntire et al., 1972). As a result, young boys often show more similarity to their mothers than to their fathers (Lynn and Cross, 1974). This means that they have greater difficulty in achieving same-sex identification than do girls (Bermant, 1972; Evans, 1971; Freedman, 1971). This partly explains why males are often more anxious than females regarding their sex-role identification (Currant et al. 1979). On the one hand, they are more severely punished for being "sissies" than girls are for being masculine, and, on the other hand, they have more difficulty breaking away from feminine influences and of finding suitable male role models (Chodorow, 1971). When the father is absent from the home, the male child has the most difficulty because of the lack of masculine influence (Biller and Bahm, 1971; Walters and Stinnett, 1971). One study showed that boys with absent fathers were found to be more dependent, less aggressive, and less competent in peer relationships than those whose fathers were present (Biller, 1971).

The extent of identification depends upon the relative influence which parents exert (Acock and Bengtson, 1978; McDonald, 1977; Tarr, 1978). High-status parents exert more influence that low-status ones (Tomeh, 1978). Mothers employed outside the home have more prestige and so exert more influence on their children than nonworking mothers. The parent with more education is able to exert more influence (Lueptow, 1980; Smith and Self, 1980; Vanfossen, 1977). Of course, the sex role concepts the child learns depend upon the patterns of role models exemplified. A girl who closely identifies with a masculine mother, becomes only weakly identified with a typically feminine personality. One brought up by a mother who is a professional career woman will get a less stereotyped concept of femininity than one whose mother is primarily a homemaker. Similarly, a boy brought up by a father who represents very traditional ideas of masculinity and of the role of the husband and father in the family will likely develop quite different concepts than one brought up by an egalitarian parent. As a result, sex role concepts are perpetuated from one generation to the next. They can be gradually changed, however, if each generation is able to analyze existing concepts so as to discard outmoded ideas and roles and to adopt improved ones.

Masculine-Feminine Concepts

Each society has its own ideas about what masculine or feminine concepts should be learned by its children. The judgments made about masculinity, i.e., the extent of "manliness," are *subjective judgments based on the accepted standards of "maleness" as defined by the culture.* These standards vary from culture to culture, or within different periods of history in the same society. In the days of George Washington, a man, especially a gentleman, could wear hose, a powdered wig, and a lace shirt without being considered unmanly. Today he would be considered quite feminine.

Similarly, the standards of "femaleness" vary. Margaret Mead (1950) found considerable differences in the concepts of "femaleness" and "maleness" in three primitive tribes. Arapesh men and women both displayed "feminine" personality traits. They were taught to be cooperative and unaggressive and emotionally responsive to others. In contrast, Mundugumer men and women both developed "masculine" traits. They were ruthless, aggressive, and positively sexed, with tender maternal emotions at a minimum. In the third tribe, the Tchambuli, the sex roles as defined by American culture were reversed: the women were dominant and impersonal, the men were emotionally dependent. Any concepts of masculinity or femininity, therefore, must always be considered tentative, since they are related to the standards by which those qualities are judged, as well as reflecting the prejudices and ideas of the persons doing the judging.

Many people develop fairly stereotyped concepts of masculinity and femininity (Albrecht et al., 1977; Broverman et al., 1972). By stereotype is meant a simplified and standardized conception that is held about something.* Howe says that "sexual stereotypes are assumed differences ... norms ... attitudes, and expectations" about men and women (Howe, 1971).

---

*The word "stereotype" first appeared in 1798 when Didot, a French printer, designed printing blocks to duplicate pages of type. The essential feature of these stereotypes, or printing blocks, was their permanence and unchangeableness (Naffziger and Naffziger, 1974, p. 252). Gradually, the term "stereotype" began to be used for any rigid concept or idea held about others, whether or not those ideas were correct.

Masculine Stereotypes

Some typical masculine stereotypes include the following. Men are supposed to be:

Aggressive	Adventurous
Dominant	Courageous
Strong	Independent
Forceful	Ambitious
Self-confident	Direct
Rugged	Logical
Virile	Unemotional
Instrumental	

These stereotypes of masculinity are considered socially desirable by some elements (but certainly not all) in our culture today. The stereotypical American businessman is supposed to be aggressive and ambitious. The man in "Marlboro Country" is rugged, tattooed, and virile (Balswick and Peck, 1971).

Some men are beginning to assume major responsibility for child care, rejecting the traditional view that it is unmasculine.

One of the best descriptions of masculine stereotypes in our culture is given by David and Brannon in their book *The Forty-nine Percent Majority: The Male Sex Role* (David and Brannon, 1976). They emphasize four dimensions of the traditional male sex role.

To be a man, *the male has to avoid all sissy stuff or anything feminine.* This rule is applied to every aspect of life. If the male buys cosmetics, these have to have names like Brut, Command, or Hai Karate. The male has to avoid hobbies and pastimes like knitting, flower arranging, or poetry. He is never to be emotional or to reveal tender emotions or weaknesses. And above all, men are never to express affection toward other men, to avoid all suspicion of homosexuality (Tognoli, 1980).

To be a man, *the male must be a big wheel: be successful, have status, be looked up to.* This means achieving wealth or fame or other symbols of success such as being able to afford fancy clothes or to drive expensive cars. Men who do not make it in business have to prove themselves in other ways: by being stronger and tougher than anyone else, by being able to seduce and dominate women, or even by only becoming the champion dart thrower at the neighborhood bar.

To be a man, *a male must be a sturdy rock with an air of toughness, confidence, and self-reliance.* The great heroes are William Holden in the movie *Stalag 17*, Bogart in *The African Queen*, Paul Newman in *Cool Hand Luke*, John Wayne, in *True Grit*, or Peter O'Toole as *Lawrence of Arabia*. Real men must sometimes hurt, conquer, humble, outwit, punish, or defeat others. Business wants the man who is aggressive. Movies, novels, television depict their heroes of violence. College football coaches praise the men who like to hit the line hard. The public reveres politicians who can make "give 'em hell" speeches. David and Brannon even complain that our society gives some social sanction to men becoming rapists. As one man said: "Its one way of having sex without having to go out and socialize for it" (David and Brannon, 1976, p. 32). This aura of sex and violence pervades much of life and is one symbol of misconceived masculinity.

In a recent study, both male and female clinical psychologists were asked to choose traits that characterized the healthy male. The respondents chose those traits that were stereotypes of masculinity. Males who were passive, dependent, emotional, cautious, quiet, or gentle were rated mentally "unhealthy" (Broverman and Broverman, 1970). This study illustrates how sterotypes of masculinity are deeply imbedded in our culture, even with professional psychologists, so that males who deviate from the pattern are considered undeveloped in "manly" traits.

Feminine Stereotypes

What are the traditional concepts of femininity as taught by middle and upper-middle strata of our society? In the past, women were supposed to be:

Unaggressive	Warm and affectionate
Submissive	Sentimental
Weak	Softhearted
Dependent—unable to do many things for herself, needed security	Sensitive
Gentle, tender	Aware of feelings of others
Kind	Emotional and excitable
Tactful	Somewhat frivolous, fickle
	Illogical
	Talkative

A "feminine" female was careful never to be too aggressive, too boisterous, loud, or vulgar in speech or behavior (Hall and Black, 1979; Kutner and Brogan, 1974). She was expected to be tender, softhearted, and sensitive and to cry on occasion or to get upset sometimes over small things (Balkwell et al., 1978; Balswick and Avertt, 1977). It was all right for her to like laces, frills, and the frivolous. She was expected to be submissive and dependent and interested primarily in her home (Dweck and Bush, 1976; Dweck et al., 1978; Flora, 1971; Soltz, 1978).

Today, there are few social groups where these stereotypes of femininity are rigidly held, indicating the significant changes that have already taken place in our concepts. The problem with stereotypes is that whenever quite rigid sex standards are applied to the members of one sex, especially since those standards really vary from culture to culture, then human values and human personalities can become completely distorted. Everyone is expected to conform, regardless of individual differences or inclinations.

Standards of femininity and masculinity are, however, in a state of flux today. Nowhere are changing standards more in evidence than in relation to marital roles and in relation to the personality requirements for marriage.

Requirements for Marriage

The concept of "new marriage" as outlined in the first chapter of this book emphasized the following:

- Marriage for love, companionship, the satisfaction of emotional needs
- The value of the individual
- Personal freedom, self-fulfillment, self-actualization, individual growth
- Equality of the sexes, a democratic power structure
- Emotional, personal involvement, open communication
- Flexible sex roles
- Sex as mutual love, pleasure

- Small family size
- Marriage as a voluntary relationship
- Permanence through marital integration rather than through legal force
- High expectations of marriage, possibility of failure increased
- Criteria of success is personal fulfillment, happiness
- Monogamy, sexual fidelity are ideal; alternative lifestyles allowed

In view of these concepts of marriage, the requirements for both men and women are quite similar. Marriage for love, companionship, and the satisfaction of emotional needs, and which is characterized by personal and emotional involvement, requires emotional sensitivity, awareness of the feelings of others, warmth, affection, sentimentality, plus kindness and tact. These traits are needed by both the husband and wife, even though they are characteristics that have been traditionally considered feminine. Similarly, a truly egalitarian marriage emphasizing personal freedom, the value of the individual, self-fulfillment, and self-actualization, where sex roles are flexible and interchangeable and where the power structure and decision-making process is democratic, requires people who are cooperative (not domineering) and who are self-confident and independent, not meek, passive, submissive, weak, or dependent: traits that are a mixture of both femininity and masculinity. A marriage where the husband and wife both share in raising the children requires a mixture of firmness, flexibility, patience, sensitivity, and an ability to express affection: traits that may be found in either men or women (DeFrain, 1979). A marriage that involves open communication needs people who are talkative—supposedly a female trait. A marriage with flexible sex roles, where both the husband and wife are successful breadwinners, demands some assertiveness, ambition, forcefulness, and adventureousness on their part—supposedly

male traits. A marriage where people maintain monogamy, fidelity, and permanence, voluntarily rather than through coercion, and where the requirements for success are so very high requires a certain kind of perseverance: a combination of female and male traits. A marriage where sex is considered a mutual expression of love and pleasure requires the typical male virility and the typical female emotional sensitivity. The new demands of a new kind of marriage require partially **androgynous** personalities: a mixture of typically male and female traits, so that the old standards of masculinity and femininity are no longer valid (Scheff and Koopman, 1978; Spence, and Helmreich, 1978). This does not mean that men and women will will ever be identical. Genetic inheritance and biological development will always be different for women and men, but sex identity is also formed by acquiring those traits that are necessary to function as a woman or a man. These acquired traits are becoming quite similar for both sexes because the roles of men and women increasingly overlap (Osofsky and Osofsky, 1972). Times change, demands change, ideals and standards of what it means to be a man or a woman eventually change too. It remains only for individual adults to change their sex roles according to their life situations rather than being limited to what is culturally defined as male or female (Abrahams et al., 1978).

Homosexuality

Concepts

Homosexuality may be described in a number of ways. From a *physical and sexual point of view*, homosexuality refers to the phenomenon in which an individual predominantly or exclusively desires genital sexual stimulation and gratification with a person of the same biological sex. This definition sharply diverges from one that describes homosexuality as *a behavioral act*. One study of 20,000 educated liberal men and women of high socioeconomic status indicated that one-third of the men and almost one-fifth of the women had had at least one homosexual experience involving orgasm (Athanasiou, 1970). This does not mean that all of these were homosexuals. All that the study stated was that large numbers of persons, some of whom were not homosexuals, occasionally became involved in homosexual experiences. This is quite common among persons who are isolated from those of the opposite sex: in prison, in remote armed services outposts, or other places.

Many people object to any definition describing homosexuals only in terms of genital preference. Instead, they prefer *a definition with a more emotional connotation:* Homosexuality is the love of one human being for another human being of the same sex (Martin and Mariah, 1972). But one objection to this concept is that even though it recognizes the emotional aspects of homosexual relationships, it omits the sexual aspects. A father and son may love one another but this does not make them homosexuals.

Another way of describing homosexuality is as *a stage of psychosexual social development* (Rice, 1981). Most children pass through three stages as they are growing up. **Autosexual** is the stage of development during the early preschool years when a child's primary interest is in himself. This is typical of the two-year-old who wants to be in the company of others but who plays alongside them, not with them. **Homosexual** is the stage of development during the primary grades in which the child's chief pleasure and satisfaction is in being with others of the same sex. **Heterosexual** is the adolescent and adult stage of development in which individual pleasure and friendship are found with those of the opposite sex. Many adolescents experience a period of sexual identity confusion in which

they experience difficulty in passing from homosexuality to heterosexuality in their orientations (Money and Russo, 1979). Most homosexuals report that they experienced a long period of ambiguity, confusion, and uncertainty in their search for identity (Shaver and Freedman, 1976). In some, identity is never fully acquired and is always subject to modification (Troiden, 1979).

Is It Natural?

Freud (1953b) first pointed out that there are both homosexual and heterosexual components in almost everyone. Freud saw no harm in sentimental friendship with others of one's own sex provided there was no permanent inversion or reversal of the sex roles and choice of sexual object. While reversal of sex roles and sexual objects is frequent, Freud nevertheless regarded the reversal as a deviation from normal sexual life and to be avoided if possible. Wilhelm Stekel, a coworker with Freud, stated: "All persons originally are bisexual in their predisposition. There are no exceptions" (Stekel, 1922). Stekel went on to say that at the age of puberty, however, the heterosexual represses his homosexuality, whereas the homosexual somehow pushes the wrong button and represses his heterosexuality instead. As a result, homosexuals are neurotic because of their unexpressed heterosexuality (Martin and Lyon 1972). This view is the one that most psychoanalysts traditionally accepted. "We consider homosexuality to be a pathologic, biosocial, psychosexual adaptation consequent to persuasive fears surrounding the expression of heterosexual impulses" (Bieber, 1962, p. 220). If homosexuality was regarded as pathological, it must be cured, and if cured, then causes must be found. Much of the research in the past was concerned with causes and cures (Weinberg and Bell, 1972).

Kinsey was one of the first social scientists to emphasize that there are degrees of heterosexuality and homosexuality. He developed a six-point scale of sexual behavior with 0 representing no homosexual desire or behavior, and 6 no heterosexual desire or behavior (see figure 6-2). He found that many human beings fall into neither of these categories, but can be rated from 1 to 5 depending upon their mixture of homosexual and heterosexual attraction and behavior. Some persons have a mixture of both tendencies, so are bisexual. Generally, these would be those who rate from 2 to 4 on Kinsey's scale (Weinberg and Williams, 1974). Some of these apparently live a typical heterosexual life with their wives and children and yet enjoy homosexual sex on the side in such places as "tea rooms"—public restrooms (Humphreys, 1970).

Just as there are different degrees of homosexuality and heterosexuality, there are different types of persons who are homosexuals. Some are definitely neurotic or even psychotic (as are some heterosexuals); others are psychologically well adjusted. Most are creative, contributing members of their society. The researchers at the Institute for Sex Research (the institute that Kinsey founded) suggest: "It is our wish that societies come to conceptualize homosexuality in less negative

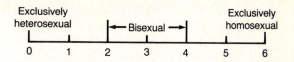

1 Predominantly heterosexual, only incidentally homosexual
2 More heterosexual than homosexual
3 Equally heterosexual and homosexual
4 More homosexual than heterosexual
5 Predominantly homosexual, only incidentally heterosexual

FIGURE 6-2. *Kinsey's continuum of heterosexuality-homosexuality*

terms, and as not being 'deviant,' thereby reducing the differentiation of human beings on the basis of sexual orientation" (Altman, 1971, p. 275). These writers observe that homosexuality is considered deviant in our society but that it is not so regarded in some other cultures. Therefore, "deviancy" is a relative term and depends upon the standard of normalcy. In a predominantly heterosexual society, homosexuality is deviancy, but it would not be so regarded in a more homosexually oriented culture. Therefore, the whole concept of homosexuality as "deviant" or "normal," "pathological" or "healthy," "immoral" or "moral" is partly a result of cultural conditioning. Table 6-1 shows a comparison

TABLE 6-1. *General population's evaluation of homosexuality, by society*

Extent to Which General Population Agrees that Homosexuality is Obscene and Vulgar	United States (N = 239)*	Amsterdam (N = 37)	Copenhagen (N = 34)
Very much	48.5%	5.4%	11.8%
Somewhat	23.0	18.9	26.5
Very little	17.1	21.9	23.5
Not at all	11.3	54.1	38.2

Source: From *Male Homosexuals: Their Problems and Adaptations* by Martin S. Weinberg and Colin J. Williams, p. 84. Copyright © 1974 by Oxford University Press, Inc. Reprinted by permission.

* Males from cities over one million; selected from the study's total sample in order to increase comparability with Amsterdam and Copenhagen. A more precise delimitation of city size was not possible from that study's code categories.

of male attitudes towards homosexuality in the United States, Amsterdam, and Copenhagen. As can be seen, in both Amsterdam and Copenhagen, homosexuals live in an environment that is much more tolerant of them than do those who live in the United States (Weinberg and Williams, 1974). One national survey of 3,000 adults in the United States revealed that nearly half of the respondents agreed that "homosexuality is a social corruption which can cause the downfall of civilization" (Hills, 1980).

Problems of Homosexuals

Certainly most homosexuals would agree that their problems are made much worse because of the attitudes of society toward them. Many have been arrested, persecuted directly and indirectly in countless ways, and forced to lead segregated, secretive lifestyles that are not conducive to personal happiness or well-being. Many homosexuals would like to admit their sexual preferences openly but are afraid of public and personal recrimination (Humphreys, 1972). As a consequence, they are often isolated, lonely, unhappy people, terribly afraid of rejection—even by other homosexuals. Some do everything possible to hide their situation; some even marry as a cover-up for their real preferences. One study showed that more than half of the male homosexuals who used public restrooms for sex were also heterosexually married (Humphreys, 1970). Homosexuals realize that discovery may mean loss of employment, dismissal from the armed services or college, or social rejection and persecution (Williams and Weinberg, 1971). This concern for secrecy has led many male homosexuals to confine their sexual experiences to anonymous, impersonal contacts in public restrooms, steam baths, or massage parlors. It is also this fear of exposure and the desire for anonymity that sometimes prevents the male homosexual from establishing more lasting relationships. Female homosexuals are better able to establish close relationships, since society is more tolerant of women being seen together. The male or female who is afraid of being seen in an open homosexual relationship, however, may end up being lonely or in participating only in casual encounters with persons not known (Harry, 1979). Of course, those who meet for sexual activity in public parks or in other spots where others can see them encourage hostility and legal action against themselves. In such cases, recrimination has been stimulated because of their own indiscretion. Those who establish more lasting, exclusive relationships, report more self-acceptance, less social awkwardness, less depression, and loneliness (Norland, 1978).

Because of the attitudes of society toward them, most homosexuals experience considerable conflict over their situation. One homosexual writes: A person cannot live in an atmosphere of universal rejection, of widespread pretence, of a society that outlaws and banishes his activities and desires, of a social world that jokes and sneers at every turn, without a fundamental influence on his personality. The net effect is to experience problems with self-acceptance and self-esteem. This is why modern gays are urging one another to step forward. They feel that the only way to gain acceptance is by an open acknowledgment of their situation and by a demand that homosexuality be accepted as normal. This solution works for the betterment of some. Research shows that those who are committed homosexuals and who accept themselves this way show far fewer psychological problems than do those who are still in conflict over their condition (Weinberg and Williams, 1974). Gays who are parents report that, for the most part, their children accept the parents' homosexuality (Miller, 1979; Voeller and Walters, 1978). In most cases, the children do not grow up to be homosexuals, which indicates that modeling and imitation alone cannot account for persons becoming homosexuals. In case of divorce, however, most courts still deny homosexuals custody of their own children (Davies, 1979; Hitchens, 1979–80).

Implications for Marriage

Heterosexuals who marry persons who are definitely homosexual, or who are bisexual with strong homosexual tendencies, may be faced with serious difficulties. They may realize the true situation only after marriage occurs. Sometimes the homosexual partner shows no interest at all in heterosexual sexual expression. At other times the interest is weak or unpredictable. In other instances, the couple have normal and regular intercourse, but the straight partner discovers his or her mate is also having homosexual relations outside the marital bond. Such discovery usually poses a threat to the marriage unless the straight partner is particularly understanding and accepting. Of course, some homosexuals, as well as heterosexuals, have **extramarital sexual relationships** for years without their mates finding out and so are still able to maintain their marriages. Occasionally, two bisexuals of the opposite sex marry one another and have intramarital and extramarital sex with the full knowledge of one another. They may be quite satisfied with the arrangement. Generally speaking, however, a heterosexual who suspects a preference for homosexual relations in a partner prior to marriage needs to be quite certain about the situation before proceeding with marriage. Similarly, the person who knows he or she is exclusively or strongly homosexual is really not being fair or wise to enter into a heterosexual marriage, since the chances of succeeding are slim. The bisexual would do well to get professional help to determine if a heterosexual marriage would indeed have a chance of succeeding.

At the present time, marriages between homosexuals are becoming more frequent, even though not legally sanctioned. The sparse literature available indicates that as many as 46 percent of homosexuals are "married" or have been "married" to another homosexual (Leitsch, 1971; Monosevitz, 1974). Whether such marriages should ever be legally recognized is a very controversial question. While some homosexual relationships, especially among females, are long lasting with deep emotional attachments, the majority of gay marriages are shortlived. Many gays feel that this is owing to the lack of legal, religious, social, and financial sanctions which hold heterosexual marriages together. Consequently, these persons feel that homosexual unions should be recognized (Jensen, 1974). Others believe this is unnecessary. It is clear that laws making homosexuality a crime are useless, however, since sexual preference cannot be legislated. What is needed is a more thorough understanding of the homosexual.

Conclusions

There are three major influences on human sexual development: (1) genetic, (2) hormonal, and (3) environmental. Gender is determined genetically at the time of conception, but physical growth and the differentiation of the sex organs into male or female take place subsequently under the influence of both the genetic code and the level and type of hormones in the bloodstream. As has been seen, sometimes males are born with either an excess of Y chromosomes, resulting in "supermales," or with an excess of X chromosomes, resulting in "feminized" males. Females are sometimes born with an X chromosome deficiency, resulting in an incompletely developed woman. Similarly, the relative proportion of male versus female hormones during prenatal growth of the fetus will partly determine the extent to which the individual develops physically into a male or female. Hermaphroditism in females results from an excess of androgens prenatally, which exert a masculinizing influence. Hermaphroditism in males results from an androgen deficiency, which results in a feminized male. If detected early, corrective surgery and hormonal therapy for either males or females have proved successful in many cases.

While maleness or femaleness has a physical basis, masculinity or femininity is primarily learned. This is best seen by the fact that a child will grow up as masculine or feminine depending on the sex assigned and the sex role in which he or she is reared. As far as sex identity is concerned, this plasticity does not persist beyond the first several years of life, for once masculinity or femininity is established, it becomes extremely difficult for the basic pattern of personality to be changed or reversed later in life. This is why it is very important that correct gender identity be established at birth. Once gender is assigned and cognitively accepted by the child and his or her parents, numerous social forces and influences begin to operate to mold the child into a masculine or feminine person.

As has been seen, however, the concepts of masculinity or femininity vary from culture to culture depending upon the norms of "maleness" or "femaleness" that have been established. Since it is society which defines what is a "man" or "woman," it is society that can change those standards as situations and needs change. As applied to marriage, this means that as egalitarian, companionship marriages replace authoritarian, traditional marriages, the requirements for being a man or a woman change too. As sex roles become more flexible and interchangeable, the necessary personality traits to fulfill those roles become partly masculine and partly feminine, adopting—as necessity arises—some of the distinguishing traits of each sex. Does this mean that it is likely that a unisex will develop? No, but it does seem likely that men will become more emotionally sensitive and less aggressive, and women will become less passive and will feel freer to express their erotic impulses and to be autonomous. Beyond these broad patterns of change, it is difficult to predict.

Female-centered households are on the increase, making it more and more difficult for boys growing up to find masculine sex role models. This fact should be taken into account by mothers who, because of circumstances, are forced to raise their boys in the absence of a father. They can encourage their sons to participate in boys clubs or groups, attend summer camps, or seek other opportunities for them to find male models. While there are some degrees of homosexuality in everyone, those who show a marked genital preference for their own sex have difficult adjustments to make in a society that emphasizes heterosexuality. While societal attitudes have become somewhat more tolerant, homosexuals in the United States are still ridiculed and persecuted to such an extent that most try to hide their preferences and wish that they too were not different. Their lives would be easier if laws were changed to decriminalize homosexuality, and if people were educated to understand that it is neither a crime nor a sin, but a pattern of sexual behavior the individual has not consciously chosen.

The following discussion took place in an undergraduate dormitory room of a large university. The participants were four sophomores Helen and Ann, who shared this room, and their male friends, Hank and Ed. The foursome were discussing what kind of men and women they most admired.

Helen: You asked me what kind of man I like. I prefer men who are rugged, he-men types. I don't necessarily mean those who have big muscles, but men who are very confident and sure of themselves, who don't let other people push them around. I like a man whom I can admire and look up to.

Ann: The trouble with that type is that they are all a bunch of jocks. Who wants to marry a guy who is all brawn and no brains? I went with one guy like that who was so egotistical and insensitive that he never considered my feelings about anything. He was so busy showing off his body that he didn't have time to think about me.

Hank: Just because a guy has a nice build and can model for a Marlboro ad doesn't mean he's dumb or insensitive or unemotional. I knew a guy in high school who weighed 230 pounds who cried like a baby when his dog died. He used to be very emotional about everything.

Helen: I think that's gross! What a sissy! I can't stand a man who cries.

Ann: What's so sissy about expressing feelings? I'd like my husband to be sensitive to what I'm thinking and feeling, to tell me he loves me, to send me flowers, and to show real emotions. If he never lets himself show real emotions, I don't see how he could feel real love either.

Ed: Would you like a husband who acted more like a woman than a man? I knew a guy down our block at home who liked to knit.

Ann: So what? Does that make him less manly? I hope my husband will want to change the baby's diapers and rock it to sleep. I hope he'll be warm and tender. That doesn't make him less of a man.

Helen: How can a man do women's work and act like a woman and be a real man? Would you guys want a wife who dressed like a man, worked as an auto mechanic, and who swore like a sailor?

Hank: Personally, I don't think that what a woman wears or the work she does or whether or not she swears determines whether or not she is a good wife. I like a woman who is a nice person, who's kind and generous, who's fun, and who cares about me. I wouldn't care if she wore overalls and was a welder and knew every swear word in the dictionary. I once met a woman wrestler who was one of the sweetest people I've ever met. If I loved her, I'd marry her.

Helen: I suppose you won't care whether or not your wife is flat-chested and looks like a scarecrow.

Ann: I'd hate to think that my worth as a wife would depend on what size bra I wore.

Ed: And I'd hate to think that my wife looked and acted like the guy next door.

Hank: But that's not the point. The problem is that the work a woman does or what a woman looks like should not be the important criteria in whether or not she's a real woman, or whether or not she would be a good wife or mother. And you can't judge "manliness" by how rugged a man looks or by whether or not he tries to hide tender feelings.

Ann: I think we ought to start emphasizing what it means to be a real person, to be really human, not whether people are masculine or feminine according to the stereotypes in our culture.

QUESTIONS

1. What personality characteristics that are traditionally masculine make it more difficult to achieve intimacy, companionship, harmony, and success in marriage? Explain.

2. How do traditional masculine stereotypes prevent men from being good fathers?

3. What personality characteristics that are traditionally feminine make it more difficult for women to achieve full equality at home and in the business world?

4. What effects do traditional feminine stereotypes have upon husbands, wives, children?

5. What are your concepts of an ideal human being? Man? Woman?

CHAPTER
7

Women's
Rights and Roles

CHAPTER OUTLINE

The Women's Movement

Chauvinism and Sexism

Legal Equality

Sex Role Differentiation and
Discrimination

Women's Sexuality

Employment and Income

Education

Marriage Roles and Housework

Child Rearing

Reproduction

Conclusions

The women's movement has had a significant impact upon marital relationships. Traditional sex roles in marriage are being challenged. Sexual standards, relationships, and behavior have undergone evolutionary changes. Women's struggle for equal educational and employment opportunities has resulted in some successes and some frustrations. Traditional ideas of child rearing are being reexamined, especially in view of women's insistence upon more group care centers for children. Even women's traditional childbearing functions are being questioned, so that many women now opt for voluntary childlessness and for elective abortions rather than compulsory motherhood.

This chapter presents a brief overview of women's historic and contemporary struggle for legal, social, occupational, educational, sexual, marital, and personal equality and some of the effects of that struggle on society, families, and individuals.

The Women's Movement

The modern day women's movement and the concept of **feminism** are not new. Wollstonecraft first published *A Vindication of the Rights of Women* in London in 1792, a year after Paine published his controversial *The Rights of Man.* Wollstonecraft was Paine's friend and came to his defense when he was tried for treason. At the time Wollstonecraft wrote, the fires of the French Revolution were raging across the channel, so her feminist's philoso-

phy was in keeping with the revolutionary spirit of the day.

The first feminist movement in the United States was launched at Seneca Falls, New York, in 1848 when the first women's rights convention was held. The convention said that "men *and* women are created equal . . . endowed . . . with certain inalienable rights." Starting with almost no political leverage, no money, and with conventional morality against them, the suffragists won the Married Women's Property Act in the latter half of the nineteenth century and won the enactment of the Nineteenth Amendment to the Constitution in 1920, which gave women the right to vote. But after women won the franchise and after the depression the movement lost momentum (Freeman, 1973).

In spite of the unprecedented employment of women during World War II, social philosophy still planted women's feet firmly in the home. As a result, even though large numbers of women worked, they were discriminated against so that their economic position in the job market declined. They were segregated in "female jobs" such as secretarial work, teaching, and other traditionally female work. The percentage of women in professional and technical jobs actually declined along with relative income. The result was a class of educated but underemployed and underpaid women workers. Women were encouraged to raise large numbers of children in nuclear families where they assumed the major responsibility for homemaking and child rearing. Those who did not feel totally fulfilled through marriage and parenthood were made to feel that something was wrong with them (Callahan, 1971). During these years, from 1930 to 1960, feminism was a dirty word.

The first sign of new life came with the establishment of the Commission on the Status of Women by President Kennedy in 1961 (Freeman, 1972). During its short life the Commission made a number of proposals, some considered radical. Then Friedan became the spokeswoman for thousands of women when she published her famous classic *The Feminine Mystique* in 1963. In this book, she examined the contemporary "back to the home" movement and then proceeded to tear apart the myth of the fulfilled and happy American housewife. According to Friedan, the "feminine mystique" was a woman who became a function of someone else (husband or children) or of something else (homemaking) and who never became her own true self through creative self-realization (through a career). Friedan complained that there had grown up a whole generation of American women

who adjust to the feminine mystique, who expect to live through their husbands and children, who want only to be loved and secure, to be accepted by others, who never make a commitment of their own to society. . . . The adjusted or cured ones who live without conflict or anxiety in the confined world of the home have forfeited their own being (Friedan, 1963, p. 300).

As one of the first spokeswomen, Friedan continues to exert a powerful influence in the contemporary women's struggle. She was the founder of NOW, the National Organization for Women, which is made up of numerous chapters that comprise the older branch of the movement (Freeman, 1973). This organization, along with others such as Women's Equity Action League and Human Rights for Women are often referred to as *moderate* or *reform* feminists. They are concerned primarily

with "women's rights" (Hole and Levin, 1971).

The younger branch of the movement consists of innumerable small groups, often loosely called *radical* feminists (Bird, 1973). They are concerned with "women's liberation": liberation from the hold of the patriarchy (Pollock, 1972). Some of the more radical groups are completely socialistic in their philosophy and are as devoted to espousing the revolutionary doctrine of the Left as they are in promoting the cause of women (Firestone, 1970). For them, the goal is to overthrow the whole capitalistic system in which men are the chief oppressors (Brownmiller, 1970). One must be cautious about labels, however. Freeman writes:

It is a common mistake to try to place the various feminist organizations on the traditional left/right spectrum. The term "reformist" and "radical" are convenient and fit into our preconceived notions about the nature of political organizations, but they tell us nothing of relevance. . . . Some groups called "reformist" have a platform which would so completely change our society it would be unrecognizable. Other groups called "radical" concentrate on the traditional female concerns of love, sex, children and interpersonal relationships (although with untraditional views) (Freeman, 1972, p. 204).

In 1973, a number of women's magazines surveyed readers' attitudes on women's issues (Skolnick, 1973). One such survey was conducted by *Redbook* magazine. The authors of the report state:

These women are far from being radicals or feminists. As the profile of those who replied to the questionnaire shows, they tend to be political moderates, to acknowledge a religious affiliation and to have chosen the conventional style of marriage and motherhood.

These rather conventional women, however, harbor some very unconventional attitudes about their status in American society. The overwhelming majority believes that women are, indeed, sec-

The women's movement has made significant progress in winning equal rights for women.

ond-class citizens, a notion that as recently as several years ago was held by only a small majority of women (Tavris and Toby, 1973, p. 68).

The vast majority of American women are not members of any formal group, but there are thousands of women and men who are in sympathy with one or more of the causes that the movements promote.

Chauvinism and Sexism

Chauvinism, *by dictionary definition, means overzealousness or blind enthusiasm for a cause. The male chauvinist is the man who continues to believe in male supremacy and who treats women as inferior beings* (Battle-Sister, 1971). He is the man who believes and acts as though women are stupid, childish, unimportant, and incapable and so should be placed in subordinate, inferior roles (Homstrom, 1973). His feelings of male supremacy justify his contentions that men should receive better jobs and more pay, hold the most important political and social positions in our culture, receive more education, and be given preferential treatment in the family.

While permeating the whole social order, these feelings are particularly persistent among lower-class males. One study of blue-collar men showed that these males did not accept females as their equals. In fact, the men harbored deep-seated feelings of hostility and resentment toward all women (LeMasters, 1972).

Men who feel this way seek to justify

their contention that women were created for the pleasure and assistance of men and that women's "natural" function is to serve men. A Council of Congregational Ministers wrote the following in 1836, 143 years ago:

The power of the woman is her dependence flowing from the consciousness of a weakness which God has given to her for her protection; for when she assumes the place and tone of man, she yields the power which God has given her for her protection and her character becomes unnatural (Soely, 1970).

It is these views against which women are protesting. If females are considered inferior, then these chauvinistic views are used to justify **sexism,** which is discrimination in many forms. In such societies, men can deny women sex or force it upon them, command or exploit their labor and control their produce, control their children or force children upon them, confine them physically and prevent their movement, use them as "things" to give pleasure, or withhold from them society's knowledge or deny them cultural attainments (Gough, 1971). The theme of Millet's book *Sexual Politics* is that men have seized the power and control of human society, denied woman's personhood, and relegated her to a position of subjugation.

But sexism is more than discrimination against women. *It is the naive, unconscious, taken-for-granted, unexamined acceptance and institutionalizing of patriarchal attitudes and behavior by both men and women.* In language, "mankind" and "he" are used for both sexes. In religion God is our "Father." In marriage, the couple is "man" and wife (not wife and husband). In committee meetings, men are appointed as chairmen, women as secretaries. In society as a whole, men are elected or accepted for positions of leadership, women are expected to follow (Bart, 1971). The eradication of sexism and the practices it supports is one of the major goals of the women's movement.

Legal Equality

In an effort to eliminate sexism and discrimination, women are seeking complete equality before the law. The passing of the Equal Rights Amendment is considered a must. This amendment says that: "Equality of rights under the law shall not be denied or abridged by the United States or by any State on account of sex." Passing of this amendment is considered vital because even though the Fourteenth Amendment guarantees equal protection under the law to all persons who are citizens, the Supreme Court has refused to rule on the issue of whether women are "persons" (Congress to Unite Women, 1972). The ERA has actually been introduced at every session of Congress since 1923. Finally it was approved by Congress, but it was not ratified by the states. Proponents vow to continue trying.

One of the significant advances in recent years was the passage of the Civil Rights Act of 1964. It included a provision under Title VII which states that sex may not be a qualification for employment in a particular job and that it is the obligation of the employer to prove that either sex is disqualified on the basis of incompatibility with the nature of the work. It further states that persons of equal training, education, and experience must receive the same pay regardless of sex. Implementation of this law still remains to be accomplished, however. There is no provision for penalty against discrimination or for not enforcing the act, though the federal government does exert considerable pressure on agencies receiving federal funds—unless the provisions of the law are followed, funds may be withheld. Since Title VII only covers employment, the ERA is still needed.

There are a wide range of other legal changes that need to be made to assure women equality before the law. One struggle has been the effort of women to win credit privileges for themselves (Steinem, 1972).

More and more lending institutions, as well as shops and stores, are being forced to extend credit to women on the basis of their own credit ratings. It is estimated that 10 percent of those applying for home loans are single women. The Federal Equal Credit Opportunity Act now prohibits credit discrimination on the basis of race, color, religion, national origin, sex, marital status, or age. Married persons now have the right to have credit information listed in the name of both the wife and the husband.

Women's groups also have pointed to other inequities. Income tax laws discriminate against single persons and childless couples (National Council on Family Relations, 1973). A wife has no legal right to a share of the husband's earnings beyond necessary expenses to run the household. She has no legal right to compensation for doing domestic work. She is under obligation to follow the husband if he moves (Skolnick, 1973). The husband may force her to have sexual intercourse with him against her will, an act which if committed against any other woman would constitute the crime of rape (Gillespie, 1972). In a country founded upon the principle of equality under the law, more than half of its citizenry do not now enjoy this privilege.

Sex Role Differentiation and Discrimination

Discrimination against women has been blamed partially on sex role differentiation and on the way children are socialized (Barwick, 1971). According to this view, as long as girls are socialized to assume one role and boys another, the sexes will never really be accepted as equal. Separation means discrimination. While the concept of "complementary but equal" in marriage sounds nice, in actual practice it leads to discrimination against women. Therefore, it is argued, differentia-

tion in sex roles must be eliminated. There should be an end to socializing children to grow up to do men's work or women's work or to assume either an instrumental or expressive role. Sex roles should be dynamic and interchangeable with both men and women able to assume any role. In other words society would be *androgynous*—both male and female in one (Osofsky and Osofsky, 1972).

The media, especially television and advertising, have come under heavy attack because of their perpetuation of traditional sex role stereotypes. Komisar writes:

Advertising begins stereotyping male and female very early in life ... Madison Avenue woman is a combination sex object and wife and mother who achieves fulfillment by looking beautiful and alluring for boy friends and loves cooking, cleaning, washing, or polishing for her husband and family....

*"Why yes, I am 'a little homemaker'—
I'm in the construction business and
I build small homes!"*

Reprinted by permission, © 1975, NEA, Inc.

Nearly half the women in the country work, but you wouldn't think so to look at American advertising. A woman's place is not only in the home . . . it is in the kitchen and laundry room. . . .

If television commercials are to be believed, most American women go into uncontrollable ecstasies at the sight and sound of tables . . . that have been lovingly caressed with . . . lemon-scented . . . furniture polish . . . or they glow with rapture at the blinding whiteness of their wash. . . .

Advertising did not create these images about women, but it is a powerful force for their reenforcement. . . .

Advertising also reenforces men's concepts about women's place and women's role and about their own roles. It makes masculine dominance legitimate (Kosimar, 1971, pp. 208, 209, 212).

Women's Sexuality

The overemphasis on women as sex objects is also a major source of contention (Brownmiller, 1970). The emphasis on a woman's physical appearance and body dimensions as a measure of her worth and acceptability is anxiety producing and demeaning and it reflects distorted values (Boston Women's Health Course Collective, 1971). Women are told repeatedly by the media that they will be valueless, lonely, unhappy unless they emulate the slim, glamorous, young model in the ads. Women's groups have called for "the elimination of the generally derogatory image of women as sex objects by the media" (Staples, 1973).

At the same time that they are objecting to being used as "playbunnies," women are rebelling against the double standards of sexual behavior and insisting on equal rights to sexual satisfaction (Becker, 1972; Seaman, 1972). The research findings of Masters and Johnson (1966) and others have emphasized women's superior orgasic capacity to that of men, a fact that has delighted feminists (Bernard, 1972a). Overall, the rediscovery of

women's sexual capacities has had a positive effect on sexual relationships in marriage, enabling husbands and wives to participate in meaningful sexual relationships on an equal basis (Bordon and Shankweiler, 1971).

Employment and Income

Employment figures include increasing numbers of married women. In March of 1979, 49.4 percent of all married women with husband present were working. Of all women with children six through seventeen years old and husband present, 59.1 percent were working. Of those with children under six years old and husband present, 43.2 percent were working (U.S. Department of Commerce, *Statistical Abstract of the United States*, 1980). These figures show only those that were employed in March. But since total labor force participation during any one year is greater than during any one month, the percentages of women who worked at some time during the year would be higher (Ridley, 1971).

The problem of female employment is not employment as such but the type of employment in which women are engaged (Suelzle, 1973). Ridley (1971) writes:

To argue that high female labor force participation rates necessarily imply that women have a high status may be in error. Nonwhite women in the United States have long exhibited higher labor force participation rates than white women. Yet, as is well known, black women in the United States have been mainly confined to occupations accorded relatively low status (p. 191).

The confinement of women to low status occupation is also true of all women. An analysis of the female participation patterns in various occupational categories indicates that women continue to be a minority in the managerial, professional, technical, and skilled occupations with the majority in office and clerical occupations (Epstein, 1970). Women also are well represented in service occupations (Equal Opportunity Commission, 1971). (See figure 7-1.) Large numbers of employed women are in five occupations—secretary-stenographers, household workers, bookkeepers, elementary school teachers, and waitresses (Lyle, 1973). An examination of table 7-1 will reveal that many occupations are still largely segregated according to sex, although that segregation is being eliminated slowly (U.S. Department of Commerce, Statistical Abstract, 1980).

Discrimination is even more evident when the income of women is compared with men in identical occupations (Mitchell, 1971). There are a number of factors that influence earnings differentials. As already discussed, men have higher status jobs than women, thus larger income. A greater percentage of men than women go on to higher education. Men are about twice as likely as women to be working full time, year around during the year. Men have about twice the work experience as women of comparable age. But if all of these factors are adjusted statistically so that women are assumed to have the same occupational status, education, working hours full time, and work experience as men, the income level of women would still be only 61 percent of the male income level (Suter and Miller, 1973; U.S. Department of Commerce, Statistical Abstract, 1980). *The conclusion is inescapable: The primary reason for the lower income of women is discrimination. Women are not receiv-*

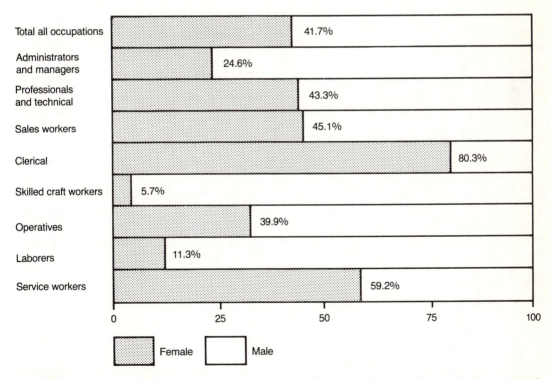

FIGURE 7-1. *Female participation by occupational group, 1979 (Source: U.S. Bureau of the Census,* Statistical Abstract of the United States, 1980 [Washington, D.C.: U.S. Government Printing Office, 1980], pp. 418–420.)

TABLE 7-1. *Percentage in different occupations who are female.*

	1972	1979
Accountants	21.7	32.9
Bank officers and financial managers	19.0	31.6
Carpenters	.5	1.3
Other construction craftworkers	.6	1.6
College teachers	21.8	31.6
Engineers	.8	2.9
Insurance agents	11.6	23.8
Lawyers and judges	3.8	12.4
Physicians	10.1	10.7
Protective service workers (police, fire, etc.)	5.7	8.8
Registered nurses	97.6	96.8
Religious workers	11.0	13.3
Restaurant, cafeteria, bar managers	32.4	35.4
Social and recreation workers	55.1	61.4
Teachers - elementary and secondary	70.0	70.8

Source: U.S. Bureau of the Census, Department of Commerce, *Statistical Abstract of the United States, 1980* (Washington, D.C.: U.S. Government Printing Office, 1980), pp. 418–420.

ing equal pay for equal work. Nationally, a woman chemist with a Ph.D. averages less income than a male chemist with a bachelor's degree (O'Neill, 1972).

Education

One of the important goals of the women's movement has been to improve the status of women by improving their educational opportunities and participation. At the present time, more women than men complete high school, but fewer women go on to take college work (Suelzle, 1973). Figure 7-2 shows a comparison for the year 1979 for those twenty-five years old and over. As can be seen, a greater percentage of females than males graduate from high school, but greater percentages of males than females graduate from college (U.S. Department of Commerce,

Statistical Abstract, 1980). Females fall farther behind with each succeeding year of college or graduate school. During the year 1979, females received 47 percent of the bachelor degrees but only 29 percent of the doctorates (U.S. Department of Commerce, Statistical Abstract, 1980).

A number of studies have been undertaken to determine why more women don't go on to take college and graduate degrees (American Council on Education, 1972; Bayer, 1972; Watley and Kaplan, 1971; Wegner and Sewell, 1970). The overwhelming answer is because they get married. While marriage need not, or perhaps should not, interrupt a woman's education, it does for many. Feldman writes of female graduate students:

There is conflict between the role of wife and the role of full-time graduate student. Married women are under great pressure to drop out. ... In comparing single and divorced women, I note that the

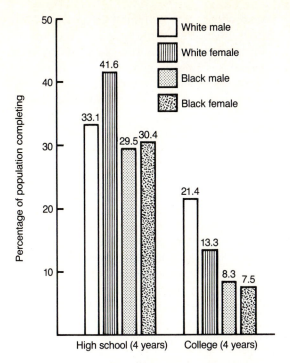

FIGURE 7-2. *Years of school completed by race and sex, 1978 (as of March 1) (Source: U.S. Bureau of the Census, Department of Commerce,* Statistical Abstract of the United States [*Washington, D.C.: U.S. Government Printing Office, 1980*], p. 149)

products of familial, educational, and personal experiences that orient them toward marriage and homemaking rather than toward careers (Angrist, 1972). They are only gradually moving into permanent, long-term careers (Alamek, 1970; Almquist and Angrist, 1970).

Most women want to develop and use all of their capabilities (Cofield, 1973; Epstein and Bronzadt, 1972). On this point most writers agree. Loring writes: " . . . self-actualization is not found by living *through* one's husband, one's children, even by the full and free expression of one's love for one's family" (Loring, 1972, p. 82). Bardwick says: "While the vast majority of educated women may define their *femininity* in terms of achieving marriage and parenthood, their *self-perception* is very likely to include needs for independent achievement" (Bardwick, 1971, p. 190). Those women who drop out of college to marry or

most committed and active graduate students are divorced women. Once divorced or separated, it is almost as if they were making up for lost time by becoming fully immersed in the student role, despite the fact that almost 70 percent of the divorced female graduate students have at least one child. . . .

Marital status has an effect upon the student roles of both men and women; greatest "success," that is, ability to adhere to a career-primacy model, obtains among married men and divorced women (Feldman, 1973, p. 231).

Of course, this does not answer the question of why women get married rather than completing higher education in the first place. The answer is extremely complicated but, as has been pointed out, part of it lies in the way women are socialized. Women are

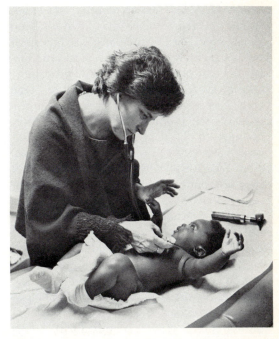

More and more women are entering professions that have been predominantly male.

to work to put their husbands through do so at the sacrifice of their own personal fulfillment, at least fulfillment through an education and the possibilities it offers.

Marriage Roles and Housework

If women are to realize the maximum opportunity for personal fulfillment, in a career as well as in marriage, not only will they have to be educated for that career, but profound changes will have to take place in the patterns of marriage relationships. Some extremists insist that personal fulfillment is incompatible with marriage, that love and marriage are traps to keep women in subservient roles. Atkinson writes: "Marriage means rape and lifelong slavery. Love has to be destroyed" (Atkinson, 1969). "Women in this movement," declares Loring, "believe that inevitably love has and will continue to cause their downfall. Second class status, loss of identity, lack of autonomy . . . all are due to love. Love has been used as a tool both by men and institutions of society to keep women in their place, and historically that place has been defined by men" (Loring, 1972, p. 78). Morgan writes: "One thing does seem clearer as time goes on; the nuclear family is oppressive to women" (Morgan, 1970, p. 32). Radical feminists who advocate these views urge women to stay single, accept lesbianism if they choose, or to find other alternative lifestyles such as in communes (Bernard, 1973). Less radical writers do not go so far (Hunt, 1974). They want to keep marriage alive but insist on egalitarian and flexible sex roles in marriage. Men, as often as women, ought to do domestic chores: housecleaning, cooking, and baby tending. Almost all writers insist that housework is the primary female enemy and that women ought to quit doing most of it (Mainardi, 1972).

In spite of modern conveniences, the volume of household tasks is considerable.

Housewives work extremely long hours. One of the frustrating things about housework is that it is repetitive, routine, and unsatisfying. The housewife can seldom say, "The task is completed," and have the satisfaction of knowing it is true. Furthermore, in terms of prestige, the occupation is near the bottom of the scale (Greer, 1971).

Research indicates that being a housewife *is* debilitating to the morale and well-being of many women. Bernard summarized research findings which show that marriage imposes more regulations and adjustment on women than men, that more wives than husbands consider their marriages unhappy, that more married women than single are bothered by depression, worries, and phobias, neurotic symptoms and physical pains and aches, and that women who have the deepest commitments to domesticity are most likely to experience depression at menopause (Bernard, 1971).

A number of answers to the problem of housework have been proposed. One is for the wife to receive a part of the husband's pay so she may at least feel financially compensated for her labors. But this does not meet the needs of the educated woman who feels that housework is demeaning. Most feminists feel that the menial chores should be shared by both husband and wife, just as the responsibility for income earning should belong to both. At the present time, however, this concept is more of an ideal than a reality in most homes. A study of fifty-three couples where both partners were working professionals revealed that only one out of the fifty-three marriages could be considered truly egalitarian, where both the husband and wife made a conscious effort to share (not just help) in cooking, cleaning, caring for the children, and providing for the family's economic needs. In all other homes, the wife was responsible for the traditional feminine tasks and the husband helped in varying degrees, while the husband was responsible for providing family status and income with the wife assisting (Poloma and Garland, 1971). What to do about housework, therefore, continues to be a source of frustration in many families (Gordon, 1972; Whitehurst, 1972b).

Other suggestions have been made, that the husband and wife each work part-time—leaving each free to do homemaking part of the time—or that the man work for six months of the year while the women takes care of the house and children—with the roles reversed for the next six months. Actually, graduate students and others often reverse roles on a temporary basis, but it is difficult to find part-time careers (not just jobs) on a daily or yearly basis that will allow more permanent role reversals to be accomplished. Since research indicates that egalitarian marriages without a high degree of role specialization are happier marriages, and since the wives are happier women, however, the effort to achieve equality is necessary and worthwhile (Bernard, 1973).

Child Rearing

There are several important emphases in the feminists' views on child rearing. *Anatomy is not destiny.* Feminists very soundly reject Freud's dictum that "anatomy is destiny." This dictum states that maternity is woman's most important goal in life and that to be fulfilled a woman *has* to become a mother. The dictum insists that women are predestined by biological considerations to be bearers of children. This is the same view as held by Pope Pius XII who said in 1946: "Now the sphere of woman, her manner of life, her native bent, is motherhood. Every woman is meant to be a mother."

"But," says New York psychiatrist Rabkin (1970), "women don't need to be mothers any more than they need spaghetti. If you're in a world where everyone is eating spaghetti,

thinking they need it and want it, you will think so too." In other words, women have become socialized to *want* children, to feel that they *ought* to have children, but there is no instinctual drive that says they have to have them.

Not all women need or should have children. For one thing, having children doesn't necessarily make a "not-so-hot marriage better, or a hot marriage, hotter still." Parenthood can be a crisis in marriage; in fact, some childless marriages are happier. For another thing, it is having children, more than any other factor, that prevents a woman from developing her own interests and her own career. Without children, a married woman has no childwork and less housework. She can leave on the commuter train each morning with her husband if she wants to. She is free to go to school, pursue a career, or do whatever she desires. Becoming a mother is an identity crisis for many women. One mother writes:

When you are married and with small children, you have a lot of things you would like to do, but can't; you don't have time or facilities. . . . Sometimes I feel lost in the shuffle, confused . . . as if I lost identity (Lopata, 1971, p. 192).

Furthermore, it is maintained that *children in our society get too much mothering.* Slater writes: "The idea of expecting the average mother to spend most of her time alone with her children in a small house or apartment is a relatively modern invention and a rather fiendish one at that" (Slater, 1974, p. 115). Even though the farm woman of past generations spent a lot of time in her home, she was rarely alone; her husband worked within calling distance and she often worked with him. There was a variety of group activities, considerable community life, and she shared the household and child-rearing responsibilities with other adults in the extended family. Schultz points out that the modern mother spends more time with her children than have any mothers at any time in history. As a consequence, many children are overindulged, remain too dependent, and suffer a loss of autonomy. Some males develop narcissistic personalities and expect the same overindulgence from wives that they received from their mothers (Homstrom, 1973). If a mother happens to be a rejecting, harsh, cruel, abusive person, the effect on the children can be disastrous. Such children benefit from the care of others beside the mother.

This *overemphasis on motherhood is disadvantageous to women themselves.* A study of 533 women, ages forty through fifty-nine, who had suffered maternal role loss (when at least one child was not living at home) showed that it was the women who were overinvolved in their maternal role who were most likely to respond with depression when their children left home (Bart, 1973).

One of the most controversial proposals of the feminists *is to transfer much more responsibility for childcare to the community* (Finch & McDermott, 1970; Zigler, 1971). The Congress to Unite Women advocated "free twenty-four-hour-a-day" child care centers for all children from infancy to early adolescence regardless of their parents' income or marital status" (Congress to Unite Women, 1972, p. 208). While most persons approve of day care centers for children of working mothers, official government policy has always insisted that the child in need of day care is one who "has a family problem which makes it impossible for his parents to fulfill their parental responsibilities without supplementary help" (Steiner, 1973). Many feminists insist, however, that childcare be available for all families, not just those with problems, ("Day Care . . .", 1970). They feel that real equality of the sexes will not take place until society relieves women of the exclusive responsibility of child rearing (Schulz, 1973).

As the situation now stands, it is difficult for parents to combine professional and child-

rearing responsibilities because there are few collective solutions to the problems encountered. Each family must find its own individual solution (Lake, 1970). Day-care homes and centers are meeting only a fraction of the need. Figure 7-3 shows that a majority of children receive care from their own parents (U.S. Department of Commerce, May 1980). Most of the children of working mothers are of school age.

The scarcity of formal childcare arrangements in the United States sharply contrasts with programs elsewhere. In France a town with more than two thousand population provides an *ecole maternelle* for children up to age six, and almost every center has infants as young as two months (Klapper, 1972). The centers are open from 7 a.m. to 7 p.m. In Israel, about 4 percent of the population live on collective farms or **kibbutzim.** Babies and

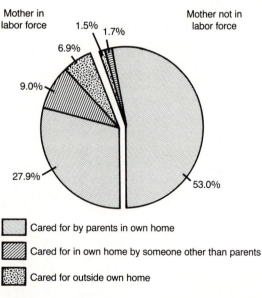

FIGURE 7-3.   *Daytime care arrangements of children 3 to 13 years old, by labor force status of mother: 1974 and 1975 (Source: U.S. Bureau of the Census, Department of Commerce,* American Families and Living Arrangements, Current Population Reports, *Series P-23, no. 104, May 1980, p. 13.)*

older children live in quarters apart from their parents and are taken care of by nurses and teachers. It must be emphasized, however, that even though both parents are employed full time, mothers do much of the feeding and care of babies during the first year, and all children visit their parents and spend much time after working hours in their parents' quarters. "Parents take a warm interest in the care and personality development of their children and spend much time with them" (Nye and Berardo, 1973). This combined care enables Rabkin and Rabkin to say that the kibbutz child "shows no signs of the emotional disturbance we would expect from a violation of our ideal mother-child relationships" (Rabkin and Rabkin, 1969).

Although research evidence is scarce and inconclusive on the effects of the French and Israeli experiences on children, tentative data to date indicate that group care *plus* interaction with parents is effective in socializing children. Nye and Berardo caution that "in these group-care programs, children have parents and, in all but the kibbutzim, children spend only the weekdays in the day-care centers. Their socialization differs greatly from those reared in orphanages" (Nye and Bernado, 1973, p. 397).

It would seem, therefore, that the choice is not between parents *or* childcare. Both are needed. Certainly, *exclusive* maternity is often "counterproductive." The mother who resents having the total responsibility discharges her own frustrations and anxieties on the child. Mitchel writes: "An increased awareness of the critical importance of socialization, far from leading to a restitution of classical maternal roles, should lead to a reconsideration of them—of what makes a good socializing agent who can genuinely provide security and stability for the child" (Mitchel, 1971, p. 274).

There is still another important need: the need for the father to share a part of the responsibility for rearing the child. Streib writes: "The major reorganization of the family requires a shifting of some of the aspects of child-rearing from women to men. Family roles and activities related to socialization in the home must be restructured with men doing much more than they have done traditionally" (Streib, 1973, p. 25). Some writers have even pointed out that "if the maternal instinct is defined as an innate tendency to want children, and to love, cherish, nurture, and protect children, then history reveals that men have had more of a maternal instinct than women" (Stannard, 1973, p. 183). This emphasis is also an important one. Research findings point to the harmful effects on the child of a nonfunctioning father, as well as a poorly functioning mother.

Reproduction

Women are also demanding full voluntary control over reproduction. This means the right to contraceptive information, and to contraceptive devices for all women of child-bearing age, plus the right to sterilization and, in case of unwanted pregnancies, the right for the individual woman to decide whether or not she wants to terminate the pregnancy by having an abortion. Feminists insist that no one, and no society, has the right to tell any woman that she has to bear a child that she herself does not want. Kurtz pretty much reflects this philosophy when she says: "Each woman's body is her own and therefore abortion must be a matter for her conscience alone" (Kurtz, 1972, p. 230). For additional information on abortion, see chapter 18.

Some women do not want any children, and shouldn't have them, and should not be made to feel guilty because they don't have them. They point to the well-documented evidence that the lowest marital satisfaction for many wives is during the "child-intensive phase" of the family life cycle (Burr, 1970; Rollins and Feldman, 1970). They also point to the problems of world population and ecology and emphasize that the decision not to have children is a socially desirable and responsible decision.

Conclusions

In evaluating the philosophy of the women's movement and the impact the movement is having on society and individuals, several points need to be kept in mind.

The movement exists because deep-seated prejudices against women permeate our culture, because women are not afforded completely equal rights, and because they are treated as second-class citizens. Many males— though certainly not all—are male chauvinists in their relationship to women and do seek to perpetuate sexist attitudes and behavior.

As persons first, and females second, women have the right to equal pay for equal work, to job opportunities in the professions, to equal educational opportunities, and to full rights under the law: politically, socially, and economically. The passage of the Equal Rights Amendment would at least provide the *legal* basis for achievement of full equality.

One of the important questions this chapter raises is whether or not the socialization process is keeping women confined to marriage and motherhood when it should be socializing them to seek personal fulfillment through careers. At the present time, the socialization process is becoming more supportive of marriage and motherhood combined with careers. It must be recognized, however, that the women who are able to have fulfilling marriages, to be good mothers, and have successful careers will always be the group of the most intelligent, capable women. It is to these groups that the women's movement has made its most successful appeal. Other women, like other men, need the chance to develop and use their potentialities to the fullest according to their choice: at home, at work, or at both, but it is as unrealistic to expect that all women will make work a career as it is to say that all women will be good mothers. Many men and women will never be able to rise above menial jobs because they neither have the ability nor the inclination. Certainly, many jobs outside the home are no more fulfilling than some jobs in the home. The emphasis on giving women options is what is important. Women want to have the unprejudiced option of having a career or not, of marrying or not marrying, and of having children or not.

If women are to succeed in all three roles, it is vital to strive for equality in marriage. True sharing of the housekeeping, child-rearing, and income-earning functions is only possible when there are equal opportunities of employment for *both* the wife and husband and when husbands are willing to do their share at home. If women share income earning, men should share housework and childcare.

The women's movement has made women and men now realize they can and should have options. What feminists are doing is to offer women and men choices, to give them the chance to seek their own destiny rather than to follow prescribed roles whether the roles are acceptable or not. To have the chance to choose is to become truly free.

CHAPTER 8

Men's Conflicting Roles

CHAPTER OUTLINE

The Husband's Changing Role

The Effect of the Male's Role on Himself

Occupational Roles and Marriage

Housekeeping and Parental Roles

Companionship Role

Roles of the Low Socioeconomic Status Husband

Conclusions

Dialogue

The modern husband-father is presented with a painful dilemma. The demands of his job for his time and talents and the demands of his family are in conflict. In such a situation, the man has three choices. He can opt for family togetherness at the expense of his career. If he decides to choose the intimate life, he may miss out on those material conforts Americans so prize. He can sacrifice his family life for job advancement. If he makes this choice, his marriage may become utilitarian, lacking those intrinsic rewards and satisfactions found in companionship marriage. Or he and his wife can realign family and vocational roles, each sharing in income earning and family governance. If this solution is chosen, it may be necessary for the husband to re-think his ideas about what the ideal husband and father ought to be. Middle-class ideas are rapidly changing and are in sharp contradiction to traditional values still held by "old world" type families. The man who wants to be a "good husband" or "good father" must then first define his terms and figure out what being a good husband or father really means. Not only that, but traditional concepts of what is an ideal wife and mother are being challenged on all sides, so that the man must also redefine his concepts of these, if he and his wife are to work out what kind of hus-band-father and wife-mother they want to be. This chapter examines the changes in the male's family role, along with the implica-tions and effect of those changes upon him-self, his wife, their marriage, their children, and their lives.

The Husband's Changing Role

Traditional Concepts

Traditionally, the ideal of a good husband was one who assumed a dominant role as head of his family. He expected his wife and children to be obedient and submissive, and he had the final authority in matters of dis-pute. The male who could not control his household was considered unmanly and ineffective.

One rationale for this philosophy was re-lated to man's superior physical strength (Ko-marovsky, 1973). Because he was stronger, it was also assumed that he had superior intel-ligence and experience. The male's role was even given religious sanction. The Bible or-dered: "Wives be subject to your husbands, as to the Lord. For the husband is head of the wife as Christ is the head of the church. . . ." (Ephesians 5:22, 23). To be sure, husbands were admonished: "Love your wives" (Ephe-sians 5:25) and do not "provoke your children to anger" (Ephesians 6:4). But the injunction was clear: It was the male's responsibility and divine right to extend his authority over his wife and children, even though his discipline was to be tempered with love and prudence.

An important role of the American male was also one of provider. He was the chief wage earner, since his wife was confined to the house and his children were dependent. A man who did not provide for his family was considered shiftless and lazy. The male who was an exceptionally good provider—especially if he was a self-made man who rose from office boy to corporation president—was the new American hero and the ideal man (Kelley, 1974).

New Concepts

Today, many males have lost or relinquished their position of dominance and authority, not only in relation to their wives but in relation to their children as well (LeMasters, 1972). This has led extremists among social critics to speak of "the crisis of masculinity," of castrated males, and feminized husbands. Actually, most mature women don't need to dominate their husbands, but want to share more equally in family decision making and deeply resent the husband who insists on trying to be the unquestioned lord and master. Furthermore, increasing numbers of husbands feel less need to be authoritarian in their family relationships.

What about the male's breadwinning function? The primary role of the modern male is still that of breadwinner. When asked: "What are the roles of the man of the family?" several hundred urban, suburban, and working wives said that the role of breadwinner was the most important. The role of father was listed second and that of husband third (Lopata, 1971). Table 8-1 shows the results of this study.

TABLE 8-1.   *The most important roles of men (as perceived by women). Percentage distributions of answers to "what are the roles, in order of importance, of the man of the family?"*

Roles, in Order of Importance	Total
Breadwinner (total)	87
1st place	64
2nd place	10
3rd place	12
4th place	1
Father (total)	65
1st place	9
2nd place	38
3rd place	17
4th place	1
Husband (total)	46
1st palce	14
2nd place	16
3rd place	14
4th place	2
Family member (total)	26
Home-owner or maintenance of residence (total)	20
Community member (total)	2
Duties to self (total)	10
Roles equal in importance	1
Number of respondents	722

Source: From *Occupation: Housewife* by Helena Znaniecki Lopata. Copyright © 1971 by Oxford University Press, Inc. Reprinted by permission.

Even though the chief role of the modern male is still that of breadwinner, he is no longer the sole provider. With almost half of all married women working at any one time, the male is certainly not the only breadwinner (U.S. Department of Commerce, Statistical Abstract, 1980). And as the wages of women increase so they are receiving equal pay for equal work, the proportion contributed by the men will decrease even further.

Other roles within the household are also changing. Clear-cut distinctions between "man's work" and "woman's work" have been broken down in some middle-class families so that typically the husband may share in housekeeping, food preparation, and baby sitting. One of the most important changes in the man's role has been in his personal relationships with his wife. For many middle-class couples, the functions of marriage have shifted from utilitarian to intrinsic functions, with the couple seeking love and companionship. With this new emphasis on intimacy and love in marriage the modern male either succeeds or fails as a husband to the extent that he and his wife have a marriage that fulfills their emotional and social needs (Bowman, 1974).

Fulfilling sexual needs has also become an important component of emotional fulfillment. The whole sexual relationship in marriage has changed from one of a dutiful wife having intercourse with her husband for his pleasure to one of the husband and wife sharing sexual experiences for their mutual enjoyment (Nye and Berardo, 1973). This means the male is now required to give pleasure as well as gain it. Granted that there is sometimes an overemphasis on either male or female sexual *performance*, which can be harmful to sexual adjustment (Masters and Johnson, 1970), nevertheless, the important point is that the male's role in intercourse has shifted drastically from recipient to provider, from a solo performance to a participant in a duet.

Reasons for Changing Roles

There are a number of reasons why the male role has changed. For one thing, *there has been a change in the way the male provides for his family*. As families moved from the farm to the city, the male spent longer periods away from home, since his work and residence were separated by considerable distances. This meant his role as provider was no longer visible to his wife and children, a fact that created misunderstandings and conflict (Bell, 1975). This meant also that the wife was deprived of her husband's companionship, that the children lacked a male figure with whom to identify, and that they were no longer as much under their father's socializing influence. As a result, it became more and more difficult for the father to maintain his authority, which then became his wife's responsibility for long periods of time. The following case history from the author's counseling notes illustrates a common trend:

Mr. B. is a fairly typical example of the modern urban male. He and his family live in the suburbs, which requires that he commute to work some thirty miles away. Usually, he leaves early and arrives home just in time to say goodnight to his two preschool children. Usually his job requires that he work Saturdays. By Sunday, he is exhausted, so that he likes to sleep late. Sunday afternoons he plays golf or watches sports on television. Though he seems fond of his children, he does not show much inclination to take an active part in bringing them up.

In such a situation, the influence of the father over the children is bound to be reduced. In other instances, the father tries to compensate for his long hours away from home by making a deliberate effort to spend time with the children when he is home. This has been especially true of middle-class fathers and especially in relationship to their sons. Daughters continue to be more neglected.

Another reason for the male's changing role has been the continuing struggle for women's rights. The women's movement has had a major influence on masculine roles. Women are no longer willing to be dependents and servants. As they have become better educated, economically more self-sufficient, and better able to enjoy the same social and legal rights as men, their status and role in the family have become more egalitarian, forcing even those men who have resisted such change to rethink their positions and relationships.

The revolution in childcare practices has also had a profound effect on the male's role as father. Since World War II, childcare practices have emphasized children's needs, self-regulation, and parental permissiveness. This has resulted in the "child-centered family" in contrast to the male-dominated family, so that children dared to talk back even to their father and flaunt their authority if they were so inclined. In recent years, there has been some shift away from overindulgence to moderate permissiveness, but the modern father is never quite able to expect the unquestioned authority over his children that his grandfather exercised.

The Effect of the Male's Role on Himself

Strain

The male's efforts to fulfill his role has taken its toll. Men have a higher criminal record, more stress and illness due to strenuous work, higher suicide rates, and shorter life expectancies than do women (Palme, 1972). One explanation is that the strain of competition and achievement create great psychological tension. The modern technological system demands unremitting discipline, since the standards of performance are not only high but often without limit. Every worker, from the man on the assembly line who gets paid piecework for each unit assembled to the top-level manager who is judged by the total output of his plant, is under constant pressure to produce (Goldman, 1973; Skolnick, 1973).

Another explanation of the strain is that the male is caught in a vise of conflicting pressures: to earn a better living for his family, yet to spend more time with his wife and children. He is supposed to be a tender and romantic lover, yet never to reveal any emotional weakness when attacked by political, business, or physical opponents. He is pressured to meet his children's emotional and physical needs and even to participate fully in all aspects of their care, yet also to be a leader in his community in Rotary, the United Fund Drive, the school board, or the church. He was brought up to be autonomous and to prize freedom, yet he is besieged on all sides by those who want him to put their interests ahead of his own desires and time. Vilar speaks cynically of what she calls the manipulated man: "No matter what a man's job may be—bookkeeper, doctor, bus driver, or managing director—every moment of his life will be spent as a cog in a huge and pitiless system—a system designed to exploit him to the utmost, to his dying day" (Vilar, 1972, p. 10). The man who feels he is caught up in a system he cannot get out of, doing a job he does not like when he would like to be free to be himself, will suffer emotionally and physically because of his inner conflict.

Self-Image

The male's self-image is especially important to his own happiness and sense of well-being. But because of the emphasis on materialism in western culture, *a man's self-concept, and especially his sense of manliness, is closely tied to his occupational role:* the pay he receives, the prestige of his job, and the status it provides him in the community (Brenton, 1971).

His self-image is enhanced if his occupation is one that society considers masculine. Different segments of society have different criteria of man's work. Laboring classes may define a man's job as one requiring strength and endurance or one in which a man gets dirty or has to take chances. Skilled laborers may define a man's work as that which requires coordination and skill in operating huge machines or complicated equipment. Upper classes may say that a man's work requires superior knowledge, professional ability, or managerial skill (Etzkowitz, 1971).

His self-image is enhanced if his occupation is one that is remunerative. The more money he makes, the more this builds the man's own prestige and sense of accomplishment (Gould, 1976). Vilar writes:

A man's salary is the yardstick of his worth. America is the only place where a badly paid professor is a bad professor, and an unsuccessful writer a bad writer. For the Latin American male, masculinity is still associated with sexual potency. For the American male, however, the association is directly with money (Vilar, 1972, p. 166).

If the male makes a lot of money, he has succeeded as a man according to the standards of his culture. Furthermore, his success gives his family greater status in the community.

The man's self-image is also enhanced if his occupation is a prestigious one. In the hierarchy of occupations, white collar jobs are more prestigious than blue collar, clean work is more prestigious than dirty work, mental work is more prestigious than physical work and professional work is more prestigious than vocational work. David and Brannon write:

One of the most basic routes to manhood in our society is to be a success. . . . Success is usually defined in terms of occupational prestige and achievement, wealth, fame, power, and visible positions of leadership. . . . The tycoon, the congressman, the movie star, and the sports hero enjoy an automatic kind of status, and will often be viewed as masculine role-models on this basis alone. There's something ineffably masculine about the word "millionaire," or even "the richest man in town" (David and Brannon, 1976, p. 19).

Obviously, males in occupations of very low prestige are more likely to have lower self-concepts and more difficulties in feeling adequate as men. The following description is taken from the author's counseling notes.

Mr. W is able to earn only slightly above minimum wages as a laborer. He and his wife and children live in an old farm house on the outskirts of town. The house is paid for since it was inherited from Mr. W's father, but it is badly in need of repair. The roof leaks; all of the paint is off; several windows are broken. The yard is filled with junk cars since Mr. W repairs them in his spare time. The children are sick frequently, very poorly dressed, often dirty, and have a high absenteeism from school. The family car is whatever piece of junk Mr. W has fixed up but hasn't yet sold.

Once Mr. and Mrs. W went to the school to talk to the principal about one of the children, but they felt very uncomfortable. Everyone seemed to be looking at them. They never went back after that. Mr. W feels especially bad when one of the kids wants money to buy tickets for a school game, or to get a pair of new jeans like the other children have. He hates to tell the kids no, that he doesn't have any money. His wife seldom complains, but just once he'd like to be able to buy her something really nice for her birthday. Mostly, he just goes to work but he knows he is Mr. Nobody and that no one else really cares.

But he cares, and it hurts.

Occupational Roles and Marriage

Income and Marital Success

Sometimes a man is in a low prestige occupation but makes very good money. Being a successful junk dealer or garbage collector are good examples. People in higher social classes will never give a man in such occupations much recognition, since to them status depends upon income *and* the prestige of the occupation. But in the lower classes, the important requirement is that the man be a good provider, no matter how he earns the money. In her study of blue collar marriages, Komarovsky (1962) found that lower-middle-class women might not know the specific occupations of their close relatives, but that it didn't matter, since a good job was one that brought in a good living, and not necessarily one that represented high achievement in a specialized vocation. Other research substantiates the fact that *income is more closely related to marital satisfaction than either education or occupation* (Hicks and Platt, 1970; Renne, 1970). Probably it's because the level of income has the most impact on the couples' daily life. Social status counts for relatively little if family income is inadequate to meet needs (Schneider and Smith, 1973). As a result, nonsupport becomes one of the major causes for divorce.

The Wife's Satisfaction

Whether the wife is satisfied with the husband's job or not is an important factor in influencing martial success. A study of existing versus dissolved marriages showed that in existing marriages, the husband's job: (1) carried a prestige level that the wife felt was adequate; (2) it supplied the kind of income and security necessary to meet the family lifestyle aspirations of the wife; and (3) there was more often a high degree of consensus between the husband and wife over the husband's occupation and the lifestyle it produced (Scanzoni, 1968).

In dissolved marriages, the wives of manual laborers were consistent in saying that the husband's job was *not* the kind that could provide either the prestige or lifestyle desired by the wife. The wives of nonmanual workers whose marriages had dissolved felt their husband earned enough, but they were still dissatisfied because their husbands spent so much time fulfilling their occupational roles that they were not able to perform their conjugal roles, particularly in providing companionship. In the vast majority of cases of dissolved marriages, there had been a high degree of dissension between the husbands and wives over the husband's occupational achievement and the lifestyle it produced (Scanzoni, 1968).

Work That Separates Couples

Some men have jobs that require them to spend many days away from home. A man in the armed services who is not able to take his wife along is one such example. The typical truck driver or traveling salesman is away all week and comes home only on weekends. A business executive may have to travel all over the country or even over the world, leaving his wife and children at frequent intervals.

Travel jobs may or may not have an adverse effect upon the marriage, depending upon the circumstances, what couples desire in marriage, and how they are able to adjust. The couple who want close companionship will be miserable if separated from one another. In fact, some men give up promotions or change jobs so they won't have to be separated from their families so much. One man remarked:

I cheerfully . . . passed up two good promotions because one of them would have required some traveling and the other would have taken evening and weekend time—and that's when Pat and I *live*. The hours with her (after twenty-two years of marriage) are what I live for (Cuber and Haroff, 1965, p. 56).

There are couples who get on one another's nerves if they are together too much. They welcome time spent apart.

One wife complained:

I nearly go crazy when my husband is home on vacation. He makes too much work for me and demands something all the time. I'm glad when he goes back to work, and especially when he's away on business. I get a lot more things done and have time to do what I want for a change.

Generally speaking, couples who have utilitarian marriages, who stay together for convenience, for the sake of the children, or for financial or social reasons rather than for companionship, don't mind enforced separations as much. In fact, some *want* to spend a lot of time away from one another. But couples who really enjoy one another's company, who have a fulfilling sex life, and who seek a vital, close relationship hate any job that keeps them apart. A high public official in an appointive position said:

I'll admit I'd rather have run for elective office. But my wife isn't comfortable with all the campaign dishonesty . . . and a full life together is more important to me than being Senator. . . . What would it profit me to try for a Senate seat and make it, if afterwards I found that our close and deeply sustaining life had been damaged in the process (Cuber and Haroff, 1965, p. 133)?

Certainly, it is more difficult to be close in marriage if the couple is often separated. The fact that traveling salesmen have one of the highest divorce rates indicates the problems associated with that occupation. One reason may be that the man on the road, with his wife at home, may seek compliant partners to satisfy his sex needs. A mother of three school children raised a provocative question:

I really don't know—should and can a sexually vigorous woman of forty renounce her sexuality for the rest of her life because her husband is away from home most of the time on business . . . (Cuber and Haroff, 1965, p. 72)?

Couples who are faithful to one another still get very lonesome and find themselves drifting apart, each developing his or her own interests to fill the nonworking hours.

Some types of work require very odd hours. Recently, a student confided to the au-

thor that she was engaged to a highway patrolman. She loved him, but she was beginning to discover that the times when she wanted to be with him the most—weekends and holidays—were the times when he was always on duty. She was beginning to wonder if she could adjust to being separated from her husband on Thanksgiving, Labor Day, Christmas, New Year's, Memorial Day, Fourth of July, and so on.

Working night hours or very irregular hours presents difficulties for other families. In one family, the wife works from 9:00 A.M. to 5:00 P.M. The husband works from 6:00 P.M. to 2:00 A.M. Allowing for commuting time, the only period during the week that the couple are together is from 3:00 A.M. to 8:00 A.M. each morning, when they are asleep. Such schedules make close contacts in marriage almost impossible.

In other instances, the husband works regular daytime hours and comes home nights, but his work requires him to do a lot of paperwork at home. Such is true of full-time students, school teachers, and of many self-employed persons, as well as professionals with a lot of responsibility (Hepker and Cloyd, 1974). One wife complained:

My husband comes home every night with a briefcase full of papers to read. Often, he burns the midnight oil until after 1:00 A.M. So we never get a chance to visit, and I hate going to bed by myself.

Work That Involves the Family

In a sense, most occupations involve the whole family. For example, if the husband is transferred, it is the whole family that is affected by the move (Hill, 1970). Some types of work, however, require more contact and direct involvement of the family. *Politicians' wives* are under considerable strain because of their husband's jobs. An article in *Time* (1974) speaks of the relentless ordeal of political wives whose personality and character are under the steady scrutiny of television and the press. Such wives are expected to manage a household and raise a family, to be the model of purity and propriety at home, yet be Everywoman outside, with a ready smile, a cheerful word, and an intelligent answer to every question. During campaigns, the politician's wife must stand aside while her husband is pawed by overzealous females, manipulated by his staff, and driven to exhaustion by public appearances. She is almost never alone with him when she can call his time her own. As a consequence, many wives feel like an appendage, without importance or identity of their own. Some like Mrs. Ted Kennedy, Mrs. Eugene McCarthy, or Mrs. Pete McCloskey (wife of a California representative) leave their husbands and name politics as the culprit.

Being married to a *clergyman* or *physician* also is difficult. The husbands are always under pressure to serve other people's needs. Some always place their occupations ahead of their families; others often place their families first. It is obvious though that *some occupations require so much of the man that it is difficult even for the most conscientious family man to perform his family responsibilities.*

Work Requiring Special Talents

Some types of jobs require special qualifications in the wife. Corporations are notorious in the demands they make upon the wives of their top-level executives. One of the principle demands is that the wife be a loyal member of the corporation "family." As one executive put it: "Management . . . has a challenge and an obligation to deliberately plan and create a favorable, constructive attitude on the part of the wife that will liberate her husband's total energies for the job" (Fullerton, 1972, p. 211). This means a good corporation wife is one who doesn't complain when her husband works late, who accepts his transfer to another city, and who never gossips about

company affairs with her women friends. She never engages in controversial political activities or intrudes on her husband's business affairs (she doesn't show up at the office, or phone her husband unless absolutely necessary). She never plays the role of the jealous wife, so trusts her husband at the office Christmas party or when he works with other women. She is agreeable and pleasant to all the company people she meets. She isn't too pushy or showy and doesn't try to outdo those who are her husband's superiors.

Her job requires her to be attractive, very neat and well groomed, but not so "chic" or daring in her clothing selections that she attracts the criticism of other wives. She has to be a willing, gracious, and capable hostess, since she is expected to entertain visiting company officials or prospective clients. In short, the corporation wife is loyal, adaptable, gregarious, and sociable, yet domestic as well.

As time goes on, fewer corporations try to mold modern wives into these traditional "help-mate" roles. Wives who seek professional advancement for themselves do not have the time, energy, or inclination to spend all of their time helping their husbands get ahead. In some cases, the roles are completely reversed, the husband's primary family role is that of giving support to his wife in her career.

Effect of Marriage on Employment Success

Marriage itself contributes to a husband's occupational success (Balswick, 1970; Marx & Spray, 1970; Tropman, 1971). Four explanations are possible. Employers generally prefer married men, especially at top managerial levels. Certain personality traits contribute both to marital and employment success. The right kind of wife can be of tremendous help to a man in getting ahead. And being married provides an added incentive for a man to work harder.

Housekeeping and Parental Roles

Sharing Household and Parental Responsibilities

Even though most husbands help their wives with the housework and caring for the children more than men used to, a complete sharing of these responsibilities is far from complete, even if the wife works full-time outside the home. One study of the roles of business and professional men indicated that fathers of preschool children devoted the largest percentage of their total time to household tasks and to the care of children, but these activities combined still took only about 8 percent of their hours. Fathers of grade school and teenage children devoted only 4 percent of their total time to household tasks and to childcare. The retired husband averaged far more time at home but spent it largely in his own pursuits rather than in sharing household tasks (Smith et al., 1969).

Another study by the United States Department of Agriculture gives a more detailed analysis of what husbands and wives actually do around the house ("How Much Does He Do . . . ?", 1971). According to this study, husbands averaged a total of one and one-half hours a day on yard and home care, car upkeep, food preparation and/or cleanup, taking care of children, and all home tasks combined. This was true regardless of whether the wife was a full-time homemaker or a full-time job holder—thirty or more hours a week. *Those women who were full-time job holders still spent an additional four and one-half daily on homemaking tasks, or three times the amount of time spent by their husbands.* This means that while egalitarian and democratic marriage ideals emphasize that the husband and wife share everything fifty-fifty, in actual practice, the wife still takes the primary responsibility for housekeeping and childcare.

There are individual variations in the way husbands perform their role. Some men are perfectly willing to do all of the outside work around the house: gardening, the lawn, painting, repairs, and so forth, since traditionally these tasks have been assigned to the men in the family (Landis and Landis, 1973). Other men will do the grass but insist that their wives take care of the flowers. These same men may be very unwilling to do cooking, cleaning, or baby tending. Other men are willing to do the heavier inside work, such as floor mopping and cleaning but leave the lighter tasks to their wives. The one job that men do not do very often is the laundry, ironing especially, but occasionally a husband is an exception (Smith et al., 1969). According to studies by Landis and Landis (1973), most men are willing to go grocery shopping for their wives—and will even dry the dishes—but the majority won't set the table, wash the dishes, or clean the house.

There are also great variations in the way different fathers perform their parental roles. One father may bathe the children every night while another never does. One will change diapers, another won't. Some fathers enjoy playing with the baby; others wait until the child is old enough to play baseball before they even notice him or her. Generally, *most* husbands are willing to spend more time with the children, but this is not the same as having the major responsibility for their day-to-day care. The majority of husbands still delegate this responsibility to their wives (Miller, 1971). This is indicated by the fact that wives almost always talk about their husbands "helping them with the children." The way this is worded indicates that childcare is not considered the father's primary role, it is done as a favor to the wife rather than as a major responsibility of them both.

There are a number of reasons for this refusal to assume major responsibility for childcare. For one thing, many men still feel that spending a lot of time in the actual care of children—washing, feeding, dressing, comforting, and playing with them—is unmasculine. Fasteau tells about a truck driver who was coaxed into spending an hour playing with his four-year-old son at nursery school. The father had obviously enjoyed doing so, but he asked very painfully upon leaving: "What'll I tell the guys at work about this" (Fasteau, 1974)? Like many others, this man felt that playing with his son was somehow sissy. For another thing, part of the feeling that care of children is inappropriate comes from the fact that it is a diversion from men's "real" work: the building of a career. The man who stays home from the office to spend more time with his children is considered unambitious.

Also, some men still feel uncomfortable with tender emotions—either their own or those of children. Such men are embarrassed at hugging, kissing, or other physical expressions of affection. They are upset when their sons cry (it is sissy). They have trouble talking with their children because they can't drop their air of authority or the need to feel superior. They tend to camouflage their true feelings toward children and express this in roughhousing: a mock punch instead of a hug. For all of these reasons, many men back off from caring for their children even though many express a real desire to be close to them.

Providing for a child's physical care is only part of what is required; the role of the father in his children's socialization is even more important. The man who is away from home for days at a time has limited opportunities to assist with family decisions and to become acquainted with his children. As a result, the children grow up almost without a father figure. Numerous studies have shown that *children whose fathers are absent a great deal show more difficulties in their sex role identification, are less likely to have strong ego identities and self-concepts, show more signs of emotional disturbance, more hostility, and generally develop less independence than those whose fathers are home* (Connell and Johnson, 1970; Nash, 1973). Since a son's pattern for the male role is ob-

Father-child companionship is an important factor in sex role development.

tained from identifying with his father, boys whose fathers are absent may develop only a very weak, often feminized, masculine identification (Biller and Bohn, 1971; Simon and Gagnon, 1970). If the mother turns to her children for emotional comfort in the absence of her husband, she encourages their overidentification and dependency on her, so that they do not develop as much autonomy.

Companionship Role

Degrees of Companionship

Contemporary marriage emphasizes getting married for love and companionship. But couples differ markedly in the degree of closeness they desire or are able to achieve. Some wives and husbands want a very close relationship with one another; others would feel smothered by this arrangement. Some prefer almost separate lives, with little sharing of careers, family, emotions, or social life. Others would feel completely rejected and emotionally starved in such a marriage.

Fulfilling Needs

A major problem arises only if the needs and desires of the two people are dissimilar. A husband who will not let himself get close to anyone and who marries a wife who is starved for love finds that he cannot fulfill his wife's needs because her desires are so much different than his. Mr. and Mrs. N had that kind of problem.

The wife was a warm, outgoing, very expressive, and maternal woman. He was cold and unresponsive emotionally. Professionally, he was a very successful surgeon. In describing her husband, the wife remarked: "I think the reason he's such a good surgeon is that he never gets emotionally involved with his patients. In fact, sometimes I think he enjoys cutting up people."

"Sometimes," the wife went on to say, "I wish that he would just put his arms around me and hug me and kiss me and tell me that he loves me, but he never does."

It is difficult for two people with such opposite emotional needs to find fulfillment with one another. Whether or not the modern husband has succeeded in his role as companion to his wife will depend partially upon how their mutual needs correspond and upon the husband's willingness and ability to assume the role of need fulfiller.

Roles of the Low Socioeconomic Status Husband

There are considerable differences between husband-wife role performances and expectations in low socioeconomic status families as contrasted with those of the middle class (Scanzoni, 1971). The following descriptions represent differences that are extreme. *Because they are extreme, they cannot be applied to all low socioeconomic families,* but they do describe a great number of such families, especially the very poor.

Marital Roles

Since the low socioeconomic status family is fairly traditional in its values, the husband-wife relationship tends to reflect traditional roles. Quite characteristic of low socioeconomic status families are (Bell, 1971b; Komarovsky, 1962, 1973; Smith et al., 1969):

- Masculine superiority and the subservience of women
- Highly segregated sex roles with a sharp division of labor between woman's work and man's work
- Emphasis upon the utilitarian roles of husband and wife with the husband's role primarily one of breadwinner and the wife's role one of breadwinner and housekeeper-mother
- Lack of emphasis on mutual satisfaction of emotional needs
- Little joint social participation outside the family

One of the tendencies of the low socioeconomic status husband is to have doubts and fears about his manhood, partly because of his uncertain economic accomplishments, and because of the concepts of masculinity with which he was raised. Therefore, he frequently overcompensates by presenting an image of stern authority, seeking to dominate his wife and children. Many times, however, he finds that his wife actually has more status and authority than he, so his efforts to exert authority are sometimes frustrating (Yarburg, 1973). Anthropologists have described this as the "cult of masculine superiority" of the lower classes, in which the men feel dominant and both the husband and wife believe that what they verbalize actually exists.

This attempt at masculine dominance tends to create hostility between the sexes and a marked segregation of sex roles. Because he is always striving to prove his manhood, the husband hesitates to perform any family chores conceived of as women's work: housecleaning, baby tending, cooking, washing, sewing, and other such chores. This is true even if the wife works outside the home. As a matter of fact, husbands of working wives sometimes help out less around the house than do husbands of nonworking wives (Allen , 1970).

But the segregation of sex roles and the emphasis upon the utilitarian functions of the family results in emotional and social isolation and deprivation. The masculine man is not supposed to show tender feelings, so the wife tends to feel emotionally deprived, rejected, and lonesome because her husband is neither expressive nor romantic nor tries to play the friend-lover role. Such wives frequently fulfill their emotional needs by escaping in true romance magazines or soap operas on television.

Thus, the wife must endure emotional as well as physical and economic deprivation. Often, she tends to overemphasize the motherhood role in her family, since she does not find other gratifications in her marriage. Her children represent some compensation for her husband's lack of attention and for her dull life. In a study of lower-class women in Philadelphia, the women were asked: "If you could only be a wife or mother (but not both) which would you choose?" The majority of women, both married and single, chose the mother's role (Bell, 1965).

At the same time, the husband tends not to look upon his wife as a friend and companion. When the husband wants companionship, he seeks it with other men outside the home: at the corner bar, out hunting, working on cars, playing poker, or attending sports events. As a result, there are relatively few instances of the husband and wife having friends in common, except for visits with the extended family. The male feels he's a good husband if he brings home an adequate paycheck. The wife, in turn, seeks her social life with relatives or the woman next door or down the block.

The Father's Role

The working-class father often plays a passive role in the child-rearing task. As a result, the children do not often confide in their father or feel close to him. Because of the lack of an adequate, mature, masculine, husband-father image, the degree of positive identification by the son with the father is often minimal in low socioeconomic families. At the same time, the image of an adequate, powerful, emotionally important mother presents a positive identification figure for the son, which makes it difficult for the son to resolve his oedipal conflict and to find an acceptable masculine role. If the father is an explosive, hostile man, the son is silenced at home but may explode when away from home by directing his hostile feelings toward other symbols of adult authority or toward siblings or peers. He may become a bully among his peers, seeking status and power. Other youths who are made to give in to their fathers may become submissive followers.

Lower socioeconomic status fathers tend to be authoritarian, evidencing quite rigid parental relationships with the children. The atmosphere tends to be one of imperatives and absolutes, physical violence, and psychological distance, if not rejection. Father-child interaction patterns are often rigid and oriented toward maintaining order, obedience, and discipline. The discipline itself tends to be impulsive, harsh, and inconsistent and emphasizes physical punishment (even of adolescents). Many times, however, the fathers are not able to maintain very good discipline because of their own lack of status in the family and the inconsistency with which they take an interest in the children. One mother remarked: "The only time my husband disciplines the kids is when they bother him while he's watching TV. He gets mad and straps them so hard I'm afraid he'll hurt them."

Most fathers mean well. They usually want to bring up their children to live decent, obedient lives. But the lower-class father tends to be concerned with overt behavior, with the immediate situation, and not with what the behavior means in regards to future development. There is little concern for personality growth or for desirable child-rearing goals such as the development of creativity, curiosity, independence, or self-direction. There is greater paternal control exercised over daughters than sons, which is why many girls use marriage as an escape from home (Gecas and Nye, 1974).

In large families especially, parents seem to lack the time and will to control and to give attention to their children as they get older. The mother is often preoccupied with a new baby; the father is struggling to make a living for the family. When problems arise, the father often explodes with anger and resentment, the mother feels hurt, bewildered, and helpless, powerless to remedy the situation. A frequent feeling on the part of both parents is: "We've done the best we could, you've made your bed, now you'll have to lie in it. There is nothing I can do." Thus, a fatalistic attitude of accepting what comes is evident in the child-rearing task (Allen, 1970; Chilman, 1975).

Conclusions

There are no easy answers to the modern male's dilemma. Each individual husband has to examine his own values and priorities to determine what he really wants out of life. Similarly, each woman needs to examine her priorities in life to determine what kind of a husband she wants and what she really expects of him in marriage. If a woman falls in love with a man whose priorities and values are different from hers, this is sufficient reason to take a long pause to reflect and to decide if marriage to him would be wise. Some men are quite content with an average salary as long as they have the love and companionship of their wife and children. It would be very unfair for a compulsively ambitious wife to marry such a man and then to spend her marriage trying to push him to greater success. She might accomplish part of her goal, but she would run the risk of destroying her marriage and possibly her husband in the process. If she can't love him as he is, she shouldn't marry him.

The future trend is toward intimacy and companionship in marriage, completely flexible sex roles, equality in relationships and decision making, and a more complete sharing of the breadwinning, maintenance, and child-rearing functions of the family. If men are expected to perform family duties and their wives are expected to earn part of the family income, the role-teaching process has to start with the very young. But how many parents make an effort to teach their sons to be housekeepers or give them opportunities to learn the basic principles of childcare? How many teach complete equality among the boys and girls in a family? How many parents are rearing their daughters to take over part of the breadwinning functions, so that husbands are freer to provide more companionship for their wives and more fathering for their children? Parents who are teaching these things are helping their children to find secure and well-defined but flexible roles in a completely egalitarian marriage.

Tom and Vera were married nine years ago and have two girls in elementary school. They came to see Dr. Miller, a marriage counselor, because they were unable to cope with the conflict over their marital and parental roles. Vera had a new appointment as an academic dean at a private liberal arts college near Hartford. Tom was an assistant professor at a nearby state college in the history department. For years the couple lived off his income alone until Vera had completed her Ph.D. and was quickly promoted from assistant dean of women to academic dean.

"I can't arrive at a satisfactory answer to the problem," Tom said. "Perhaps you can provide a solution. It seems that neither of us has as much time as we need to do the housekeeping and look after our small girls. Vera has her career and I have mine. I want to advance as much as she does. I don't feel that I should relax in the development of my career so that I can assume household duties she no longer has time for."

"Don't think that I'm being inflexible," said Vera, "but I don't feel that I've shirked my responsibilities. You've never taken an interest in what the girls do. You hate housework of any kind. Well, I accepted that before I began working full time. But now I work just as hard as you do and provide the largest income to the household upkeep, so I don't see why I also have to be a full-time housekeeper as well!"

Turning to Dr. Miller, she added, "Tom seems to have a problem; perhaps it's my fault—I don't know. The point is that he really doesn't want to help around the house."

"Hey, wait a minute, that's not true. I have my career. You knew that when we got married."

Dr. Miller turned to Vera. "Is he correct? I mean, do you think that his career places special demands on him so that he can't help?"

"No more than mine," Vera retorted.

Dr. Miller asked Tom why he couldn't arrange some time for housework.

"It's very difficult to keep a schedule," Tom replied. "I have a full-time course load and I'm in the final stages of my book, which I have to finish or I'll be out of work. It's not that I mind housework or assuming some responsibility. It's that I can't do it all the time and Vera knows that."

"What of the children?" Dr. Miller asked.

"What of them?" asked Tom.

"Was Vera correct in saying that you neglect the children?" Dr. Miller asked.

"I take them out on weekends," Tom replied, "and sometimes I read them stories at night when I'm not at the library."

"That's not very frequent," said Vera.

"What do you want me to do?" Tom shouted. "I can't relate to them as well as you."

"You see what I mean, Dr. Miller," Vera said. "Every husband that I know tries to help out a little on a regular basis around the house. Tom is the only one who doesn't."

"That's not true," Tom said.

"Not regularly, you don't."

Dr. Miller inquired of Vera whether her views of Tom's household role had always been that way.

"No."

"What do you mean?"

"Before we had our girls he was very helpful in spite of his teaching and research. After the girls came, he became totally self-absorbed. He can't take me to restaurants or night clubs. I even have to make repairs around the house."

Tom groaned in objection.

Dr. Miller asked Tom whether Vera's description was accurate.

"I do things around the house," Tom said. "She just wants me on a regular schedule. She knows that that is impossible until I have my book out and have secured tenure."

"I don't think that you'll change," Vera said.

QUESTIONS

1. The problem of homemaking has become a vexing one for modern couples, particularly in homes where both parents work. Problems over childcare arise in nearly every such marriage. In what ways is modern society responsible for the picture of the husband so preoccupied with his work that the wife must carry the burden of exclusive childcare?

2. In what ways do Tom's attitudes reveal traditional male chauvinism and sexism?

3. What do you think of Vera's views?

4. What possible resolutions of the problem have the couple explored?

5. Must there be an either/or resolution of the conflict in which one person gives all? Explain.

6. What might be some creative resolutions of Tom and Vera's problem?

7. What services might the couple use beyond themselves?

8. What services exist in communities which might help families involved in dual careers?

CHAPTER 9

Dual-Career Marriage

CHAPTER OUTLINE

The Husbands and Wives

Benefits of a Dual-Career Marriage

Job Establishment

Childcare

Effects on Children

Strains

Conclusions

Dialogue

A **dual-career marriage** is one in which both the husband and wife pursue careers and maintain a family life together (Rapoport and Rapoport, 1971). The word "career," as used here, refers to a job that requires a high degree of commitment and a continuous developmental life (Pendleton et al., 1980; Rapoport and Rapoport, 1978). The individual pursues a career by undergoing extensive education and preparation, and then by moving from one job level to another, until he or she achieves expertise and a position of responsibility.

By its very nature, a career requires a fairly continuous pattern of involvement (Bebbington, 1973; Holmstrom, 1973). It usually requires full-time employment, especially if one is working for someone else. The greater the responsibility and the higher the position achieved, the greater is the commitment of time involved—leaving less and less time to devote to mate and children. The majority of married women who work do not pursue a career. They fill a position for a limited period of time, usually after marriage and before children are born. They may then stop working when the children are small and return to work when the children ar older. But because of the expected interrupted work pattern, many of these women are underemployed—filling positions below their level of training and ability because they know they are not going to make careers of their work. At the present time, only about one in six married couples in the United States have both spouses working at year-round, full-time jobs (Rawlings, 1978).

The dual-career marriage then is actually a minority pattern in spite of the millions of working wives and mothers. As a minority occurrence, the dual-career marriage is also difficult to achieve from a strictly managerial point of view. It is difficult to rearrange husband-wife and father-mother role relationships and responsibilities; it is difficult to find adequate childcare help in a society that expects parents to assume the major burden; and it is difficult to maintain the expected husband-wife intimacy and companionship so that the marriage itself becomes a viable relationship.

In spite of difficulties, there are those couples who are able to succeed in pursuing careers and in being good mates and adequate parents. Other couples try to succeed at all three roles and fail. Both the successes and failures of others are helpful in understanding the satisfactions, adjustments, and problems of dual-career marriage (Huser and Grant, 1978; Jones and Jones, 1980; St. John Parsons, 1978).

The Husbands and Wives

Wives

Career women tend to be energetic, competitive, and ambitious, and have a need for personal recognition and achievement (Rice, D. G., 1978). Quite typically the marriage rate among career women is lower than among women in general. A study of women with successful careers in business revealed that half had married and half had not. Many who did marry remained single until at least age thirty-five (Hennig, 1970). Other research of women who received their doctorates indicates that many did not marry until they were in their forties, and even by then only a little more than half were married (White, 1970). Frequently, they turn down men who are opposed to careers for women. Often they have long courtships to see how their two careers will mesh (Holmstrom, 1973).

The issue of the wife's career does not always come up prior to marriage. In marriages where the couple are younger, this may be because the wife decides only *after* she is married to pursue a career. In marriages where the couple are older and both are working, it may just be assumed that the wife will continue in her long-established career. In Holmstrom's (1973) study of twenty two-career families, most of the husbands said that prior to meeting their wives they had not thought much about whether they wanted to marry a woman devoted to homemaking or one who had career interests. Those who had thought about it said they preferred a woman with intellectual interests and a professional orientation.

Apparently, establishing a two-career marriage does not always happen by deliberate choice and planning, especially on the part of the husband. Perhaps even without formal discussion, the wives are able to sense that their fiancés will approve of their career after marriage, so they feel free to go ahead.

The majority of women work, but most do not pursue full-time careers.

Certainly, after marriage, *all wives agree that it is absolutely essential that they have the complete support and understanding of their husbands.*

The vast majority of career women say that having children is important to them (Epstein and Bronzaft, 1972). Holmstrom (1973) found only one out of twenty women who was completely negative about the idea of having children. The remainder placed a great value on children, even those who remained childless. They said: "We wanted children, there was no doubt about it." "We definitely wanted a family."

In spite of their desire for children, career women are atypical in several ways:

1. They tend to have small families, with fewer children than the average couple (Bryson et al., 1978; Tickamyer, 1979).
2. There is usually a long interval between marriage and the birth of their first child (Skinner, 1980). Holmstrom (1973) found that over half of the couples waited five or more years before having their first child.
3. Because of the delay of both marriage and childbearing, most of the wives have their first child at a relatively late age, usually not until their late twenties or their thirties.

As a consequence, many career wives do not even begin their families until the age at which other women complete their families. This means that if their careers are to continue relatively uninterrupted, the wives have to get care for their children from the time the children are born.

Decisions concerning the number of children desired are definitely influenced by career plans (Notman, 1973). Career plans also influence the timing and spacing of children. One woman commented about the spacing of her children:

I make calculated guesses of when I can get time off. I calculate on time off before I get pregnant—I mention that in ten months or so there may be a child coming and see what can be arranged (Holmstrom, 1973, p. 22).

As far as they can consciously plan, the majority of career women do not believe that "biology is destiny." This does not mean that all decisions concerning bearing children are determined by careers alone. One woman may space her children, fitting pregnancies into her work schedule; another may have all her children close together so they will have more companionship with one another, and she can return to the labor force with fewer interruptions. *But it does mean that career women do not lead lifestyles merely as a passive consequence of the number and arrival times of their children. They plan both their children and their careers, because their plans for life make room for both.*

Two important studies of dual-career families by Bebbington (1973) and by the Rapoports (1971) showed that dual-career wives more often came from higher social class backgrounds than did their conventional counterparts. About half of their mothers were employed during their childhood. A majority of the remaining mothers were occupationally oriented, and they were frustrated or ambivalent at being kept at home. Some of the mothers were unusually ambitious on behalf of their daughters. These factors combined to orient the daughters to adopt career roles.

Another striking feature of the wives was the fact that about half were only children with the majority of the remainder being eldest children in their families. Research indicates that first-born children tend to undergo intensive socialization and to gain cognitive stimulation from interacting with adults. In this case, first-born daughters were effectively socialized to accept their parents' ambitions for them (Bebbington, 1973).

In the case of only children, or those who were separated from siblings by a large age gap, one gets a picture of an "only-lonely" child syndrome (Rapoport and Rapoport, 1978). Many dual-career wives also tended to have prolonged separation from parents because of attending boarding school, because of war, or because their mothers worked. There were seldom other adult relatives living with the family to provide companionship while parents were gone. Researchers also reported there was a greater percentage of career than noncareer wives who experienced tension in relationship to their parents while they were growing up. Tension in relationship with the father was very common. In some other cases, the daughters encountered disturbing relationships outside the family. In these instances, career orientation was felt to be a defense against the insecurities of their own family and childhood experiences. "One gets a picture of uncertainty and a desire for security and self-realization" (Rapoport and Rapoport, 1971, p. 27).

It is obvious that career orientation was an outgrowth of both positive and negative childhood experiences and that family background, relationships, and socialization were extremely important in the career orientations of wives who were surveyed (Rapoport et al., 1971).

Husbands

There does not seem to be very much difference between the early experiences of husbands in dual-career marriages, and those of husbands in traditional marriages (Rapoport and Rapoport, 1971). Dual-career husbands do not necessarily come from high socioeconomic backgrounds. In fact, many come from poor families and are motivated to rise above poverty. They also tend to have greater family harmony in their backgrounds than do their wives.

The attitude of the husbands toward their wives having careers ranges from relaxed detachment and willing acceptance because "I knew what I was getting into," to positive in-

volvement and facilitation of their wives' career roles. Holmstrom reports several characteristics of husbands of career wives (Holmstrom 1973, p. 135):

1. Husbands took their wives' work seriously, often showing deep admiration and respect for their wives' accomplishments.
2. Husbands wanted their wives "to be happy" or "to be the kind of person she was."
3. Husbands not only showed positive attitudes toward their wives' career, but they translated this into concrete, practical acts of support.

These dual-career husbands changed their own behavior and way of life to accommodate two careers. They took their wives' needs into account before moving. They considered their wives' time when setting up schedules. They helped with domestic and child-rearing duties. Holmstrom tells of one husband who taught his wife's classes the first week after they had a baby, of another who waged a battle on his wife's behalf to change a rule regarding women's employment, and of another who fought off criticism of his wife because of her career.

All research shows that the husband's attitude is an important factor in making a dual-career marriage workable (Bailyn, 1970; Heckman, 1974; Jones, 1971; Linn, 1971). One wife said:

I might say . . . that my present husband has the best attitude toward working that a husband possibly could. . . . When you're up against it and you need help and support, then you've got to have this from a husband who wants you to do what you're doing, rather than putting up with it (Holmstrom, 1973, p. 137).

Because of the importance of the husband's attitude, career wives caution: "Be careful whom you marry. The choice of a husband is very important in making a career possible; if you don't have a husband who supports you and is interested in your work, you can't survive."

Dual-career husbands tend to be secure, well-adjusted men whose identities are not threatened by their wives working, nor by the nontraditional division of labor within the household. The husband who has to feel psychologically superior to his wife, who feels threatened if his wife achieves a position of prominence, who has strong feelings of competitiveness, or who has to "put-down" his wife cannot tolerate a dual-career marriage. In the case of a female graduate student, her husband's immaturity became so intolerable that she divorced him. The wife commented:

It was very destructive to me. He was a person who could never resist taking things apart.... Every single time I would think of something (for a master's thesis) I'd start to talk with him about it and in half an hour there wouldn't be anything left of it. And it wasn't just that. This was the way just about everything went, my opinions about everything (Holmstrom, 1973, p. 147).

In another case, the husband felt so threatened by giving up traditional masculine sex roles that he refused to assume his share of domestic responsibilities and tried to keep his wife submissive and subservient by denying her any independence of thought and action. His wife couldn't stand it any longer and walked out. One study showed that men whose mothers never worked outside the home felt more threatened by their wives working than did those whose mothers had been employed.

Obviously, the husband in a dual-career marriage must be nontraditional in his sex role concepts, but he must also be certain of his identity as a person so that his wife's intelligence and success are no threat to him.

Benefits of a Dual-Career Marriage

There are some real satisfactions and gains in a dual-career marriage. These can be grouped under four headings: *financial, self-expression, sharing, and benefits to children.*

Financial

The financial rewards in a dual-career marriage are considerable, especially if both persons are earning salaries as professional people. The relatively high income enables couples to accumulate savings, establish independent pension plans, and to provide financial security against possible disaster. In addition, the standard of living is relatively high, with couples able to provide for expensive leisure activities and holidays. Because they work so hard, couples usually feel they need to pamper themselves with rewarding vacations. In addition, the extra expenses for clothes, transportation, domestic help, and childcare because both are working, make it necessary for couples to have a relatively high income.

But this relatively high income can be of direct benefit to the wife if a housekeeper can be hired. When the wife comes home tired, she can sit down and relax, put her feet up, and come to dinner when she is called just like her husband. This chance to relax and this freedom from some household chores is one of the many pluses of having too good incomes.

Self-Expression

One frequently mentioned reason why any highly qualified woman wants a career in addition to a family is because of a need for creativity, self-expression, achievement, and recognition (Herrigan and Herrigan, 1973; O'Neill and O'Neill, 1972). A woman who is trained for a profession wants the satisfaction of using that training (Hall and Gordon, 1973). Many such women are dissatisfied in confining their energies to their husbands and children: in just being John's wife or Susan's mother. Such women find a large part of their identity in their career role (Gannon and Hendrickson, 1973). Many feel that they would experience a real loss if the satisfactions of a career were removed.

There are also indirect benefits to the husband and the family. A woman who is getting satisfaction from her career is a happier wife and mother. If the wife comes home strained, anxious, and exhausted because of her work, however, this can contribute to marital dissatisfaction and be harmful to the children. Thus, whether the husband, wife, and children benefit or not, depends in part on the woman's work, what it does for her and to her, and how she reacts to it.

Sharing

The most successful dual-career marriages are those in which the husband and wife treat one another as equal partners. As a result, they not only share in earning the income, but also in caring for children, and in performing such household tasks as cooking, dishwashing, clothes washing, food shopping, and doing household repairs (Scanzoni, 1980). Wives are far less satisfied and under more strain in those marriages where the responsibility for homemaking tasks rests primarily on their shoulders (Pendleton et al., 1980).

Benefits to Children

Children also benefit from the mother working. Career mothers report that their children develop greater independence and resourcefulness, that they assume more responsibility for family tasks (Propper, 1972) and that their pride in the accomplishments of both parents reinforces their feelings of importance, enhances their status and sense of identity, and provides a greater range of role models for children of both sexes. The children of career mothers have a broader, less stereotyped concept of the female role than do the children of nonworking mothers (Nye and Berardo, 1973).

Job Establishment

Career Pursuit

One of the problems of establishing a two-career family is the expectation of the way in which a career should be pursued (Snow, 1971). A professional person is generally expected to be single-minded about his or her career and to subordinate all other activities to it. This means placing career ahead of family. As a result of these pressures to "give all" for one's career, it becomes difficult to have two full-time careers in the same family and leave time and energy for anything else.

Moving

The pressure to move about frequently while one's career is becoming established presents another difficulty for the two-career family (Gilliland, 1979; Wallston et al., 1978). *This expectation of frequent moves is based primarily on the assumption that there is only one such professional per family and this person is the husband* (Voydanoff, 1980). The wife and children are supposed to tag along. Or if there were a choice between the husband's and wife's career, traditionally it has been expected that the wife would follow the husband (Heckman et al., 1977). Under such circumstances, it would become difficult for the wife to pursue an uninterrupted career, so the competing job requirements of two careers may threaten to separate the couple geographically and maritally. The more mobile the professionals, the more their work will threaten to disrupt their relationship (Epstein, 1970).

It is not always easy for both partners to find suitable employment in one area, especially in less populated areas where there are fewer opportunities. Also, some firms and employers have rules against **nepotism**: hiring two people from the same family, even though the Health Education and Welfare's Office of Civil Rights has declared this discriminatory (Pingree et al., 1978). This rule falls hardest on the husbands and wives who are in the same field, since employers are especially reluctant to hire two people in the same administrative department or section. If the rule is enforced, it is usually enforced against the wife. She is the one who is denied employment, permitted to work only part-time to circumvent the rule, or forced to work outside her field.

In her study of dual-career families, Holmstrom (1973) found that fifteen out of twenty couples said that the issue of moving had arisen since their marriage. In every case, the wife's decision about where to live was influenced by the career needs of her husband. Whenever a move occurred, the couple either negotiated simultaneously for a set of positions or the wife followed the husband. Sometimes the wife wanted to move but could not because the husband could not or would not move. In twelve out of fifteen cases, however, the husband's decision about where to live was also significantly influenced by his wife's career. The couple negotiated for a set of positions, taking into account the occupational needs of both, or the husband followed the wife, or the couple decided to postpone the move. Sometimes one remained behind to finish up some work, then rejoined the other later.

Travel

The issue of travel arises in dual-career marriages because professional jobs often require attending out-of-town meetings or conferences or consulting with others in different locales. Professional wives are expected to travel on brief business trips, usually from two to ten days. Some have to travel monthly or even more often; a few have to make extended trips abroad. Holmstrom (1973) reports that six out of twenty wives went alone to Europe, Africa, or Asia, for periods of time from three weeks to almost a year. During the longest separations, the family was periodically reunited. Since five of the six women had preschool or grade school age children, the husband cared for them while the wife was away. Generally, the husbands traveled even more than their wives; some were away for long periods of time each year.

Occasionally, couples commute long distances when home base for their careers are in different locations (Gerstel, 1979; Gross, 1980; Kirschner and Walum, 1978). They may work all week in separate places and get together weekends. Actors and actresses commonly follow this pattern. One well-known congresswoman, Martha Griffiths of Detroit, Michigan, spends weekdays in Washington, D.C. when Congress is in session and flies to Detroit each weekend. Occasionally, her husband flies to Washington to be with her. It is reported that they spent over $5000 in air fares during one year. While such arrangements are not common, they illustrate to what lengths some couples are willing to go to maintain their marriages and careers at the same time. Most couples tolerate and endure the separation without really liking it. Couples report that they feel lonely, and have more difficulty being emotionally close and intimate (Kirschner and Walum, 1978). While away, they miss their children and often feel guilty that they aren't caring for them. The one left home often resents the added burden of running errands, and caring for the house and children alone (Gross, 1980). The only advantage is the increased freedom to work hard at one's job while away from home.

Time Off

One problem women face has been in obtaining maternity leave or a leave of absence for other special family reasons (Voydanoff, 1980). Employers are usually lenient with men when family troubles arise and they need time off but have frowned on women who ask for temporary leave for personal reasons. Among the twenty women in Holmstrom's study, half had taken less than three months total time off to have their children. The mother who had taken the least amount of time off commented:

I think two days is the maximum length of time I missed with any of the children. . . . A few of them were born over the weekend. And only one was born during the week and I didn't even miss much with that one . . . because it turned out there was a snow storm and [everything] was closed that week, so I just missed two days on that one. I never missed more than that with any of them (Holmstrom, 1973, p. 56).

As more employers become willing to grant leave of absences, women will find it much easier to combine motherhood with a career. One woman in Holmstrom's study was able to take off five years to raise her one and only child.

Childcare

The Nuclear Family

The difficulties in combining a career with parenthood become apparent after the first child is born. Part of the problems arise because in the nuclear family the husband, wife, and children live in their own household separate from their relatives, so there is no other family member available to care for the children while the parents are working (Slater, 1970).

Individual Solutions

One solution being considered by increasing numbers of career couples is to remain childless. Those who do have children end up finding their own solutions to the childcare problem. Wealthier parents hire a nurse, a governess, or some other full-time person to live in and take care of the child on a twenty-four-hour-a-day basis. Actually, this is one of the better solutions to a difficult problem if one can afford the enormous expense and if the right person can be found. The wrong person can be extremely harmful to children. Another solution of the wealthy is to send their children to private boarding schools and to camp in the summer.

Parents who work days, seldom travel, and are usually home weekends, often end up getting a regular baby sitter every day during the week and then taking care of their own children during other times. The total effect on the child will depend upon the regularity and the quality of care provided. The more that different baby sitters are employed and the more often the physical and geographical locale for the care is changed, the more likely that such arrangements will have a disturbing, upsetting effect upon young children (Bem and Bem, 1972). Young children gain security through established routines and from familiar faces and surroundings, so most parents strive to hire the same people all the time and to care for their children in the same place. If the child is cared for one week at home, another week at the baby sitter's, and perhaps for a period of time at nursery school, the frequent changes of environment and persons can become a very disturbing factor. As children get older, however, they learn that they can be happy in several places and well cared for by several different people. These children have few tears on the first day of school and less homesickness when they go to college.

Institutionalized Solutions

Another difficulty arises because there are really no satisfactory institutionalized solutions provided in American culture (Bronfenbrenner, 1970). The parents can send their child to a day-care center, if one is available (which is unlikely in many communities), but care is provided only during the day. The child must still be taken to the center and back home each day, an arrangement that further complicates the lives of any two busy career people, especially if they have to drive miles each way. What happens when the parents are out of town? Usually one or the other parent is available, but providing transportation is only part of the problem. The parent who is home must still get the child ready for nursery care and care for him or her after the nursery has closed. What if that parent has an important evening meeting? Obviously, a baby sitter is still needed and one who can get home by herself or himself.

Effects on Children

Reactions of Mothers

What are the effects on the children when both parents work? The answer is that *working or not working, even in full-time careers, is not the criteria for determining whether the effect on the* *children is harmful or helpful* (Ferriss, 1971; Keidel, 1970; Rutter, 1972). There are too many other factors that are important to the child's total mental health. For example, part of the effect on the children depends upon the effect that working or not working has on the mother. If the mother feels her work is important, if she likes her work and is satisfied with it, the effect on the marriage and on the child is likely to be positive (Ridley, 1973; Yarrow et al., 1973).

Age of Children

Another important factor that determines the effect on children is the age of the children at the time parents are separated from them (Schwarz, 1974). Up until children are about six months of age, because they can readily form attachments with different adults, the negative effects of the absence of both parents are relatively slight (Rice, 1979). As long as babies get the necessary attention—body warmth and contact, being held and carried about, being rocked and patted, getting something to suck and the necessary nutrition, physical care and protection, and the opportunity to listen to pleasant voices—they seem to thrive irrespective of who takes care of them, whether it is the child own parents or a caring substitute. Children of this age are said to be "care oriented" and not yet "person oriented."

Gradually, however, *as children begin to become attached to the person or persons who tend to them, it becomes more and more important that the same adult—or adults—return again and again* (Callahan, 1971). Observations of children who were over seven months of age who had different nurses while in hospitals showed that the children began to cry and turn away from the adults, not wanting to eat and showing in other ways that they were not adjusted. The warmer the child's relationship with its parents, the harder it was for the child to be separated from them at this developmental stage (Skard, 1965). Even in group nurseries where several persons care for the children, each child generally had one person to whom it is more attached. It is not harmful, however, for the children to have a few other adults in addition to the main person. What is harmful is if the children have no regular substitute parent or if different adults are frequently introduced to them. Skard explains: "If persons who are very different take care of the child in this period, this will mean a particular stress . . . because so much will be unexpected and different" (Skard, 1965). (See Rice, 1979 for a full discussion.)

Length of Absence

Young children from six to seven months of age and older are particularly upset if they are separated from their parents for long periods (several weeks) continuously, especially if they have no substitute parent on whom they can fix their emotions. For this reason, separation should be brief— only a few hours at first. Whenever mother is gone children will feel secure if they can rely on another familiar person (such as the father or a mother substitute) for protection and care.

For preschool children from about three years of age up to first grade, children need adults of both sexes, so either maternal or parental deprivation can cause stress. Because children of this age have better memories than at young ages, however, parents can stay away for longer periods, even for several months, as long as they return. Children may be affected negatively, but they get over it more quickly than at younger ages. Here again, dependable ties to a few adults are important. Friendship with others of their own age also contributes to the child's total development. For this reason, nursery school and kindergarten experiences

for several hours each day can be helpful. Then from school age onward, ties with adults gradually loosen as the child gains more independence.

Substitute Care

One of the crucial considerations, of course, is the kind of substitute care provided the child when parents are gone (Chantiny et al., 1973; Papousek, 1973). Every child needs warm, loving care by an adult who will meet the developmental needs of his or her age. This care can be given by a capable parent substitute for periods of time appropriate to the child's age, provided the care is consistent and adequate (Seaman, 1972; Wortis, 1971). There have been a great many children who have been raised by grandmothers, grandfathers, or by other parent substitutes who have not been adversely affected. There are also children who have been almost irreparably harmed by such persons as well as by inadequate parents. The crucial consideration, therefore, is the quality and consistency of the substitute care provided.

Parent–Child Relationship

The overall quality of the relationship of the parents with their children is also important (Yorburg, 1973). Research indicates that employed women frequently spend more undivided time with their children than do women who remain at home. Employed women and/or their husbands may take their children more places, and they may talk and play with them more often. They may show them more tenderness and concern. This is especially true of college-trained parents. These educated parents tend to compensate for time away from children by more planned, shared activities than is true of parents with less education (Rogers, 1973; Rossi, 1975; Yarrow, 1973).

Strains

Overload

The strains of a dual-career marriage are considerable. One source of strain is overwork (Keith and Schafer, 1980). The demands of the marriage, children, career, and home are great and often leave couples tense and exhausted. Couples deal with this problem differently. If husbands expect their wives to assume the burden of responsibility, the wife is over-worked, and may feel resentful at having so much to do (Poloma and Garland, 1971).

Most couples try to hire some sort of domestic help on a regular basis. Couples report considerable difficulty in getting competent help, however. Some become so discouraged with hired help that they just decide to split the work between them. Most try to purchase various labor-saving machines to cut down on the time required. Others use other means for increasing the efficiency of housework and of streamlining tasks. For example, some couples buy more fully prepared foods. Others are careful to buy clothing that never needs ironing. Others report that they had to lower their standards of housekeeping and cleanliness. Some, however, are disturbed by their own

Dual-career marriages are a source of both strain and rewards.

untidiness (Holmstrom, 1973). Some couples assign definite chores to children in the family (Rapoport and Rapoport, 1971).

Scheduling

Most couples admit that they have to budget their time very carefully. If job requirements allow the individual considerable flexibility in controlling his or her own schedule, it is easier to mesh job and home responsibilities. If an individual works for himself or herself, scheduling may be considerably easier. Such was the case of Dr. M, a licensed veterinarian.

Dr. M maintained an office in the basement of her own home and posted office hours only during those periods of time when her children were in school or on Saturday when her husband was home to take care of the children. Generally, she found that she worked about thirty hours a week and could very successfully combine such a career with marriage and raising a family.

Husbands and wives also try to mesh their schedules so that one or the other is available to care for children and so that they will be able to spend time together as a couple. Most couples admit that they have to give up a number of activities just to have time for necessary things. Career couples usually do not entertain as often as some others do. The wife does not as often play the hostess role for her husband. There is not as much time or need for involvement in community activities or in such things as gardening or leisure time reading.

Relationships with Others

The Rapoports and Fogerty (1971) report that in dual-career marriages there is a tendency for more friends to come from the wife's work environment and for the wife's friends to be-

come prominent. This may be because of the need for social support to sustain the dual-career pattern and because such support is more likely to come from the wife's associates. This can lead to trouble if the husband becomes at all jealous of his wife's friends.

Dual-career couples tend to have minimal relationships with kin because of other commitments and demands. Most couples have guilt feelings about not fulfilling relatives' expectations and try to deal with relatives in such a way as to prevent hurts as much as possible.

Identity and Competitiveness

Career husbands and wives each sacrifice a great deal to make it possible for the other to pursue a career. For this reason, if each does not accept the high value that the other places on career pursuit, conflict is bound to arise. Or if two people compete, each trying to outperform the other, the relationship may become tense. If two people are certain of their own identities and secure within themselves, they are able to work out compromises so that each is not threatened by the demands and successes of the other.

Conclusions

At the present time, dual-career marriages are still very clearly in the minority. While almost half of married women work, the majority do not pursue careers throughout their lives. It is easy to understand why. The wife is under constant pressure to sacrifice her career for the sake of her husband's career or for the sake of her children, and both the husband and wife are under considerable strain to manage everything at once.

But the dual-career marriage is no "freak of nature," it is quite probably a testing ground for things to come. As sex roles become more flexible and interchangeable, as more career opportunities are opened to women (Perrucci, 1974), as the concept of equality of the sexes becomes realism as well as idealism, as the financial demands of families become more difficult for the husband alone to fulfill, as society begins to offer more collective solutions to childcare problems, as greater numbers of educated women seek personal fulfillment through careers, marriage, and child rearing, the number of dual-career couples will no doubt increase.

Is this a "good thing" or a "bad thing?" For whom, and according to what standards? As seen, the possibilities for a happy marriage can be greater or lesser. The effect on children can be harmful or helpful, depending upon the circumstances. Certainly dual-career marriages present problems and strains, which have to be taken into consideration. This means that couples considering dual careers would do well to examine the experiences of others in making their own decisions, in solving problems, or in minimizing difficulties. It

may be that even the choice of a career itself should be made according to whether the career is possible in a dual-career situation. Certainly one's choice of a mate ought also to take into account attitudes and feelings toward dual careers.

It is hoped that society also will come to recognize that it has responsibilities toward dual-career families. For example, one of the problems that big business and government face is the high rate of absenteeism and turnover of working mothers. Yet, if employers adopted more flexible policies regarding working hours, part-time work, or in relation to maternity leaves and childcare (Graham, 1970; Harris, 1970), and offered collective solutions to childcare problems (such as nurseries where the mother works), those rates could be reduced considerably (Willett, 1971). Right now, some businesses still expect everything else to revolve around them and the family to make all of the sacrifices. The fact that most wives and mothers, and some husbands, aren't willing to make these sacrifices is really a credit to them.

The following points of view reflect the concern of many couples today. The account below is taken from a counseling interview of one couple, Al and Alice Todd, with a therapist. Alice regards herself as flexible in her dual role as housewife and a professional working woman. She is a department store buyer. For the last eight years she has been married to Al, a sales manager who, because of his job, frequently travels. They have a two-year-old son, Johnny.

Al: It took me almost eight years but I think that I've been able to achieve success in my work, but it's caused conflict between Alice and me. She complains that we never get to see one another. It's probably true. We're separated a lot. She has her career and I have mine.

Therapist: Alice, how do you feel about Al's traveling a lot and entertaining customers so much?

Alice: Uneasy. Lonely sometimes. I've never really accepted it. I don't like to interfere, but how can we have any companionship if we're never really together?

Therapist (to Al): How do you see the situation?

Al: Alice is right. I'm not home very much, especially when I'm on the road. Sometimes, I feel I don't know Johnny at all. I'd like to have more time with him and with Alice, but she knows I can't help it with this job.

Therapist: Isn't there any way you two can arrange some time together?

Al: We could except that Alice works too. It seems when I am home she's busy with her work. She goes to New York several times a year to buy clothes. She has to attend fashion shows and innumerable sales meetings at the store. Last year she was gone paractically the whole month of my vacation.

Therapist: What do you two do about Johnny? Who takes care of him?

Alice: Fortunately, we have a wonderful live-in housekeeper and baby sitter. Johnny just adores her, and she is awfully good with him.

Therapist: Can't you at least arrange weekends and vacations together?

Alice: Weekends, I'm so busy getting caught up with everything, and after that I'm so tired that I don't feel like going out with Al even though he wants to sometimes. Maybe, if we tried harder, we could arrange our vacations the same month, but it's difficult since we never know what's going to happen at work.

Therapist: What do you two want most out of your marriage that you're not getting?

Al: I want a woman who's a wife to me in every way, who has time for me, and especially one who will go to bed with me at least once a week.

Alice: I want a husband who takes more of an interest in his home and family and on whom I can depend for companionship and for helping out when I need him.

Therapist: Those are both worthy goals, so let them be the things that we try to work out together.

QUESTIONS

1. What kind of a wife does Al want? How does Alice differ from his expectations? What factors prevent her from living up to his expectations of her? Should she change her job? Explain.

2. What kind of a husband does Alice want? How does Al differ from her expectations? What factors prevent him from being the type of husband she wants and needs? Would his changing jobs be an answer to the problem? Explain.

3. In what way are Al's and Alice's goals in marriage similar? What circumstances, relationships, or attitudes need to be changed before their goals can be reached?

4. What should be the role of the therapist in counseling with this couple?

Marital Relationships

The Intimate Life: Its Satisfactions and Adjustments

CHAPTER OUTLINE

Marital Satisfaction over the Family Life Cycle

Correlations with Marital Satisfaction

Marital Adjustment

Early Adjustments

Adjustments during Parenthood

Adjustments during the Postparental Years

Adjustments after Retirement

Adjustments by Widows and Widowers

Conclusions

Dialogue

What constitutes a "good" marriage? What standards are used to evaluate marital success? One criteria which has been used is *marital stability:* the absence of separation or divorce. Our society tends to feel that an unbroken family is a "better" family than a broken one, but a lot of people stay married and are miserable, and they and their children suffer because of the disturbing environment in which they live.

At other times, *marital happiness* has been used as the criteria. But it is a vague, undefined dimension that is too personal and subjective a phenomenon to be used as a measure of marital "goodness" or "success" (Glenn and Weaver, 1978). Also, a given person may show a pattern of peaks and valleys of happiness. Even a person in a very unhappy marriage will usually have some moments of happiness.

This chapter discusses the intitmate life from two points of view—*marital satisfaction* and *marital adjustment. Marital satisfaction may be defined as each person's evaluation of the extent to which each marital partner feels he or she receives from the other partner the feelings, attitudes, services, and goods needed.* Admittedly, this is a highly subjective set of criteria, but since no two couples are completely alike in terms of needs and marital expectations, using personal evaluations seems wiser than trying to establish more objective standards of what consitutes a "good" or "bad" marriage.

There is the fact that no couples are completely satisfied; there are always some gaps between expectations and fulfillment. Therefore, a second concept is needed, that of *marital adjustment, which emphasizes the dynamic nature of marriage: the necessity to give and take in the continuing evolution of the husband-wife relationship.* For this reason, it is a realistic concept, emphasizing that marriage not only offers some fulfillments but that it also offers some frustrations, thus requiring flexible realignments and adaptations if the total relationship is to exist. *Marital adjustment, therefore, may be defined as the process of modifying, adapting, or altering individual and couple patterns of behavior and interaction in order to achieve satisfaction.* This means that adjustment is only a means to an end, not an end in itself. The end goal is satisfaction.

This means that adjustment and satisfaction have to be considered together. Research has shown that marital satisfaction and marital adjustment correlate very highly with one another. Therefore, both aspects need to be kept in focus in discussing what marriage is all about.

Marital Satisfaction over the Family Life Cycle

The Family Life Cycle

The family life cycle has been used as a helpful device for comparing the changes in family structure, composition, and behavior that accompany the inevitable progression from birth to death (Feldman and Feldman, 1975; Spanier and Sauer, 1979; Tamashiro, 1978). The cycle has been used also to show changes in marital satisfaction during various stages from the beginning to the end of marriage.

The most commonly used family life cycle is one divided into eight stages as follows (Duvall, 1971):

    I. *Beginning families.* Married couple without children

    II. *Childbearing families.* Oldest child: birth to 30 months

    III. *Families with preschool children.* Oldest child: 30 months to 6 years

    IV. *Families with school children.* Oldest child: 6 to 13 years

    V. *Families with teenagers.* Oldest child: 13 to 20 years

    VI. *Families as launching centers.* First child gone to last child leaving home

    VII. *Families in the middle years.* Empty nest to retirement

    VIII. *Aging families.* After retirement

Figure 10-1 shows the comparative length of time in each of the eight stages. Note that the length of stages II through V is based on the age of the oldest child. Quite obviously, the cycle does not apply to childless couples or to those who delay marriage and childbirth to much later than these averages, or to those who divorce and remarry (Nock, 1979; Norton, 1980; Walker, 1977). Variations have been found also among those of different educational levels (Spanier and Glick, 1980). Stage VII represents the period of time from the last child gone until retirement. The length of this **empty nest period** has been extended greatly due to improving survival rates and fewer children (Glick, 1977). Stage VIII in this figure represents the total number of years from retirement until the death of both spouses. On the average, the life expectancy of both white and black husbands at retirement at age sixty-five is thirteen more years. Ordinarily, wives of husbands who live to age seventy-eight will be widowed for the last two or three years of their lives (U.S. Department of Commerce, Statistical Abstract, 1979). A wife whose husband dies at age sixty-five

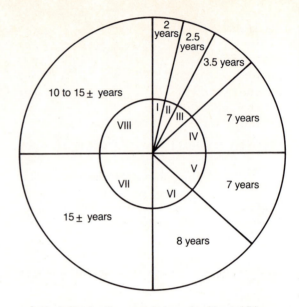

I   *Beginning families*—married couple without children
II *Childrearing families*—oldest child: birth–30 months
III *Families with preschool children*—oldest child: 30 month–6 years
IV *Families with school children*—oldest child: 6–13 years
V *Families with teenagers*—oldest child: 13–20 years
VI *Families as launching centers*—first child gone to last child leaving home
VII *Families in the middle years*—empty nest to retirement
VIII *Aging families*—after retirement

FIGURE 10-1. *The family life cycle by length of time in each of eight stages (Source: Fig. 7-2 [p. 148] in* Marriage and Family Development, *5th edition, by Evelyn Millis Duvall. Copyright © 1957, 1962, 1967, 1971, 1977 by J. B. Lippincott Company, a division of Harper & Row, Publishers, Inc. Reprinted by permission of Harper & Row Publishers, Inc.*

may be widowed for eighteen years. As can be seen from the figure, *the number of years that couples have to live together after the last child leaves home is as great as the total number of years of marriage that have gone before* (U.S. Department of Commerce, May 1980).

Changes in Marital Satisfaction

How does marital satisfaction change during these various stages of the family life cycle?

The studies are quite consistent in showing a decline in marital satisfaction during the early years of marriage, particularly following the birth of the first child and continuing to the end of stage III or IV (preschool or school age children). A few studies show the decline extends to the end of stage V (teenage). Practically all studies show an overall increase in marital satisfaction after stage IV or V (after school age or teenage). Some also show another slight decline in satisfaction prior to stage VIII—retirement (Burr, 1970; Feldman, 1973; Rollins and Cannon, 1974; Spanier, Lewis and Cole, 1975; Uhlenberg, 1974). Figure 10-2 gives a comparison of results of studies in three separate communities. As can be seen from the figure, and from other studies, *the general trend is for marital satisfaction to be somewhat curvilinear; to be high at the time of marriage, lowest during the child-rearing years, and higher again after the oldest child is beyond teenage* (after stage V) (Schram, 1979). Apparently, bearing and rearing children interferes with marital satisfaction (Laws, 1971; Thompson, 1980).

The common assumption that couples, and particularly wives, are affected negatively by the children leaving home cannot be substantiated by research. In fact, data from six United States national surveys indicate that *women whose children have left home are happier, enjoy life more themselves, and have greater marital satisfaction than do women whose children are still at home* (Glenn, 1975). Among women forty to forty-nine years of age, a 1973 survey showed that 93 percent of postparental women indicated that they had "very happy" marriages, as compared to only 57 percent of parental women. Similar results were obtained for women fifty to fifty-nine years of age as well (National Opinion Research Center, 1973).

When the question is raised as to why marital satisfaction is at an ebb when the children are of school age, the most plausible explanation seems to be that the demands placed upon the couple during these years are at their greatest. The couple are under increased financial pressure because of the needs of a growing family. Usually, job responsibilities outside the home are at a maximum. The children make increasing demands as they get older. Community responsibilities also increase during the middle years of marriage. In more technical language, "*the number and intensity of social roles of an individual gradually increase until the middle years*" (Riley and Foner, 1968). As a result, the couple experience greater role strain because of the discrepancy between role expectations and perfor-

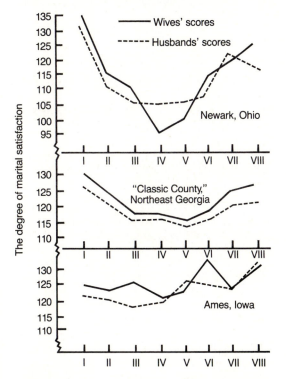

FIGURE 10-2. *The degree of marital satisfaction (Source: Adapted from G. B. Spanier, R. A. Lewis, and C. L. Coles, "Marital Adjustment*over the Family Life Cycle: The Issue of Curvilinearity"* Journal of Marriage and the Family 37 [May 1975]: 271–273. Copyrighted 1975 by the National Council on Family Relations. Reprinted by permission.)

*The authors use the Locke-Wallace Marital Adjustment Scale to measure the degree of satisfaction.

mance (Burr, 1973). This role discrepancy results in less satisfaction with the marital relationship. After the children are grown, however, role expectations and strain decrease in these later years, resulting in a concomitant increase in marital satisfaction (Hicks and Platt, 1970).

Correlations with Marital Satisfaction

There are a number of important factors which are related to marital satisfaction (Lewis, 1975; Miller, 1976). Marital satisfaction has been found to be greatest among those:

Marital satisfaction involves fulfilling one another's needs.

- *Of higher occupational status, income and educational levels.* These factors are interrelated but the most important factor is income and whether or not the couple are satisfied with the amount earned (Geismar, 1973; Hicks and Platt, 1970; Renne, 1970).
- Who are *satisfied with their jobs* (Brinkerhoff and White, 1978; Jorgensen, 1979).
- Who are *mentally and physically healthy* (Cole, Cole and Dean, 1980).
- Who spend the greatest proportion of *leisure time in joint activities* (Kraus, 1971; Orthner, 1975; West and Merriam, 1970).
- Who have *good verbal and **nonverbal** communication* (McCubbin, 1979; Snyder, 1979), who talk more, understand one another, show sensitivity of one another's feelings, say positive things about one another, discuss a wide range of subjects, and who keep open the channels of communication.
- Who *express more affection* (Fineberg and Lowman, 1975).
- Who *trust one another* (Wachowiak and Bragg, 1980).
- Who *conform to the marital role expectations of one another* (McNamara and Bahr, 1980) and who show *role flexibility.*

- Who *fulfill one another's emotional needs* (Crosby, 1973).
- Husbands and wives *who have an **egalitarian** relationship* (Bean, Curtis and Marcum, 1977).

Marital satisfaction is least among those:

- Who are *heavy or excessive drinkers.*
- Who are *social isolates* with few friends.
- Who are in *conflict over child bearing.*
- Who *disagree on finances.*
- Who are *sexually dissatisfied* (Renne, 1970; Snyder, 1979).

Marital Adjustment

Meaning of Adjustment

Marital adjustment is the process of modifying, adapting, or altering individual and couple patterns of behavior and interaction to achieve maximum satisfaction in the relationship. According to this definition, adjustment is not an end in and of itself. It is a means to an end. The end is satisfaction in and with the marriage. It is quite possible for couples to "adjust" to one another but still be quite unhappy and dissatisfied with the relationship. For example, people who like sex may accept the fact that their mates seldom want to go to bed with them. They learn to adjust to this situation, but this does not mean they really like it or that they are satisfied with this accommodation. Or people may learn to "adjust" to their mate's bad temper and try to overlook it, but this does not mean they approve. They have learned how to avoid overt conflict, but this adjustment gives them very little real comfort or joy.

Couples are motivated to try to adjust for different reasons. Some couples "adjust" for the sake of marital stability: to avoid splitting up the family through divorce. Other couples adjust for the sake of marital harmony so as to avoid conflict and quarreling (Skolnick, 1973). Their goal is to keep peace at all costs, even at the cost of ulcers, estrangement, or of never really communicating with one another. Other couples adjust because of their mutual esteem and love for one another.

Sometimes a particular adjustment may not be the best that one would like, but it may be said to be successful to the extent that it provides the highest-positive satisfaction possible under the circumstances (Edmonds, Withers, and Dibattista, 1972). Obviously adjustment is not a static achievement to be done once and for all. It is a dynamic, ongoing process throughout married life.

Marriage Adjustment Tasks

All couples discover that they have to make adjustments in one or more areas. These areas of adjustment might be called *marital adjustment tasks* (Clayton, 1975), and may be divided into nine areas as shown in Table 10-1.

Early Adjustments

During Courtship

The couple are first confronted with some of these marital adjustment tasks early in courtship. They begin to learn how to fulfill ego needs, to discover and adjust to temperamental differences, and to develop varying degrees of physical and personal intimacy. They may begin to develop relationships with future in-laws and with mutual friends and to establish a degree of companionship and communication in working, playing, talking, and being together. They begin to explore ideologies, values, and philosophies of life. They begin to arrive at a balance of power in their relationship and to make workable decisions affecting one another. Conflict arises occasionally and they begin to discover whether or not they can cope with it satisfactorily. Certain things, such as some of the material and economic tasks of marriage do not concern them until they establish a mutual residence. Until the couple begin to make a definite commitment to one another, they only have a minimum of actual responsibility toward one another.

After Marriage

After marriage, however, the couple are required to make a tremendous number of adjustments and to assume heavy responsibilities. This often leads to a period of disillusionment and disenchantment in naive, immature couples who have not realized what marriage really involves. Some couples are not aware until the honeymoon that marriage is such an intimate relationship. The primary focus during the honeymoon is on sexual expression and relationships, on learning to express affection, and on developing physical and emotional intimacy. Of course, many cou-

TABLE 10-1. *Marriage adjustment tasks*

Intimacy
  Adjustments to personal habits: cleanliness, dress, manners, eating and sleeping habits, habits relating to smoking, drinking, drugs
  Adjusting to temperamental differences
  Developing physical and emotional intimacy
  Learning to fulfill ego needs of one another
  Learning to express affection
  Satisfying needs for love, physical contact
  Finding, using acceptable means of birth control

Material Concerns and Economics
  Selecting a residence: geographical area, community, neighborhood, type of housing
  Equipping and maintaining a household
  Finding, selecting, and maintaining employment
  Adjustments to type, place, hours, conditions of employment
  Establishing husband-wife roles in relation to material concerns in and outside the home
  Agreement on division of labor

Power, Decision Making
  Achieving desired balance of status, power
  Learning to make, execute decisions
  Learning cooperation, accommodation, compromise
  Learning to accept responsibility for actions

Extrafamily Relationships
  Establishing relationships with parents, in-laws, relatives
  Learning how to deal with families
  Establishing, maintaining husband-wife job-related relationships
  Establishing, performing community, voluntary responsibilities

Children
  Adjusting during pregnancy and childbirth
  Reorientation of roles, responsibilities, allocation of time, resources

Companionship
  Learning to think it terms of "we" rather than "I"
  Getting used to living together
  Learning to work, play, talk, eat, sleep together
  Learning to share space, time, belongings, ideas, interests, work
  Learning to communicate ideas, worries, concerns, needs
  Achieving privacy and togetherness

Social Life
  Selecting, relating to friends
  Learning to plan, execute joint social activities
  Learning to visit, entertain as a couple
  Deciding on type, frequency of social activities as individuals and as a couple

Conflict
  Learning to understand conflict causes, circumstances
  Learning to cope with conflict constructively
  Learning when, how to obtain help if needed

Mores, Values, Ideology
  Understanding and adjusting to individual mores, ethics, values, beliefs, philosophies and goals in life
  Establishing mutual values, goals, philosophies
  Accepting one another's religious beliefs and practices
  Decisions in relation to religious affiliation, participation

ples have slept together before marriage, but even for some of these, being together constantly and sleeping together in the same bed every night is a very different experience. For some couples, this is a completely new adventure, something neither has experienced before. Sometimes sexual intercourse at the beginning of the marriage does not prove to be the wonderful experience that was expected.

This may leave the couple disappointed, bewildered, doubtful, or hurt (Vincent, 1974).

Tremendous Trifles

In the beginning, couples notice very minute detail about the way the other person walks, talks, dresses, eats, sleeps, bathes, and so on (Henton, 1970). Everything one does comes under the close scrutiny and observation of the other. The newness of the experience makes the two people very observant and sometimes critical. One young husband described the first week with his wife.

One of the things that used to annoy me was the routine my wife went through every night before bedtime. After getting undressed, she would spend an hour putting her hair up in curlers and putting cold cream on her face. Then she had to place a full glass of water by the bed and make certain she had plenty of cigarettes, since she also smoked in bed. Usually, she had a snack before bedtime, had to listen to the 11:00 o'clock news, and do several other things as well. By the time she got through with all this, I was either asleep, too tired to make love, or quite annoyed with what seemed unnecessary delays.

Other couples complain about a variety of little things: One husband complained because his wife never wanted to sleep with a window open whereas he liked a lot of fresh air. One meticulous wife discovered that her husband never liked to take a bath or to use deodorant. Another discovered that her husband always threw his dirty socks and underwear in a corner of the room. One husband was annoyed because his wife always lounged around the house in her bathrobe until after lunch. Gradually, couples begin to get used to one another, to overlook some of these little things, and to learn how not to annoy one another. Early in the marriage, however, these "tremendous trifles" can be quite aggravating (Bowman, 1974).

Material Roles

One of the major adjustments relates to husband-wife roles in relation to material concerns and money. Earning an adequate income is not easy. If the couple hold stereotyped concepts, this burden falls heaviest on the husband, who begins to realize

what an enormous responsibility he has accepted. One husband told his counselor:

After we got back from our honeymoon . . . I sat with my head in my hands. I wanted Janet. I still do. But I felt like the walls were closing in. Already we owe thousands—on a car, furniture, the whole bit. I see myself in ten years with a mortgage, a power lawn mower and kids that need braces. It's like *my* life is over (Maynard, 1974, p. 136).

The traditional wife suddenly realizes that she has the daily responsibility for cooking and homemaking. Modern women may never have done these things regularly at home, so this becomes a major chore. As one wife said: "I spent the first year of our marriage with my nose in a cookbook." Of course, where the husband and wife observe less traditional sex role separation, they can be of real help to one another in earning the income and in performing household duties. Still they both have assumed heavy responsibilities in getting married or have considerable adjustments to make before performance is adequate. Most young couples feel like this one: "We both had a lot of growing up to do after we got married."

Independence, Decision Making

Some young people have never lived away from their parents before marriage. Some of these get quite homesick and want to go back home quite often to visit parents. A major task is that of becoming emotionally independent from parents and to learn to depend on one another for guidance, moral support, and emotional fulfillment (Gendzel, 1974; O'Neill and O'Neill, 1972). Learning how to make joint decisions becomes an important part of the early months of marriage. In so doing, the couple work out their own balance of status and power and the process by which decisions are made. When differences and conflict arise, the couple are confronted with the task of dealing with conflict constructively so as not only to solve problems but to strengthen rather than to weaken their relationship.

Friends and Social Life

Selecting and relating to friends and establishing the type and frequency of social life sometimes causes trouble. A common complaint is: "I don't like his (or her) friends." Being married does not mean one has to give up all of one's old friends, but neither does it mean that one can maintain the same social life one had while single. A common complaint of young wives is typified by the following: "After we were married my husband wanted to spend most of his spare time with his buddies and to run around with them just like he used to." Yet these same wives may be expected to give up seeing many of their old friends and to stay home and take care of a house and children.

Sharing and Cooperation

It is not easy for individuals who have been single and independent for a number of years to begin to think in terms of "we" instead of "I." Even such things as time schedules, decisions about when to go to bed and when to get up in the morning involve some degree of cooperation and consideration for one another (Adams and Cromwell, 1978; Darnley, 1978). Couples now share belongings, space, work, and time and have much to get used to in adjusting to individual differences. Throughout it all, they also need some individual privacy and spaces in their togetherness. Mace and Mace liken such adjustments to those required of two porcupines settling down to sleep on a cold night. If the porcupines get too close, their quills prick one another. If they get too far apart, they can't ben-

efit from one another's body heat. So the porcupines shift back and forth, first together, then apart, until they arrive at positions in which they can achieve the maximum amount of warmth with a minimum amount of hurt (Mace and Mace, 1974).

Adjustments during Parenthood

Parenthood as Stress

"First pregnancy," says psychiatrist Eldred, "is a nine-month crisis. Thank God it takes nine months, because a child's coming requires enormous changes in a couple's ways of adjusting to each other" (Maynard, 1974, p. 139). In recent years, there has been less of a tendency to refer to the addition of a first child as a crisis and more of inclination to refer to it as a period of stress and transition (Bell et al., 1980; Boss, 1980; Miller and Sollie, 1980). The amount of stress will vary from couple to couple. *The more stressful a couple's marriage before parenthood, the more likely they will have difficulty in adjusting to the first child.*

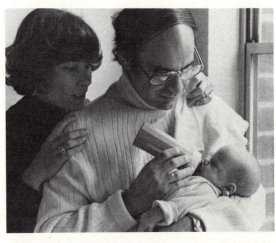

Parenthood involves major adjustments for both the husband and the wife.

Middle-class parents seem to find the transition to parenthood more stressful than do lower-class parents (Russell, 1974).

Sometimes stress arises if the pregnancy was not planned (Hobbs, 1977). Even couples who plan the pregnancy begin to realize little by little that tremendous adjustments are required. Roles have to be realigned, heavier responsibilities assumed, and social activities curtailed. The adjustment from two people living on two incomes to three people living on one income, as is often the case, is most difficult to make.

Part of the stress comes from the fact that most couples are inadequately prepared for parenthood. As one mother stated: "We knew where babies come from, but we didn't know what they were like." One study showed that 81 percent of middle-class women reported absolutely no experience in caring for infants at the time of the first child as compared to 63 percent of her working-class respondents (Jacoby, 1969). Another study showed that men who had been prepared for parenthood by attending classes, reading books, and so forth found far greater satisfaction in being a parent than those who had not been so prepared (Russell, 1974).

Part of the stress arises, also, because of the abrupt transition to parenthood. Rossi writes:

The birth of a child is not followed by any gradual taking on of responsibility, as in the case of a professional work role. It is as if the woman shifted from a graduate student to a full professor with little intervening apprenticeship experience of slowly increasing responsibility. The new mother starts out immediately on twenty-four-hour duty, with responsibility for a fragile and mysterious infant totally dependent on her care (Rossi, 1968, p. 35).

For this reason, it is of tremendous help to the mother if her husband will share this care with her. Direct assistance from relatives in the early days after birth can also minimize stress.

Stress will vary from child to child depending upon each child's temperament and how easy each child is to care for. Some children never give any trouble. Others, such as hyperactive or sick children, require an abnormal amount of care (Balkwell and Halverson, 1980; Roberts and Miller, 1978).

Adjustments of the Wife

Parenthood affects the wife and husband differently. The wife has to carry the child for nine months, accompanied by varying degrees of physical discomfort or difficulties and sometimes by anxiety about impending childbirth. Women who have a good job may deeply resent having to take time off from work to bear and care for a child. *Some women suffer an identity crisis at this point* similar to that of men who are retiring. The necessity of giving up their job—if only temporarily—plus the addition of long hours of constant physical work and being confined to the home with a demanding infant creates an intellectual and social void in the lives of women who have participated in multidimensional social roles before their children are born. *Some women complain of being tied down:* "My life is not my own. The demands of the children take time and I have less time for myself. When I worked, there was no nervous strain. I wish I could get out more." Other women complain about the lack of privacy: "Someone is always around." Other women feel that they have been "lost in the shuffle" or are "vegetating" because of the endless repetition of physical tasks and their isolation from social interaction. *One of the biggest changes for the mother is the addition of much work and responsibility.* One mother remarked: "I never realized how much work is involved in caring for one small child."

One important change is in the realignment of the woman's wife-mother roles. Even middle-class women in companionate marriages experience a decrease in the time, attention, and social activities previously shared with the spouse. Many couples report that having a baby gave them something in common and "brought them closer together," but their combined attention is now focused on the child rather than on one another, so even though they feel a common bond through their child, there is usually less husband-wife companionship and communication (Rosenblatt, 1974). Some husbands feel rejected, especially during times when sexual relations are medically discouraged or when the wife is too tired to pay attention to her husband's desires.

Some wives too feel rejected, especially if they feel unattractive during and after pregnancy. Wives worry about their personal appearance and loss of figure (Russell, 1974). One study emphasized that a woman accepts pregnancy well when it brings her closer to her husband, but she rejects pregnancy when she feels it serves to exclude her from her husband. If the husband is fully employed so that the wife feels confident of her husband's ability to provide for the baby, she also feels better about having a child (Meyerowitz, 1970). Other women enjoy their motherhood role and report that having a baby has been one of the great sources of satisfaction in their lives.

Adjustments of the Husband

After the first surge of phallic pride—"I did it"—expectant fathers approach impending fatherhood with essentially three different reactions. *Romantic men* approach fatherhood in a spirit of self-absorption and awe, seeing it as putting aside their carefree youth and accepting adult responsibility. *Resentful men* react to fatherhood as a burden requiring additional resources or interfering with their freedom, their good times with their wives, or with professional advancement. Some of these

men, angry because of the pregnancy, even take out their hostility on their wives. *Family-oriented husbands* welcome their responsibility as conferring a new and valued status. Such men identify closely with all stages of pregnancy, are excited when they first feel the baby kick, enthusiastically prepare the room for the baby, and complete some of the other arrangements before the actual birth (Maynard, 1974).

For all first-time fathers, however, the period following birth constitutes a prolonged period of strain. New fathers reported interrupted sleep and physical weariness. Most men complain about the amount of work required and about being tied down. In one study, 53 percent indicated having a baby increased their money problems and the amount of work required (Russell, 1974). *Young husbands, especially, find parenthood to be more of a crisis than do those who are older and who have been married longer.* Husbands who are insecure may be more jealous of the time their wife has to spend taking care of the baby and may grow to resent their own offspring.

Adjustments during the Postparental Years

Time Span

The **postparental years** usually refer to the ages after the last child leaves home and until the husband's retirement. As shown in figure 10-1 found earlier in the chapter, if the woman gets married at the average age of twenty-one and has children, she is fifty-one when the last child leaves home. The husband who married at age twenty-three and has children will be fifty-three when the last child leaves. Some writers prefer the term the "empty-nest" years, since once children are born, one is always a parent.

Fact and Fiction

The picture that one gets of this period from fictional literature is quite depressing. The woman is depicted as going through **menopause,** spending large sums of time and money at the local beauty or figure salon trying to look youthful and beautiful, is readjusting her life to fill the gap after the departure of the children, or is trying to keep busy with her clubs and volunteer service to keep from being too depressed and lonely because her children are gone and her husband is away so much. The man is depicted as experiencing an identity crisis. He is shown as beginning to fear he may have failed in accomplishing his professional goals in his career, in spite of the fact that he is working harder than ever and earning more. He is aware that he is growing gray, paunchy, and short of breath, is beginning to have doubts about his sexual prowess and potency and so may start chasing younger women or start thinking about divorcing his wife. *The stereotype of middle age has been one of lost companionship, sexuality, and purpose in life for the aging female and of the overworked, disillusioned, woman-chasing male* (Peterson, 1970; Somerville, 1972).

According to recent research, however, such fiction is largely fancy and only partly fact (Harkins, 1978; Robertson, 1978; Targ, 1979). It is true that some women are going through the menopause during these years, but often with a minimum of physical or psychological disturbance, thanks to greater understanding and better medical care. The biggest adjustment for the wife whose whole life has been wrapped up in her children is in filling the gap after the children leave. One woman comments:

My daughters were both nineteen when they married. I didn't want them not to marry, but I missed them so much. I felt alone. I couldn't play golf. I couldn't even play bridge. I don't have a profes-

sion, and I couldn't take just any job. I just didn't have a chance to learn anything (Einzig, 1980, p. 58).

While these comments are not unusual, even *greater numbers* of women breathe a sigh of relief after the last child leaves (Rubin, 1979). At last, these women are now free to live their own lives. Many go back to school, take up postponed careers, establish businesses, and become involved in hobbies and personal interests or in community affairs of one kind or another. These women can now enjoy the pleasures of their own lives, and/or of being grandmothers with only a minimum of responsibility. And as far as looking old is concerned, many middle-aged women are slim, youthful looking, attractive, poised, and full of energy and vitality. They may not feel the need for sex quite as often as when younger, but some are enjoying intercourse more than ever before—without fear of pregnancy.

The *husbands* of this age are at the height of their careers, taking more responsibility and making more money than ever before. The decrease of financial burdens and the increase of income enables the couple to take longer and more expensive vacations, to buy expensive jewelry or automobiles they couldn't afford when younger, and to eat at the expensive restaurants without having to cope with the children or hire a baby sitter. Many men join tennis clubs or jog to keep in shape, go to their doctors regularly to get help with diets or with reducing their cholesterol level, and have long ago stopped smoking when they learned it was bad for their health. Hair dyes and better cut clothes enable some to look younger and to feel better about themselves. With understanding and love, the average couple still enjoy an active sex life well into their seventies. They don't feel too great a loss when the children leave, especially if they have reason to be proud of them and their accomplishments (Lewis, Frenau, and Robert, 1979). It's nice to brag to friends about children who turned out all right.

There is considerable evidence to show that *adults in the postparental period are happier than are those earlier or later in life*. The period has been described as "a time of freedom." This new-found freedom was described by one wife in this way:

There's not as much physical labor. There's not as much cooking and there's not as much mending and, well, I remarked not long ago that for the first time since I can remember my evenings are free. And we had to be economical to get the three children through college. We're over the hurdle now; we've completed it. Last fall was the first time in twenty-seven years that I haven't gotten a child ready to go to school. That was very relaxing (Deutscher, 1964, p. 55).

One husband showed his relief at not having such a great financial burden. "It took a load off me when the boys left. I didn't have to support 'em anymore" (Deutscher, 1964, p. 55). It would appear, therefore, that *while there are adjustments to be made during the empty-nest years, there are increased opportunities to enjoy life as a couple.*

Adjustments after Retirement

The major problems facing the retired couple may be grouped into seven categories:

1. Lower income
2. Loss of identity and social status
3. Realignment of husband-wife relationships, roles, routines
4. Health and medical problems
5. Relations with grown children
6. Housing and living conditions
7. Sexual relations

Income

The most immediate problem facing the retired couple is the reduction of income. In 1978, the median income of families whose head was age sixty-five or older was $10,140. This total represents a considerable drop in income for most of these persons when the figure is contrasted with the $17,640 income of all families, regardless of age of head (U.S. Department of Commerce, Statistical Abstract, 1979).

Identity and Social Status

Along with the loss of income often comes a loss of identity and social status. People find status through their occupation. When they leave that role, they have the feeling that they have lost their main identity. As Bell says: "A former mechanic is no longer a mechanic—he is occupationally nothing" (Bell, 1975, p. 332). Those who have found identity through avocations, marriage, their children, or in other ways adjust more easily (Brenton, 1971).

Husband–Wife Relationship

People who retire from their occupation begin to spend more of their time at home with their mate. This may put a strain on the marriage because the couple must interact more than in the past. Some wives complain of additional work when they and their husbands retire. The couple sometimes gets on one another's nerves. Studies show that retired husbands take on a few additional household tasks, but overall they don't share more than when they were working (Arling, 1974). Much of a retired husband's time at home is spent in his own pursuits. So while the retired couple are together more, retirement does not ensure that the husband will spend that much additional time in household chores.

On the more positive side, one of the advantages of retirement is that couples who enjoy one another's company are now able to spend more time together. They are free to pursue mutual interests, to travel, or just to be better companions. Retirement can mean years of carefree fun and relaxation.

Health and Medical Problems

As people get older, their bodies slowly deteriorate, they become more prone to various illnesses, and they go more often to doctors and hospitals. While the aged account for about a twelfth of the population, they occupy about one-fifth of all hospital beds.

Older people dread physical problems that will impair their mobility, their senses, and their capacity to perform minimal tasks that make them independent of others for personal care. Older people who are able to drive a car more often remain in good spirits and more often report that their health is good than do those who are housebound (Shanas, 1968). Those who suffer from arthritis or other crippling diseases, who have physical impairments so they can't walk very well, can't go up or down stairs, have trouble doing household chores, washing and dressing themselves, or putting on their shoes become more dependent on others, more isolated from outside social contacts, and become more depressed about their lot in life. Investigations of the relationship between mental health and physical illnesses show that *physical disability, including sensory loss, stands out strongly as the most important factor associated with mental illness* (Shanas, 1968). Living arrangements, whether at home, in the home of a child, or in a hospital or nursing home, are less important to mental health than the extent of physical disability.

The most vivid indication of the declining mental health of the aged is reflected in their suicide rates. In the United States, about 22 out of every 100,000 people in their forties kill themselves, but at age 80 the rate is 697 in every 100,000. "Most of these suicides are the normal reaction to a hopeless, irreversible situation that is found to be unbearable" (de Beauvoir, 1972, p. 276).

Of course, there are wide individual variations in the reaction of older people to their illnesses. Some become preoccupied with the state of their bodies, noticing every ache, pain, and symptom. Other people who may suffer as much physical discomfort try not to think about it and continue to enjoy life greatly. They enjoy what has been called "body transcendence" in contrast to those with "body preoccupation."

Mrs. Slayton is an eighty-year-old widow. She lives alone. She is hard of hearing, badly crippled by arthritis, and reports that she has difficulty in going out of doors, washing and bathing, dressing, and putting on her shoes. She often feels as though she is about to fall. Mrs. Slayton says that a neighbor has to help her dress. The housework is done by her daughters, who live about ten minutes' distance. Despite her impairments, Mrs. Slayton says that her health is good for her age. She spent no time in bed during the past year and has not seen the doctor for several months (Shanas, 1968, p. 212).

Mrs. Slayton is optimistic about her health, partly because she is not preoccupied with it. This is unusual considering her condition and the fact that she lives alone. *Usually, people alone have more serious health problems and higher mortality rates than do those of comparable ages who are married and living with spouse* (Carter and Glick, 1970). Elderly married couples are more able to provide necessary care and assistance for one another than is a person living alone.

Relations with Grown Children

A national survey revealed that the nearest child of over three-fourths of the aged respondents was located within a thirty-minute drive and that two-

thirds had seen one of their own children in the twenty-four-hour period preceding the interviews (Stehouwer, 1968). A study of older persons living in two small Wisconsin communities found only a third who did not have at least one child living in their own community. Of those with children in the same town, two-thirds saw at least one child each week. Only one-tenth of all the elderly studied did not have at least one child living in their home state. Elderly migrants to retirement communities in Florida or Arizona tend to be somewhat more isolated, but even among these, 36 percent of the elderly migrants to Florida and 43 percent of those to Arizona see their children more than once a year. Those who saw their children infrequently were also unlikely to see them often even if they lived in the same community (Bultena and Marshall, 1970).

Most elderly people see their children frequently, but only a minority turn to their children for help in meeting many daily responsibilities. Several studies have shown that older people are more likely to turn to their daughters rather than their sons for help. Help comes in many forms: living with their children (about 10 percent of married elderly couples and about 17 percent of previously married elderly individuals live with a married child), economic support, personal care, transportation, gifts of cash and food, performing housekeeping, yard, and home chores, or providing help for outings and holidays (Shanas, 1967). Understandably, most older people don't like to have to turn to their children for help or be dependent on them. They much prefer independence. Of course, sometimes it is the older person providing the help: help with grandchildren, gifts of food, cash, clothing, household furnishings, assistance with home repairs, yard work, or housework. Generally speaking, *white-collar parents more often provide help to their children than do blue-collar parents. Blue-collar parents more often need help from their children than do white-collar parents*

(Shanas, 1967). About 18 percent of all old people in the United States have no surviving children.

Housing and Living Conditions

It is usually of great importance to the elderly to be able to keep their own home. This allows independence, and relationships with children are usually more satisfactory with separate residences. A home allows the elderly to lead their lives as they choose, and this is important. Furthermore, the elderly prefer to remain in one place among familiar faces and surroundings. Younger people often enter occupations in which they have to move a great deal. If they have their parents with them, the parents are forced to tear out important roots of the past (Montgomery, 1972). Statistics from 1978 revealed that almost three out of four households maintained by persons sixty-five years old and over were owned by them. In the remaining households, the oldsters were renting (U.S. Department of Commerce, 1978b). Of course, large numbers of older people (about one out of ten men and one out of five women sixty-five and older) are not heads of households, since they go live with married children (U.S. Department of Commerce, May 1980).

There is an increasing trend for older people to sell their homes and move to *retirement communities*. But these are usually those who are leisure minded, in good health, and who have considerable financial resources (Montgomery, 1972). *Housing developments for the elderly* have also become a booming business, but little research is available on the effects of segregating people by age groups. Usually older people prefer to have young people around them. A number of elderly Americans (almost a million) live in *nursing homes* or *convalescent facilities*. The trend is increasing, so that nursing homes now provide more beds than hospitals. Some of these homes have high standards of cleanliness and management and strive to provide for some of the social and emotional needs of residents, as well as offering custodial care. Such homes do provide for necessary care of the elderly who are not able to care for themselves, who are chronically ill, and whose needs are too great for family members to meet. But even in the best of homes, the elderly are in a highly segregated setting with other old and/or infirm people. Their lives are often distorted and frequently sad, as they see one resident after another die. Some homes are shocking in the care and treatment provided. Many are understaffed, with patients continually tranquilized or under restraint to keep them quiet. Some lack basic sanitation, provide inadequate nutrition, nursing, or medical care. Such abuses have led to the passage of corrective legislation and licensing in some states. As might be suspected, residence in nursing homes or homes for the aged is rare for elderly persons whose marriages are intact (Carter and Glick, 1970).

Sexual Adjustments

As people age, sexual needs decline, but the majority of married couples between sixty and seventy years of age are still sexually active (Pearlman, 1972). Between seventy and seventy-nine years of age, a little less than half of the couples are still having intercourse. Other research shows more decline in sexual activity among aging women that among aging men. One major reason, however, is that a large number of older women do not have a spouse or one with sexual interest. As a consequence, large numbers masturbate. Few elderly people engage in postmarital coitus (Pfeiffer, Verwoerdt, and Davis, 1973). This is not necessarily because of a lack of interest, but because of strong societal sanctions against such activity.

Masters and Johnson indicate that the sexual activity of women over age seventy is strongly influenced by male attrition. The male, in turn, is strongly influenced by a fear of **impotency.** Any male may have temporary impotence, but if he is of normal health, does not become anxious by an occasional failure, and realizes "that loss of erective prowess is not a natural component of aging," the average male can remain potent and enjoy sex well into his seventies. The aging male and female may not want intercourse as often as they did when they were younger, but giving it up is not necessary in most cases. *If a couple's sex life has been enjoyable during their earlier years, the chances of its still being enjoyable in later years are greatly enhanced* (Masters and Johnson, 1966).

Adjustments by Widows and Widowers

A couple who are married and have children in the 1970s and whose marriage is not broken by divorce or separation can expect to live together for forty-four years. The median age of these married women with children at the death of one spouse (either she or her husband) will be sixty-five years (Glick, 1977). A woman who is age sixty-five when her husband dies may have a life expectancy of sixteen more years. A man who is age sixty-seven when his wife dies at age sixty-five has a life expectancy of about twelve more years. This is a long time to be a widow or widower and requires significant adjustments for those involved. Altogether, about 16 percent of all men and 53 percent of women age sixty-five have lost their spouse through death (U.S. Department of Commerce, 1977).

Because of the greater longevity of women than men, the number of widows exceeds widowers at all age levels. Table 10-2 shows the ratios at different ages (U.S. Department of Commerce, 1979, p. 38). Partly as a result of these ratios, the remarriage rates of widows is lower than

TABLE 10-2.   *Ratio of widows to widowers at different ages*

Age	Ratio of Widows to Widowers
45–54	6.5 to 1
55–64	6.7 to 1
65–74	5.0 to 1
75 yrs. and over	4.4 to 1

Source: Adapted from U.S. Department of Commerce, Bureau of the Census, *Statistical Abstract of the United States: 1979* (Washington, D.C.: U.S. Government Printing Office, 1979), p. 38.

among widowers. As might be expected, the younger a person is when a mate dies, the greater the chances of remarriage. More than 75 percent of women widowed before age thirty remarry but, of those who are widowed after age fifty, only 6 percent remarry. Also, women who have many children when widowed are less likely to remarry than those who have fewer children (U.S. Department of Commerce, 1977).

Bereavement

No matter how long the death of a spouse has been anticipated through prolonged illness, it comes as a shock. In fact, those who have watched their loved ones suffer through chronic illness and finally die are more negatively affected than those whose spouses are bereaved after a short illness (Gerber, 1975).

There are usually three stages of grief (Hiltz, 1978). The *first stage* is a short period of shock during which time the surviving spouse is stunned and immobilized with grief and disbelief. The *second stage* is a period of intense suffering during which the individual shows both physical and emotional symptoms of great disturbance. The *third* stage is a gradual reawakening to an interest in life. Physi-

cal upset during the second stage may include disturbed sleep, stomach upset and loss of appetite, loss of weight, emptiness in the stomach, loss of energy and muscular strength, shortness of breath, sighing, or tightness in the chest. Emotional reactions may include anger, guilt, depression, anxiety, or preoccupation with thoughts of the deceased. During intense grief, persons need an outlet such as talking with friends or family about their loss. If this opportunity is denied, as it often is since grief and death are uncomfortable subjects, recovery from the loss is more difficult and prolonged (Parkes, 1972).

One of the most common reactions to bereavement is to "purify" the memory of the deceased by mentally diminishing all negative characteristics of that person. One woman who had hated her husband remarked: "My husband was an unusually good man" (Lopata, 1973). If idealization of the dead continues, it can prevent the formation of new intimate friendships (Atchley, 1975). Extended bereavement can result in a sentimentalized, nostalgic, and morose style of life (Bischof, 1976).

Men and women may respond differently to bereavement. Men find it more difficult to express grief but are able to accept the reality of death more quickly than women, although women are more able to continue work during bereavement than are men. Men more often than women describe their loss as the loss of part of themselves. Women respond in terms of having been deserted, abandoned, and left to fend for themselves (Glick, Weiss, and Parker, 1974).

The negative impact of bereavement and loss of mate cannot be minimized (Heyman and Gianturco, 1973). Damage to the self often accompanies widowhood, if the spouse was a significant other. The degree and duration of damage to the self depends upon the intensity of the involvement with the departed spouse and the availability of significant others.

Relationships with Friends and Family

People usually do not go through bereavement alone. Family and friends help out for awhile, but the extent to which widows or widowers recover and start rebuilding their lives will depend partially upon the extent to which they form meaningful relationships, especially with friends (Arling, 1976).

Older people, especially widows, have a consistently high degree of contact with other family members, including married children (see the previous section of this chapter). Usually, the elderly female is closer to her children, especially daughters, than is the elderly male. One disadvantage, however, is that the woman is more likely to be dependent on them for material aid. The more dependent elderly people become, and the more that helping roles are reversed, the lower is their morale (Kent and Matson, 1971). Arling explains:

In old age, the flow of assistance shifts and adult children begin to give more aid to their parents than they receive in turn. Even though contact with kin might not have declined, the functional importance of the older person within the family has decreased, and commensurately, the aged individual has lost the supportive role and taken one of dependency (Arling, 1976, p. 75).

As a consequence, Arling found that widows with children living close by had no higher morale than respondents who either had no living children or had none within an hour's drive. Similarly, the frequency of contact with children had no significant association with morale. Those having family members nearby were just as likely to worry and to feel lonely.

One of the reasons for this finding was that even though the children regularly visited their widowed mothers, affective ties were not always close, so the married children could give relatively little emotional support. Also, children and their elderly mothers had contrasting interests, so often

did not make good companions. Another study of widows in Chicago revealed that only about 10 percent received any economic support or physical services (such as transportation, house repairs, or yard work) from siblings or other relatives. Only about one in ten shared social activities with them. So having relatives close by did not necessarily mean that they could be counted on for emotional, physical, or social support, or if support were given, that the oldsters were happier (Lopata, 1978b).

All research findings stress the positive importance of peer support in helping widows and widowers adjust. Morale is very positively associated with involvement with friends. The reason is that friends are usually of similar ages, can share common interests, and generally are equal in their ability to exchange assistance, thereby preventing the negative psychological consequences of emotional or material dependency (Hochschild, 1973b).

Problems of Widows

An in-depth study of Wyly and Hulicka of seventy-two women of middle socioeconomic status, all widowed for less than five years, showed that the most frequently cited problem was *loneliness* (Wyly and Hulicka, 1977). Widows miss their husbands as companions and partners in activities (Kivett, 1978). This problem is accentuated if the woman has low income and is not able to afford many social activities outside the home. Younger widows report that participation in social activities is a problem because so many activities are couple oriented. Sexual frustration is common among the widowed (Goddard and Leviton, 1980).

The problem of loneliness is accentuated also because over half of widowers and widows live alone (U.S. Department of Commerce, 1975a). Aloneness, however, does not always mean loneliness. Many people grow accustomed to living alone and become involved with friendship groups, so loneliness declines.

A second problem cited by the widows in Wyly's and Hulicka's study was that of *home maintenance* and *car repair.* Other problems cited frequently by younger widows were *decision making, child rearing,* and *managing the family finances.* Widows in the oldest group frequently mentioned such problems as *learning basic finance, lack of transportation,* and *fear of crime.* The only advantages of widowhood, mentioned by the younger women, were increased independence and freedom of choice (Wyly and Hulicka, 1977).

Financial problems continue to plague both widows and widowers. In every age category, however, widowed females earn less than widowers. The females who are most impoverished are widows older than sixty-five years of age, even though they might have been receiving social security or pensions of some sort (Sass, 1970; Tissue, 1979). Blacks and other minorities in rural areas or areas of urban blight are the poorest of all. If they are to have the basic necessities of life, a variety of social supports are needed (Lopata, 1978a; Scott and Kivett, 1980).

The complaints of widows indicates that one of their biggest adjustments relates to *role changes.* Young widows particularly are puzzled by role expectations and by vague and contradicting expectations concerning appropriate behavior. They experience considerable uncertainty over when to terminate the mourning period, when to begin dating again, and how long to wait before considering remarriage. Since they usually have dependent children, they have to assume the total role of childcare and socialization, as well as the roles of provider, homemaker, community liaison, and maintaining ties with the extended family. Most widows of all ages experience a loss of sexual role, but this hits younger women somewhat harder than the very elderly. Since widowhood requires a greater number of necessary changes in role definition for younger women than for older women, young women have a greater difficulty with the adjustments of widowhood. Older women see widowhood as normal for them, so they are able to find a more definite social position in the community.

Widowhood, at all ages, however, changes the basic self-identity of many women. This is especially true of traditionally oriented women for whom the role of wife was central to their lives. The woman who has put her role as wife at the top of the list has to reorient her thinking to find other identities. The woman who had put her role of mother primary, and who still has dependent children at home when widowed, is not forced to change her role as drastically—except as provider if that role falls on her shoulders. Therefore, the specific role changes that are required when a woman is widowed depend upon what roles were emphasized prior to widowhood. The career wife without children, who was not very close to her husband may not have to change her role performance much at all. In fact, she may welcome the increased freedom.

Widowers

Whether widowers have easier or harder adjustments to make than do widows is a matter of some dispute (Berardo, 1970). Men with dependent children may have a hard time caring for them if they are not used to the responsibility. Bischof feels that widowers without parental responsibilities, however, have a greater degree of freedom than do widows without dependent children (Bischof, 1976). The loss of their wife does not directly affect their occupation or income, unless of course the wife is earning a considerable share of the family income. Their only disruption is learning to cook, keep house, and take care of themselves, although many men can already do these things. If they can't, they may be able to hire help. In such cases, the major adjustment is the loss of companionship and love of their wife.

Conclusions

There are several important conclusions that may be emphasized from the material in this chapter. One, it is not at all unusual for young couples to go through a period of disillusionment and disenchantment after marriage, especially if they have held overly romantic views of marriage in the first place. The problems of adjustment that all couples face are numerous and often take a considerable amount of time and experience before they are resolved. Most couples report less satisfaction later in marriage than in the beginning, but they still feel glad to be married.

Two, parenthood adds many positive dimensions to a relationship, but it also produces much stress. One possibility might be for couples to give themselves several years to adjust to one another and to work out important marital problems before they even consider having children. The more harmonious their marriage, prior to childbirth, the greater likelihood their relationship will be satisfying after the first child arrives. Furthermore, the more mature the couple are before becoming parents, the easier it will be to deal with the stresses of parenthood.

Three, the empty-nest years can be some of the most satisfying of the couple's life, especially if the wife is prepared for her postparental role. She is fortunate if she can continue in a career she enjoys. If she needs additional education to do what she wants, she can go back to school. If she and her husband have neglected their marriage, some marital bonds may have to be reestablished at this time.

Four, the retirement years are crisis years for many persons. Probably the most difficult problems arise because of lack of money. If couples have sufficient income, they can remain fairly independent by being able to hire help and assistance as needed. Several ways of increasing income are suggested. The ceiling could be taken off maximum allowed earnings for those who are under social security. The number and coverage of private pension plans could be increased. Changes could be made in laws so as to benefit the elderly. As it is now, the laws almost force people to live at poverty levels.

Another major problem of the elderly is housing. Many older people want to keep their own home, but high taxes and costs force them to sell. Instead of government-subsidized housing for the elderly, one alternative is government subsidies for the elderly in their own homes in the form of tax breaks, help with mortgage payments, taxes, heating costs, or by other means. Since most elderly people want to live near their own children, another alternative would be subsidies for those children who construct separate—but adjacent—apartments or living quarters for their aged parents. Expanded medical benefits and services through medicare might be considered to meet some of the needs for better health care. Certainly, better solutions can be found than are currently operative.

Amy and Frank Sands have lived together for twenty-nine years and are the parents of two daughters, both college graduates who have lived away from home for a few years now. Frank is fifty-one years old and actively involved in running a construction business he started himself. Amy is forty-nine, attends classes in sculpture. The couple are fairly wealthy, although for years Frank was the only source of income for the family. A recent interview revealed tensions that were new to their lives in the postparental years.

Interviewer: How have you been getting along now that the girls are gone?

Amy: Usually very well as far as Frank and I are concerned. We've always had a good marriage and been very happy together. As a matter of fact, since the girls moved out, we enjoy one another even more. We go out more—to plays, concerts, and places like that. It's wonderful not to have to cook or to stay home because we're expecting the girls to pop in the door at any moment. I feel free as a bird for the first time in years. It's a good feeling.

Interviewer: What seems to be the problem then?

Amy: I don't have enough to do, especially when Frank is at work. During those years when the girls were growing up, I devoted my life to them. I was always there when they needed me, but now that they don't need me any more, I don't know what to do with myself.

Interviewer: Don't you have any outside interests apart from your home?

Amy: I'm enrolled in a sculpturing class but that's only one day a week. I enjoy it but there must be more to life than that.

Interviewer: There is, depending upon what you want to do. How about getting a job?

Amy: I've never worked since we were married. I never believed in it. I don't know who'd hire me; I don't know how to do very much.

Frank: She's always been interested in art, and she's really brilliant and knowledgeable in it.

Amy: Frank always says that but he's exaggerating. I do like to paint—oils mostly—and now I'm getting interested in sculpturing, but I wouldn't say my work is brilliant.

Frank: I've been trying to persuade her to let me talk to the curator of the local gallery to see if he would be willing to have a one-woman art show with her paintings. She has dozens at home.

Interviewer (to Amy):   How do you feel about it? Would you be willing to let Frank inquire?

Amy: Naturally I'd be thrilled, but I don't think anything will come of it. I'm not a professional artist, but I suppose it won't hurt to try—if you think I could.

Interviewer: I'm sure you could. Why not let the curator be the judge of your work? I'm sure you realize, Amy, that you have a wonderful opportunity to enter a new phase of your life. Your goal of raising two daughters has been accomplished; now you have a chance to establish new purposes. Maybe your art will be an answer for you. If not that, then something else. The important thing is to always have something that you enjoy and through which you feel fulfilled.

Frank: What about me?

Interviewer: What do you mean? Aren't you willing for Amy to begin accomplishing new things?

Frank: Of course I am, but I'm not talking about her, I'm referring to me personally. To tell you the truth, I'm sick and tired of going to the office every day. I'm tired of the construction business. I've made plenty of money, so that's no problem. But I'd like to do something besides work my ass off for a change.

Interviewer: What would you really like to do?

Frank: I'm not sure. Sometimes, I think about selling the business and finding something else. I'm not sure what I'd enjoy the most, but I'd sure like to make a change. As long as Amy is going to, perhaps I can too.

Interviewer: I'm sure you can if that's what you want. One of our goals could be for you—as well as Amy—to reevaluate your life and to explore what you do want to do. To do that you'll have to ask yourself: "What things do I consider most important to me now at this stage of my life? Are there any things I've always wanted to do but never had a chance? If I could do anything I wanted to do, what would it be? What can I do that will give me the most satisfaction and that will enable me to provide the kind of life and companionship Amy wants as well?

Frank: Those are big questions. You've certainly given us both plenty to think about.

Interviewer: At least you have a start. I'll see you both next week.

QUESTIONS

1. How common is the middle-age crisis that both Frank and Amy are going through? Do you know others who are or who have gone through the same thing? Describe their situations.

2. Is it idealistic to expect that Amy and Frank can completely reorient their lives once they've reached middle age? Explain. What are some impediments or barriers that keep many couples from doing likewise?

3. What can men and women do while younger to prevent middle age from becoming a time of crisis?

4. Do men go through a stage of life comparable to the menopause that women experience?

5. What type of men and women have the hardest time adjusting to changes in their lives at middle age?

6. Do you believe that anyone over thirty is "over the hill"? Explain your feelings.

7. Do you consider your parents old? Why? Why not? In what ways do you want your life to be similar to theirs? In what ways do you want a different life from the one your parents have had?

CHAPTER

11

Power, Decision Making, and Communication

CHAPTER OUTLINE

Marital Power Patterns

Power in Decision Making

Sources of Power

Communication in Marriage

Barriers to Communication

Improving Communication Skills

Conclusions

Marital power as discussed here refers to control or authority in marriage, especially as related to decision making. The philosophy of new marriage that has been outlined in this book emphasizes the need for a democratic power structure in the family where the husband and wife both have an important voice in decision making as equal partners. This concept is most in keeping with middle-class ideals in the United States. It is the philosophy that feminists are advocating and is the one most in harmony with the concepts of modern college youths. Furthermore, research substantiates the value of this philosophy: United States couples who share in decision making are likely to have a high degree of marital satisfaction (Centers, Raven, and Rodrigues, 1971; Landis and Landis, 1973; Laws, 1971). Because many persons have been interested in promoting an egalitarian philosophy, there has been a need to find out what is happening in United States marriages. Has reality kept pace with idealism? Are United States marriages really democratic? Who has the power in the decision-making process? What factors determine whether or not the couple have equal power or whether the power resides in the hands of one spouse more than the other?

Though power may be exercised in many ways and over many different aspects of married life, as discussed here it relates only to who has the control over the decision-making process. Do the husband and wife have equal or dissimilar power in making decisions? Why?

There has been increasing concern also about communication in the family. Part of this impetus has come out of the T-group or encounter group movement, which uses sensitivity training, nonverbal communication, marathon groups, and other activities as "laboratories in human relations training," "to enhance interpersonal competence," and "to facilitate interpersonal exchange" (Altman and Taylor, 1973). These groups have shown the importance of openness and relatedness among participants in breaking down barriers that separate people, helping them to find real intimacy and to really communicate and understand one another. Many of these principles can also be applied in helping couples learn how to communicate in marriage as well.

Marital Power Patterns

There are four basic types of marital power patterns as related to decision making (Clayton, 1975).

1. *Husband dominant.* A traditional patriarchal family form in which power is exercised by the husband.
2. *Wife dominant.* A matriarchal family form in which power is exercised by the wife.
3. *Egalitarian or syncratic.* A democratic family from in which a fairly equal distribution of power is shared between the husband and wife.
4. *Autonomic.* A form in which the husband and wife are equal in power but which they choose to exercise individually and separately. A husband or wife who makes decisions without consulting the other come under this category.

Relationship to Marital Satisfaction

Generally speaking, marital ideology in the United States emphasizes an egalitarian exercise of family power: "Husbands and wives are equal and should share everything 50-50 including decisions." But to what extent does or will this philosophy contribute to marital satisfaction? The research indicates that *egalitarian patterns result in high marital satisfaction* (Laws, 1971). Landis and Landis (1973) reported that 47 percent of the couples they studied had a 50-50 pattern of dominance and these received the highest happiness rating. The next highest happiness scores went to those who reported that the husband was dominant or tended to be dominant. Four percent of the couples reported the wife was dominant or tended to be dominant. These couples received the lowest happiness scores. Other studies in the United States reveal similar results; marital satisfaction is high when there is an egalitarian marriage, lowest when the wife is dominant. One study of decision-making patterns in low income families showed that 72 percent of the respondents were in intact marriages if decision making was egalitarian or democratic, but only 27 percent of their marriages were intact if decision making was **autocratic** (Osmond and Martin, 1978).

It should be pointed out that a few studies such as those by Centers (1971) and others report that marital satisfaction is highest when power is exercised autonomically or when the husband is dominant. Some husbands who prefer to be dominant grew up with younger sisters and their wives grew up with older brothers, resulting in a classic family structure for teaching masculine ascendancy. In those cases where the wife is dominant, she may have had only younger siblings while her husband had older ones, leading to a situation where this exercise of power was preferred by both the husband and wife. Thus, patterns of preference were conditioned by the structure of the families in which the individuals grew up.

Power in Decision Making

Who Makes the Decisions

One measure of power in the family is who makes what family decisions. A study of 800 United States families representing a cross section of socioeconomic groups from a large urban area showed that the joint decisions were made by the husband and wife in 46 percent of the instances indicated on a list of nine decisions and as reported by the wives and by their adolescent children (Kandel and Lesser, 1972). No significant differences were found in the replies of the mothers or their teenagers. Another study of a cross section of white and black families in Detroit showed that joint decisions were made by the husband and wife in 37 percent of the instances (Blood and Hill, 1970). Table 11-1 shows the percentages of husbands and wives in the two studies who shared in making each of the decisions mentioned. As can be seen, some decisions, such as those involving vacations, selection of house or apartment, or what the children should be allowed to do, were equilateral in a majority of instances. Other decisions, such as whether or not the wife should work and how much money to spend for food, were made unilaterally by the wife in the majority of instances, while still other decisions, such as what car to get or what job the husband should take, were made unilaterally by the husband in the majority of cases. Overall, these and other studies reveal that there are no clear-cut consistent patterns of authority across all areas (Douglas and Wind, 1978). *The only conclusion that may be made is that overall, these studies reveal that the husband had more power in decision making than did the wife.*

TABLE 11-1. *Percentage of husbands and wives sharing decisions*

Both Husbands and Wives Share Decision about:	Percentage of Couples	
	Large Urban Area (N = 800)	Detroit (N = 731)
Where to go on vacation	75	70
What apartment, house to take	61	59
What child should be allowed to do	61	—
What doctor to see	52	46
Whether to buy life insurance	51	42
Whether wife should work	37	18
How much money to spend on food	36	33
What car to get	31	25
What job husband should take	8	3
Mean	46	37

Source: Adapted from D. B. Kandel, and B. S. Lesser, "Marital Decision-Making in American and Danish Urban Families: A Research Note," *Journal of Marriage and the Family,* 34 (February 1972): 136. Copyrighted 1972 by the National Council of Family Relations. Reprinted by permission; Adapted from R. O. Blood, Jr. and R. Hill, "Comparative Analysis of Family Power Structure: Problems of Measurement and Interpretation," In *Families in East and West,* edited by R. Hill and R. Konig, Paris: Mouton, 1970, p. 530. Used by permission of publisher and author.

Sex Differences and Stereotypes

Any evaluation of overall power will depend somewhat upon who answers the questions (Turk and Bell, 1972). In the studies by Kandel and Lesser (1972) and Blood and Hill (1970), responses were elicited from wives only. It has been suggested that *when both husbands and wives are questioned, some discrepancies exist in husbands' and wives' reports about their respective roles in decision making, that women tend to overestimate the power of their husbands and that the husbands report less power for themselves than their wives claimed for them (Granbois and Willett, 1970; Safilios-Rothschild, 1970). Safilios-Rothschild writes:*

There are some decisions which are less disputed between the spouses, both of them more or less agreeing that they are "feminine" decisions such as child bearing, purchase of furniture and household items, and the purchase of food, or masculine decisions such as purchase of life insurance, purchase of the car, and the husband's job. On the other hand, the degree of disagreement in some decisions such as the use of available money, what doctor to consult, the use of leisure time, the choice of friends, and the purchase of clothes is statistically significant (Safilios-Rothschild, 1969, p. 293).

It is evident here that *sex role stereotypes influence not only the actual decision-making process but also the evaluation of that process.* Those decisions that were traditionally masculine or feminine were more often reported as such by both spouses, but in other decisions that were not as clearly masculine or feminine, there were greater differences between the spouses as to who actually made the decisions.

Studies of decision making of farm husbands and wives in Wisconsin (Wilkening and Bharadwaj, 1967) and of Iowa farm and nonfarm families (Burchinal and Bauder, 1965) illustrate the influence of sex role stereotypes in the decision-making process. The Iowa study showed that some decisions tended to be the husband's prerogative and others the wife's prerogative. Thus, in relation to family finances, the husband more often made the decisions concerning how much life insurance to buy or when to borrow money, whereas the wives more often made the decisions about how much to spend on food. In relation to work, the husbands more often made decisions regarding changes in their job. The Wisconsin study also showed some specialization between husbands and wives in decision-making patterns. Husbands were more involved in such decisions as whether to buy major farm equipment, whether to buy or rent more farm land, whether to borrow money for the farm, what specific make of machinery to buy, how much fertilizer to buy, or whether to try out a new crop variety. Wives were more involved in such decisions as whether to take a job in town, how much money to spend for food, when to invite people for dinner, when to make household repairs, when to buy major household equipment, whether to paint or paper in the home, and decisions relating to the children such as when children visit friends and how much money children get for allowances. Interestingly enough, these farm wives were often involved in whether to buy a different car, probably because the car was so often used by the wife. Also, the wives were more often involved in areas pertaining to buying a car, household maintenance, food and entertainment, wife's working, and child training than their husband's wanted them to be, indicating more of a patriarchal attitude on the part of the husbands than the wives were willing to accept.

These findings indicate that *any evaluation of husband-wife power in decision making is dependent partially on what areas of decision making are studied.* When Centers and others (1971) added six decision areas to those originally studied by Blood (1972), they found that the husband's power was less. The six added decision areas were:

1. Whom to invite to the house or to go out socially with
2. How to decorate or furnish the house
3. Which TV or radio program to tune in
4. What the family will have for dinner
5. What clothes will be bought
6. What type of clothes the spouse will buy

The reason for the indicated drop in the husband's power is that some of these six new decision areas were considered the wife's prerogative.

Sources of Power

Other Factors Influencing Power

There have been numerous other efforts to sort out those factors influencing husband-wife power in decision making. These factors may be grouped under eleven categories.

1. role patterning
2. cultural norms
3. control of valued resources
4. socioeconomic class norms
5. physical power
6. personality and age factors
7. primary interest or presumed competence
8. relative love and need
9. stage of family life cycle
10. children
11. circumstances (Bahr and Rollins, 1971; Centers, Raven, and Rodrigues, 1971; and Eshleman, 1978)

Role patterning relates to stereotype sex role expectations and has already been discussed.

Cultural Norms

Cultural norms exert a big influence on the exercise of power in making family decisions. Traditionally, the husband was supposed to make the decisions, with the wife assuming a passive role. Because this was the expected pattern, people were conditioned to believe that this was the "right way." The husband's power was legitimized by society and the wife's power was denied. Some cultures still teach these norms.

Control of Valued Resources

One theory holds that the more individuals control resources of value to themselves and to their mates, the greater their power in decision making (McDonald, 1980). A person with superior education, status, background, occupation, or income would exercise more power in the decision-making process (Burr, Ahern and Knowles, 1977). Research has revealed many truths in the theory—but also some exceptions—so that the theory cannot be universally applied in every instance (Bahr, 1972; Safilios-Rothschild, 1967). The following conclusions may be drawn on the basis of the evidence to date, however.

The influence of education on power in decision making is variable depending upon the cultural context and relative differences between the husband and wife (Kandel and Lesser, 1972). In the United States, the more education a husband has, the greater his power. *Both low and high education white-collar husbands and high education blue-collar husbands continue to gain power if they exceed their wives' education, and they lose it if they fall short. The exception to this is a minority of low education blue-collar husbands who tend to have more power even when their wives have superior education* (Gillespie, 1971). Komarovsky (1964) attributes the greater power of some blue-collar husbands to more prevalent patriarchal attitudes among the less educated, to

the husband excelling in other personal resources in some cases, or to male prestige factors among the less educated.

In the United States as well as in other industrialized countries, *a wife's employment outside the home, either part-time or full time, tends to increase her decision-making power.* She gains power as she gains occupational prestige status (Hiller and Philliber, 1978; McDonald, 1979). Her power also increases as she gains more resources—more income and more ownership of property (Osmond, 1978; Safilios-Rothschild, 1970; Salamon and Keim, 1979; and Udry, 1974). One study showed that the more the wife's income equalled that of her husband, the more likely the spouses were equal partners (Scanzoni, 1980).

Socioeconomic Class Norms

Marital power patterns are significantly related to socioeconomic class norms. Lower socioeconomic or working-class families are more likely to be husband dominated than are middle- or upper-class families. This holds true for both white and black families.

Traditionally, the black family has been characterized as a *matriarchy* with the power ascribed to the mother of the family (Jackson, 1972; Scanzoni, 1971; Staples, 1971; Staples, 1973; Ten Houten, 1970; Yancey, 1972). Recent research indicates, however, that it is not race that makes the difference, but class. Middle-class black families have been found to be more egalitarian than middle-class white families (Willie and Greenblatt, 1978). Other studies have similarly concluded that the black matriarchy is a myth and egalitarian decision-making patterns predominate (McDonald, 1980; Staples, 1970). Conversely, the Chicano family has been characterized as a *patriarchy* dominated by macho males. This is characteristic only of working-class families, however. When socioeconomic class is taken into consideration, an egalitarian pattern of conjugal decision making is the most common mode (Cromwell and Cromwell, 1978). The stereotyped classifications of matriarchy for blacks and patriarchy for Chicanos must be rejected.

Physical Power

It has been suggested also that physical violence and coercion may be a source of power in some families. One woman reports of her husband:

He is a big man and terribly strong. One time when he got sore at me, he pulled off the banister and he ripped up three steps (Landis and Landis, 1973, p. 227).

This woman realized what her husband could do to her if he decided to strike her. The physical beating of a wife is used by some males as one technique for punishing or keeping control. One occasionally hears of wives who use physical violence against their husbands as a way of getting their own way.

Personality and Age Factors

Personality characteristics have some influence on decision-making powers in the family (Doherty and Ryder, 1979). Dominant males have their own way more frequently than less dominant ones, and wives of less dominant males have more influence in decision making. Husbands and wives with high scores in authoritarianism tend to be found in families where one spouse is dominant over the other. *The combination of husband-wife traits is also important.* Patriarchal attitudes are more prevalent among the less educated, so wives in these marriages would find it easier to accept authoritarian husbands. In her book, *Blue-Collar Marriage,* Komarovsky quotes one wife as saying:

He [my husband] is very sure in the way he moves and does things and says things. Many of the boys I went to school with act as if they don't know what they want. He's very easy about what he does and it is because he is so sure. You want to please him. He says things definitely and everybody likes it—the children, his friends. I like it very much myself (Komarovsky, 1964, p. 228).

Other wives, of course, would find such attitudes bordering on conceit or authoritarianism and would react negatively. It depends on what one seeks in a mate, and this depends partially on the personality pattern one has been taught to accept.

Considerable *age differences between spouses are also a significant factor in influencing power structures, with the older spouse exerting influence over the younger one* (Scanzoni and Polonko, 1980).

There are differences too in the way males and females strive to exert their power and influence. Safilios-Rothschild found that men more often than women used one-sided persuasion or verbal techniques to influence decisions. Women less often used verbal persuasion and more often used nonverbal techniques such as anger, crying, pouting, or the silent treatment as influence techniques. "Educated women tended more often to use sweet talk and affection" as a way of exerting influence, as well as more verbal techniques.

Primary Interest or Presumed Competence

The theory that holds that primary interest or presumed competence is a factor in decision making assumes that the person who is most interested or most involved with a particular choice will be more likely to make the decision. The second aspect of the theory is that the person who is most qualified to make a particular decision will be more likely to do so (Conklin, 1979). Often these two aspects, interest and competence go together. If the wife will be using the kitchen utensils more than her husband and is thus more interested in which ones to buy and if she has had more experience in the use of different utensils, presumably she will be the one who will exert the most influence in making this decision. If the husband does most of the driving and knows more about cars, presumably he will take more interest and exert more influence in this decision. In some homes, one or the other spouse is so dominant that he or she never gives the other an opportunity to decide anything. One wife comments:

I have never been able to feel that I could decorate or furnish our house the way I wanted. My husband always insists on having his way about everything. He has to select the pictures he wants. He wants oriental rugs, so he bought those. He even tells me how to clean them. I can't think of one thing that I have ever been able to do myself.

Relative Love and Need

The theory of relative love and need is closely related to the idea of primary interest. This theory states that *the spouse who is most in love and has the most need has less power in the relationship than the other* (McDonald, 1980). The reason is that dependency results in loss of power. The person who is most dependent has the most to lose if the relationship breaks up, so feels less right to orchestrate power.

Stages of Family Life Cycle

The theory holding that stages of a family's life cycle are a factor assumes that the realtive power of the husband and wife varies with each stage of the family life cycle. The power of the wife is medium during the honeymoon stage and in the early years of marriage. It decreases with the birth of the first child and continues to decline after the birth of subsequent children, the wife's power being least when she has the most small children. It seems clear that as the number of dependents increases, the wife's bargaining power declines. It increases again, however, as the children grow, declines when

her motherhood role has ended, but reaches a higher level after her husband's retirement (Lewis, 1973; Rogers, 1973). All of the studies agree that *the wife's power is lower following successive births and while her children are young and dependent* (Safilios-Rothschild, 1970). One wife comments:

I had three children the first five years we were married. Then I found out that my husband was running around with other women. I asked him about it, but he said I had to take him the way he was, that this was what he was going to do, and that if I didn't like it I could get the hell out. But where was I to go? I had three kids to think of. I couldn't even get a good job since I didn't have any special kind of training. I was stuck.

It is precisely this helpless dependency that many modern women are finding unacceptable and that motivates them to want financial and occupational independence.

Children

Very little research has been done on the influence of children on family decision making. Strodtbeck has suggested that *by adolescence a child's censure of his parents may be fully as effective a control mechanism as the parent's censure of him or her* (Weill, 1971). Even the younger child has both verbal and nonverbal methods of influencing parents: shaming, belittling, coaxing, nagging, explaining, temper tantrums and other displays of anger, crying, yelling, threats to run away, pouting, or withdrawal of love and affection. Many parents are afraid of alienating their children and give in easily whenever the children want or don't want something. Very insecure parents, or parents of unplanned children, handicapped children, illegitimate children, stepchildren, children from divorced homes, or adopted children sometimes feel sorry for the children, or even guilt in relation to them, so bend over backwards to be fair. In so doing, they let the children take advantage of these feelings. Of course, the opposite may be true; some children are completely overlooked so that they make no difference at all in the actions or decisions of the parents.

Circumstances

Sometimes family circumstances change suddenly or a crisis occurs that results in a realignment of power structure (Bahr and Rollins, 1971). Physical incapacitation of one spouse or illness may force an otherwise submissive partner to take a more active role (Power, 1971). If a husband loses his job and remains unemployed over a long period of time, his power and authority may diminish.

Egalitarian couples, because they are more fluid and flexible, are able to shift and exchange roles in order to meet the demands of a stressful situation. Such couples give and take and help each other make decisions when the situation demands it. Families with a very dominant person are very vulnerable to crises or stress. When that person becomes incapacitated, family functioning collapses, unless the other person can take over.

Communication in Marriage

What It Involves

Communication between human beings may be defined as a message one person sends and another recieves (Knox, 1975). It is also the process of transmitting feelings, attitudes, facts, beliefs, and ideas between them. It is not limited to words but also occurs through listening, silences, facial expressions, gestures, touch, body stance, and all other nonlanguage symbols and clues used by persons in giving and receiving meaning. In short, it may include all the means by which people exchange feelings and meanings as they try to understand one another and as they try to influence one another (Bienvenu, 1970).

In order for communication to take place several things have to happen. Once people become aware of particular thoughts, feelings, or desires they begin to make a choice: whether to *disclose* these, fully or in part, or to keep them to themselves (Miller, Corrales, and Wackman, 1975). If they choose to disclose them, they have to decide on appropriate times and places (Culbert, 1970). And since all relationships have boundaries and they ordinarily want to avoid under- or overdisclosure, they establish their own procedures as well as their styles of communication (Miller and Peterson, 1974; Raush, 1974). How something is disclosed is often as important as what is disclosed. The amount of disclosure is itself important, however, since it bears a direct and linear relationship to marital satisfaction (Jorgensen and Gaudy, 1980). Whether disclosure actually takes place or not will depend partly on the honesty and the skill of the persons doing the disclosing (Berger and Benson, 1971; Miller, Nunnally, and Wachman, 1975).

But something else is needed—*receptivity* on the part of the listeners. They must be attentive, interested in listening, concerned about receiving the messages. Whether or not they receive accurately and without distortion will depend on the clarity with which the messages were transmitted and also on their skill in receiving. Their responsibility is to strive to understand accurately the messages that are being sent.

An important part of communication is *reciprocity* or *symmetry*, which is the free flow of information back and forth (Corrales, 1974). The persons doing the disclosing need *feedback* from the receivers to ascertain whether or not the messages have been accurately perceived and to learn the receivers' reactions to them. It then becomes the responsibility of the receivers to become the disclosers: to indicate their reactions, feelings, thoughts, and desires and to transmit these to the other persons.

In significant relationships, disclosure tends to encourage disclosure. The reverse is also true; if one partner tends to withhold information or lash out at the other, the other is likely to respond in the same manner (Jourard, 1971). It is important, therefore, that an *empathetic exchange* takes place so that each person discloses and receives in *a reciprocal* or *symmetrical* way.

Importance in Marriage

One of the major dimensions of any human adjustment problem is the extent and nature of the communication among the parties involved. *Many authorities contend that good communication is the key to family interaction and the lifeblood of the marital relationship* (Powers and Hutchinson, 1979). One couple writes:

There is no area of our married life that isn't affected by communication: our bed, our job, our children, our social life, our leisure time, our relationship with relatives and friends. All could become potential areas of discontent and friction when there isn't good communication between us (Herrigan and Herrigan, 1973, p. 149).

There is considerable reasearch evidence to substantiate these statements. Some researchers have found that *for wives, especially, good communication is more related to general satisfaction with marriage than is sexual satisfaction* (Benard, 1972c: Wachoiak and Bragg, 1980). Researchers talk about the psychologically deserted wife who is denied the comfort of discussing her problems with her husband and whose constant lament is "he never talks to me" (Mace and Mace, 1974; Mornell, 1979). This does not mean, however, that all communication is helpful to marriage. As discussed in the last chapter, *the act of communicating does not always lead to a resolution of problems.* Talking things over and expressing feelings may make things worse (Levenson, 1972). As one author expressed it: "Engagement . . . can result in escalation (Raush et al., 1974, p. 307). Couples who openly share negative feelings the other can't handle may increase tension and alienation (Billings, 1979). As a result, some couples avoid such disclosure, feign agreement, or deliberately lie as a means of maintaining marital harmony. Just communicating is not enough, communication must be constructive or *selective* (Bateson, 1972).

Verbal and Nonverbal Communication

Verbal communication—the use of language and words—is more strongly associated with good marital adjustment than is nonverbal communication. One reason is that nonverbal communication, the language of signs and signals, is more subject to misinterpretation (Kahn, 1970).

Barbara comes downstairs dressed only in her bikini panties and bra. Her husband, Chuck, interprets this as a signal that she's interested in going to bed. Right away, he becomes aroused and starts to make advances. She becomes annoyed: "Will you leave me alone. I'm trying to get my dress out of the dryer." It is obvious that Barbara's signal was only that she was without her dress and needed to get it, but Chuck interpreted it as asking for him.

One of the most important uses of words is in what Berne calls "the stroking function" (Berne, 1964, p. 13). By this he means words that soothe, that give recognition, acceptance, and reassurance and that fulfill emotional needs. Words can heal hurt egos or satisfy deep longings. What husband is immune to the words: "I think you're a handsome, wonderful man." Words are also used to solve problems, to convey information, or to reveal emotions. One of the most important functions is to provide companionship or, as expressed by John Milton, "In God's intention a

The ability to communicate is the most important factor in a satisfying marriage.

meet and happy conversation is the chiefest and the noblest end of marriage."

Rosenbaum (1979) suggests that couples avoid especially those tactics that remind the other of a disapproving parent. These tactics include ordering, commanding, warning, threatening, preaching, lecturing, disapproving, blaming, name calling, probing and cross-examining.

Nonverbal communication is in many forms. *Body language* includes such things as *posture, facial expressions, still or tense muscles, blushing, movement, panting breath, tears, sweating, shivering or quivering,* an *increased pulse rate,* or a *thumping heart.* "The message 'I love you' may be communicated in a gesture (outstretched arms), facial expression (pleasant smile), tone of voice (whisper), speed of

speech (slow), eyes (attentive), and touch (gentle)" (Knox, 1975, p. 162). The *manner of dressing* or *the use of cosmetics* are forms of communication. Emphasizing the mouth with cosmetics highlights sex appeal; playing up the eyes gives an ethereal or spiritual message. "A man's face is his autobiography," Oscar Wilde has said, whereas "a woman's face is her work of fiction." Whatever story she tells, the fact that she tells *that* one is significant.

Direct actions are another form of communication so that the florist can remind us: "Say it with flowers." Some nonverbal communication is *symbolic communication.* Thus, a surprise gift of perfume may be symbolic of infinite care and love (Otto, 1972).

Sometimes the messages transmitted verbally and nonverbally contradict one another. The O'Neills write:

Bill may say to his wife, "I'm listening, I'm listening," but his body is hunched over attentively in front of the television set. Arthur may tell his wife, "I love you," over and over, but she has good cause to wonder if he means it when he never listens to her attentively, gives her only a peck on the cheek, and is perfunctory in bed (O'Neill and O'Neill, 1972, p. 100).

Barriers to Communication

Barriers to communication may be grouped under five categories: (1) *physical and environmental,* (2) *situational,* (3) *cultural,* (4) *sexual,* and (5) *psychological.*

Physical and Environmental Barriers

There is a close relationship between physical proximity and social interaction. In general, closer physical distances are associated with more intimate relationships. This means that such factors as the size and arrangements of living spaces and the location of furniture in those spaces has an influence on interaction. The closer people sit around a table the more likely they will be friendly, talkative, and intimate. Whether couples sleep together in the same bed or in separate bedrooms influences the extent of their interaction.

It has been shown also that *physical confinement is associated with accelerated self-disclosure, particularly in intimate areas of exchange.* This means that the longer couples are together the greater the possibility that intimacy will develop. Of course, there is also the possibility that conflict and tension will develop (Altman, Taylor, and Wheeler, 1971).

Situational Barriers

Situations can also enhance communication or make it more difficult. If employment separates

"*I'm sorry, dear, I must have lost consciousness. What were you saying?*"

Drawing by Chon Day; © 1982 The New Yorker Magazine, Inc.

couples frequently or for long periods of time, the tendency is for communication to break down with a resultant loss of intimacy. Or, when couples live together with others in the same spaces, *lack of privacy* becomes a major factor in making intimate communication more difficult. The *situational context* changes during different periods of marriage and affects communication. For example, it has been found that husbands make far more effort to give emotional support to their wives during *pregnancy* but, following childbirth, feel that their wives do not require this special support. As a result, the increased closeness reported during pregnancy then declines, resulting in the increased dissatisfaction that some wives feel after childbirth (Raush, 1974).

Cultural Barriers

Wide cultural differences impose difficulties in communication (Hawkins, Weisberg and Ray,

1977). Such factors as *educational and age differences* affect the ability of the couple to communicate with one another. The graduate student and elementary school graduate think on different levels and about different things. One graduate student commented:

During these years I've been in college, my wife and I have drifted apart. I learn all about these new things in school, come home and tell my wife about them. But she isn't interested and doesn't know what I'm talking about.

One possibility, of course, would be for the wife to enroll in college too.

Couples with *divergent ethnic backgrounds* also have more difficulty understanding one another. Words have different meanings, as do actions. People are also *socialized differently.* Persons who are taught to be more reserved have more difficulty communicating in marriage than do others, One wife of a blue-collar husband comments:

He can clam up and not talk for a long time. Sometimes I ask what are you so clammy for, spit it out and you'll feel much better, but he'll answer me coarsely or just say, "Oh yeah." Sometimes I can worm it out of him, but I believe in leaving him alone (Komarovsky, 1964, p. 157).

Sexual Barriers

Part of the barriers to communication are a result of masculine-feminine differences. Men and women are socialized to be interested in different things (Christensen, 1971). Not as many wives as husbands are interested in talking about the Sunday afternoon football game. One husband confessed that he was bored with his wife:

What does she have to talk about? Dirty diapers and stuff. I don't care about that. She talks about the children, but we both see what is happening.

We are both there, it's no use talking about it all the time (Komarovsky, 1964, p. 149).

This same husband liked to read so that when he came across an interesting situation he tried to "talk her into reading the magazine, but she doesn't like reading, so I stopped bringing up these things" (Komarovsky, 1964, p. 149). Men and women are also socialized to express different degrees of sensitivity. When those who are emotionally sensitive and responsive try to communicate with those who are not, the results can be frustrating (Coults, 1973).

Psychological Barriers

The most important barriers to communication are psychological: fear of rejection, ridicule, failure, or alienation or lack of trust between two people (Larzelere and Huston, 1980). As one person expressed it, "I'm afraid. I'm afraid that others won't like me." Komarovsky writes:

In some cases the chief cause of estrangement lies in the personality of one mate who finds any close relationship threatening for a variety of psychological reasons. These persons would have probably been withdrawn no matter whom they married (Komarorsky, 1964, p. 159).

She goes on to say, however, that generally it is not just the personality of one mate but the interplay of the two personalities that impairs communication. Husbands and wives will not share experiences if they are unrewarding, threatening, or downright painful They need to be sure of an empathetic reply.

Improving Communication Skills

Skill in communication involves five aspects:

1. A positive feeling between spouses where they value and care for one another and are moti-

vated to want to develop sympathetic understanding

2. A willingness to disclose one's own attitudes, feelings, and ideas

3. An ability to reveal these clearly and accurately

4. A talent for being a good listener and for receiving messages accurately

5. A reciprocal relationship where disclosure and feedback originate with both partners and there is a free flow of information from both directions

Concern and Empathy

Communication is most possible when couples really show they care about one another. *Couples who frequently make positive statements about one another have much higher marital adjustments than do those who are very negative or disparaging in what they say* (Murphy and Mendelson, 1973). In addition, *supportive communications* stimulate reciprocal supportiveness, increasing the degree of marital integration (Alexander, 1973a; Alexander, 1973b; Gibbs, 1971). It is not just the communication itself that is important but also the *spirit behind the message* and a couple's feelings for one another. The tone of voice used and the words selected are also important. Most authors also talk about the importance of **empathy** — experiencing the feelings, thoughts, and attitudes of another person.

Self-Disclosure

Communication depends partially on the willingness of the persons involved to disclose their real feelings, ideas, and attitudes. People cannot really get to know others unless they are willing to talk about themselves. Some people can be classified as high revealers, others as low revealers. High revealers are more prone to reveal intimate facets of their personalities and to do so earlier in their relationships than

are low revealers. They are also able to make a more accurate assessment of the intimate attitudes and values of their friends than are low revealers (Taylor, 1968). In general, dyads where both persons are high revealers are more compatible than are pairs of low revealers.

Other research has shown a direct correlation between *dissatisfaction in marriage and the lack of disclosure of feelings to one's partner* (Levinger, and Senn, 1973). Satisfied couples less often discuss negative feelings pertaining to their mates, however. The negative feelings they disclose usually relate to external events such as a bad day at work. Feelings about their spouses are usually positive and pleasant. Thus, as in other facets of communication, *it is not just the fact of disclosure that builds satisfaction but the fact of selective disclosure of feelings which seems more beneficial to marital harmony than indiscriminate catharis.*

Clarity

Couples differ in their abilities to convey messages clearly and accurately. Low socioeconomic status couples have few verbal skills and so are not as able to communicate on this level. They make greater uses of nonverbal techniques. But learning to say what one means and interpreting accurately can be learned. Clarity and accuracy are enhanced by the following:

1. *Avoiding "double-level" messages* where words say one thing and actions and innuendos another.

2. *Speaking clearly and to the point,* saying what one really means, avoiding vagueness, tangentiality, ambiguity and indirect approaches that are easily misinterpreted (Meryman, 1973).

3. *Avoiding both exaggerating or understating the case* one is presenting. Some people are prone to embellish or elaborate on the truth. Other people reveal only part of the facts presented so that false impressions are created. Some people play

so fast and loose with basic facts that it is hard to decipher the real from the imaginary.

4. *Avoiding flippant, kidding remarks that mask one's real feelings and opinions.* How many times have the remarks been heard: "I didn't really mean that. I was only joking. Don't take everything so literally."

5. *Asking the other person to repeat what one has said* if there is any doubt that he or she has not heard accurately.

6. *Talking about important things when there is a minimum of distraction and when the other person can focus his or her attention completely on what is being said.*

Good Listening

Good communication also involves open listening and hearing and being able to receive what has been said. Sometimes people pretend to listen when they do not. This can become a habit that discourages the speaker from talking. Other people find it useful not to listen to those things which make them uncomfortable or which they don't want to hear. They figuratively "turn off their hearing aid" (Bernard, 1972c).

George D always started to play with the children every time his wife tried to talk to him about spending too much money on his hobbies. This made Mrs. D furious, because she knew he was trying to shut her out so she could not get through to him.

Some people are so interested in talking themselves they don't really listen. They are so concerned about what they're going to say next they aren't really listening to what is being said.

Feedback and Reciprocity

Feedback involves responding to what the other person has said as well as disclosing one's own feelings and ideas. In technical terms, feedback involves receiving the output of a computer and feeding it additional information to correct its errors. In human communication, *feedback involves paraphrasing the other person's statement to make sure it is understood, asking clarifying questions, and then giving one's own input or response telling how one feels about the matter.* The advantage of feedback is that it helps to assure a clear understanding as the conversation progresses. With feedback, self-disclosure may enhance real intimacy and growth.

Conclusions

In commenting on the discussion in this chapter relating to power and decision making in marriage, several points need to be emphasized. For one thing, decision-making patterns are influenced strongly by the cultural context in which the marriage exists and by the family backgrounds of the couple. This is why studies of different socioeconomic or ethnic groups in the United States reveal significant differences in status patterns.

For another thing, the trend in the United States is toward egalitarian patterns, but one still finds a degree of male dominance in low socioeconomic status families and marked segregation of decision-making powers according to prevailing sex role concepts. As wives gain more education, and particularly when they work outside the home, they achieve greater equality in making family decisions. Wives are most powerless when they are most dependent, with young children, but they regain some measure of lost power as their children grow and they can become more independent. Black middle-class families have more egalitarian power structure than do white middle-class families.

There is a close relationship between marital satisfaction and selective communication. Some couples learn to use both verbal and nonverbal language in positive ways to share experiences, ideas, or feelings to build companionship and to bind up shattered egos and restore depleted psychic reserves. Communication, at its best, can be one means whereby couples can give and receive emotional satisfaction, tenderness, understanding, sympathy, and love. But creative, constructive communication is an art to be learned (Wampler and Sprenkle, 1980). Some couples apply themselves diligently to learning and practicing the art, until their relationship has been tuned to a fine degree of empathetic intimacy. Others spend many years together, but remain strangers—isolated, lonely, and frustrated because they have not been able to penetrate the barriers that keep them apart.

CHAPTER 12

Marital Conflict

CHAPTER OUTLINE

Some Sources of Conflict

The Focuses of Conflict

Cause and Effect

Some Positive and Negative Values
of Conflict

Methods of Dealing with Conflict

Family Violence

Conclusions

A certain amount of conflict and discord may be considered a normal part of every marriage (Rodgers, 1973). Two people will never agree on everything. Tensions build up and misunderstandings occur in the process of living. The numerous decisions that couples must make and the disappointments, frustrations, and adjustments they must face will result, at some time, in a hurt look, an angry word, or a more overt quarrel. Some couples have more conflict than others; some are able to deal with it more constructively than others, but the potential for conflict is there, in every human relationship.

Mace and Mace (1974) compare the relationships of marriage to that of two people who are confined in a delineated space. If the space were a mile square field, the couple could coexist fairly well. If they wanted to talk or needed one another's help, they could easily get together. If they wanted to be alone or had a quarrel, they could quickly get out of sight and sound of each other. But reduce this space to 150 square feet—the area of an average bedroom—and there would be a very different situation. Now the two people would be fully conscious of each other during every waking moment. They would see and hear every move, cough, sneeze, grunt, and groan. If a disagreement arose, there would be no chance to get away to gain perspective or to cool off. Solving the problem would be painful. Mace and Mace conclude: "That's what intimacy means—great when two people are in harmony with one another, terrible when they're in conflict."

But while some conflict may be inevitable, it does not mean it is always desirable or helpful. Conflict can destroy love and even an otherwise good marriage. But it can also relieve tensions, clear the air, and bring two people closer together than ever before. It depends upon the total circumstances, the focus of the conflict, the way it is handled, and the ultimate outcome (Altman and Taylor, 1973; McGary, 1975).

There is a need, therefore, to understand as much as possible about conflict. What are its causes? What are its functions in marriage? What are some of the ways couples use in dealing with conflict? Which ways help and which ways hurt the marriage? What factors influence a couple's conflict-solving abilities? How can conflict become a more constructive means for bringing a couple closer together?

Some Sources of Conflict

Conflict may have its origin in 1. **intrapsychic sources** 2. **intrasomatic sources** 3. **interpsychic sources** 4. **situational or environmental sources** (Crosby, 1973; Nye, Carlson, and Garrett, 1970; Raush, 1974)

Intrapsychic Sources

Intrapsychic or inner sources of conflict refer to those that originate within the individual when inner drives, instincts, and values pull against each other. The conflict is, basically, not with one's mate but with one's self, so that inner tensions arise because of the inner battle. As a result of these inner tensions, the individual has disagreements or gets into quarrels in situations that stimulate that tension.

Mr. M was brought up by parents who rejected him and made him feel unwanted and unloved as a child. As a result, he became the kind of man who was afraid to show love for his wife or to let her get close to him. He needed her, and wanted her attention and companionship, but whenever she tried to develop a close, loving, intimate realtionship, he became anxious and fearful and would end up rejecting her or pushing her away. She was very hurt, and became frustrated and angry, which, in turn, made him mad. They always ended up in a fight when they started getting close to one another.

Whenever any person has irrational fears, anxieties, or neurotic needs, these can be the basic sources of husband-wife friction. For example, a wife who has a deep-seated fear of losing her husband becomes terrifically jealous of other women, even if her husband only has superficial contacts with them. She gets in an argument with her husband whenever she sees him talking with any member of the opposite sex. Or a husband who is very unsure of his own manhood seeks numerous extramarital affairs with other females to try to assure himself that he is manly. Because of his need to prove himself, he also has a need to tell his wife about his affairs. The result is much conflict and considerable estrangement whenever such an episode occurs.

In each of these examples, the basic cause of the conflict lies deep within the psyche of the individuals involved. Usually, the anxieties have their origins in childhood experiences and early family relationships. For this reason, troubles that arise in marriage because of these previous experiences are difficult to deal with. Permanent solutions can be found only when the internal tensions within the individual are relieved.

Intrasomatic Sources

Intrasomatic sources refer to inner tensions having a physical origin. Physical fatigue is one such source. Fatigue brings irritability, emotional upset, impatience, distorted reasoning, and a low frustration tolerance. It causes people to say and do things that they wouldn't do ordinarily. *Hunger* and a *low level of blood sugar* are also potential sources of tension. This means that before breakfast or dinner are poor times to try to settle arguments. Every parent learns that children are fussy when they are hungry, but many don't realize that adults are the same way. *Physical illness* also causes upsets. A painful headache may be just as much a source of conflict as a serious disagreement. *Emotional illness* also is a major source of friction and arguments (Bullock, 1972). Mentally ill people often behave in disruptive, bizarre ways, with the result that their marriages are often disrupted (Rushing, 1979). Even emotionally healthy men and women have fluctuations of mood that influence their behavior (Bardwick, 1971).

Interpsychic Sources

Interpsychic sources of conflict are those that occur in relationships between people. Sometimes the conflict between a husband and wife has its origins in their individual contacts with others outside the family. Thus, a man who has a very deep resentment toward his mother—and upsetting contacts with her—may take out his hostilities on his wife who reminds him of her. A wife who is resentful of the way she is treated by her boss vents her anger on her family after she gets home.

Frustration of either biological or emotional needs is perhaps the most important cause of conflict. Most mature people learn that they can't always find immediate self-gratification of all of their needs, since other people also have needs that may conflict with theirs. But when frustration is repeated often enough, or is continual, tension mounts until it boils over in more overt conflict. The effects of frustration are cumulative, and the most patient, understanding person may reach a point where anger or resentment can no longer be contained. Miller and Siegel write:

Whether . . . [frustration] arises from the blocking of a biological or primary drive, from interference with the expression of personal and social goal striving, or from the paralysis associated with conflict, frustration serves to arouse the individual, to increase his level of tension. He is stressed. The extent to which tension is raised depends on the intensity of the drives involved and on the strength of the obstacle. . . .

The immediate effect of increased tension is to generate greater effort to overcome the obstacle, whatever it may be. . . . Each [person] posesses a certain tolerance for frustration; some of us more, some of us less. When this personal threshold is exceeded, tension becomes catastrophic or overshelming in its intensity. Aggression, withdrawal, or total disorganization results (Miller and Siegel, 1972, pp. 81, 82).

Situational, Societal, or Environmental Sources

Situational, societal, or environmental sources of conflict include such things as living conditions in the household, societal pressures on family members, or unexpected events that disturb family functioning. Research has shown that having more than two children produces increased strain on marital roles so that stress and conflict increase (Nye, Carlson, and Garrett, 1970).

A large number of other situations influence conflict. Williams tells of one husband who returns home from work at the close of an intensely difficult day.

During the course of the day he lost two big business deals, learned he was being transferred to another department and that the transmission was going out of his comparatively new car. Upon re-

turning home he turns into his driveway and suddenly confronts two bicycles, a tricycle, a go-cart, and a basketball, all of which are directly in his way. He can't park on the street and there isn't a child in sight. He angrily steps from the car, throws the objects quickly and roughly into the yard, gets back into his car, guns the motor, and screams to a stop inches from the garage door.

Following the commotion, his two youngest children innocently appear on the front doorsteps. Instead of his usual friendly tousle of the hair and greeting, father flies into a rage. He yells at the top of his voice about toys and other objects in the driveway, spanks both of them with anger, and tells them to go to their room. By this time he is in the house and begins screaming at his wife about he rough day he has had and her inability to discipline the children.

Little does he know about the day she has had. The washer broke down, the sewer clogged. John fell off the jungle gym and had to be rushed to the emergency room of the hospital to have his arm checked, and she learned that her mother had terminal cancer. One other problem to complicate her day is that she is to host the monthly bridge club that night (Williams, 1974, p. 223).

In this example, a whole series of events occurred that caused frustration, strain, and conflict to increase geometrically.

Sometimes a marital relationship remains in a state of relative equilibrium until some traumatic event occurs to disrupt the relationship. One study of couples who had lived together in basically neurotic relationships for a number of years showed that specific events could disrupt this neurotic equilibrium by interfering with the neurotic need gratification patterns of the couples. One wife seemed to get along fairly well with her husband as long as he paid a lot of attention to her by berating her for sexual affairs prior to marriage. When he stopped because he wanted "to treat her better than before," she had an affair with a man next door to give him new evidence of her sexual promiscuity. The wife's real motive was that she had missed the only attention her husband had shown through his prior criticism of her sexual affairs. In the case of another couple, conflict started when active steps were taken to remove the husband's psychotic mother from their home. In another case, the husband and wife started having conflict when the wife expressed a desire to stop having children after the birth of the tenth child (the same number her mother had). The husband did not wish to stop having children until after the twelfth child (McGee and Kostrubala, 1964).

In each of these instances, a specific event triggered the conflict, although the seeds of tensions were already present in the relationship. Unexpected events such as unemployment, change of jobs, war, disaster, illness, an unplanned pregnancy, death or a forced separation or move may be enough to trigger a crisis. Couples who are emotionally insecure or unstable usually have far more difficulty coping than do other couples (McCubbin et al., 1980). One study showed that couples who have high levels of tension between them, have even more conflict when they are together because of vacations, retirement, illness, or reduced hours of employment (Rosenblatt et al., 1979).

The Focuses of Conflict

Importance of Interaction Patterns

All couples have marital problems, but *unhappily married couples have some problems that are different, and they have more problems than happily married couples.* Unhappily married couples are more likely to complain of neglect, lack of love, affection, sexual satisfaction, understanding, appreciation, and companionship than are the happily married. Furthermore, their self-image is attacked, for their mate magnifies their faults, makes them feel worthless, belittles their efforts, and makes false accusations. These complaints become the focus of the conflict that ensues. Lack of communication and withdrawal also perpetuate the difficulties (Mueller, 1970; Tallman, 1970).

The intimate interaction patterns and relationships between mates far outweigh other major focuses of conflict. One reason is because couples begin to feel hurt, resentful, and frustrated when they are not meeting one another's sociopsychological needs. Relationships with kin, the community, or others outside the family do not affect the couple as much as their relationships with one another. When 108 couples who had come for marriage counseling were asked what they considered to be their *basic* problem in marriage, 38 percent of the husbands and 46 percent of the wives indicated they had one or more unsatisfied sociopsychological needs, such as the need for understanding, communication, love, affection, or companionship, as their basic problem (MacMillan, 1969).

Cause and Effect

Other research indicates that it is difficult to sort out cause and effect of conflict because of the interrelationship of multiple problems. A husband's lack of sexual interest in his wife has been found to be correlated with quarreling, lack of communication, his social habits, infidelity, his wife's loneliness and his mental health problems and can be an indicator of his general alienation (Krupensky, Marshall and Yule, 1970). A wife's lack of sexual interest in her husband correlates with her dislike of her husband and personal indifference, lack of communication, and her mental health difficulties. Her frigidity appears as an indicator of a nervous, upset, and alienated wife who has difficulty coping in a situation of stress. Similarly, this same study showed that economic difficulties were related to all other factors (McMillan, 1969).

Couples who aren't able to solve their conflicts can benefit from counseling.

Every marriage counselor knows that *the problems couples complain about in the beginning of counseling may be only symptoms, or the focal point of conflict. The real causes of difficulties often run much deeper.* Sometimes, couples themselves may not realize the basic reasons for their difficulties. These causes often are found only in the underlying psyche of the individuals or in the pattern of their interpersonal relationship with one another.

Some Positive and Negative Values of Conflict

Conflict as Reality Testing

Conflict can have some positive results. *One possible benefit is to establish the relationship on a more realistic basis.* Many persons who get married are young and immature. Until the couple really have to grapple with problems, they can't really know if their ability to resolve differences is sufficient to develop a working and satisfactory relationship.

As one author has suggested, *the process of bonding must occur* (Sprey, 1971). That is, couples discover what they have in common to tie them together; they establish interdependence and work out their respective places and roles in the relationship. Bonding is the process of "binding members together, keeping them together, and causing them to interact" (Turner, 1970). The more involved two people become, the greater the possibility of a close bond, but the more vulnerable they become to strains encountered through intimacy. There is always the possibility, of course, that no permanent bonds will develop, but this can never be known until the relationship is tested. As one couple put it:

We've been through an awful lot together since we got married. In the beginning, we didn't really know whether we were compatible or not. Now, we know we are and that our marriage can survive anything.

Conflict as Acceptance

Some writers hypothesize that conflict is a natural and continuing state in marriage, so to speak of *conflict resolution* is unrealistic, and instead of striving for *consensus-equilibrium*, couples need to talk about *conflict management.*

Conflict management accepts the ongoing necessity of dealing with the family differences. According to this point of view, family stability is achieved by the settlement of problems in terms which make possible the continuation of differences and even fundamental disagreements. Disagreements are respected and accepted and hostility and marital dissatisfaction are thus minimized. Marital stability is achieved through this form of conflict management.

The above viewpoint is still largely theoretical and untested. It emphasizes that when disagreement is accepted as normal, it is possible for two people who disagree to still live together in a spirit of cooperation. But this view seems to place conflict largely on an intellectual plane. Conflict is conceptualized as lack of consensus.

Conflict as Catharsis

Many mental hygienists and psychologists would disagree with the above theory because they believe that conflict arises out of the frustration of desires and needs. They view conflict as primarily negative feelings and emotions arising out of *blocking* or *deprivation*. From this point of

view, it would be impossible for a relationship to remain harmonious so long as much negative feeling in the form of resentment and hostility remains. The value of conflict, therefore, is *ventilation: a means whereby negative feelings and emotions can be drained off and replaced by more positive emotions.* This concept has been used in psychotherapy for years. It involves encouraging persons who are disturbed to talk out or to act out their feelings to get them out in the open where they can look at them, understand them, and channel them in less destructive directions. This *therapeutic approach*, which emphasizes the importance of *leveling* or of *letting it out*, is based on the idea of **catharsis.** *Catharsis theories*, also called *ventilation theories*, assume that all persons have built into their nature a greater or lesser tendency toward aggression that cannot be bottled up (Berkowitz, 1973). If they attempt to repress this tendency, it will only result in a more destructive explosion at some later time. Hence it is better to "let it out" through a series of minor explosions than to let negative feelings accumulate until they become a potential bomb. The authors of *The Intimate Enemy* state in their book that "couples who fight together are couples who stay together—provided they know how to fight properly" (Bach and Wyden, 1968). The authors go on to note that 80 percent of the couples who come to them don't fight at all; they avoid conflict. The result is emotional divorce.

Verbal and Physical Aggression

In commenting on *The Intimate Enemy* Straus writes:

In fairness, it must be pointed out that Bach and Wyden's book makes a sharp distinction between procedures for rational conflict and what they call "kitchen sink" or "Virginia Woolf" type fighting, characterized by insults and personal attacks designed to hurt the husband or wife. However, although Bach and Wyden reject Virginia Woolf type fights, they do advocate dropping inhibitions and "outmoded notions of etiquette"—what I will call "civility" later in this paper. Their emphasis on "leveling," "honesty," "having it out," "overcoming inhibitions," and venting aggressive feelings contradicts their rejection of Virginia Woolf type fights (Straus, 1974, p. 13).

Actually, in his audiotape course on "therapeutic aggression" Bach makes much stronger statements about expressing aggression. During one group session on "aggressive dating" Bach urged the women participants, "Don't be afraid to be a real shrew, a real bitch! Get rid of your pent-up hostilities! Tell them where you're really at! Let it be total vicious, exaggerated hyperbole" (Bach, 1973; Bach and Wyden, 1975)! Other authors urge symbolic acts of physical aggression such as punching pillows, biting a plastic baby bottle, smashing a board. One author insists that the only way to have a vital marriage is to maintain a fairly high level of tension but without physical attacks (Charney, 1972). The emphasis is on *leveling*, "gut-level communication" and "letting it all hang out."

In evaluating this approach to dealing with conflict, it must be admitted that such methods have proved to be helpful psychotherapy for those with hostile feelings and emotional problems. But *venting one's hostilities on the psychiatrist's couch, in the counseling center, or in other psychotherapeutic environments, and in the presence of a trained therapist, is far different from doing the same in one's own home where the hostilities are directed toward one's spouse or children.* In therapy, the hostilities toward family members are given verbal expression or, in the case of children, physical expression (such as symbolically shooting baby sister with a gun) in the presence of the therapist, but not actually in the physical presence of that person. To tell a therapist, "I hate my wife" is far different than telling the wife, "I hate you." In the first instance, the hostilities have been drained off, harmlessly,

so that when the husband gets back home he feels less hateful, but in the second instance, even though the husband feels better, the wife feels worse and will usually retaliate in some fashion, which may result in the increase of hostile feelings between the two people. Recent reveiws of the effects of catharsis in the family situation suggest that *"almost none of the research with any pretensions to scientific rigor supports the idea of catharsis and some show the reverse, i.e., opportunities to observe or give vent to anger, hostility, and violence tend to produce greater subsequent levels of aggression and violence"* (Berkowitz, 1973; Hokanson, 1970; Steinmetz and Straus, 1973; Steinmetz and Straus, 1974). The reason is that the family is an intimate, closely confined group, with members intensely involved with one another. If excessive hostility is directed to other family members, they feel angry, hurt, or misunderstood. If this reactive emotion is not dealt with, additional disagreements arise and tension mounts, sometimes to intolerable levels. Furthermore, family members can't get away from the source of friction without splitting up the family, if only temporarily.

In a revealing piece of research, Straus found a strong, positive association between the level of verbal and physical aggression between husbands and wives. He discovered that *as the level of verbal aggression increases, the level of physical aggression accelerates even more rapidly.* Figure 12-1 shows the relationship. The facts as presented provide no evidence of the beneficial effects of "leveling," "letting it out," releasing inhibitions, or expressing one's anger toward one's mate. On the contrary, the results suggest that "gut-level communication," rather than helping to *avert* physical aggression, *is associated* with physical violence (Straus, 1974). Furthermore, *the more often aggression is expressed, the more often it is likely to occur in the future.* The persons are learning to assume aggressive roles.

What about more intellectual, rational approaches to problem solving? Straus's evi-

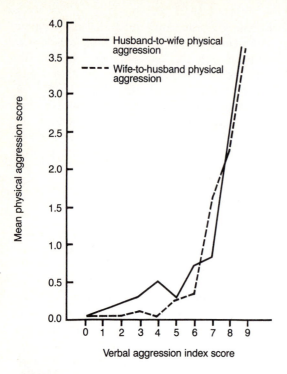

FIGURE 12-1. *Relationship between verbal and physical aggression (Source: From M. A. Straus, "Leveling, Civility, and Violence in the Family,"* Journal of Marriage and the Family *36 [February 1974]: 17. Copyrighted 1974 by the National Council on Family Relations. Reprinted by permission.)*

dence suggests that *families that take the calm, rational, intellectual, emotion-suppressing approach show much lower levels of physical violence.* This is even more true for working-class families than of those of middle-class socioeconomic status. This means that intellectual approaches that observe "civility" and "etiquette" in interpersonal relationships are more helpful in the long run in promoting marital harmony and stability (Harris, 1972).

Other Negative Effects of Aggression

There are other negative effects of excessive verbal and physical aggression. One of these

is *guilt.* Part of this arises, no doubt, because of the way people are reared: "Don't hit; it's not nice." "You ought to be ashamed of yourself for getting angry." As a consequence, many couples suffer from what has been called the "guilt-over-conflict syndrome" (Sennett, 1973). To these persons, conflict indicates a type of moral failure. But guilt can have a positive result if it stimulates couples to search for positive ways of solving problems.

Another consequence of excessive conflict is *fear and anxiety.* Children who have been brought up in families with excessive conflict and fighting grow quite tense, upset, and extremely anxious in the presence of overt hostility. They likely carry these feelings into their married life, so that when they become involved in arguments or quarrels, they become very upset and nervous. One wife commented:

I really can't take any more fights with my husband. When I was growing up my parents fought constantly, so that now I just get numb all over. I feel upset for days afterward. It takes me a long time to get over it.

Another possible negative effect of conflict, particularly unresolved strife, is *alienation.* Saying mean things that hurt, belittle, or degrade another stimulates anger, resentment, and hurt. Not all arguments help a couple. Some quarrels result in a widened gulf between them, a loss of love and positive feelings toward one another, and estrangement and separation. One husband remarked: "After Judy and I quarrel, we end up not talking to one another for a week."

It seems obvious that the effect of conflict on marriage can be either positive or negative. This means that conflict can be functional or dysfunctional, productive or unproductive, constructive or destructive, depending upon how it is handled.

Methods of Dealing with Conflict

It is not the existence of conflict, per se, that is important to the family, but the methods of managing and resolving the conflict (Straus, 1979). Some couples have a lot of conflict, but keep it under control, and resolve their tensions and problems. Other couples are never able to minimize tension or solve anything. So small problems grow into very big ones.

Avoidance

Some couples try to deal with conflict through *avoidance*. That is, they try to prevent conflict by avoiding persons, situations, and issues that stimulate it. The following comments illustrate avoidance techniques.

"My husband really growls when he gets up in the morning, so it's better if we don't say anything."

"My wife and I try to avoid controversial issues."

"My wife is very sensitive about her kinky hair, so I never say anything."

"If I complain about my husband's drinking, it just leads to an argument, so it's better not to say anything."

It is evident from each of these comments that couples were trying to avoid conflict.

Sometimes a person becomes too upset to think straight. In such instances, positive solutions can be found only after the intense negative feelings have subsided. Physical activity through work or recreation, distraction by going to a movie or by visiting a neighbor, or discussion with a counselor may be necessary to drain off negative feelings to the point where the individual can talk more rationally with his or her mate.

What about conflict in front of the children? Disagreements that concern the children may have to involve them, such as what time to come in nights, doing family chores,

school work, appropriate dress, and others. But in these instances, children have to learn that there is a fair way and foul way to fight, that conflict can be constructive or destructive, that there are certain rules to the game that should be observed even when mad. But *to involve children in unrestrained, unmanageable, uncontrolled fights can be as highly destructive to them as to their parents.* When children are small, to expose them to frequent and/or violent arguments will stimulate a great deal of fear and insecurity, and it is certainly detrimental to their mental health.

Children growing up in an atmosphere of tension, become anxious, tense, and insecure people. One study showed that the more children were exposed to family fights, the lower their self-concept. This was as true in intact as in broken families (Raschke and Raschke, 1979).

In some instances, however, couples try to avoid discussing controversial issues even though important to the marriage. In these cases, keeping quiet might be counterproductive. By so doing, the couple avoid conflict, but they also never solve the problem.

Mr. and Mrs. P had in-law problems ever since they were married. Mr. P's mother expected them to spend all of their holidays with her. Mrs. P thought this unfair and objected, but this made her husband so angry that she never dared bring up the subject again. The problem continued for years of marriage, unresolved, even though it continued to bother Mrs. P. As a result, she became very hostile toward her husband's mother, was often upset and ill after each visit.

The problem in this instance was not overt conflict, which was avoided, but unresolved differences with resultant resentment and hostility within Mrs. P. By refusing to solve the basic problem, increased alienation was the result.

Couples who never face important issues in their efforts to avoid controversy gradually with-

draw from one another. There is a gradual disengagement and alienation where couples stop communicating and caring about one another. As a result, there is increased lonliness, less reciprocity in settling issues, a loss of intimacy, and a decline in other forms of interaction, such as sexual intercourse (Altman and Taylor, 1973).

One of the most common complaints of wives is that their husbands won't talk to them about problems. Such husbands seek to prevent conflict by avoiding issues. As a result, the wives become even more frustrated, and put pressure on in their efforts to confront their husbands with the problems, or they widthdraw more and more and the problems are not solved (Welby et al., 1978).

Constructive Conflicts

There are two basic types of quarrels in marriage: the one *constructive* and the other *destructive* (Duvall and Hill, 1972). *Constructive arguments are those that attack the problems, stick to the issues without being sidetracked, and lead to a more complete understanding, to consensus, compromise, or other acceptable solutions to the problem* (Gottman, Markman and Notarius, 1977). They minimize negative emotions, build respect and confidence, and bring a couple closer together. They take place in a friendly and trusting atmosphere in a spirit of goodwill where honest disagreements may be discussed and understood and where the argument progresses according to fair rules. The

Conflict can be constructive or destructive, depending upon how it is managed.

following is an example of a constructive quarrel.

He (testy):   The bank called and said we're overdrawn again.

She (skeptical):   Gee, darling. I can't believe it. I thought we had plenty of money in our account. Have they made an error?

He: I don't know, but let me see the bank book.

She (after retrieving the checkbook from her purse):   We had plenty of money in last week.

He (examining the book):   Didn't you write a check for the insurance? I don't see it.

She (shocked):   Oh my gosh. I forgot to deduct the $340. No wonder we're overdrawn. I wrote another check to the oil company on top of that.

He (sighing):   What am I going to do with you?

She (putting her arms around him and kissing him):   Love me.

He (squeezing her hard):   I do. I sure do.

While the problem in the above example was not a serious one, it could have resulted in a heated argument if not handled correctly. As it was, the discussion stuck to the point without bringing in extraneous issues or belittling anyone, it was conducted in a friendly, rational manner so the wife could admit her mistake without any threat, the husband accepted her explanation—and her—and the result was a feeling and expression of closeness and love.

If couples are able to think rationally about a problem, there are six steps involved in constructive problem solving. These steps are:

1. Identification and definition of the problem
2. Collection of information about the problem
3. Production of alternative solutions
4. Deciding among alternatives
5. Taking action
6. Evaluating the action

Destructive

Destructive arguments are those that attack the ego of the other person rather than the problem. They seek to shame, belittle, or punish the other person through name calling or by attacking sensitive spots in a spirit of hatred, revenge, or contempt. They are characterized by real lack of communication and by suspicion, and they often rely on interpersonal strategies that involve threat or coercion. The argument brings up many side issues that are beside the point, and it seeks to relieve individual tensions of the attacker at the expense of the other person. Destructive arguments increase resentment and hostility toward the other person, undermine confidence, trust, friendship, and affectionate feelings, result in loss of companionship, and engender greater alienation. The following phrases are examples of destructive ways of quarreling.

"How would you know? You never went to college. You're just a dumb slob."

"Don't you ever do anything right? You're so clumsy."

"Other husbands earn enough to pay their bills, but not you. You're too lazy."

"You're the worst housekeeper I have ever seen"

"Do you always have to be so obnoxious?"

"I refuse to give you your dinner until you fix my vacuum cleaner."

"If you don't sleep with me, then to hell with your allowance."

"I just don't believe you."

In these examples of destructive quarreling, efforts were made to shame and hurt the other person through deprecating remarks, coercion, and threats to try to force compliance. There was a great deal of distrust, contempt, and hostility revealed in the husband-wife relationships.

One of the characteristics of destructive

arguments is the way they get off the track and bring in irrelevant issues. The following is a recapitulation of a family fight in the Smith domicile on a Sunday morning following a Saturday night dance. *The scene:* around the kitchen table. *The characters:* Sue and Bill Smith.

Sue (sarcastically):   You were quite a ladies' man at the party last night.

Bill (casually):   What do you mean?

Sue (raising her voice):   Get off it. You know damned good and well what I mean. You danced with Joan half the night. I thought you'd squeeze her so hard you'd smash her boobs.

Bill (cuttingly):   Well, at least she's got some to squeeze; that's more than some people I know.

Sue (starting to yell):   Look who's talking, lover boy. You couldn't even make it last night, could you? What's the matter, losing your zip?

Bill (angrily):   Not really, you're getting so goddamn fat, you're disgusting to look at. Why in the hell don't you go see your doctor and lose some weight?

Sue (very sarcastically):   Speaking of doctors, your mother says it's time for your annual checkup. Can't you even go to your doctor without mama reminding you? When are you going to grow up and do something yourself for a change? I never heard of a grown man who calls his mama every day the way you do.

Bill (stomping out of the room):   You s.o.b., everytime we get into a discussion, why do you have to bring in my mother? I'm going to play golf.

Sue (yelling after him):   Maybe you can score at the country club. You sure can't in bed.

Certainly, this quarrel did not solve any problems. Sue was jealous and hurt by her husband dancing with Joan, but he did nothing to relieve her anxiety or hurt. Instead, he attacked her ego by trying to belittle her. She struck back, did the same thing, bringing up completely different problems. Such a quarrel

only increased their misunderstanding, tensions, hostilities, and alienation in relation to one another.

Threat and Submission

Authoritarian means of problem solving use *coercion, threats, and manipulation* to gain ascendancy and to force compliance and submission. *The intent is not to develop understanding but to win, which means to force the other person to submit or to acknowledge compliance or defeat.* Coercive methods may involve verbal commands and threats such as a threat to leave, to get a divorce, a threat of exposure, a threat to withdraw love or support, a threat to punish, or a threat to use physical force or violence. Such methods assume that one person has the right to force his or her will on the other in a superior-inferior relationship. These methods don't work, of course, if one person remains defiant and refuses to submit. If control is obtained by forcing the other person to submit, the immediate quarrel is ended but at the expense of the wishes and desires of the submissive person. In the long run coercion only increases the conflict. One study showed that those who are able to influence control and to manipulate their spouses may resolve the conflict, but at the expense of the other person's feelings (Chafetz, 1980). One wife who had decided to divorce her husband remarked: "He always has to have everything his way without regard for my wishes or feelings. He's made me feel like a complete nobody. I have to leave if I'm going to be a real person." Another study showed that discordant husbands (those with a great amount of discord with their wives) used more coercion and less cognition in problem solving than did harmonious husbands (Raush et al., 1974). In the case of two domineering, authoritarian people, problems can never be solved and continual conflict is the result. The more each person is willing to "give in," the more easily conflict is resolved (Osmond and Martin, 1978).

In one well-known research experiment, opposing couples were given the following options: (1) both were given the option to threaten, (2) one was given the option to threaten unilaterally, and (3) neither was given the option. The results showed that under the no-threat condition both parties gained in their efforts to negotiate. In both other instances, both parties were defeated, and the worst losses in negotiation occurred when opportunity was given to threaten unilaterally (Deutsch and Krauss, 1960).

Role Induction, Modification, and Reversal

Role induction involves trying to get a spouse to change while remaining the same oneself. It is really the attempt to exert authority over the other person through various methods such as *coercion, coaxing, evaluation, masking,* and *postponing. Coaxing* involves asking, pleading, nagging, tempting, promising. *Evaluation* involves praising, blaming, showing, approving, or disapproving as a means of winning the point or changing the other person's ideas or behavior. *Masking* is the deliberate withholding of pertinent information to distort a situation. It may involve pretending, censoring, evading, or lying about the situation in order to win one's own way. *Postponing* is sometimes tried in the hope that there will be a change of attitude later.

Role modification involves a change in role expectations and a willingness to modify one's own role. Thus, resolution is obtained through multilateral exploration of alternatives leading to *compromise,* and to *accommodation* or *concession. Accommodation* or *concession* is an agreement to disagree. It is necessary if couples can't really agree. The only way they can live without conflict is to resign themselves to the fact that further attempts to influence the partner are not worth the conflict they provoke (Blood, 1974).

Role reversal involves assuming the role of the other person in trying to understand his or her point of view. A wife or husband who asks questions to clarify and understand the other's point of view is using this technique. The goal is to achieve empathetic insight, although the consequences of the process may lead subsequently to role induction or to role modification.

Negotiation and Contracting

Negotiation and *contracting* with married couples is becoming increasingly popular as a therapeutic means for stimulating behavioral modification in couples who are having difficulty (Olsen, 1972a; Patterson and Hops, 1972, Patterson, Hops, and Weiss, 1975; Rappoport and Harrell, 1972; Stuart, 1973; Weiss, Hops, and Patterson, 1973). The basic principles, however, are not new at all and are used frequently by couples themselves in trying to work at solutions to their own conflicts. *Negotiation* is the process by which a couple reach accord by means of trade, barter, or any form of exchange. Its goal is to establish reciprocal trade, a "this for that," so that each spouse does something or gives something in exchange for something else (Weiss, Birchler, and Vincent, 1974). Thus, in its simplest form:

If the husband washes dishes in evening, then he gets backrub from wife. No dishes, no backrub (Weiss, Birchler, and Vincent, 1974, p. 325).

In an effort to avoid the problem of "who goes first," a parallel exchange can take place that insures that *both* partners initiate changes in behavior. Thus,

If H washes dishes, W gives H backrub. If W makes gourmet meals, H picks up children from activity.

No dishes, no backrub.
No meal, no taxi service (Weiss, Birchler, ard Vincent, 1974, p. 325).

Sometimes outside rewards or penalties are promised. That is, the rewards or penalties are not contingent on the *other* person's behavior. For example:

H agrees to wash dishes three nights,
and W agrees to cook three gourmet meals.
If dishes, then backrub.
If meals, then three movies (Weiss, Birchler, and Vincent, 1974, p. 326).

Note that in this example, if H or W keeps the promise, he or she is rewarded by a positive consequence other than a change in the other person's behavior.

Marriage counselors who use negotiating and contracting in clinical practice feel that the exclusive use of penalties rather than awards is not wise. It is sometimes effective if a combination of rewards and punishments is used. For example:

H agrees to three evenings per week at home with W.
W agrees to daily instruction sessions with children.
If H keeps his promise, he gets to go fishing once a week.
If H does not keep promise, he must do dishes.
If W keeps promise, she gets one unit of outside-activity free time.
If W doesn't keep promise, she has to clean oven thoroughly (Weiss, Birchler, and Vincent, 1974, p. 327).

If negotiation has been successful, the couple can enter into a formal or informal contract (Knox, 1975). The following contract was drawn up by John and Mary.

John's Agreement. I agree to spend every Sunday afternoon with Mary for six consecutive weeks. *Reward:* If I do, I can buy new fishing rod. *Punishment:* If I don't, I have to give up the following Wednes-

day night poker game with my friends. I also agree to Mary's contract provisions.

Mary's Agreement. I agree to vacuum the carpet at least once a week for six consecutive weeks. *Reward:* If I do, I get to buy a new dress. *Punishment:* If I don't, I will have to give up my bridge club the following Wednesday night. I also agree to John's contract provisions.

The above contract is a good one because both rewards and penalties are not contingent upon the other person's behavior.

Negotiation and contracting may seem rather childish at first, but they have been used by counselors as one way of modifying behavior by encouraging and rewarding desirable behavior and punishing undesirable behavior. It has been found, however, that such methods are not advisable for couples expressing deep resentment toward one another in relation to the proposed action. Trying to force the action may only increase the resentment. In cases where there is a fairly good relationship between couples who need incentives to do what they ought to do, these incentives can serve as stimuli to desirable behavior, provided the couple do not have any serious objections (Weiss, Birchler, and Vincent, 1974). Also, it is questionable whether these strategies are useful in those instances where both partners are severely limited in resources, that is, limited in their abilities to comply.

Family Violence

Definitions

Violence in the family generally refers to any rough and illegitimate use of physical force or aggression of one family member in relation to another. Violence may or may not result in physical injury of another person. Thus, a husband who throws and breaks dishes, destroys furniture, or "punches out walls" when he is angry may not injure his wife or children, but he is certainly being violent.

Family violence is not easily defined since there are disagreements among individuals over what is a legitimate and illegitimate use of force. Unlike Sweden where a parent can be imprisoned for a month for striking a child, many Americans believe that spanking children is normal and necessary, and "good." In fact, a high percentage of families use corporal punishment to discipline their children (Steinmetz, 1978). This privilege has been extended to bus drivers and school teachers in many states. Yet, many spankings verge on beatings. Some men and women believe that it is acceptable for a man to hit his wife under some circumstances (Gelles, 1980). Most wife beaters deny they have "beaten" their wives: "I just pushed her around a little bit, but I didn't really hurt her," is a common assertion, yet many of these wives are badly injured. Even the authorities hesitate to interfere in family quarrels, because of the difficulty of distinguishing between legitimate force and illegitimate violence in the family. As violence increases, however, public toleration seems to be declining and people are demanding preventative and remedial action.

Spouse and child abuse are more limited and specific terms, usually referring to acts of violence which have a high probability of injuring the victim. An operational definition of child abuse, however, may include not only physical assault which results in injury, but also malnourishment, neglect, and sexual abuse. Wife abuse may not only include "battering," but sexual abuse and marital rape as well (Gelles, 1980).

A Cycle of Violence

Studies of family violence show that individuals who have experienced violent and abusive childhoods are more likely to grow up and become child and spouse abusers than individuals who have experienced little or no violence in their childhood years (Conger, Burgess, and Barrett, 1979). Violence begets violence, which means it is passed on from generation to generation. Most "batterers" have experienced abuse from their own parents. The greater the frequency of violence, the greater the chance that the victims will grow up to be violent parents or partners (Gelles, 1980). Galdston expressed the belief that "children who have received significant exposure to violent behavior before the age of two are likely to have identified with this pattern of response in a fashion that proves to be essentially irreversible, although a great deal can be done subsequently to contain it" (Galdston, 1975, p. 375). He notes that intervention before eighteen months greatly enhances the possibility of modifying the child's violent behavior.

Factors Related to Violence

Early studies of child abuse attempted to show that abusive parents suffered from *mental or emotional illness*, that the reason people abused their spouses or children was that they evidenced various psychiatric defects: psychoses, neuroses, or psychopathic problems of one kind of another. Empirical evidence shows, however, that child abusers are not more or less emotionally ill than any randomly selected groups of parents, and that spouse abusers may be exemplary citizens in all other aspects of their lives (Steinmetz, 1978).

Family violence may be related to *stress* of one kind of another. *Unplanned pregnancies* or *premarital pregnancies* cause emotional stress and strain limited financial resources of both the mother and father. Wives report being the victims of beatings before and after the birth of their child. Attacks during pregnancy are especially brutal with wives being kicked or punched in the stomach.

Financial problems, unemployment, or job dissatisfaction which are perceived by husbands as incompetency in fulfilling their roles as providers are linked to child abuse and wife beating. *Social isolation* also raises the risk that severe violence will be directed at children or between spouses. Families who lack close personal friendships and who are poorly integrated into the community lack support networks during times of stress. They also feel less influenced by the social expectations of friends and family. Certainly, a battered wife is less likely to become friendly with neighbors because of embarrassment or fear of discovery, but this only compounds her problem (Steinmetz, 1978).

Domestic violence may be found among families of all *socioeconomic status* groups. Studies of corporal punishment show no social class differences in the frequency with which it is employed. Physical abuse between spouses is also a part of middle- and upper-class marriages. The horror stories include that of a physician who jumped on his wife's spine causing paralysis, because she had left a door open allowing air-conditioned air to escape; a divorce lawyer who designed a special weapon to beat his wife that would not make marks; and a space-age scientist who hit his wife in the stomach so severely that she vomited for several days (Langley and Levy, 1977). Abuse seems more frequent among lower-class families, however, partly because of an underrepresentation of reported violence among middle-class families, and because lower-class families must more often rely on social controls such as the police and social service agencies. Middle- and upper-class families have more resources to mediate stress, such as greater financial resources, greater access to contraception and abortions, greater access to medical and psychological personnel, more opportunities to utilize baby sitters, nursery schools, and camps to provide relief from child-rearing responsibilities (Dibble and Straus, 1980).

A lot of family violence is related to *alcohol and drug abuse*. Some people never get abusive until under the influence. The question arises: do they drink or take drugs and lose control because of the alcohol or drugs, or do they drink or take drugs to give them an excuse for their abusive behavior? Either one or both may occur.

Parent-child interaction is reciprocal, so that one affects the other. Children with certain characteristics have a greater potential for being recipients of parental abuse than do others. Those who are hardest to take care of and who impose the greatest stress on the parents are most likely to be abused, as are those who are perceived to be "different." These include *premature babies and those of low birth weight* who are more likely to be restless, fretful, and require intensive care. It includes *children with physical handicaps or those who are mentally retarded whose development is delayed*. Couples with larger-than-average families, especially if the *children are unwanted* are more likely to abuse them. If there is a lack of emotional attachment behavior between parent and child, the children are more likely to be abused (Gelles, 1980).

Prevention and Intervention

There are three major treatment approaches to help child-abusing families: the *psychiatric approach* uses individual and group therapy. The *sociological approach* emphasizes family planning programs, abortion services, family life education and counseling, and support services such as day-care centers, nursery schools, and homemaker services. The *social situation approach* tries to modify distressing social situations and to change interaction patterns among family members.

Violence against spouses uses crisis shelters and transition houses, "hot line" services, police intervention teams, legal intervention, trained social service workers, family therapy services and teams, and many organizations.

Authorities, such as medical personnel and the general public are being encouraged to report cases of child or spouse abuse so that intervention is begun as soon as possible. The natural inclination of people "not to interfere" allows much abuse to go unreported and untreated.

Certainly, a society that places few restrictions upon violence in the mass media, or that does not consider many types of family violence to be immoral, has little hope of reducing the level until it is able to change its permissive attitudes toward it.

Conclusions

The basic question this chapter raises is what to do with tension and conflict. As has been seen, some conflicts develop from tensions within the individual, either intrapsychic or intrasomatic. Other tensions originate from without—from interpsychic realtionships or environmental sources. Tensions that arise should not be ignored. Attempts at complete repression may result in their building up to the point where they will create real harm for the individual and for the marital relationship. They have to be dissipated. But how?

All couples strive to deal with their tensions in ways that are acceptable to them. Some learn to live with conflict as though it were a natural and normal state, but this is a disturbing, upsetting way to live and is completely unacceptable for many people. Couples are faced with a dilemma, therefore. They can't completely suppress their ten-

sions; neither can they be completely free to express them as they want. If they choose the latter course, they discover that quarreling becomes habitual and that verbal aggression may grow into physical aggression.

One possibility is for couples to discuss important and controversial matters only at those times and in those places where the conditions make for an easier solution to their problems. Another is to overlook unimportant subjects that are not worth arguing about. Still another possibility is to discover helpful ways of relieving tensions other than through overt conflict. Such ways include physical activity and exercise, work, distracting hobbies and activities, sleep, sex, or seeking counseling to dissipate tensions.

Overall, the most effective way to deal with differences is through rational discussion, which becomes possible when the couple relate to one another as equals, seek consensus, understanding, and acceptance (or at least compromise and accommodation if consensus is not possible). Authoritarian methods involving threat, coercion, or role induction impede progress toward an equitable solution. Empathy is developed through careful questioning, listening, role reversal, or through a willingness to modify roles. In the long run, solving conflicts is a crucial test of the couple's love and consideration for one another. If they are able to communicate and to try to understand, they will more likely be able to deal with most of the difficulties with which they are confronted. A more complete discussion of communication and decision making is given in the next chapter.

CHAPTER
13

Money and Its Management

CHAPTER OUTLINE

Money and Marriage

Why People Go into Debt

Money Management

Housing

Consumer Economics

Conclusions: Getting the Most for Your Money

Dialogue

The way people use money is a reflection of their basic values. The proportions spent on different things reflect not only needs, but priorities, and so reveal what couples value most. People differ in the way they manage money. Some people are careless in their handling of money because they don't really care about it; it's unimportant to them, so they spend very little time and effort in managing it carefully. Others place a great value on money and do everything they can to earn and save as much as possible. They seem determined to get ten cents of value for every nickel they spend. Other persons place little value on money itself but only on what it can buy. One couple remarked: "Money is important to us, but only because it can make life better for us" (Thal and Holcombe, 1973).

The way in which couples manage money can be a revelation of basic character: their degree of maturity, responsibility, and unselfishness and their ability to cooperate. People who buy things they don't need often do so as a means of gaining status or prestige or to allay fears and anxieties (Neisser, 1972). Others never spend money at all, preferring instead to save and hoard it "for their old age." The classic example of extreme insecurity is the elderly person who dies alone in a shack, living like a pauper, with $50,000 tucked away under the mattress.

Other people reveal basic emotional needs in their efforts to use money to gain power or love. They use money to manipulate and force others to do their bidding or to buy affection. For some parents, material indulgence of children becomes a substitute for neglect.

Whatever their value system or basic character, all persons can benefit themselves or others by improving their money management skills. Even if they don't care much about money, necessity forces them to learn to manage on what they have, and willingness to do so shows consideration for other family members. The better managers they become, the better they are able to follow the order of priorities they have established and the more they are able to get and give what they want in life.

Money and Marriage

Financial Needs

Couples quickly discover that two can't live as cheaply as one. Table 13-1 shows the percentage of families at different income levels. In this case, the figures represent gross income (before deductions). The median income level was $19,684 in 1979, meaning that 50 percent of all families were above and below that figure (U.S. Department of Commerce, Statistical Abstract, 1980). By 1985, based upon a 8 percent annual gain, median family income should rise to around $30,232 per year (U.S. Department of Commerce, March 1980).

In spite of the rise in family income, however, real income or purchasing power now remains constant, or is decreasing. Because of inflation, the cost of living has increased, by percentage, as much or more that wages have increased during the last five years, so families are no better off now than they were five years ago (Portrait, 1979).

to more expensive private colleges (Rockfeller, 1972).

Poverty and Family Life

Obviously, millions of persons will never reach median income levels. In 1979, 10 percent of persons living in families were below the poverty level, which was $7,412 for a nonfarm family of four (U.S. Department of Commerce Statistical Abstract, 1980). For these families, daily life is a struggle just to pay the bills for rent, groceries, a pair of shoes, a winter coat, or a TV set (Komarovsky, 1964).

Much has been said in recent years about mothers of dependent children who live on ADC checks. When the program began, the death of of the father was the most common cause for being in need of aid. Today, however, more than 60 percent of ADC cases are due to estrangement of parents—divorce, separation, desertion, or unmarried motherhood. While each state determines the level of payments, most provide support far below basic subsistence levels because of unfavorable public attitudes toward these mothers. As a result of these "budgets of despair," the mothers get behind in their rent payments, the families eat little meat, vegetables, and fruit (even with food stamps), and they have little or no money for transportation or recreation. In a study in Detroit, when families were asked what they did when they ran out of money, two-thirds said they borrowed either from relatives and friends or storekeepers, and one-third said they just "stayed run out." Some "let the bills go"; others resorted to schemes like cashing in bottles, stealing, or prostitution (Lebeaux, 1972).

The effects of poverty on the family are many: increased tensions and unhappiness in the marital relationship, high rates of **illegitimacy,** desertion, separation, or divorce, with children brought up without a stable father figure in the home and cultural and social de-

The way people spend money is a reflection of their basic values and a test of their ability to work out differences.

Various estimates have been given on how much it costs to bear and rear a child to maturity. Regardless of price levels, the costs may be figured roughly as requiring three years of the father's income. Thus, four children will take twelve years of the father's earnings (Landis, 1975). In terms of 1985 costs, the cost of giving birth will be around $4,000 with subsequent costs (not including costs for a college education) calculated at around $100,000. Thus, a family with two children can expect to spend more than $200,000 to rear them to maturity. If college costs are included, total costs will be closer to $250,000 to raise both to maturity and to send them to a state university for four years. The total would be closer to $300,000 if the children go

TABLE 13-1. *Income levels and percent distribution of families in each level*

Income Levels	Percent of Families at Each Income Level 1979	Income Levels Per Year	
		1979	1985 (Projected)
All income levels	100		
Less than $5,000	6.9		
$5,000 to $9,999	13.5		
10,000 to 14,999	15.6		
15,000 to 19,999	22.3		
20,000 to 24,999	14.4		
25,000 to 34,999	19.2		
35,000 and over	15.5		
Persons below poverty living in families	10.1		
Median Income		$19,684	$30,232

Source: Adapted from U.S. Bureau of the Census, Department of Commerce. *Statistical Abstract of the United States, 1980* (Washington, D. C.: U.S. Government Printing Office, 1980).

prevation with accompanying lower aspiration and educational levels. Limited resources leave few opportunities for contacts with the outside world, with resultant isolation and provincialism. Increased problems and the lack of resources result in much higher rates of mental and physical illnesses (Komarovsky, 1964). Limited alternatives and feelings of helplessness and powerlessness leave little hope for the future or little prospects for getting ahead (Rytina, Form, and Pease, 1970). The poor are at the mercy of life's unpredictable happenings: sickness, injury, loss of work, or trouble with the law. The lack of status of the low-income husband creates more tension and antagonism between the husband and wife. This, in turn, stimulates him to try to overcompensate by becoming more authoritarian at home or more sexually promiscuous outside of marriage. Sometimes he tries to escape the pressures through desertion, alcohol, or drugs. One wife remarked: "The reason he drinks so much here is that he can't stand to think he's been a flop." Low income mothers tend to view motherhood as their chief satisfaction in life in compensation for the lack of companionship in marriage and the poverty of their lives (Dill, 1980; Schulz, 1969).

Money and Marital Satisfaction

Family income has a close relationship to marital satisfaction (Feldman and Feldman, 1975; Geismar, 1973; Hicks and Platt, 1970; Renne, 1970). In fact, the male's level of income has an influence on his willingness to marry in the first place (Cutright, 1970). In one study of low socioeconomic status families in urban Washington, D.C., Lewis (1965a; 1965b) found a relationship between marital harmony and payday. Couples seemed happier just before payday than at any other time. After the pay arrived, tension increased as couples argued how the money was to be allocated. Then after the money was gone, tension decreased until the next payday.

Marital satisfaction is not necessarily

greatest, however, when income is the highest (Jorgensen, 1979). For most couples, the self-satisfaction and status of the husband and the satisfaction and feelings of security of the wife are dependent only upon their feelings that income is adequate (Feldman and Feldman, 1975; Renne, 1970). If the husband feels he cannot do his part in supporting his family, he experiences frustration and failure, since one of the measures of a successful husband in American culture is his adequacy as a breadwinner (Lopata, 1971). In almost half of all families, of course, the wife is also a breadwinner, thereby taking part of the pressure off the husband. If the wife is not earning as much as she feels she needs, and if she and her husband feel their earnings aren't adequate, their marriage satisfaction is lessened because of financial pressures and tension over money (Renne, 1970).

The management of money even more than the level of income is a major source of discord in the marital relationship. One study of couples who requested counseling from various family service agencies showed that more than half reported severe problems with money. The most frequently reported reasons for difficulty were immature or unrealistic attitudes toward earning, saving, or spending money and the emotional use of money to control or punish a spouse or to compensate for inadequacies, guilt, or the inability to give love (Greene, 1970; Lobsenz and Blackburn, 1969).

Money is used frequently as a tool for personal attacks. Kieren, Henton, and Marotz write:

One partner may use his or her spending habits as a tool to attack the other for dissatisfactions in their relationship. ... A wife may continually go on spending sprees in order to punish her husband for his sexual indifference to her.... In another example, a husband may keep tight control over money because he sees this as a way to legitimize his power in the family. ... Emotionally immature spouses who see money as a means of compensating for their personal limitations will in all proba-

Without agreement on how decisions will be made, money management can be an important source of marital discord.

bility encounter difficulty in money management (Kieren, Henton, and Marotz, 1975, p. 227).

The authors go on to say that money can be a valuable resource to the marital system, but it can also be a source of irritation to that system.

Masculine-Feminine Differences

One of the reasons couples have disagreements over money is because of traditional masculine-feminine differences in socialized priorities (Herrigan and Herrigan, 1973). A traditional wife who was brought up to feel that she is primarily responsible for the home and children and for family care is going to be more interested in decorating the house, buying clothing for the children, paying the milk bill, or investing in a new sewing machine. The traditional husband may be interested in impressing others at work with his new car or clothes or in getting a boat or snowmobile. His wife can't understand why he wants to get ski equipment for the children when she would rather spend the money on music lessons. In these examples conflict arises because the husband and wife have different priorities according to the way they were socialized. *If the husband and wife were socialized to have similar values, however, their conflicts over the way their money is spent will be minimal.*

If both the husband and wife are employed, the couple may disagree over the use of their two paychecks. Some couples put one check into a savings account. Others use one of the checks for important things they couldn't afford otherwise: a down payment on a house, new furniture, or a vacation. In some cases, both checks are needed to pay basic living expenses.

Some people who earn the money feel a special right to it. "It's my money, I earned it." In such cases, if the other person feels that the money should be spent and used by all, conflict is bound to result. Some of these problems can be minimized if both are wage earners as well as family managers. The working wife gains an appreciation of what it takes to earn money; the husband helps with homemaking, learns how much food costs, and finds out how hard it is to make the money last when one is trying to manage a home and family. Flexible roles help each to understand the other's problems.

Why People Go into Debt

No matter how much money they make, some couples are always in debt. They estimate that if they had a little more each month they would be able to balance their budget, but when "the little more" is obtained, the couple still can't make do. They never seem able to meet all their obligations. The more that income increases, the greater the debtedness incurred (Bagarozzi, and Bagarozzi, 1980).

The families that are most in debt are not the poor but those in middle-income brackets. The poor less often have mortgages, charge accounts, or large installment debts, although they might if they were able to establish credit. Level of income is not the reason why couples do or do not go into debt. The reasons relate more to the lifestyle of the couple and their ability to manage their money wisely.

There are essentially four reasons why couples go into debt: because of 1) credit spending, 2) crisis spending, 3) careless or impulsive spending, and 4) compulsive spending.

Credit Spending

Many couples go into debt because of excessive and unwise use of credit. Credit can be a helpful thing; few couples can afford to pay cash for a home, automobile, or other large puchase. But habitual and unthinking use of credit often leads to excessive indebtedness that couples can ill afford. Before they realize it, they are in debt so deeply, with so many regular charges, time payments, and revolving charges, that they may be able to extricate themselves only by backruptcy.

Crisis Spending

Many people go in debt because of crisis spending (Moen, 1979). That is, unexpected but important events occur that throw the family budget off completely, and couples are forced to go into debt to meet the emergency. Unemployment is the most common crisis (Anderson, 1980; Moen, 1979; Thomas, McCabe, and

Berry, 1980). Uninsured illness is another one. Consider the following example:

Steve and Barbara were getting along very well on the husband's wages of $15,000 a year. They paid cash for everything and always managed to live on their income. Then their child became seriously ill, an illness that required hospitalization for almost six weeks. By the time the child was well, the couple were more than $5,000 in debt. The husband struggled valiantly to pay off the obligation by getting a second job, but still had half of the debt left after one year. Meanwhile, the increased pressures and tensions were so disruptive of the marital relationship that the couple were divorced six months later.

Careless or Impulsive Spending

Many couples go into debt because they buy things carelessly or impulsively. As a possible consequence, they pay more than is necessary, get merchandise of inferior quality that doesn't last as long as it should, or they get things they don't need. Mrs. M relates:

My husband and I decided to buy wall-to-wall carpeting for the downstairs of our house. We looked at a lot of different carpets: wool, nylon, polyesters, rayon, even cotton shag. They were all so expensive. Finally, we decided on a rayon carpet that was several dollars a yard cheaper than the acrylics. This was the biggest mistake we ever made. It was completely worn out in two years, and now we have to get another one. I've learned my lesson; I'm not going to buy something just because it is cheap.

Some couples see things they want and buy them without ever stopping to think whether or not they can afford them. Mrs. G says:

My husband loves to go to auctions. Whenever he reads about someone selling the contents of their home in an auction, he always shows up. He loves

"At what point would you say we stopped pursuing the finer things in life and settled for just keeping our heads above water?"

Reprinted from *Dynamic Years;* Drawing by Joseph Farris

the crowds and the excitement, but he gets carried away. Once he brought home a cement mermaid. I don't know what he expected to do with it since we don't have a fish pond or swimming pool. But he like it. It's still down in the family room where he put it.

Couples who buy without careful planning or thought waste money needlessly.

Compulsive Spending

Other people are compulsive buyers. They can't say no. Their buying habits may be an expression of their emotional insecurity; they can't say no to a salesperson for fear of hurting that person's feelings or because they are afraid the person won't like them. Or they buy to try to gain status and recognition. Some people try to make up for basic insecurities by collecting things.

My husband Frank is a compulsive collector. He spent a fortune on his coin collection, would travel hundreds of miles to see a rare coin, and would always end up outbidding everyone else to buy it. He showed his collection to everyone who came into the house and derived great satisfaction out of owning a coin that other collectors had never seen.

Of course, if Frank could afford it, there was nothing wrong with buying an outstanding coin collection, but the basic problem was that he couldn't afford it. He had two mortgages on his house and was deeply in debt. His wife called him "incurable."

A lot of purchases are made to satisfy deep-seated needs for recognition or status rather than out of physical necessity. One husband relates:

We don't have much else, but we're the only family on the block to own two color TV sets, a fact of which we're very proud.

Money Management

Management Systems

Four different systems exist for managing money in the family (Kelley, 1974). One system is for *the wife to exercise complete control.* She makes the major decisions, pays the bills, and gives her husband an allowance or spending money. This system is often preferred by the husband who is financially irresponsible or who doesn't want to be bothered with the responsibility of money management. One husband commented:

I admit I don't know how to handle money. That's why I let my wife have the paycheck and pay all the bills. If I try to do it, things get all balled up. I forget to pay the bills. They come, I put them down some place and then can't find them. Or I see something I want and spend too much on it before all the bills are paid. Our checking account used to be overdrawn all the time. Now, my wife manages the money and the account is always in balance. My wife is a whiz at it. She takes care of everything. If I need money, I ask her.

The second system is for *the husband to exercise control.* He pays all the bills, decides on how much is spent on what, and doles out allowances to his wife for "housekeeping money" and to his children for incidentals. One modern variation of this system is for the husband to allot a portion of family income to his wife, who is responsible for certain expenditures and bills.

The third method is *joint control*, where the husband and wife have joint bank accounts, both have free access to the accounts, and where most decisions are shared, including the responsibliity for making purchases and paying bills. The wife may or may not work, but if she does her wages become joint property, as are the husband's earnings. There is no separate "his money" or "her money." All is "their money."

The fourth method is *autonomous control*, where the husband and wife keep their wages, financial planning, accounts, and expenditures completely separate. He has his money; she has hers. They each may be responsible for a certain proportion of all expenses, or they each may have particular areas over which they are responsible. The only joint decision is over who pays what and how much. One counselor relates:

Barbara J was a career woman. When she married, she insisted on keeping all finances and accounts completely separate, each person contributing 50 percent of all expenses. However, she earned slightly less than her husband, so she would run out of money before he did. When this happened, she might borrow from her husband, but she always insisted on paying him back. She paid for everything she needed for herself: her own car, clothes, and personal expenses. She did not want to be financially dependent on her husband in any way.

The chief advantage of this system is that the wife can feel independent. One disadvantage is that the couple become dependent on two incomes.

Most couples adopt variations of these four systems. The husband may control some things, the wife others. They may plan jointly in some cases, in other instances they prefer to manage their money separately. In her study of urban and suburban housewives in or around the Chicago area, Lopata (1971) found that 37 percent said their husbands handled all finances, 21 percent said it was their own responsibility with no help from their husbands, 37 percent said they and their husbands handled their money jointly, the remainder used a variety of systems. Of those couples controlling their money jointly, about half did it together and about half divided the labor.

The basic theoretical question remains: Who should handle the money? Actually who does it is not as important as the skill with which it is managed and the extent of the re-

sponsibility and agreement of both spouses in relation to its use. *The person who has the most interest and skill in money management might be the one to exercise the most control, as long as the other person is in agreement.* Marital adjustment is smoother when couples adopt a "we" attitude in relation to making financial decisions (Landis and Landis, 1973; Mace, 1972c).

Establishing Goals

Few families have so much money that they can do without a system of priorities in their spending plans. *The first step in effective management is to make a list of basic goals so the couple can decide how to plan their finances to accomplish their objectives* (Pershing, 1979). Goals can be arranged under four headings: long-term goals (over five years), medium-term (two-five years), short-term (one year), and immediate (one month). Objectives can be placed under appropriate headings together with estimated costs. If desired, goals can be listed in order of decreasing priorities.

Budgeting

Budgeting is the allocation of expenses on a regular basis (McGary, 1975). This requires an examination of personal values plus knowledge of actual costs. How much is required for food, clothes, shelter, and so forth? How much do the couple have and want to spend on entertainment, eating out, or personal improvement? Expenses may be allocated under major headings that the couple establish for themselves.

The actual amounts allocated under these different categories will depend partially upon level of income. The lower the income, the greater the percentages that have to be allocated for housing and food and the lower are the usual percentage allocations for taxes, savings, insurance, and donations. Higher income families spend smaller percentages of their total incomes on food and housing, but greater percentages on clothing, transportation, taxes, and savings.

There are some expenses of course that are *fixed*. These include all financial commitments already made or occurring on a regular basis. Other expenses are *flexible* and vary according to a couple's needs and priorities (Landis, P., 1975). Since the flexible expenses can be controlled to a certain extent, the couple have to decide on the allocations among the various categories. Again, the actual decisions will reflect the couple's values and priorities.

Record Keeping

The first allocations will be tentative. *The next step is to keep careful financial records of where the money goes.* To do this, some sort of bookkeeping system has to be set up. The most convenient system utilizes the same categories as in the budget, so that entries may be made under the categories. Daily entries can be made along with notations by each indicating what money was spent for. The husband and wife may want to keep individual expense books to jot down daily entries so they won't forget them, until such time as they can transfer the information to the account pages. It is not necessary to account for every penny, such as the way personal allowances and expense money are spent, but overall amounts can be recorded.

Analyzing Expenditures

After records have been kept over a period of time, the couple can begin to analyze expenditures by categories (Kieren, Henton, and Marotz, 1975). Is the money going where they want it to go? How do actual expenditures compare with budget estimates? The couple will discover

that the regular, fixed expenses cause little trouble. It's the variable expenses which create difficulties. Sometimes a whole lot of little things add up to a far greater amount than the couple imagine. Unexpected expenses arise which have not been anticipated. These are the things which upset the budget. By analyzing expenditures, however, the couple can determine what things they want to cut out so they can have more money available for something else. Budget estimates need to be revised periodically to reflect actual needs, priorities, and changing income.

Housing

Buy or Rent?

Housing expenses constitute one of the single largest items in the family budget at all income levels (U.S. Department of Commerce, May 1980). Considerable thought needs to be given, therefore, to the type of housing chosen. Should a couple buy or rent? If this decision were made strictly on the basis of monthly cost, one would have to say that usually renting is the cheaper choice. There are considerations other than just monthly costs, however. Table 13-2 shows some of the advantages and disadvantages of home ownership versus renting.

Housing and the Family Life Cycle

Generally speaking most couples start out their married life in *rented quarters,* usually because they don't have sufficient funds for a down payment for a house or for the monthly expenses. Then as their family grows and as they can afford to do so, they buy a house to take care of the expanding needs of their family. A little more than three out of four families in the United States today own their own home (Rawlings, 1978). Some families buy a

TABLE 13-2. *Home ownership or renting: advantages, disadvantages*

HOME OWNERSHIP

Advantages	*Disadvantages*
1. Builds equity in house, so ownership is a form of savings.	1. May require expensive down payment that many couples can never accumulate.
2. Provides a tax shelter since taxes and interest are deductible.	2. Monthly payments ordinarily greater than renting even though part of this money is recovered at time house is sold.
3. Usually more space, outside yard.	3. Sometimes hard to sell. Lack of fluidity of investment sometimes forces homeowner who has to move to sell at a loss.
4. More privacy than apartment.	
5. Greater freedom to live as one wishes.	
6. Value appreciates, helping to offset negative effects of inflation.	4. Requires expense, time-consuming maintenance.
7. Pride in owning property.	5. Overall price is so high, it is beyond reach of majority of Americans.
8. Fixed price and payment schedule that does not increase over the years (unless loan is drawn up with escalation clause).	6. Interest rates are high and expensive over the years.
9. Usually found in better neighborhoods than apartment buildings.	7. Requires considerable knowledge of construction quality, housing values, and costs if couple are to avoid a poor buy.
	8. May have to buy in locations a long distance from place of work.

APARTMENT RENTAL

Advantages	*Disadvantages*
1. Allows for flexibility of movement. Can move on thirty-day notice if lease allows escape clauses with minimum penalty for leaving before lease is up.	1. More limited as to geographical area in which to live since apartments are restricted to certain zones.
2. Do not have to assume a long-term cost.	2. No accumulation of equity.
3. Lower initial cost, lower costs per month.	3. Lack of privacy, may be noise and confusion.
4. No expensive and time-consuming maintenance.	4. Usually smaller, less convenient living space.
5. Gives couples time to evaluate community, neighbors, and costs before they make any decisions.	5. Subject to restrictions on building use and to rules for governing property. May not allow children, pets.
6. Opportunity to invest and to make profit on money that would otherwise go to down payment of house.	6. May be subject to nonrenewed lease or to eviction.
7. Minimum investment in furniture and furnishings. Can rent fully furnished apartments. Laundry services often available.	7. Raise in rent uncertain from lease year to lease year. Hard to calculate future costs.
8. Usually located closer to business area, shopping centers, schools.	8. Less control over who neighbors are.
9. Close to other people so opportunity to meet others. Children have friends to play with.	9. Subject to performance of landlord in maintaining property.
10. Sometimes provides recreational facilities: playgrounds, tennis courts, swimming pool.	

number of different houses during their married life, striving to make a profit on each house they sell, and buying larger and more expensive houses as they can afford to do so. Frequent moving is hard on children and adults, however, so many couples avoid it if at all possible. As couples grow older, some move into smaller living quarters requiring less expense and maintenance. Figure 13-1 shows a comparison of the types of house for three different generations of families in 1970 in the Minneapolis-St. Paul area (Hill, 1970). As can be seen, the parent generation was most often housed in *single family dwellings*, and a great percentage of them owned their own homes. More of the grandparent than the parent generation occupied *multifamily dwellings*, and fewer percentage owned their own homes, primarily because they could no longer afford home ownership.

Newer Trends in Housing

Partly because of the rapidly increasing costs of housing, a greater percentage of families live in multifamily structures today than a decade ago. Figure 13-2 shows a comparison for the years 1960, 1970 and 1978. As can be seen, there has been a significant decrease in percentage of families living in single-family dwellings and a marked increase of those living in apartments of five or more units (U.S. Department of Commerce, Statistical Abstract, 1979).

Also, there are increasing percentages of families that live in *mobile homes*. The mobile home now comes in a great variety of sizes and luxuriousness and is meeting an increasing need for low-cost housing. As mobile homes have grown in size, it is not as easy to transport them as was originally the case, but

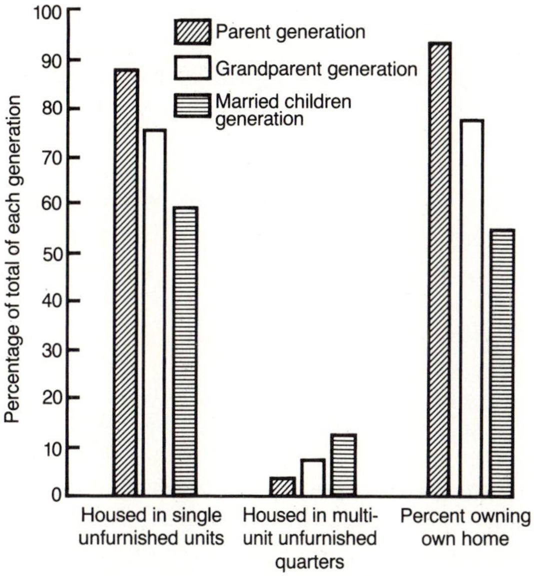

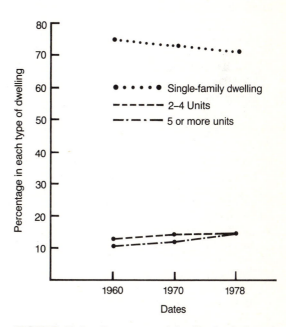

FIGURE 13-1. *Types of housing for three different generations of families, Minneapolis-St. Paul. (Source: Adapted from R. Hill et al., Family Development in Three Generations [Cambridge, Mass.: Schenkman, 1970], p. 52. Reprinted by permission.)*

FIGURE 13-2. *Percentages of families in single and multi-family dwellings. (Source: U.S. Bureau of the Census, Statistical Abstract of the United States, 1979 [Washington, D.C.: U.S. Government Printing Office, 1979], p. 787.)*

most still have the advantage of being movable—at least by truck—when such is necessary. It may be better for prospective buyers to purchase low-cost *modular homes* or *compact houses*. New compact houses have been developed by architects for families of medium income who can afford monthly payments.

Two of the latest housing developments are *condominiums* and *cooperative apartment houses*. The condominium is a single-family unit in a multiunit dwelling, where each of the residents enjoys exclusive ownership of this individual unit, plus retaining an individual interest—with all other comdominium owners—in the common facilities and areas of the building and grounds, used in common by all the residents. The owners usually elect representatives to a governing board that determines fees for outside maintenance and services. Sometimes the developer retains ownership of parking lots, garages, swimming pools, and other extras, for which he charges users increasingly expensive fees. Prospective buyers need to exercise caution to be certain they aren't going to be assessed high fees over which they have little control after they have purchased their units (Norcross, 1976).

The *cooperative apartment* is one in which residents have an interest in the equity, usually shares of stock in a corporation owning the building, and a lease entitling them to occupy a particular apartment within the building. If they move, they sell their interest in the corporation. Management is conducted cooperatively by elected trustees of the corporation according to state law (Norcross, 1976).

Consumer Economics

The Use of Credit

Credit buying is expensive. Interest rates on most revolving charge accounts, Visa, or Mastercard accounts are 1½ percent per month on the unpaid monthly balance, or 18 percent per year. *Pawnbrokers* typically charge 36 to 50 percent interest so are one of the most expensive sources of credit. *Small loan companies* are also expensive, often charging 30 to 36 percent true annual interest. *Credit unions* are usually a good source of money for members, with rates usually around 12 percent per year. Borrowing on one's own *savings account* is also possible, and less expensive, with banks usually charging only 2 percent more interest than they are paying on the account. Loans on *life insurance policies* are a good source of credit in an emergency, and the loans are usually for reasonable rates. Some states have recently passed laws allowing insurance companies to charge far more interest than they have been able to up to now. But the amount that can be borrowed is equal only to the cash value and not the value of the policy. One of the most common sources of credit is the *local bank*, which usually charges less interest than one would have to pay by obtaining credit from a store where merchandise is purchased. But even at banks, interest rates are high and variable, so one should shop around. Surveys of bank interest rates in various large cities across the United States have revealed wide discrepancies in rates in the same city or state (Spread, 1976).

Buying a Car

For most people, an automobile represents the second largest purchase they will ever make (a house is the most costly). Yet because of rapid depreciation, the value declines almost to nothing in a comparatively short time. For this reason, a car is the most wasteful and extravagant of all purchases. Investment in a home can usually be recovered with profit years later, but not so with a car. A car is expensive, and even if it is never used its value declines rapidly (Saxton, 1972). For this reason, a car is the poorest "investment" one can make. It may be necessary, but it is a costly necessity. At 1979 prices, it is estimated that it now costs 31 cents per mile to drive a standard size, medium priced sedan for 10,000 miles per year. These figures assume the car is traded every three years.

Based on actual costs it is far cheaper to buy a second-hand car than a new one, provided one gets a good used car at a fair price with reasonable mileage and not too old. But how old? On the average, annual maintenance costs become greater than the annual depreciation about half way through the fourth year. Therefore, a person who buys a two-year-old car to drive for three years avoids the big depreciation costs of the first two years and the rise in repair costs after the fifth year. Of course, these are only averages (Consumer, 1974). Consumers Union *Buying Guide* for the current year can be consulted for precise steps to take in buying a used car. The *Buying Guide* outlines eight on-the-lot tests and eight driving tests to make before buying a used car (Consumer, 1974). It is helpful also to have another reliable garage or auto diagnostic center go over the used car before buying to be certain there are no undiscovered defects.

Savings and Investments

Saving regularly is a good habit for any family to acquire. It takes six years at 12 percent interest compounded annually to double one's money. Investments in certificates of deposit, interest-bearing bonds, money-market funds, or other high yield savings pay much higher rates of interest than savings accounts. The interest earned on one's money has to be greater than the annual rate of inflation for a savings plan to be a good investment, otherwise one's capital in terms of purchasing power never grows and, in fact, may decrease.

Conclusions: Getting the Most for Your Money

A number of suggestions have been given in this chapter relating to sound money management, selecting and financing adequate housing, the use of credit, buying a car, and saving and investing. Little has been said directly, however, relating to buying food, clothes, furniture, and other needed household items. There are a number of things individual consumers can do to get the most for their money. The following are suggestive.

1. *Shop where you secure good quality at low price.* Some stores consistently charge more than others for the same quality goods. A car owner may spend more for gasoline at one station than another. One building contractor may charge double the price of another to do the same work. A corner grocery store may consistently charge from 5 to 40 percent more on various items than does a large food chain.

2. *Take advantage of seasonal sales and markdowns on needed items.* Generally speaking, stores offer preseason and postseason sales. Thus, one might be able to get a good buy on an airconditioner in either February or August.

3. *Do food shopping when individual items are offered as a leader item at drastically reduced prices.* Use food coupons also to save on needed items.

4. *Buy staples in sizes with the lowest per unit cost.* This may be a giant size or a smaller size. Stores no longer offer consistently the best buys only in the largest sizes.

5. *Watch for the best values in private brands or in lesser known brands rather than buying widely advertised national brands.* For example, some drugs can be ordered by generic names rather than by brand names.

6. *Seek basic quality rather than deluxe features.* Thus, the same appliance may fall into three price categories: economy, standard, and deluxe (Margolius, 1970).

7. *Check the recommendations of consumer research services before you buy to insure getting good quality at the best prices. Consumer Reports* and *Con-*

sumer Bulletin are the two best known magazines. *Changing Times* and *Kiplinger Magazine* also specialize in family finance and consumer education. The United States government publishes biweekly consumer news in its *U.S. Consumer* magazine, put out by Consumer News, Inc.

8. *Pay cash to avoid paying interest and carrying charges* or pay off accounts before interest is added on.

9. *Consider buying discontinued models, second-hand items, or seconds.*

10. *Be willing to spend time and effort in learning as much as possible about family economics* since it is this type of working knowledge that is necessary to the successful and practical functioning of the family.

The Bargain Hunter

Tim has a new law practice with a good, well-established firm. His wife Jeri has been teaching elementary school for two years. They have two children, a girl and a boy, ages three and four years of age. Their combined annual income last year was $37,000, but increasing debts have created acute tensions in their six-year marriage. The young couple consulted Dr. Scott, a marriage counselor, who interviewed Tim and then Jeri individually before getting them together for subsequent sessions.

At the initial meeting, Tim exclaimed: "Jeri is neurotic. I think that she's the main problem insofar as money is concerned."

"Be more specific! What do you mean?"

"I work hard to provide for our needs. I mean, I want the best for us; she knows that. But her spending makes me furious. She goes out and buys stuff she thinks we need—two color television sets, a humidifier, two air conditioners, and a portable bar. We need more and more money to sustain ourselves. We're in so much more debt now as compared to last year that I'll either have to take a second job or take out a second mortgage on our house. She does nothing but marvel over some bargain she's discovered. But it only means that we're forced during the summer to economize on vacations for our two kids. She says we can always use what she buys, but I simply can't take it any longer."

Jeri appeared in the counselor's office the next day, aggressive and indignant. "You charge a lot for conversation," she said.

"You disagree with my fee?"

"I don't consider myself a patient."

"Your husband is concerned about your indebtedness, particularly about your spending habits. How would you evaluate your situation?"

Jeri became defensive. "We have a respectable income, and my purchases seem possible," she replied. "Tim doesn't have time to search for good buys. He doesn't feel as secure as I in making decisions about what we need. I mean, you know, he always likes what I've bought, but I can't recall one single item that he's bought on sale. He can't save money like I can. That's not his talent. He's good at making money."

"Do you really need two color television sets?"

"Sure, many times the kids want to watch their program and Tim wants to watch a football game. I got both sets at a discount of 10 percent off, and I knew we'd always be able to use the second one."

QUESTIONS

1. The handling of money matters is often a good indicator of individual maturity and the quality of the marriage relationship. Evaluate Tim's and Jeri's level of maturity and the quality of their marriage as revealed by their spending habits.

2. That many people buy for the sake of a bargain is well known to every retailer. Does Jeri have a mistaken pride in her ability to obtain a bargain? Explain.

3. What excuse does Jeri give and what are the real reasons for her compulsive spending?

4. How does Tim contribute indirectly to Jeri's spending impulses?

5. If you were Dr. Scott, how would you summarize the reasons for the couple's financial difficulties?

6. What might the couple do to improve their financial management?

CHAPTER 14

Couple, In-Law, and Kinsfolk Relationships

CHAPTER OUTLINE

In-Law Adjustment and Marital Happiness

The Kind of In-Laws People Like

In-Laws People Dislike

The Roots of Conflict

When Parents and Married Children Live Together

The Extended Family Network

Conclusions

Dialogue

Large numbers of couples have in-law problems, but this is only part of the picture. Parents and in-laws may be a source of friction, especially to young couples, but they are also a source of support and help. Many young couples admire their elders and do not want to be cut off from them. In fact, most desire and maintain regular and frequent contacts. An analysis of aid patterns shows that there is currently considerable intergenerational exchange of services, moral support, and financial aid. Residential patterns reveal few couples living with relatives, but a high degree of interaction and dependence upon one another.

In-Law Adjustment and Marital Happiness

Importance

How important are in-laws in their effect upon marital success of failure? Studies reveal that in-law disagreements are more common in the early years of marriage (Landis and Landis, 1973). Some young couples are able to work out their relationships with in-laws so that a good understanding with in-laws is reached. Others are not able to make acceptable adjustments and their marriages fail for this and other reasons. Still others settle into a permanent state of friction with their in-laws. This friction may not break up the marriage, but it can cause much unhappiness (Leslie, 1973).

When the in-law relationships of happily married couples and of engaged couples were compared with those who were having marriage counseling or who were divorced, the happily married couples had better in-law relationships than those having counseling or who were divorced. The engaged couples *believed* that they had more agreement concerning in-laws than did the happily married couples (see Figure 14-1). Actually, it takes time both to discover and to solve in-law problems, so it is likely that some of the couples who were engaged would find out about in-law problems only after marriage (Landis and Landis).

The Kind of In-Laws People Like

About one-fourth of all couples have a very fine relationship with their in-laws. Couples give the following reasons for liking their in-laws (Duball, 1954):

They are the kind of people we admire: sincere, interesting, young in spirit, good-natured, pleasant and fun, generous, tolerant and understanding.

They do many things to help us: they take care of the baby; they help us when we're sick, when my husband is in the service; they give us so many things like furniture, clothes, and money.

They are more like parents to us than our own parents. (Orphans and persons from broken homes may be especially close to their in-laws.)

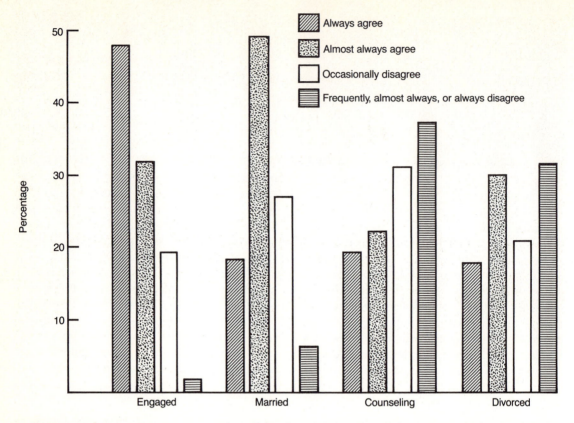

FIGURE 14-1. *Degree of agreement on in-law relationships (Source: Judson T. Landis and Mary T. Landis,* Building a Successful Marriage, *6th ed., © 1973. Adapted by permission of Prentice-Hall, Inc., Englewood Cliffs, N.J.)*

They are loved because they are the parents of my spouse who is a fine person.

We're in-laws ourselves so we can appreciate what it means. (Such couples object to stereotyped prejudices against in-laws, which they feel are very unfair.)

In-Laws People Dislike

In her book, *In-Laws: Pro and Con,* Duvall (1954) groups undesirable traits of in-laws into a number of categories. Of all complaints, the one noted more frequently than any other about the mother-in law is that she meddles, interferes, and intrudes on privacy. She is also

criticized frequently for being possessive, overprotective, and demanding and for nagging and criticizing. *More than half of all complaints about the mother-in-law are in these three categories: being meddlesome, possessive, and nagging.* This "mother-in-law syndrome" indicates that some are too close to their children, and too frequently intrude into their lives. These types of mothers have trouble in letting their children go and grow, and their interference is generally resented.

Sisters-in-law are also condemned for meddling, nagging, and criticizing. But they are also sometimes accused of being indifferent and aloof or thoughtless, inconsiderate, and selfish. Some are also childish and im-

Relationships with in-laws are especially important in the early years of marriage.

mature, jealous and envious, or gossipy. These types of sisters-in-law may have trouble sharing their younger brother with his wife and may also be competitive and immature persons who carry their sibling rivalry into adulthood.

Most people don't find *brothers-in-law* difficult to get along with, but when they do they often find them incompetent and lazy, childish and dependent, or thoughtless and selfish. There seems to be a tendency for brothers-in-law to use their relatives in inconsiderate ways. Like sisters-in-law, they are also sometimes criticized for being too indifferent and aloof.

The top-ranking difficulty with *fathers-in-law* is their being meddlesome, followed by nagging, critical, possessive, and overprotective. They are also often accused of being old-fashioned and intolerant, resistant to change, and self-righteous and smug. They sometimes evidence quite annoying overt behavior: boastfulness, talkativeness, and drinking. The

combined picture is of those who continue to be possessive and to interfere with their children's lives or who are quite convinced that their own ideas are right and others wrong. Some are accused of being too indifferent and aloof, however, and of ignoring their children.

The Roots of Conflict

There are many reasons for in-law conflicts. Sometimes the problem is with the parents-in-law. More frequently, it is with the couple themselves who in most cases are more critical of their in-laws than the in-laws are of them.

Conditioning

Many couples are conditioned to expect trouble. Children hear mother-in-law jokes at a young age even before they are old enough to un-

©Joseph A. Dawes. Reprinted from *Dynamic Years*

derstand them. By the teens, the children laugh with others when jokes are made about her. By the time of marriage, they already expect that the mother-in-law will be all the terrible things they have been taught. This early conditioning brings many brides and grooms to the altar who are already bristling with hostility and ready to defend themselves at all costs (Bowman, 1974). As a result, the expectation of trouble may become a self-fulfilling prophecy (Bell, 1975). The man or woman who has been prematurely prejudiced against mothers-in-law is genuinely surprised, and even apologetic when he or she finds her likeable (Neisser).

Immaturity of the Couple

Immaturity of the married couple may contribute to conflict with in-laws. In fact, there is a negative correlation between age at marriage and in-law adjustment. Those who marry young take longer to achieve a good understanding

with in-laws and have more frequent disagreements than do those who marry later. Couples who are twenty-four years of age or older seem to make the most satisfactory in-law adjustments (Landis and Landis, 1973). Figure 14-2 shows the relationship between the age of wives at marriage and in-law adjustments. As can be seen, three times more wives who married at ages seventeen to nineteen reported poor in-law adjustments than did those who married at age twenty-four or older.

It is not surprising that young couples are more vulnerable to in-law problems than older couples. If the young are still rebelling against their parents, they may transfer a part of this revolt against authority to their in-laws (Goodrich, Ryder, and Raush, 1968). Some insist upon absolute independence because they are unable to handle the interference of parents who do not respect their judgment or ability to work out problems themselves. A

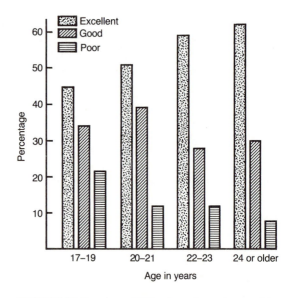

FIGURE 14-2. *Age of 544 wives at marriage and in-law adjustment (Source: Judson T. Landis and Mary T. Landis,* Building a Successful Marriage, *6th ed. © 1973. Adapted by permission of Prentice-Hall, Inc., Englewood Cliffs, N.J.)*

lack of confidence and experience invites more parental interference or help. A young husband may not be able to carry the full financial responsibility for his family. It shifts back to the parents. A young wife has a tendency to "run home to mother" when marital problems arise (Klemer, 1970).

It takes time for young couples to shift their primary loyalties from parents to one another. If the marriage is to succeed, however, the couple's first loyalty is to one another (Duvall, 1974). Time also is required to get used to the different patterns and habits of the other family members. Good relationships with new parents-in-law require maturity, time, and patience so young couples seldom adjust to their in-laws without difficulties.

The following examples illustrate the problems of immature couples in dealing with in-laws (Rice, 1966).

A young husband: My wife complains of being homesick. She calls her mother up nearly every day and wants to spend every weekend with her folks.

A wife: My husband ignores me when his mother is around. He seems so wrapped up in her that I feel left out.

Parental Resentment

Some parents create problems because they resent the mate their son or daughter married.

He's not of our faith.

Her family are rather common people. John married beneath him.

Why couldn't he have picked some fine Italian (or Irish, German, Swedish, Spanish) girl?

Some parents find it hard to accept a son- or daughter-in-law who comes from a different national, religious, economic, or social background. Others resent anyone a son or daughter marries because the mate "is not the right one" or "is not good enough." In these cases, the intolerance of the parents is the primary problem.

Conflict sometimes develops during courtship and continues after marriage. A study of 1,079 college students showed that the majority of parents tried to influence the courtships of their sons and daughters (Kephart, 1972). However well-meaning the parents, the children often resent their "interference" and come to expect trouble after marriage. Or when unpleasant relationships develop during courtship and the problems are never solved, the difficulty remains during the marriage.

A wife: When my husband was courting me, I tried in every way to get his parents to like me, but they would never accept me. They seemed to resent everything I did. I knew I was going to have in-law problems after marriage and we certainly did.

Couples able to work out their in-law problems before marriage find the going a lot easier than those in the preceding examples.

Parental Immaturity and Interference

Parents who are emotionally insecure and who have difficulty adjusting to the loss of their child create problems by being overprotective and meddling. This is particularly true of parents with a history of overprotection—who find it difficult to let go and to let their children grow up. They continue to try to protect their children, to run their lives, and to offer advice and assistance. Sometimes the dependent children encourage this overprotection and continue to look to parents for guidance rather than to their mates. In such cases, the mates rightly feel left out and find it unbearable to have to play "second fiddle" to their in-laws (Williamson, 1972).

When Parents and Married Children Live Together

The percentage of adult offspring making a home with an aged parent has steadily declined (Hess and Waring, 1978). At the height of the housing shortage after World War II, 9 percent of all couples were without their own house or apartment and had to double up with others (Glick, 1975). *Today, only 1 percent have to or do double up.* This fact, together with the lower birth rate, has reduced significantly the number of persons in the average household. In 1910 the average household consisted of five persons, but today it is slightly less than three (U.S. Department of Commerce, February 1980a).

Most young couples do not want to live with their parents after marriage, but the younger they are when they first get married, the greater the likelihood that they will do so for awhile, since they cannot afford living quarters of their own. This doubling up adds to the stress of family relationships (Blood, 1969).

When doubling up is necessary, a variety of living arrangements is used. If doubling up takes place under one roof—but in a house where there are two apartments—the situation is hardly more stressful than if the two families lived next door. When families live in the same house or apartment, they must share more spaces—kitchen, bathroom, living room, garage, and other areas—and there is a greater likelihood of conflict. Some families even end up sharing the same sleeping quarters. If at all possible, it is helpful if each couple has at least one room they can call their own, and to which they can retreat for privacy (Blood, 1972).

It may not be possible, however, to be completely separate (Komarovsky, 1964). Couples find it necessary to develop a clear understanding of financial obligations ahead of time. Who is to pay for what and how much? The same thing applies to the division of household and yard work. What are each husband and wife expected to do? If the young couple is living in their parents' house, a common complaint of parents is that their children are messy, that they aren't careful of walls, rugs, or furniture, or that they abuse privileges they have been granted. The persons owning the house feel that they are entitled to set the rules and regulations for living there (Rice, 1966).

The Extended Family Network

Attitudes toward Kinsfolk

In spite of the possibilities of in-law conflicts, most young couples want close contact with their families. In fact, members of the younger generation value interaction with their parents and grandparents even more than do older adults (Hill, 1977). After a couple have children, contact with grandparents is a very important part of the children's lives (Robertson, 1977). In a study of 120 young married couples, 120 parent families, and 120 grandparent families living in close proximity to one another, Hill et al. found the most positive attitudes toward contact with **kinsfolk** among the youngest generation (Bytheway, 1977; Hill, R., 1977). Some couples also admitted they would find it difficult to get along without the help provided by their parents or grandparents (Clavan, 1978).

Frequency of Visiting

When the actual frequency of visiting was tabulated, it was found that 70 percent of married children saw their parents weekly or more frequently. About one-third of the grandchildren and grandparents visited each other at least weekly. Figure 14-3 shows the percentage of

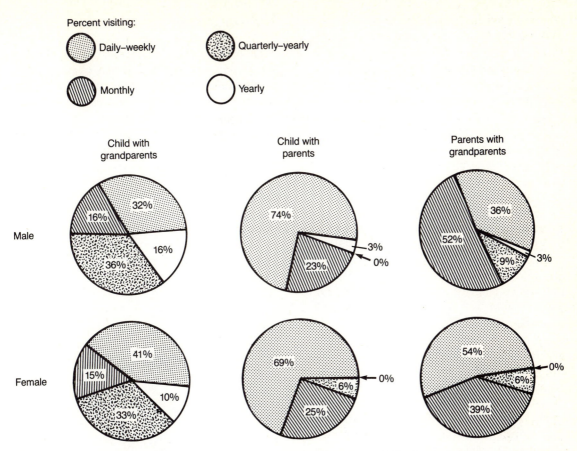

FIGURE 14-3. *Intergenerational visiting according to gender (by percentage). Percentage totals do not always add to 100 because of rounding. (Source: Adapted from J. Aldous, "Intergenerational Visiting Patterns: Variations in Boundary Maintenance as Explanation,"* Family Process 6 *[September 1967]: 235–251.)*

those visiting at specified intervals (Aldous, 1967; Hill, 1970). These and other data show that kinship intergenerational visiting patterns are a mainstay of couples' social activities when they live close enough to one another so it is possible to get together (Adams, 1970; Uzoka, 1979; Winch and Greer, 1968).

Social Variables

The degree to which married children and their relatives continue contacts is not uniform in all levels of society, however (Udry, 1974). *Lower- and working-class families* maintain closer contact than do middle-class and professional families. *Low income farm wives* visit more often with relatives than do high income farm wives (Straus, 1969). There is some doubt, however, as to whether or not farm families, in general, interact more with realtives than do urban families (Adams, 1968; Bultena, 1969). In one study in Wisconsin, *urban offspring* saw their parents more frequently than did rural offspring (Bultena, 1969).

Black families have a greater number of extended family networks than do white families, even when the two groups are matched for socioeconomic level, geographical mobility, and family size (Hays and Mindel, 1973; Kilpatrick, 1979; Martin, 1978). Black families have apparently developed a more pervasive and encompassing family structure which meets more needs with more intensity than that found among white families (Kilpatrick, 1979). The integration of extended kin forms a support network for survival in black urban communities. Researchers have commented especially on the importance of the grandmother in black families where the father is absent (Scanzoni, 1971; Staples, 1973; and Staples, 1971). The maternal grandmother frequently socializes and nurtures her grandchildren and runs the house while the mother works (Clavan, 1978).

Mexican-Americans also have large extended families (Keefe, Padilla, and Carlos, 1979; Sena-Rivera, 1979). This does not mean that trigenerational families are the norm. Rather it means that relatives live in close proximity to one another. Economic interdependence is strong among both the most affluent and the least affluent. Interdependency for personal services is universal and taken for granted among and within generations. There is a hierarchy among family members, which is somewhat authoritative and follows generational and eldest male lines. Such authority is voluntarily granted and accepted by other family members, however. Most important, there is an emotional interdependence which appears to be a mainstay of all families (Sena-Rivera, 1979).

Recent immigrants are more likely to maintain closely knit family groups than are those who do not emigrate. Generally speaking, *minority status* tends to result in residential compounding and in stronger kin ties for the sake of mutual aid and survival in a hostile environment. Vietnamese immigrants to the United States are examples (Adams, 1970).

Differences by Sex

It has been found that women maintain closer contact to kin of all sorts than do men (Adams, 1970; Booth, 1972). The women keep in touch with kin more frequently, they know more kin, consider them more important, and are more involved in kinship obligations and activities than are males (Berardo, 1967). They represent the family in kin contacts and relay what goes on with kin to their husbands. When parents face a crisis, they are more likely to call upon a daughter than upon a son. When parents move in with an offspring, it is ordinarily with a daughter (Adams, 1970). One study of the support systems of female Puerto Rican single parents who are coping success-

Frequent contact with an uncle or other men in the extended family can be beneficial to children without a father present.

fully showed that they relied primarily upon their mothers and sisters for help, and secondarily upon boyfriends or former husbands and neighbors (Nutall, 1979).

Aid Patterns

Another way to evaluate the extent of intergenerational contacts is by analyzing the extent and types of aid given between parents and their children. As parents get older many expect and need more help from their married children (Wood and Robertson, 1978). This is especially true of the oldsters who are widowed or divorced, who have low incomes, or who have poor health (Seelbach, 1978). As friends are lost, and as dependencies increase, the family may become socially and instrumentally more important for the older individual. This has led to the emergence of a "modified-extended" family structure which provides these traditional family functions within the modern, industrial context (Seelbach, 1978).

The United States also has large numbers of older people who were foreign born who grew up on farms and villages. They were brought up on a system of intrafamily caretaking and will call on a child for assistance rather than a friend or neighbor (Hess and Waring, 1978).

In times of crisis, married couples more often turn to immediate relatives than to professionals (Croog, Lipson, and Levine, 1972; Kelley, 1974). In one study of 293 males recuperating from heart attacks, parents, in-laws, and siblings were rated fairly equal in the level of help provided. Other, more distant relatives were less helpful. Neighbors and friends, along with immediate family members, were also very helpful in providing services and moral support. Parents and siblings were the ones who most often provided financial aid (Croog, Lipson, and Levine, 1972). Table 14-1 shows the percentages of patients reporting significant help offered by kin and nonkin sources. The table does not include all kin and nonkin, but only those the patients rated as offering significant help.

A study of family interdependence among three generations by Hill and his col-

TABLE 14-1. *Percentage of patients reporting significant help offered by kin and nonkin sources.*

	Type of Help		
	Services	Moral Support	Financial Aid
Kin			
Parents	30.5	67.1	25.6
Siblings	34.0	71.8	21.3
In-laws	34.1	33.8	13.4
Other relatives	20.3	77.0	8.1
Nonkin			
Friends	33.6	72.5	9.5
Neighbors	54.8	58.0	3.2

Source: Adapted from S. H. Croog, A. Lipson, and S. Levine, "Help Patterns in Severe Illness: The Roles of Kin Networks, Non-family Resources, and Institutions," *Journal of Marriage and the Family* 34 (February 1972): 36. Reprinted by permission.

leagues (1970) showed that *a modern extended family network relies on the middle or parent generation as the bridge across the generations.* This means that it is the middle generation who gives to both the younger and older generations more than they receive. They give grandparents emotional gratification and assistance with problems of illness and household management. They give their married children economic assistance and help with childcare. Thus, *both the older and younger generations turn to the middle generation for help, with the result that this group gives disproprotionately.* The married children generation received the most help, the parent (or middle) generation the least. But overall, Hill et al. found that *70 percent of all instances of help given to these three generations was given by other family members.* Other research indicates that single, divorced, or widowed family members are even more integrated into external networks than are the married (Gibson, 1972).

Conclusions

Even though married couples do not often live with their parents or grandparents, kinship remains the strongest tie to bind people together. The modern family is a "modified-extended" family (modified because of separate residences) with a network which transcends geographical boundaries and generational lines. Mutual aid patterns, emotional supports, and social exchanges fulfill the needs of couples, children, and oldsters, many of whom would otherwise feel isolated from the larger society of which they are a part.

DIALOGUE
The Mother-In-Law

Suki, fighting her bitterness with caustic-tongued humor, bristled as she related her story to the counselor. "My mother-in-law has been staying with us for about seven months, although I thought she was only visiting for a short while. My major objection is that she interferes in our lives and tries to run our affairs. Even though she lives with us in our house, she knows that we have to listen to her because she helps us out financially. I mean the grip that she has on Kenneth sometimes makes me nauseous."

"You mean that she pays a lot of your expenses?" the counselor asked. "Is she that wealthy?"

"She has a substantial amount of money," Suki replied. "Of course, when she passes away, it all goes to Kenneth."

"What is your husband's attitude about his mother?"

"The main problem is that I married a man who never outgrew his need for his mother. She still babies him. He has to buy her gifts. One day Kenneth burst into the house with chocolates and said to Ala, 'I thought you needed a treat!' But he didn't bring me one. A few weeks later he brought home two tickets to go to the Berlioz concert, and that kind of thing goes on all the time. Not only that, but—would you believe this—she even asked if she could wear my best scarf to the concert since she knew that I wasn't going. Of course, she and Kenneth never invited me. Kenneth can't see how much his mother stands between us and interferes in our relationship. It's very hard to respect a man who is so much under his mother's thumb.

"And she's not easy to live with, since she's so spoiled. She expects me to pick up after her, to be deferential towards her at dinner parties—to always treat her with kid gloves and to cater to her. She *has* to have her own way."

"I would like to involve both your mother-in-law and Kenneth in counseling," the counselor remarked. "Would you be willing to see if they would come in?"

"Certainly, I'll call you," Suki promised. She did telephone the next day to say that her mother-in-law and Kenneth would be willing to talk to the counselor. The counselor suggested that he talk to each of them separately before meeting with all of them together. Suki agreed.

Ala came in first. She was a pleasant, matronly sort of woman with grey-tinted hair. She began by admitting that she was sometimes overly concerned about her only son. "But he's such a good boy, and he's been sickly for years. He has a very weak heart, and he works so hard—you know—to support his family. He'd do anything for Suki and Sandy, their little boy. But Suki doesn't like me until she and Kenneth need money. After that, I'm a nonperson. If Kenneth doesn't buy Suki something or isn't taking her out all the time she really gets offended. Usually, she gets upset at me. I'll tell you something, my husband—he's dead now—did pretty well in real estate and I never lacked for money, but I was never as demanding as that girl. She never listens to me; no, she has her own mind. I try not to interfere when they fight. I don't think she really loves him; she just wants to be taken care of. I know the type. She never does anything that I say. You'd think that she'd show more respect for me."

The counselor's next interview was with Kenneth. "There's a lot of friction between your wife and mother," he began. "How do you see the situation?"

"I think the basic problem is that Suki is jealous. She and my mother don't get along because she resents everything that I do for my mother. But Suki has to realize that my mother is all alone. She has nobody but me. What am I going to do, throw her out on the street? And she is good to us; she buys us everything and pays a lot of our bills."

"Do you think Suki has any reason for being jealous?" the counselor asked.

"Not really," Kenneth answered. "I love my wife, but my mother is old and one day she'll be gone. I'd hate to think that I didn't pay any attention to her while she was alive. I don't want that on my conscience."

QUESTIONS

1. How would you analyze this situation? What are the basic causes of the difficulty?

2. Evaluate the points of view and problems of each person: Suki, Ala, and Kenneth.

3. Who or what has to change before the situation can be improved? What can and should Suki do? Kenneth do? Ala do?

4. After marriage, who should come first, one's spouse or parent? Give the reasons for your answer.

5. What should be the counselor's role in this situation?

CHAPTER 15

Sexual Adjustments and Difficulties

CHAPTER OUTLINE

The Functions of Sexual Intercourse

Sex and Happy Marriage

Sexual Anatomy and Physiology

Male-Female Differences
and Similarities

Sexual Adjustments

Sexual Dysfunction

Causes of Sexual Dysfunction

Conclusions: Getting Help

Dialogue

Sexual expression is an important component of the total relationship of marriage. As such, it affects the whole marriage and is, in turn, affected by all other aspects of the relationship. It also involves interdependent physical and emotional stimuli and responses. One's emotions and feelings affect physical responses, and physical conditions and responses affect feelings. Most sexual adjustments, therefore, require an understanding of both physical and emotional aspects of sexual response.

Most couples can look forward to a great deal of pleasure, happiness, and love as derivatives of their sex life. Many couples run up against some problems in adjustment, however. Some of these are quite minor; others are very serious—or become quite serious because they are never adequately defined or solved. It is helpful, therefore, to know what some of the most common problems are and to realize that most can be satisfactorily overcome with some knowledge and help.

The Functions of Sexual Intercourse

What are the purposes of sexual intercourse? This question may be answered differently by different persons or groups (Mace, 1972d). One important function is *pleasure*. For centuries most Asians emphasized this purpose as did the ancient Hebrews, Greeks, and Romans (Vatsyanana, 1962). The more puritani-

cal elements of western culture have tried to deny this function. Some cultures applied a double standard of behavior for men and women. Men acknowledged that sexual expression was pleasurable for them but denied that it was for women (Seaman, 1972). Modern research has shown, however, the fallacy of such views (Lehrman, 1970; Masters and Johnson, 1966). Both men and women today are learning to enjoy sex, to thrill to the rhythmic pulses of orgasms, to respond to the physical sensations of being touched and caressed (Comfort, 1972; Hamilton, 1971; Hollender, 1971; "M," 1971).

Sexual intercourse, however, has a more profound function: as a means of *expressing and bestowing love*. This is not to say that sex can't be enjoyed without love—it can. Sex which is more than physical, which is an expression of love, is preferable to most couples. Popular literature would have couples believe that all they have to do to have a happy sex life is to have sexual intercourse frequently, engage in uninhibited love play, have mutual **orgasms,** and show variety and imagination in their technique (one book suggests making love in a bathtub of Jell-o), and they will be satisfied (Commission, 1970). Such is simply not true. Couples can find physical stimulus and release and even come to a mutual agreement about the mode and manner of their sex life but still find "something lacking" (Winick and Kinsie, 1973). The something lacking is often warmth of feeling, depth of emotion, and closeness of spirit. The "something" can only be described as emotional and spiritual: oneness, tenderness, a kind of secure awareness that one is accepted and loved without limit and that one has expressed the deepest feelings of affection of which one is capable.

One distortion of the purposes of sexual expression is to say that women want and need these emotional and spiritual components to sex but that men do not. This is as false as to say that women are capable only of spiritual love but not physical pleasure. True, more men than women will have sex without love. When given a choice, however, most men and women prefer closeness, tenderness, real concern, sympathetic understanding, and affection in their sexual relationships (Hollender, 1971).

The task of the couple, therefore, is to cultivate love and then to learn to use the body as a means of expressing inner feeling and emotion. When sex is more than just physical expression and response, it becomes more satisfying to human beings (Lowen, 1972).

Another important function of sexual intercourse is *procreation*. In fact, the view that sex was solely for procreation was the accepted dogma of some branches of the Christian church (Westoff and Westoff, 1971). Both Augustine and Aquinas taught that each and every act of sexual intercourse ought to allow the possibility that conception can take place. Augustine even said that every act of intercourse ought to be procreative in intention. It was not until the Ecumenical Council of 1965 that this doctrine was repudiated by the Vatican. The council meeting at the Vatican in Rome spoke of "conjugal love" and declared that "love is uniquely expressed and perfected through the marital act (Guttmacher, 1969). This declaration emphasized the emotional purposes of sex as well as the physical. Today, the procreative functions of sex have been deemphasized, recognizing that couples may have intercourse hundreds of times but consciously use sex as a means of conception on only a fraction of these occasions.

Sex and Happy Marriage

In any sexual relationship, physical expression and emotional feelings affect each other (Ard, 1974; Shope, 1968). It is easier to give oneself to a loved person than to a stranger or to someone one dislikes (McCary, 1973). Areas that affect the total marriage also influence the couple's sex life, and vice versa (Belliveau and Richter, 1970).

A satisfying sex life, then, is most possible within a happy marriage, but it also contributes to the success of the marriage (Bell and Bell, 1972). One study showed that 60 percent of the wives who rated their marriages as very happy reached orgasm 90 to 100 percent of the time in coitus, whereas 38 percent of the wives who rated their marriages as very unhappy never or rarely reached orgasm (only 1 to 9 percent of the time in coitus). There were, however, 4 percent of the wives who rated their marriages as very happy who never had orgasms and 38 percent of the wives who rated their marriages as very unhappy who practically always reached orgasm (Gebhard, 1966).

Some tentative conclusions may be drawn from this study. *Orgasm response alone does not insure wives a happy marriage, nor does happy marriage insure wives orgasm response, but it is harder to be happily married without orgasm response, and it is harder to have orgasm without a happy marriage.* The results of this study should not be surprising since sex is one of the strongest drives with which humans are endowed. The body craves sex physically just as it craves food to satisfy hunger. Also, most individuals crave physical closeness, love, and affection (Bell and Bell, 1972).

Ordinarily, most married couples develop an intense need (both physical and emotional) for sexual expression and feel frustrated, angry, hurt, rejected, ignored, or unloved when this need is denied repeatedly. Few persons are upset by occasional frustration, but most persons become deeply resent-

Satisfying sex and happy marriage tend to go together.

ful when denied sexual expression frequently in marriage. If sexual expression is withheld because of anger, the withholding further increases the tension between them. The more tension, the less they feel like making love. It's a vicious circle that may destroy the marriage if it continues over a long period of time. The couple who have intercourse because they feel loving, however, find that coitus stimulates further love (Udry, 1968).

Sexual Anatomy and Physiology

Male and Female Reproductive Systems

One of the things that helps couples find sexual satisfaction is to have some basic knowl-

edge of sexual anatomy and physiology (Chernick and Chernick, 1970; McCary and Flake 1971). Figure 15-1 shows a cross-sectional diagram of the male reproductive system. Figure 15-2 shows a front and cross-sectional diagram of the female reproductive system.

Erogenous Zones

The diagrams do not show all of the **erogenous zones** of the body—the areas that are sexually responsive to physical stimulation and touch. On the woman, the most sensitive area is on and around the clitoris (Melody, 1970). The breasts also, and especially the nipples, are sensitive to the touch. The area of the labia around the vaginal opening begins to be

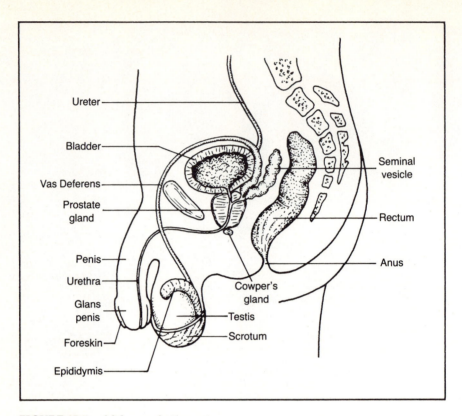

FIGURE 15-1. *Male reproductive system*

more and more sensitized as sexual excitement progresses. Some women also respond to caressing of the mons pubis, the inner thighs, the buttocks, or the anus. The tongue and lips are also very sensitive. In fact, most women thoroughly enjoy being caressed over the entire body, along with embracing and kissing, but usually the most sexually stimulating caressing is of the breasts and clitoral area (Clark, 1970b). The feelings of some women are quite diffuse, which means that they require a period of wooing, bodily contact, and love play before they are physically and emotionally ready for intercourse itself.

The most sensitive area of the man is the penis itself, especially the ridge of corona of the glans, and the tip of the glans. Most of the sexual feelings, once aroused, are concentrated in this narrow area. Most men, how-

ever, also enjoy having the testicles, the inner thighs, buttocks, anus, chest, abdomen, and entire body caressed, although since the most intense feelings are concentrated in the genital area, this area should be given primary attention if sexual excitement is to be increased most rapidly. The man's lips and tongue, like those of the woman, are highly sensitive to touch.

Stages of Sexual Response

In order to gain a better understanding of the total process of sexual stimulation and resolution, it is helpful to have a clear understanding of the actual physical changes that take place in the body during the sexual act. According to the research of Masters and

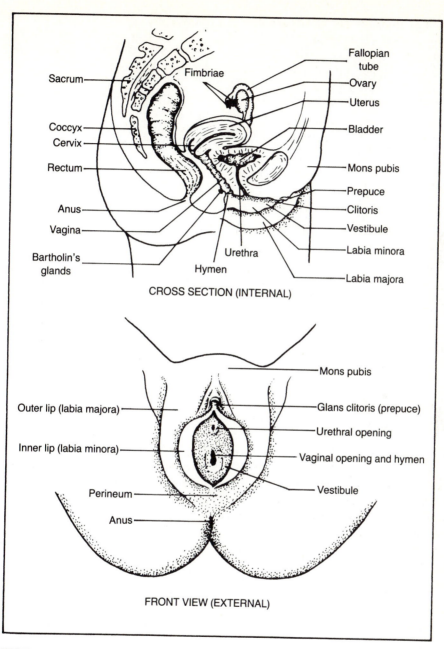

FIGURE 15-2. *Female reproductive system*

Johnson (1966), the stages of sexual response may be divided into four phases: the *excitement phase*, the *plateau phase*, the *orgasmic phase*, and the *resolution phase*. The excitement phase extends from the beginnings of sexual stimulation until the individual reaches a high degree of sexual excitation. The duration of this phase may be prolonged or shortened depending upon the intensity of the stimulation and individual reactions to it. Cessation of stimulation or the presence of objectionable psychological factors may even abort the process. If effective sexual stimulation is continued, sexual tensions are intensified and the individual reaches the second or plateau phase of the sexual cycle, from which he or she may move to orgasm. If sexual stimuli or the drive to culminate the activity in orgasm is inadequate and sexual stimuli are withdrawn, the individual will not achieve orgasm and sexual tension will gradually subside.

The orgasmic phase is limited to those few seconds during which sexual tension is at its maximum and then suddenly released. Women usually vary more in the intensity and duration of orgasm than do men. After orgasm, the person enters the last or resolution phase of the sexual cycle, during which sexual tension subsides as the individual moves back through the plateau and the excitement phases to return to the unstimulated state.

Physiological Responses

As sexual excitement increases, both men and women show similar physical responses:

• *Erection.* The man's penis, the woman's clitoris, the nipples of the female breast (a majority of men also evidence nipple erection), and the woman's labia become engorged with blood, which causes swelling, enlargement, and erection.

• *Increase in heart and pulse rate, blood pressure, respiration, and perspiration.* The heart, pulse, and respiratory rates may more than double; the blood pressure may increase anywhere from 20 to 80 percent. About a third of men and women evidence perspiration during the resolution phase.

• *Sex flush.* There is a noticeable reddening of the skin of the body, usually in the form of a red, splotchy rash, gradually spreading over more and more of the body as excitement increases. About three out of four women, and one out of four men show this reaction.

• *Myotonia.* Myotonia is muscular tension of both voluntary and involuntary muscles. As excitement increases, there is a tensing and flexing of the muscles of the arms, legs, abdomen, face, neck, pelvis, buttocks, hands, and feet. During orgasm, there may be severe involuntary muscular contractions throughout the body, gradually subsiding during the resolution phase. These contractions during orgasm are especially strong in the vagina, uterus, and pelvic region of the female and in the penis, vas deferens, seminal vesicles, and prostate gland of the male.

• *Vasocongestion.* One of the most important changes in the female is in the vagina. The outer one-third becomes engorged with blood, reducing the opening, with the outer muscles contracting around the penis. At the same time, the vaginal length increases and the inner portion balloons out, increasing considerably in width. Women who use diaphragms for contraception have to be certain they are fitted quite tightly otherwise the ballooning out of the inner vagina under sexual excitement loosens the diaphragm, allowing sperm to pass around the edges, or the diaphragm itself to become dislodged. Under sexual excitement, the uterus increases in size by 50 percent and pushes outward during the contractions or orgasm, expelling any fluids that may be inside. If orgasm is during the menstrual period, increased flow may result for a brief period of time.

The most important change in the penis is erection and increase in width and length. It is not uncommon for an erection to come and go several times if the excitement phase is prolonged. It is also affected by fear, anxiety, changes in temperature, loud noises, changes in lighting, or other distractions. The testes also enlarge by at least 50 percent due to engorgement with blood during sexual excitement.

Summary of Response Patterns

There are two observations that should be made about these phases of sexual response. One, the responses of the male and female are very similar, even though the actual sexual organs are different. Both male and female show vasocongestion of the sex organs when stimulated and both have erectile tissue that enlarges and becomes firm. Both show evidence of sex flush—the reddening of the skin of the body. Both show myotonia—muscular tension. Both show an increase in heart rate, blood pressure, and respiration. Both perspire during the resolution phase.

Two, the physiological responses to stimulation are similar regardless of the method of stimulation, whether manually by **masturbation,** by mutual love play, or by intercourse (Clark, 1970a). The only real difference is in the degree of excitation. Sometimes the orgasm is deeper or shallower than at other times, and the physiologic responses more or less intense (Fisher, 1973). Many times the degree of physical response is greater through masturbation than through intercourse, but this varies with different individuals and with the same individual at different times (Lydon, 1970). The important point that Masters and Johnson and others have made is that an orgasm is an orgasm, regardless of the method of stimulation (Lydon, 1974). There is no physical difference between the so-called *vaginal orgasm* (one achieved by stimulation of the vagina) and the *clitoral orgasm* (one achieved by the stimulation of the clitoris). Of the two organs, however, the clitoris is by far the most sexually sensitive organ of a woman's anatomy, not the vagina. In fact, the nerve endings in the vagina lie deep beneath the surface, so that often no feeling occurs

until sexual excitement is already well advanced. The important point is that female sexual arousal comes far easier by clitoral than by vaginal stimulation (Kinsey, 1953; Scully and Bart, 1973). It must be recognized, however, that intensity of orgasm can vary with any method of stimulation. Also, since orgasm is more than physical, reaching a climax during intercourse in a loving relationship is more emotionally satisfying than is self-masturbation, at least for most persons, even though the physiological responses are the same.

Male-Female Differences and Similarities

Before the Masters and Johnson research, most writers emphasized the sexual differences between men and women. Gradually, however, research is showing that fewer differences exist than was once thought.

One difference has been in the sources of sexual stimulation of men and women. Kinsey (1948; 1953) and others observed that men were aroused by erotic writing and pictures, talking about sex, by looking at women with shapely figures, going to burlesque shows, observing sexual activities of humans or animals, or looking at nude photographs. Women were not as much aroused by these sources as by reading love stories or seeing romantic movies. Men have always been considered *erotic* and women *romantic*. Not too long ago, however, Sigusch did a significant research study in Hamburg and found that when exposed to erotic photographs women tended to verbally judge them to be less arousing than did men, but "the women showed almost the same degree of sexual-physiological reactions and activation of sexual behavior as the men" (Sigusch, 1970, p. 23). Apparently both men and women were responding to social cues. Those cues said that women were not supposed to be stimulated by the pictures, when, in fact, they actually were aroused. Men were socialized to accept the fact that they were aroused, which is what they reported. Apparently, there is not as much difference between the sexes in this regard as was once thought, and, when it does exist, it may have its foundation in the socialization process.

Other researchers have found women were more stimulated by psychological stimuli than once believed. Mosher and Greenberg (1969) found that college women were sexually aroused by reading erotic material. Loiselle and Mollenauer (1965) found that women showed greater response to nude males than to nude female figures. Kinsey (1953) found that 2 to 3 percent of women were more responsive to psychological stimuli than men, and one-third of women were regarded as the same as men in this respect.

Another male-female difference has been the emphasis on the relative time required for arousal to orgasm for men versus women. Kinsey observed that the average male was able to have an orgasm in four minutes of intercourse, but this required ten to twenty minutes for women. But when properly stimulated through masturbatory techniques, the average woman was able to climax in less than four minutes, about the same length of time required for men. The important point is that the reason it took longer for the female to achieve climax was because she was not properly stimulated before and during copulation so that climax could take place. Once the husband gains control of his ejaculation and the couple know how the wife can be most easily aroused prior to and during intercourse, she is able to reach an orgasm easily (Gebhard, 1966).

One important male-female difference was "discovered" by Masters and Johnson (1966) even though Kinsey and others had mentioned it years before. It was that some females are capable of a rapid return to orgasm

after an orgasmic experience. Furthermore, these females are capable of maintaining an orgasmic experience for a relatively long period of time. In other words, some females are capable of multiple and more prolonged orgasms, whereas the average male may have difficulty in achieving more than one, unless some time has elapsed in between (Bell, 1972; Laws, 1971). Figure 15-3 shows individual differences in response patterns.

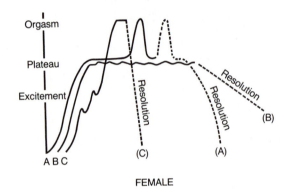

A, B and C are three different female sexual response patterns, Female C— one orgasm, Female A—two orgasms, Female B,—no orgasms.

FEMALE

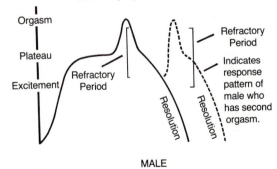

The refractory period represents the last, irregular contractions during which sexual tension rapidly subsides.

MALE

FIGURE 15-3. *Human sexual response cycles* (**Source:** *From W. H. Masters, and V. E. Johnson,* Human Sexual Response [*Boston: Little, Brown, 1966*], *p. 5. Reprinted by permission.*)

It must be emphasized, however, that there are great individual variations (Marmor, 1971). Some wives frequently desire multiple orgasms to be satisfied. Others seem satisfied with one. The husband needs to follow his wife's lead; she can indicate to him what her needs and desires are (Avery, 1971). It may be that as wives become more and more uninhibited, they will be the ones primarily concerned with their husbands' satisfying them (Chartham, 1970).

Sexual Adjustments

There are three important time factors that relate to sexual adjustment. One, it takes time to adjust to one another and to learn to respond sexually. Two, response is enhanced if couples are able to have an adequate and uninterrupted period of time to make love on each occasion. Three, suitable intervals of time between love-making experiences have to be worked out.

Time and Timing

The first important consideration is for couples to give themselves time to adjust to one another and to learn to make love. Some people are brought up to be quite modest about their bodies (Fromme, 1972; Sherman, 1971; Vincent, 1969). Others are never allowed to ask questions about normal bodily functions or about sex (Mace, 1970; Wright and McCary, 1969). These persons enter marriage with negative feelings and inhibitions that make it more difficult to give themselves freely in an uninhibited sexual relationship. When people have been taught to inhibit their sexual responses, it takes time before negative feelings can be overcome (Kaplan and Sager, 1971).

How long does it take couples before they are able to make a satisfying sexual adjust-

ment? In a 1971 study of married college women, Landis and Landis found that approximately half the wives experienced orgasm within the first month of marriage, one-fourth more within the first year of marriage, and the remaining fourth took one or more years or had never experienced it (Landis and Landis, 1973, p. 281).

If both the husband and wife have had prior orgastic experience through masturbation, the chances are greater that coital orgasm will occur. Kinsey found that of females who had masturbated to orgasm before marriage, only 13 to 16 percent failed to have coital orgasm during the first year of marriage, whereas of those who had never masturbated to orgasm before marriage, 31 to 37 percent failed to reach orgasm during coitus the first year of marriage. The implication is that masturbation contributes to orgasmic responses, a fact that has also been found true in clinical practice.

Not only do couples need time after being married to make a happy sexual adjustment, but *when they have intercourse, they also need an uninterrupted period of time to make love* (De-Martino, 1970). It's disadvantageous to be pressured to "hurry up." An important study by the Institute for Sex Research points to the relationships between orgasm and the time devoted to precoital foreplay. Table 15-1 shows the relationship. The implication of this study is that there is a positive correlation between duration of foreplay and the wife's orgasm rate. When only one to ten minutes of foreplay was involved, only two-fifths of the wives reached orgasm nearly always, but when foreplay was twenty-one minutes or more, nearly three-fifths of the wives achieved this orgasm rate (Gebhard, 1966). This means that most wives don't appreciate the mate who is in too great a hurry.

Furthermore, *couples need to work out suitable intervals of time between lovemaking experiences.* The majority of couples under forty are happy with two to four times a week (Pearl-

TABLE 15-1. *Female orgasm rate and duration of precoital foreplay in marriage*

Percent of Coitus Resulting in Orgasm	Average Duration of Foreplay in Minutes			
	0 Min.*	1–10 Min.	15–20 Min.	21+ Min.
0	(2 cases)	3.9%	7.6%	7.7%
1–39	(1 case)	19.5	12.6	7.7
40–89	(1 case)	34.6	28.9	25.6
90–100	(2 cases)	41.9	50.6	58.9
Total Number	(6 cases)	179	79	78

Source: From P. H. Gebhard, "Factors in Marital Orgasm," *Journal of Social Issues* 22, no. 2 (1966): 88–95.

* Too few to indicate percentages

man, 1972). But the couples are cautioned not to try to adjust to any national average. They have to develop their own schedule (Bell, 1971a; Levinger, 1970; Weinberg, 1971).

A problem arises, however, when there is a marked difference between the partners in the frequency with which intercourse is desired (Bell, 1972). An almost total absence of desire is certainly not normal. One wife remarked:

My husband has not made love to me for a whole year. I've tried everything: buying sexy nightgowns, getting him drunk, serving him dinners by candlelight, and trying to seduce him when he's asleep. But nothing works. Sometimes I don't think I can stand it any longer.

It is disruptive to the total relationship when couples have to argue over whether or not to have intercourse. One wife comments:

My husband and I fight constantly, as he thinks you must have sex three or four times a week. He would rather have sex than eat. I am of the opinion that there's more to life than that. I am not against sex, but twice a week is more than enough. It would be different if he enjoyed it, but he seems to force himself (Lamb, 1974, p. 8).

Of course, the level of sexual appetite varies. Overwork, physical or nervous exhaustion, physical illness, or lack of sleep may lower the sexual drive (O'Connor et al., 1974). The onset of disturbing emotional states such as depression may cause a marked disinterest in sex (Bullock, 1972). The aging process usually results in some decline in desired frequency of sexual relations, although there are individual exceptions (Kaplan and Sager, 1971; Pfeiffer, 1968; Verwoerdt, 1969). The frequency of desire is also determined, in part, by past gratification experience. Those who have found sex very gratifying in the past are more likely to desire sexual relations more often now and in the future (Barton, Kawash, and Cattell, 1972).

The sexual appetite of a particular couple may be irregular (Bardwick, 1971). Some people are cyclical in their sexual desires. In females, desire may depend on the time of the month in relation to **menstruation.** In twenty-eight separate studies conducted over a number of years, thirteen of the studies showed that the peak of a woman's sexual desire occurs just after the menstrual flow begins. Nine studies showed the peak to be just before the flow, and six showed it to be midway in the cycle (Cavanaugh, 1969; Shader and Ohey,

1970). Bardwick (1970; 1971) explained this increased sexual desire before and during menstruation as a result of the relative increase in the ratio of male versus female hormones during the period, and as a symptom of the tension and irritability that occurs premenstrually when female hormone levels are at their lowest level.

When couples differ in desired frequency of sexual relations, cooperation and consideration are necessary. If the couple are not able to work out the problem, counseling help may be needed. Mace (1972d) suggests that masturbation be used as one means of taking up the slack and overcoming the problem of nonmatching sexual patterns. Specifically, he suggests that if one wants intercourse when the other is not able to respond that the one wanting intercourse guide the other in masturbating him or her to orgasm. Mace doesn't recommend noncoital sex as a way of life for married couples (although in certain instances it can be that), but he does feel it can be a source of sexual pleasure and release when intercourse is not possible.

Overcoming Inhibitions

One of the uncertainties in the beginning is how uninhibited to be. Certainly the wife ought to feel as free to initiate intercourse as the husband and to indicate to him by word and behavior when she feels like making love (Brissett and Lewis, 1970). Most couples enjoy exploring every part of each others' bodies. The majority (60 to 80 percent) also use the mouth and tongue as instruments of stimulation, touching various erogenous zones orally, as well as with the fingers, hand, or genitals (Bell and Connolly, 1973). Most couples enjoy experimenting with a variety of positions in intercourse, using different techniques of sexual arousal, changing times of the day or night, and trying a number of different settings (Herrigan and Herrigan, 1973; Zehv, 1969). There are no set rules; they can let their lovemaking lead them to do things that are acceptable to both. Usually the longer two people are married, the more uninhibited they become. It goes without saying that keeping all parts of the body scrupulously clean by daily washing and bathing enhances uninhibited lovemaking. The genital regions especially need daily washing (McCary, 1973).

Defloration of the Hymen

If a woman's **hymen** is intact, and she is concerned, she should consult her physician, who may want to examine her and advise her about initial defloration. Only in exceptional cases is it necessary for the physician to rupture the hymen surgically.

There are several suggestions that will help in the initial defloration through intercourse (Lowry, 1969). One, arousal almost to the point of orgasm before intromission (insertion of the penis) facilitates penetration and the rupture of the hymen. The vagina will be well lubricated if the woman is aroused. Two, the male can use a **vaginal jelly** on his penis before inserting it. Three the male needs to enter cautiously and gently, pushing gently back and forth until intromission is achieved. If the hymen is ruptured at that time, usually a little bleeding takes place but the amount varies. If intercourse is too painful, perhaps both may want to finish their orgasm by manual stimulation on this occasion. The woman may be sore for several days afterward so may or may not feel like intercourse, but manual stimulation to orgasm is sometimes substituted for intercourse. As soon as the torn hymen is healed, however, intromission may be resumed. Most women find intercourse hurts a "little" for some period of time after the hymen is ruptured, but this gradually subsides as the vaginal walls stretch and become more used to receiving the penis. If pain persists, a physician may be consulted.

Sexual Dysfunction

The human reproductive system, which includes the sex organs, is an amazing system. Consider, for example, the fact that mere thoughts can produce sexual reactions. A man can start thinking about sex and have an erection. A woman can dream about a man making love to her and have an orgasm. A look at a sensuous photograph may increase the rate of respiration or blood pressure.

Under most circumstances, the body functions quite predictably. If a woman's breast is caressed, the nipples become engorged and firm. If a man's penis is stimulated in a pleasurable way, it becomes erect. If it is stimulated enough, an ejaculation occurs. These are predictable reactions to sexual stimuli.

Sometimes, however, difficulties arise so that the sex organs do not respond as expected. The penis is rubbed and it doesn't get hard. A couple copulate for a period of time, and don't reach a climax. Obviously, something is wrong. The expected response is not produced by a particular stimuli.

When this happens, the condition is called a **sexual dysfunction,** which really means a malfunctioning of the human sexual response system. It means a person hasn't reacted as one would normally expect. Some of the problems discussed in this chapter represent examples of male dysfunction; others are of female dysfunction. Let's get an overall view first of some common male sexual dysfunctions.

Male Sexual Dysfunction

The four most common types of sexual dysfunction in males are **premature ejaculation, impotence, ejaculatory incompetence,** and **low sexual drive.**

Premature ejaculation has been defined as the inability to delay ejaculation long enough for the woman to have orgasm 50 percent of the time (Bel-liveau and Richter, 1970). This definition assumes that the woman is not consistently nonorgasmic for reasons other than the rapidity of the male's ejaculation. The intent of the definition is to emphasize that the male is unable to exert voluntary control over his ejaculatory reflex and that once he is sexually aroused he reaches orgasm too quickly. It is the most common sexual dysfunction in males.

The ability to control ejaculation is helpful for proficiency in lovemaking and thus for successful sexual adjustment. The couple must be able to engage in sex play and in intercourse until both partners are sufficiently aroused for orgasm to take place. If the male climaxes, and his penis becomes flaccid before the woman is sufficiently aroused, he will have to rely on other means of stimulation to bring her to orgasm. The fact remains that premature ejaculation curtails the wife's sensuous enjoyment, and certainly the husband's (and wife's) pleasure is heightened and intensified if he can prolong the period of intense excitement prior to orgasm. At best, prematurity restricts the couple's sexuality and, at worst, it is highly destructive if the couple become anxious and worried about their sexual life or angry and rejecting and begin to avoid one another.

Some men are concerned only with their own satisfaction and are quite content to cease all lovemaking once they have ejaculated, leaving their wives dissatisfied, tense, and rejected. Other men ejaculate even before they can insert their penis into the vagina, making coitus impossible since their erection subsides quickly. Thus, ejaculation may be "premature" in varying degrees. One encouraging aspect is that premature ejaculation is one of the easiest of male sexual dysfunctions to treat (Semans, 1956). Out of 186 cases treated by Masters and Johnson (1970), only four were not cured. Those with this difficulty should seek professional help.

Impotence means the inability to create and

maintain an erection for a sufficient period of time to satisfactorily complete sexual intercourse (Carlton, 1980). Impotence should not be confused with **sterility.** A man who is sterile is unable to conceive children. When he is impotent, he is unable to produce an erection so that coital connection can take place, or he is unable to maintain an erection long enough to complete the sexual act. Mrs. G. told of her marital disappointment.

From the very beginning of our marriage, I noticed that Bob had trouble getting hard. Sometimes he would, and sometimes he wouldn't. I could never tell ahead of time when it would happen. Sometimes he would get hard, but only for a minute or so—long enough for him to finish, but not me. Sometimes he would wake up in the morning with an erection; we'd hurry up and begin, but as soon as he entered, he'd get soft again. It's very frustrating. I asked him if he used to have that trouble, and he said he never did until he married me. He tries to make me believe that it's my fault, that I'm doing something wrong, but I think there is something wrong with him.

In recent years, physicians have become increasingly aware of the problem of impotence. Doctors at college student health centers report increasing numbers of men coming in for treatment. It may be that the increasing numbers brought to the attention of physicians is a result of more men being willing to talk about their difficulty and to get help. Fortunately, the condition is treatable in the great majority of cases (Masters and Johnson, 1970).

Disagreements over sexual expression can become a major source of tension in marriage.

Ejaculatory incompetence is an inability of the male to ejaculate while his penis is in the woman's vagina. The severity of this dysfunction varies considerably. At one extreme is the male who has never experienced an orgasm, but this form is rarely encountered in clinical practice. At the other extreme is the man who occasionally finds himself unable to ejaculate. Mild forms of the disorder may be highly prevalent, as attested by the increasing number of patients applying for treatment. In this dysfunction, the male is able to respond to sexual stimuli with erotic feelings and a firm erection. Even though he desires orgastic release and his stimulation is more than enough to trigger a climax, however, he cannot ejaculate (Ovesey and Meyers, 1970). This condition is in contrast to that of the impotent man who may be able to ejaculate with a limp penis if he is sufficiently stimulated.

Strangely enough, there are very few references in the literature to the fact of *low sexual drive* in men. Female frigidity is discussed at length, but there is little discussion of frigid men who have a low sexual drive, who seldom take any interest in sexual expression. Perhaps this is because it is just assumed that all men have an ample sexual drive, and a persistent desire for intercourse. They don't. There are significant numbers of males who can go for days, weeks, or even months without intercourse, and never raise any objections. Every physician, marriage counselor, and sex therapist gets dozens of female clients whose chief complaint is that their husbands are not interested in making love with them (Peterson and Peterson, 1973). The following example is typical of these complaints:

My husband and I are in our late thirties. We're both in good health as far as we know. We seem to get along pretty well except for one thing—my husband spends every night after supper watching television. He watches every program until at least two in the morning; sometimes I find him asleep in the chair, even after the station has signed off. I've asked him, even begged him, to come to bed early, but he never will. So I go to bed by myself. I'm all alone and feel rejected. I'd like my husband to make love to me, but he seldom does. It's getting so he doesn't seem interested more than once a month. What's the matter with him that he is so uninterested in sex? I'm reasonably attractive, and have a nice figure, but it doesn't seem to help (Rice, 1978a, p. 181).

It was learned from the sexual history of this couple that the husband had an exceptionally low sexual drive from the very beginning of marriage. In the case of other husbands, they may be interested early in marriage, but the interest declines slowly. As one wife exclaimed: "We had a fantastic sex life on our honeymoon, but it has been going down hill ever since" (Rice, 1978a, p. 182).

Sexual disinterest on the part of the husband is *not* normal. The first step is for the couple to seek professional help to discover the cause, then to get the right kind of medical or counseling help to remedy the situation.

Female Sexual Dysfunction

The four most important female sexual dysfunctions are: **general sexual dysfunction, orgasmic dysfunction, dyspareunia,** and **vaginismus.**

General sexual dysfunction in females is a lack of desire for, or a lack of pleasure in, sexual relations (Hastings, 1963; McGuire and Steinhilber, 1970). Such women may have little or only a minimal interest in sexual activity or, if they participate, derive little if any erotic pleasure from the experience. On a physiological level, they show little physical response; light lubrication inside the vagina and little vasocongestion (Kaplan, 1974). Often, they have an aversion to sex, consider it frightening, an ordeal, or disgusting, and try to avoid sexual contact.

The dysfunction may be situational, that is, a woman may be unresponsive in a particular situation or with a certain person but not on other occasions or with another man. Also, there are degrees of sexual interest and responsiveness, and different persons have dissimilar standards by which they judge. A husband who wants intercourse daily—but whose wife only desires it twice a week—may refer to her as frigid. Standards do differ. Or perhaps she doesn't love him and finds it difficult to respond to him. If she had a husband to whom she were more attracted, she might be very responsive. Complete and permanent lack of sexual interest is actually quite rare.

Orgasmic dysfunction in women is the inability to reach a sexual climax (Kohl and Kaplan, 1974). Some women can reach an orgasm under certain circumstances or with a particular person but not in other situations or with another person. Some women are able to reach an orgasm through masturbation, oral-genital stimulation, by use of a vibrator, or by other stimulative techniques, but not through coitus. Other women may have an occasional, "random" orgasm, but are otherwise nonorgasmic. Still other women are orgasmic in lesbian relationships but not in heterosexual encounters, while some others seem to have a low sexual drive and difficulty in reaching a climax that is seemingly unrelated to negative conditioning or to specific traumatic experiences.

There are also women who have trouble having an orgasm but who have a strong sexual drive. They enjoy sexual foreplay, lubricate copiously, and enjoy the sensation of phallic penetration. They show no significant inhibition of erotic feelings, of the vasocongestion component of sexual response, nor are they sexually anesthetic. But they remain at or near the plateau phase of sexual response and have great difficulty reaching a climax even though their stimulation has seemingly been sufficiently intense to release the orgasmic discharge. Only a minority of women have never had an orgasm. Most are able to at some time.

Dyspareunia (pronounced dis-pä-rú-nē-u) is *painful coitus*. In this condition, penile entry into the vagina is painful and pelvic thrusts are painful. If orgasm occurs, it is painful. So instead of being pleasurable, intercourse becomes an ordeal (Reuben, 1969).

Physical causes of dyspareunia are quite common, one being insufficient lubrication. The remedy for this condition is longer love play prior to coitus and the use of lubricating jelly or cream. Initial intercourse and the defloration of the hymen may be painful for some women, for others not. Intercourse may become painful, particularly if it is quite frequent, because of mechanical irritation of the vaginal lining and urethral opening. One woman writes:

I am a newlywed four months and I should be quite used to making love since we do it every day. We can make love once, with no trouble, but if we do it the second or third time, I feel like pins are sticking into me and intercourse becomes painful to the point of tears. We enjoy sex, but this is becoming a problem. Also, I keep getting infection after infection.

This woman is suffering from what is commonly referred to *as honeymoon cystitis*. Frequent intercourse has irritated the urethra, plus bacterial infections have occurred. This together causes pain, particularly after repeated coitus.

The excessive use of acid foams, creams, jellies, or suppositories as contraceptive measures may also add to the irritation (see chapter 17). Some women react painfully to rubber or plastic condoms or diaphragms or to excessive douching. In other instances, coitus is painful because of lesions or scar tissue formed in the vaginal opening as a result of childbirth, rape, a crude abortion, or a **hysterectomy.** Polyps, cysts, or tumors of the reproductive system can cause painful intercourse, as can a displaced or prolapsed uterus. Medical opinion suggests that if dyspareunia persists over a period of time, small undetected lesions in the vagina are the cause in 85 percent of the cases. Various types of vaginal infections, such as streptococcus and fungal infections are also seen quite frequently. These possibilities should be checked with a physician (Lehrman, 1970; Mace, 1972d).

Dyspareunia also has *emotional causes.* If medical examination does not reveal any physical problems, then tension, fear, and anxiety may be suspected. If the woman is nervous or afraid of being hurt, if she is trying to repulse her sexual partner, or if she feels guilty or tense for any reason, the vaginal opening constricts and the muscles grow taut. The tenseness itself results in pain, so the woman does not have to pretend; it does hurt. In some instances, of course, the woman may counterfeit pain as a way of avoiding intercourse.

"It hurts" is a common complaint to gynecologists. The pain may be severe or slight, the degree depending upon its origin and the woman's condition. While such a difficulty is not unusual, it is not "natural." Except for intercourse in the early days of marriage, or under certain other conditions, such as too soon after childbirth, it should not be painful. Pain indicates that something is wrong and needs attention, usually that of a physician.

Vaginismus is a powerful and painful contraction of the muscles surrounding the vaginal tract (Ellison, 1972). Muscle spasms occur, and in severe cases any attempt to introduce the penis into the vagina will produce agonizing pain and make penetration impossible. In less severe cases, the spasms delay intromission or make it more difficult.

Causes of Sexual Dysfunction*

In general, all sexual dysfunctions have either physical or emotional causes, or both. For pur-

* Part of the material in this section is taken from the author's book *Sexual Problems in Marriage.* Philadelphia: The Westminster Press, 1978. Used by permission.

poses of clarity of discussion, the causes will be grouped into five categories: *ignorance, inadequate stimulation, psychological blocks, negative feelings toward one's partner or a disturbance in the relationship,* and *physical causes.*

Ignorance

A lack of knowledge and understanding of sexual anatomy, sexual response, and lovemaking techniques may be the reason why couples have problems. People aren't born with an understanding of male and female differences or of how to make love. Sexual instinct and urges are inborn, but a knowledge of lovemaking is not. It must be learned.

Inadequate Stimulation

Sexual responses may not occur because the individual has not been stimulated properly in the right places, in an appropriate way, for a long enough time (Sherfey, 1973). One wife complained:

I really don't enjoy sex with my husband, because I don't get anything out of it. The reason is Chuck never really tries to arouse me by kissing me or playing with me. I've tried to tell him that I need time to get worked up, that he has to caress me and pet with me first, but he gets worked up so quickly that he wants to hurry and enter before he comes. Afterward, he's not interested.

In this situation, the husband was too inconsiderate of his wife's feelings to take the time to arouse her sufficiently before coital connection took place.

Insufficient arousal through foreplay is one of the primary causes of orgasm dysfunction in women (Hite, 1977). Reference has already been made to the research study that showed the relationship between duration of foreplay and a wife's orgasm rate (Gebhard, 1966). This same study also showed the relationship between the duration of penile intromission (the length of time the penis was in the vagina) and the female orgasm rate. When intromission was less than one minute, wives achieved orgasm in only slightly more than one-quarter of the occasions when they made love, while intromission of one to eleven minutes resulted in an orgasm rate of more than 50 percent of all the coital connections (Gebhard, 1966). Arousal takes time. Lovemaking that is rushed because of the pressure of time may be completely frustrating.

Couples who are willing to experiment and to communicate with each other have an easier time overcoming problems. They can experiment by caressing different places to find out for themselves what is most stimulating. They can tell the other what places to caress and how, until they become knowledgeable of the best means of arousing the other. The couple usually discover, for example, that quite vigorous manual stimulation or too heavy pressure applied to their sexual organs, particularly at the start of love play, may have a numbing effect rather than an arousing effect, whereas the same general type of caressing, but with a more delicate, deliberate touch, may have a most stimulating result. The point is, each couple have to learn where, how, and for how long to stimulate each other to achieve the desired result.

Psychological Blocks

Psychological blocks to sexual response may include any type of negative feelings, fear, anxiety, stress, depression, embarrassment, guilt, disgust, or hostility (Kaplan, 1974). These blocks prevent individuals from participating fully in a sexual experience, or prevent them from "letting themselves go" so they respond fully to each other (Peters, 1975). *Fear* is one of the negative feelings that can inhibit sexual response (Lazarus, 1975). Fear may be of pregnancy, of being hurt, of failure, or rejection or ridicule, or of discovery (Weiss, 1973).

Fear of being hurt is quite common, especially in a new bride, or especially during pregnancy or after childbirth. The wife who is afraid that intercourse may harm her unborn child finds it difficult to relax enough or to give herself fully enough really to enjoy sex. Vaginismus is really a physical reaction to fear, so that penetration cannot take place.

Fear of pregnancy can prevent spontaneous participation, which is one important reason why adequate contraception is a necessary prequisite to a good sexual adjustment. Fear of failure can also be a strong enough feeling to motivate a husband or wife to avoid intercourse entirely (Flowers, 1975). The husband who was impotent on one occasion, who becomes fearful of repeating the failure, may try to avoid sexual relations (Cooper, 1971; Ehrlich, 1975; Ginsberg, Frosch, and Shapiro, 1972). Or the wife who was not able to have an orgasm becomes fearful that the same thing will happen again, so she begins finding excuses so she won't have to make love to her husband. One common reaction of both husbands and wives is to blame the other person for one's failure. The unmarried couple who park along a dark roadside to make love, but who are afraid of being caught in the act by the police or by a passing friend, may find their lovemaking to be completely futile. They can't relax enough to respond.

Anxiety about any number of things may be sufficient to block response. The mother who is worried about a sick child may not be able to concentrate on making love. The husband who is worried about unpaid bills, or about finding a job may have the same trouble (Greiff, 1975). One husband told of his and his wife's problem.

My wife and I have a fantastic sexual life except when we have company sleeping over in the next room. Our bed is old and it squeaks something awful. We get along fine with our lovemaking until I get on top and start thrusting up and down too hard, then the bed begins squeaking so loud you can hear it all over the house. When that happens, forget it. My wife turns off like she jumped into a tube of ice cubes. It's no use after that. When we're alone though, it never happens. She gets excited and forgets all about everything.

Couples who live in cramped quarters where there is a lack of privacy may become very anxious about making noise and so be unable to enjoy sex. One wife used to like intercourse until her oldest teenager walked in on her and her husband when they were all undressed, without any covers on the bed, and just as they both were reaching a climax. For several months afterward, the wife had trouble relaxing, even after her husband put an inside lock on their bedroom door.

Various *emotional illnesses* may impair sexuality. When people are emotionally depressed, sex is the farthest thing from their minds. Men or women who are under chronic stress or fatigue may lose sexual motivation. It has been found, for example, that men under chronic stress show a consistent decline in the testosterone level in their blood. Since testosterone is the male hormone which stimulates sexuality, a decline in the level results in a diminishing of sexual interest and capacity.

Embarrassment may also be a strong deterrent to sexual response. Some people have been brought up to be overly modest about their bodies (Rainwater, 1964). Their parents never allowed anyone in the family to see anyone else nude (not even the baby). Toilet procedures always took place behind closed doors. Dressing and undressing was strictly private, with the sexes segregated. Children were punished for even handling their genitals. Anything that had to do with sex was considered dirty, so that any normal curiosity was suppressed. The children may have been overly protected while growing up, to be certain to keep contacts with the opposite sex quite minimal. Courting opportunities were either denied or closely supervised. As a result, such persons enter marriage feeling very ashamed or guilty about anything having to do with the body or sex. If the children grow

up feeling that "nice boys or girls don't think or talk about sex," they may find extreme difficulty adjusting to the intimacies of married life (Calderone, 1971; Gadpaille, 1971). There are husbands or wives who have never seen each other dressing or undressing or nude, who have never had intercourse unless it was in complete darkness. Some of these persons are so inhibited that they won't go to a physician for assistance, won't read literature that could help, or won't talk about sex with each other, which could help even more. Until the couple are able to overcome part of their modesty and embarrassment, they will continue to have difficulty (Blazer, 1964).

Guilt may be strong enough to block sexual response. Individuals who are taught that extramarital sex is wrong, but who violate their own ethical principles, may be so guilt-ridden that they subsequently have problems.

Negative Feelings toward One's Partner, or a Disturbance in the Relationship

People respond best to those they love, admire, and trust. Contrary feelings can influence their ability to give themselves to one another. This is why the quality and the emotional tone of a couple's relationship are important to their sexual life. A sensitive wife who is disgusted by her husband's crude language or behavior may be turned off by his advances, as is the wife who can't stand her husband when he is drunk or smelling like a brewery. The fastidious husband or wife may be so disgusted by unpleasant odors, or by other evidences of lack of personal cleanliness, that making love under such circumstances becomes almost impossible.

Couples whose relationship to each other becomes hostile, angry, or resentful may find more and more difficulty responding to each other sexually (Charney, 1972; Greene, 1970). A minority of couples is able to separate sex from other aspects of their relationship, so that they can be quite hostile toward each other and still have sex together. In such cases, however, sex becomes just erotic response without any emotional feeling, or, if any feeling is there, it may be negative, so that sex becomes a means of expressing anger, hostility, or of inflicting punishment or pain on the other. Certainly, under these circumstances, it is not an expression of tender feelings of affection and love.

One factor that has been found to be important to the wife in relation to her ability to have an orgasm is the extent to which she feels secure in her relationship to her husband. If a woman trusts her husband and knows that she can depend upon him, she is more likely to be able to relax completely and to give herself up to the sexual experience. This is particularly true of middle-class females who become dependent upon their husbands, find their sense of identity bound up with them, and who tend to equate sex with love. Chilman comments:

Since the male is almost always stronger than she is, since he enters her body, since she may get pregnant by him, it would seem essential for her to be able to trust him and to depend upon him. The less readily she can do this, the less likely she may be to participate freely and lovingly in the sexual experience (Chilman, 1974, p. 128).

Research has also shown that females are more likely to be consistently orgasmic if they have strong, stable fathers who have taught their daughters through example that they can trust and depend upon the important males in their life (Fischer, 1973).

Physical Causes

Some sexual problems have a physical origin. One most frequent cause of sexual problems is the taking of certain drugs, particularly drugs that have a sedative effect. *Alcohol* is probably the most common sedative. It may have a stimulating effect in small quantities,

since its first effect is to release inhibitions that prevent response when the couple is sober. For this reason, some couples have sex only when they have been drinking. They find that alcohol relaxes them, minimizes anxieties, and makes them less inhibited. A wife who is very bashful or shy, for example, may really be able to "let herself go" sexually only after she has had a drink. The same is true of *marijuana*, which, like alcohol, is an intoxicant. It releases inhibitions, so that couples do things under its influence that they would never do ordinarily.

In quantity, however, alcohol's next effect is as a sedative that dulls sensations and blocks responses, so that complete participation is impossible (Wilson and Lawson, 1978). Consuming quantities of alcohol is one of the principal causes of impotence in males. Over a period of time, it may cause damage to the nerves that control erectile response. Such a condition is quite prevalent in chronic alcoholism. Smoking large quantities of marijuana over a period of time may reduce the male hormone, testosterone, found in the bloodstream. Whether this results in impotence or lower sexual drive in some males is a matter of dispute. There is some evidence that it may. It is known that mild doses may have a stimulating effect, especially on persons who tend to be sexually inhibited otherwise.

Similarly, small doses of sedatives such as *barbituates* may release inhibitions temporarily, resulting in an increase in sexual appetite or response, but large doses act as depressants of sexual behavior and response. Chronic abuse of such sedatives diminishes human sexuality. *Narcotics* such as heroin or morphine act as analgesics, having a depressive effect on the central nervous system and on sexual response.

Stimulants such as *amphetamines*, taken in small doses, may enhance the sexual interest, performance, and abandonment of some persons. Habitual use leads to a physical addiction, however, and to a decrease in sexual interest and performance. The "speed freak" is a severely addicted person who is usually very sick and certainly not interested in sex.

There are numerous other drugs that affect sexual response (Goodman and Gilman, 1970). *Anticholinergic drugs,* which are used in treating peptic ulcers, glaucoma, or other eye disorders, inhibit the transmission of the nerve impulses that control erection and may therefore cause impotence. Similarly, *antiadrenergic drugs,* used in treating hypertension or vascular disorders, block nerve impulses and so may cause impotence or ejaculatory failure (Kaplan, 1974). *Sex hormones* may also affect sexuality (Fox et al., 1972; Greenblatt, 1975; Jakobovits, 1970; Kolodny, 1975; Miller, 1968). The female hormone *estrogen* found in birth control pills may over a period of time decrease sex desire in women, as with other hormones that exert an antiandrogenic effect (O'Connor, 1974; Trainer, 1965). Thus, the steroids *cortisone* and *ACTH* commonly used in treating allergies may oppose the stimulating action of androgen on the brain and sexual organs. The person who is on any type of medication should find out if that drug has an inhibiting effect on sexual interest and response. There are some drugs, such as tranquilizers like *Valium* used to treat anxiety and as muscle relaxers, that may have no direct sexual effects in recommended doses but may indirectly increase sexual interest as the anxiety diminishes. Of course, when abused, these transquilizers will inhibit sexual response patterns. Under all circumstances, people should check with their physicians.

Numerous physical illnesses also affect one's sexual life. *Hepatitis* diminishes sexual interest. *Diabetes* may affect the erectile response of men. *Multiple sclerosis* may cause impotence or orgastic problems. Numerous *local diseases* of the female genitals may cause dyspareunia, or painful intercourse. *Severe malnutrition* or *vitamin deficiencies* in either males or females may affect arousal capacity and orgasm. *Heart* and *lung diseases* and various

types of malignancies may decrease sexual desire and impair arousal capacity. In all cases of sexual problems that may be caused by ill health, people should get expert medical advice to determine what needs to be done. In any type of sexual problem, physical factors ought to be checked out before emotional or psychological causes are suspected (Kaplan, 1974).

Conclusions: Getting Help

Masters and Johnson (1970) estimate that as many as 50 percent of all couples have some sort of difficulty with sexual adjustment in marriage. Sexual difficulties, left untreated, can wreck a marriage. This is even more tragic because most of the difficulties might have been cleared up by obtaining help (O'Connor and Stern, 1972).

Basically, there are four types of help: (1) medical, for physical problems, (2) psychoanalysis and psychotherapy when longer term counseling help is needed for deep-seated emotional problems, (3) marriage counseling that deals with the total marital relationship, and (4) sex therapy that emphasizes sensate-focus or symptom-focus approaches that concentrate on the immediate sexual problem (Adams, 1980; Hartman and Fithian, 1972). This latter type of help assigns couples sexual tasks that enable the couples to learn how to caress or "pleasure" one another in a nondemanding way until they are able to respond to one another. Whatever type of help is needed, and it sometimes involves a combination of one or more of the above approaches, most therapists agree that conjoint therapy, involving both the husband and wife, is desirable since sexual functioning necessarily affects them both. Couples who are having problems should decide to get help together. For a more complete discussion of problems and their treatment, see the author's book *Sexual Problems in Marriage* (Rice, 1978a).

Robin Knox is talking with her husband Jim about his sexual passivity with her. The Knoxes have been married more than seven years. "You know, since the first year of our marriage," Robin said, "you've acted as though you didn't care whether you made love to me or not."

Jim (trying to change the subject):   Let me get a drink. I'm exhausted.

Robin: Do you realize that it has been over a month since we had intercourse?

Jim: I haven't been counting. I've been too busy. You know how hard I've been working to get the Hilton contract. Once the deed is set, I'll have more time to think about other things.

Robin: But Jim, before the Hilton contract, it was the Allied products deal, and before that you had some other excuse. Am I supposed to wait around for years before my husband finds time to make love to me?

Jim: You remember what happened the last time. Just as I was getting turned on, you started an argument and I couldn't get warm after that.

Robin: Don't forget that you had been drinking a lot. That happens to a lot of men when they've been drinking.

Jim: I can tell you it's not going to happen again.

Robin: What do you mean?

Jim: I mean if you're going to be so much of a bitch, I can do without you.

Robin: Don't you love me anymore?

Jim: I don't know. I used to.

Robin: I still love you. But I need you, don't you see that?

Jim: I still love you too.

Robin: But you never do anything about it. I want you to hold me and caress me. I want you to make love to me.

Jim: I can't explain it, Rob. I try to do the right thing. I tried. I'm sorry. I do love you.

Robin: That's an evasion. I don't believe you really love me. If you do, I want you to show me right now.

Jim: You know I have to meet Pete about the contract. Maybe if you had more to do, you'd think about something else for a change.

Robin: How can I think about something else when I'm frustrated all the time? Let's face it Jim, you've got a problem. If you were a man, you'd do something about it.

Jim (angrily):   The only thing I want to do is to get away from you. (He leaves, slamming the door after him.)

QUESTIONS

1. Give your analysis of Jim's and Robin's problem. What is the problem from the point of view of Robin? Of Jim? What are the basic difficulties as you see them?

2. What are some probable causes of the difficulties?

3. What does Robin do that makes the situation worse?

4. What does Jim do to compound the problem?

5. Is Robin oversexed? Explain.

6. Is Jim undersexed? Explain.

7. What is the likelihood of marital breakdown in the Knox household?

8. What might the couple do about their problem?

CHAPTER

16

Divorce and Remarriage

CHAPTER OUTLINE

Facts and Figures on Divorce

Divorce and the Law

The High Cost of Divorce

Children and Divorce

Adult Adjustments after Divorce

Remarriage

Conclusions

Dialogue

The United States now has the highest divorce rate of any country in the world (Glick, 1975; Glick, 1977). Numerous and conflicting explanations have been given as to why this is so: the declining influence of the church, the breakdown of morals, more lenient divorce laws, changes in marriage functions and roles, or a decline of interest in traditional family forms. Probably all of these have to be considered as forming a kaleidoscope picture of the reasons. But whatever the explanations, the increasing numbers of persons involved in divorce have stimulated numerous new books on the subject that describe everything from how to do it yourself divorce to making divorce a more creative experience. With the books has come increasing interest in changing the divorce laws that in their old forms have created much suffering for millions of couples and their children. Increasing numbers of state legislatures have changed their laws and there is pressure in every state to offer **no-fault divorce.**

All of the statistics, laws, court cases, and individuals' efforts involve human beings: husbands, wives, and children who are trying to make the best of difficult situations each in his or her own way. There is a need, therefore, to take a careful look at this picture; at the facts of divorce and some of the reasons, at our divorce laws old and new, and at the involvement of children in divorce, their reaction to it, and its effects on them. There is a need also for a more sympathetic understanding of what couples go through and the difficult adjustment with which they are faced after a divorce has been granted. And finally,

since the great majority of divorced persons remarry, what do they face in the new situation? What are the problems of second or third marriages? Are such marriages successful? What are the adjustments parents and children have to make in order "to live happily ever after?"

Facts and Figures on Divorce

Rising Divorce Rates

The most meaningful divorce statistics are obtained by indicating age-specific rates, that is, rates per 1,000 married women of certain ages. The divorce rate in 1979 was 22 per 1,000 married women fifteen and older. Figure 16-1 shows the trends in first marriage rates and divorce rates for women fifteen years old and older and remarriage rates for women fourteen years old and older (U.S. Department of Commerce, Statistical Abstract, 1980). As can be seen, the rate of divorce has risen dramatically at the same time that the rates of first marriage have decreased. There does seem to be some indication, however, that the rise in divorce rates is now leveling off (U.S. Department of Health and Human Services, August 1980).

Age Factors

Divorce rates vary greatly according to the age of the wife. Divorce rates are highest among women fourteen to twenty-four, with

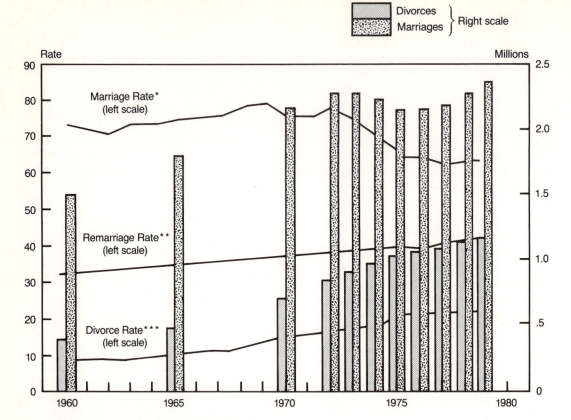

Figure 16-1. *Marriages, remarriages, and divorces: 1960 to 1979 (Source: Adapted from U.S. Bureau of the Census, Department of Commerce.* Statistical Abstract of the United States, 1980 *[Washington, D.C.: U.S. Government Printing Office, 1980], p. 58)*

the probability of divorce decreasing as the women gets older (England and Kuntz, 1975).

Socioeconomic Factors

Divorce rates vary according to a number of socioeconomic factors (Hicks and Platt, 1970). In general, men with a college education have a greater chance of their marriage surviving during the first five years than do men with

less education. These differences in rates among those with more versus those with less education and income, however, generally disappear after ten years of marriage (Glick and Norton, 1971).

Family Background

Persons who grow up in unstable and unhappy homes are less likely to marry and if they do marry, their marriages are more likely to end in divorce than are those who grow up in stable and happy homes (Riley and Spreitzer, 1974).

Variations by States

Divorce rates vary greatly from region to region of the United States. Generally speaking, the rates increase going from the East to the West. This variation has been attributed in part to the "frontier atmosphere" of the western states but particularly to their higher migration rates, which result in relaxed norms and lower social costs attached to divorce. The lower divorce rates in New England can be attributed also to the high percentage of foreign born and Catholics in the total population, coupled with the low migration rate (Fenelon, 1971).

Duration of Marriage

The median number of years of first marriage before divorce is 6.6 years (U.S. Department of Health and Human Services, July 1980). The duration of first marriage is greater for whites than for blacks (U.S. Department of Commerce, 1976). These median figures, however, tell only part of the story. The probability of divorce is greatest two to four years after first marriage for males and one to four years for females. Considering the fact that months may pass between the beginning of marital discord and the time couples separate with serious thought of divorce, the first year or so of marriage is certainly the hardest. About 10 percent of U.S. divorces come in the second year, about 8.6 percent the third year, and the rate diminishes after that. Forty percent of all broken marriages last ten or more years; 13 percent last more than twenty years (Freed and Foster, 1972).

Drawing by Joseph Farris; © 1982 The New Yorker Magazine, Inc.

Number of Children

Since half of all divorces occur in the first seven or eight years of marriage, it is inevitable that large numbers of children—especially young children—should be involved. Nearly two out of three divorces involve couples with children. The *average* number of children involved per divorce is now about 1.2, which means that more than one million children were involved in divorces that took place in 1979 alone (U.S. Department of Commerce, 1980). It is now estimated that more than 30 percent of all children of school age are not living with a father and a mother who are in a continuous first marriage (Glick, 1975). In some cases, of course, one parent is deceased or the parents are separated, but in the majority of instances the parents are divorced. Such situations are no longer unique and promise to become even more commonplace in the years ahead.

Divorce and the Law

Grounds for Divorce

Marriage involves a legal and civil contract that is binding upon the parties for as long as the contract remains in force. The contract may be broken, but only under those circumstances the states have established as legal grounds. Since laws of marriage and divorce are under state jurisdiction, the grounds for divorce vary from state in state. In states without no-fault laws, the most commonly recognized grounds for divorce are adultery, desertion, impotence, cruelty (physical or mental) conviction of a felony, habitual drunkenness or narcotics addiction, nonsupport, and incurable insanity (occurring after marriage). A minority of states recognize such grounds as incompatibility, indignities, the presumption of death, obtaining a foreign or out-of-state di-

vorce, or simply "the discretion of the court." Living separate and apart is now an important ground in over half of all states, because it sometimes does not require "fault" as a condition of divorce (Mayer, 1971). Irreconcilable differences, breakdown of the marriage, and incompatibility without fault are also becoming more common as grounds in no-fault divorce (Bohannan, 1971).

In addition, there are other grounds for annulment and/or divorce in many states. These include incestuous marriage (to close relative), under-age marriage, pregnancy by another at time of marriage (unknown to husband), insanity or mental incapacity at the time of marriage, **fraud** in marriage, **duress** (force in inducement of marriage), **bigamy,** and **venereal** or other "loathsome" **diseases.** In addition, there are a variety of other minor grounds for divorce and/or annulment in a few states (Mayer, 1971).

In states without no-fault divorce laws, about three-fourths of all divorces are granted on three legal grounds: cruelty (physical or mental), desertion, and nonsupport. In some states, 90 percent or more of decrees are granted on one particular ground. Incompatibility is usually the ground given in Alaska or Oklahoma, indignities in Wyoming.

No-Fault Divorce

In 1960, the National Conference of Commissioners on Uniform State Laws promulgated the new Uniform Marriage and Divorce Act (Kargman, 1973). This act is not a law; it is a model for state legislatures to accept or deny in part or completely. It rejects fault grounds as a precondition for access to courts and recommends instead the rights of the individual who petitions for a divorce on the grounds of "irretrievable breakdown" of the marriage (Monahan, 1973).

Some states such as Colorado, Iowa, Michigan, or Oregon now have no-fault grounds

No-fault divorce can minimize the harmful effects of divorce on children.

for divorce as the only ground (Foster, 1973–1974). Other states, such as California and Florida, recognize irreconcilable differences in addition to incurable insanity or mental incompetence. Other states merely added no-fault grounds (Weitzman, Kay, and Dixon, 1974). In these states, one spouse can still threaten to sue for divorce on grounds other than the no-fault ground if his or her demands are not met. As long as this is possible, divorce can still be a bitter contest between two partners who are each out to hurt or to win from the other (Anonymous, 1973). Goode's (1965) study of women in divorce showed that half of a typical group of divorcees either wished to remarry or punish their ex-husbands years after the divorce occurred.

The possibility for vengeance is removed when no-fault divorce is the only alternative offered. Under the new California law, divorce is referred to as the "dissolution of marriage." The law removes all fault (the question of who is to blame) and reduces the grounds to (1) irreconcilable differences, or (2) incurable insanity (Fullerton, 1972). A petition for dissolution may be granted if the petitioner can give affirmative answers to the following questions put by the judge:

1. Do you want to dissolve your marriage?
2. Are there irreconcilable differences between you and your spouse?
3. Have these caused an irremedial breakdown in your marriage?

Because of community property law, in California the property is usually divided equally, unless the couple request otherwise (Cox, 1972). If the petitioner seeks spousal support (not called alimony), several other questions are raised: Are you working now? Have you worked in the past? Is there any reason you cannot work either part- or full time? The final decision is based upon the needs of the petitioner, ability to pay, the standard of living, and similar considerations.

The California law did not solve all problems (Robbins, 1973). The sensitive issue of child custody is supposed to be settled by what is considered the "best interests of the child," although the sentiment favors the mother when the child is young (Gough, 1970). The petition for divorce itself can still be contested. If needed, the court can call in witnesses to establish the existence of irreconcilable differences. Although the testimony is for the purpose of giving information rather than finding fault, it can still lead to some ugly testimony. The California law did not establish a family court system as was recommended by the Governor's Commission. Experience with reconciliation bureaus and conciliation counseling, however, has shown that few marriages can be saved after they reach the courts, but such a system would be helpful in resolving such matters as awarding spousal support and child custody (Foster, 1970). To avoid a California "divorce mill," a six-month residency requirement was established.

One of the most criticized provisions of the California law was the establishment of an **interlocutory period** of six months, which means that this period of time must elapse between the decree of dissolution and the final granting of it. The intent is to offer a "cooling off" period, but this should come before the decree, not after (Gough, 1970). The end result of delaying final action is usually to prolong the agony of the couple, to add to the expense of the divorce, to add to the tension between the spouses, and to delay the time when they can begin to readjust their lives as divorced persons. Most authorities are against any interlocutory provisions in a decree.

No-fault divorce is a great improvement over the older adversary system, but some critics say that divorce should be awarded to any person without any possibility of its being contested. Cantor writes: "No one should have the right to force the legal continuation of a marriage that has ceased to exist in fact" (Cantor, 1970).

There are those that feel that such an approach would make divorce too easy, but as it is, divorce is extremely easy to get if it is not contested. It usually requires only a superficial hearing in court that requires ten to thirty minutes. But it is in the process of trying to work out the agreement that the harm comes. Couples fight bitterly, using the promise not to contest as the leverage for benefits. It is the possibility of contest that creates such havoc. The interests of children and the lives of people are traded in the negotiation. Eliminate the possibility of contest and you eliminate much of the fighting (Bohannan, 1971).

The Adversary Approach

The majority of states still allow an adversary approach to divorce. This means that one party must bring charges against the other, proving that the other is guilty of cruelty, desertion, nonsupport, habitual drunkenness, or some other fault. One of the spouses must be proven guilty, while the other must be blameless (Wells, 1975). If the accused proves his or her innocence, or if the court finds that both spouses are guilty, the divorce may not be granted. In some states, no matter how incompatible are the couples, no matter how miserable they are living together, if both spouses are at fault, the divorce can be denied. Some states, recognizing the folly of not granting a divorce when both parties were guilty, introduced the *doctrine of comparative rectitude*, which recognizes that the court may grant a divorce to the party least at fault.

The worst part about the adversary approach is that it forces spouses to become combatants, to attack one another like gladiators, with each trying to win over the other. This creates tremendous hostility and anger, even when couples are trying to settle amicably (Wylie, 1975).

There are other ways that the law prevents amicable agreements. If one party knows of any offense of the other and forgives the other of the act by reconciliation, or by continued cohabitation, then this forgiveness—known legally as **condonation**—can be used as a defense against divorce and as a basis for denying a divorce. The important argument against condonation as a legal tool in divorce cases is that it may prevent reconciliation. If the future of the marriage is in doubt, the offended spouse may be persuaded not to forgive and forget but to use the offense as a weapon against the other.

If couples get together to work out an agreement in relation to the divorce, they may be charged with **collusion**, which is against the law and grounds for denying the divorce. As a result, couples are further encouraged to fight one another rather than to settle amicably. In those states where divorce laws are very strict, couples may be forced into **connivance**, which is also illegal. Connivance means that one party gives assent to or encouragement of the conduct of the other. For example, a wife hires a prostitute to seduce her husband then arranges for a photographer to take pictures. Such arrangements were commonly made in states like New York, where adultery used to be the only ground for divorce. In such cases, however, if the court finds out about the connivance, the divorce may be denied.

One of the results of the adversary approach is that pressure is applied against one party to grant concessions in exchange for not delaying a divorce or for not contesting it. The consequence is bargaining. The divorce itself becomes an object of trade in exchange for alimony, child custody, visitation rights, or the allocation of property.

The High Cost of Divorce

Property and Finances

Nowhere is the injustice of adversary divorce laws more evident than in matters relating to property and money. One crusader for women's right has pointed out that wives may be astonished to learn in many states, unless they have joint deeds to property, they are legally entitled at divorce only to whatever income and property they themselves have earned or acquired. A minority of states have "community property" laws that entitle a wife, upon divorce, to an equal share of family income and property (Wylie, 1975). In actual practice, many husbands turn over the house to their wives, especially if children are involved, but by law, many wouldn't have to (Warner, 1974).

The husband is responsible for the continuing support of his wife and children while they are waiting for the divorce to be granted. Since some states require the couple to live apart for a period of time before the divorce, the husband has to support two residences, which gets expensive. Most couples have to reduce their standard of living drastically (Freed, 1973). If the wife is at all vindictive, or if the divorce drags out for months or years, the husband may find himself deeply in debt by the time the divorce is granted. One husband relates:

When my wife found out I wanted a divorce, she ordered a new refrigerator and washing machine, bought a new car, began to charge hundreds of dollars worth of clothes at different stores, and ran up the bills so that by the time of the divorce, I had to pay $11,000 worth of her charges. The judge accepted the fact that these were ordinary and necessary expenses.

As a result of such vindictiveness, some husbands try to shut off all charge accounts to protect themselves. Husbands, also, can be vindictive, especially if their wives have money. One actress announced that she paid her husband $75,000, as part of her divorce settlement, in exchange for her freedom.

Alimony, Child Support

Alimony and child support, referred to as "the high cost of leaving" are usually expensive. Normally, a husband with two small children pays one-third to one-half of his after-tax income in alimony and child support (Porter, 1975). Of course, costs vary depending upon the family's standard of living, whether or not the wife is able to work, the size of her independent wealth, the number and ages of the children, and the overall financial status of the husband. Some women now reject alimony as demeaning and a symbol of feminine dependency. Others try to sue their husbands for as much they can. In some states, a wealthy woman may be ordered to pay alimony to her husband, particularly if he is not able to work. Alimony payments are usually made only until the former spouse remarries, and child support payments are made until children are of legal age. Sometimes, an escalator clause is added, which boosts payments as the husband's income goes up. Often, the husband agrees to finance his children's college education if he is able. If the husband remarries, however, he is still obligated for whatever payments are being made to his former wife and children. This means he must now help support both his new family and his old one.

Legal Fees

Most husbands are surprised to learn that they may be responsible for the legal fees of both lawyers (their own and their wife's). Fees vary according to income bracket and the amount of time and work a case demands. In the simplest, uncontested divorce of those in the under $10,000 to $20,000 income bracket, fees may run from $500 to $2,500 for each lawyer. In higher brackets, if there is a fair amount of wrangling and property, fees may rise to $7,500 or more. Most families never recover their former standard of living. Porter writes:

Whatever your financial situation, a divorce is one of the most costly economic ventures you can undertake—with expenses which few to-be-divorced couples weigh in advance (Porter, 1975, p. 715).

Children and Divorce

Children as Pawns

In the most tragic cases, children become pawns in the battle. As one appalled judge put it, children "are treated as negotiable debris from the marriage, not much different from the hi-fi set or the family car" (Wylie, 1975). Couples may fight over custody, each trying to win the children. In one case, the wife agreed to let her husband have the children in exchange for a $50,000 payment. In another, the wife wouldn't agree to a divorce unless the husband promised to give her the custody of the children and to move at least 1,000 miles away. Since judges often consider the wishes of older children in deciding what parent the children will live with, each parent may try to get the children to side with him or her or to turn the children against the other. One husband relates:

My wife has done everything she can to turn my son against me. She told him so many lies, which he believed, that whenever anyone comes to the door of the house where my wife and son are living, my boy answers the door with a shotgun in his hands, just in case it's me at the door.

Much of the upset and turmoil that children experience because of divorce arises because parents are upset or because the children are forced to take sides. The children love both parents; which one are they to believe or to defend? If they weren't upset before, they become so if couples continue to fight one another. If parents become embittered, these hostilities become deeply disturbing (Morrison, 1974). The whole adversary bargaining process is wrong because it prevents justice, it destroys whatever semblance of friendly feelings might still exist between couples, and because it often works great harm on children (Cantor, 1972).

Child Custody

Traditionally, custody of the children has been granted to the mother, unless it can be established that she is unfit (Bohannan, 1971). Actually, the children might be closer to the father; he might be the one who can better afford them and who can better care for them. Most wives have to work after the divorce, as does the husband. More and more, therefore, the overriding consideration is what the court considers the best interests of the children (Dulea, 1975).

In some cases, joint custody is awarded with both parents responsible. The children may reside alternately with each parent, or primarily with one, and visit the other often. The theory is for the children to have complete access to both parents. Such arrangements require great maturity and forbearance of both parents, otherwise numerous squabbles create continual tension.

Visitation Rights

Ordinarily, visitation rights are given to the parent not given custody. Those rights may be unlimited—to visit the children at any time—or they may be restrictive—limiting visitation only to several hours or days a month or a year. A vindictive spouse can make life even more miserable by managing to "be away" with the children when it's time for the other parent to visit, by "poisoning" the children's minds against the other parent, by refusing to allow the children to phone or write, or by using visitation rights as a club to wield over the other person's head.

One of the hardest adjustments of the parent not given custodial rights is to be away from his or her children (Rose and Price-Bonham, 1973). One Marine corps sergeant was sued for divorce with the wife asking for custody of their two sons. When informed by his attorney that the wife is ordinarily given custody, the sergeant expressed his anguish:

Parting with either of my two sons would be like his death to me. If they (the lawyers and the court) part them, they might as well kill me. . . . I stand to lose my own son through a dirty, nasty experience in court. I have never been afraid of a thing in my life, but I'm afraid of the court (Wylie, 1975, p. 224).

Faced with the possibility of losing their children, some fathers are driven to violence. In one case, a man drew a gun during a session in the judge's chamber, severely wounding his wife and killing the judge (Wylie, 1975). Attempts to take children away create much resentment between spouses and parental custody battles are very disturbing to children.

Effects on Children

In spite of the harmful effects of a bitter divorce, a "good divorce," which is uncontested, fairly amicable, and with a minimum of bitterness, may be better for the children than an unhappy marriage (Shideler, 1971). Three independent surveys by Nye and Berardo (1973), Landis (1962), and Burchinal

(1962) comparing children from happy, broken homes with children from unhappy, unbroken homes showed either few differences or that the children from the broken homes had made better personality adjustments, showed less stress, less psychosomatic illness, and less deviancy than those from the unhappy, unbroken homes. An analysis of eleven studies of the relationship between broken homes and juvenile delinquency showed the correlation between the two factors was small (Rosen, 1970).

Not all studies agree with these. A study of 5,376 juveniles showed that children from broken homes were more than twice as likely to be charged with offenses as would be expected by their number in the population (Chilton and Markle, 1972). In another study, Rosenberg (1965) found that New York high school juniors and seniors from broken homes showed less self-esteem and more psychosomatic symptoms than those from unbroken homes. The unbroken homes in these two studies, however, were not necessarily unhappy and the self-esteem of the children in Rosenberg's study was greatly affected by the age of the mother at the time of the divorce. The younger the mother when divorced, the greater the loss of self-esteem by the children. Younger mothers were not as able to cope with the upset of the divorce and with the added responsibility of bringing up their children themselves. The greater the trauma of the mother over the divorce, the more negative will be the effect on the children (Rose and Price-Bonham, 1973).

Divorce does not always have the tragic impact upon children that was once suspected. The long-term effect depends a lot on how happy their situation is after the divorce (Morrison, 1974). Children who are forced to live in an unhappy home, broken or unbroken, will be affected negatively. Children will find relief in a divorce that removes them from a highly conflicting family but will be distressed by a divorce if they had not been

previously aware of parental conflict. As one girl remarked:

I didn't even know my parents weren't getting along. When they told me they were getting divorced, it came as quite a shock.

For this reason, it is important to help the children understand the reasons for the divorce.

Helping children to understand completely may take months or years. One adult said she did not really understand why her parents were divorced until she got married herself (Westman and Cline, 1973). The important thing is for parents to be open, to be willing to discuss and to explain, yet to do so without recrimination. Children resent one parent trying to get them to hate their other parent (Schulhofer, 1973).

Reactions of Children

The reactions of children to a divorce vary, depending upon the circumstances. They may go through a period of *mourning and grief*, and the mood and feeling may be one of *sadness and dejection*. One seven year old described divorce as "when people go away" (Rice, 1979). Other common reactions are a *heightened sense of insecurity*. Children feel that "if you really loved me, you wouldn't go away and leave me." Some become very afraid that their other parent will also leave, and the child may become very possessive with that parent. One mother remarked: "Since the divorce, Tommy has been very upset when I go to work or when he goes to school. I think he's afraid that he'll come home and not find me there" (Rice, 1979, p. 304).

Another common reaction is to *blame themselves*. If one major source of couple conflict is over the children, the children feel they are responsible. Some children feel that the departing parent is abandoning them because they haven't been "good boys or girls." Another common reaction of children is *to try to bring their parents together.* They "wish that everyone could live together and be happy." The longing for a reunited family may go on for a long time, until children fully understand the realities of the situation and the reason for the separation.

After children get over the initial upset of divorce, one common reaction is *anger and resentment,* especially against the parent they blame for the divorce. Sometimes this is directed against the father—especially if they feel he has deserted the family. The child feels: "I hate you because you have gone off and left me." When the father comes to visit, he may be surprised to find that his children remain cold and aloof. The reason is that they have been hurt, so they have erected defenses, have shut off their emotions, and have tried to remain unfeeling (Rice, 1979).

The resentment or hostility may also be directed at the mother, especially if the children blame her for the divorce. One five year old blamed her mother for her father's absence: "I hate you, because you sent my daddy away." (Actually, the mother hadn't wanted the divorce.) An older girl, age twelve, asked her mother: "Why did you leave my father all alone?" It was obvious that the girl did not understand the reason for the divorce (Rice, 1979, p. 305).

Children have other adjustments to make. They have to adjust to the absence of one parent, often one on whom they have depended deeply for affection and for help. One teenage girl remarked:

The hardest thing for me was to get used to living without my father. I never really realized how much I needed him until he left. I used to talk to him about a lot of things, and he would understand. He took me places, and even helped me with my homework—especially with math. Mom is working, and always seems so busy. It's not the same with her.

Older children may also be required to assume much more responsibility for family functioning: cooking, housekeeping, even earning money to support the family. This is usually a maturing experience for them, but it is an adjustment. Some children, used to having everything, have a hard time realizing that money is short and that they can't buy the clothes and other things they used to.

Special adjustments are necessary, of course, when the parent caring for the children begins to date again and to get emotionally involved with another person. Now the children must share their parent with another adult. If the parent remarries, as the majority do, the children are confronted with a total readjustment to a stepparent (Rice, 1978b).

Adult Adjustments after Divorce

The problems of adjustment after divorce may be grouped into a number of categories (Bohannan, 1971):

- Getting over the emotional trauma of divorce
- Dealing with the attitudes of society
- Loneliness and the problem of social readjustment
- Finances
- Realignment of responsibilities and work roles
- Sexual readjustments
- Contacts with ex-spouse
- Kinship interaction

Emotional Trauma

Under the best of circumstances, divorce is an emotionally disturbing experience. Under the worst conditions, it may result in a high degree of shock and disorientation. Krantzler (1974) refers to divorce as an emotional crisis triggered by a sudden loss. He speaks of the emotional turmoil before and during divorce, the shock and crisis of separation, a time of mourning as the relationship is laid to rest, and a period of disruption as one attempts to regain balance. Sometimes the emotional trauma of divorce comes primarily from a drawn-out and bitter legal battle (Kay, 1970). In these cases, the actual divorce decree comes as a welcome relief from this long period of pain.

The trauma is greater when one spouse wants the divorce and the other doesn't, when the idea comes unexpectedly, when there is very little time to consider the idea, when one continues to be emotionally attached to the other after the divorce, or when friends and family disapprove of the whole idea (Goode, 1965).

There seems to be a definite relationship between age at the time of divorce and the amount of trauma. Younger people in marriages of long duration experience the highest trauma. For older people the pattern is reversed, divorce after a long marriage seems less traumatic (Goode, 1965). For most couples, the decision to divorce is viewed as an "end of the rope" decision, which is reached, on the average, during a period of about two years. The time of greatest trauma is usually at the time of final separation, not at the time of the final decree, but then comes a long period of realization that the relationship is over emotionally as well as legally (Krantzler, 1974). The fact that the suicide rate for divorcees is three times that of married women and four times as great for divorced males as for married men indicates that being divorced is no emotional picnic.

Attitudes of Society

Part of the trauma of divorce is experienced because of the attitudes of society toward divorce and divorced persons (Brandwein, Brown, and Fox, 1974; Honig, 1974; LeMasters, 1973; Miller, 1970; and Staples, 1971). In the eyes of some, divorce represents moral failure, evidence of personal inadequacy, or of deviant behavior, which society condemns (Kay, 1970). It takes a lot of courage to make known publicly that one has failed, because it exposes that person to social ridicule and condemnation. As a result, some persons never get divorced when in fact they should. Or if they do, they retreat from family and friends for a considerable period of time (Carter and Glick, 1970). Some discover that the people they thought they could count on have deserted them. "Friends," one woman remarked bitterly, "they drop you like a hot potato" (Bohannan, 1971, p. 487).

Research indicates that the majority of divorced persons are ashamed that they have been divorced and try to keep it from new friends. Their children too feel stigmatized and try to hide the fact of divorce, primarily because of the attitudes of teachers and other parents. All of these attitudes make the fact of divorce harder to live with. Negative attitudes are lessening as divorce becomes more common, but such feelings still exist.

Loneliness and Social Readjustment

Even if two married people did not get along, they kept one another company. At least they knew that someone else was in the house. After divorce, they begin to realize what it is like to live alone. This adjustment is especially hard on those without children or whose children are living with the other spouse. Holidays are especially hard on those who are lonely. Krantzler (1974) relates: "I celebrated Christmas one day late with my daughter. As on Thanksgiving, I was alone on Christmas and wept without shame over my solitary state and for the past I would never know again" (p. 24).

One of the things divorced persons complain about the most is the difficulty in rebuilding their social life. "I can't seem to meet any women who are right for me." "How on earth do you get back into circulation after nine years of marriage?" "Where are all those divorced men I used to hear about?" Numerous authorities suggest that the friendship and companionship of other people is one of the most essential ingredients for a successful readjustment after divorce, so getting involved with others is important (Goode, 1971; Hunt, 1971).

Finances

Most divorced persons suffer financial hardship and are forced to lower their standard of living. Men who are forced to pay heavy alimony and child support payments may have little money for years (George and Welding, 1972). Wives who have never worked or who have no special education or skills, and who now have the custody of one or more children, find themselves completely impoverished (Ferris, 1971).

The former husbands of many of these women do not provide much help. Various studies indicate that only about one-third of ex-husbands contribute at all to the support of their ex-wives and children (Kriesberg, 1970). One study in Wisconsin showed that only 38 percent of fathers were in full compliance with the support order. Four years after the divorce, 67 percent of the fathers had ceased providing any money (Citizens Advisory Council, 1972). As a consequence, many mothers with children need welfare assistance (Stein, 1970). The effect of all this is a lowered standard of living, with less income and the need to move to poorer housing and a poorer neighborhood, often with more delinquency, poorer schools, and other concomitant social conditions that affect the family (Weisman and Psykel, 1972).

Realignment of Responsibilities and Work Roles

The divorced woman with children is faced with the prospect of an overload of work. Now she must perform all family functions, which were formerly shared by two persons. If she works outside the home, she is faced with an eighteen-hour day, seven days a week, and 365 days a year. She also has to readjust her parenthood role to include taking over functions formerly fulfilled by her husband. Some women lack the training and experience to assume the role of authority, protector, and counselor for the children (Bern and Bern, 1971). As a consequence, the children listen to them less, so these mothers have more problems controlling and guiding the children.

The roles of the divorced man also change, especially if he is a traditional male who was used to depending upon his wife for household care and personal maintenance. Krantzler confesses his chauvinistic and sexist longings.

How could I have taken for granted those chores which my wife had performed all these years, and which I now had to struggle with unassisted? . . . The dirty linen was constantly out of control. . . . My cooking was lousy. . . . Everytime I walked into the apartment, it seemed to punish me for walking out on the comfortable home of my past. How I longed for someone to take care of me (Krantzler, 1974, p. 12).

If, in addition, a father also has custody of his children, his responsibilities are total. So whether male or female, the solo parent has to fulfill all family functions and has no relief from his or her burden.

Sexual Readjustments

A 1973 study revealed that most divorced persons are sexually quite active. Hunt found only 9 percent of divorced women who were not sexually active. Those who were active had a median of 3.5 sexual partners per year. Divorced males had a median of 8 different sexual partners per year. Apparently, the complaint of sexual frustration that was common among divorced people a decade ago has been partially eliminated. In addition, formerly married men and women make frequent use of masturbation as a way of releasing sexual tensions when other sexual outlets are not available (Masters and Johnson, 1970).

This does not mean, however, that all of these sexual contacts are emotionally satisfying. Some divorced persons speak of meaningless sex, using sex to find companionship, to prove sexual attractiveness, or as an escape from problems. Divorced women complain frequently that they are often the targets of sexually aggressive males who believe that because they are experienced they are likely to be promiscuous (Fireston, 1970).

Contacts with Ex-Spouse

The more upsetting the divorce has been and the more vindictive the spouse, the less the other person wants to have any postdivorce contact. This is particularly true in cases of remarriage. Most second wives or husbands object to contacts with former spouses, because such contacts usually lead to resentment and conflicts. This is especially true if a bitter ex-spouse tries to cause trouble for the new couple.

When contacts are maintained, it is usually in relation to the children and/or support money (Mead, 1970). When the children have problems, both parents become concerned and sometimes correspond or talk to one another about these problems. In this case, an amicable relationship helps them to work things out. Often, however, couples have to turn to the courts to settle disputes after the divorce.

Most of the postdivorce disputes are in relation to visitation rights, child support, or alimony. Some cities have "Fathers Day" in court, when fathers are taken to task for not making payments on time. Other disputes may occur if a former husband seeks to reduce alimony payments or a wife to increase them.

In contrast to these situations, there are some couples that remain friends. One woman commented:

My former husband and I get along better now than when we were married. He came over for dinner the other night, I cooked, and we had a pleasant evening. It's strange, but when we were married, we fought all the time. Now we are really good friends.

Amicable relationships are easier on the children, but they are not frequent. Occasionally, couples end up remarrying. Westman and Cline (1973) mention one extreme case where a couple had separated from each other seventeen times with three divorces and eighteen reconciliations.

Kinship Interaction

Contacts with parents and siblings usually remain about the same after a divorce. One study showed that almost one-fifth of the individuals increased their contacts with their relatives after the divorce, primarily because of affectional needs, sometimes because of the need for assistance (Spicer and Hampe, 1975). Bernard writes:

Assistance, such as money or clothing, was vital, but having people who could give advice, encouragement, and understanding was even more central to the respondents' morale (Bernard, 1971, p. 39).

Remarriage

Who Remarries and When

At the present time, about one in four marriages are second marriages for one or both of the couple (Glick and Norton, 1971). In the next decade, close to one in three marriages may be second marriages. About 87 percent of all divorced men and about 86 percent of all

Over 80 percent of divorced couples remarry.

divorced women eventually remarry (Carter and Glick, 1970). About one-fourth of the remarriages take place within a year, one-half within three years, and three-fourths within nine years of the divorce. The median duration between the divorce and second marriage is 3.1 years for males and 3.4 for females. Black men and women usually wait longer to remarry than do whites. The median age of remarriage is in the early thirties for women and in the middle thirties for men (United States Department of Health, Education and Welfare, 1973b). Of course, the younger people are when they get divorced the greater their chances of remarrying.

The majority of those remarrying are divorced rather than widowed. Divorced men have a remarriage rate five times greater than widowers; divorced women have a remarriage rate twelve and a half times greater than widows. Part of these differences are due to the younger ages of the divorced as compared to those whose mates are deceased. Only after age fifty-five do the numbers of widows and widowers remarrying exceed the numbers of divorced remarrying (United States Department of Health, Education and Welfare, 1973b).

Partners

Most persons marry those of like marital status. More than 90 percent of single men and women marry other single persons. More than half of divorced men and women marry divorced partners, and about half of widowers and widows select each other (United States Department of Health, Education and Welfare, 1973b).

How Successful?

The research on marriage and divorce contains little data on the outcome of remarriage, and some contradictory findings have yet to be resolved. Two such issues involve whether remarriages are more unstable than first marriages of divorced persons. The only really valid method of resolving these issues is to follow the marital history of a representative population group. This was done by Riley and Spreitzer (1974) with a sample of 1,445 white males and 520 white females from three different sections of the country who were in the forty-five to fifty-four age bracket. This sample had somewhat higher rates of separation and divorce than found in the general population because it represented those who had applied for disability benefits with social security (disability introduces stress into the marital relationship.) The data are significant for the population studied, however, and show that the second marriages of both the divorced and widowed were no more likely to end in divorce or separation than were first marriages. Other data are also beginning to show that remarriages, especially of males, are no more likely to end in divorce than are first marriages (Glick and Norton, 1971).

Quality of Remarriages

Divorce statistics only tell part of the story about remarriages. What about their quality? Most studies indicate that remarriages are happier. Ninety-two percent of the remarried women in Goode's (1965) study indicated that their second marriages were better than their first. One of the reasons is that remarried couples are older, more experienced, and highly motivated to make their marriages work. "The most distinguishing characteristic of second marriages," says a New York marriage counselor, "is sweat. They really work at it" (Rollin, 1973, p. 493).

Stepchildren

This does not mean that remarriages are problem free. One of the biggest problems arises when there are children living at home. Adolescent stepchildren, particularly, have difficulty in accepting their new stepfather or stepmother (Rice, 1978). One reason is they are jealous of the attention their own parent gives his or her mate (who is the stepparent). Another reason is that they feel their primary loyalty is toward their own parents and that the stepparent is an intruder. This was dramatically illustrated in the case of a new wife who was greeting her husband's older daughter for the first time. Naturally, the woman was anxious to make a good impression. "I'm your new mother!" she cooed. "The hell you are," replied the daughter and stamped out of the room (Bowerman and Irish, 1973, p. 494). This case is not unusual. One of the typical reactions of a stepchild to a stepparent is rejection. "You're not my father," or "you're not my mother." This apparent rejection is hard for the stepparent to take and sometimes leads to a battle of wills, a contest over authority, or to resentment and bitterness. If children are infants when parents divorce and remarry, they usually grow up accepting the stepparent as substitute mother or father.

Adjustments with stepfathers are usually easier than with stepmothers, primarily because stepmothers play a more active role in relation to the children and spend more time with them than do the stepfathers (Duberman, 1973). Also, fairy tales and folklore have developed the stereotype of the cruel stepmother, a myth that is hard to overcome. Problems are also greater if the parent without custody tries to get a child to dislike the stepparent. If there are stepsiblings living together, trouble may also ensue if the natural parents show favoritism to their own children. If this happens, resentment and jealousy are likely to occur.

In contrast to these examples, others might be given to show very satisfactory stepchild-stepparent relationships. One mother spoke of her husband's relationship with her child:

He's always referred to her as his daughter rather than as his stepdaughter. He never made any issue of her being a stepchild. There are times when I think she is closer to him then she is to me. He is more her father than her real father ever was or is now (Duberman, 1973, p. 285).

Relationships between stepsiblings also can be quite harmonious.

Our boys are the same age to the day. They are just like brothers. His son and my son are more alike than the two real brothers are. They all refer to each other as brothers; they are like one family (Duberman, 1973, p. 286).

Out of a total of eighty-eight couples who had remarried and had stepchildren, Duberman found that 64 percent of the families could be voted excellent as measured by a parent-child relationships score. However, in these reconstituted families with two groups of children—hers and his—the relationship between the stepsiblings was excellent in only 24 percent of the cases and rated poor in 38 percent. Apparently, stepparents and stepchildren have an easier time adjusting to one another than do stepsiblings. (For additional information, see my book, *Stepparenting* (Rice, 1978b).)

Conclusions

This chapter raises a number of important questions. Should couples preserve a marriage for the sake of their children? Should divorce laws be made more strict or more lenient? Should couples be able to get a divorce on demand without contest and with a minimum of effort and expense? Should payment of alimony be allowed?

One of the most important factors in divorce is its effects on children. What can divorcing couples do to minimize the trauma for children? What is the best way for couples to handle the whole situation? How can the laws and court procedures be changed to benefit children?

Often, family members, friends, and even the children of divorcing parents are not cognizant of the emotional upset and the enormous problems of adjustment that divorce brings to the couple. How can friends and family help them? What should be the roles of family members? How can children help their parents who are getting a divorce? How do the attitudes of society make a divorce a more upsetting experience? How do welfare laws affect divorce and its consequences?

When couples remarry, as the majority do, what factors affect their marriage the most? Should couples have to wait a certain period of time before getting married again? How can parents best help children and stepchildren to adjust to the new situation? Why do stepmothers and stepfathers have such a wicked image? What can be done to change this image?

After four years of marriage, Ron and Meredith Clifton decided that they wanted a divorce. The couple lived in eastern Massachusetts. Since the state legislature had enacted a no-fault divorce provision, which added "irretrievable breakdown of the marriage" to the seven fault grounds already in effect, the Cliftons filed under what they assumed was the most amicable ground for dissolution of the marriage. But they soon discovered that no-fault divorce was more complicated than they had expected. This excerpt from a recorded conversation between Meredith and her lawyer, Mr. Smith, reveals some of the problems that can arise.

Meredith: I have the impression that Ron has changed his mind. I thought everything was settled three months ago. Why am I here?

Lawyer: A problem has arisen, Meredith. You see, even a no-fault divorce can be disputed. Your husband has objected to the settlement you requested. He doesn't want to pay your household improvement expenses above $1,500, nor bills incurred on your credit cards.

Meredith: That stinker! He's being vindictive. Now that things are nearly over he's trying to get in one last dig by fouling up the agreement. He's the one who convinced me to apply for a no-fault divorce. I should have known! He agreed to everything before we filed, so long as I didn't sue him for cruelty. I don't understand. Didn't he sign the agreement? How can he get away with this?

Lawyer: You both signed the sworn affidavit claiming no-fault. You did not file a separation agreement, and now since you cannot yet agree on a financial settlement, we must discuss the next step.

Meredith: I guess we'll have to go to court to see what the judge says.

Lawyer: That's not so simple. Do you still want a no-fault divorce?

Meredith: Sure, but what are you driving at?

Lawyer: The difficulty, you see, is that under fault, if the parties cannot agree on the terms of divorce, the court imposes the terms. Under no-fault, the couple has to work out the terms.

Meredith: But we may never be able to agree on terms.

Lawyer: In that case, you may have to file for a new hearing to change the divorce to fault.

Meredith: That will take us forever to settle.

Lawyer: No, in fact, it would be quicker, though less happy than no-fault. When uncontested, no-fault takes eighteen to twenty months and in difficult cases two years. After the complaint and affidavit are filed, we would have three months to file a separation agreement. The hearing would come up in thirty days after that. If matters were satisfactory to the court, there would be a ten-month waiting period and another six months before the divorce became final.

Meredith: And under fault, how long?

Lawyer: A fault divorce would come up for a hearing in two-and-a-half months. If granted, the divorce would become final six months after that, according to Massachusetts law. What you must weigh before making a decision is the trauma of a fault contest upon yourself and the children against the probability of reaching some agreement with Ron under no-fault. But even with an agreement, you'll still have to wait sixteen months after the hearing before a no-fault divorce is final.

Meredith: That's maddening. If I have to, I'll prove it's his fault. When we began all this I felt that neither of us was innocent. I could see that both of us were to blame for letting our marriage fail.

Lawyer: Do you believe he'll fight?

Meredith: I don't know. It'll be a lot more expensive. I need some time to think about it. I don't see him. I don't talk to him. I don't know him anymore. Why must we keep on punishing each other?

QUESTIONS

1. What are the pros and cons of no-fault versus fault divorce in Massachusetts as revealed by the above conversation?

2. What are the pros and cons of no-fault versus fault divorce in your state (assuming your state has a no-fault provision)?

3. Under what circumstances is no-fault advantageous? Under what conditions is it not? Why?

4. Should it be necessary for Ron and Meredith to fight it out in court? What are possible effects upon them and the children? What should they do?

5. What protection is provided children under no-fault legislation?

6. Are legal fees a significant factor in deciding upon fault versus no-fault divorce? Explain.

7. Evaluate the total expenses of a divorce under no-fault versus fault legislation.

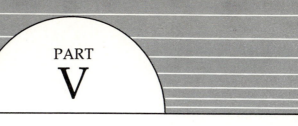

Parenthood

CHAPTER 17

Family Planning, Pregnancy, Prenatal Care, and Childbirth

CHAPTER OUTLINE

The Importance of Family Planning

Hormonal Control: The Pill

Chemical and Spermicides

Mechanical Devices

Sterilization

Attempts at Birth Control Without Devices

Which Method?

Successful Family Planning

Birth Defects

Pregnancy

Prenatal Care

Preparation for Parenthood

The Hospital, Labor, Delivery

After Childbirth

Conclusions

Planned parenthood means having children by choice and not by chance. It means that a couple have only the number of children they want and can take care of and at the time they want them (Bahr, Chadwick, and Stauss, 1975). But to do this effectively requires sound knowledge of birth control methods and motivation to use them.

But the thought of becoming parents raises some important concerns. Couples are concerned about having healthy babies. They want to know if they can conceive healthy children. If they have any health or medical problems or physical defects, they want to know if their children will be affected. Increased knowledge about the effects of maternal illnesses, age of the mother, nutrition, drugs, radiation, emotional factors, and birth injuries to a child cause couples to worry. This worry was only recently expressed by a young woman who asked: "If you have taken LSD, will this have any effect upon future children?" It is a thoughtful question and one many people are asking.

Couples also continue to ask some of the same questions their grandparents asked. How do you know if you're pregnant? What can you do about **morning sickness**? What are some of the major complications of pregnancy? What about sex relations when you're pregnant?

In addition to these traditional concerns, couples want information on prepared childbirth and on the various childbirth methods. Many young husbands want to be actively involved in the process, instead of waiting out the ordeal of childbirth pacing the waiting room. Expectant mothers ask for information on physical conditioning and exercises, and on infant care. Couples are questioning hospital and nursery room policies and want to know about newer developments such as the **Leboyer method** of childbirth and about **rooming-in.** A revived interest in breast feeding is developing also.

These are important concerns and indicate the seriousness with which many couples contemplate their future as prospective parents.

The Importance of Family Planning

There are important reasons why family planning is necessary. One is to protect the health of the mother, another to safeguard the welfare of children. Family planning is necessary also for the good of the marriage and the family. Having too many children or having them too early in the relationship imposes strains on the marriage (Cutright, 1971; Figley, 1973; Renee, 1970). In recent years, much emphasis has been placed on the humanitarian and ecological importance of family planning (Corman and Schaefer, 1973). At the present rate of population growth, which is about 2 percent per year, the world will double in population every thirty-five years. The world now has more than 4 billion people. Can it support double that number by the year 2015? Family planning then becomes, of necessity, one of the most important human-

"Since you ask, I had you, Samantha, because the birthrate was falling; and you, David, as revenge on society; and you, Mark, as a bid for lost youth; and you, Jason, were a mistake."

© Punch/Rothco

itarian problems with which any couple is faced.

Hormonal Control: The Pill

Use and Action

Oral contraceptives contain two synthetically produced female sex hormones that are chemically similar to ones the woman already produces in her body. These natural hormones are **estrogen** and **progesterone** (**progestin** is the artificially produced equivalent). When these two hormones are present in sufficient quantities in the woman's blood stream, conception is prevented in four ways (Beacham and Beacham, 1972; Garcia, 1970):

1. **Ovulation** is prevented in about 90 percent of the menstrual cycles.
2. When a woman takes a birth control pill, the *cervical mucus* remains thick, sticky, and sparse throughout the month, blocking the entrance to the uterus and making penetration by the sperm difficult.
3. The pill also alters the *endometrium*, the inner lining of the uterus so that successful implantation and nourishment of a possible fertilized ovum is difficult.

4. And finally, the hormones may actually affect the transport of the egg cell down the Fallopian tube (Guttmacher, 1973).

Effectiveness

All of these effects make the birth control pill the single most effective chemical contraceptive used. Since some users are careless, however, the actual pregnancy rate for combination pills is seven unplanned pregnancies per 1,000 women per year (Guttmacher, 1973).

Advantages

The pill is convenient and easy to use (Westoff and Westoff, 1971). Uneducated, low socioeconomic status women can take the pill reliably and faithfully. This is important, since no contraceptive is effective if it is not used.

Types and Administration

There are several types of pills. *Combination pills* contain estrogen and progestin (a synthetic progesterone derivative). The woman begins taking her pill on the fifth day of her period, counting the first day of menstruation as day one. She takes the pill for twenty-one days, then omits the medication for seven days. Some brands have a different color pill, a placebo (sometimes containing iron), which the woman takes each day for the 7 days, before recommencing the twenty-one-day regimen. Usually menstruation begins about seventy-two hours after ceasing the regular pill. It continues for four or five days before the regular pill is taken again. Since the pill is a prescription drug, it should never be taken without a prior physical examination and a doctor's prescription and guidance (Arnstein, 1973; Pierson and D'Antonia, 1974).

A *morning-after pill* is seldom given because it has not been approved by the Food and Drug Administration for general use. This pill, which may be administered orally or by injection, consists of heavy dosages of estrogen compounds that are given daily for three to five days following intercourse. The effect of this medication is to prevent implantation of the fertilized egg or zygote in the uterine wall. Physicians will begin this treatment as late as seventy-two hours after coitus, although most prefer to begin within twenty-four hours.

While postcoital estrogen is quite effective in preventing pregnancy, it is not recommended by doctors as a routine contraceptive because of possible severe side effects: gastrointestinal upset, vomiting, nausea, possible long-term toxicity, or prolonged menses (Guttmacher 1973). Authorities worry too about possible links with cancer, particularly in women with a family history of breast or cervical cancer.

A newer form of pill, called the **minipill** because it contains only progestin, is now being sold. This pill is taken every day for twenty-eight days, but the small dosage does not prevent either ovulation or menstruation. Yet the likelihood of impregnation is greatly reduced, either by altering the sperm cells within the tubes or by interfering with the passage of the egg down the tube. Minipills do produce fewer side effects, but they have a higher failure rate (Ecstein et al., 1972; Mears et al., 1969). More research needs to be done on them to determine the future possibilities of their use. They are prescribed very infrequently at the present time.

Risk of Thromboembolism

One of the most serious worries about using the pill is the worry that it may cause blood clots (*thrombosis*) and possible transference of clots through the blood stream (*embolism*) to some distant organ. The most common sites for clot formations are the veins of the pelvis and leg. If these clots travel to vital organs, such as the lungs (*pulmonary embolism*) or the brain (*cerebral thrombosis*), grave illness or death can occur. What are the possibilities?

Research findings in the United States consistently show a strong association between the pill and thromboembolism although the risks are small (Tindall, 1971). The original evidence was disturbing enough to result in hearings before a Senate investigation committee, however, and in a marked reduction in the dosage of estrogen in the pill, since it was found that lower dosages resulted in less risk (Inman et al., 1970; Westoff and Westoff, 1971). One of the important findings is that there is a marked increase in risk with age. Deaths per 100,000 users attributable to the pill from blood-clotting diseases including *coronary thrombosis* is 1.3 for women 20 to 29; 4.8 for women 30 to 34; 7.8 for women 35 to 39, and 46.4 for women 40 and over ("About New Report on 'The Pill'," 1975). On the basis of these findings the FDA sent a warning bulletin to doctors suggesting they advise patients older than forty to change to some other contraceptive. Not enough data is available yet to determine the risks of the minipill, which contains no estrogen (Ecstein, et al., 1972; Mears et al., 1969).

Risk of Cancer

Research into the full relationship of the pill to various forms of cancer is not expected to show conclusive results for a number of years. In the meanwhile, all the FDA can say on the basis of available evidence is that the relationship between estrogen in the pill and cancer "can neither be confirmed nor refuted at this time" ("About New Report on 'The Pill'," 1975; Peel and Potts, 1969; Vessey, Doll, and Sutton, 1972). It is known that the administration of estrogen to women who already have breast cancer may cause the cancer to grow (Kistner, 1969). Aggravating already existing cancer, however, and causing it to start, are two different things. The former has been proved. The latter has not been proved or disproved at the present time.

No link has been established between the use of combination pills and endometrial cancer (cancer of the inner lining of the uterus). Progestins alone have been used successfully throughout the world to achieve remission of endometrial cancer already present. Estrogen will cause a more rapid growth of already existing *fibroid* (nonmalignant) *tumors* of the uterus. For this reason, estrogen is contraindicated in cases of detectable existing malignancies. Women who take estrogen alone during and after *menopause* are five to fourteen times more likely to develop endometrial cancer. For this reason, the Food and Drug Administration is reviewing the facts to determine if new guidelines are needed for use of estrogen. *Cancer of the cervix* differs from cancer of the breast or of the endometrium in that it demonstrates no response whatsoever to estrogens or progestins (Kistner, 1969).

Birth Defects

There is increasing evidence that if women take the pill in the early stages of pregnancy birth defects of male **fetuses** can result (Kistner, 1969). Therefore, doctors want to make certain the woman is not already pregnant before she starts taking the pill.

Sexual Drive and Frequency of Intercourse

The effect of taking the pill on sexual drive and frequency of intercourse is variable (Peel and Potts, 1969). There seems to be some evidence that long-term usage of the pill may decrease sexual drive. In answer to a questionnaire distributed by the American College of Obstetricians and Gynecologists, 31 percent of the doctors blamed the pill for a reduction in the sex drive of their patients, while 24 percent reported that it increased the libido of patients. Masters and Johnson report a reduction in women's sex drive after taking the pill for eighteen to thirty-six months. They suggest that other methods be substituted from time to time to give the woman's system a chance to restore its hormonal balance.

Overall, the frequency of sexual relations of women on the pill seems to increase (Westoff, Bumpass, and Ryder, 1971). This is due to the alleviation of the fear of pregnancy and elimination of the mechanical unpleasantness of other birth control methods.

Fertility

One of the questions that arises is the effect of the pill on subsequent fertility after the patient stops taking it. Generally, the woman reverts back to her pre-pill condition. A minority of women who have been on the pill become more fertile after ceasing to take it, usually because of more regular menstruation and ovulation. One study compared women who had been on the pill with those who used other methods of contraception and found that those who had been on the pill waited an average of 2.3 months to conceive. The other women waited an average of 2.1 months (Westoff and Westoff, 1971).

Other Side Effects

Other side effects of the pill are variable, differing with different persons and with different brand names of the pill. Many of the unpleasant effects disappear after a patient becomes adjusted to the pill or after the doctor adjusts brands or dosage. Some side effects include nausea, breast tenderness or discharge, fluid retention, increased appetite and weight gain, increased vaginal discharge, increased vaginal or urinary tract infections, nervous reactions such as depression, hypertension, irritability, elevation of blood pressure, or migraine headaches. The pill may also cause a slight increase in blood sugar, a decrease in folic acid (one of the B-complex vitamins) and of vitamin B-6. In some cases, persons have to be taken off of the pill because unpleasant side effects become too serious or can't be eliminated. One positive effect is an increase in levels of both copper and iron and fewer incidences of iron-deficiency anemia (Kistner, 1969).

The individual physician will decide who should or should not take the pill based upon information received from giving a thorough medical examination and after taking a complete medical history of each patient (Kogan, 1973).

Chemicals and Spermicides

Foams, Creams, Jellies

Contraceptive foams, creams, or *jellies* are chemicals that are used to prevent conception. They work in two ways: by blocking the entrance to the uterus and by immobilizing and killing the sperm. To be most effective, they are inserted in the very back of the vagina, over the cervix, and not more than five to fifteen minutes before ejaculation (McCary, 1973) (see figure 17-1). Additional applications must be made each time intercourse is repeated. The foam that comes in an aerosol can is the most effective of the three types since it spreads more evenly and blocks the cervix more adequately than the other types. Estimates of failure rates run from 32 to 50 percent, with the lower rates achieved with the foam (Westoff and Westoff, 1971). Some

women can't use the chemicals because of burning and other adverse reactions. Urinary tract infections also become a problem for some women.

Douching

Douching is used to try to flush sperm from the vagina. At best, douching is not a very effective means of contraception since (1) the sperm may already have entered the cervix or (2) the jet of water may push them up into it. Douching has one of the highest rates of failure of any contraceptive technique (Guttmacher, 1973).

Mechanical Devices

IUD

The IUD or *intrauterine device* is usually made of plastic but sometimes of metal and is placed in the uterus to prevent pregnancy. It comes in various sizes and shapes: coils, rings, loops, bows, double S, T'shape, springs, and others (Zipper et al., 1971). The IUD must be inserted by a physician who first exposes the cervix with a vaginal speculum, loads an inserter with an IUD, and then threads the device through the cervical canal and into the uterine cavity where it is deposited. The device is "unwound" into a straight line while in the inserter, but when released in the uterus, resumes its former shape (Guttmacher, 1973).

Just how the IUD works is not known for certain. Several possible explanations have been offered. One is that the egg cell is fertilized but prevented from implanting itself in the wall of the uterus (Davis, 1971). Another possibility, for which evidence is accumulating, is that the IUD causes demonstrable changes in the uterine fluids that affect sper-

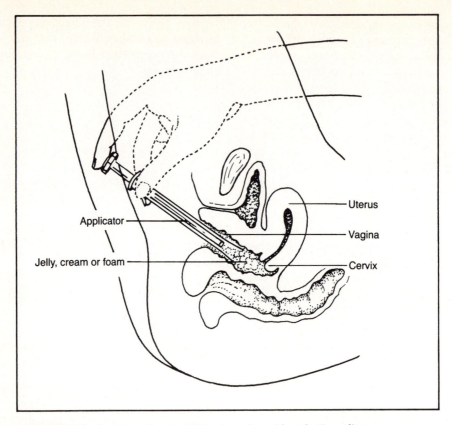

Applicator

Jelly, cream or foam

Uterus

Vagina

Cervix

FIGURE 17-1   *Insertion of spermicidal preparation with a plastic applicator*

matozoa adversely, destroying them before they can fertilize the egg cell (Davis, 1972; Moyer and Mishell, 1971; Tatum, 1972). Another explanation, not yet demonstrated, is that the IUD increases tubal activity causing the hastening of the passage of the ovum through the Fallopian tube so that the egg is never prepared for fertilization (Davis and Lenski, 1970). However it works, the failure rate is about 2 to 10 percent the first year, the exact percentage depending upon whose figures one accepts (Guttmacher, 1973; Westoff and Westoff, 1971). The highest percentages occur when a woman expels the IUD without realizing it. The rate of failure is only 2 to 3 percent when the woman retains the IUD. Overall, 20 to 40 percent of women either

expel the IUD or have it removed because of side effects (Pierson, 1971).

Condom

The *condom* or "safe" is usually made of thin, strong latex rubber or, less frequently, of animal gut and is inserted over the end of the penis and then unrolled to enclose the penile shaft. Condoms come in different styles (and now even in different colors). Some have a teat on the end to receive the ejaculate. If the condom doesn't have this feature, it can be unrolled on the penis so as to leave a half-inch space or overlap at the end to receive the semen. Other models come packaged singly in fluid, which provide lubrication and allow the penis to be inserted into the vagina easily. If a condom is not lubricated, a contraceptive jelly or cream may be used to aid intromission and to prevent the condom from tearing on insertion.

Condoms are the best method, except abstinence, of preventing the spread of veneral disease. They are a fairly reliable method of birth control, with a failure rate of about 5 to 15 per hundred couples. When failure occurs it is due to one or more of several reasons: the condom has a hole in it; it ruptures; it slips off; or it is reused (Tietze, 1970). If not thoroughly cleansed before being reused, live sperm may remain on the condom. Condoms are used by 7 to 17 percent of all married couples practicing contraception and, more frequently, by couples outside of marriage (Guttmacher, 1973; Westoff, 1972). The biggest objection comes from men who complain that they dull sensation during intercourse.

The Diaphragm

The *diaphragm* is a thick rubber or latex dome-shaped cap stretched over a collapsible metal ring, designed to cover the mouth of the cervix. It comes in a variety of sizes and must be fitted by the physician to each individual woman. A snug fit is especially important, since its effectiveness as a contraceptive depends on its forming an impenetrable shield over the entrance to the uterus (see figure 17-2). If the fit it not right, the sperm can get around the edges of the diaphragm and enter the cervix. For this reason, the largest diaphragm a woman can wear comfortably is advised, since under sexual excitement the back portion of the vagina enlarges (Masters and Johnson, 1966). After childbirth, a woman always requires a larger size diaphragm. Also, a size change may be in order whenever a woman gains or loses fifteen pounds. To add to its effectiveness, about a spoonful of sper-

micidal cream or jelly is smeared in the cup fitting against the cervix and about the rim to create a protective seal. For additional protection, foam should be inserted into the vagina after the diaphragm is in place. The diaphragm should not be removed until at least six hours after intercourse. With the jelly or cream and foam, the failure rate is from 4 to 10 percent. Without the foam, but with the spermicide around the rim, the failure rate may be 12 to 18 percent (Westoff and Westoff, 1971).

Sterilization

Vasectomy

Male sterilization or **vasectomy** has become increasingly popular as a means of birth control. It is now estimated that almost a million vasectomies are performed in the United States each year (Fleishman and Dixon, 1973; Presser and Bumpass, 1972). It is a simple operation, requiring only fifteen to thirty minutes in the doctor's office, is relatively inexpensive, and is effective in 99 percent of the cases (Guttmacher, 1973). When failure occurs, it is due to a spontaneous rejoining of the two severed ends of the vas deferens, which grow together again, to a failure on the part of the doctor to tie an accessory vas (some men have three or four), or to a lack of precautions in using other contraceptives until an examination of sperm reveals a count of zero. Sometimes doctors suspect that failure has been due to infidelity on the part of the wife rather than failure of the surgical technique.

There are a number of misconceptions regarding vasectomies. A vasectomy does not involve **castration,** which is the removal of the testicles. In vasectomy, the male continues to ejaculate semen, but it contains no sperm. His physical ability to have sexual relations is

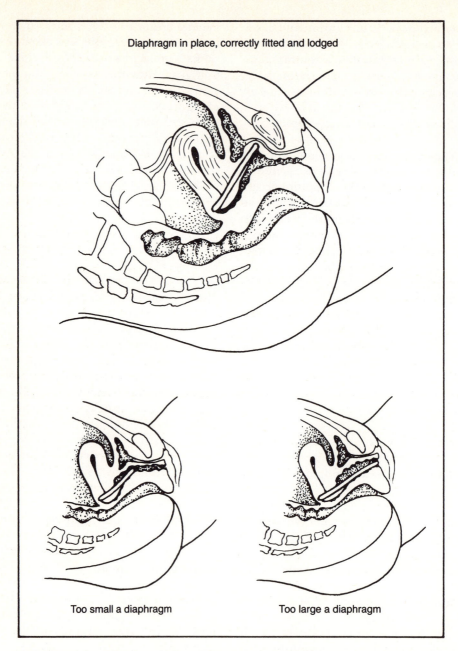

FIGURE 17-2. *Diaphragm in place, correctly fitted and lodged*

not in any way affected; he still has erection, orgasm, and ejaculation as usual; his masculinity is in no way affected; his voice, body hair, musculature, beard growth, and so on remain unchanged; male hormones are still produced and released by the testicles into the blood stream as usual (Fleishman and Dixon, 1973).

Vasectomy should be considered permanent, since the chances of rejoining the vas through surgery (*vasovasostomy*) are unpredictable. Experiments are being conducted in inserting various obstructions into the tubes, which can later be removed, to allow the sperm to pass once again. One clinic is experimenting with inserting a screw valve that can be turned on or off by the physician (Guttmacher, 1973).

An overwhelming majority of males who have vasectomies report they are glad they did and would recommend it to their friends. A large percentage (from 38 to 78 percent) expect and in fact report an increase in sexual desire and activity. From 1 to 2 percent of the men report a decrease in sex drive and activity. Many (22 to 60 percent) report no change. A little more than half of the males in one study reported that marital harmony had improved since their vasectomy (Fleishman and Dixon, 1973; Roberto, 1974). In spite of contrary evidence, some males do feel that vasectomy may lessen their masculinity and sexual drive (Mullen et al., 1973). Many psychiatrists recognize that vasectomy is psychologically harmful to some males or a source of worry to their wives. Other couples have strong religious compunctions against sterilization, making it morally unacceptable to them. For these reasons, couples will want to consider their decision very carefully.

Salpingectomy

Salpingectomy, or **tubal ligation,** is female sterilization by severing and or closing the Fallopian tubes so that mature egg cells and sperm cannot pass through the tube (Haskins, 1972; Smith and Symmonds, 1971). Since the ovaries and the secretion of female hormones are in no way disturbed, there is no change in the women's femininity, physique, menstrual cycle, sexual interest, or sexual capacity. In most cases, her interest in sex and her sexual responsiveness improve because of removal of the fear of unwanted pregnancy. Hypothetically, salpingectomy is reversible in 50 to 66 percent of the cases, but it is not easily accomplished since it requires a second major operation. Few women ever request it.

In recent years, a new technique, **laparoscopy,** has been used extensively (Barton, 1972). With this method, the physician introduces a tubular instrument through the abdominal wall, usually through the navel, and cuts and electrically cauterizes the open ends of the Fallopian tubes (Wylie, 1972). The method is successful, is far simpler since the woman can leave the hospital the day of the operation or the following morning, and there are no cosmetic scars remaining.

Attempts at Birth Control Without Devices

The Rhythm Method

The *rhythm method* of birth control relies upon timing coitus so that it occurs only during the so-called "safe period" of the month: that period when the woman is most likely to be infertile (Bouvier, 1972). Although authorities differ in their time estimates, one can say with fair certainty that the ovum can be fertilized no longer than forty-eight hours after it is released and that the sperm can fertilize an ovum no longer than forty-eight hours after being ejaculated (McCary, 1973). The average woman ovulates fourteen days before her next menstrual period, with a common range of twelve to sixteen days. A few women ovulate regularly outside this common range, other women occasionally. Some are very irregular as to when they ovulate (Rock, 1970). Ovulation has been known to occur on any day of the cycle, including during menstruation itself. It is suspected that women may occasionally ovulate twice during a cycle, perhaps because of the stimulus of sexual excitement itself. While not completely substantiated in humans, coitus-induced ovulation is a distinct possibility (Clark and Zarrow, 1971). For these reasons, there really is no completely "safe period" of the month when a woman can't get pregnant.

Careful attention to one's individual cycle, by whatever means, can only minimize the possibility of pregnancy. Figure 17-3 illustrates schedules of fertile and infertile periods on a regular twenty-six- and on a thirty-one-day cycle and of a woman whose cycle is irregular from twenty-six to thirty-one days.

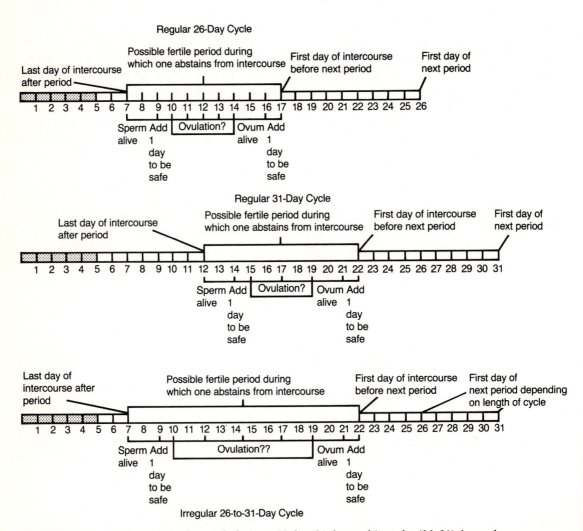

FIGURE 17-3. *Fertile and infertile periods during a 26-day, 31-day, and irregular (26–31) day cycle*

Since the woman who is irregular on a twenty-six- to thirty-one-day cycle never knows when ovulation occurs, nor when her next period will be, she will have to abstain for fifteen days instead of the usual ten. A woman whose cycle is irregular from twenty-four to thirty-one days can never find any "safe" period except during menstruation, since she has to abstain for nineteen days out of every month. Of course, these are only statistical calculations. As has been mentioned, one can't really be sure of any infertile period during any cycle. For this reason, the average failure rate is 30 percent (Westoff and Westoff, 1971). As can be seen from the figure, possible times for intercourse are severely limited, especially on the irregular cycle (Brayer, Chiazze, and Duffy, 1969).

Coitus interruptus refers to the practice of withdrawing the penis from the vagina before ejaculation occurs. While this method is better than nothing, its success depends upon a high degree of self-control on the part of the male (Segal and Tietze, 1971). Under sexual excitement, the normal male reaches a point beyond which ejaculatory control is impossible (Masters and Johnson, 1970). If he doesn't withdraw in time, he will ejaculate whether he wants to or not. Also, before orgasm, the male discharges a small amount of lubrication fluid that has been secreted by the Cowper's glands. The male is not aware of when this *preejaculate* is discharged, and since it often contains sperm cells that have been residing in the urethra, the sperm may be deposited before the man withdraws (Masters and Johnson, 1966; Sjovall, 1970). While the **sperm count** is low and fertilization is less likely than in actual orgasm, it can occur. Depending upon the care and timing of the man, withdrawal has a failure rate of 18 to 23 percent (Westoff and Westoff, 1971). One nationwide survey showed that the number of couples using withdrawal was less than 3 percent (Westoff, 1972). The greatest disadvantage to *coitus interruptus* is its interference with sexual satisfaction and pleasure of both the man and woman.

Noncoital Stimulation

Couples use a variety of techniques of stimulation to orgasm other than through intercourse. *Mutual masturbation* has been used for years as a substitute for intercourse. If the man gets semen on his fingers and introduces sperm into the vaginal canal, however, conception can happen (McCary, 1973). *Interfemoral stimulation* is a method whereby the male places his penis between the woman's closed thighs and rubs back and forth along the length of the clitoris. Climax may be reached in this way, but if the male ejaculates near the vaginal orifice, there is a possibility the sperm may find their way inside. *Oral-genital stimulation* is sometimes used, not only as a method of precoital love play but also as a technique of arousal to orgasm. It is as possible to transmit veneral disease through this means as through regular intercourse, since the mucous membranes of the mouth and tongue come into contact with the genitals.

Which Method?

The Ideal Contraceptive

To be ideal, a contraceptive would be: (1) 100 percent effective, (2) inexpensive, (3) convenient to use without any fuss or bother and without interfering with lovemaking, and (4) without any risk or adverse side effects. As of now, there is no one method that is ideal. In deciding on a method, a couple should consult their physician, weigh all factors one against the other, and make a choice based upon information that is as complete as possible.

Weighing the Risk

The Population Council has published a report that compares the risk of death due to the use of various contraceptives, including deaths from pregnancies that result from contraceptive failure ("Birth Control Deaths," 1976). Figure 17-4 illustrates the findings of this report. As can be seen, the IUD has the lowest risk factor throughout the life cycle, but it is useful only for those women who can retain one. The IUD, pill, condom, and diaphragm (with jelly) have about the same risk for women fifteen to twenty-nine years of age, at which time the risk from the condom and diaphragm more than doubles from twenty-nine and thirty-nine years of age. (The overall risk factor is still minimal, however). After age twenty-nine, the risk from the pill increases tremendously, and it becomes quite high for women after age forty. The risk of death from pregnancy is greater than that of using any method of birth control, except the risk involved in using the pill after age forty. Note also the increasing risk of abortions, especially after age twenty-nine. As can be seen, the use of chemical and spermicidal methods alone are not included in this graph, nor are sterilization techniques. The latter are among the most effective and safest methods, but their great disadvantage is their irreversibility and possible negative psychological effects for some persons. Therefore, the method to use is up to the couple in consultation with its physician (Scarlett, 1972). Many persons use a combination of methods at different times in their marriage.

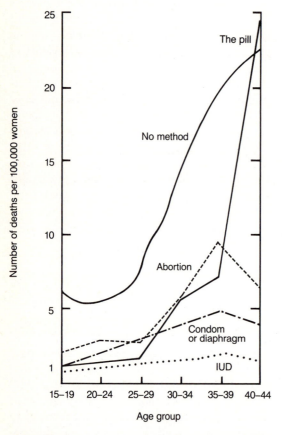

FIGURE 17-4. *Annual number of deaths per 100,000 women caused by various contraceptive methods (including deaths from pregnancies that result from contraceptive failure.) (Source: The Population Council.)*

Cost Factors

Cost factors are quite important for those with minimal resources or for choosing methods as a part of public policy (Kelley, 1972). Porter (1975) has calculated relative costs of each major type of birth control, assuming sexual intercourse 100 times a year over a thirty year period. Checkups and followups relating to each method are included in these costs. These include annual checkups after the first year for users of the diaphragm, IUD, and the pill. Sterilization of the male is by far the cheapest method except for rhythm or withdrawal. The pill is by far the most expensive. Mechanical and chemical contraceptive methods are in between in cost.

Successful Family Planning

First, successful family planning, requires shared responsibility of both the husband and wife.

Second, the primary reasons for contraceptive failure is lack of use or improper use. No method will work if not used. This means proper use every time, not just part of the time (Miller, 1973).

Third, unhealthy attitudes about sex itself, which leads to excessive guilt, shame, modesty, or fear, interfere with effective birth control practice, since negative feelings make it more difficult for couples to deal with the mechanics of birth control.

Fourth, the husband and wife need to talk about birth control, how they feel about the various methods, and their attitudes toward sterilization once they have the children they want (Jaco and Shephard, 1975).

Fifth, family planning and sexual satisfaction go together. What helps one, helps the other. Dislike or fear of intercourse makes it harder to use birth control, but use of birth control may help overcome this dislike or fear. Special thoughtfulness on the part of both husband and wife—each striving to understand the other's desires and fears—is most important to birth control success.

Birth Defects

Frequency

The great majority of babies are born healthy and normal. Occasionally, however, a child is born with a *congenital deformity;* that is, one that is present at the time of birth. Presently, one in sixteen is born with some sort of serious physical defect of body formation (Jones et al., 1970; The National Foundation, 1977).

Causes

Birth defects have three different causes: 1) *heredity,* 2) *a faulty environment* which prevents the child from developing normally, and 3) *birth injuries.* About 20 percent of all birth defects are inherited; that is, they are caused by faulty genes, examples of which are *Down syndrome, sickle cell anemia, muscular dystrophy,* and *cystic fibrosis.* Most of the remainder are due to a faulty environment or to a combination of factors, some being caused by injuries during the birth process itself (The National Foundation, 1977).

Genetic Counseling

Couples who have inherited disabilities or who have a family history of some type of disability might want to get **genetic counseling** before having children, to discover the possibility of passing on their defect to their children. This would be especially wise if the disorder were serious and/or found in both the prospective mother and father. Sometimes one child has a defect and the parents want to know the chances of another child having the same disorder (Rose and Burdette, 1966).

One couple came to New York University Medical Center after their first child was born with a cleft lip and palate. A genetic and hormonal assay revealed that the chance was one in fifty that their next child would have a cleft lip and palate. The couple decided to take the risk (Rusk, Swinyard, and Swift, 1969, p. 145).

Early genetic diagnosis can prevent an otherwise potentially serious defect from becoming a problem. If possible birth defects are suspected prenatally, a sample of amniotic fluid may be withdrawn with a needle, the baby's chromosomes examined and chemical tests made, and a diagnosis made as to the possibility of a deformed child being born. If deformities are present, an abortion may be considered.

A large number of defects are caused by a combination of heredity and environment. *Harelip* is one example. It may be related to hereditary factors, to the position of the embryo in the uterus, to the blood supply, or to some drugs given during pregnancy (Jones, Shainberg, and Byer, 1970). Difficulties because of the *RH factor* are another example.

Environmental Conditions

There are a number of environmental conditions that may have an influence on birth defects. These conditions may include.

- Illness of the mother
- Age of the mother
- Nutritional deficiencies
- Ingestion of drugs by the mother
- Exposure to X-rays and radiation
- Position of the fetus within the uterus itself
- The mother's emotional state

Illness of the Mother

One of the most important and well-known illnesses that can affect the baby in the early months of pregnancy is *rubella*, or German measles. The best estimate is that 12 to 15 percent of the fetuses will be seriously damaged if the mother gets the illness during the first three months of pregnancy. If the illness strikes when the mother has been pregnant about six weeks, the fetal risk may be as high as 50 percent (Hardy, 1969; Maeck and Phillips, 1972; Smithells, 1971). Other virus infections such as *infectious hepatitis, cytomegalovirus* (a flu-like disease) and *herpes virus* may cause

damage ranging from serious to mild (Guttmacher, 1973).

New treatments have made some other diseases during pregnancy less severe. Pregnant women who were found to be *tubercular* used to have an abortion and then would go to a sanitorium for months or years. Now the woman can be treated at home with a combination of drugs (Guttmacher, 1973). Both *gonorrhea* and *syphilis* can be quite serious if left untreated. If an expectant mother has syphilis, her child may die in the uterus or be born gravely ill with the disease. If treatment with penicillin is begun early enough, however, damage is prevented and both the mother and child are cured of the disease.

Age of the Mother

The age of the mother is related to the incidence of birth defects (The National Foundation, 1977). *Down Syndrome*, for example, occurs only one in 1,000 in mothers younger than thirty, but one in 100 in mothers at age forty, and one in forty-five when the maternal age is forty-five or over. Other fetal abnormalities, not transmitted through heredity but that have environmental origins, increase in incidence with maternal age. These include *spina bifida* (incomplete closure of the lower spinal canal), *microcephaly* (pin head), *congenital heart defects,* and *hydrocephalus* (water on the brain) (Guttmacher, 1973). Too young an age also contributes to a higher incidence of birth defects, however, primarily because of the large numbers of infants born prematurely to these women (U.S. Department of Health, Education, and Welfare, 1970).

Nutritional Deficiences

Lack of vitamins, minerals, and protein in the diet of the expectant mother may cause damage to the embryo, has been associated with *stillbirths*, **miscarriages,** and *major deformities.* The extent of the damage depends upon the time, duration, and the severity of the nutritional deficiencies. A lack of vitamin A or calcium may result in improperly developed teeth. A serious protein deficiency may cause mental retardation, **premature birth,** low resistance to infections, or low fetal weight (Guttmacher, 1973).

Drugs

Much more is discovered each year about the effect of drugs on the fetus. Drugs taken by the mother are absorbed into the infant's bloodstream. If the mother is a heroin addict, for example, the baby becomes an addict too (Wilson et al., 1973; Zelson, 1973; Zelson et al., 1971). For this reason, expectant mothers are now advised not to take any form of medication or drugs—even aspirin—without prior approval of the doctor. *Antimetabolics* and those used to treat an overactive thyroid, for example, may cause malformations in the embryo. Even the antibiotic, *aureomycin,* may later cause yellow teeth in the offspring. There is some evidence that *LSD* has been associated with chromosomal damage and birth defects, although a definite causal relationship has not been established (Dishatsky, 1971; Wikler, 1971). A review of the literature reveals that evidence of damage is strong, especially if the drug is taken during pregnancy (Boyd, 1971; Jacobson and Stubbs, 1968; Smart and Bateman, 1968). Damage to chromosomes due to the use of large quantities of marijuana is still a matter of dispute (U.S. Department of Health, Education and Welfare, 1974).

The more *tobacco* an expectant mother smokes, the greater the tendency for the baby to be born with a weight deficit, the greater tendency to be born prematurely, and the greater likelihood of miscarriage and still

birth (U.S. Department of Health, Education and Welfare, 1971). *Alcohol* can have very negative effects, especially if the mother is a heavy drinker or an alcoholic. There have been a few cases of newborn babies suffering from *delirium tremens,* when their mothers were severely alcoholic. Even a nonalcoholic mother drinking too much at one time, or drinking small amounts regularly, may damage the fetus, so she should completely abstain unless given specific permission from her doctor.

X-Rays and Radiation

Radiation or *X-ray treatment* during pregnancy may seriously damage a fetus, but only if the pregnant mother has inadvertently received an excessive amount of radiation such as in treating a pelvic tumor. The earlier in pregnancy the radiation is administered, the greater the likelihood of damage.

Fetal Position

Some birth defects may be caused by the particular position in which the fetus grows in the uterus. *Clubfoot* may have this origin (Jones, Shainberg, and Byer, 1970).

Mother's Emotional State

The mother's emotional state also has an effect on her child. If she is nervous and upset, *adrenalin* is not only pumped into her own system, but it passes into the system of the fetus as well. As a result, her infant is more likely to be hyperactive and irritable and to eat and sleep poorly. Prolonged nervous and emotional disturbance of the mother during the later months of pregnancy may cause feeding difficulties and an irritable and hyperactive autonomic nervous system in the infant, In fact, the infant can be born neurotic (Kennedy, 1971).

Birth Injuries

Some birth defects are caused by birth injuries during labor and delivery. *Cerebral palsy,* which affects one child in every 215, is one of the most notable examples. About 3 percent of cerebral palsy cases are caused by *forceps delivery* and about 60 percent from *brain hemorrhage* and *contusions* and from *oxygen starvation* during a difficult natural delivery (Landis, 1975).

Pregnancy

Signs and Symptoms of Pregnancy

One of the first questions every prospective mother asks is, "How can I tell when I'm pregnant?" The signs and symptoms of pregnancy may be divided into three categories. *Presumptive signs* are those that indicate a possibility of pregnancy. They are the first noticed by the individual woman, but since they are subject to her individual, subjective interpretation, she may only presume pregnancy but cannot be completely certain without further substantiation. The presumptive signs are:

- Cessation of menstruation
- Morning sickness
- Increase in size, tenderness, and fullness of the breasts along with development of dark coloration of the areolae (the area around the nipples)
- Frequent urination
- Quickening or feeling of movement by the mother
- Overpowering sleepiness (McCary, 1973)

Probable signs of pregnancy are more objective than presumptive signs, since they must be interpreted by the physician. Some of them occur later in pregnancy than the presumptive signs, but still are not absolute proof. The probable signs include:

- Positive pregnancy tests (chemical tests are 97 percent accurate)
- Darkening of vaginal tissues and of cervical mucous membranes (they get purplish in color—called *Chadwick's sign*)
- Softening of cervical tissue (*Hegar's sign*)
- Enlargement of abdomen and uterus
- Mapping of fetal outline
- Intermittent contractions of uterus
- An increase in basal body temperature (A level of 98.8° to 99.9°F for more than sixteen days is highly suggestive of pregnancy.)

Positive signs of pregnancy are indisputable, since no other condition except pregnancy causes them. There are five of them: the examiner feels the fetus move, hears the fetal heartbeat, detects the fetal skeleton by X-ray, gets an electrical tracing of the fetal heart, and maps the fetal outline by means of special ultrasonic equipment (Bowman, 1974). When these signs are discovered, the mother and her physician *know* she is pregnant.

Pregnancy Tests

Since most women don't want to wait several months to determine if they are pregnant, pregnancy tests are administered. There are now a number of different tests. *A-Z tests* use animals: a mouse, rat, rabbit, toad, or frog. The tests are quite accurate at approximately three weeks after implantation or six weeks after the last menstrual period. *Chemical tests* are simpler and faster and have all but superseded the older animal tests (McCary, 1973).

Calculating the Birth Date

The duration of the pregnancy is ordinarily estimated at 280 days, or forty weeks from the beginning of the last period. This is approximately equivalent to 267 days from the time of conception. Of course, these are average figures. One study showed that 46 percent had their babies either the week before or the week after the calculated date and 74 percent within a two-week period before or after the anticipated day of birth. Occasionally, pregnancy is prolonged more than two weeks beyond the calculated date and usually an error in calculation is involved. At the most, 4 percent of pregnancies are actually carried two weeks or more beyond the average time (Guttmacher, 1973).

The expected date of confinement may be calculated using *Naegele's formula* as follows: Subtract three months from the first day of the last menstrual period, then add seven days. Thus, if

The date of first day of last period was December 16

Subtracting three months gives the date September 16

Adding seven days gives the birth date as September 23

This is really a shortcut for counting 280 days from any fixed date. In other words, a woman ordinarily delivers nine months and seven days from the beginning date of her last menstrual period (Guttmacher, 1973).

Prenatal Care

Medical Care

Ordinarily, the fetus is well protected in its uterine environment, but the expectant mother will want to put herself under the care of a physician as soon as she suspects she is pregnant. Time is of the essence, since the first three months of development are crucial to the good health of the child.

Minor Side Effects of Pregnancy

No pregnancy is without some discomfort. Expectant mothers may experience any one or several of the following discomforts to varying degrees: *Nausea* (morning sickness), *heartburn, flatulence, hemorrhoids, constipation, shortness of breath, backache, leg cramps, uterine contractions, insomnia, minor vaginal discharge,* and *varicose veins* (Hern, 1971; Sherman, 1971). The physician will give suggestions regarding the best ways of minimizing these discomforts.

Major Complications of Pregnancy

Major complications arise only infrequently, but when they do they present a more serious threat to the health and life of the baby than do the minor discomforts already discussed. Major complications may include any one of the following.

- *Pernicious vomiting.* That which is prolonged and persistent.
- *Toxemia.* Characterized by high blood pressure; water logging of the tissues (*edema*) as indicated by swollen limbs and face or rapid weight gain; *albumin* in the urine, headache, blurring of vision, hypertension; and *eclampsia* (convulsions).
- *Threatened abortion.* As indicated by vaginal bleeding.
- *Placenta praevia.* Happens about once in 200 pregnancies and is the premature separation of the placenta from the uterine wall, usually because the placenta is growing partly over or all the way over the opening of the cervix.

- *Tubal pregnancy.* The fertilized ovum attaches itself to the wall of the Fallopian tube and grows there rather than within the uterus. Sometimes the pregnancy, termed *ectopic*, is situated in the ovary, abdomen, or cervix. All such pregnancies have to be terminated by an operation.

- *Rh factor.* The expectant mother with Rh negative blood who carries a fetus with Rh positive blood can have problems.

- *Illnesses of the mother.* Depending upon the illness, can create major complications.

Sex Relations

Masters and Johnson have reported the results of a study of the changes in sexual tensions and performances through the three trimesters of pregnancy. The female subjects were divided into two groups: (1) those going through a first, full-term pregnancy (referred to as *nulliparous* women) and (2) those going through a second or more full-term pregnancy (referred to as *parous*). As a group, the nulliparous women showed a marked reduction in sexual interest and in effectiveness of sexual performance during the first trimester of pregnancy, a marked increase during the second trimester, and during the third trimester a loss of sexual interest as well as a marked decline in sexual intercourse because of medical contraindications for periods of from four weeks to three months. As a group, the parous women showed no change in sexual tensions or in effectiveness of sexual performance during the first trimester of pregnancy, a marked increase during the second trimester, and during the third trimester, a marked decrease in sexual interest and performance, primarily because of chronic exhaustion from the pregnancy and from taking care of other children, and/or because of prescribed medical contraindications for periods of from four weeks to three months.

Among both the nulliparous and parous groups, 70 percent of the women had been told by their physicians that intercourse was medically contraindicated during the last four weeks to three months. Many wives did not believe that sexual continence was really necessary, and expressed concern with the prescribed period. A majority of these women made deliberate attempts to relieve their husbands during the period of prescribed continence.

What about sexual interest and activity after childbirth? Forty-seven percent of the women in Master's and Johnson's study described low or negligible levels of sexuality when interviewed early in the third postpartum month. The reasons for low levels of sexuality were fatigue, weakness, pain, irritative vaginal discharge, or a fear of permanent physical harm if coitus were resumed too soon. Fifty-three percent reported varying levels of sexual interest. The nursing mothers reported sexual stimulation from the sucking activity of their infants and wanted to begin having intercourse with their husbands as soon after childbirth as possible. All the women interviewed, except those for whom intercourse was medically forbidden for three months, returned to full coital activity within six weeks to 2 months after delivery. Despite the fact that intercourse was forbidden for at least six weeks by most physicians, there frequently was a return to prepregnancy coital activity within three weeks of delivery, especially among higher tensioned women, and by those who were actively nursing.

What about the reaction of husbands? Thirty-nine percent had withdrawn slowly, almost involuntarily, from active coital demand upon their wives during the end of the second trimester or early in the third trimester. Some were afraid of injuring the fetus; others just weren't interested. Only one-third of the men whose wives were medically prohibited from having intercourse from four weeks to three months prior to confinement understood, agreed with, and honored the prohibition. One-third did not understand the reasons, were not sure the doctor had said it, or wished they had had it explained to them. Twenty-five percent of all the husbands sought release outside of marriage during the postpartum continence period. All of the husbands interviewed expressed concern over how soon after delivery intercourse could be resumed without physical harm or emotional distress to their wives.

Mental Health

Some effects of the mother's emotional state upon her infant have already been discussed. Prolonged nervous and emotional disturbance of the mother may result in a *hyperactive, irritable, neurotic child* (Kennedy, 1971). Emotional disturbance may also have negative effects upon the mother herself. Women who suffer from *pernicious vomiting* during pregnancy have been found to be under considerable emotional stress, usually because of conflict between wanting and not wanting the unborn child (McDonald, 1968). Vomiting may be an unconscious rejection of the pregnancy.

Investigations have revealed a close relationship between personality and emotional factors and *habitual abortion*. Women who are prone to bearing *premature infants* may show similar upset. Emotional factors have also been shown to be related to *difficult* and *prolonged labor* and to such physical complications of pregnancy as *toxemia*, which has already been discussed (McDonald, 1968).

A number of factors may precipitate the mother's anxiety and tension. Anxiety and fears that originated in the mother's family background may be precipitated by the crisis of pregnancy. The mother may experience conflict if the pregnancy is unplanned and unwanted. Some inexperienced mothers worry about their ability to take care of their baby and about the enormous responsibilities with which they are suddenly confronted.

Part of the emotional upset during pregnancy may be due to physical causes such as hormonal changes (Salk, 1974; Sherman, 1971).

All of these data add up to the fact that pregnancy is not always the euphoric, blissful experience that romantic literature describes. It should be a happy, healthful time, but it can also be a period of stress and anxiety, especially for the immature and unprepared. Bell writes: "It does sometimes happen that the arrival of pregnancy interrupts a pleasant dream of motherhood" (Bell, 1975, p. 453). This is why preparation for childbirth and for parenthood is so important.

Preparation for Parenthood

Prepared Childbirth

The term *prepared childbirth* as used here means physical, social, intellectual, and emotional preparation for the birth of a baby. It means physical care of the body to provide the ultimate physical environment for the growing fetus, and it means physical conditioning so the body is prepared for labor and childbirth. It means social preparation: of the home, the husband, and the children so the proper relationship exists within the family in which the child will be growing up. It means intellectual preparation: obtaining full knowledge and understanding of the process of birth and what to expect before, during, and after the hospital stay. It also means adequate instruction in infant care. It means psychological and emotional conditioning so that fear, anxiety, and tension are kept to a minimum and so that childbirth can be as pleasant and pain free as possible.

The term prepared childbirth, as used here, does not insist upon labor and delivery without drugs and medication, although it may include that if the mother desires. In other words, the emphasis is not just on *nat-*

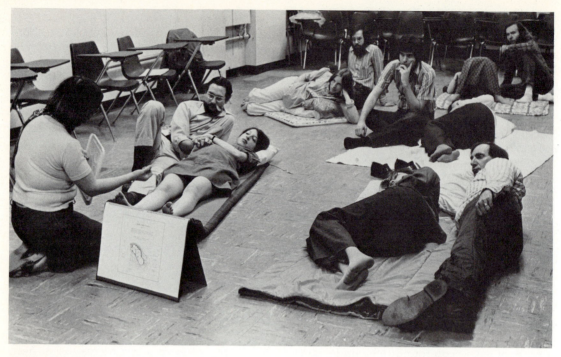

Prepared childbirth means physical, social, intellectual, and emotional preparation for the birth of a baby.

ural childbirth (in a sense all childbirth is natural), but on whether or not the woman, her husband, and family are really prepared for the experience of becoming parents.

Methods

Dick-Read, an English obstetrician, pioneered the concept of prepared childbirth through publication of a paper in 1933 and then later a book, *Childbirth Without Fear*. He believed that fear caused tension, which inhibited the process of childbirth. He felt that if women could be educated to understand what was happening to their bodies so that tension and fear were eliminated, and if they could also be conditioned for the experience, that pain during childbirth could be eliminated in all but a minority of cases. Furthermore, women who

delivered without drugs had perfectly healthy babies and were able to resume their duties sooner after delivery than those who had had anesthesia (Bean, 1974).

The important elements of the Read method include:

1. Education about birth including deconditioning from earlier fears, myths, and misconceptions
2. Physical conditioning exercises and learning voluntary muscle relaxation and proper breathing
3. Emotional support for the mother by husband, nurses, and doctor during pregnancy, labor, and delivery

The Read approach is a fairly passive method emphasizing relaxation and proper breathing as each contraction comes.

The **Lamaze method** originated in Russia and was introduced to the western world in

1951 by Lamaze, (1967) a French obstetrician (Boston Women's Health Course Collective, 1971). The important elements of the Lamaze method include:

1. Education about birth, including teaching the importance of releasing uninvolved muscles
2. Physical conditioning through exercises
3. Learning controlled breathing and how to "let go": how to relax the muscles and release muscular tension. The psychological technique for pain prevention is controlled breathing
4. Offering emotional support to the wife during labor and delivery, primarily by teaching the husband how to coach her during the process. The importance of the husband-wife relationship and communication are emphasized. So in this method as well as the Read method, the attendance of the husband in childbirth education classes is essential (Bean, 1974)

Another method of prepared childbirth, referred to as a *psychosexual* method was developed by Kitzinger in England. Her method is called psychosexual because she shows the husband how to help his wife relax by touching various parts of her body with his hand. Kitzinger also teaches women how to gain better control over the openings in the pelvic floor and over the muscles inside the vagina, thus allowing descent and delivery of the baby. This is done by prescribed exercises.

Some groups and childbirth education classes combine elements of the Dick-Read, Lamaze, and Kitzinger method (Boston Women's Health Course Collective, 1971). The important element of the philosophy is that the woman is in control of how she wishes to experience birth. Classes do not teach that medication or anesthesia will or will not be used. They are taught that drugs and anesthesia should be requested if needed. One woman commented:

Gosh I feel so grand! . . . I just lie here like a nut smiling out the window and wondering how two deliveries could be so different. You know, the first was hell for me. And now the marvelous experience sets me in good stead and frame of mind for any future babies (Bean, 1974, p. 10).

Critique of Prepared Childbirth Methods

Prepared childbirth, by whatever method, is not without its critics, especially if a particular advocate emphasizes that drugs or medication of any kind should not be used. A majority of obstetricians accept most of the other concepts of prepared childbirth and feel that it is an ally. "The patient is calm and relaxed. Without fear, she has less pain," one said. Part of the value of prepared childbirth is not only the benefit of psychological suggestion but of physical conditioning.

Organizing the Home for the Baby

Prepared childbirth includes a number of things that have to be done ahead of time at home. Where will the baby sleep? What equipment is needed? What arrangements are to be made for feeding, bathing, and changing the baby? A second task is to obtain necessary baby clothing and supplies. A third is to arrange for assistance until the mother is feeling well again. It is important to have help with the housework, cooking, and caring for other children, so as to leave the new mother free to care for the baby. A fourth task is to arrange for a doctor for the baby. A fifth task is to prepare other children, if any, for the birth of the new baby, including discussing the facts of life at their level of understanding. Including other children in on the "secret" helps them to feel a part of the experience and minimizes jealousy and misunderstanding.

The Hospital, Labor, Delivery

When Labor Begins

Real labor is rhythmic in nature and recurs at fixed intervals, usually beginning at about fifteen to twenty minutes apart and decreasing to three- to four-minute intervals when labor is well under way. In addition, the total length of each muscular contraction increases from less than half a minute to more than a minute. One of the signs that labor is about to begin or has already begun is the discharge of the blood-tinged mucus plug that has sealed the neck of the uterus. The plug is dislodged from the cervix and passes out of the vagina as a pinkish discharge; it is termed the **show.** Its appearance may anticipate the onset of labor by a day or more, or it may indicate that dilation has already begun.

Sometimes the first indication of impending labor is the rupture of the bag of water (*amniotic sac*), followed by a gush or leakage of watery fluid from the vagina. In one-eighth of all pregnancies, especially first pregnancies, the membrane ruptures *before* labor begins. When this happens, labor will commence in six to twenty-four hours if the woman is within a few days of term. If she is not near term, labor may not commence for thirty or forty days or longer. This delay is actually necessary, because the longer the baby has to develop completely, the greater the chance of being born healthy. About half the time, however, the bag of water doesn't rupture until the last hours of labor.

Duration of Labor

Bean (1974) reports a study of 10,000 patients who delivered at Johns Hopkins Hospital. The study showed the total length of labor of each patient from the onset of the first contraction until the extrusion of the afterbirth.

The median number of hours of labor for *primipara* women (first labor) was 10.6, for *multipara* (refers to all labor subsequent to the first) was 6.2. One woman in a hundred may anticipate that her first child will be born in less than three hours. Every ninth woman requires more than twenty-four hours.

Going to the Hospital

The doctor will give instructions as to when he or she wants to be notified. Most want to be called as soon as rhythmic contractions are established. Her doctor will also determine when the mother should go to the hospital. Admission procedures vary somewhat after arrival at the hospital.

The Father's Role

Medical opinion is also changing gradually in relation to the role of the father. Since fathers are encouraged to attend classes with their wives and to act as coaches during labor and delivery, many couples are insisting that the father be present during labor and even at the delivery. These considerations need to be worked out between patient and physician beforehand to avoid misunderstanding.

Stages of Labor

The actual process of labor can be divided into three phases. The first is the *dilation stage*, during which the force of the uterine muscles pushing on the baby gradually opens the mouth of the cervix, which increases from less than four-fifths of an inch in diameter to four inches. This phase takes longer than any other. There is nothing the mother can do to help except relax as completely as possible to allow the involuntary muscles to do their work. Dilation progresses faster if the mother is not tense. When dilation is complete, the baby's head can start to pass through.

The second stage begins upon completion of dilation and ends with the birth of the baby. It involves *the passage of the baby through the birth canal.* During the phase when hard contractions begin, the mother alternately relaxes and pushes to help force the baby through the birth canal. After the baby is tended to the obstetrician again turns his or her attention to the mother for the third stage of labor.

The third stage involves *the passage of the placenta or afterbirth.* The mother may be kept in the delivery room for an hour or so after delivery while her condition is checked. When her condition is considered normal, she is usually placed in a recovery room for awhile before being returned to her own room.

The Leboyer Method

In his book, *Birth Without Violence,* The French obstetrician Leboyer emphasizes gentle, loving treatment of the newborn. Not all of his ideas are accepted by American obstetricians, but those ideas include dim lights, gentle voices, and delaying cutting the cord until the naked newborn is soothed, massaged, and stroked while resting on the mother's abdomen. After the cord is cut, the baby is bathed in water similar in temperature to the environment inside the mother.

The theory behind the method is that bringing a newborn into a world of blinding lights and loud voices, where it is jerked upside down, spanked and treated roughly, and immediately separated from its mother, is a terrifying, traumatic experience after the quiet, secure, warm, and silent world of the womb. "Why do we do it?" Leboyer asked. "Because we never really thought of the infant as a person. The newborn is a sensitive, feeling human being, and in the first few mo-

ments after birth, he should be treated that way. We must introduce him to the world gradually" (Braun, 1975, p. 17).

Advocates of the *Leboyer method* are highly enthusiastic. "I've been absolutely amazed by the results," says Davis, a family doctor in Carson City, Nevada. "I've delivered at least thirty-five babies with the Leboyer method in the last five months—and I can't say enough about it. These babies are so different from the others, so graceful in their movement. They seem to be reaching out instead of protecting themselves" (Braun, 1975, p. 19).

There is still a lack of research evidence to back up the claim that the Leboyer method is superior, but some results of studies in Paris have leaked out and indicated that "Leboyer children are noticeably different—in their overall attitude and behavior, and more specifically, their unusually avid interest in the world around them" (Braun, 1975, p. 19).

After Childbirth

Mother-Infant Contact

There is important evidence to show that mother-infant contacts during the early hours and days of life are important. Studies at Case-Western Reserve University in Cleveland confirmed the maternal feeling that the emotional bonds between mother and infant are strengthened by intimate contact during the first hours of life. One group of mothers was allowed sixteen extra hours of intimacy during the first three days of life—an hour after birth, five hours each afternoon. At one month of age and again at a year, these mothers were compared with a control group that had gone through the usual hospital routine. The differences were striking. The mothers who had more time with their babies fondled them more, sought close eye contact, responded to their wails. The researchers concluded that keeping the mother and baby together during the first hours after birth strengthened a mother's "maternal sensitivities" and that prolonged infant-mother separation during the first few days would have far-reaching negative effects (Salk, 1974).

It is an understandable desire for new parents, fathers as well as mothers, to want to hold their baby, yet policies and rules at some hospitals keep parents and baby separated during much of the hospital stay. Fathers are only permitted to see their baby through the nursery room window. The mother is brought her baby on a fixed schedule only at feeding time, even if the infant has been crying for an hour because it was hungry before. As a result, the parents are frustrated and their child is denied the benefits of "contact comfort," which psychologists emphasize is so important in the development of love (Harlow and Suomi, 1970).

Rooming In

In order to avoid this separation, a minority of hospitals are equipped with *rooming in* facilities where the baby is cared for most of the time by the mother in her own room or in a room the mother shares with several others. A big advantage to rooming in is that the new father can share in the baby's care also, so that childcare becomes family centered from the beginning. Another big advantage is that new mothers learn much about infant care while still in the hospital, thus avoiding the panic and anxiety in realizing that they are given the total responsibility all at once (Salk, 1974).

Breast Feeding versus Bottle Feeding

One of the questions every mother faces is whether or not to breast-feed her baby. Actually, if the decision to breast feed is made during pregnancy, the mother can massage her nipples and toughen them for the experience. If not made then, the doctor will at least want to know at the time of delivery. In making her decision, there are several considerations, one being how the mother feels about nursing. Both bottle and breast-fed babies may do well emotionally, depending upon the parents' relationship with their child. Each child needs physical contact and warmth, the sound of a pleasant voice, and the sight of a happy face. A warm, accepting mother who is bottle-feeding her baby helps her infant feel secure and loved. The important thing is the total parent-child relationship, not just the method of feeding.

All babies need a certain amount of sucking, apart from their nutritional needs. Infants derive a great deal of emotional security from the experience. This need may be met through bottle- or breast-feeding.

Whatever type of milk is given has to be of sufficient quantity and has to agree with the baby. Most doctors would agree that there is nothing nutritionally better for the baby than mother's milk, provided the supply is adequate. Babies less frequently develop allergies to the mother's milk than to cow's milk (Salk, 1974). They receive antibodies against infection from breast milk. Sometimes, however, the mother's supply is not adequate, or her nipples become cracked and sore so that nursing is too painful. Because of the effort involved, nursing mothers may become excessively fatigued by three months postpartum (Sherman, 1971). Such problems can usually be overcome, one being to supplement the breast with a bottle.

Some women find breast-feeding to be a challenge, and they become very upset if for some reason or other they can't manage it. Others really want to but let medical personnel dissuade them, for which they are sorry afterwards. Individual mothers ought to follow their best instincts and do what they really want to do and what seems best for the baby.

Conclusions

The majority of American couples look forward to having children. True, more and more are making a conscious decision to remain childless, but this still involves only about 4 percent of all couples. The remainder want to raise a family as one of their major life goals.

Since one child in every sixteen is born with a serious physical defect, and 20 percent of these defects are inherited, couples who suspect that they themselves are carriers of defective genes will probably want to seek genetic counseling before having their first child. Since 80 percent of all birth defects have environmental causes or are due to birth injuries, it means the defects are preventable. Constantly improving medical knowledge enables couples to deal with such problems as rubella, venereal disease, or Rh-negative factors. Awareness of the possible harmful effects of faulty nutrition, drugs, or radiation on unborn children can help couples to avoid these risks.

One of the most important facts in having a healthy baby is to get early prenatal care once pregnancy is suspected. Most of the complications of pregnancy and/or childbirth that become serious do so because of ignorance and neglect.

Most couples are inexperienced and uncertain. They are quite vulnerable to both suggestion and domination. What helps most is a considerable amount of instruction and preparation ahead of time, so they enter this experience with knowledge and understanding and a minimum of worry and anxiety, because they have prepared themselves for the experience of becoming parents.

CHAPTER 18

Infertility, Adoption, Unwed Pregnancy, and Abortion

CHAPTER OUTLINE

Infertility

Adoption

Unwed Pregnancy

Abortion

Conclusions

Dialogue

Enabling couples to have the number of children they want means providing medical assistance to help childless couples overcome problems associated with **infertility.** It means offering adoption services to couples who find they would otherwise remain permanently childless. It means offering contraceptive information and medical help to prevent unplanned pregnancies and giving counseling and assistance to the woman who finds herself pregnant out of wedlock. It means providing abortion counseling and services in other cases of unwanted pregnancies. All four of these problems: infertility, adoption, unmarried pregnancy, and abortion present difficult challenges to professional people who seek to assist other persons in dealing with their human situation. Each problem presents a different kind of challenge to the persons or couples who are faced with the dilemmas. This chapter takes an honest look at these problems, both from the point of view of the individuals experiencing them and from the viewpoint of professionals who are working with them and assisting them in overcoming difficulties.

Infertility

Definitions

The words *infertility* and *sterility* are often used interchangeably to describe the inability to conceive or to effect pregnancy. Strictly speaking, *sterility* describes a condition in which one has zero capacity to produce egg cells or sperm cells. *Infertility* usually means involuntary childlessness due to difficulties in conceiving. It is a kinder word, since it does not necessarily imply a permanent or a biological inadequacy. Neither sterility nor infertility should be confused with *impotence* or lack of *virility*. Impotence refers to the male's inability to maintain an erection; virility describes his sexual vigor (Folkman and Clatworthy, 1970).

Incidence

One-third of all couples in the United States experience some difficulty in having a child, either because they are unable to conceive or because the wife has difficulty carrying the child long enough to produce a live birth (McCary, 1973; Westoff and Westoff, 1971). *Approximately one couple in ten would never be able to have children without medical help* (Guttmacher, 1973). *With help, about half of these 10 percent do have children* (Rao, 1974).

There are a number of factors that influence conception rates. One is frequency of intercourse. Couples who have sexual intercourse several times per week are more likely to achieve pregnancy in less than six months than couples practicing coitus once or less often per week. Age is another factor influencing conception rates. When couples want to conceive, the younger the husband and the wife the more likely the wife can get pregnant. Of course, since coital frequency is related to age, frequency influences conception rates as well as chronological age itself.

How long does it ordinarily take for couples to achieve pregnancy? In one study, Guttmacher found that one-third of couples were able to achieve pregnancy the first month, more than half within the first three months. Fifteen percent required four to six months; thirteen percent seven to twelve months, and 8 percent one to two years. More than 6 percent of those who eventually had a baby took two or more years to achieve pregnancy. The median time for conception was two and one-half months. Generally speaking, if couples are younger than thirty-five years of age, they should wait a full year before consulting a physician. If they are older than thirty-five, they should see a doctor after six months of unsuccessful attempts. Psychological and physical factors that work against conception grow stronger with time, so the older couple should get help sooner. For the younger couple, a reasonable period of time (one year) improves the chances of fertility.

Getting Help

If help is to be obtained, the active cooperation of both the husband and wife is essential, since either one may be the cause of infertility. Some men object to getting help. They feel that if the cause lies with them it is a reflection on their manliness. The male who is secure in his manhood is not threatened by an examination to determine the cause of infertility. The important thing is to explore all possible causes and to find out what is wrong and if the problem can be remedied.

Causes Involving the Couple

Some causes of infertility involve both the husband and the wife. Infrequent intercourse has already been mentioned as one. Infertility may also be caused by too frequent intercourse (McCary, 1975). Couples who have intercourse several times a day, every day for weeks at a time, do not allow the husband's sperm count to build up sufficiently for impregnation to occur.

Infertility is often due to a combination of fairly simple factors. Some vaginal lubricants are spermicidal, for example. Even Vaseline, in quantity, may injure sperm cells or act as a barrier to prevent the sperm from entering the cervix. The couple may have had intercourse only during those times of the month when the wife was least likely to get pregnant. Poor nutrition may have a direct effect on fertility. Anemia, fatigue, or emotional stress may exert an indirect influence because they tend to decrease the frequency of intercourse. The doctor will want to get complete medical histories, give general physical examinations, and investigate the couple's sexual life before beginning specific and separate tests for the husband and the wife.

Infertility in the Husband

After the general physical examinations and history taking, the physician usually begins by examining the husband since the male is easier to test. There are four biological requirements before the husband can impregnate his wife.

First, he must be able to produce healthy live sperm in sufficient numbers. *Second,* he must secrete seminal fluid in proper amounts and with the right composition to transport the sperm. A sperm count is made with the aid of a microscope and an assay made of the vigor, mobility, and normalcy of the sperm. The semen is also examined to see if there is sufficient volume and adequate consistency to support the sperm.

The *third* prerequisite if the husband is to be able to impregnate his wife is an unobstructed "throughway" from the testicle to the end of the penis so that sperm can pass. If the vas deferens is blocked anywhere, the sperm cannot be ejaculated. The *fourth* prerequisite for the husband to be able to impregnate his wife is the ability to achieve and sustain an erection and to ejaculate within the vagina. If the husband is completely or partially impotent, intromission is difficult or impossible.

Infertility in the Wife

If the tests on the husband reveal that he is fertile, the wife must then be examined. The first question is whether or not she is ovulating: producing a normal egg cell. There are a number of tests that have been developed to detect ovulation. If one or more of these tests reveal that ovulation is not taking place, treatment is begun immediately, usually in the form of hormone or drug therapy to stimulate the ovaries and to improve the woman's general health. Since it is difficult to regulate dosage, there is the tendency for the hormone to stimulate the development of more than one egg cell, thus producing multiple births (Shearman, 1969).

If ovulation has been found to be normal, the next step is to find out if there is any blockage of the Fallopian tubes down which the ovum must travel. Here also, several tests are available.

Sometimes abnormalities of the uterus prevent conception or carrying a baby to full term. Occasionally, the problem may be with the cervix itself, which acts as a bottleneck in preventing the sperm from reaching the ovum. In some cases, the chemical climate of the vagina is too acid, thus immobilizing the sperm. Once the union of sperm and egg has taken place, infertility is not at an end. An estimated 10 percent of pregnancies end in miscarriages.

Artificial Insemination

If the husband is fertile but has a low sperm count or fairly immobile sperm, or for some reason or another the delivery of the sperm is not possible through intercourse, conception may still be possible through **artificial insem-ination** with the husband's seminal fluid. This is called *AIH, artificial insemination husband,* or *homologous insemination.* If necessary, semen may be frozen and stored over a period of time and then a quantity injected into the vagina or through the cervical opening during those times of the month when the woman is most likely to be fertile. Generally, AIH is only successful in 5 percent of the cases, because the husband's sperm is usually incapable of effecting pregnancy in the first place (Pierson and D'Antonio, 1974).

AID is *artificial insemination donor,* or *heterologous insemination,* using the semen of a donor whose identity is known to the doctor but not to the couple. In such cases, the donor is selected with care.

Certainly, both the husband and the wife should be sure they want to have a baby this way and that they are mature enough to surmount emotional reactions that may arise (Novak et al., 1970). There may also sometimes be legal complications or religious objections. For those who can carefully accept this method of fertilization and its consequences, however, it is highly successful, producing pregnancy in fertile women about 80 percent of the time (McCary, 1973).

Adoption

Changing Philosophies

One possibility for the couple who are not able to bear their own child is to consider adoption. The philosophy of adoption has changed over the years. In earlier times, there were more orphans and unwanted waifs than there were adoptive parents. Adoption was rare then and was considered an act of philanthropy. Little good was expected of the children. People took them in "to work around the house" as unpaid servants but seldom considered them as family members. Today, however, adoption is no longer considered an act of charity; rather, it is deemed a privilege for both parents and children, with the primary motive of providing a permanent substitute family for a child deprived. In light of this philosophy, the emphasis is no longer on finding a child for the family but on finding a family for a child.

Adopted and Unadopted Children

In recent years, there have been increasing numbers of couples, especially among middle-class whites, who want to adopt children. In 1974, 149,000 children were adopted but 95,000 of these were adopted by relatives. Of the remaining 54,000, 43,000 were placed by social agencies and 11,000 were placed through private arrangement (Bonham, 1977; U.S. Department of Commerce, Statistical Abstract, 1980). Of course, large numbers of children are in foster homes or public institutions, but only a small percentage of these children are available for adoption.

The primary source of children for adoption are unwed mothers who decide to give up their children. Other children come from relatives, from remarriages (where the second husband adopts the wife's children), or from neglected or dependent children of parents who are not able to take care of them. But even though both the percentage and total number of children born out of wedlock has increased, more unwed mothers are keeping their children and thus there are fewer babies than adoptive couples. This is not true, however, for black babies or for those of some ethnic groups. There are more black babies awaiting adoption than there are parents for them (Aldridge, 1974; Herbert, 1973). Some black parents, who would otherwise be eligible, are "screened out" by policies that emphasize home ownership, money, prestige, and education rather than a family's ability to nourish, love, and rear a child. The time and red tape involved in completing adoption, the probing into the personal lives of prospective parents, prohibition against single parent adoptions, and against such things as more than one child sleeping in a room have resulted in many blacks refusing to go through the procedure of adoption (Fisher, 1971; Herzog, 1971).

Changing Policies

Partly because of the shortage of children and partly as a result of rethinking traditional ideas about adoption, agencies are becoming more willing to place children with handicaps or physical defects. Also, attitudes have changed somewhat toward letting single, unmarried persons adopt children, or toward approving interracial or international adoptions. Many people who adopt children of another nationality and race are not those who would ordinarily adopt. They are those who are concerned about children who would not otherwise find a home.

Questions Couples Face

Parents who are considering adoption would be wise to make a thorough examination of their own motives. They might ask: Why do we wish to adopt a child? Are we able to love and completely accept a child who is not of our own flesh and blood? If parents have other children, they need to ask: How will our bringing an adopted child into our home affect our other children? How will our adopting a child affect our marriage? Are we seeking to adopt a child to try to spruce up a faltering marriage? Realistically, couples need to face the question: Are we likely to be considered eligible to adopt a child? Are we young enough and able to care for a child financially? Will we be able to fulfill the qualifications an agency is seeking? Couples might also ask: Would we be willing to adopt an older child or one with a handicap?

Adoption through a Licensed Agency

An essential step in the adoption procedure is the termination of the rights and responsibilities of the biological mother (Bain, 1974). The unwed mother is given every opportunity to decide whether she wants to keep or give up her baby. This is a decision only she can make. If she is hurried or pushed into giving up her child, she may later be sorry. If she gives up her infant, her rights are terminated by a court, and the custody of the child given to a qualified adoption agency.

Some agencies will not consider applicants who are simultaneously applying to other agencies, so it is wise for a couple to find out the policies before making multiple applications. After the couple makes application, the agency makes a careful study of the adoptive home and couple. The investigation may take from a month to a year, after which the agency makes its recommendations to approve or disapprove the application. Couples who have been approved by an agency still have to wait until a child is available that the agency is willing to match up with them. At the present time, the waiting period may be two to five years.

After a child is placed in the adoptive home, it is kept under observation by social workers who visit periodically. Ordinarily, a one-year probation passes before the agency makes its recommendation to a court and judge and the adoption can become final. After the decree, a new birth certificate is issued for the child, giving it the last name of the adoptive parents and the first and middle names they have chosen.

Private or Independent Adoption

Large numbers of couples are not able to obtain a child through an authorized agency. As a result, many turn to private sources to obtain a child. Some 71 percent of all adoptions in the U.S. are arranged privately. Sixty-four percent are adopted by relatives, and 7 percent are other adoptive parents (Bonham, 1977; U.S. Department of Commerce, Statistical Abstract, 1980.) Many of these adoptions are arranged through family clergy, doctors, or lawyers who act as the intermediary between the adoptive couple and the natural mother. Consent of the biological mother and court approval are required.

A definite distinction ought to be made between "black market" placement—those who "sell" babies to make a profit—and independent or private placement where profit is not the motive. There is, of course, a "gray market" somewhere in between, but it usually operates according to state law. Paying money for a child or selling one is a serious crime, punishable by law. The adoptive parents can pay medical, hospital, legal, and, in some cases, "cost of living" expenses, but other money paid may be illegal and may be challenged by a court. For this reason, couples would be wise to get legal help and adhere strictly to the procedures of adoption as required by law. Some states forbid adoptions except through adoption agencies.

Private adoption involves special risks, especially if the letter of the law is not followed by well-intentioned, but naive, parents. A common error is to obtain a child only to find the child is not legally available for adoption because the mother or perhaps a new husband is unwilling to consent to the adoption. The rights of biological mothers are not terminated until the final decree is signed. So adoptive parents can never be certain they can keep the child even though the child resides in their home. The biological mother may change her mind at any time up until the final decree. Also, the judge may not grant permission. Prospective adoptive parents who need to obtain the biological mother's consent may discover she has left the state. Without the required papers, it may take years to prove abandonment of the child by the mother so that the adoption can go through. In the meantime, adoptive parents live in fear that the mother will reclaim her child, and the child, meanwhile, is without legal protection. *The most important requirement, therefore, is that the adoptive parents have the written consent of the biological mother, and this signature must be obtained after the birth of the child, not before.* Some states specify several days. A mother younger than eighteen may have to have the consent of her parents in some states. In every state, a married woman must also have the consent of her husband, even if he is not the father.

One disadvantage of private adoptions is that it is not always possible to maintain anonymity. If the biological mother knows who the adoptive parents are and where they live, she may be tempted to visit her child at some time and to reveal her identity. Some states do not permit intermediaries and require the mother to place her child for adoption herself. One study of private adoptions in Florida showed that serious problems, including extortions and threats to abduct the child, were most likely to follow cases where the mother or her relatives had made the placement without the aid of an intermediary such as a minister, doctor, or lawyer.

Private adoptions are fraught with danger, so couples need full legal counsel. They may discover the bills are padded or that they have to pay two attorneys' fees if they reside in one state and the child was born in another. Obstetrical and hospital bills may be considerable. By the time all legal fees are paid, including cost-of-living fees, the cost may run into thousands of dollars.

Relationships between Child and Adoptive Parents

Adoptive parents often worry about their performance as parents, or they wonder how the child selected will turn out. What about the adjustments of adopted children? How do these children get along? One study of 100 adult adoptees showed that 64 percent were very close to their parents. Only 14 percent reported casual, distant, or very distant relationships (Jaffee and Fanshel, 1970). Another study of couples who had adopted older children showed that more than half of the parents felt it had been an extremely satisfying experience (Kadushin, 1970). Most authorities recognize, however, that it is a hard job raising adopted children.

One of the most important requirements is for parents and adopted children to be open, honest, and communicative with one another. The adopted child should be told of his or her adoption while still young, but in a matter-of-fact natural way without giving undue emphasis to the fact that he or she was "chosen." The important emphasis is not how the adoptive parents got the child but that they love him or her. Most adopted children will wonder at some time in their lives about their real parents—who they were, why they couldn't keep them. One eleven-year-old boy commented: "My parents must have been no good." His adopted mother replied:

I don't know very many specific facts about the people you were born to. But I do know this: no matter what unfortunate thing happened that meant they didn't keep you, there were surely some very fine things about them. I know that, because I know you so well, and a boy like you has some wonderful people among his ancestors (Landis and Landis, 1973, p. 460).

Unwed Pregnancy

Illegitimacy Rates

The National Center of Health Statistics estimates that during 1978 there were 544,000 illegitimate births in the United States. Out of this total, 249,000 illegitimate babies were born to teenagers aged nineteen and younger (U.S. Department of Commerce, Statistical Abstract, 1980). Between 1970 and 1978, there was a 25 percent increase in the number of illegitimate births to women aged nineteen and younger, even though the overall birth rate to teenagers was dropping during these years. If not for the number of hasty marriages that turned premarital conceptions into legitimate births, these figures would have been more than double, since it is estimated that close to one million teenagers become pregnant out of wedlock each year (Sarrel, 1974; Westoff, 1976).

Why?

The question may be raised: Why do so many unmarried women become pregnant? The basic reason is because of the increase in premarital sexual intercourse (Zelnick and Kantner, 1972).

Another reason that illegitimacy rates are high is because the majority of females who are having premarital sexual experience are doing so without the protection of adequate birth control measures (U.S. Department of Health, Education and Welfare, 1972; Zelnick and Kantner, 1972). (See chapter 2.) Some of these are almost completely ignorant about the basic facts of contraception or of conception. Some adolescents are afraid of going to a doctor for birth control pills or for other medically prescribed protection for fear their parents will find out (Westoff, 1976). Some women are afraid of the pill because "I might get cancer." Some males who object to the condom talk their partner into intercourse

without any adequate means of contraception. Some men use sexual relations in a completely exploitative way without regard for the woman or the consequences involved.

Some men and women object to any birth control measures because of vaguely conceived moral reasons. Others feel that arranging for contraceptives ahead of time is too premeditated. Some individuals get pregnant out of wedlock because they want to do so, one common motive being to force marriage.

Some women are motivated to get pregnant by very subtle or unconscious motives they do not fully comprehend. One of the most common motives is a desire for love. After her third trip to a home for unwed mothers, one young woman remarked:

I know how I got pregnant and why I'm here. But the trouble is, I don't seem to be able to do anything about it. At least when I have sex, I have the feeling that for a few minutes, someone really loves me. All I want is someone to love.

In other cases, a woman is motivated to have a baby whom she can love.

In other situations, pregnancy may be a means of rebelling against parents or of finding one's own identity in an attempt to become a grown-up person. For some, it represents a means of escape from an unhappy home situation (Westoff, 1976). For others, pregnancy is an expression of hostility toward parents and a way of getting even with them or of hurting them. In spite of these instances, however, only one-fourth of unmarried pregnant women say they wanted to get pregnant and are happy about it. Most are shocked and extremely upset when they first discover they are pregnant.

In discussing the reasons for out-of-wedlock pregnancies, one must also recognize the influence of cultural factors (U.S. Department of Commerce, Statistical Abstract, 1980). Illegitimacy is much higher among the poor and undereducated, and among those from broken homes and disorganized neighborhoods, than among higher socioeconomic, intact families (U.S. Department of Commerce, Statistical Abstract, 1980). This is due to a number of factors: to the greater sexual exploitation of lower socioeconomic status women, to their less efficient use of contraceptives, and to the fact that they less often get legally divorced in case of an unhappy marriage. Once pregnant, they less often terminate their pregnancies through abortions or are less often pushed into marriage because of pregnancy. Also, among such groups, bearing a child out of wedlock does not carry the same social stigma it does in other circles (McCary, 1973).

It has been shown that illegitimacy tends to run in families, indicating that family circumstances, parental example, and social learning exert marked influences (Geismar, 1973). A woman is more likely to have an illegitimate baby if her mother or grandmother had an illegitimate child, and she is even more likely to do so if both her mother and grandmother bore illegitimate children (Vincent et al., 1969).

The traditional picture of unwed mothers as "oversexed," promiscuous females is certainly not an accurate one (Ryan, 1971). They are often trying to escape unhappy family and environmental circumstances. Many establish a longstanding relationship with their partners prior to pregnancy and believe that they are in love with them at the time of their sexual union (Fink, 1970; Reiss, 1970). Involvement becomes a means of overcoming alienation and of satisfying a deep longing for closeness and love (Westoff, 1976).

Tragic Results

From most points of view, illegitimacy is a tragedy. The unwed mother, particularly if she is an adolescent, is a high-risk patient with an increased incidence of prenatal complications, prematurity, and infant mortality (Menken, 1972; Sarrel, 1974). Once she bears a first child out of wedlock, she is likely to bear other illegitimate children at short birth intervals (Haney et al., 1975; Presser, 1971). If pregnant while still in school, her chances of completing her education are slim (Rice, 1981). If she is a teenager and marries because of pregnancy, the chances of her marriage remaining intact after five years are less than one in five. If she keeps her baby but does not marry, she often becomes trapped in a self-destructive cycle consisting of failure to continue her education, repeat pregnancies, failure to establish a stable family life, and dependence on others for support.

This self-destructive pattern was documented by a study done in New Haven, which described the "unwed mother syndrome." Among 100 females aged seventeen or under, whose records were followed for five years after initial pregnancy, only nine had married, only five had managed to complete their high school education, only five did not have a repeat pregnancy. Ninety-five amassed a total of 249 additional pregnancies, and sixty of the young women living with their 240 children were being supported by welfare agencies (Sarrel and Davis, 1966).

Help for Unwed Expectant Mothers

Unmarried pregnant women need help of various kinds. The immediate need is for counseling to assist them in evaluating their situation and to look at alternative courses of action. One alternative is to have an abortion (Lieberman, 1971). As an isolated approach, however, an abortion probably does little to help the woman work out basic conflicts about herself. She may have a psychological need to become pregnant. If so, the same thing may happen again. There is need, therefore, for a total counseling approach to help her understand the factors that led to her pregnancy and to find other ways of meeting her needs and dealing with her problems (Bernstein, 1971).

If the decision is made to have the baby, the woman needs prenatal care and, later, obstetrical, postnatal, and pediatric assistance. One of the hardest decisions for the woman who bears her child is the decision of whether or not to keep the baby or to give it up for adoption. Today, it is estimated that more than four out of five unmarried women who bear children decide to keep and raise them (Arnstein, 1973; Westoff, 1976). Many do not realize the responsibilities they are assuming and quickly find that they need help from a variety of community agencies.

One of the important needs of the young woman is for continued education. Although it has been declared unconstitutional for the school to bar the pregnant teenager from the classroom permanently (she may return after termination of the pregnancy), many are forced by school attitudes and policies to leave school with no provision for continuing their education during the pregnancy (Mackey and Milloy, 1974). Some schools require the female to wait up to a year after the birth before she can return. Others allow her to return but will not allow any participation in extracurricular activities or in graduation exercises. Some women can find no care for their child while they are in school or, lacking financial resources, cannot afford to do so. As a result, the great majority of women become discouraged about returning to school and so never complete their education (Braen, 1971; Brown, 1972; Cromwell and Gangel, 1974).

Recently, communities and their school systems have been taking a fresh look at the problem, realizing that punitive action has not reduced the number of pregnancies and may indeed have only further damaged the lives of young mothers and their infants. One result has been the establishment of compre-hensive community programs for pregnant teenagers that include not only continuing educational opportunities in regular classrooms or in special classes for pregnant women but also complete medical, psychological, and social services as well (Howard, 1971). As a result of such programs, medical problems have been sharply reduced, educational continuity has been maintained, and family life strengthened rather than weakened with the arrival of the baby.

Help for Fathers and Parents

Counseling services may include the unwed father and the parents of the woman as well. The unwed father may have strong feelings of guilt and conflict leading to extreme emotional trauma and depression. Some men attempt to rationalize their feelings by projecting all of the blame on the woman. Others adopt a supportive role and are willing to share all responsibilities, including financial (Pannor et al., 1971). The more emotionally involved the man has been, usually the more concerned he is with the woman's welfare.

Parents too need help with their feelings. They react in various ways. Some are convinced that intercourse took place only once—since their daughter had no interest in sex—or the parents are certain the pregnancy was all the man's fault. Some parents go to extremes in hiding the pregnancy from siblings or other family members and want to rush their daughter to an abortion clinic, out of town to a residence home for unwed mothers, or to a distant relative. A few parents completely reject a daughter and will have nothing to do with her from that point on because of "what she has done to her mother and father." Other parents, including those of the male, try to urge or to force the couple into marriage "to save face" or "to give the baby a name."

Abortion

Need for Understanding

Large numbers of persons are faced sometime in their lives with whether or not to get an abortion or at least with the question of whether or not to support abortion legislation. Abortion raises some difficult questions to which there are no simple answers. Abortion issues may be divided into five categories, which are discussed here: (1) legal, (2) physical and medical, (3) moral, (4) social and realistic, and (5) psychological and personal considerations.

Legal Considerations

On January 22, 1973, the United States Supreme Court ruled that a state could not inhibit or restrict a woman's right to attain an abortion during the first trimester of pregnancy (thirteen to sixteen weeks), and that the decision to have an abortion was the woman's own in consultation with her doctor (Doe v. Bolton, 1973; *New York Times,* 1973; Roe v. Wade, 1973; Sarvis and Rodman, 1974). The major ground for the court's decision was the woman's right to privacy. The court did not say, however, that a physician *has* to perform abortion if the woman demands it (she can go to another one who will), nor did it guarantee her the absolute right to an abortion regardless of circumstances or the period of her pregnancy.

The court further declared that during the second trimester of pregnancy—when abortion is more dangerous—that "a state may regulate the abortion procedure to the extent that the regulation relates to the preservation and protection of maternal health" (Roe v. Wade, 1973). Reasonable regulation might include such things as outlining the qualifications or licensure of the person who performs abortions or the licensing of the facility where the abortion is performed. The

court went on to say that the state's interest in protecting the life of the fetus arises only after viability (after twenty-four to twenty-eight weeks, when the fetus is potentially capable of living outside the mother's womb), so that the state "may go so far as to proscribe (forbid) abortion during that period except when it is necessary to preserve the life or health of the mother" (Reed, 1975, p. 205). The reasons the court rejected the state's interest in protecting human life from the moment of conception were: (1) that the "unborn have never been recognized in the law as persons in the whole sense" (2) that the rights extended to the unborn, in law, are contingent upon live birth and, therefore, (3) a state's interest in protecting fetal life cannot override the woman's right to privacy (Sarvis and Rodman, 1974).

Since the ruling, states have had the option of writing new abortion laws in keeping with the court's decision or of operating without an abortion statute. As countermeasures, right to life forces have become more organized and are now seeking to nullify the Supreme Court action by introducing constitutional amendments that either give the embryo a constitutional right to life from the time of conception or implantation or that return the decision to pass restrictive legislation to the states (*Family Planning/Population Report,* 1973). In rebuttal, right to choose advocates have pointed to the undesirable consequences that would follow a constitutional amendment granting personhood and equal protection under the law from the time of conception (McCoy, 1973, Schardt, 1973). In view of deep passions on both sides, the legal aspects of the abortion controversy have not been laid to rest and will undoubtedly continue at both the state and national levels.

Physical and Medical Considerations

Certainly, from every viewpoint if a pregnancy is to be terminated, it should be terminated as soon after conception as possible (Mace, 1972). This is of special necessity from a biological and medical point of view. By the end of the eighth week after conception, the name **embryo** is changed to *fetus*. It is one inch long, has full arms and legs, well-formed fingers and toes, a crude brain that is at work, a heart that beats, bloodstream of its own, and a simple digestive system. After twelve weeks, the fetus is three and a half inches long, and can move about in its waterfilled sac, although the movements are still so faint as not to be felt by the mother until the sixteenth to the twenty-second week (Guttmacher, 1973).

During the first three months of pregnancy, the most common method of abortion now used is the **suction curettage** or **vacuum aspiration** method (Harting and Hunter, 1971; Novak, 1970). The suction method reduces the risk of perforation, minimizes blood loss, and lessens trauma as compared with the traditional **D and C.** Both of these methods are usually performed only if the pregnancy is twelve weeks or less duration. After twelve weeks of pregnancy, the physician usually asks the woman to wait until the sixteenth week so that the *salting out* method can be used. Many physicians and hospitals refuse to give abortions to women who are more than twelve weeks pregnant ("After a Conviction," 1975).

Hysterotomy (not to be confused with hysterectomy) is less frequently done to terminate second trimester pregnancies. It is really a miniature *cesarean section* whereby under anesthesia the uterus is incised, the fetus is removed, and the opening sewn up. It is most often performed when sterilization is also desired, since the Fallopian tubes can be severed and tied while the abdomen is open (Guttmacher, 1973). Research is under way at the present time on new types of drugs called **prostaglandins,** which induce spontaneous labor (Bergstrom, 1972; Speidel and Ravenholt, 1971).

Moral Considerations

Much of the controversy about abortion has centered around the moral issues involved. For many individuals and churches, abortion is wrong because it represents the murder of a human being (Adamek, 1974). Their point of view is that the soul enters the body at the moment of conception so that at whatever stage of growth, the new life is a human. The Christian Church in the first centuries after Christ forbade abortion under all conditions from the moment of conception (Mace, 1972).

Proponents of this view worry also that justifying abortion may lead to euthanasia under other conditions. "If you say, 'The embryo can be killed because it doesn't yet have a human identity or doesn't have a name, and it can't speak for itself,' you can also say, 'We can kill this old man because his mind is wandering, he doesn't know who he is, and he has even forgotten his name.'"

Opponents of this view argue that to say that a group of human cells, however highly differentiated at the early stage of growth, is a person is to stretch the point. There is no consciousness, nor any distinctly human characteristics and traits. Advocates of this view point to the teachings of the thirteen-century church father, Thomas Aquinas, who said that there was neither life nor ensoulment until the fetus moved and, therefore, abortion was not sinful in the first sixteen weeks of pregnancy. This view lasted for three centuries following Aquinas; then the church fixed ensoulment at forty days after conception, following Aristotle's teaching. Abortion during the first forty days of pregnancy was not considered sinful until the Council of Trent in 1869 when it was once more ruled that life begins at the time of conception and that abortion at any time is a grave sin. This view was reaffirmed by the Second Vatican Council and made official Catholic doctrine by Pope Paul in December 1965 (Mace, 1972). In recent times, Protestant thought has become more liberal, permitting abortion under certain circumstances.

Members of the Right to Life movement, and others, emphasize the rights of the unborn child. They emphasize the right to life of the fetus, and that no individual or state should deprive the fetus of its constitutional and moral right to live (Louisell and Noonan, 1970; Sarvis and Rodman, 1974). Legally, of course, the Supreme Court has never established the fact that the fetus is a person, enjoying full protection under the Constitution and the Bill of Rights. Right to choose proponents emphasize that the moral and legal rights of other parties must also be considered, not just those of the fetus (Mace, 1972). What about the rights of the mother, the father, other family members? Should these lives be sacrificed for the sake of the child? Is it right to let the fetus live but to let the mother die so that her husband and other children are deprived of her love? The Constitution guarantees equal protection under the law. Is it moral to force a woman to bear a baby she doesn't want, can't care for, or that might be deformed? Is it moral to insist that an unwanted child be born into the world and then to suffer all of its life because it was never wanted (Lieberman, 1971)? Who has the right to decide? The Supreme Court ruling establishes the legal principle that the mother's right takes precedence, at least in the first trimester of pregnancy. It is obvious that the moral dilemmas raised by the abortion issue are not easy to solve.

Social and Realistic Considerations

Those advocating the right to choose emphasize the realistic position that strict laws against abortion, such as those that permit abortions only when the mother's physical life is threatened, have never worked. If a woman is determined not to have her baby, she will attempt, however foolishly (and sometimes futilely), to abort her own child (Swartz, 1973). Or she will go to an unqualified person and get an illegal abortion that may threaten her own life as well as abort the fetus. Various estimates place the number of illegal abortions before 1967 at around one million per year or about 20 percent of total pregnancies. Maternal death rates from illegal abortions in New York City were about nineteen times higher than those from legal abortions. Legalized abortion, therefore, saves lives by reducing the number of illegal attempts (Guttmacher, 1973).

Strict laws against abortion discriminate against the poor and against deprived minority groups. The low income woman who gets pregnant is either forced to bear her child, to try to abort her own child, or to go to a completely unqualified abortionist, whereas the wealthier woman can afford to pay a competent physician or to fly to another country where abortion is legal (Steinhoff, 1973). As a result, deaths from illegal abortions are concentrated among the poor. Furthermore, the physician tends to treat the low income pregnant woman differently than he does the higher income woman. The low income female is stereotyped as "bad," "stupid," "a tramp," or "a loose woman" and is treated in a public clinic, whereas the high income female who has "been careless" or who has "made a mistake" receives the attentive care of the private physician (Stewart, 1971). Legalizing abortion and establishing clinics and services make better care available to everyone. Data from New York City during the first nine months after the liberalization of its laws showed that the problem of differential access according to race was largely eliminated (Steinhoff, 1973).

In reply to these social and realistic considerations, right to life groups emphasize their fears that without any restriction, except the individual woman and her conscience, an "abortion mentality" develops so that abortions become too commonplace and are performed too easily or for reasons that are not serious. The evidence seems to justify part of this concern. The majority of abortions today are not for medical reasons, but for personal, social, and economic reasons that have to do with the woman's life situation and not with her health (U.S. Department of Health, Education and Welfare, 1971a). A 1970 study in Honolulu among 272 abortion patients summarized the reasons cited by them as to why they wanted an abortion (Steinhoff et al., 1972). The results are shown in table 18-1. The average age of the women was twenty-two and one-half years; more than half were single and could not or did not want to marry the father. Many abortions were first pregnancies. Of course, whether or not these reasons cited are considered "unimportant" or not is partly a matter of opinion. One fact is significant, however, and that is that these women did not want to bear the child, and that in itself is a very important consideration.

Most thoughtful advocates of abortion agree that it should only be a backup measure, not the primary method of birth control, and they urge fuller usage of contraceptives among all sexually active persons (Ballard and Gold, 1972). Physicians worry too about the long-term medical effects of aborting first pregnancies (Wynn and Wynn, 1972). There is some indication that abortion, especially repeated abortion, may be associated with a later inability to conceive or to carry a child to full term and with various birth complications (see Sarvis and Rodman, 1974, pp. 130–132 for a summary of research findings). One answer is a fuller and more efficient use of contraceptives so that repeated abortions are not necessary.

Psychological and Personal Considerations

Right to life proponents have often pointed to the negative psychological effects on the woman who has had an abortion. But the incidence of psychological aftereffects is a major subject of dispute. Both sides cite facts to support their views. Those advocating the right to choose point to the fact that many women are far more depressed before the abortion is performed than they are afterward. When abortions were illegal, much of the anxiety was over the illegality of the act: feelings that have now been eliminated. Also, hostility and resentment toward the woman herself from medical personnel, hospital staff members, even friends and family, can be responsible

TABLE 18-1. *Reasons for abortion most frequently cited by patients*

Reason	Number of Patients	Percentage of Patients
I am not married	116	36.0
I cannot afford to have a child at this time	83	25.7
A child would interfere with my education	50	15.5
A child would interfere with my job or other activity	39	12.0
I think I am too young to have a child	30	9.0

Source: Adapted from P. G. Steinhoff, R. G. Smith, and M. Diamond, "The Characteristics and Motivations of Women Receiving Abortions," *Sociological Symposium,* no. 8 (Spring 1972): 83–90. Reprinted by permission.

Family planning includes being able to have the number of children wanted at the time desired.

an abortion (Fleck, 1970; Smith, 1972). For this reason, abortion counseling, which assists the woman in working through her feelings ahead of time (and afterwards if needed), is a must. But this counseling must not be for the purpose of trying to persuade the woman to make one decision or another, but rather to assist her in making the best decision she can live with (Brashear, 1973; Smith et al., 1971). Each individual is different. For some, abortion provides great relief with little if any disturbance. For others, the experience is upsetting. In one follow-up study of 380 abortion patients at State University Hospital in Syracuse, New York, 65 percent of the women were moderately or very happy about their abortion, while 15 percent were moderately or very sad (Osofsky, 1971). The key factor seems to be whether the woman wants an abortion or whether she is reluctant (Kimball, 1970; Margolis, 1971). Being refused an abortion and forced to bear an unwanted child can lead to psychiatric symptoms. But the woman who has health problems and has to have an abortion, or who is persuaded to have an abortion against her better judgment, is also more likely to show negative psychological reactions following the operation (Levene and Regney, 1970; Pare and Raven, 1970). This is why if the decision is hers, adverse psychological reactions are minimized.

Conclusions

This chapter discusses several important problems. Infertility continues to plague many couples but, with medical help, only about 5 percent of all couples who want children remain childless. Many of these couples turn to adoption as one solution to the problem only to discover a shortage of adoptable babies at least among whites. It seems ironic that at a time when unwed pregnancies, especially among teenagers, are at an all-time high, there is also such a shortage of adopta-

for some of the emotional disturbance of patients. Marder (1970) gives several examples of harassment from medical personnel whose general attitude is one of resentment, "You've had your fun and now you want us to take care of you."

In contrast, right to choose proponents point to the realistic fact that some women do suffer psychological scars as an aftermath of

ble babies. The major reason, of course, is because of the increasing numbers of single women who are keeping their babies. One suspects that many do not have any comprehension of the difficulties they will encounter in raising their children. If they did, more might consider other alternatives. As it is, many turn to relatives for help. Since the baby belongs to the mother, however, unless she legally surrenders her right to it, no one—relatives or others—should try to persuade her either to keep or to give up her child against her will. Since so many of these unmarried mothers, and their children, become wards of the state, it means that the state should take every opportunity to provide counseling help for the prospective mother to assist her is making her decisions responsibly and with full knowledge. It means too that every effort should be made to assist her in completing her education, in training her for employment, and in other ways preparing her to become a financially independent adult.

Much more needs to be done in providing family life education, including full contraceptive education to all young people. The problem of the unmarried woman who becomes pregnant begins when couples first indulge in sexual intercourse without adequate contraceptive knowledge or protection or without motivation to use the best means of birth control available. A society that emphasizes sexuality, but does not also emphasize protection against unwanted pregnancy, is being unrealistic and irresponsible. Either society has to wage an all-out campaign against premarital intercourse or make an all-out effort to insure that unwed pregnancy doesn't happen when intercourse takes place.

It seems ironic, too, that so many babies are being aborted when thousands of couples go childless. One can argue the pros and cons of abortion, with both sides presenting convincing arguments, but let us hope that the decision to have an abortion will never be made frivolously, without any deep thought about the issues involved. Ultimately, the decision has to be the mother's, but society's obligation is to help her make that decision as wisely as possible. Certainly, the Supreme Court decision allowing her the power of choice will do much to prevent unwanted children from being born into the world.

Some mothers will elected to bear their children and give them up for adoption. Others will bear them and raise them themselves. Others will make a conscientious and wise decision to abort. The most that society can do is to offer the kind of supportive counseling and services that will best benefit those making the decision.

"No, I didn't realize what is was going to be like. All you know is that you feel love for a child and want it as your own. You don't know what the problems will be. You don't think of problems." Judy was talking to her second husband Bruce. She was trying to describe her slow realization that both she and her first husband Paul had been unprepared to be adoptive parents.

Paul had been a lecturer at a large metropolitan university. He and Judy were married for eight years during which time two children, a boy and a girl, were born. Judy had finished a doctorate in English literature but was unable, for more than a year, to get a teaching job. At this point, even though the couple were financially strained, they had decided to adopt five-year-old Gerald, an American Indian child.

"I was attracted by the challenge," she told Bruce, "and let's face it, by the sense of responsibility and social purpose that an orphan like Gerald inspires in you. I suppose I knew that I'd have to make an extra effort to make him feel at home. I was going to devote myself to making him feel as one of our family."

Yet well into the probation period of their adoption, she began to get clues that something was wrong with Gerald. She had found a part-time job teaching a course on women in literature at a local college and had placed Gerald in a day care school. For awhile, he seemed quite well adjusted. But toward the beginning of the Easter holidays Gerald had developed an acute rash on his legs, arms, and scalp. He became fretful and irritable at the school and often cried when Judy left him off.

"Then we discovered him washing his hands one evening in the bathroom," she said. "The little thing had been washing himself with a wet cloth after his bath. I asked him what he was doing and he said he was trying to get himself clean. 'But Gerald,' I said, 'you're already fresh and clean.' He said, 'No, Mommy,' He pointed to my arm—he wanted to be clean as me: he meant as white as I am."

"Paul and I weren't getting along very well then either. He objected to almost everything in relation to my career. He was never able to accept me as a partner in the marriage when I was working. His efforts to help Gerald also created problems. I mean, he made a lot of his Indian son. He would dress him in Indian garb and read him stories about frontier days and Indian life. It was well intentioned, but his relationship with Gerald was so starkly different from that with the other children that Gerald didn't really seem his child at all."

"How did the other children react to Gerald?" Bruce asked.

"They really liked him," Judy replied. "They were protective and affectionate. There was no problem with them. Finally, however, Gerald developed sores all over his arms and legs from scratching the rash. The doctor who examined him said it was nerves, so we took him to a child psychiatrist."

"What did the psychiatrist say?" Bruce asked.

"The psychiatrist advised us to use an ointment and prescribed sound mild sedative. She suggested that tensions between Paul and me might be affecting

Gerald. She also suggested to Paul that he try to be less ethnic oriented in his relationship to the child. I don't think that she understood Paul's intentions or the reasons for his wanting to give Gerald pride in his roots. There was a great deal of tension; we were stared at in public whenever we took Gerald out. People would say things that probably affected Gerald's self-image. Paul, in his usual direct way, was only trying to help Gerald. But sophisticated as we both were, we had no idea how conscious we were making the child of his different status in our family."

Shortly after their visit to the psychiatrist, the adoption agency decided against finalizing the adoption. Gerald was taken back and placed in a foster home to await further placement.

"It was the most painful experience of my life,"Judy said. "We all cried. I didn't want to see him go. I am sure that things will be better for him, but I was depressed about it for a long time."

"Perhaps it was for the best," said Bruce, hugging her with a gentle squeeze. "It was an impossible situation, with you and Paul as you were."

"I don't know," Judy said, "I wish we could have kept him."

"You couldn't help it," Bruce said, "it wasn't your fault."

QUESTIONS

1. What is your view of parents of one race or ethnic group adopting a child from a different group?

2. Is it possible for parents of one race to bring up successfully the children of another race?

3. React to Paul's efforts to give Gerald knowledge of his cultural heritage. How might Paul have handled the situation so as not to create problems?

4. Evaluate the adoption agency's decision to take Gerald back. Did they do the right thing?

5. If Judy and Paul had a happy marriage, could the situation have been saved? What could have been done?

CHAPTER
19

Parenthood

CHAPTER OUTLINE

Philosophies of Child Rearing

Parental Roles

Meeting Emotional Needs

Fostering Cognitive and Intellectual Growth

Socialization and Discipline

One-Parent Families

Conclusions: No-Parent Families or Both-Parent Families?

Being parents has many rewards and pleasures (Russell, 1974). For some persons, to live alone—even with a loving mate—is unthinkable (Spock, 1975). They want children as a creative expression of themselves: to love and to be loved by them. They find their own lives enriched by having children (Berelson, 1975). These are romantic feelings, but nevertheless very real and very much a part of being parents. Parents are supposed to be completely altruistic and want children for their own sakes and not for what the children can do for them. But at the same time, there are joys and pleasures. Without some benefits, not many parents would be unselfish enough to be glad they had children.

But learning to become parents is not an easy task. New parents soon learn that taking care of an infant involves long hours of physical labor and many sleepless nights. One mother commented: "No one told me a baby wakes up four or five times a night." Parents soon learn also that their life as a couple isn't the same. They don't have the same freedom of movement and the opportunities to do what they want to do. Furthermore, the parental task is a twenty-four-hour job seven days a week for years and, once begun, is irrevocable. You can't give the baby back. "I think I made a mistake," was one mother's first reaction as she came out from under the anesthetic (Clark, 1972). A baby changes things; it changes everything, so couples need to give considerable thought to the responsibilities involved (Salk, 1974). If they devote themselves to learning how to be the best possible parents, they and their children are better able to enjoy the experience.

Philosophies of Child Rearing

Changing Emphases

Child-rearing philosophies—like fashions— seem to go in cycles (Kephart, 1972). Yesterday's parents, feeling their own parents were too strict, turned to self-demand schedules, child-centered homes, progressive education, and more indulgent concepts of child rearing. Now some parents are worried that today's children are too spoiled so are reacting to what they feel has been overpermissiveness. It is evident that child-rearing philosophies change from one generation to the next and that parents often have to sort out conflicting advice.

Husband-Wife Differences

Husbands and wives often differ with one another on their basic philosophies of child rearing, a situation that can create marital conflict and confusion for the child (Chilman, 1975; Gecas and Nye, 1974; Landis and Landis, 1973; Le Masters, 1970). Each parent tends to feel that the way he or she was reared is the "right way" and that other methods will not achieve as good a result. Parents may sometimes repudiate the methods by which they themselves were reared, and resolve to do differently with their own children. But when such parents begin to have difficulties with their children, they tend to revert back to the old methods their parents used on them (Christensen and Johnsen, 1971). One mother expressed her frustration:

I was brought up by a mother who believed that if she spared the rod she would spoil the child. We had spankings, hard ones, and plenty of them. We didn't dare talk back or argue with her. But when she wasn't around we were little devils, and did all sorts of sneaky things.

I decided I was going to bring up my daughter differently, that I would talk things over with her, and try to reason. But sometimes I get mad and hit her just like my mom did me. It's frightening.

Differences in Children

No one method can be considered "best" for all children. Children are individuals; what works for one may not work for another. One child may need very firm guidance, another is devastated by a mild reprimand. It is necessary, therefore, for parents to learn to be flexible, to adjust their philosophies and methods to the individual child. What is important is the quality of the parent-child relationship, the total climate of the family setting rather than the particular philosophy of child rearing that is followed (Christensen and Johnsen, 1971).

Parental Roles

Meeting Children's Needs

The parental role sounds simple: it is to meet the needs of children so they can grow. Within all children are "the seeds of growth," that is, a natural inclination to develop to maturity. Parents don't have to teach children to grow physically, for example. The tendency to grow is so strong that only by extreme physical deprivation can parents prevent physical development, and even then, some development takes place. This means that the parental task is to discover the *physical needs* of their child and to fulfill those needs.

Similarly, the parental task is to fulfill *emotional needs* so children can grow to become emotionally secure and stable persons. If children's needs for love, affection, security, understanding, and approval are given, they are more likely to develop positive feelings. But if their emotional needs are deprived, the children may become fearful, hostile, insecure, anxious, and rejecting persons.

Children also have *social needs.* They are born naturally gregarious persons. They want to be with others, generally like other people, and ordinarily try to please them and be accepted by them. But these natural tendencies are unsophisticated. Children want friends but don't know how to relate; they want others to like them but don't know how to please. Their need, therefore, is for socialization—to build on their normal desire to belong and to relate by learning group mores, customs, manners, and habits so they can fit into the group. The parental task is to provide their children the necessary opportunities for socialization so that they can become a part of society.

The capacity for intellectual growth is also inborn. Children are born naturally curious. They want to learn about everything. They desire a variety of new experiences by which this learning can take place. The parental role is to fulfill these *intellectual needs* by providing sensory stimulation and a variety of learning experiences involving observation, reading, conversation, and a maximum amount of contact with others and with the natural world. As long as the environment in which children are placed is a stimulating one, as long as the curiosity of children is encouraged, their cognitive development pro-

The parental role is to meet the needs of children so that they can grow.

ceeds at an unbelievably fast rate. But once their surroundings become sterile, unchanging, and uninteresting, or their human contacts and experiences limited, growth stops or slows down because of intellectual deprivation.

Children also have the capacity for moral growth. They are born trusting persons and only become disbelievers and mistrusting when they learn they can't depend upon people around them. They are born with a capacity for the development of a sensitive conscience and with an ability to distinguish different moral values once these are taught. But their ability is only a potential one; it has to be developed through educated reasoning, by imitating the example of others, and through the trial and error of living. The parental role here is to fulfill their children's *moral needs:* for trust and for values to live by.

Sometimes, of course, children's needs aren't met, either because parents can't or won't fulfill them. The children aren't given proper food and rest; they aren't loved; they aren't socialized; they are deprived intellectually and spiritually. When this happens growth stops or slows down, so the children remain physically, emotionally, socially, intellectually, or morally retarded. *Growth takes place by fulfilling needs; retardation occurs because of deprivation.*

Sharing of Responsibilities

If there are two parents with children, the children benefit if both parents share in meeting their needs. The needs of dependent children are not easily met by the mother or father alone, especially if there is more than one child. To expect the mother alone to fulfill the exhausting parenting role is unfair.

Such a mother is overcommitted (LeMasters, 1970). Even if she has only one child and is not working outside the home, she still can't totally fulfill the needs of her child, since her child needs social contacts with adults and with peers. If the mother is alone and separated from the child's father for one reason or another, she may want to draw on outside help frequently and regularly to supplement the help she can give (Geismar, 1973).

A child benefits by being cared for by more than one parent. Every parent has strengths and weaknesses. Most fathers can contribute something positive to a child's life. The best fathers are almost indispensible (Stannard, 1973). One mother relates:

I do an awful lot for the children, but there are some things that John can do better. He can put the baby to bed, rock her, and get her to sleep a lot calmer and easier than I can. I'm too impatient. He teaches our oldest son how to fish, roller skate, and play baseball. I never could do these things. And John is very affectionate. He hugs and kisses Maurine and holds her. I do too, but not like John. She is in seventh heaven when she is in his arms. You don't have to tell me that my children need their father. I know they do.

One must not omit the fact that the father also benefits from caring for his children (Miller, 1971). Changing a baby's diaper is not a very exciting thing to do, but shared companionship during the process may develop a father-child closeness that enriches the father's life as well as the child's.

The modern father's minimal participation in the day-by-day care of children has been well documented and discussed in other chapters of this book (see chapters 7 and 8) (Kotelchuck, 1972; Lopata, 1971; Miller, 1971; Poloma and Garland, 1971; Rebelsky and Hanks, 1971; and Stannard, 1973). Geismar's (1973) study of 555 young families in Newark, New Jersey, who had just had their first child revealed that in only seven families (1.3 percent) was there a fairly equal allocation of physical childcare functions. The mother carried out the physical care alone in 36 percent of the families and received some help from the father in 34 percent. While middle-class fathers took a more active role than lower class fathers, this study as well as others revealed that the major responsibilities for childcare still fell most heavily on the mother.

This situation is slowly changing. There is increasing recognition that fathers can and should participate in the child-rearing facets of family life and that if they do not, their children miss much and they themselves are missing out on a chance for self-actualization (Clayton, 1975).

Meeting Emotional Needs

The Infant's Emotional Needs

The basic emotional needs of infants are for security, trust, love and affection, and self-esteem. The psychoanalyst Erikson (1959) found through psychotherapy with children that developing trust is the basic *psychosocial task* during the first years of life. If infants are well-handled and nurtured and loved, they develop trust and security and a basic optimism. Badly handled, they become insecure and mistrustful. During the first year of life, parents can best meet these needs by fostering their children's feeling of dependency, helping them feel totally secure. This is accomplished in several ways. The home environment is important. If it is fairly relaxed, free of tension and anxiety, if it is a pleasant, happy place, children develop a feeling of well-being just by living there. The emotional tone that parents convey is also important. Warm, loving, pleasant parents who are themselves calm and relaxed convey these feelings to their children. Being able to depend on parents for need fulfillment, whether it be for food when hungry or for comfort when upset, also develops children's sense of security and trust. Physical contact and closeness is also important. Children feel secure when held close to one's own warm body, when they can feel their hand on one's face, or feel the comfort of loving arms. Even when sleeping, children feel more secure wrapped in a blanket than lying exposed to the world. Mention has already been made in the previous chapter of the importance of sucking as a means of gaining security. Children usually need several hours of sucking daily apart from their nutritional requirements. Above all, children need to feel they are wanted and accepted, that their parents truly like them and approve of them. These feelings, when transmitted to them, build their own sense of self-esteem.

Emotional Attachments

Research has shown that children begin to make emotional attachments to other people very early in their development. By three weeks of age, a live human face elicits more excitement than a moving drawing of a face. A baby will smile readily at the sight of a human face by the time he or she is five or six weeks old (Smart and Smart, 1972). Some infants are able to recognize their mother by one month of age; 81 percent can by three months, and all normal infants can by five months. Confidence in the mother as evidenced by signs of expecting her to soothe or comfort is shown by half of babies studied at three months and in 75 percent of babies at nine months.

Even though babies are able quite early to distinguish the mother from other persons, infants develop emotional attachments to persons in general before they become attached to one person. A study of sixty infants focused on their protest at being separated from objects of attachment by ascertaining the extent of their crying and whimpering (Schaffer and Emerson, 1964). The situations were everyday, ordinary occurrences, such as being left alone in a room, being left in a pram (this was a British study) outside a store, and being put down from arms or lap. It was found that half of the specific attachments, including attachments to mother, occurred most often between twenty-five and thirty-two weeks. Strongly attached infants were found to have mothers who responded quickly to their indications of need. Individuals showed variations from time to time in the strength of their protest over separation. If the infant was left outside on the street with other persons around and things happening, the protest was less than if the infant was left alone in a room. If the infant was ill, in pain, fatigued, or afraid at the time, the protest was stronger in seeking the mother's presence. When the attachment object returned, such as the father returning from work, the infant demanded more attention for awhile. Figure 19-1 shows the development of the infant's attachments at different ages (Schaffer and Emerson, 1964).

These findings mean that if a parent has to absent herself or himself from a child in the early months of the infant's life, the child will not usually be too upset if there is a competent substitute, especially one to whom the infant has also formed an attachment (Bell, 1970). Upset can be avoided by leaving children only with sitters to whom they have become attached. When a new sitter is hired, a parent should also stay until the child gets used to that person.

Effects of Separation and Rejection

One investigation of separations because of hospitalization showed that when children between about eight months and three years of age were left by their mother, they were likely to cry and protest, showing acute distress in trying to find and regain the mother

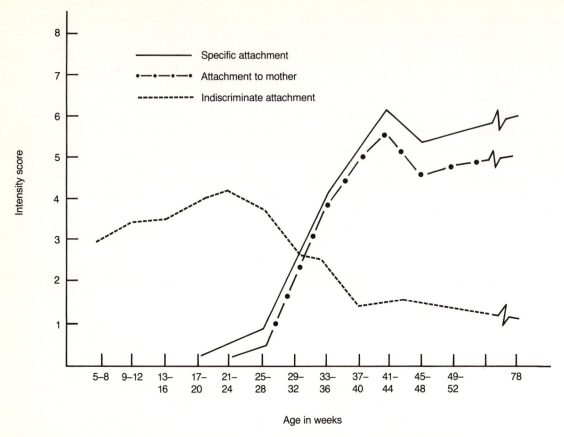

FIGURE 19-1. *Development of infants' attachments (Source: Adapted from H. R. Schaffer and P. E. Emerson, "The Development of Social Attachments in Infancy,"* Monographs of The Society for Research in Child Development *29 [1964]:3. Reprinted by permission of The Society for Research in Child Development, Inc.)*

(Bowlby, 1969). The initial phase gave way to quiet despair, followed by more attention to the environment and interaction with other people. When children were separated from parents and then went home, they showed more anger and aggression and more whining and clinging (Ainsworth and Bell, 1970). If the parents gave extra opportunities for proximity and contact, recovery was more rapid. The parents who reject or ignore their children only encourage their children's attachment behavior.

Older infants may be left for several hours at a time without upset, provided they have acceptable substitute care from a person to whom they are also attached. If one parent is away a lot, however, it is reassuring to the child to have the care of the other parent, or, if this is impossible, then the same substitute parent each time. If both parents have to work, it is helpful if their hours can be staggered so only one is away at once, at least for part of the day. Part-time work of one or both may enable at least one parent to be home while the other works. If both have to work the same hours, then a regular parent substitute on an individual basis may be the best they can do. Separation, in the form of rejection rather than physical separation as such, can also be upsetting (Salk, 1974).

Group Care

Some authorities feel that group care is more appropriate after two-and-one-half to three years of age—at the time the child needs contacts with peers (Salk, 1974). If day care at younger ages is necessary, however, it is less upsetting if a child is cared for at the center by the same adult each day. There are authorities who feel that during the first three years of life, group care is never as adequate as individual care and that substitutes for parents can never take the place of the care of at least one parent (Salk, 1974; Stannard, 1973). For some contrary opinions and a fuller discussion of day care, see chapters 7 and 9.

Fears of Spoiling

One of the most frequent worries of new parents is that they will spoil their children. Because of this fear, they sometimes don't give children as much care as they really need. The fact remains that no child is spoiled by love, by being given appropriate affection and attention as needed. Children who are starved for affection do either of two things. Either they withdraw and become calloused and indifferent to whether they are loved or not or they become even more demanding (Ainsworth, 1970). Current psychology suggests that the syndrome of spoiling, cl racterized by excessive demands, sulking, pouting, crying, or temper tantrums to get one's own way occurs not as a result of lavish affection "but rather from (1) a lack of emotional support and affection and (2) a family environment that is authoritarian or that fails to be demonstrative in its affectional interaction" (Saxton, 1972, p. 425). Emotional deprivation increases anxiety and stimulates further de-

mands from the child. Of course, children can be spoiled by overprotective, overpermissive, inappropriate indulgence.

Autonomy

One of the emotional needs of children beginning at about age eighteen months and continuing for more than two years is the need for autonomy, that is, the need to assert independence and self-will and to assert their rights to be individuals (Erikson, 1959). This stage has been called "the terrible twos" when two-year-olds will resolutely fold their arms to prevent their parents from holding their hands as they cross the street. "No, I don't want to" becomes a familiar sound throughout the house during this period.

If children are to function as individuals, they want to learn to do things for themselves: to walk, to pick up and manipulate objects, to feed themselves, to hang on to things to prevent falling. As soon as children can move around, they will push adults away, protest against them. This is the child's way of trying to become a person. "Me do" is the key phrase during this period (Smart and Smart, 1972).

Since children of this age are not as capable as they would like to be, frustration and anger are frequent and temper outbursts increase. Figure 19-2 shows the results of a classic study by Goodenough (1931) from *Anger in Young Children*. As can be seen, there was a marked peak in anger outbursts during the second year and a decline thereafter. Physical factors were found to influence anger responses. Children showed more anger responses before mealtime, or when ill, even with slight colds or constipation.

The parent's role is to encourage independence in such things as eating, playing with toys, walking and so forth and to guide through substitution, distraction, and tactful control, trying to avoid direct confrontations

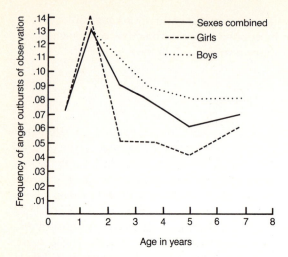

FIGURE 19-2. *Number of anger outbursts in ten hours by age and sex (Source: Adapted from F. L. Goodenough,* Anger in Young Children *[Minneapolis: University of Minnesota Press, 1931]. Reprinted by permission.)*

as often as possible. Children whose autonomy is encouraged tend, as preschoolers, to show more favorable personality characteristics such as a sense of self-worth, resistance to discouragement, and a capacity to tolerate parental deprivation than do children whose parents do not permit such autonomy (Smart and Smart, 1972).

Fostering Cognitive and Intellectual Growth

Cognition

The word *cognition* is derived from the Latin *cognoscere,* "to know." It refers to individuals becoming acquainted with the world and objects in it, including themselves. They do this by taking in information through the senses of vision, touch, taste, hearing, and smell, processing this information and acting on it. This process goes on daily so that the infant is developing cognitively all the time (Duvall, 1971; Furth, 1970; Piaget and Inhelder, 1969).

Parental Contributions

Parents can assist in this development in two major ways. One way is by providing secure human relationships from which exploration can take place. Cognitive development proceeds faster when the child feels emotionally secure (Ainsworth and Bell, 1970). The emotional climate of the home, the degree of affectionate interchange in the family, the emotional closeness between parent and children, and the extent of parental compatibility and agreement over discipline have all been found to correlate with intelligence test scores during childhood and adolescence. The degree of emotional security and cognitive growth are very much related.

In addition to providing a secure base, parents can enhance cognitive development: by offering a stimulating and intellectually rich environment. This means talking and singing to babies, playing music, offering objects that vary in shape, texture, size, and color, propping babies up so they can see, taking them places so as to expose them to a variety of sights, sounds, and people, offering toy and play materials to look at, hold, squeeze, suck, bite, taste, smell, hear, examine, climb onto, crawl under, push, pull, drag, ride, swing, jump, float, and splash.

Sensorimotor Deprivation

Children who are culturally deprived do much poorer on IQ tests because of cognitive retardation. The theory of Head Start is to compensate for this cultural deprivation by offering an environment rich in sensorimotor experiences. While Head Start helps, the one disadvantage of the program is that it is offered too late. Intervention by eighteen months is recommended for infants who are markedly culturally deprived. Infant education programs may involve individual tutors at home or giving mothers special training in enriching their children's experiences at home. Results from studies show significant improvement in IQ of children who have been exposed to this type of compensatory education (Painter, 1969).

Language Development and Cultivation

In the beginning, human babies utter vowel-like sounds that are expressions of emotional distress or of comfort. The median time for uttering the first word is around eleven months. By twelve months the average vocabulary is two words. From twelve to eighteen months, babies begin to combine words. The earliest sentences are usually two words: a noun and a verb or predicate word, such as "Daddy all gone." Between nine and twelve months, babies show they understand words and respond and adjust to them. A baby may open its mouth in response to the word "cracker" or accept a glass of water in response to the word "drink" (Rebelsky et al., 1967).

The rapidity of language development has a definite relationship to environment and human relationships. Slowness in starting to talk, defective articulation, and stuttering are all associated with certain kinds of disturbing parent-child relationships. Parents who read stories to their children enable them to produce significantly more sounds and so learn to talk earlier than do other infants. Both the amount and warmth of the vocalization of mothers with their infants are related to vocalization of their children. "These studies offer convincing proof that the infant's early experiences with people's talking have definite effects on his own language behavior" (Smart and Smart, 1972, p. 129).

Socialization and Discipline

The Family's Role in Socialization

Socialization is the process by which persons learn the ways of a given society or social groups so that they can function within it. The dictionary says it is "to make fit for life in companionship with others." Children are taught the ways and values of their society through contact with already socialized individuals, initially the family. The family is important because it has children first, maintains contact with them over a longer period of time than any other group, and through close emotional associations is able to exert a maximum influence in their lives (Bell, 1975). Both adult and older sibling members act as role models in providing examples for children in the development of their personality, attitudes, and behavior.

If parents choose to absent themselves from the home a great deal, other adults may exert more socializing influence on small children than do the parents. As the children get older and are able to maintain contacts with their peers, the peer group may take over and begin to exert more influence in developing values. Bronfenbrenner (1969) suggests that in many urban and suburban homes, where the parents of school-age children are not often home and the children themselves are with their peers most of the time, peer contacts exert the greatest influence on values. Ordinarily, it is adults who are able to teach such values as cooperation, unselfishness, consideration for others, and responsibility. Peer values often emphasize aggressive, antisocial behavior (Bronfenbrenner, 1975). Thus, by default through their own noninteraction with their children, adults are exposing their children to other influences. In a recent interview, Bronfenbrenner commented:

If parents begin to drop out as parents even before the child enters school, you then begin to get children who become behavior problems because they haven't been "socialized. . . ." They haven't learned responsibility, consideration for others. You learn that from adults. There's no way that you can learn it from kids of your own age (Bronfenbrenner, 1975, p. 49).

Socialization means "to make fit for life in companionship with others."

Numerous parents try to be home when their children come home from school, they take an active role in the education and training of their children, and they are important influences in their children's lives. But Bronfenbrenner is pointing to an important trend: the trend for fewer and fewer parents to spend the necessary time with their children so they can make their influence felt. When this happens, other persons or groups assume this important role of the family.

and in accord with the rules and regulations established by the group.

In the beginning, control over the child is established by external authority, but gradually children are encouraged to adopt these principles for themselves so that the standards they strive to follow become a part of their own lives, not because they have to but because they want to. When this happens, these *internalized truths* become their own standard of conduct (Elkind, 1970; Kay, 1969).

Meaning and Goals of Discipline

The word *discipline* comes from the same root as does the world disciple, which means "a learner." Discipline, therefore, is a process of learning, of education, a means by which socialization takes place. Its purpose is instruction in proper conduct or action rather than a means of punishment. The ultimate goal of discipline is to sensitize the conscience and to develop inner self-controls, so that individuals live according to the standards of behavior

Principles of Discipline

If discipline is to accomplish its goal of developing inner controls, there are a number of principles that, if followed, enhance this development. These may be summarized as follows: *Children respond more readily to parents within the context of a loving, trusting relationship of mutual esteem.* Heise writes: "The degree of love and the degree of control exercised in a parent-child relationship are seen to interact" (Heise, 1972, p. 30).

Discipline is more effective when it is consistent rather than erratic (Deur and Parke, 1970).

Learning is enhanced if responses involve rewards and punishments, that is, if reenforcement is both positive and negative (Eshleman, 1974).

Discipline is more effective when applied as soon after the offense as possible.

Severe punishment, especially if it is cruel and abusive, is counterproductive because it stimulates resentment, rejection, and similar harsh, cruel behavior on the part of children.

Discipline becomes less effective if it is too strict or too often applied. A parent who continually criticizes a child no matter what the child does is teaching the child that it is impossible to please the parents.

All children want and need external controls in the beginning, since they are not yet mature enough to exert self-control over their own behavior. Appropriate methods of discipline will vary according to the child's age and level of understanding. At very young ages discipline may be accomplished through wise management: providing interesting toys and activities, equipping sections of the residence such as a play room or play yard, or childproofing the house by keeping dangerous things out of reach. Young children may be disciplined through distraction and offering substitute activities. Sometimes the wisest discipline is through environmental manipulation: removing the child from the situation or the situation from the child. Parents can discuss issues with older children and arrive at joint decisions, whereas instruction to preschoolers necessarily involves more imperatives. Even then, explanations and reasons are helpful, depending upon the children's level of understanding.

Methods of discipline to be avoided are those that threaten the child's security or his development and self-esteem. In some cases, parents threaten to give children away if they aren't good or to call a policeman to put them in jail. Such threats create great harm since they undermine children's trust in their parents. Similarly, threats to withdraw love if children aren't good is a harmful means of disciplining, but it is one that middle-class parents often employ in subtle ways to control their children's behavior (Maslow, 1970). It may work to control behavior, but it is devastating to the child's security if regularly employed.

One-Parent Families

Occurrence

So far, the discussion in this chapter has implied that there are two parents at home who are able and willing to meet children's needs. In many families this is not the case. In 1979, 19 percent of all families with children living at home were maintained by one parent. Of this total number, 90 percent were maintained by mothers, only 10 percent were maintained by the fathers. These figures continue to grow. Between 1970 and 1979, there was a 5 percent increase in the number of one-parent families (Rice, 1979; U.S. Department of Commerce, July 1980). Rising divorce rates mean that these families will increase even more in the years ahead. This means that the one-parent family represents a major segment of the population, especially among black families (Lincoln, 1971; Staples, 1973) and especially among the poor (Le Masters, 1970). Figure 19-3 shows the proportion of all families with children present that are one-parent families (U.S. Department of Commerce, July 1980).

Special Problems of the Female–Headed Family

One of the most important problems of the female-headed family is limited income (Blueston et al., 1971; Brandwein et al., 1974). The

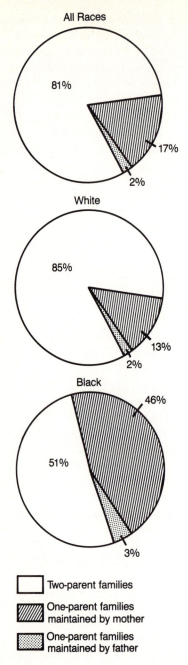

FIGURE 19-3. *One-parent families as a proportion of all families with children present: 1979 (Source: Adapted from U.S. Bureau of the Census, Department of Commerce, "Household and Family Characteristics: March 1979,"* Current Population Reports, *Series P-20, no. 352, July 1980.)*

median income of families headed by a woman is less than half the income of families with a male head (Nye and Berardo, 1973). As a consequence, about 60 percent of these mothers are on welfare (Stein, 1970 U.S. Department of Health, Education and Welfare, January 1973a). Other help comes from the families of these mothers (Sussman, 1971).

Another major problem of these women is that of inadequate childcare (see chapter 7) (Kriesberg, 1970; Schlesinger, 1973; U.S. Women's Bureau, 1973). Day-care centers are sparse or nonexistent, with only 6 percent of children of working mothers in group care (Brandwein et al., 1974). Additional mothers might work if good day care were available (Hedges and Barnett, 1972; Oldham, 1971).

The mother who is left alone to bring up her children herself may have difficulty performing all family functions well. One woman states:

I found managing the household finances difficult, as my husband had looked after them. Household repairs were another problem. I had difficulty deciding if I were making the right decisions as we had always decided everything together.... Suddenly I had to do everything alone (Schlesinger, 1972, p. 363).

There may be little time or energy left to perform household tasks, which means either the house is dirty, little time is available for food preparation, or the physical and emotional care of the children is neglected (Burgess, 1970; Glasser and Navarre, 1974).

The mother must also deal with her own emotional needs for affection and adult companionship. She often feels isolated from the mainstream of social life, which is organized for couples. One widow remarked: "I still haven't got used to it. You can be alone in a big crowd" (Schlesinger, 1972, p. 364). Some of these mothers turn to their children for emotional gratification. Maternal possessiveness and overprotection are quite common, with the result that the children become overdependent. Delayed marriage or lack of autonomy may be the result (Biller, 1971; Blood, 1972; Glasser and Navarre, 1974).

Many solitary parents seek social outlets outside of the home through a variety of groups. *Parents without Partners* was organized not only to help parents with problems with their children but also to meet the social and emotional needs of adults who are alone (Clayton, 1971).

The adjustments of the female single parent differ, depending upon the reason for the absence of the husband (LeMasters, 1970). The *deserted mother* is more likely to have severe financial problems because the withdrawal of economic support is sudden and no support payments have been previously agreed upon. Psychologically, desertion is more traumatic than divorce because it is more unilateral, more sudden, and less planned. Furthermore, the mother is less free to go with other men and is not legally free to remarry. Overall, the more traumatic the experience for the woman, the harder it is for the children. The *separated mother* has greater advantages than the deserted mother since presumably the arrangement has been arrived at by mutual agreement. She has some of the disadvantages of the deserted mother—she is not free to marry and her courtship status is ambiguous. One woman remarked:

I am in an anomalous position; I don't belong to anybody; I am a social misfit. It weighs heavily against meeting anyone with a view to remarriage. I am not anything. I am just a woman that is not living with her husband. . . . I would like to be finished and be free of him. I am nowhere and I don't see getting out of it. He does not want a divorce; he does not want to remarry (Schlesinger, 1972, p. 365).

Under these circumstances, it is pretty difficult for the woman to reorient her life.

The *widowed mother* has one big advantage in the favorable attitudes of family, friends, and community toward her. This helps her self-concept and gives her emotional support. The emotional upset of the loss of spouse, however, is difficult to overcome (Schlesinger, 1972). Once she gets through the period of bereavement, she has the usual financial and social problems and the problems of childcare.

The *unmarried mother* has many disadvantages. Many of these women are immature and dependent on others. They suffer from a lack of education and income, the possibility of sexual exploitation and subsequent pregnancies, isolation from unmarried friends of their own age, and societal sanctions against them.

Special Problems of the Male-headed Family

Solo fathers usually do not suffer poverty to the same extent as do solo mothers (Schlesinger, 1972). Most have a greater income than do their female counterparts but still not as large an income as do married men (U.S. Department of Commerce, Statistical Abstract, 1980). Many solo fathers hire help. Others become adept at the various tasks of home management: shopping for food and clothes, preparing meals, doing the family laundry, and cleaning the home. For other men, a stove or iron remains a mystery forever. If the children are of preschool age, however, all fathers are faced with the same dilemma as are solo mothers who must work, that of finding adequate childcare services. This is a strain on a limited income, so such fathers have a difficult time financially. Even if the man can afford household help and childcare, he experiences a profound change in his daily life: he now must make provisions for his own daily maintenance and care and that of the children. Many of the things he took for granted, such as someone doing the laundry, he must now do himself.

Psychologically, men who have lost their

wives suffer from the same syndrome as women who have lost their husbands—loneliness, sorrow, perhaps bitterness or a sense of failure (if divorced), plus a feeling of being overwhelmed by their responsibilities for their children. It is no wonder that so many men solve their problems by searching for a new partner and remarrying.

Effects of Paternal Absence on Sons

The important question that plagues both parents and professionals is whether or not children grow up to be maladjusted because of the lack of two parents in the home. The findings reveal that the earlier a boy is separated from his father, and the longer the separation is, the more affected the boy will be in his early years (Blanchard and Biller, 1971). One study of fifth-grade boys who were father absent before age two were found to be less trusting, less industrious, and to have more feelings of inferiority than boys who became father absent between the ages of three to five (Santrock, 1970a). Father absence also affects the development of masculinity. Father-absent boys are more likely to score less on measures of masculinity (Biller and Bahm, 1971), to have unmasculine self-concepts and sex-role orientations and to be more dependent, less aggressive, and less competent in peer relationships than their father-present counterparts (Santrock, 1970b).

As boys grow older, however, the earlier effects of father absence decrease (Santrock and Wohlford, 1970). By late childhood lower-class father-absent boys appear to score at least as high as their father-present counterparts on certain measures of sex role preference and sex role adoption. By adolescence there is relatively little difference among lower-class father-present and father-absent boys with respect to many facets of sex role

awareness, preference, and adoption (Biller, 1971).

The effect of father absence is dependent partially on whether or not boys have other male surrogate models. Father-absent boys with a father substitute such as an older male sibling are less affected than those without a father substitute (Santrock, 1970b). Male peers, especially older peers, may become important substitute models for paternally deprived boys. Young father-absent male children seek the attention of older males and are strongly motivated to imitate and please potential father figures (Biller, 1971).

Effects of Paternal Absence on Daughters

The effect of paternal absence on daughters has not been as extensively studied as has been the effect on sons. The reasoning has been that children make a same-sex identification so daughters would be affected less by the father's absence than would be sons. Girls aren't affected as much when they are young, but they are definitely affected during adolescence. Lack of meaningful male-female relationships in childhood can make it more difficult to relate to the opposite sex. One study showed that fatherless girls when they grew up had more difficulty in achieving satisfactory sexual relationships with their husbands than did father-present girls (Jacobson and Ryder, 1969). Case studies of father-absent girls are often filled with details of problems concerning interactions with males. In one study of a group of girls who grew up without fathers, Hetherington (1973) found few effects during preadolescence, but during adolescence the girls of divorced parents who had lived with their mothers were inappropriately assertive, seductive, and sometimes sexually promiscuous. Having ambivalent feelings about men because of their negative memories of their fathers, they pursued men in inept and inappropriate ways. They began dating early and were likely to engage in sexual intercourse at an early age. Girls whose fathers were dead were excessively shy and uncomfortable around men, probably because they did not have as much experience in being around men as did girls who grew up with males at home.

Paternal absence may have a negative effect on a girl's feminine development. Father absence during adolescence has been associated with low femininity interests and less feminine self-concepts (Landy et al., 1969). Father-absent girls may have trouble dealing with their aggressive impulses; they are more likely to have emotional problems, a high degree of anxiety, or to evidence delinquent behavior than are father-present girls. They frequently show school maladjustments, excessive sexual interest, and social acting-out behavior. They are often overly dependent on their mothers, which is associated with low peer status (Biller, 1971).

In summary, therefore, fathers appear to play a significant role in encouraging their daughter's feminine development. The father's acceptance and reenforcement of his daughter's femininity greatly facilitates the development of her self-concept. Interaction with a competent father also provides the girl with basic experiences that help in her relationship with other males. Girls who have positive relationships with their fathers are more likely to be able to obtain satisfaction in their later heterosexual relationships (Biller, 1971).

This does not mean, of course, that a father-present home is thereby always better for the children than a father-absent home. Some fathers, though home, are ineffectual models. One study showed that fathers who were home spent less than one minute a day verbalizing to their infants (Rebelsky and Hanks, 1971). Another showed that 75 percent of professional fathers took no routine role in childcare (Kotelchuck, 1972). In such families, father absence would not have as much effect as in homes where the father spent more time with his children.

Some fathers are also inappropriate models. The father who presents an image of an irresponsible, immature, alcoholic, cruel, or promiscuous male may be exerting an influence that is primarily negative. If there is a father at home who is rejecting, paternal deprivation may be a significant cause of emotional problems and/or antisocial behavior. Some fathers tend to ignore their daughters (Josephson 1969). One cannot say that the influence in the lives of their daughters was very positive. Females who have been devalued and rejected by their fathers are more likely to become homosexual than are those who have had a warm, affectionate relationship with them (Biller, 1971).

The effect of paternal absence on the mother is crucial in determining the influence on the children (Brandwein et al., 1974). Many father-absence studies have failed to take into account the mother's changed position following a divorce, separation, or the death of her husband. (See critical analysis by Herzog and Sudia [1971] and by Billingsley and Giovannoni [1971].) If the mother is quite upset, if her income is severely limited, if her authority and status in the eyes of the children is significantly reduced, if she must absent herself frequently from the home because she has to work, or if she has inadequate care for her children when she is gone, the children are going to be affected, not because of their father's absence, as such, but because of the subsequent effect on their mother and their relationships with her. The children may be affected by their mother's upset and/ or absence, not by their father's absence as such. As has also been seen, the presence of surrogate father figures exerts a modifying influence on both boys and girls (Herzog and Sudia, 1971).

Conclusions: No-Parent Families or Both-Parent Families?

Basically, couples today have a number of important choices to make as these relate to children. The decision to become a parent involves a responsibility for meeting children's needs. If people are unwilling to accept this responsibility, they should not become parents. Why should children be brought into the world only to be deprived of satisfaction of their needs?

This does not mean that the total burden for childcare should or can be borne by the mother. Too many men want children, but they expect that their wives will take care of them. Meanwhile they go about their own business and pleasures, ignoring their all-important role as father. When women were home most of the time, more fathers were also home. The needs of children were met by both parents. Then, as fathers began to go away from home to work, the children missed their fathers, but the mother was there to take up part of the slack.

Today, however, both parents may be absent from the house, either because both are employed outside the home or because both seek their social life apart from their home. There are those who feel that the basic problem with today's family is that so many mothers are working. Many of these persons feel that the solution is to keep the mother at home. But if the father has dropped out of the childcaring role, today's problem is not that the mother is gone but that both parents are gone. Even when fathers are home, they are not spending time with their children. Meanwhile, the frantic wife and mother is trying to do everything she always did, plus go out to work. Obviously, she can't do everything. Of course, there are large numbers of mothers who aren't working, particularly among the middle- and upper-middle classes, and who are busily engaged in their own pursuits and who never have time to spend with their children either.

As a consequence, the emotional needs of many children are not being met, so they are seeking intimacy with their friends. Children are not socialized as much by parents; the school and peer groups are taking over more and more of the socializing functions. As a result, many of the attitudes, values, and customs children are learning are in conflict with those that parents would like them to learn. Parents are concerned about the values their children are learning from their peers, but some parents are not willing or able to spend the time to teach *their own* values. Recent summaries of test scores have shown that the cognitive development of children is being retarded. One explanation is the lack of family stimulation, plus basic insecurities in children because of emotional deprivation that affects their intellectual development.

One answer is to offer more societal supervision of children. This is desperately needed. Some parents who are raising their children alone aren't negligent; many are very conscientious, but they need help. Another answer is to turn increasing attention to a needed shift in the male role. Women are now reexamining and reorienting the female's role. But males have not increased their family responsibilities significantly, except for their breadwinning function. As a result, there is a gap in parental care, and children are suffering because of it. When *Playboy, Esquire, Fortune,* and other traditionally male magazines begin to print as many articles about being good fathers as they print about being good lovers, males will be more influenced to accept their fatherhood roles. Also, much of the research relating to marriage and parenthood involves only the females in the family. Attention must now focus on the husband and father to find out more about what has happened and about what needs to be done. Somehow, American males have to be convinced that being a good father and an attentive husband has as much value as economic success, sexual prowess, a low golf score, or an afternoon of football on television. Their wives are leaving them by the thousands, since many of the wives are realizing that they can get along just as well without them. It would seem that an alternative answer to living apart is to learn to live together and to truly share the total task of raising the children and maintaining the family.

Nontraditional Marriages

CHAPTER
20

Variant Marital Forms

CHAPTER OUTLINE

Marriage as a Personal Contract

Marriage as a Renewable Contract

Marriage as a Contract by Stages

Extramarital and Comarital Sex

Swinging

Intimate Friendships

Group Marriage

Communes

Voluntary Childlessness

Attitudes of College Students

Conclusions

Dialogue

High divorce rates and marital dissatisfaction have stimulated much thought about how to improve traditional marital forms. One idea is for each couple to draw up a detailed personal contract, outlining in detail the rights, duties, and promises made in relation to such things as marital roles, sex, money, in-laws, children, birth control, and other aspects of married life. The intent of such a contract is to guarantee the rights and outline the duties of the husband and wife and to assure that sexist prejudices and discrimination are eliminated.

One of the most serious questions that has been raised is whether the marital agreement as a civil contract should be binding for life. Numerous writers have proposed instead that the marital contract be for a limited period of time—two to five years—and subject to renewal. In order to eliminate mismatched and hasty marriages, other writers have suggested that marriage take place in stages. These proposals usually suggest a period of probation for several years before the marriage becomes finalized.

Some couples are experimenting with other variant marital forms. Some have adopted entirely new lifestyles in rural **communes.** Others hold on to their positions and employment while they experiment with **group marriages** or urban communal living. Others are rejecting a lifetime of social mores and are experimenting with sexually open marriages or exchanging partners with close friends or even with strangers. People grow restless and leave the establishment behind them while they make the trek to "Morning Glory Commune" or to other "utopian" gatherings that promise freedom and fulfillment and a life completely different from the one they left behind.

These are significant happenings that need to be understood. This chapter reveals what modern research has found out about these variant family forms that are emerging.

Marriage as a Personal Contract

All persons who get legally married enter into a civil contract. This means that their marriage is not just a personal affair. It is also of social concern, so each state has set up laws that define one's eligibility to marry and that govern the contract once it is made (Albrecht and Bock, 1972; Bowman, 1974). Once legally established, the two members of a marital contract cannot voluntarily alter or break the contract. The contract can only be severed by official action of the state in accordance with established laws (Bell, 1975).

In recent years there has been an increasing use of personal marriage contracts in addition to the usual legal agreements (Sussman, 1974b). Part of the impetus has come from the women's movement, whose members seek complete sex-role equality in marriage (see also chapter 7). The feeling has been that if a couple draws up a written agreement prior to marriage, or even after marriage, outlining husband and wife roles, relationships, and responsibilities, the marriage is more likely to be an egalitarian relationship (Pierson and D'Antonio, 1974; Weitzman, 1978). When a couple supports and signs such an agreement, husbands are more likely to share in household chores, to look upon their wives as equal partners, and to be relieved of the entire responsibility of earning family income. Advocates also point out that issues are clarified and conflicts are minimized (Sussman, 1974a). There are even marriage counselors who use the contract principle of negotiation and reciprocity to assist couples in working out their problems (Skolnick, 1973; Weiss et al., 1974).

Personal marriage contracts are not new. Religious wedding rites end in a formal agreement with the couple exchanging vows. *The real difference between traditional agreements and the type of personal marriage contract referred to here is that the latter is usually more extensive, outlining more detailed rights, duties, and roles of both husband and wife.* Also, the personal marriage contract is usually written by the individual couple themselves (Shulman, 1970). Other parties are required as witnesses if the couple seek legal sanction of their actions. Many courts will now enforce contracts found to be fairly and freely entered, recognizing that such contracts can promote marital happiness. The courts will, however, disallow contracts in which shrewd and calculating spouses take advantage of others. The point is, the courts no longer automatically declare antenuptial contracts invalid. They weigh the fairness in individual instances (Krauskopf, 1979).

Areas of Concern

In their study of personal contracts at Case Western Reserve University, Sussman and colleagues (1974b) suggest the following categories of provisions in the contract as both salient and relevant. These categories are those the researchers found most frequently in their surveys of contracts.

Economic. This major category could include a discussion of ownership of property acquired before and after marriage. Will assets be held and managed separately or be merged and jointly managed? The division of assets and income acquired after marriage would also be discussed. Will part or all of assets and income be pooled? If part is pooled, how is the proportion determined? Will the couple contribute half each or proportionately to income? What if one is involuntarily unemployed due to layoff, illness, or pregnancy? The researchers suggest that, to avoid placing either partner in a dependent position, the person losing a job be considered as having already contributed a proportional share.

Children. This category would discuss the decision to have or not to have children, the shared or assigned responsibility for birth control, and the attitude toward abortions, taking into account especially the woman's decision. The contract would also cover the responsibility for financial support of children during marriage and possibly in case of divorce, irrespective of custody.

Career and Domicile. This category discusses the intention of the partners to maintain their individual careers outside the home, with equal importance attached to careers of wife and husband. The researchers suggest that some husbands waive their legal right solely to determine the couple's domicile, that equal importance be attached to the careers of wife and husband, that moves be decided jointly with consideration given to the overall advantages and disadvantages to the marriage of the move, and that the amount of income not be the controlling factor in deciding a move (Sheresky and Mannes, 1973).

Relationships with Others. This category would include a discussion of friendships, time devoted to individual interests and to each other, an agreement regarding sexual fidelity.

Division of Household Responsibilities. This category would discuss how household responsibilities are divided. Three possibilities were suggested: (1) both partners share everything equally, (2) both partners share equally but the division be flexible and periodically realigned to take into account individual schedules and changing preferences, or (3) jobs and schedules be rigidly outlined on a day-to-day, almost hourly, basis (Shulman, 1970).

Renewability, Change, and Termination of Contract. This category discusses the provisions and means for periodic reevaluation of the contract. It was suggested that reevaluation be made whenever either party desired it, at least yearly on the anniversary of the contract, and after the birth of a child. In case of unresolved conflicts, the partners would agree to arbitration by an objective third party. Provisions for contract termination could be discussed, but it was suggested that the contract be terminated at the desire of either partner and be uncontested. Breach of a substantial provision of the contract could also constitute grounds for termination. If the woman has foregone further education and career to stay home and care for children and household, it is suggested by the researchers that if the contract is terminated that the wife receive a lump sum payment in compensation. If either partner has paid the educational expenses of the other, the receiving partner would be obligated to repay the expense.

Other Provisions. Other provisions occurring less frequently include a discussion of the woman's name after marriage, religion, relations with in-laws or families of previous marriages, or items dealing with decision making (Sheresky and Mannes, 1973 p. 11).

Other writers divide the categories differently. One writer suggests that marriage imposes both rights and duties and in four major areas—*sexuality, children, domestic and economic services,* and *property* ("Making a Marriage," 1973). The rights and duties in these four areas could be spelled out in the personal contract.

More radical writers have suggested that the marital contract include even such things as a declaration of marital intent, the past history and present status of the two people, future expectations with respect to support, residence, religion, work, sex life, the children, present assets, the future ownership of property, and matters of estate. The chief argument given in favor of writing such a comprehensive contract is that it will enable the couple themselves to make the rules before there is trouble.

Rationale for a Personal Contract

The chief advantage of a personal contract prior to marriage is that it can serve as a springboard for fruitful discussion. Couples need to understand their individual ideals and marital expectations and to discuss finances, roles, sex, children, and other aspects and to work out these many things before marriage. So while the rationale for the discussion is to work out the contract, the real focus is on the couple and how they relate to one another in these different areas. Proponents of a personal contract emphasize that this is one way that difficulties can be avoided; the couple learn to talk about everything with one another, they enhance their decision-making capability, and they develop negotiating skills and their own personal and social identities. They derive real security from knowing what to expect in the future (Charney, 1972).

One of the chief advantages of having a per-

sonal contract in marriage is that it can motivate the couple to reexamine and realign sex roles and to effect innovative changes in roles and behavior. In this sense, a contract is an external control device to effect task allocations. One couple found that the only way they could keep from drifting into traditional roles was to sit down and write everything out. They decided to define their roles so that they shared completely the responsibility for their household and for raising their children. The wife writes:

When our agreement was merely verbal, it didn't work; our old habits were too firmly established. So we made a formal agreement instead, based on a detailed schedule of family duties and assignments. Eventually, as the old roles and habits are replaced, we may be able to abandon the formality of our arrangement, but now the formality is imperative. Good intentions are simply not enough (Shulman, 1970).

The contract can also become a communicative tool for dealing with situations. As problems emerge, contract making becomes part of the means of finding solutions, since the contract itself can specify negotiation procedures.

Pitfalls

One disadvantage of the contract is that it is hard to legislate human behavior. It may be that persons will agree to provisions that are not compatible with their real nature or that are beyond their capability of keeping. Yet their spouses fully expect that the agreement be kept because the contract says so.

A contract might be used to control or force behavior (O'Neill and O'Neill, 1972). One couple reports that after the contract was signed, it was hung on the refrigerator and the wife became a nag trying to enforce it. This couple found that "contracts are harder to keep than

to write." For this reason, they dropped their written agreement and now reach verbal agreements as they go along (Eshleman, 1974).

Another disadvantage is that it is hard to anticipate all marital problems and contingencies ahead of time. No matter how extensive the contract, it never covers everything. Furthermore, marital relationships change over different periods of the family life cycle. The problems of a working young couple without children are different from those of an older couple with four children and a wife in ill health. How can the contract written prior to marriage adequately define roles a few years hence? It can't, which means that *to be meaningful at all a contract has to be rewritten after every major change in the couple's situation.* The couple can agree that both the husband and the wife will work and will contribute their equal share to family expenses, but what if the husband is laid off at work. How does the contract apply? If this contigency has not been anticipated, the contract has to be rewritten.

Whether a contract is a help or a hindrance will depend a lot on the maturity of the people writing and using it. The fearful, immature, selfish person may use the contract to protect his or her own ego, to satisfy neurotic needs, or to win advantage. A completely irresponsible person may never abide by any agreement; he or she has never learned to accept any obligation. The contract may or may not exert a motivating influence to accept responsibility or to constrain undesirable behavior.

Will the contract be interpreted literally or figuratively? Some people interpret everything literally, so that if a contract isn't spelled out in detail, they won't follow it. Thus, a contract literally interpreted can become as much of a source of conflict as the disputed situation. Whenever the contract becomes more important than the relationship, the contract has ceased to serve a useful purpose.

At the present time, the personal benefits and social functions of a contract are a matter of long-term study. Will a personal contract provide the moral imperatives for workable relationships among family members? Will periodic contract evaluation result in productive evaluation of the marital relationship itself? Will a contract reduce divorce rates because it forces couples to deal with problems before they become unsolvable? Would a compulsory prenuptial contract prevent large numbers of marriages from ending in divorce? These are questions that cannot be answered with certainty right now (Sussman, 1974a).

Marriage as a Renewable Contract

One of the most interesting proposals in recent years is the idea of marriage for a limited period of time, subject to renewal (White and Well, 1975). A couple would be licensed for a term of say five years, at the end of which period they could separate without legal action or could renew their license for another five-year period. This would provide legalized marriage but would not require an expensive often bitter court battle to "get divorced" in case they should decide not to remain married any longer. The marital vows would be "until the end of our term" rather than "until death do us part."

This type of arrangement offers more security than living together without any legal marriage, and it insures that the couple can't rashly or impulsively break up whenever there is a blowup or an argument. But it also avoids the frightening prospect of being locked into a lifelong contract that is hard to keep yet difficult to break. It also provides real incentives for the couple to try to make their marriage work, since they know another negotiating and contract period is coming up.

Satir's Five-Year Renewable Contract

The family therapist Virginia Satir (1967) introduced a plan for marriage as a statutory five-year renewable contract. The plan was presented at the annual meeting of the American Psychological Association in 1967. Satir's primary reasoning was that there needed to be "an apprentice-period . . . in which potential partners have a chance to explore deeply and experiment with their relationship, experience the other and find out whether . . . fantasy matched reality." Thus, in Satir's view, the first five years are years of trial and experimentation before the couple decides to live together for an additional time.

Adult Protection

Historically, marriage laws have been used primarily to protect dependent women and children. But with many women developing independence and no longer wanting to be dependent, some aspects of marital law need to reflect these changing times. Not long ago, a bill was actually introduced in the Maryland State Legislature to make marriage a three-year contract, with an option to renew every three years by mutual consent. In this bill, any disagreements over alimony, child custody, and the like would be settled by a court (Kelley, 1974; "Renewable Marriage," 1971). Though the bill did not pass, nevertheless its introduction reflects a change in traditional views of marriage.

Marriage as a Contract by Stages

It has also been suggested that there be different stages to the marital contract, which could be entered into in steps of progressively greater commitment. The first advocate of this concept was Judge Ben Lindsay (1927), who in the year 1926 proposed a testing period before marriage became finalized.

Russell on Trial Marriage

The philosopher Bertrand Russell became one of the strong supporters of Lindsay's view. In espousing this "new kind of marriage," Russell outlined three ways in which it could be distinguished from ordinary marriage:

First, that there should be for the time being no intention of having children, and that accordingly the best available birth control information should be given to the young couple. Second, that so long as there are no children and the wife is not pregnant, divorce should be possible by mutual consent. And third, that in the event of divorce, the wife would not be entitled to alimony (Russell, 1961).

Russell felt that this new kind of marriage, which he called *companionate marriage*, would eliminate incompatible couples, particularly those who might be sexually incompatible. He wrote: "It seems absurd to ask people to enter upon a relation intended to be lifelong, without any previous knowledge as to their sexual compatibility. It is just as absurd as it would be if a man intending to buy a house were not allowed to view it until he had completed the purchase" (Russell, 1961). He also argued that marriage should never be considered consummated until the first pregnancy.

Mead on Two-Step Marriage

The anthropologist Margaret Mead (1966) caused quite a stir some time ago with her proposal for marriage in two steps. The first step was *individual marriage*, which was a union between two persons who were committed to one another for as long as they wanted to remain together. This first step would be marriage without children during which time the couple would have a chance to know one another more intimately than possible through a brief love affair. Individual marriage would be considered a serious commitment, requiring legal and religious sanction and ceremony, in which each person would look forward to a life-time relationship, though not yet be bound to it. The couple would be concerned deeply for the happiness and the well-being of one another. If this first step did not work out, the husband would not be responsible for alimony.

The second step was *parental marriage*, which would be allowed only after a good background of individual marriage. It would be hard to contract and the couple would have to demonstrate their economic ability and, perhaps, their emotional qualifications to raise a child. If parental marriage did break up, divorce would be arranged to offer maximum protection for the children.

Mead emphasized several points in offering her rationale for marriage in two steps. One, a good marriage is the necessary prelude to responsible parenthood so that when children are born they will be loved and cared for. Two, under the present system of dating and courtship, couples are entering into early marriage and becoming parents before they work out their relationship as husband and wife. Three, using early marriage as a means of solving the sex problems of youth has been a mistake. Early marriage may or may not provide sexual satisfaction, but even if it does, the young couple are faced with the many other problems of adjustment and are trapped in marriage before they are ready for it. The couple ought to be committed when they marry, but early commitments should not be irrevocable. Individual marriage would provide the first step without final commitment.

Scriven's Three-Step Plan

The philosophy professor Michael Scriven elaborated on Mead's two-step plan. He proposed three steps to marriage: (1) *preliminary marriage*, which would be legitimized cohabitation entered into contractually for one year without the need for subsequent commitment; (2) *personal marriage*, similar to Margaret Mead's individual marriage except that it could be entered into only after a year's trial of preliminary marriage; and (3) *parental marriage*, the first step to be taken only after successful personal marriage (Berger, 1971).

Packard on Confirmation

Vance Packard (1968) in his book, *The Sexual Wilderness*, suggested a two-year confirmation period after which marriage would be dissolved or become final. He felt that the first two years of marriage were the hardest, so that this period of time would be adequate for the couple to determine if they were really suited to one another.

Extramarital and Comarital Sex

Sexual Exclusiveness

The concept of monogamy in Judeo-Christian society emphasizes the need for sexual exclusiveness in the marital relationship. Once married, a person may not engage in any sexual relationship with any person whatever other than his or her marriage partner (McMurtry, 1973). A violation of this principle constitutes an act of adultery, which is forbidden by religious commandment. This exclusivity is also still buttressed by civil statute, which considers adultery a crime, although it is rarely prosecuted (Bernard, 1973a). It is also

still considered grounds for divorce in the majority of states (see chapter 16). Public opinion is also against extramarital intercourse. A recent national survey showed that 65 percent of respondents felt that extramarital sexual relations were always wrong (Gallup, 1979). An additional 16 percent said that they were almost always wrong, and 11 percent said they were wrong only sometimes. Only 4 percent said they were not wrong at all. Among those eighteen to twenty-nine years of age, only 6 percent said they were not wrong at all (Gallup, 1979).

Extramarital Sex

As sometimes happens, however, social practices do not always follow social norms, at least for a significant minority of the population. A study of 100 middle-class, middle-aged couples from two suburban areas of a large metropolitan city in the Midwest showed that 28 percent of the marriages were affected by at least one instance of extramarital coitus (Johnson, 1970). A more comprehensive study of 2,262 professional married women whose names were taken from the roster of the National Council on Family Relations showed that 26 percent of the women had at least one extramarital experince (Bell et al., 1975). Age was shown to be a significant factor in this study, primarily because a younger age was related to a more liberal value system and lifestyle. Figure 20-1 shows the relationship between age and the percentage of these women who had had an extramarital coital experience.

The authors of both of these studies caution that these were limited samples and from them one cannot generalize about the rates of extramarital coitus in the general population. Other research would indicate that the rates of extramarital coitus vary among different cultural groups (Edwards and Booth, 1976;

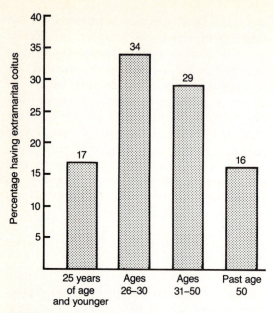

FIGURE 20-1. *Age and the percentage of professional women in the NCFR who had extramarital coital experience (Source: Adapted from R. R. Bell, S. Turner, and L. Rosen, "A Multivariate Analysis of Female Extramarital Coitus,"* Journal of Marriage and the Family *37 [May 1975]: 375–384. Copyright 1975 by the National Council on Family Relations. Reprinted by permission.)*

Reiss, 1971; Reiss, 1980; Whitehurst, 1972a). All studies show that the rates among males are higher than among females but also that the rates among females are increasing (Bell, et al., 1975). The point is that the social norm of sexual exclusiveness in marriage is still the norm most widely accepted, but it is one that is not practiced by a significant minority of American men and women (Edwards, 1973).

One result of this discrepancy between the norm and the practice has been for many persons to keep their extramarital sexual involvements secret. Clandestine love affairs are common. The theory has been, "What others don't know won't hurt them." This concept is reflected in the description Rogers (1972b) gives of the accommodation one cou-

ple made to their jealousy toward each other over their extramarital affairs:

Eric experiences a full measure of primitive jealousy when he knows she [Denise] is having sexual relationships with another man. And Denise, though ashamed of her feelings, is hurt when he is sexually involved with another woman, a hurt she feels even though she has been similarly involved with other men. . . .

So they have come to a somewhat peculiar accommodation. If either feels such attraction to another person that he/she wants it to come to a climax in a sexual relationship, so be it. But they will keep these matters private from each other, simply because openness brings too much pain and hurt (Rogers, 1972b, pp. 195–196).

Consensual Adultery

It is precisely this hypocrisy and dishonesty that has led an increasing number of writers to talk about the need for more honesty in marital relationships, even if this honesty includes an admission of a desire for sexual relations outside the marital bond. This new honesty has been discussed under various lables. Clayton (1973) makes a distinction between what he calls **clandestine adultery, ambiguous adultery,** and **consensual adultery.** *Clandestine adultery* describes the extramarital sexual relationships, already mentioned, that the adulterer strives to keep secret from the spouse, because if he or she knew about it, that person would disapprove. *Ambiguous adultery* is marked by an extramarital relationship about which the spouse knows but does not fully approve. The spouse chooses to adapt to the mate's extramarital involvement rather than issue an ultimatum demanding its end. *Consensual adultery* is extramarital sexual relationships about which the spouse knows and approves. Here adultery is viewed as part of the lifestyle of both spouses.

Comarital Sex

The new term for extramarital sex with the knowledge and permission of one's mate is **comarital sex,** or *consensual sex* (Smith and Smith, 1973). *Comarital sex* is sexual intimacy with an extramarital partner, single or married, to which a monogamous heterosexually married couple openly agree prior to the involvement (White and Wells, 1975).

There are, however, different degrees of involvement in comarital sexual activity. Comarital sex that includes an exchange of partners by married persons for sexual purposes and that does not include any emotional involvement at all is "recreational sex" and is commonly referred to as **swinging** or *mate swapping* (Libby, 1973). If the sexual activity is part of a larger group sexual experience, the activity becomes group sex (Ford, 1973). Comarital sex that takes place in an established and rich relationship has been categorized as **intimate friendships** (Ramey, 1972).

Effect on Marriage

Extramarital sexual relationships affect couples in a variety of ways (Glass and Wright, 1972). Some marriages are never the same afterward. The offended spouse can neither forget nor forgive. Feelings of love, trust, and commitment are replaced by anger, resentment, distrust, fear, doubt, or indifference. One has been betrayed, so it is difficult to trust or care in the same way again. As a result, many such couples get divorced.

The opposite extreme, of course, are those marriages that are not affected at all. One or other of the spouse is having an affair, but the other doesn't care. These are often marriages where the emotional bonds between the couple are already broken, so the extramarital relationship is just evidence of the fractured marriage (Burkstel, 1978).

In between those couples who care deeply and those who do not care at all are those who say they love and care for one another and don't want to break up their marriage. Some of these say they still want to sleep with someone else (Reiss et al., 1980). Many of these persons see nothing wrong with extramarital relationships. Some of these had multiple partners before marriage, and continue these patterns after marriage. Several writers suggest that some who are promiscuous are engaged in a desparate quest—the search for a caring parent, for love they never found as children (Scarf, 1980; Strean, 1980).

More commonly, the extramarital affair is a symptom of problems in the marriage that have never been resolved. The person becomes involved outside of marriage to try to meet needs that have not been satisfied. The affair precipitates a crisis, so the couple is forced to take a look at the problems that have needed attention all along. Adequate counseling help is usually needed to help the couple straighten things out.

Swinging

Participation

There is really no accurate estimate of the number of couples involved in swinging (Bell and Silvan, 1970). Estimates range between 1.7 and 5 percent of middle-class and high socioeconomic status couples (Johnson, 1971; Spanier and Cole, 1972).

Becoming Involved

Swingers use various methods to make contact with one another: ads in local newspapers, personal referral of other couples, contact in "swing clubs," bars, or at parties (Varni, 1973). The husband more often than the wife initiates the involvement (Athanasiou, 1970; Bartell, 1971; Bartell, 1970; Smith and Smith, 1970). In one study, the husband's suggestion was usually met with a negative reaction by the wife who felt revulsed and/or that something was wrong with her marriage. (Varni, 1973). At this point the husband began trying to convince his wife. This resistance stage might last for several months during which the husband might invite a swinging couple in for a chat. If the husband were successful, the wife resigned herself to trying out swinging. Every woman in this study approached her first experience with varying degrees of anxiety and misgiving. The men were anxious too, but less so than the women. If nothing traumatic happened in the first experience, the couple were likely to try again. It was particularly important to continual involvement in swinging that the couple felt the marriage had not been damaged and that they were able to enjoy the experience. After the wives went through a period of acceptance, one study showed that the next stage for some was one of enthusiasm, during which they began to relish comarital sex, sometimes to an even greater extent than their husbands. In some cases, husbands began to worry and urged discontinuance when they discovered how much their wives enjoyed sex with other men (Gilmartin and Kusisto, 1973).

Characteristics of Swingers

Swingers compartmentalize sex, separating it from other aspects of their life, and from marriage and love, seeking to emphasize only the physical aspects of the experience as an end in itself (Denfeld and Gordon, 1970). They seek sexual variety and sensual experience, part of which may involve feeling attractive,

virile, sexy, and desired by other persons (Varni, 1973). Swingers tend to be highly educated, low on religious affiliation, and less controlled by agents of social control, such as church, family, and kin. In a comparison of 100 swinging couples with 100 control couples, one study found that the only major difference between swingers and controls was that the former reported less gratifying and more strained relations with parents during their formative years and they interacted with relatives and neighbors less frequently than controls. The picture one gets is of persons who avoid close, interpersonal contacts with family and friends (Gilmartin and Kusisto, 1973).

Effect on Marriage

In one comparison of swinging couples with other control couples, 49 percent of swinging husbands and 34 percent of swinging wives had been divorced and remarried, with comparable figures of only 15 percent and 14 percent of control husbands and wives. Some husbands or wives who had been married before, divorced, and remarried were divorced originally because they found their first partners too conventional for them. They married their present partners after selecting someone whose major values and interests were similar to their own (Gilmartin and Kusisto, 1973).

Dropouts from Swinging

Many couples try out swinging and then give it up, encountering difficult problems. A survey among 473 marriage counselors who had counseled swinging dropout couples revealed a number of reasons for the dropping out. Table 20-1 shows the reasons listed in order of decreasing frequency. Additional ones not shown in the table included pregnancy, venereal disease, feelings of being excluded,

TABLE 20-1. *Problems or reasons for dropping out of swinging*

Problems	Number of Couples	Percentage
Jealousy	109	23
Guilt	68	14
Threatening marriage	68	14
Development of emotional attachment with other partner	53	11
Boredom and loss of interest	49	11
Disappointment	33	7
Divorce or separation	29	7
Wife's inability to "take it"	29	7
Fear of discovery: community, children	15	3
Impotence of husband	14	3
Totals	467	100

Source: From D. Denfield, "Dropouts from Swinging: The Marriage Counselor as Informant," in *Beyond Monogamy,* edited by J. R. Smith and L.G. Smith (Baltimore: The Johns Hopkins University Press, 1974). Copyright © 1974 by The Johns Hopkins University Press. Used by permission.

and difficulty in finding suitable couples (Denfeld, 1974).

As can be seen, jealousy and guilt were the major reason for couples dropping out. Husbands reported more jealousy than wives. A number became concerned about their wives' popularity and their wives' sexual endurance capabilities. A number of wives dropped out because they were fearful of losing their mate. Dropout couples reported that swinging weakened rather than strengthened their marriage; fighting and hostilities became more frequent after swinging. In some cases, the development of an attachment to swinging partners led to divorce and/or new marriages. In other cases, lying, cheating, and clandestine meetings between extramarital partners were discovered, which was in violation of swinger's rules. Some wives were repulsed by swinging, which they were forced into for their husband's benefit. Once involved, 3 percent of the husbands found themselves impotent. Fear of discovery by the children or the community was another reason for dropping out of swinging.

Some 192 counselors in this study were involved with current swingers, most of whom came to the counselors because of difficulties with swinging. Active swingers reported similar problems to those reported by dropouts, but the actives reported more fears of discovery, of venereal disease, and of rejection. It is evident from these counselors' reports that swinging left some couples psychologically damaged and hurt or destroyed some of the marriages of others.

Intimate Friendships

Swinging and Intimate Friendships

Swingers are interested in sexual variety, but many discover that relationships based solely on sex are unsatisfying and they replace swinging with *intimate friendships*. According to Ramey (1972b), an "intimate friendship is an otherwise traditional friendship in which sexual intimacy is considered appropriate behavior." Unlike swinging, intimate friendships involve some degree of commitment and responsibility toward the other person. Couples are interested in person-to-person relationships, and the object is to form relationships where sex is but one part of a complex level of emotional and social interaction. Some of these relationships develop with friends of long standing; other persons are introduced into intimate friendships by mutual friends. Some develop a close union with one or a few couples (and in a few cases with singles) in a *closed group*. Closed groups, as the name implies, are closed as to membership. Other persons form looser bonds with a greater number of people in an *open group* (Ramey, 1975). Open groups develop among individuals and remain open to other persons: married, single, and in some cases, bisexual.

Motivations

When asked to check their most important reasons for maintaining intimate friendships, 380 upper-middle-class persons listed the reasons as summarized in Table 20-2 (Ramey, 1975, p. 519). Items are listed in decreasing rank order with the percentage of those indicating reasons or strong reasons added together. Closed group members saw intimate friendships as a compromise between monogamy and unrestricted intimacy outside the husband-wife relationship.

Effects

When asked the effect of joining the intimate friendship group on their primary relationship, 30 percent said the effect was very positive, 30 percent said it was somewhat positive, 19 percent said it was equally positive and negative, and 13 percent said it was somewhat negative; 2 percent said it was very neg-

---

TABLE 20-2. *Reasons for participating in intimate friendship groups*

Reasons	Percent Strong Reasons
More personal freedom	40
Sex accepted as normal between friends	25
Adds depth to social relationships	36
Sexual exploration in nonjudgmental setting	38
Strengthens bond with spouse	42
New personality aspects emerge relating to more people	25
New experiences	23
Being loved more	21
Feeling desired and wanted more	30
Sense of belongingness	38

Source: From J. W. Ramey, "Intimate Groups and Networks: Frequent Consequence of Sexually Open Marriage," *The Family Coordinator* 24 (October 1975): 519. Copyrighted 1975 by the National Council on Family Relations. Used by permission.

ative. Forty-one percent felt they thought their primary relationship was never threatened, but 60 percent reported that one of their problems was "pressure" on the primary relationship (Ramey, 1975).

Group Marriage

Definition and Description

Group marriage represents an even closer involvement than intimate friendships. In their book on group marriage, the Constantines define it as "a marriage of at least *four* people, two female and two male, in which each partner is married to all partners of the opposite sex" (Constantine and Constantine, 1973, 1974a, p. 29). They make a distinction between group marriage and what they call **multilateral** marriage, which they define as consisting of "three partners, each of whom considers himself/herself to be married (or committed in a functionally analogous way) to more than one of the other partners" (Constantine and Constantine, 1973a). The three or more individuals may represent any distribution by sex as long as they share in a community of sexual and interpersonal intimacy (Constantine and Constantine, 1974b). If each of the married relationships is represented by a line, the whole marriage is a many sided or multilateral figure, hence the name "multilateral marriage." A multilateral marriage involves a deep love by each member for all other members, an "ideal" which is usually not achieved in practice. In this type of marriage, homosexual relationships may be involved—although much less frequently than heterosexual relationships. Multilateral marriage often involves couples who are themselves monogamously married before they enter into the group relationship. A decision to marry another person would be made, not

by the male (as in polygynous marriages), but by the group. The same principle holds true for polyandry as distinct from a multilateral triad with two or more men and one woman (Crosby, 1973; Eshleman, 1974).

Ramey uses the term *pair-bonds* to describe "a reciprocal primary relationship involving sexual intimacy" (Ramey, 1972b, p. 436). Pair-bonded couples see themselves as mates. Thus, Ramey defines group marriage as one where "each of three or more participants is pair-bonded with at least two others." Ramey did not find any groups with more than seven individuals. The Constantines (1974a) found more tetrads (two men and two women) than any other size group, with six the maximum number. Triads with either two men and one woman or two women and one man were also common.

Motives and Reasons

Why do persons enter into group marriage? Participants in the Constantine (1973a) study checked the following items as the most important reasons for entering group marriage. The reasons are listed in order of decreasing importance.

- Personal fulfillment
- Opportunity for personal growth
- New aspects of personality emerging in relating to more people
- Richer environment for children
- Sense of "community"
- Multiple adult models for children
- Variety of sexual partners
- Greater intellectual variety

Eighty-three percent of the participants checked "personal fulfillment" as among reasons for trying multilateral marriage, and 75 percent checked "variety of sexual partners." The desire for companionship, security, love, and especially for closeness, in which one can find fulfillment through intimate, reciprocal relationships was a powerful need. Participants sought community and a desire to love and live intensely with others through an expanded identification with a larger family (Dass, 1971).

While the majority are not rebelling, seeking escape, or trying to improve what they consider to be unsatisfactory marriages, a small number of couples do have problems as their motivation, especially problems with insecurity or with sexual inadequacy.

Typical was the case of Eleanor who felt her marriage to Malcolm did not give her the security she desired. Apparently, she felt that two partially committed husbands were better than one. Actually, the group heightened her sense of insecurity when she saw Malcolm become deeply involved with the other woman and realized her own lack of involvement with either the other man or woman. The result for Eleanor was painful, and her jealousy added to the frictions and tensions of the group (Constantine and Constantine, 1973a, p. 111).

Overall, it is generally true that couples who enter group marriage as a means of solving marital difficulties usually have trouble. Things often get worse rather than better. The Constantines add an additional word:

As a consciously chosen transition mechanism to divorce, or as an alternative to divorce, multilateral marriage is *not* to be recommended. For these deliberate ends other means are almost certainly less emotionally expensive than multilateral marriage (Constantine and Constantine, 1972a, p. 462).

There are some motivations that seem to be more common to either the wife or the husband. In his report of conversations with eighty upper-middle-class couples who explored, over a three-year period, the feasibility of entering group marriage or communal living, Ramey reported that wives concern

about "(1) the sense of isolation that comes with raising children, (2) overdependence on the husband for adult contact, and (3) less than optimal development and use of their talents and training" (Ramey, 1972a, p. 694). Wives who left budding careers to raise children, who had few relatives or friends to fall back on, who lacked any real community of interest with neighbors, felt isolated and alone. Many of these women felt that living with others would provide companionship and built-in baby sitters so they would feel freer to seek personal fulfillment. The men among Ramey's eighty couples were concerned about the two problems unique to men in our society; freeing themselves from the rat race and from financial insecurity, and achieving higher living standards.

Money

To what extent do group marriages work out financially? In the Constantines' study, most groups said too little money was a problem. Those with adequate money usually looked for mansion-like houses that could be adapted to multifamily living. Others made do with smaller conventional houses they already had or could afford. Some remodeled garage spaces. Most homes were mortgaged legally to only one couple, partly to avoid embarrassment and difficulty with the banks.

As might be expected, there were some couples who had conflicts over money. In one case, one couple filled their living room with art objects by running up substantial debts, while their companions were frugal. As a result, the frugal couples resented the sacrifices they had to make for the lavishness of the other couple.

Money management varied from group to group, but most said that one-half to two-thirds of each couple's income was pooled, with the remainder kept as personal money. Pooled income was usually used to meet all or almost all of household expenses. The majority of groups purchased small or major assets from pooled income. In most cases, consensus was required for major economic decisions.

Sex

The desire for sexual variety is listed as one of the reasons for establishing group marriage. Bed partners are decided by different means. In the beginning, many groups set up a fixed standard of rotation of partners, allotting three or four days with each partner. The theory was that a rotating schedule eliminated repeated decision making. Actually, it often served to hide real feelings and preferences, rather than to eliminate these, so it provided a means of making choices rather than a way of eliminating problems. One group occasionally used a deck of cards to pair off couples. Another group had the women controlling sleeping arrangements one month and the men choosing the next. Bedroom arrangements vary, with the most prevalent setup that of one bedroom and one bed per two people. Group sex occurs infrequently.

Jealousy

While participants try hard to eliminate jealousies, sexual encounters often stimulate fears, anger and rage, or despondency (Constantine and Constantine, 1973b). Realistically, of course, this is one of the most important problems couples face, so while many groups learn how to deal with it as part of the group marriage itself, the majority of groups are never completely free of the problem (Constantine and Constantine, 1973c).

Children

One of the arguments for group marriage that is most often mentioned is its benefit to children. Whitehurst writes:

Mothers (and fathers) often fall short of the ideals of parenthood. . . . Conditional love, achievement-ethnic norms, and status anxiety are pressures and conditions which help children within a definite and fairly rigid normative system. . . . This . . . means that on the average there is a problem in the child rearing system. . . . This problem is alleviated in quite a neat fashion with the norms of the counterculture family movement. . . . The commune system, with its multiple adults, visibility, and heavy norm of child-loving, makes it virtually impossible to mistreat a child (Whitehurst, 1972b, p. 396).

To date, there has been relatively little research to back up the claims that group marriage is beneficial to children (Constantine and Constantine, 1972b). It is evident that differences over child-rearing styles are mentioned as frequent factors contributing to the dissolution of group marriages.

Organization, Decision Making, and Leadership

Many of the problems of group marriage arise because of the complexity of getting along with a number of different people. Six persons living together involve fifteen separate relationships (Hunt, 1974). The more individuals, the less likely that they will all be compatible. Their personalities are different; their thought patterns, temperaments, needs, habits, attitudes, and lifestyles vary. And since time is limited, the possibility of relating separately to each individual is problematical. As a consequence, communication is listed as the number one problem in multilateral marriages. The larger the group, the less the available "air time" for each individual to talk to solve problems. When decisions are made by consensus, a great deal of time and energy may have to be expended before agreement is reached (Constantine and Constantine, 1973a).

Structure is needed in group marriage to make decisions, establish rules, and to carry out group functions. In fact, the multilateral family requires more explicit structure and more rules to get things done than does the nuclear family. Cleaning and cooking schedules, sign-up sheets, rotational systems for baby sitters are common. Some families have weekly meetings; most find that regularly scheduled meetings are essential. Usually during the difficult formative period, many rules and regulations are needed to deal with problems. But as people become more adept at dealing flexibly and sensitively with others, rules are gradually relaxed.

Group Integration and Tenure

Ideally, all members of a group marriage would have a deep, committed love for one another, but such an ideal is hard to achieve. Sometimes the love and commitment of one person toward another is not reciprocal. Very commonly, members discover they cannot love every marriage partner equally, that beneath the insistence on equal love, individuals have definite preference for particular sexual partners or for particular persons for certain activities (Constantine and Constantine, 1973a).

Part of the problem is that some couples do not know one another well enough before they form a group. Ramey (1972b) insists that a trial period is essential to the success of a group. Taking a joint vacation or renting a summer house together were two specific suggestions he made.

How long do groups last? When couples enter the marriage, they usually intend that it be permanent (Constantine and Constantine, 1972b). In actual practice, most break up eventually. Among dissolved groups, the Constantines (1972a) found that the median duration was sixteen months. Table 20-3 shows the percentage of groups in the Constantine (1973a) study that were still intact after specific periods of time. These figures would suggest that group marriage is a relatively unstable form. This fact leads Ellis (1974) to suggest that it is highly unlikely that group marriage will ever replace monogamous mating or that a majority of Westerners will voluntarily choose it instead of our present system.

Communes

The Communal Movement

Living communally is not a new development. The nineteenth century alone pro-

TABLE 20-3. *Percentage of group marriages still intact after specific periods of time*

	End of 3 Months	End of 1 Year	End of 3 Years	After 5 Years
Percent still intact	93	94	17	7

Source: Adapted from Larry L. Constantine and Joan M. Constantine, *Group Marriage* (New York: Macmillan, 1973), p. 67. Reprinted by permission.

duced some 130 communes in the United States of which there are clear records (Haughey, 1972). Most of these were utopian in character with a desire to retreat from the larger society and return to a simple, less complicated existence. The *Oneida community*, the *Shakers*, and the *Hutterites* are examples of these early communes (Caplow, 1973).

The modern communal movement, however, dates from the birth of the hippie community in the Haight-Asbury section of San Francisco in the middle 1960s (Cavan, 1972, Perry, 1970). The image fostered by the mass media was a scene different from anything that had occurred before in America, with open sexuality and psychedelic drugs at the center of the new counterculture. A secret group known as the "Diggers" was organized to serve the crush of wandering young people who had journeyed to the Haight. The Diggers' philosophy was "Love and Peace," emphasizing an existentialist here and now framework, hedonism, warm interpersonal relations, noncompetition and nonexploitation, and an appreciation of the domestic, the mundane, and the natural (Conover, 1975).

But the Diggers weren't just idealists; they tried to put their philosophy into practice by creating such institutions as crash pads, free stores, free clinics, and communes (Smith and Luce, 1971). The latter emerged as an intelligent way of taking advantage of the large old houses that dominated the Haight-Asbury neighborhood.

The "flower children's" dream was shattered, however, by the summer of 1968, caught in a cross-fire between the mass media that both attacked and publicized it, and drugs, venereal disease, and hepatitis that destroyed its vitality and health (Haughey, 1972). After that last summer, the Hippies were gone from the Haight.

But the period since 1968 did not see the end of the communal movement. In fact, since then the movement has grown, with increasing cultural diversification, diffusion, and institutional innovation. Conover (1975) estimated there were at least 3,000 communes and many more intentional communities. Based on more direct observation, Jerome (1974) estimated there were 50,000 contemporary communes and intentional communities in 1974 and that as many as 750,000 Americans lived in these groups, not counting religious communes. Obviously, this would include many informal groups of students and others just living together collectively.

Motivations and Philosophies

People join communes for a variety of reasons. One is that the establishment culture, with its emphasis on the work ethic, materialistic success, exploitation, consumption, and competition, does not present an image of attractiveness for many modern youths (Slater, 1970). The middle-class lifestyle is perceived as sensually dulled, cold and manipulative, exploitive rather than generous, and devoid of community and brotherhood (Skolnick, 1973). As a result, there is a desire "to escape the increasing alienation and individual isolation in our society." People "long to escape from punch-card dehumanization to a place where they can permanently *belong*" (Rogers, 1972a, p. 156). Many have a longing for community, for meaningful relationships, for companionship, love, and gentleness, and for a simpler life that is closer to nature (Zablocki, 1971). Communal members emphasize that life is meant to be joyous, spontaneous, and free from the artificial game playing that goes on in middle-class society. There is "a strong inner search for the meaning of one's life, an openness and willingness to communicate and encounter, coupled with a compelling desire for personal growth and development" (Otto, 1971, p. 17). Sometimes, of course, this inner awareness is sought through the use of mind-expanding, psychedelic drugs (Dass, 1971; Weil, 1972).

Political corruption and social injustice have led some to become social activists and others to drop out because they feel they are powerless to change the system. The exploitation of natural resources, the pollution of the environment, and the brainwashing of the consumer have led others to emphasize ecology, organic farming and natural foods. The remarks of one member of New Buffalo commune in Taos County, New Mexico, are typical of the feeling.

The stuff you get in markets is *poison.* . . . Most of the world is polluted: the air, the water, the people, the animals. Man, we gotta get back to the more natural food, more natural life (Hedgepath, 1972, p. 324).

There is also a deep respect and reverence for nature and the ecological system, so that many commune members emphasize the rehabilitation of land and the conservation of all natural resources. Some commune members have been active in movements to establish parks and game preserves and in the fight against the politically influential who have no appreciation of the beauty of nature.

There has also been disillusionment with traditional religious institutions at the same time that people are experimenting with new faiths (Medvill 1972; Veysey, 1973). Disenchantment with hypocritical and double standards of sexual behavior has led to greater openness and sexual freedom (Westhues, 1972). Casual nudism is very common in many of the communes, with members seeking to emphasize the innocent glory of the human body and of the flesh (Lamott, 1973). There are many also who desire opportunities for sexual experimentation and expression that are forbidden in the larger society. The communal movement is one outgrowth of youth's alienation from established society (Yankelovich, 1974).

Variety of Communes

Numerous efforts have been made to arrive at some system of classification (Kanter, 1972; Zablocki, 1972). Ramey (1972b) classifies communes into three major types: **religious, utopian** and **evolutionary,** plus one trial variety, the *student commune*, which is temporary. *Religious communes* are organized around religious philosophies and goals, are usually highly structured, have an authoritarian leader, and emphasize self-sustenance, withdrawal from society, and a work ethic. *Utopian communes* include several different types. Some are the "hippie communes" already described, with a dropout orientation, a "do your own thing" philosophy, with little structure or organization (Lamott, 1973). The rural groups are the back-to-the land, organic food, vegetarian, hand-labor groups. Some of the groups are political revolutionaries. Others merely seek to withdraw from society. The most successful are highly structured and organized around a strong, charismatic individual.

Evolutionary communes are usually organized in urban areas and appear to attract academic, professional, and managerial people older than thirty who desire person-to-person intimacy in a communal setting. They usually have "straight" jobs, have no intention of giving up their middle-class comforts, and desire to pool resources for investment, shelter, purchasing, and to provide schooling for their children. Table 20-4 summarizes the characteristics of these three types of communes (Ramey, 1972b).

The *student commune* of which Ramey speaks may be the crash pad variety or just a group of students sharing living quarters. These loosely organized coed living arrangements all have one thing in common: they are temporary. In every urban and university center, there are countless such students sharing space, rent, food costs and preparation,

TABLE 20-4.   *Types of communes*

Utopian Commune	Evolutionary Commune	Religious Commune
Dropout orientation	High achievers	Highly structured
Do your own thing	Highly mobile	Authoritarian leader
Loosely organized	Straight jobs	Work ethic
Usually subsidized	Upper middle-class	Usually self-sustaining
Youth oriented	Opinion leaders	Withdraw from society
Sometimes revolutionary	Most over 30, many	Family oriented
Usually short-lived	postchildren	

Source: From J. W. Ramey, "Emerging Patterns of Innovative Behavior in Marriage," *The Family Coordinator,* 21 (October 1972): 449. Copyrighted 1972 by the National Council on Family Relations. Reprinted by permission.

housecleaning duties, and recreational activities (Mazur, 1973).

The communal movement has many facets and branches; it is not a monolithic structure that is easily described (Berger, 1972b; Fairfield, 1972; Roberts, 1971). But it is not a dead movement. What started out as a youth-centered, hippie, countercultural movement, including many temporary street communes and crash pads, has now fully blossomed to include more intentional communities of older adults. Conover (1975; 1973a; 1973b) predicts the continued vitality and growth of communes and intentional communities. Some specific examples of various types of communes will be given in the next section in order to give the reader a clearer understanding of the movement.

Examples of Rural Communes

Crow Farm is a completely anarchistic, hippie-type commune, located on 310 acres in Oregon. It has a "dropout" orientation, a "do your own thing" philosophy, and is completely without structure or organization. It was financed by loans and parents in the amount of $75,000. The men do odd jobs such as tree pruning; the women contribute their welfare checks, take care of the babies, and do the household work. The commune has thirty to fifty people including transients and has a rapid turnover. The men of the commune are described by Estellachild:

The men come in a few simple varieties. The first is the Bill C., mathematician with 2 wives and 7 kids, too good to work with his hands, but not too good to fuck everything that moves. At the same time always making it clear by putting you down that he had the market for brains....

The second type of "man" was the big Jim C. variety. He was a macho alcoholic (as were at least 6 other men). He has sired 6 children but will never be a father. I have seen his wife thrown around and come close to a concussion. The men are basically this macho type with one exception. Fucking became the major occupation. No one was capable of getting anything else done.... Meanwhile the house and the kiddies were women's work (Estellachild, 1972, p. 333).

She goes on to describe the purposelessness of the life: "Gluttony, drunken brawls, three to five nights a week, constant high key frenetic living as well as the sexual frenzy, lack of any creative activity, reading, writing, discussions, religious or revolutionary activity contributed to my misery" (Estellachild, 1972, p. 334). Any efforts at women's liberation, to establish equality of sex roles, or to organize basic chores in this community were squelched by the men.

In sharp contrast to this commune, *Twin Oaks* is a highly structured, rural commune of some fifty members, set on 200 acres of rolling farmland in central Virginia (Conover 1975). The older branch has had a continuous existence of seven years, with the last four years relatively stable with only a modest turnover in membership. The ideology of Twin Oaks is based on B. F. Skinner's novel *Walden Two* (Kinkade, 1973). Since most members have come from the alternate culture, there is a lot of individualism and experiential hedonism but without drugs.

The commune has survived primarily because of its organization. All income, ownership of major items, and expenditure are communal. Important decisions are made by an elected group of "planners" and "community planners," one of whom is retired every six months, at the same time a new one is elected. Women are represented as equally as men. The income of Twin Oaks is derived from a small hammock factory, building construction, contract mailing, farming, and a variety of minor enterprises. Women and men have equal access to all work, which is shared on the basis of a complex labor credit system that assigns credit for labor on the basis of psychological desirability. Any member with a work skill is expected to teach it to any other member who asks.

Gender equality is observable in several ways. Everyday clothes are owned and managed by the commune with shirts and pants the typical apparel of both genders. Bathrooms and outhouses are generally shared with deemphasis of privacy and nudity norms. The names of children are chosen before birth, are unisexual, and are awarded in serial order.

Sexual practices vary. Couple formations

may be strongly monogamous or temporarily monogamous. There are some threesomes, and a number are celibate or quasicelibate individuals. The majority of members practice free love, with jealousies occurring frequently (Conover, 1975).

Problems of Rural Communes

The rural commune that tries to be economically self-sufficient is faced with the same financial problems as the small farmer—how to make sufficient income from farming to sustain life. Many young people who establish rural subsistence communes have no concept at all of how to farm. The only land they may be able to buy is marginal farm land that others have tried and abandoned. Then, if work is not organized or the garden isn't weeded and tended because everyone feels that everyone else is responsible, crop failure is the result (Gardner, 1973).

Even if the group is able to grow enough to eat over the winter, the fixed expenses of running a farm are very high. Most groups find they can't survive on subsistence farming alone so develop small crafts or manufacturing and produce such things as candles, leather objects, or pottery. The Bruderhof community has a substantial income from manufacturing school furniture and play equipment, marketed under the name, *Community Playthings* (Rudikoff, 1974; Zablocki, 1971). Members of other groups are forced to seek employment off the farm wherever they can find it.

Open communes that do not limit membership are plagued with an influx of visitors who sap the resources of the group (Houriet, 1971). *Wheeler Ranch* and *Morningstar*, and a few of the New Mexico communes, were so inundated by refugees from Haight-Asbury that they could no longer cope (Rudikoff, 1974). Furthermore, open admissions allow alcoholics, drug addicts, the psychotic, and the misfit of every description to arrive along with mature, serious-minded individuals. Problem persons can create havoc in communal life. Furthermore, a rapid turnover of members breaks down the stability of the group and makes ongoing functioning more difficult (Estellachild, 1972).

Relationships of the rural commune with the surrounding community are often strained, primarily because such a group is visible and different. Casual nudity attracts the curious and the attention of local law enforcement officials. A fight between blacks and whites at *Morningstar* hippie commune crystallized local hostile sentiments, and as a result the district attorney announced he was closing the commune (Lamott, 1973). Communal children in public schools also draw the criticism of other parents and community leaders who are worried that their own children will be corrupted.

Members of rural communes face some of the same personal problems as would any group of people trying to live together. Members discover that there is still a need for some autonomy and a degree of privacy.

In one commune, with central living quarters, members found they simply could not cope with the all-day-long howls and wails of two disturbed children aged four and six, who continually annoyed the group, particularly on the many rainy days when everyone was shut up in the house together (Gardner, 1973). As a result, most members decided to move out. Jealousies, irritations, and basic incompatibilities arise, which indicates how difficult it is for people to live together.

Urban Communes

Urban communes are as varied as are the rural communes (Bradford and Klevanky, 1975). *Cambridge Commune* is a small urban commune of nine adults (two of whom are full-time movement organizers) and four children, organized for fellowship and political outreach (Heckman, 1973). Many of the original members had known one another for years. The majority of members have relatively stable sources of income, only part of which is pooled. When they started, members donated dishes, pots and pans, dishwasher, various large pieces of furniture, clothes, and so on while retaining anything else they wanted for private use.

Decisions are made by consensus. Rules are kept to a minimum, but there are some governing such matters as the division of labor, the proportion of maintenance costs (i.e., mortgage payments) that everyone is to pay, and so on. Everyone—male and female—cooks once a week on a specified night, although tradeoffs are frequent. Everyone has an additional task such as buying food or being a general handyman around the house. Tasks rotate every two months. Members admit that no amount of legislation will force anyone to do their task. The only thing that works is mutual trust and willingness of everyone to do his or her part.

The economic and functional benefits of communal living attract many couples with young children who desire to share equipment, household care and maintenance, cooking, and child rearing. Such arrangements are particularly advantageous to working mothers and their husbands.

One of the characteristics of urban communes of middle-class adults is their emphasis on organization and structure. These people are used to leading orderly lives, so they carry this same kind of orderliness into their group life. Those groups that lack structure and leadership do not survive very long. When responsibilities are not assigned, tasks never get done. The contradiction between the ideal of individual freedom and the ideal of group solidarity and responsibility is a very real one. Without organization, groups disintegrate because of disputes over private property, privacy, and over who is to do what tasks when.

The meals have to get cooked and the dishes washed. . . . Something's got to be done about the flies in the kitchen and mice in the cupboard . . . and money set aside for the rent or mortgage and taxes (Berger, 1972a).

Communal groups that survive are either under the control of charismatic, authoritarian leaders or have definite procedures by which decisions are made and tasks accomplished. Small, well-integrated groups may find it possible to arrive at decisions by consensus; larger groups may use democratic procedures and elected representatives to make decisions (Shey, 1977).

The long-term effects on children of being brought up in an urban commune is still a matter of study (Blanton, 1980; Weisner, 1979). Child-rearing practices within the communes are affected by the fact that parents always have an audience whenever they discipline their children. Communal parents report greater self-consciousness about rule making and rule enforcing when others are there to observe them. They express more concern with demonstrating consistent, reasoned discipline, with controlling anger. Some parents overreact and try to exercise greater control over their children than they would ordinarily (Kanter et al., 1975).

The presence of other adults means that parents lose some control over their own children's experiences, environment, and relationships. Other adults also have the right to make and enforce rules, to make demands on the children, to provide for experiences and relationships with them. As a result of multiple rule makers, children have to learn to get along with many persons, each of whom is involved with rule making and rule enforcing and each of whom may have different expectations than another person. Children hear constant repetition of "don't stand on chairs"

or "pick up your things." As a result, they complain of "too many bosses" or "too many people saying 'stop that'" (Kanter et al., 1975).

Voluntary Childlessness

Voluntary childlessness is another alternative family form that is attracting widespread attention and increasing numbers of followers.

Arguments against Having Children

Couples who are voluntarily childless and those who would like to see more couples

More and more couples are opting for voluntary childlessness.

consider the possibility use some convincing arguments against having children (Katz, 1972; Peck, 1971; Rollin, 1970; Silverman and Silverman, 1971). Problems of overpopulation continue to increase (Movius, 1976). Other couples frankly admit that they don't want to accept the gamble. One wife writes:

Something prevents us from making the final decision to go ahead. I believe this something could be called fear. For one thing, life is so good right now that we hesitate to change it in any way.... We view children as an unknown risk.

The prospect of taking care of the physical needs of an infant, helping him to grow properly, providing him with values and raising him to be a well-adjusted useful adult is a most rewarding one, true. But to me it is also a very frightening one. All along the way loom pitfalls, and the possibility of errors.

What if, in spite of our best efforts, our child turned out to have severe emotional problems, to be a drug addict or a criminal (Michels, 1970, pp. 166, 167)?

Another of the principle arguments against having children is the restriction on freedom which rearing children entails. Having children means readjustment of one's total lifestyle to take into account their needs and activities. A mother from Ann Arbor, Michigan, commented: "Suddenly I had to devote myself to the child totally. I was under the illusion that the baby was going to fit into my life, and I found that I had to switch my life and my schedule to *fit him*."

It's a simple fact that no children means no childwork and less housework. No children means freedom for the couple to do what they please together. A young wife who decided to remain childless writes:

But it's not just that we can travel when we like or move to another country if we choose. It's not just that we can be truly involved with projects we believe in or personal plans that delight us. It's not just that we can leave on a spontaneous Saturday morning drive and not return till Monday—or stay up late or visit friends on the spur-of-the-moment

or decide to take in a midweek concert, as though every night were Saturday night. It's all of these and more. We are the first generation that can choose to live as free individuals, not simply nurturers of our genetic copies, and it is a joyous choice (Katz, 1972, p. 163).

There is no question that the woman who is seeking self-fulfillment through a career of her own finds it much easier by not having children. Movius calls voluntary childlessness "the ultimate liberation."

Career-oriented wives may increasingly consider the child-free state as a liberating alternative. Freed from child care responsibilities, a woman who is committed to a career may benefit from greater mobility, fewer family commitments and more time for professional development (Movius, 1976, p. 57).

In one extensive study in twelve modern capitalist, socialist, communist, and dictator countries, the working wife and mother was consistently found to be busier than the head of state (Lear, 1973). Another study of professional women with doctor's degrees showed that these women spent three to five hours per day on household tasks and childcare, this in addition to the time devoted to their careers (Astin, 1969). Few women can maintain this schedule over the years without becoming exhausted.

One of the motherhood and marital myths is that married women with children are happier than childless couples. The feeling has also been that children strengthen marital bonds. As shown in chapter 10 marital satisfaction is at its lowest ebb during the child-rearing years (Burr, 1970; Rollin and Cannon, 1974; Spanier et al., 1975).

By many standards, large numbers of people should not become parents, judging from the thousands of cases of child abuse in the United States each year (Handel, 1970). Many persons have neither the interest nor the aptitude to be parents, "with a resultant performance which is at best marginally competent and at worst blatantly irresponsible" (Veevers, 1974, p. 399).

Pressures to Bear

Certainly, childless couples report that there are tremendous pressures on them to have children. Wives report that they are stigmatized to some extent because they do not have children. Other persons try to make them feel that they are abnormal, selfish, immoral, irresponsible, immature, unhappy, unfulfilled, or nonfeminine. Wives report that family members and friends generally accept their childlessness for the first twelve months. Then after the first year the pressure to have a baby grows, reaching a peak during the third or fourth years. After the fifth year, the pressure diminishes; family and friends give up trying to persuade (Veevers, 1973b).

The pressures come from all sides, one source being society itself. The social norm is that married people should have children, that they should want to have them, and that they should rejoice at the prospect of becoming parents (Veevers, 1974b; Veevers, 1973a). Parenthood is considered a social obligation. Peck suggests:

Everything in our society—from the tax laws to television shows to women's magazines to the most casual conversation—is oriented toward parenthood. It's very difficult to even consider whether you shouldn't have children when everyone is pressuring you to "have kids and find out what you're missing" (Peck, 1971).

Without realizing it, parents put a lot of pressure on their married children to have children of their own. "When are you going to have a baby?" (They never ask, "Are you going to have children?") Friends too can be counted on to exert their share of pressure. "Every woman should have the experience of having a baby." A number of voluntarily childless wives receive considerable pressure

from their physicians, whether the doctor's advice is sought or not (Pohlman, 1970).

The Decision Not to Have Children

In her study of fifty-two voluntarily childless couples, Veevers (1974a; 1974b; 1973a; 1973b) found that only one-third of the couples had agreed *before* marriage not to have children. With the other two-thirds, remaining childless came not as an agreement ahead of time, but as a series of postponements which took place in four stages.

In the *first stage*, couples postponed having children for a definite period because of work, graduating from school, traveling, buying a house, saving a nest egg, or adjusting in marriage.

During the *second stage*, the couple remained committed to parenthood but postponed the event indefinitely because they said they "couldn't afford it now," they "needed to feel more ready," and other reasons.

In the *third stage*, there was open acknowledgment that they might remain permanently childless, since they had already experienced many of the social, personal, and economic advantages of remaining childless.

In the *fourth stage*, the couple had made a definite decision not to have children. For some, this involved a change in attitude or a recognition that an implicit decision had already been made and that it now ought to be acknowledged openly.

Most of the couples in this study were well defended against the pressures to have children. They considered many of their friend's arguments with detached amusement and were no longer hurt or intimidated by them. Many said they told friends that they were "willing to consider adoption" and that this took the pressure off of them since others now considered that they were "normal" and "well adjusted" (Veevers, 1973b).

Childlessness as an Alternative

It should be no more cause for alarm for a couple to decide *not* to have any children than to decide *to have three*. Certainly, many couples who become parents regret it deeply. Planned parenthood implies "the right of every child to be wanted," "the right to every child you want," and "the right not to want children at all" (Veevers, 1973b, p. 400). Parenthood is not an obligation but a privilege, especially since the world is already too crowded. Cer-

TABLE 20-5. *College students' ratings of alternate forms of marriage*

Study A. College Students' Interest in Alternative Forms of Marriage			Study B. College Students' Willingness to Participate in Alternate Marital and Family Forms		
	Percentage Indicating Interest				
Type of Arrangement	*No Inter.*	*Some Inter.*	*Type of Marital and Family Form*	*Male Ratings**	*Female Ratings**
Living together permanently without marriage	28	72	Egalitarian marriage	2.46	1.74
			Long-term cohabitation	3.25	4.19
Contractual marriage for limited period subject to renewal	30	70	Traditional marriage	3.38	4.36
Communal	57	43	Five year evaluation and renewal	4.01	4.10
Comarital—extramarital sex by agreement	62	38	Rural commune— shared sex	4.20	4.92
Mate swapping	67	33	Childfree marriage	4.22	4.49
Polygamous—polyandry or polygyny	73	27	Remain single	4.51	4.71
Group marriage	76	24	Consensual extramarital sex	4.91	5.40
Homosexual	90	10	Spouse swapping	5.05	5.65
			Group marriage	5.18	5.67
			Serial monogamy	5.23	5.50
			Role reversal	5.36	4.72

* In Study B., respondents were asked to rate each item on a 6-point Likert scale in which 1 was defined as "very willing to participate" and 6 was defined as "very unwilling to participate."

Study A. *Source:* Adapted from M. White and C. Wells. "Students' Attitudes toward Alternate Marriage Forms," in *Renovating Marriage*, edited by R. N. Whitehurst and R. W. Libby (Danville, Calif., Consensus, 1973), p. 287.

Study B. *Source:* L. D. Strong, "Alternative Marital and Family Forms: Their Relative Attractiveness to College Students and Correlates of Willingness to Participate in Nontraditional Forms," *Journal of Marriage and the Family* 40 (August 1978): 495.

tainly the women's movement is not "anti-marriage" or "antichildren" as such. Rather, women and couples are urged to consider the fact that childlessness is a viable alternative and that parenthood should not be compulsory. In a world where alternative lifestyles are growing in number and acceptance, voluntary childlessness might also be considered by some as an option.

Attitudes of College Students

How do college students feel about various alternate marriage and family forms? *Various studies reveal a decided preference for conventional marriage* (Strong, 1978; White and Wells, 1975; Yost and Adamek, 1974). A survey of a representative sample of undergraduate students at Kent State University showed that 68 percent of the students were conventional and another 16 percent were conservative in their attitudes toward different family forms (Yost and Adamek, 1974). More than 90 percent of the students wanted to enter into marriage with legal ties rather than without them. Students were least accepting of homosexuality.

A comparison of this study with two others among representative undergraduate student populations revealed similar results: conventional family forms were the most widely accepted (Strong, 1978; White and Well, 1975). Those forms most unlike conventional marriage (homosexuality, group marriage, polygamy, mate swapping, and consensual extramarital sex) were the least accepted. Table 20-5 shows the results. There was considerable interest in living together without marriage and in contractual marriage for a limited period of time. Note that Study A indicates students' *interests* in alternate forms of marriage, whereas Study B indicates students' *willingness to participate* in alternate forms. The results of the two studies, however, were strikingly similar.

Conclusions

It appears that a major revolution in marital and family expectations has not occurred. Rather it may be that we are experiencing some desire to experiment, and some decline in commitment to marital permanence. But, overall, students show a decided preference for legal monogamy and for sexual exclusivity (Strong, 1978).

Jim and Betty (both age twenty-four) have agreed to write their own individual marriage contract. The contract will be automatically terminated in five years and the couple will then have the option of renegotiating a new marriage agreement. This interesting proposal, still considered an experimental marriage by most people raises questions among proponents as well as opponents. The couple whom I taped were idealistic and almost evangelical about the idea. Accompanied by a college chaplain (Dr. B) and Betty's parents, the couple met at the office of a lawyer (Mr. A), who was writing the contract. These are excerpts from that discussion.

Betty began by explaining to Mr. A and Dr. B why she and Jim had decided to write a five-year marriage contract. "The most important reason," she explained, "is that neither Jim nor I want to feel ourselves trapped by the other for life. After five, six, or ten years of marriage, our needs may change. Neither of us wants to own the other person. We want to be open and free. I want to be able to grow as a person. Jim wants freedom and the opportunity to change also. If I find that I can't stand to live with him, and would prefer to live with somebody else, then I shouldn't have to be victimized by the present divorce setup. The same right should be his. A marriage contract for five years will give us more control over our future lives."

"How did you get the idea for this pact?" asked Mr. A. "Was it something you decided yourselves, or did someone suggest it to you?"

"No one suggested it directly," replied Jim. "We had a discussion and decided not to commit ourselves for life. Many people are living together without marital vows. Many older married people really suffer because they find that getting a divorce is too difficult. Personally, I'm for marriage, but I know that it's not a security blanket. Someday, Betty or I may meet someone more appealing. And then our marriage ought to end."

"I wonder if you need me?" asked Mr. A. "I mean why get married at all? Why not simply live together? That way you can break it up without any legal hassle if and whenever you want to."

Betty cut in at this point: "We could still have the same problems! The fact is that marriage or living together—either way—involves our feelings. Marriage is a psychological contract even more than a legal one. So either way, we'd want to agree on the ground rules."

"Besides," Jim added, "our commitment to one another is serious, not impulsive. We don't know what will happen; we may someday want to have children. Being legally married would protect our kids from legal hassles over documents, inheritances, and so on."

"I don't dispute that one bit," said Mr. A. "But let us say that after five years you decided not to renew your contract? How would you feel about supporting the children then?"

"Of course, we'd be legally bound to support them," Jim said, "But even before that, we'd want to be legally married as a declaration to one another of our mutual commitment."

Betty's parents had been silent all this time. Her father asked: "Where is love and trust in your contract?"

Betty responded: "Love can't be meaningful without some formal understanding of what we are doing. It's true, of course, you can't make love last with a contract. But our marriage contract recognizes that we may not love one another forever."

"And trust," Dr. B asked, "How does that work if you expect to fail?"

"I don't understand what you mean," Betty replied, "Fail?"

Dr. B answered, "I mean you're implying that your marriage won't last, that it may fail. Nobody guarantees that living together in a loving, committed marriage will be without pain. It will be a struggle. A good marriage always has been. What troubles me is that I fail to sense in what you've said any awareness that you must consciously affirm a strong commitment to love one another. Love can't live on mere guidelines for living together. You need to be able to depend upon one another, to trust one another enough to commit yourselves totally."

"How are you suggesting that we prove that we trust one another any more than we do?" asked Jim.

"Well," the chaplain replied, "trust doesn't mean much if it doesn't ask for a real commitment—if you're not risking anything by it. If you really love one another, you shouldn't have the option of getting out of the marriage. You wouldn't want the option."

"I don't think either of us has doubts now about the marriage," said Jim, "but we do have doubts about the future."

"You're missing his point," said Betty's mother. "You still have to feel now that you can depend upon one another. If your contract is only for five years, how can you do that?"

"What is important," said Mr. A "is that the contract makes clear to both of you, right now, the duties, obligations, and rights of this proposed marriage. That's all."

QUESTIONS

1. Give your opinions of the points of view of Jim and Betty, and Dr. B.

2. What do you think about a marriage contract for five years? What might be the effects on the marriage, the couple, any children?

3. What might be the impact of a five-year contractual marriage upon the future of American family life?

4. Can you describe any advantages of a personalized contractual marriage agreement over a conventional marriage agreement?

5. What are the most significant disadvantages of a contractual marriage agreement?

6. What factors are necessary preconditions for the observance of the guidelines in a contractual marriage?

7. Do you believe that a contractual marriage promotes more or less openness and growth for couples than a conventional marriage? Explain.

Epilogue:

The Future

It is interesting to speculate about the future and what family forms will exist in the year 2000 and after. I should like to conclude this book with a look into the future.

Monogamy and the Nuclear Family

There are those who say that monogamy is outdated, that it is dead, and that the nuclear family is sick and will inevitably be replaced. I cannot agree. Monogamous marriage and the nuclear family are in a state of flux and change, but changes that are occurring ought to make these forms more meaningful than ever. This does not mean we are going to witness a return to traditional marriage and family living. It means that we are in the process of revitalizing monogamy, realizing its intrinsic worth in meeting human needs. It means we are seeking ways and means of making the nuclear family a viable family form by decreasing its isolation from other persons and society, but it does not mean that we will witness a return to the traditional extended family or a mass stampede to establish polygamy, group marriages, or to live in communes. In my opinion, these things are not going to happen since the variant family forms are more unstable than is monogamy itself. There

are some changes, however, that I feel are far more likely.

Women and Marriage

One change is that a few, but an increasing minority of women will elect *not* to choose marriage as the *summum bonum* of life. According to Bernard (1972b; 1974), marriage is poor status for some women. Most research indicates that women are unhappier in marriage than are men, a greater number indicate that they are dissatisfied in their marriages, and that unemployed married women have poorer mental health than married men or single women (Athanasiou, 1970). Many modern women are rebelling against marriage itself, at least in the form in which they experience it, because of the subservient role in which it places them. As they become more educated and financially independent, they are discovering that they don't need to be married to have fulfilled lives. As a result, greater numbers are electing to postpone marriage indefinitely, perhaps forever. Perhaps as more women achieve complete equality within marriage itself, women who now oppose marriage because they feel it stifles their career, or their self-actualization and fulfillment will once more join the throngs to the altar. In the meantime, some are electing not to be married just as some who are married are electing not to become mothers (Bernard, 1974). Marriage will always be enormously more popular than nonmarriage, but the fact that some feel nonmarriage is superior to marriage is a revolutionary idea whose time has come for a small group of persons.

Sex Roles

The struggle of women for sexual equality and sex role flexibility is a difficult one, but it is succeeding. More and more schools, especially educational institutions that prepare persons for the professions are admitting equal numbers of men and women. This means that professions that are now male dominated, such as law, medicine, science, and engineering will include increasing proportions of women. This means also that when women are no longer forced to assume economically dependent roles in relation to men, they will no longer be willing to accept a subservient role in their families. Equality of opportunity, educationally and economically, will lead to increasing equality in all other aspects of life.

Of necessity, this means increasing flexibility and an overlapping of sex roles in the family. There will no longer be a sharp division of labor between men's work and women's work. There will be "our work," which both husbands and wives will perform. While divisions of that work are necessary, husbands and wives will show increasing flexibility in who performs what work and when. This should have three important beneficial effects. Women will have increasing opportunities for self-expression and creative employment. Men relieved of part of the heavy economic burden of supporting the family will have more time to be husbands and fathers. Both women and men will share responsibilities for decision making in the family, as equal partners.

Childbirth and Rearing of Children

Because of the increasing professional employment of women, voluntary childlessness will become more common. The 4 percent of women who don't want children will likely increase, but not by significant proportions. Being parents will always be more popular than not being parents. The average number of children will probably decrease even further, however, so that zero population increase will become a reality. Improved methods of birth control and the availability of abortions should result in fewer unplanned and unwanted children. More parents will want the children they have. The decrease in family size, especially among low socioeconomic groups should enable these parents to take better care of their children.

The important question is: What about the rearing and socialization of children? Who will do it if both parents are employed? Will the family lose its child-rearing function? There are two trends that seem likely. One, there will be increasing numbers of childcare centers established so that more children will receive professional care. Two—and this is still a real question mark—business and industry will be forced to establish shorter and more flexible work schedules to allow at least one parent to be home for part of the day. Already, a few leading companies like Northwestern Mutual Life Insurance, Union Mutual, Control Data Corporation, and Nestlé Company are experimenting with allowing workers to select the times when they go to work, as long as they work the usual number of hours. It is probable, therefore, that two trends will develop simultaneously: more childcare centers and more opportunities for working parents to adjust schedules to be with children. If society takes over most of the socialization process, as happens now in many socialistic countries, parents will exert less and less influence. But if, instead, parents are given the opportunity both to seek personal fulfillment and to be able to rear their own children, with only some outside assistance, both parent and children will benefit. Certainly, the present situation is intolerable; neither society nor parents are giving adequate care to all children.

Housing and Living Arrangements

Part of the answer to the childcare problem will be solved by future trends in living arrangements. Already, increasing numbers of Americans are living in multifamily dwellings, especially in apartments, co-ops and condominiums. This trend will likely increase as individual dwellings become more expensive and economically prohibitive. The fact that greater numbers of families will live together under one roof does not mean the demise of the nuclear family. It will mean greater opportunity for nuclear families to interact and cooperate in many ways, including social, economic, and childcare cooperation. Already, groups of families are showing increasing tendencies for cooperation. The traditional emphasis on individualism will decline as social realities force philosophical and practical changes.

Intimacy and Divorce

But it will mean, too, that couples will seek emotional sanctuary in one another. Couples will desire and strive for even more opportunities to be alone and to find intimacy. Those who aren't able to find emotional fulfillment in their marriages will be unlikely to remain together "for the sake of the children." Divorce will become even more accepted by larger society, with percentages of those divorced increasing even further for a time before the rates level off and then finally decline as solutions to the problem of family instability are found.

This means there will be an increase in serial monogamy—in a series of shorter-term monogamous marriages. This means there will be great personal satisfaction and fulfillment for those adults whose marriages are long-lasting, since unfulfilling marriages will not survive. Some other adults will at first fail and later succeed in marriage. Other adults will never find the fulfillment for which they are seeking.

For a time, because of increasing marital disorganization, children and youths will be forced to turn to peers for meaningful friendships. The present need and trend among youths to seek physical, social, and emotional intimacy with peers will likely continue. Only gradually, as the family becomes more stabilized, will children find more emotional satisfaction at home.

Sexual Expression

As youths seek greater intimacy and emotional involvement with one another and as social controls, especially of parents, are relaxed, sexual involvements before marriage will increase. Premarital sexual intercourse among youths will become even more common. The present trend toward nonmarital cohabitation will probably continue, with increasing numbers of youths living together with full sexual intimacy prior to marriage. This should have several important effects: it will decrease the sexual pressure to marry young so that the median age of marriage should continue to increase. This does not mean legal marriage will go out of style. Rather, it means marriage will be delayed, so that when it does take place, it is more likely to succeed. It should mean also that youths will be wiser and better able to choose a mate when they do decide, so that this should increase their chances of happier marriages. Eventually, these trends will help to correct the present increase in divorce rates.

The increase in premarital sexual intercourse does not mean an increase in either comarital or extramarital sexual expression. Like the Swedes, Americans will become more inclined to "sow their wild oats" before marriage and thereafter be more inclined to remain faithful and sexually monogamous after marriage. It is my feeling that the reason for much of today's comarital and extramarital sexual experimentation has been that these persons, now middle-aged, were reared in an atmosphere of sexual repression. Today's permissiveness allows them opportunities for experimentation that were denied them when they were younger. Today's youths are experimenting now but will not necessarily become more promiscuous after marriage. The overwhelming social and personal pressure to be sexually monogamous once married I believe will continue. Other alternatives present too many complications.

The Elderly

Today's solutions for institutional care of the elderly are not very satisfactory. Nursing homes and homes for the aged are increasing in numbers as the nuclear family becomes less willing or less able to care for the elderly. But often these developments are motivated by economic considerations, by promoters who want to take advantage of government subsidies of housing to make a profit. Custodial care of the elderly is forced upon them, but they really don't like it or want it. As the proportion of elderly persons in our society increases, they will become a much more important political and social pressure group, so that we are likely to see some drastic changes in society's provisions for the aged. Already, increasing numbers of older people are organizing cooperatives, social and educational groups, housing projects, etc. The time may come when homes and other institutions for the aged will be run by the elderly themselves, not for profit but for their own benefit.

Summary

In the long run, monogamous marriage will not only survive, it will become more viable, stable, and fulfilling to its members. The nuclear family will be forced to adjust to living with increasing numbers of other nuclear families, so it will become less individualistic and less isolated and more social in its outlook and lifestyle. But the basic need for marriage for love and companionship will be the driving force that will motivate couples to continue to march down aisles across the land to say, "I do."

Bibliography

"About New Report on 'The Pill.'" *U. S. News and World Report* (December 29, 1975).

Abrahams, B., Feldman, S. F. and Nash, S. C. "Sex Role Self-Concept and Sex Role Attitudes: Enduring Personality Characteristics or Adaptations to Changing Life Situation?" *Developmental Psychology* 14 (June 1978): 393–400.

Acock, A. C. and Bengtson, V. L. "On the Relative Influence of Mothers and Fathers: A Covariance Analysis of Political and Religious Socialization." *Journal of Marriage and the Family* 40 (August 1978): 519–530.

Adamek, R. J. "Abortion, Personal Freedom, and Public Policy." *The Family Coordinator* 23 (October 1974): 411–419.

Adamek, R. J. "College Work, Work Commitment, and Female Perceptions of Self, Ideal Woman, and Men's Ideal Woman." *Social Forces* 3 (Summer 1970): 97–112.

Adams, B. N. *Kinship in an Urban Setting.* Chicago: Markham, 1968.

Adams, B. N. "Isolation, Function, and Beyond: American Kinship in the 1960's" *Journal of Marriage and the Family* 32 (November 1970): 575–597.

Adams, B. N. and Cromwell, R. E. "Morning and Night People in the Family: A Preliminary Statement." *The Family Coordinator* 27 (January 1978): 5–13.

Adams, V. "Sex Therapies in Perspective." *Psychology Today* 14 (August 1980):35,36.

"After a Conviction—Second Thoughts about Abortions." *U.S. News and World Report* (March 3, 1975): 78.

Ainsworth, M. D. S., and Bell, S. M. "Attachment, Exploration, and Separation: Illustrated by the Behavior of One-Year-Olds in a Strange Situation." *Child Development* 41 (1970): 49–67.

Albrecht, R. E., and Bock, E. W. *Encounter: Love, Marriage and the Family.* Boston: Holbrook, 1972.

Albrecht, S. L., Bahr, H. M., and Chadwick, B. A. "Public Stereotyping of Sex Roles, Personality Characteristics, and Occupations." *Sociology and Social Research* 61 (January 1977): 223–240.

Aldous, J. "Intergenerational Visiting Patterns: Variations in Boundary Maintenance as an Explanation." *Family Process* 6 (September 1967): 235–251.

Aldridge, D. P. "Problems and Approaches to Black Adoptions." *The Family Coordinator* 23 (October 1974): 407–410.

Alexander, J. F. "Defensive and Supportive Communications in Family Systems." *Journal of Marriage and the Family* 35 (November 1973a): 615–617.

Alexander, J. F. "Defensive and Supportive Communications in Normal and Deviant Families." *Journal of Consulting and Clinical Psychiatry* 40 (1973b): 223–231.

Allen, G., and Martin, C. "What's Your Intimacy Quotient?" In *Choice and Challenge.* Edited by C. E. Williams and J. F. Crosby. Dubuque, Iowa: Wm. C. Brown, 1974.

Allen, V. "Personality Correlated of Poverty." In *Psychological Factors in Poverty*. Institute for Research on Poverty, Monograph Series. Chicago: Markham, 1970.

Almquist, E. M. and Angrist, S. "Career Salience and Atypicality of Occupational Choice among College Women." *Journal of Marriage and the Family* 32 (May 1970): 242–249.

Altman, D. *Homosexual: Oppression and Liberation*. New York: E. P. Dutton, Chapter 7.

Altman, I. and Taylor, D. *Social Penetration: The Development of Interpersonal Relationships*. New York: Henry Holt, 1973.

Altman, I., Taylor, D. A., and Wheeler, L. "Ecological Aspects of Group Behavior in Social Isolation." *Journal of Applied Social Psychology* 1 (1971): 76–100.

Ambrose, L. "Misinforming Pregnant Teenagers." *Family Planning Perspectives* 10 (January/February 1978): 51–53, 57.

American Council on Education. *College Dropouts: A National Profile*. ACE Research Reports, vol 7, no. 1. Washington, D. C.: American Council on Education, 1972.

Ammons, P. and Stinnett, N. "The Vital Marriage: A Closer Look." *Family Relations* 29 (January 1980): 37–42.

Anderson, R. N. "Rural Plant Closures: The Coping Behavior of Filipinos in Hawaii." *Family Relations* 29 (October 1980): 511–516.

Aneshensel, C. C. and Rosen, B. C. "Domestic Roles and Sex Differences in Occupational Expectations." *Journal of Marriage and the Family* 42 (February 1980): 121–131.

Angrist, S. S. "Variations in Women's Adult Aspirations during College." *Journal of Marriage and the Family* 34 (August 1972): 465–468.

Anonymous. "Does No Fault Divorce Portend No Fault Alimonies?" *University of Pittsburgh Law Review* 3 (1973): 486–499.

Arafat, I. S. and Yorburg, B. "On Living Together with Marriage." *Journal of Sex Research* 9 (1973): 21–29.

Araji, S. K. "Husbands' and Wives' Attitude-Behavior Congruence on Family Roles." *Journal of Marriage and the Family* 39 (May 1977): 309–320.

Ard, Fr. B. N. *Treating Psychosexual Dysfunction*. New York: Jason Aronson, 1974.

Arling, G. "The Elderly Widow and Her Family, Neighbors, and Friends." *Journal of Marriage and the Family* 38 (November 1976): 757–768.

Arnstein, H. S. *What Every Woman Needs to Know About Abortion*. New York: Scribner's, 1973.

Astin, H. S. *The Woman Doctorate in America*. New York: Russell Sage Foundation, 1969.

Atchley, R. C. "Dimensions of Widowhood in Later Life." *Gerontologist* 15 (1975): 176–178.

Athanasiou, R., Shaver, P., and Tavris, C. "Sex." *Psychology Today* 4 (1970): 39–52.

Atkinson, T. "The Oppressed Majority Demands Its Rights." *Life*, December 12, 1969.

Avery, A. W. et al. "Teaching Family Relations to Dating Versus Non-Couples: Who Learns Better?" *The Family Coordinator* 28 (January 1979): 41–45.

Avery, C. E. and Johannis, T. B. *Love and Marriage, A Guide for Young People*. New York: Harcourt Brace Jovanovich, 1971.

Bach, G. R. *The Intimate Enemy*. New York: Avon, 1968.

Bach, G. R. "Therapeutic Aggression." (Set of ten cassettes.) Chicago: Human Development Institute, 1973.

Bach, G. R. and Deutsch, R. M. "Intimacy." In *Love, Marriage, Family: A Developmental Approach*. Glenview, Illinois: Scott, Foresman, 1973, pp. 157–161.

Bach, G. R. and Wyden, P. "The Art of Family Fighting." In *Confronting the Issues*. Edited by K. C. W. Kammeyer. Boston: Allyn and Bacon, 1975, pp. 314–320.

Bagarozzi, J. I. and Bagarozzi, D. A. "Financial Counseling: A Self-Control Model for the Family." *Family Relations* 29 (July 1980): 396–403.

Bahr, S. J. "Comment on 'The Study of Family Power Structure: A Review, 1960–1969.'" *Journal of Marriage and the Family* 34 (May 1972): 239–243.

Bahr, S.; Chadwick, B. A.; and Stauss, J. H. "The Effect of Relative Economic Status on Fertility." *Journal of Marriage and the Family* 37 (May 1975): 335–342.

Bahr, S. J. and Rollins, B. C. "Crisis and Conjugal Power." *Journal of Marriage and the Family* 33 (May 1971): 360–367.

Bailyn, L. "Career and Family Orientations of Husbands and Wives in Relation to Marital Happiness." *Human Relations* 23 (1970): 97–113.

Bain, K. "Adoption: United States Philosophy and

Team Approach." In *Marriage and Family in the Modern World: Readings.* Edited by R. S. Cavan. New York: Crowell, 1974, pp. 449–453.

Balkwell C., Balswick, J., and Balkwell, J. W. "On Black and White Family Patterns in America: Their Impact on the Expressive Aspect of Sex-Role Socialization." *Journal of Marriage and the Family* 40 (November 1978): 743–747.

Balkwell, C. and Halverson, C. F., Jr. "The Hyperactive Child as a Source of Stress in the Family: Consequences of Suggestions for Intervention." *Family Relations* 29 (October 1980): 550–557.

Ballard, W. M., and Gold, E. M. "Medical and Health Aspects of Reproduction in the Adolescent." *Clinical Obstetrics and Gynecology* 14 (June 1972): 350–351.

Balswick, J. O. "The Effect of Spouse Companionship Support on Employment Success." *Journal of Marriage and the Family* 32 (May 1970): 212–215.

Balswick, J. and Avertt, C. P. "Differences in Expressiveness: Gender, Interpersonal Orientation, and Perceived Parental Expressiveness as Contributing Factors." *Journal of Marriage and the Family* 39 (February 1977): 121–127.

Balswick, J. O., and Peek, C. W. "The Inexpressive Male: A Tragedy of American Society." *The Family Coordinator* 20 (October 1971): 363–368.

Bandura, A. "Social-learning Theory and Identificatory Processes." In *Handbook of Socialization Theory and Research.* Edited by D. A. Goslin. Chicago: Rand McNally, 1969, pp. 213–262.

Bardwick, J. M. "Psychological Conflict and the Reproductive System." In *Feminine Personality and Conflict.* Edited by E. L. Walker, pp. 3–28. Belmont, California.: Brooks/Cole, 1970.

Bardwick, J. M. *Psychology of Women. A Study of Bio-Cultural Conflicts.* New York: Harper, 1971.

Barry, W. A. "Marriage Research and Conflict: An Interpretive Review." *Psychological Bulletin* 73 (1970): 41–54.

Bart, P. "Portnoy's Mother's Complaint." In *Marriages and Families.* Edited by H. Z. Lopata, pp. 222–228. New York: D. Van Nostrand, 1973.

Bart, P. B. "Sexism and Social Science: From the Gilded Cage to the Iron Cage, or, the Perils of Pauline." *Journal of Marriage and the Family* 33 (November 1971): 734–745.

Bartell, G. *Group Sex.* New York: Wyden, 1971.

Bartell, G. "Group Sex among the Mid-Americans." *Journal of Sex Research* 6 (1970): 113–130.

Barton, J. J. "Laparoscopy in Gynecologic Practice." In *Obstetrics and Gynecology Annual, 1972.* Edited by R. M. Wynn. New York: Appleton-Century-Crofts, 1972, pp. 351–372.

Barton, K.; Kawash, G.; and Cattell, R. B. "Personality, Motivation, and Marital Role Factors as Predictors of Life Data in Married Couples." *Journal of Marriage and the Family* 34 (August 1972): 474–480.

Bartz, K. W., and Nye, F. I. "Early Marriage: A Propositional Formulation." *Journal of Marriage and the Family* 32 (1970): 258–267.

Bateson, G. *Steps to an Ecology of Mind.* New York: Ballantine, 1972.

Battle-Sister, A. "Conjectures on the Female Culture Question." *Journal of Marriage and the Family* 33 (August 1971): 411–420.

Baum, M. "Love, Marriage, and the Division of Labor." In *Family, Marriage, and the Struggle of the Sexes.* Edited by H. P. Dreitzel. New York: Macmillan, 1972, pp. 83–106.

Bayer, A. "College Impact on Marriage." *Journal of Marriage and the Family* 34 (November 1972): 600–609.

Bayer, A. E. "Sexual Permissiveness and Correlates as Determined through Interaction Analyses." *Journal of Marriage and the Family* 39 (February 1977): 29–40.

Beacham, D. W., and Beacham, W. D. *Synopsis of Gynecology.* 8th ed. St. Louis: Mosby, 1972.

Bean, C. A. *Methods of Childbirth.* New York: Dolphin, 1974.

Bean, F. D., Curtis, R. L. and Marcum, J. P. "Familism and Marital Satisfaction among Mexican Americans: The Effects of Family Size, Wife's Labor Force Participation, and Conjugal Power." *Journal of Marriage and the Family* 39 (November 1977): 759–767.

Bebbington, A. C. "The Function of Stress in the Establishment of the Dual-Career Family." *Journal of Marriage and the Family* 35 (August 1973): 530–537.

Beck, D. F. "Current Challenges to the Traditional Family and Some Newly Emerging Alternative Forms for Family Living." Mimeographed. New York: Family Service Association of America, 1972.

Becker, I. "Men, Beware Women." In *Encounter: Love, Marriage, and Family.* Edited by R. E. Albrecht and E. W. Bock, pp. 89–94. Boston: Holbrook, 1972.

Bell, C. S. et al. "Normative Stress and Young Families: Adaption and Development." *Family Relations* 29 (October 1980): 453–458.

Bell, R. R. "Female Sexual Satisfaction as Related to Levels of Education." *Sexual Behavior* (November 1971): 8–14.

Bell, R. R. *Marriage and Family Interaction.* 4th ed. Homewood, Illinois: Dorsey, 1975.

Bell, R. R. "The One-Parent Mother in the Negro Lower Class." Paper read at the meeting of the Eastern Sociological Society, New York, 1965.

Bell, R. R. "The Related Importance of Mother and Wife Roles among Black Lower-Class Women" in *The Black Family.* Edited by R. Staples. Belmont, California: Wadsworth, 1971, pp. 248–255.

Bell, R. R. "Some Emerging Sexual Expectations among Women." In *The Social Dimension of Human Sexuality.* Edited by R. B. Bell and M. Gordon. Boston: Little, Brown, 1972, pp. 158–165.

Bell, R. R., and Bell, P. L. "Sexual Satisfaction among Married Women." *Medical Aspects of Human Sexuality* (December 1972): 136–144.

Bell, R. R., and Connolly, J. "Non-coital Sex in Marriage." Toronto: National Council of Family Relations, October 1973.

Bell, R. R. and Coughey, K. "Premarital Sex Experience among College Females, 1958, 1968, and 1978." *Family Relations* 29 (July 1980): 153–357.

Bell, R. R., and Silvan, L. "Swinging—The Sexual Exchange of Marriage Partners." Paper presented at the meeting of the Society for the Study of Social Problems. Washington, D.C., August 1970.

Bell, R. R.; Turner, S.; and Rosen, L. "A Multivariate Analysis of Female Extramarital Coitus." *Journal of Marriage and the Family* 37 (May 1975): 375–384.

Bell, S. M. "The Development of the Concept of Object as Related to Mother-Infant Attachment." *Child Development* 41 (1970): 291–311.

Belliveau, F., and Richter, L. *Understanding Human Sexual Inadequacy.* New York: Bantam, 1970.

Bem, S. L., and Bem, D. J. "Training the Woman to Know Her Place." In *The Future of the Family.* Edited by L. K. Home. New York: Simon and Schuster, 1972, pp. 202–223.

Bender, S. J. "Sex and the College Student." *Journal of School Health* 43 (May 1973): 278–280.

Benson, L. *The Family Bond: Marriage, Love, and Sex in America.* New York: Random House, 1971.

Berardo, F. M. "Kinship Interaction and Communication among Space-Age Migrants." *Journal of Marriage and the Family* 29 (August 1967): 541–554.

Berardo, F. M. "Survivorship and Social Isolation: The Case of the Aged Widower." *The Family Coordinator* 19 (January 1970): 11–25.

Berelson, B. "The Value of Children: A Taxonomical Essay." In *Current Issues in Marriage and the Family.* Edited by J. G. Wells, New York: Macmillan, 1975, pp. 168–176.

Bergen, G. R. and Bergen, M. B. "Quality of Marriage of University Students in Relation to Source of Financial Support and Demographic Characteristics." *The Family Coordinator* 27 (July 1978): 245–250.

Berger, B. M., et al. "Child-rearing Practices in the Commune Family." Unpublished progress report to National Institute of Mental Health, 1972a.

Berger, B. M. "The Communal Family." *The Family Coordinator* 21 (October 1972b): 419–427.

Berger, D. G., and Wenger, M. G. "The Ideology of Virginity." *Journal of Marriage and the Family* 35 (November 1973): 666–676.

Berger, M., and Benson, L. *Family Communication Systems: Instructor's Handbook.* Minneapolis: Human Synergistics, 1971.

Berger, M. E. "Trial Marriage: Harnessing the Trend Constructively." *The Family Coordinator* 20 (January 1971): 38–43.

Bergstrom, S., et al. "Prostaglandins in Fertility Control." *Science* 175 (March 17, 1972): 1280.

Berkove, G. F. "Perceptions of Husband Support by Returning Women Students." *The Family Coordinator* 28 (October 1979): 451–457.

Berkowitz, L. "The Case for Bottling Up Rage." *Psychology Today* 7 (July 1973): 24–31.

Bermant, G. "Behavior Therapy Approaches to Modification of Sexual Preferences." In *Readings on the Psychology of Women.* Edited by J. M. Bardwick. New York: Harper, 1972, pp. 254–258.

Bern, S. L., and Bern, D. J. "Training a Woman to Know Her Place: the Power of a Nonconscious Ideology." In *Roles Women Play: Readings toward*

Women's Liberation. Edited by M. H. Garskov. Belmont, California: Brooks/Cole, 1971.

Bernard, J. "The Fourth Revolution." In *Encounter: Love, Marriage, and Family.* Edited by R. E. Albrecht and E. W. Bock. Boston: Holbrook, 1972a, pp. 94–108.

Bernard, J. *The Future of Marriage.* New York: Bantam, 1972b.

Bernard, J. *The Future of Motherhood.* New York: Penguin, 1974.

Bernard, J. "Infidelity: Some Moral and Social Issues." In *Renovating Marriage.* Edited by R. W. Libby and R. N. Whitehurst. Danville, California: Consensus, 1973a, pp. 75–94.

Bernard, J. "Marriage and the Nuclear Family as Target." In *The Changing Family: Adaptation and Diversity.* Edited by G. F. Streib. Reading, Massachusetts: Addison-Wesley, 1973b, pp. 25–36.

Bernard, J. "No News, but New Ideas." In *Divorce and After.* Edited by P. Bohannon. Garden City, New York: Doubleday, 1970, pp. 3–29.

Bernard, J. "The Paradox of the Happy Marriage." In *Woman in Sexist Society.* Edited by V. Gornick and B. K. Moran. New York: Basic, 1971, pp. 85–98.

Bernard, J. *The Sex Game: Communication between the Sexes.* New York: Atheneum, 1972c.

Bernard, S. "Fatherless Families: Their Economic and Social Adjustment." Paper in Social Welfare no. 7. Waltham, Massachusetts: Florence G. Heller Graduate School for Advanced Studies in Social Welfare, Brandeis University, 1971.

Berne, E. *Games People Play: The Psychology of Human Relationships.* New York: Grove, 1964.

Bernstein, R. *Helping Unmarried Mothers.* New York: Association Press, 1971.

Bieber, I., et al. *Homosexuality: A Psychoanalytic Study.* New York: Basic, 1962.

Blenvenu, M. J., Sr. "Measurement of Marital Communication." *The Family Coordinator* 19 (January 1970): 26–31.

Biller, H. B. *Father, Child, and Sex Role: Paternal Determinants of Personality Development.* Lexington, Massachusetts: Heath, 1971.

Biller, H. B., and Bahm, R. M. "Father Absence, Perceived Maternal Behavior and Masculinity of Self-concept among Junior High School Boys." *Developmental Psychology* 4 (1971): 178–181.

Billings, A. "Conflict Resolution in Distressed and Nondistressed Married Couples." *Journal of Consulting and Clinical Psychology* 47 (April 1979): 368–376.

Billingsley, A., and Giovannoni, J. M. "One Parent Family." In *Encyclopedia of Social Work (16th Issue).* Vol. I. Edited by R. Morris. New York: National Association of Social Workers, 1971.

Bird, C. "The New Woman." In *Love, Marriage, Family: A Developmental Approach.* Edited by M. E. Lasswell and T. E. Lasswell. Glenview, Illinois: Scott, Foresman, 1973, pp. 116–120.

"Birth Control Deaths." *Newsweek* (March 1, 1976): 60.

Bischof, L. J. *Adult Psychology.* 2d ed. New York: Harper, 1976.

Blanchard, R. W., and Biller, H. B. "Father Availability and Academic Performance among Third-Grade Boys." *Developmental Psychology* 4 (1971): 301–305.

Blanton, J. "Communal Child Bearing: The Synanon Experience." *Alternative Lifestyles* 3 (February 1980): 87–116.

Blau, Z. *Old Age in a Changing Society.* New York: Franklin Watts, 1973.

Blazer, J. "Married Virgins: A Study of Unconsummated Marriages." *Journal of Marriage and the Family* 26 (May 1964): 213–214.

Blood, R. O., Jr. *The Family.* New York: Free Press, 1972.

Blood, R. O., Jr. "Resolving Family Conflicts." In *Marriage and Family in the Modern World.* 4th ed. Edited by R. S. Cavan. New York: Crowell, 1974, pp. 303–312.

Blood, R. O., Jr., and Hill, R. "Comparative Analysis of Family Power Structure: Problems of Measurement and Interpretation." In *Families in East and West.* Edited by R. Hill and R. Konig. Paris: Mouton, 1970, pp. 525–535.

Bluestone, B.; Murphy, W.; and Stevenson, M. H. *Low Wages and the Working Poor.* Two Volumes. Detroit: Institute of Labor and Industrial Relations, University of Michigan-Wayne State University, 1971.

Blumberg, P. M., and Paul, P. W. "Continuities and Discontinuities in Upper-Class Marriages." *Journal of Marriage and the Family* 37 (February 1975): 63–77.

Bohannan, P. *Divorce and After.* Garden City, New York: Doubleday, 1971.

Bohannan, P. "The Six Stations of Divorce." In *Love, Marriage, Family.* Edited by M. E. Lasswell and T. E. Lasswell. Glenview, Illinois: Scott, Foresman, 1973, pp. 475–489.

Bohannan, P. "Some Thoughts on Divorce Reform." In *Current Issues in Marriage and the Family.* Edited by J. G. Wells. New York: Macmillan, 1975, pp. 235–245.

Bonham, G. S. "Who Adopts: The Relationship of Adoption and Social Demographic Characteristics of Women." *Journal of Marriage and the Family* 39 (May 1977): 295–306.

Booth, A. "Sex and Social Participation." *American Sociological Review* (April 1972): 183–193.

Booth, A. and Welch, S. "Spousal Consensus and Its Correlates: A Reassessment." *Journal of Marriage and the Family* 40 (February 1978): 23–32.

Boss, P. G. "Normative Family Stress: Family Boundary Changes Across the Life Span." *Family Relations* 29 (October 1980): 445–450.

Boston Women's Health Course Collective. *Our Bodies, Our Selves.* Boston: New England Free Press, 1971.

Bouvier, L. F. "Catholics and Contraception." *Journal of Marriage and the Family* 34 (August 1972): 514–522.

Bowen, M. In "Cohabitation Research Newsletter, Issue no. 2." Edited by E. D. Macklin. Mimeographed. Ithaca, New York: Cornell University, College of Human Ecology, April 1973.

Bower, D. W. and Christopherson, V. A. "University Student Cohabitation: A Regional Comparison of Selected Attitudes and Behavior." *Journal of Marriage and the Family* 39 (August 1977): 447–452.

Bowerman, C. E., and Irish, D. P. "Some Relationships of Stepchildren to Their Parents." In *Love, Marriage, Family.* Edited by M. E. Lasswell and T. E. Lasswell. Glenview, Illinois: Scott, Foresman, 1973, pp. 495–501.

Bowlby, J. *Attachment and Loss.* Vol. 1.: *Attachment.* London: Hogarth, 1969.

Bowman, H. A. *Marriage for Moderns.* 7th ed. New York: McGraw-Hill, 1974.

Boxer, L. "Mate Selection and Emotional Disorder." *The Family Coordinator* 19 (1970): 173–179.

Boxer, L. "Survival Rates among Religiously Homagamous and Interreligious Marriages." *Social Forces* 41 (May 1963): 353–362.

Boyd, P. R. "Drug Abuse and Addiction in Adolescents." In *Modern Perspectives in Adolescent Psychiatry.* Edited by J. G. Howells. New York: Brunner/Mazel, 1971, pp. 290–328.

Bradford, D. L., and Klevansky, S. "Non-Utopian Communities—the Middle-Class Commune." In *Confronting the Issues.* Edited by K. C. W. Kammeyer. Boston: Allyn and Bacon, 1975, pp. 90–107.

Braen, B. B. "The School-Age Pregnant Girl: The Problem and an Attempted Solution." *Clinical Child Psychology, Newsletter* 10 (1971): 17–20.

Brandwein, R. A.; Brown, C. A.; and Fox, E. M. "Women and Children Last: The Social Situation of Divorced Mothers and Their Families." *Journal of Marriage and the Family* 36 (August 1974): 498–514.

Brashear, D. B. "Abortion Counseling." *The Family Coordinator* 22 (October 1973): 429–435.

Braun, J. "The Struggle for Acceptance of a New Birth Technique." *Parade Magazine* (November 23, 1975).

Brayer, F. T.; Chiazze, L., Jr.; and Duffy, B. J. "Calendar Rhythm and Menstrual Cycle Range." *Fertility/Sterility* 20 (1969): 279–288.

Brehm, J. W., et al. "Psychological Arousal and Interpersonal Attraction." Mimeographed, 1970.

Brenton, M. "New Ways to Manliness." In *Womankind: Beyond the Stereotype.* Edited by N. Reeves. Chicago: Aldine, 1971.

Brindley, C., et al. "Sex Differences in the Activities and Social Interactions of Nursery School Children." In *Comparative Ecology and Behaviour of Primates.* Edited by R. P. Machael and J. H. Crook. New York: Academic, 1972.

Brinkerhoff, D. B. and White, L. K. "Marital Satisfaction in an Economically Marginal Population." *Journal of Marriage and the Family* 40 (May 1978): 259–267.

Brissett, D., and Lewis, L. S. "Guidelines for Marital Sex: An Analysis of Fifteen Popular Marriage Manuals." *The Family Coordinator* 19 (January 1970): 41–48.

Bronfenbrenner, U. "Liberated Women: How They're Changing American Life." Interview conducted for *U.S. News and World Report* (June 7, 1975): 49.

Bronfenbrenner, U. "The Split Level American Family." In *Perspectives in Marriage and the Family.* Edited by J. R. Eshleman. Boston: Allyn and Bacon, 1969, pp. 521–535.

Bronfenbrenner, U. *Two Worlds of Childhood: U.S. and USSR.* New York: Russell Sage Foundation, 1970.

Broschart, K. R. "Family Status and Professional Achievement: A Study of Women Doctorates." *Journal of Marriage and the Family* 40 (February 1978): 71–76.

Broverman, I., and Broverman, D. M. B. "Sex-Role Stereotypes and Clinical Judgments and Mental Health." *Journal of Consulting and Clinical Psychology* 34 (1970): 1–7.

Broverman, I. K., et al. "Sex-role Stereotypes: A Current Appraisal." *Journal of Social Issues* 28 (1972): 59–78.

Brown, B. B. "Married Students in Public Schools: A Texas Study." *The Family Coordinator* 21 (1972): 321–324.

Browning, R. "Summum Bonum." *The Complete Poetic and Dramatic Works of Robert Browning.* Boston: Houghton Mifflin, 1895.

Brownmiller, S. "Sisterhood is Powerful." *New York Times,* March 15, 1970.

Bryson, R., Bryson, B., and Johnson, M. F. "Family Size, Satisfaction, and Productivity in Dual-Career Couples." *Psychology of Women Quarterly* 8 (Fall 1978): 67–77.

Bukstel, L. H. et al. "Projected Extramarital Sexual Involvement of Unmarried College Students." *Journal of Marriage and the Family* 40 (May 1978): 337–340.

Bullock, R. C., et al. "The Weeping Wife: Marital Relations of Depressed Women." *Journal of Marriage and the Family* 34 (August 1972): 488–495.

Bultena, G. "Rural-Urban Differences in the Familial Interaction of the Aged." *Rural Sociology* 34 (1969): 5–15.

Bultena, G., and Marshall, D. G. "Family Patterns of Migrant and Nonmigrant Retirees." *Journal of Marriage and the Family* 32 (February 1970): 89–93.

Bumpass, L. L., and Sweet, J. A. "Differentials in Marital Instability: 1970" *American Sociological Review* 37 (1972): 754–766.

Burchinal, L. G. "Characteristics of Adolescents from Unbroken, Broken, and Reconstituted Families." *Journal of Marriage and the Family* 26 (February 1964): 44–51.

Burchinal, L. G., and Bauder, W. W. "Decision-Making and Role Patterns among Iowa Farm and Nonfarm Families." In *Journal of Marriage and the Family* 27 (November 1965): 525–530.

Burgess, E. W.; Locke, H. J.; and Thomas, M. M. *The Family.* 4th ed. New York: Van Nostrand Reinhold, 1971.

Burgess, J. K. "The Single-Parent Family: A Social and Sociological Problem." *The Family Coordinator* 19 (April 1970): 137–144.

Burr, W. R. "Satisfaction with Various Aspects of Marriage over the Life Cycle: A Random Middle Class Sample." *Journal of Marriage and the Family* 32 (February 1970): 29–37.

Burr, W. R. *Theory Construction and the Sociology of the Family.* New York: John Wiley, 1973.

Burr, W. R., Ahern, L., and Knowles, E. M. "An Empirical Test of Rodman's Theory of Resources in Cultural Context." *Journal of Marriage and the Family* 39 (August 1977): 505–514.

Byrne, D. "A Pregnant Pause in the Sexual Revolution." *Psychology Today* 11 (July 1977): 67–68.

Bytheway, B. "Problems of Representation in the Three Generation Family Study." *Journal of Marriage and the Family* 39 (May 1977): 243–250.

Calderone, M. "Eroticism as a Norm." *The Family Coordinator* 23 (October 1974): 337–341.

Calderone, M. S. "Sex Education for Children." *Sexology* (April 1971): 71.

Call, V. R. A. and Otto, L. B. "Age at Marriage as a Mobility Contingency: Estimate for the Nye-Berado Model." *Journal of Marriage and the Family* 39 (February 1977): 67–79.

Callahan, S. C. *The Working Mother.* New York: Macmillan, 1971.

Cannon, K., and Long, R. "Premarital Sexual Behavior in the Sixties." *Journal of Marriage and the Family* 33 (February 1971): 36–47.

Cant, G. "Is the Pill Safe?" *Nature/Science Annual.* New York: Time-Life, 1971, pp. 33–44.

Cantor, D. J. "A Matter of Right." In *Marriage and Family in a Decade of Change.* Edited by G. B. Carr. Reading, Massachusetts: Addison-Wesley, 1972, pp. 95–100.

Cantor, D. J. "A Matter of Right." *The Humanist* (May/June 1970).

Caplow, T. "Goals and Their Achievement in Four Utopian Communities." In *Communes: Creating and Managing the Collective Life.* Edited by R. M. Kanter. New York: Harper, 1973, pp. 108–124.

Carlson, E. "Family Background, School and Early Marriage." *Journal of Marriage and the Family* 41 (May 1979), 341–353.

Carlton, E. *Sexual Anxiety: A Study of Male Impotence.*

Totowa, New Jersey: Barnes and Noble Books, 1980.

Carter, H., and Glick, P. C. *Marriage and Divorce: A Social and Economic Study.* Cambridge, Massachusetts: The Harvard University Press, 1970.

Cattell, R. B., and Nesselroad, J. R. "Likeness and Completeness Theories Examined by 16 Personality Factor Measures on Stable and Unstable Married Couples." *Journal of Personality and Social Psychology* 7 (1967): 351–361.

Cavan, R. S. "Jewish Students' Attitudes towards Interreligious and Intra-Jewish Marriage." *American Journal of Sociology* 76 (May 1971): 1064–1071.

Cavan, R. S., and Cavan, J. T. "Cultural Patterns, Functions, and Dysfunctions of Endogamy and Intermarriage." *International Journal of Sociology of the Family* (May 1971): 10–24.

Cavan, S. *Hippies of the Haight.* St. Louis: New Critics Press, 1972.

Cavanaugh, J. R. "Rhythm of Sexual Desire in Women." *Medical Aspects of Human Sexuality* (February 1969): 29–39.

Centers, R.; Raven, B. W.; and Rodriques, A. "Conjugal Power Structure: A Re-examination." *American Sociological Review* 36 (April 1971): 264–278.

Chafetz, J. S. "Conflict Resolution in Marriage." *Journal of Family Issues* 1 (September 1980): 397–421.

Changing Times. Kiplinger Washington Editors, 729 H St., N.W., Washington, D.C.

Chantiny, J.; Kagan, B.; and Crowell, D. "Day Care of Infants in Family Settings." *American Journal of Orthopsychiatry* 43 (1973): 218–220.

Charny, I. W. *Marital Love and Hate.* New York: Macmillan, 1972.

Chartham, R. *Sex for Advanced Lovers.* New York: New American Library, 1970.

Cherlin, A. "Cohabitation: How the French and Swedes Do It." *Psychology Today* 13 (October 1979): 18–19.

Cherlin, A. "Postponing Marriage: The Influence of Young Women's Work Expectations." *Journal of Marriage and the Family* 42 (May 1980): 355–365.

Chernick, A. B., and Chernick, B. A. "Role of Ignorance in Sexual Dysfunction." *Medical Aspects of Human Sexuality* (February 1970): 114–121.

Chilman, C. S. "Families in Poverty in the Early 1970's: Rates, Associated Factors, Some Implications." *Journal of Marriage and the Family* 37 (February 1975): 49–60.

Chilman, C. S. "Some Psychosocial Aspects of Female Sexuality." *The Family Coordinator* 23 (April 1974): 123–131.

Chilman, C. S., and Meyer, D. L. "Single and Married Undergraduates' Measured Personality Needs and Self-rated Happiness." *Journal of Marriage and the Family* 28 (February 1966): 67–76.

Chilton, R. J., and Markle, G. E. "Family Disruption, Delinquent Conduct and the Effect of Subclassification." *American Sociological Review* 37 (February 1972): 93–99.

Chodorow, N. "Being and Doing: A Cross-Cultural Examination of the Socialization of Males and Females." In *Woman in Sexist Society.* Edited by V. Gornick and B. K. Moran. New York: Basic, 1971, pp. 173–197.

Christensen, H. T., and Johnsen, K. P. *Marriage and the Family.* 3d ed. New York: Ronald, 1971.

Christensen, H. T. and Johnson, L. B. "Premarital Coitus and the Southern Black: A Comparative View." *Journal of Marriage and the Family* 40 (November 1978): 721–732.

Citizen's Advisory Council on the Status of Women. *Memorandum: The Equal Rights Amendment and Alimony and Child Support Laws.* Washington, D.C.: U.S. Government Printing Office, January 1972.

Clark, Joanna. "Motherhood." In *Readings on the Psychology of Women.* Edited by J. M. Bardwick. New York: Harper, 1972, pp. 131–134.

Clark, J. H., and Zarrow, M. X. "Influence of Copulation on Time of Ovulation in Women." *American Journal of Obstetrics and Gynecology* 109 (April 1971): 1083–1085.

Clark, L. "Is There a Difference between a Clitoral and a Vaginal Orgasm?" *Journal of Sex Research* 6 (1970a) 25–28.

Clark, L. "What Gives Women Sex Pleasure." *Sexology* (January 1970b) 46–49.

Clavan, S. "The Impact of Social Class and Social Trends on the Role of Grandparent." *The Family Coordinator* 27 (October 1978): 351–357.

Clayton, G. "The Contemporary Experience of Adultery: Bob and Carol and Updike and Rimmer." In *Renovating Marriage.* Edited by R. W. Libby and R. N. Whitehurst. Danville, California: Consensus, 1973, pp. 95–115.

Clayton, P. N. "Meeting the Needs of the Single Parent Family." *The Family Coordinator* 20 (October 1971): 327–336.

Clayton, R. R. *The Family, Marriage, and Social Change.* Lexington, Massachusetts: Heath, 1975.

Clayton, R. R. "Premarital Sexual Intercourse: A Substantive Test of the Contingent Consistency Model." *Journal of Marriage and the Family* 34 (May 1972): 273–281.

Clayton, R. R. and Bokenmeier, J. L. "Premarital Sex in the Seventies." *Journal of Marriage and the Family* 42 (November 1980): 759–775.

Clayton, R. R. and Voss, H. L. "Shacking Up: Cohabitation in the 1970's." *Journal of Marriage and the Family* 39 (May 1977): 273–283.

Cofield, E. "Education and Women's Rights." In *Youth Culture and Counter-Culture.* Edited by K. B. Garner. Conference Proceedings of the Southeastern Council on Family Relations. Greensboro, North Carolina: Southeastern Council on Family Relations, 1973, p. 14.

Cole, C. L., Cole, A. L., and Dean, D. G. "Emotional Maturity and Marital Adjustment: A Decade Replication." *Journal of Marriage and the Family* 42 (August 1980): 533–539.

Comfort, A. *The Joy of Sex.* New York: Crown, 1972.

Commission on Obscenity and Pornography. *The Report of the Commission on Obscenity and Pornography.* New York: Bantam, 1970.

Committee on Maternal Health, Food and Nutrition Board, National Research Council. *Maternal Nutrition and the Course of Pregnancy.* Washington, D.C.: National Academy of Sciences, 1970.

Conger, R. D., Burgess, R. L., and Barrett, C. "Child Abuse Related to Life Change and Perceptions of Illness: Some Preliminary Findings." *The Family Coordinator* 28 (January 1979): 73–78.

Congress to Unite Women. "We Are Often Accused of Not Being Specific Enough in our Demands. Here Then Is a Clear Listing of What Women Want. For Starters." In *Intimate Life Styles: Marriage and Its Alternatives.* Edited by J. S. DeLora and J. R. DeLora. Pacific Palisades, California: Goodyear, 1972, pp. 268–270.

Conklin, G. H. "Cultural Determinants of Power for Women with the Family: A Neglected Aspect of the Family Research." *Journal of Comparative Family Studies* 10 (Spring 1979): 35–54.

Connell, D. M., and Johnson, J. E. "Relationship between Sex-Role Identification and Self-esteem in Early Adolescents." *Developmental Psychology* 3 (1970): 268.

Conover, P. W. "An Analysis of Communes and Intentional Communities with Particular Attention to Sexual and Gender Relations." *The Family Coordinator* 24 (October 1975): 453–464.

Conover, P. W. "The Alternative Society: Its Sources and Futures." *Technological Forecasting and Social Change* 5 (1973a): 295–304.

Conover, P. W. "The Potential for an Alternate Society." *The Futurist* 8 (1973b): 111–116.

Constantine, L. L., and Constantine, J. M. "Dissolution of Marriage in a Nonconventional Context." *The Family Coordinator* 21 (October 1972a): 457–462.

Constantine, L. L. and Constantine, J. M. "Group and Multilateral Marriage: Definitional Notes, Glossary, and Annotated Bibliography." In *Sourcebook in Marriage and the Family.* Edited by M. B. Sussman. 4th ed. Boston: Houghton Mifflin, 1974a, pp. 66–76.

Constantine, L. L., and Constantine, J. M. *Group Marriage.* New York: Collier, 1973a.

Constantine, L. L., and Constantine, J. M. "The Group Marriage." In *Love, Marriage, Family.* Edited by M. E. Lasswell and T. E. Lasswell. Glenview, Illinois.: Scott, Foresman, 1973c, pp. 446–454.

Constantine, L. L., and Constantine, J. M. "Group Marriage for the Future?" In *Marriage and Family in the Modern World.* Edited by R. S. Cavan. 4th ed. New York: Crowell, 1974b, pp. 351–355.

Constantine, L. L., and Constantine, J. M."Sexual Aspects of Group Marriage." In *Renovating Marriage.* Edited by R. W. Libby and R. N. Whitehurst. Danville, California: Consensus, 1973b, pp. 182–191.

Constantine, L. L., and Constantine, J. M. "Where is Marriage Going?" In *Intimate Life Styles: Marriage and Its Alternatives.* Edited by J. S. DeLora and J. R. DeLora. Pacific Palisades, California: Goodyear, 1972b, pp. 391–395.

Consumer Bulletin. Consumers' Research, Washington, New Jersey 07882.

Consumer Reports. Mt. Vernon, New York: Consumers Union of the United States.

Consumer Reports: The 1975 Buying Guide Issue. Mt. Vernon, New York: Consumers Union of the United States, 1974.

Coombs, R. H. "Value Consensus and Partner Satisfaction among Dating Couples." *Journal of Marriage and the Family* 28 (May 1966): 166–173.

Cooper, A. J. "Treatments of Male Potency Disorders: The Present Status." *Psychosomatics* 12 (July 1971): 235–244.

Corman, L., and Schaefer, J. B. "Population Growth and Family Planning." *Journal of Marriage and the Family* 35 (February 1973): 89–92.

Corrales, R. "The Influence of Family Life's Cycle Categories, Marital Power, Spousal Agreement, and Communication Styles upon Marital Satisfaction the First Six Years of Marriage." Unpublished doctoral dissertation. University of Minnesota, 1974.

Coutts, R. L. *Love and Intimacy.* San Ramon, California: Consensus, 1973.

Cox, F. "Separation, Divorce, and Remarriage." In *American Marriage: A Changing Scene.* Edited by F. Cox. Dubuque, Iowa: Wm. C. Brown, 1972, pp. 220–227.

Critelli, J. W. "Romantic Attraction and Happiness." *Psychological Reports* 41 (December 1977): 721–722.

Croak, J. W., and Barbara, J. "A Four Year Comparison of Premarital Sexual Attitudes." *Journal of Sex Research* 9 (May 1973): 91–96.

Croake, J.; Kelley, J. F.; and Colten, N. *Unmarrieds Living Together: It's Not All Gravy.* Dubuque, Iowa: Kendall/Hunt, Publishing, 1974.

Cromwell, R. E., and Gangel, J. L. "A Social Action Program Directed to Single Pregnant Girls and Adolescent Parents." *The Family Coordinator* 23 (January 1974): 61–66.

Cromwell, V. L. and Cromwell, R. E. "Perceived Dominance in Decision-Making and Conflict Resolution among Anglo, Black, and Chicano Couples." *Journal of Marriage and the Family* 40 (November 1978): 749–759.

Croog, S. H.; Lipson, A.; and Levine, S. "Help Problems in Severe Illness: The Roles of Kin Networks, Non-Family Resources and Institutions." *Journal of Marriage and the Family* 34 (February 1972): 32–41.

Crosby, J. F. *Illusion and Disillusion: The Self in Love and Marriage.* Belmont, California: Wadsworth, 1973.

Cuber, J. F., and Harroff, P. B. *The Significant Americans: A Study of Sexual Behavior among the Affluent.* New York: Appleton-Century-Crofts, 1965.

Culbert, S. A. "The Interpersonal Process of Self-Disclosure: It Takes Two to See One." In *Sensitivity Training and the Laboratory Approach: Readings About Concepts and Applications.* Edited by R. T. Golembiewski and A. Blumberg. Itasca, Illinois: Peacock, 1970, pp. 73–79.

Currant, E. F. et al. "Sex-Role Stereotyping and Assertive Behavior." *The Journal of Psychology* 101 (March 1979): 223–228.

Cutright, P. "Income and Family Events: Getting Married." *Journal of Marriage and the Family* 32 (November 1970): 628–646.

Cutright, P. "Income and Family Events: Marital Stability." *Journal of Marriage and the Family* 33 (May 1971): 291–302.

Danziger, C. *Unmarried Heterosexual Cohabitation.* San Francisco: R & E Research Associates, 1978.

Darnley, F. "A Response to 'Morning and Night People in the Family: A Preliminary Statement.'" *The Family Coordinator* 27 (January 1978): 14, 15.

Dass, B. R. *Be Here Now.* New York: Crown, 1971.

David, D. S., and Brannon, R., eds. *The Forty-nine Percent Majority: The Male Sex Role.* Reading, Massachusetts: Addison-Wesley, 1976.

Davidson, J. K., Sr. and Leslie, G. R. "Premarital Sexual Intercourse: An Application of Axiomatic Theory Construction." *Journal of Marriage and the Family* 39 (February 1977): 15–25.

Davies, R. C. "Representing the Lesbian Mother." *Family Advocate* 1 (Winter 1979): 21–23, 36.

Davis, H. J. "Intrauterine Contraceptive Devices: Present Status and Future Prospects." *American Journal of Obstetrics and Gynecology* 114 (September 1972): 134–151.

Davis, H. J. *Intrauterine Devices for Contraception: The IUD.* Baltimore: Williams and Wilkins, 1971.

Davis, H. J., and Lenski, J. "Mechanism of Action of Intrauterine Contraceptives in Women." *Obstetrics and Gynecology* 36 (September 1970): 350–358.

Davis, J. D. "When Boy Meets Girl: Sex Roles and the Negotiation of Intimacy in an Acquaintance Exercise." *Journal of Personality and Social Psycholgy* 36 (July 1978): 684–692.

Davis, P. "Contextual Sex-saliency and Sexual Activity: The Relative Effects of Family and Peer Group in the Sexual Socialization Process." *Journal of Marriage and the Family* 36 (February 1974): 196–202.

"Day Care: The Boom Begins." *Newsweek* (December 7, 1970): 95.

Dean, D. G. "Romanticism and Emotional Maturity:

A Preliminary Study." *Marriage and Family Living* 23 (February 1961): 44–45.

Dean, G. and Gurak, D. T. "Marital Homogamy the Second Time Around." *Journal of Marriage and the Family* 40 (August 1978): 559–570.

de Beauvior, S. *Old Age.* Great Britain: Cox and Wyman, Ltd., 1972.

DeFrain, J. "Androgynous Parents Tell Who They Are and What They Need." *The Family Coordinator* 28 (April 1979): 237–243.

DeLamater, J. and MacCorquodale, P. "Premarital Contraceptive Use: A Text of Two Models." *Journal of Marriage and the Family* 40 (May 1978): 235–247.

DeLamater, J. D. and MacCorquodale, P. *Premarital Sexuality: Attitudes, Relationships, Behavior.* Madison, Wisconsin: University of Wisconsin Press, 1979.

DeLissovoy, V. "High School Marriages: A Longitudinal Study." *Journal of Marriage and the Family* 35 (May 1973): 245–255.

DeMartino, F. "How Women Want Men to Make Love." *Sexology* (October 1970): 4–7.

Denfeld, D. "Dropouts from Swinging: The Marriage Counselor as Informant." In *Beyond Monogamy.* Edited by J. R. Smith and L. G. Smith. Baltimore: Johns Hopkins, 1974, pp. 260–267.

Denfeld, D., and Gordon, M. "The Sociology of Mate Swapping: Or, The Family That Swings Together Clings Together." *Journal of Sex Research* 6 (1970): 85–100.

Deur, J. L., and Parke, R. D. "The Effects of Inconsistent Punishment on Aggression in Children." *Developmental Psychology* 1 (1970): 403–411.

Deutsch, M., and Krauss, R. M. "The Effect of Threat upon Interpersonal Bargaining." *Journal of Abnormal and Social Psychology* 61 (1960): 181–189.

Deutscher, I. "The Quality of Postparental Life: Definitions of the Situation." *Journal of Marriage and the Family* 26 (February 1964): 52–59.

Dibble, U. and Straus, M. A. "Some Social Structure Determinants of Inconsistency Between Attitudes and Behavior: The Case of Family Violence." *Journal of Marriage and the Family* 42 (February 1980): 71–80.

Dick-Read, G. D. *Childbirth without Fear.* New York: Harper, 1953.

Dill, D. et al. "The Impact of the Environment on the Coping Efforts of Low-Income Mothers." *Family Relations* 29 (October 1980): 503–509.

Dishatsky, N. I., et al. "LSD and Genetic Damage." *Science* 172 (1971): 431–439.

Doe v. Bolton, 410 U.S. 179 (1973).

Doherty, W. J. and Ryder, R. G. "Locus of Control, Interpersonal Trust, and Assertive Behavior among Newlyweds." *Journal of Personality and Social Psychology* 37 (December 1979): 2212–2220.

Douglas, S. P. and Wind, Y. "Examining Family Role and Authority Patterns: Two Methodological Issues." *Journal of Marriage and the Family* 40 (February 1978): 35–47.

Dramatic Rise Reported in Proportion of Unwed Couples Living Together." *Family Planning Perspectives* 12 (May/June 1980): 164.

Dressel, P. L. "Assortive Mating in Later Life." *Journal of Family Issues* 1 (September 1980): 379–396.

Driscoll, R.; Davis, K. E.; and Lipetz, M. E. "Parental Interference and Romantic Love: The Romeo and Juliet Effect." *Journal of Personality and Social Psychology* 24 (1972): 1–10.

Duberman, L. "Step-Kin Relationships." *Journal of Marriage and the Family* 35 (May 1973): 283–292.

Dullea, G. "Salk Divorce Case Different." *Maine Sunday Telegram* (November 9, 1975): 12B.

Duvall, E. M. "Adolescent Love as a Reflection of Teen-agers' Search for Identity." In *Love, Marriage, Family.* Edited by M. E. Lasswell and T. E. Lasswell. Glenview, Illinois: Scott, Foresman, 1973, pp. 92–95.

Duvall, E. M. *Family Development.* 4th ed. Philadelphia: Lippincott, 1971.

Duvall, E. M. *In-laws: Pro and Con.* New York: Association Press, 1954.

Duvall, E. M. "Marriage Makes In-Laws." In *Marriage and the Family in the Modern World: Readings.* Edited by R. S. Cavan. New York: Crowell, 1974, pp. 338–341.

Duvall, E. M., and Hill, R. "How Can You Cope with Conflict Constructively?" In *Encounter: Love, Marriage and Family.* Edited by R. E. Albrecht and E. W. Bock. Boston: Holbrook 1972, pp. 349–355.

Dweck, C. S. and Bush, E. S. "Sex Differences in Learned Helplessness: I. Differential Debilitation with Peer and Adult Evaluators." *Developmental Psychology* 12 (March 1976): 147–156.

Dweck, C. S. et al. "Sex Differences in Learned

Helplessness: II. The Contingencies of Evaluation Feedback in the Classroom and III. An Experimental Analysis." *Developmental Psychology* 14 (May 1978): 268–276.

Eckland, B. K. "Theories of Mate Selection." In *Sourcebook in Marriage and the Family*. Edited by M. B. Sussman. 4th ed. Boston: Houghton Mifflin, 1974, pp. 313–323.

Ecstein, P., et al. "Clinical and Laboratory Findings in a Trial of Norgestrel, a Low-dose Progestogen-only Contraceptive." *British Medical Journal* 3 (July 1972): 195–200.

Edmonds, V. H.; Withers, G.; and Dibattista, B. "Adjustment, Conservatism, and Conventionalism." *Journal of Marriage and the Family* 34 (February 1972): 96–103.

Edward, M. P. "College Students' Perceptions of Experimental Life Styles." Master's Thesis. Stillwater: Oklahoma State University, 1972.

Edward, M., and Stinnett, N. "Perceptions of Styles." *Journal of Psychology* 87 (1974): 143–156.

Edwards, J. N. "Extramarital Involvement: Fact and Theory." *Journal of Sex Research* 9 (August 1973): 210–224.

Edwards, J. N., and Booth, A. "Sexual Behavior in and out of Marriage: An Assessment of Correlates." *Journal of Marriage and the Family* 38 (February 1976): 73–81.

Ehrlich, R. M. "Impotence Associated with Prostatitis." In *Medical Aspects of Human Sexuality*. Edited by H. I. Lief. New York: Williams and Wilkins, 1975.

Einzig, J. E. "The Child Within: A Study of Expectant Fatherhood." *Smith College Studies in Social Work* 50 (March 1980): 117–164.

Elkind, D. *Children and Adolescents: Interpretative Essays on Jean Piaget*. New York: Oxford University Press, 1970.

Ellis, A. "Group Marriage: A Possible Alternative?" In *Beyond Monogamy*. Edited by J. R. Smith and L. G. Smith. Baltimore: Johns Hopkins, 1974, pp. 170–181.

Ellison, C. "Vaginismus." *Medical Aspects of Human Sexuality* (August 1972).

England, J. L., and Kuntz, R. P. "The Application of Age-Specific Rates to Divorce." *Journal of Marriage and the Family* 37 (February 1975): 40–46.

Epstein, G. F. *Woman's Place: Options and Limits in Professional Careers*. Berkeley: University of California Press, 1970.

Epstein, G. F. and Bronzaft, A. I. "Female Freshmen View Their Roles as Women." *Journal of Marriage and the Family* 34 (November 1972): 671–672.

Equal Employment Opportunity Commission. *Equal Employment Opportunity Report, 1971. Job Patterns for Minorities and Women in Private Industry*. Vol. 1. Washington, D.C.: U.S. Government Printing Office, 1971.

Erikson, E. *Identity and the Life Cycle*. New York: International Universities Press, 1959.

Eshleman, J. R. *The Family: An Introduction*. 2d ed. Boston: Allyn and Bacon, 1978.

Eshleman, J. R. "Mental Health and Marital Integration in Young Marriages." *Journal of Marriage and the Family* 27 (May 1965): pp. 255–262.

Estellachild, V. "Hippie Communes." In *Intimate Life Styles: Marriage and Its Alternatives*. Edited by J. S. DeLora and J. R. DeLora. Pacific Palisades, California: Goodyear, 1972, pp. 332–337.

Etzkowitz, H. "The Male Sister: Sexual Separation in Society." *Journal of Marriage and the Family* 33 (August 1971): 431–434.

Evans, R. B. "Parental Relationships and Homosexuality." *Medical Aspects of Human Sexuality* (April 1971): 164–177.

Fairfield, R. *Communes, U.S.A.: A Personal Tour*. Baltimore: Penguin, 1972.

"Family Life." Mimeographed. University Park, New Mexico: New Mexico State University, Cooperative Extension Service, March 1975.

Family Planning/Population Report (June 1973).

Farley, F. H. and Davis, S. A. "Personality and Sexual Satisfaction in Marriage." *Journal of Sex and Marital Therapy* 6 (Spring 1980): 56–62.

Fasteau, M. F. *The Male Machine*. New York: McGraw-Hill, 1974.

Feinmann S. and Gill, G. W. "Sex Differences in Physical Attractiveness Preferences." *The Journal of Social Psychology* 105 (July 1978): 43–52.

Feldman, H., and Feldman, M. "The Family Life Cycle: Some Suggestions for Recycling." *Journal of Marriage and the Family* 37 (May 1975): 277–284.

Feldman, S. D. "Impediment or Stimulant? Marital Status and Graduate Education." In *Changing Women in a Changing Society*. Edited by J. Huber. Chicago: University of Chicago Press, 1973, pp. 220–231.

Fenelon, B. "State Variations in United States Divorce Rates." *Journal of Marriage and the Family* 33 (May 1971): 321–327.

Ferrell, M. Z., Tolone, W. L., and Walsh, R. H. "Maturational and Societal Changes in the Sexual Double-Standard: A Panel Analysis (1967–1971; 1970–1974): *Journal of Marriage and the Family* 39 (May 1977): 255–271.

Ferris, A. *Indicators of Trends in the Status of American Women.* New York: Russell Sage Foundation, 1971.

Feshbach, S. and Malamuth, N. "Sex and Aggression: Proving the Link." *Psychology Today* 12 (November 1978): 111 ff.

Figley, C. R. "Child Density and the Marital Relationship." *Journal of Marriage and the Family* 35 (May 1973): 272–282.

Finch, S., and McDermott, R. *Psychiatry for the Pediatrician.* New York: W. W. Norton, 1970.

Fineberg, B. L., and Lowman, J. "Affect and Status Dimensions of Marital Adjustment." *Journal of Marriage and the Family* 37 (February 1975): 155–160.

Fink, P. J. "Dealing with Sexual Pressures of the Unmarried." *Medical Aspects of Human Sexuality* (March 1970): 42–53.

Firestone, S. *The Dialectic of Sex: The Case for Feminist Revolution.* New York: William Morrow, 1970, pp. 16–45.

Fischer, A. "The Occurrence of the Extended Family at the Origin of the Family of Procreation: A Developmental Approach to Negro Family Structure." *Journal of Marriage and the Family* 30 (May 1968): 290–300.

Fisher, C. C. "Homes for Black Children." *Child Welfare* 1 (1971): 108–111.

Fisher, S. *The Female Orgasm: Psychology, Physiology, Fantasy.* New York: Basic, 1973.

Flake-Hobson, C., Skeen, P. and Robinson, B. E. "Review of Theories and Research Concerning Sex-Role Development and Androgyny with Suggestions for Teachers." *Family Relations* 29 (April 1980): 155–162.

Fleck, S. "Some Psychiatric Aspects of Abortion." *Journal of Nervous and Mental Disease* 151 (July 1970): 42–50.

Fleishman, W., and Dixon, P. L. *Vasectomy, Sex and Parenthood.* Garden City, New York: Doubleday, 1973.

Flora, C. B. "The Passive Female: Her Comparative Image by Class and Culture in Women's Magazine Fiction." *Journal of Marriage and the Family* 33 (August 1971): 435–444.

Flowers, C. E. "Sex Relations after Hysterectomy." In *Medical Aspects of Human Sexuality.* Edited by H. I. Lief. New York: Williams and Wilkins, 1975.

Folkman, J. D., and Clatworthy, N. M. *Marriage Has Many Faces.* Columbus, Ohio: Merrill, 1970.

Ford, R. "Group Sex and Sexually Free Marriages." In *Renovating Marriage.* Edited by R. W. Libby and R. N. Whitehurst. Danville, California: Consensus, 1973, pp. 240–253.

Forrest, J. D. et al. "Abortion in the United States, 1976–1977." *Family Planning Perspectives* 10 (September/October 1978): 271–279.

Foster, H. H. "Divorce Reform: Brakes on Breakdown." *Journal of Family Law* 13 (1973–1974): 443–494.

Foster, H. H., Jr. "Reforming a Divorce Law." *The Humanist* (May/June 1970).

Fox, C. A., et al. "Studies on the Relationship between Plasma Testosterone Levels and Human Sexual Activity." *Journal of Endocrinology* 52 (January 1972): 51–58.

Frankl, V. "The Depersonalization of Sex." *Synthesis* 1 (1979): 9–13.

Freed, D. J. "Economic Effect of Divorce." *Family Law Quarterly* 7 (1973): 275–344.

Freed, D. J., and Foster, H. H., Jr. "Divorce American Style." In *Encounter: Love, Marriage, and Family.* Edited by R. E. Albrecht and E. Wilbur Bock. Boston: Holbrook, 1972, pp. 180–205.

Freedman, M. *Homosexuality and Psychological Functioning.* Belmont, California: Brooks/Cole, 1971.

Freeman, J. "The Origin of the Women's Liberation Movement." In *Changing Women in a Changing Society.* Edited by J. Huber. Chicago: University of Chicago Press, 1973, pp. 30–49.

Freeman, J. "The Women's Liberation Movement: Its Origins, Structures, and Ideas." In *Family, Marriage, and the Struggle of the Sexes.* Edited by H. P. Dreitzel, pp. 201–216. New York: Macmillan, 1972.

Freud, S. A. *A General Introduction to Psychoanalysis.* Translated by Joan Riviere. New York: Permabooks, 1953a.

Freud, S. "Three Essays on the Theory of Sexuality." *Standard Edition.* Vol. 7. London: Hogarth, 1953b.

Friedan, B. *The Feminine Mystique.* New York: Dell, 1963.

Fromm, E. *The Art of Loving.* New York: Harper, 1956.

Fromme, A. "Toward a Better Sexual Orientation." In *Sociological Perspectives in Marriage and the Family*. Edited by M. W. Weil. Danville, Illinois: Interstate, 1972, pp. 312–317.

Fullerton, G. P. *Survival in Marriage*. New York: Holt, Rinehart and Winston, 1972.

Furth, H. G. *Piaget for Teachers*. Englewood Cliffs, New Jersey: Prentice-Hall, 1970.

Gadpaille, W. J. "Father's Role in Sex Education of His Son." *Sexual Behavior* (April 1971): 3–10.

Galdston, R. "Preventing the Abuse of Little Children: The Parents' Center Project for the Study and Prevention of Child Abuse." *American Journal of Orthopsychiatry* 45 (1975): 372–381.

Gallup, G. H. *The Gallup Poll. Public Opinion 1978*. Wilmington, Delaware: Scholarly Resources, Inc., 1979.

Gannon, M. J., and Hendrickson, D. H. "Career Orientations and Job Satisfaction among Working Wives." *Journal of Applied Psychology* 57 (1973): 339–340.

Garcia, C. "Clinical Aspects of Oral Hormonal Contraception." In *Manual of Family Planning and Contraceptive Practice*. Edited by M. S. Calderone. 2d ed. Baltimore: Williams and Wilkins, 1970, pp. 283–330.

Gardner, J. "Cold Mountain Farm." In *Marriage Means Encounter*. Edited by G. Roleder. Dubuque, Iowa: Wm. C. Brown, 1973, pp. 181–190.

Gebhard, P. H. "Factors in Marital Orgasm." *Journal of Social Issues* 22, no. 2 (1966): 88–95.

Gecas, V., and Nye, F. I. "Sex and Class Differences in Parent-Child Interaction: A Test of Kohn's Hypothesis." *Journal of Marriage and the Family* 36 (November 1974): 742–749.

Geismar, L. L. *555 Families: A Social-Psychological Study of Young Families in Transition*. New Brunswick, New Jersey: Transaction Books, 1973.

Gelles, R. J. "Violence in the Family: A Review of Research in the Seventies." *Journal of Marriage and the Family* 42 (November 1980): 873–885.

Gendzel, I. B. "Dependence, Independence, Interdependence." In *Choice and Challenge*. Edited by C. E. Williams and J. F. Crosby. Dubuque, Iowa: Wm. C. Brown, 1974, pp. 97–103.

George, V., and Welding, P. *Motherless Families*. London: Routledge and Kegan Paul, 1972.

Gerber, I., et al. "Anticipatory Grief and Aged Widows and Widowers." *Journal of Gerontology* 30 (1975): 225–229.

Gerstel, N. R. "Marital Alternatives and the Regulation of Sex: Commuter Couples as a Test Case." *Alternative Lifestyles* 2 (May 1979): 145–176.

Gibbs, J. R. "Notes on TORI Theory." La Jolla, California. Unpublished manuscript, 1971.

Gibson, G. "Kin Family Network: Overheralded Structure in Past Conceptualizations of Family Functioning." *Journal of Marriage and the Family* 34 (February 1972): 13–23.

Gillespie, D. L. "Who Has the Power? The Marital Struggle." *Journal of Marriage and the Family* 33 (August 1971): 445–458.

Gilliland, N. C. "The Problem of Geographic Mobility for Dual Career Families." *Journal of Comparative Family Studies* 10 (Autumn 1979): 345–358.

Gilmartin, B. G., and Kusisto, D. V. "Some Personal and Social Characteristics of Mate-Sharing Swingers." In *Renovating Marriage*. Edited by R. W. Libby and R. N. Whitehurst. Danville, California: Consensus, 1973, pp. 146–165.

Ginsberg, G. L.; Frosch, W. A.; and Shapiro, T. "The New Impotence." *Archives of General Psychiatry* 26 (March 1972): 218–220.

Glass, S. P. and Wright, T. L. "The Relationship of Extramarital Sex, Length of Marriage, and Sex Differences on Marital Satisfaction and Romanticism: Athanasiou's Data Reanalyzed." *Journal of Marriage and the Family* 39 (November 1972): 691–704.

Glasser, P., and Navarre, E. "Structural Problems of the One-Parent Family." In *Marriage and Family in the Modern World: Readings*. Edited by R. S. Cavan. New York: Crowell, 1974, pp. 342–351.

Glen, M. L. "Intimacy and Oppression." In *Marriage and Family in a Decade of Change*. Edited by G. B. Carr, Reading, Massachusetts: Addison-Wesley, 1972, pp. 109–111.

Glenn, N. D. "Psychological Well-Being in the Postparental Stage: Some Evidence from National Surveys." *Journal of Marriage and the Family* 37 (February 1975): 105–110.

Glenn, N. D. and Weaver, C. N. "A Multivariate, Mutlisurvey Study of Marital Happiness." *Journal of Marriage and the Family* 40 (May 1978): 269–282.

Glenn, N. D. and Weaver, C. N. "A Note on Family Situation and Global Happiness." *Social Forces* 57 (March 1979): 960–967.

Glick, I. O.; Weiss, R. S.; and Parkes, C. M. *The First*

Year of Bereavement. New York: John Wiley, 1974.

Glick, P. C. "A Demographer Looks at American Families." *Journal of Marriage and the Family* 37 (February 1975): 15–26.

Glick, P. C. "The Future of the American Family." *Current Population Reports.* Special Studies, Series P-23, no. 78. Washington, D.C.: U.S. Department of Commerce, Bureau of the Census, January 1979.

Glick, P. C. "Updating the Life Cycle of the Family." *Journal of Marriage and the Family* 39 (February 1977): 5–13.

Glick, P. C., and Norton, A. J. "Frequency, Duration, and Probability of Marriage and Divorce." *Journal of Marriage and the Family* 33 (May 1971): 307–317.

Glick, P. C., and Norton A. J. "Marrying, Divorcing, and Living Together in the U.S. Today." *Population Bulletin* 32 no. 5. Washington, D.C.: Population Reference Bureau, 1977. Reprinted, courtesy of the Population Reference Bureau., Washington, D.C.

Glick, P. C. and Spanier, G. B. "Married and Unmarried Cohabitation in the United States." *Journal of Marriage and the Family* 42(February 1980): 19–30.

Goddard, H. L. and Leviton, D. "Intimacy-Sexuality Needs of the Bereaved: An Exploratory Study." *Death Education* 34 (Winter 1980): 347–358.

Goffman, E. "Genderisms." *Psychology Today* 11 (August 1977): 60–63.

Gold, D. and Berger, C. "Problem-Solving Performance of Young Boys and Girls as a Function or Task Appropriateness and Sex Identity." *Sex Roles* 4 (April 1978): 183–193.

Goldman, D. R. "Managerial Mobility, Motivations, and Central Life Interests. *American Sociological Review* (February 1973): 119–126.

Goleman, D. "Special Abilities of the Sexes: Do They Begin in the Brain?" *Psychology Today* 12 (November 1978): 48ff.

Good, H. G. *A History of Western Education.* New York: Macmillan, 1947.

Goode, W. J. *Women in Divorce.* New York: Free Press, 1965.

Goode, W. J. *The Contemporary American Family.* Chicago: Quadrangle, 1971, pp. 221–235.

Goodenough, F. L. *Anger in Young Children.* Minneapolis: University of Minnesota Press, 1931.

Goodman, L. S., and Gilman, A., eds. *The Pharmacological Basis of Therapeutics.* London: Macmillan, 1970.

Goodrich, W.; Ryder, R. G.; and Raush, H. L. "Patterns of Newlywed Marriage." *Journal of Marriage and the Family* 30 (August 1968): 383–389.

Gordon, M., ed. *The Nuclear Family in Crisis: The Search for an Alternative.* New York: Harper, 1972.

Gordon, M., and Skankweiler, P. J. "Different Equals Less: Female Sexuality in Recent Marriage Manuals." *Journal of Marriage and the Family* 33 (August 1971): 459–466.

Gottman, J., Markman, H. and Notarius, C. "The Topography of Marital Conflict: A Sequential Analysis of Verbal and Nonverbal Behavior." *Journal of Marriage and the Family* 39 (August 1977): 461–477.

Gough, A. R. "Divorce without Squalor: California Shows How." *The Nation* (January 12, 1970).

Gough, K. "The Origin of the Family." *Journal of Marriage and the Family* 33 (November 1971): 760–771.

Gould, R. "Measuring Masculinity by the Size of a Paycheck." In *The Forty-nine Percent Majority: The Male Sex Role.* Edited by D. S. David and R. Brannon. Reading, Massachusetts: Addison-Wesley Publishing Co., 1976, pp. 113–118.

Graham, P. A. "Women in Academe." *Science* 169 (September 25, 1970): 1289.

Granbois, D. H., and Willett, R. P. "Equivalence of Family Role Measures Based on Husband and Wife Data." *Journal of Marriage and the Family* 32 (February 1970): 68–72.

Greeley, A. M. "Religious Intermarriage in a Denominational Society." *American Journal of Sociology* 75 (May 1970): 949.

Greenblatt, R. B. "Steroid Replacement and Libido." In *Medical Aspects of Human Sexuality.* Edited by H. I. Lief. New York: Williams and Wilkins, 1975.

Greene, B. *A Clinical Approach to Marital Problems: Evaluation and Management.* Springfield, Illinois: Charles C. Thomas, 1970.

Greene, R. *Human Hormones.* Weidenfeld and Nicolson, 1970.

Greenwalk, H. "Marriage as a Non-Legal Voluntary Association." In *The Family in Search of a Future.* Edited by H. A. Otto. New York: Appleton-Century-Crofts, 1970, pp. 51–56.

Greer, G. *The Female Eunuch.* New York: McGraw-Hill, 1971.

Greiff, B. "Occupational Setback and Impotence." In *Medical Aspects of Human Sexuality.* Edited by H. I. Lief. New York: Williams and Wilkins, 1975.

Gross, H. W. "Dual-Career Couples Who Live Apart: Two Types." *Journal of Marriage and the Family* 42 (August 1980): 567–576.

Gunderson, M. P. and McCary, J. L. "Effects of Sex Education on Sex Information and Sexual Guilt, Attitudes, And Behaviors." *Family Relations* 29 (July 1980): 375–379.

Gunderson, M. P. and McCary, J. L. "Sexual Guilt and Religion." *The Family Coordinator* 28 (July 1979): 353–357.

Guttmacher, A. *Birth Control and Love.* New York: Bantam, 1969.

Guttmacher, A. F. *Pregnancy, Birth and Family Planning.* New York: Signet, 1973.

Hall, D. T., and Gordon, F. E. "Career Choices of Married Women: Effects on Conflict, Role Behavior, and Satisfaction." *Journal of Applied Psychology* 58 (1973): 42–48.

Hall, J. R. and Black, J. D. "Assertiveness, Aggressiveness, and Attitudes toward Feminism." *The Journal of Social Psychology* 107 (February 1979): 57–62.

Hamilton, E. "Emotions and Sexuality in the Woman." In *The New Sexuality.* Edited by H. A. Otto. Palo Alto, California: Science and Behavior, 1971.

Hampe, G. D., and Ruppel, H. J., Jr. "The Measurement of Premarital Sexual Permissiveness: A Comparison of Two Guttman Scales. *Journal of Marriage and the Family* 36 (August 1974): 451–463.

Handel, G. "Sociological Aspects of Parenthood." In *Parenthood: Its Psychology and Psychopathology.* Edited by J. E. Anthony and T. Benedek. Boston: Little, Brown, 1970, pp. 87–105.

Haney, C. A., et al. "Some Consequences of Illegitimacy in a Sample of Black Women." *Journal of Marriage and the Family* 37 (May 1975): 359–366.

Hansson, R. O., Jones, W. H., and Chernovetz, M. E. "Contraceptive Knowledge: Antecedents and Implications." *The Family Coordinator* 28 (January 1979): 29–34.

Hardy, J. B. "Rubella and Its Aftermath." *Children* 16 (May–June 1969): 91–96.

Harkins, E. B. "Effects of Empty Nest Transition on Self-Report of Psychological and Physical Well-Being." *Journal of Marriage and the Family* 40 (August 1978): 549–556.

Harlow, H. F., and Suomi, S. J. "Nature of Love—Simplified." *American Psychologist* 25 (1970): 161–168.

Harris, A. S. "The Second Sex in Academe." *AAUP Bulletin* 56 (September 1970): 294.

Harris, T. A. *I'm OK—You're OK.* New York: Harper, 1972.

Harry, J. "The Marital Liaisons of Gay Men." *The Family Coordinator* 28 (October 1979): 622–629.

Harting, D., and Hunter, H. J. "Abortion Techniques and Services: A Review and Critique." *American Journal of Public Health* 61 (October 1971): 2085–2105.

Hartman, W. E., and Fithian, M. A. *The Treatment of Sexual Dysfunctions.* Long Beach, California: Center for Marital and Sexual Studies, 1972.

Haskins, L. "Oviduct Sterilization with Tantalum Clips." *American Journal of Obstetrics and Gynecology* 114 (October 1972): 370–377.

Hassett, J. "A New Look at Living Together." *Psychology Today* (December 1977): 82–83.

Hastings, D. W. *Impotence and Frigidity.* Boston: Little, Brown, 1963.

Haughey, J. C. "The Commune—Child of the 1970's." In *Intimate Life Styles: Marriage and Its Alternatives.* Edited by J. S. DeLora and J. R. DeLora. Pacific Palisades, California: Goodyear, 1972, pp. 328–332.

Hawkins, J. L., Weisberg, C., and Ray, D. W. "Marital Communication Style and Social Class." *Journal of Marriage and the Family* 39 (August 1977): 479–490.

Hawkins, J. L., Weisberg, C., and Ray, D. W. "Spouse Differences in Communication Style: Preference, Perception, Behavior." *Journal of Marriage and The Family* 42 (August 1980): 585–593.

Hays, W. C., and Mindel, C. H. "Extended Kinship Relations in Black and White Families." *Journal of Marriage and the Family* 35 (February 1973): 51–56.

Heckman, J. "Cambridge Commune: The Cat Is Everyone's." In *Communes: Creating and Managing the Collective Life.* Edited by R. M. Kanter, New York: Harper, 1973, pp. 76–79.

Heckman, J. J. "Effects of Child Care Programs on Women's Work Effort." *Journal of Political Economy* 82 (1974): S136–S163.

Heckman, N. A., Bryson, R., and Bryson, J. B. "Problems of Professional Couples: A Content Analysis." *Journal of Marriage and the Family* 29 (May 1977): 323–330.

Hedgepath, W. "Maybe It'll Be Different Here." In *Intimate Life Styles: Marriage and Its Alternatives.* Edited by J. S. DeLora and J. R. DeLora. Pacific Palisades, California: Goodyear, 1972, pp. 321–327.

Hedges, J. N., and Barnett, J. K. "Working Women and the Division of Household Tasks." *Monthly Labor Review* 95 (April 1972): 9–14.

Heer, D. M. "The Prevalence of Black-White Marriage in the United States, 1960 and 1970." *Journal of Marriage and the Family* 36 (May 1974): 246–258.

Heise, D. R. *Personality and Socialization.* Chicago: Rand McNally, 1972.

Hennig, M. "Career Development for Women Executives." Unpublished Doctor of Business Administration dissertation. Cambridge, Massachusetts: Harvard University, 1970.

Henton, J. "Problem Solving through Conflict in Marriage." Unpublished Ph.D. thesis. University of Minnesota, 1970.

Henze, L. F., and Hudson, J. W. "Personal and Family Characteristics of Cohabiting and Noncohabiting College Students." *Journal of Marriage and the Family* 36 (November 1974): 722–727.

Hepker, W., and Cloyd, J. S. "Role Relationships and Role Performance: The Male Married Student." *Journal of Marriage and the Family* 36 (November 1974): 688–696.

Herbert, A. "The Problem and Strategies for the Adoption of the Minority Group Child." Paper presented at the NAACP Conference on the Black Child, Atlanta, September 7, 1973.

Hern, W. M. "Is Pregnancy Really Normal?" *Family Planning Perspectives* 3 (1971).

Herold, E. S., and Foster, M. E. "Changing Sexual References in Mass Circulation Magazines." *The Family Coordinator* 24 (January 1975): 21–25.

Herold, E. S., Goodwin, M. S., and Lero, D. S. "Self-Esteem, Locus of Control, and Adolescent Contraception." *The Journal of Psychology* 101 (January 1979:) 83–88.

Herrigan, J., and Herrigan, J. *Loving Free.* New York: Grosset and Dunlap, 1973.

Herzog, E., et al. *Families for Black Children: The Search for Adoptive Parents.* Washington, D.C.: U.S. Office of Health, Education and Welfare, Office of Child Development, Children's Bureau, 1971.

Herzog, E., and Sudia, C. E. Office of Child Development, Children's Bureau. *Boys in Fatherless Families.* Washington, D.C.: U.S. Government Printing Office, 1971.

Hess, B. B. and Waring, J. M. "Changing Patterns of Aging and Family Bonds in Later Life." *The Family Coordinator* 27 (October 1978): 303–314.

Hetherington, E. M. "Girls without Fathers." *Psychology Today* (February 1973): 47–52.

Heymann, D. K., and Gyianturco, D. T. "Longterm Adaptaton by the Elderly to Beréavement." *Journal of Gerontology* 28 (1973): 359–362.

Hicks, M. W. "An Empirical Evaluation of Textbook Assumptions about Engagements." *The Family Coordinator* 19 (January 1970): 57–63.

Hicks, M. W., and Platt, M. "Marital Happiness and Stability: A Review of the Research in the Sixties." *Journal of Marriage and the Family* 32 (November 1970): 553–574.

Hill, R. "Hill's Response to Bytheway." *Journal of Marriage and the Family* 39 (May 1977): 251–252.

Hill, R., et al. "Family Development in Three Generations." Cambridge, Massachusetts: Schenkman, 1970.

Hiller, D. V. and Philliber, W. W. "The Derivation of Status Benefits from Occupational Attainments of Working Wives." *Journal of Marriage and the Family* 40 (February 1978): 63–69.

Hills, S. L. "Homosexuality in a Changing Society." In *Demystifying Social Deviance*, by S. L. Hills. New York: McGraw-Hill, 1980, pp. 165–195.

Hiltz, S. R. "Widowhood: A Roleless Role." *Marriage and the Family Review* 1 (November/December 1978): 1–10.

Hitchens, D. "Social Attitudes, Legal Standards and Personal Trauma in Child Custody Cases." *Journal of Homosexuality* 5 (Fall/Winter 1979/80): 89–95.

Hite, S. *The Hite Report: A Nationwide Study on Female Sexuality.* New York: Dell Pub. Co., Inc., 1977.

Hobbs, D. F. and Wimbish, J. M. "Transition to Parenthood by Black Couples." *Journal of Marriage and the Family* 39 (November 1977): 677–689.

Hochschild, A. R. "A Review of Sex Role Research." *American Journal of Sociology* 78 (January 1973a): 1011–1029.

Hochschild, A. R. *The Unexpected Community*. Englewood Cliffs, New Jersey: Prentice-Hall, 1973b.

Hogan, D. P. "The Effects of Demographic Factors, Family Background, and Early Job Achievement on Age at Marriage." *Demography* 15 (May 1978): 161–175.

Hokanson, J. E. "Psychophysiological Evaluation of the Catharsis Hypothesis." in *The Dynamics of Aggression*. Edited by E. I. Megargee and J. A. Hokanson. New York: Harper, 1970.

Hole, J., and Levin, E. *Rebirth of Feminism*. New York: Quardrangle, 1971.

Hollender, M. H. "Women's Wish to Be Held: Sexual and Nonsexual Aspects." *Medical Aspects of Human Sexuality* (October 1971): 12–26.

Hollingshead, A. B. *Elmtown's Youth*. New York: John Wiley, 1949.

Holmstrom, L. L. *The Two-Career Family*. Cambridge, Massachusetts: Schenkman, 1973.

"Homosexual Women Have a Hormonal Difference." *Psychology Today* 11 (February 1978): 106.

Honig, M. "AFDC Income. Recipient Rates, and Family Dissolution." *The Journal of Human Resources* 9 (1974): 303–322.

Hooper, J. O. "My Wife, the Student." *The Family Coordinator* 28 (October 1979): 459–464.

Hornick, J. P. "Premarital Sexual Attitudes and Behavior." *The Sociological Quarterly* 19 (Autumn 1978): 534–544.

Hornick, J. P., Doran, L., and Crawford, S. H. "Premarital Contraceptive Usage among Male and Female Adolescents." *The Family Coordinator* 28 (April 1979): 181–190.

Houriet, R. *Getting Back Together*. New York: Coward-McCann and Geoghehan, 1971.

"How Much Does He Do around the House?" *Changing Times*, 25 (April 1971): 41.

Howard, M. "Comprehensive Community Program for the Pregnant Teenager." *Clinical Obstetrics and Gynecology* 14 (1971): 473–488.

Howe, V. "Sexual Sterotypes Start Early." *Saturday Review*, October 16, 1971.

Huang, L. J. "Research with Unmarried Cohabiting Couples: Including Non-Exclusive Sexual Relations." Unpublished manuscript. Illinois State University, 1975.

Hudson, J. W., and Henze, L. F. "A Note on Cohabitation." *The Family Coordinator* 22 (October 1973): 495.

Humphrey, F. G. "Study Says Adultery Is Serious Problem." *Portland Press Herald*, April 11, 1977.

Humphreys, L. *Out of the Closets: The Sociology of Homosexual Liberation*. Englewood Cliffs, New Jersey: Prentice-Hall, 1972.

Humphreys, L. *Tearoom Trade; Impersonal Sex in Public Places*. Chicago: Aldine, 1970.

Hungerford, M. J. *Childbirth Education*. Springfield, Illinois: Charles C Thomas, 1972.

Hunt, M. "The Future of Marriage." In *Choice and Challenge*. Edited by C. E. Williams and J. F. Crosby. Dubuque, Iowa: Wm. C. Brown, 1974, pp. 5–22.

Hunt, M. M. "Help Wanted: Divorce Counselor." In *The Contemporary American Family*. Edited by W. J. Goode. A New York Times Book. Chicago: Quadrangle, 1971, pp. 226–235.

Hunt, M. M. "Sexual Behavior in the 1970's." *Playboy* (October 1973): 204.

Husbands, C. T. "Some Social and Psychological Consequences of the American Dating System." *Adolescence* 5 (Winter 1970): 451–462.

Huser, W. R. and Grant, C. W. "A Study of Husbands and Wives from Dual-Career and Traditional-Career Families." *Psychology of Women Quarterly* 3 (Fall 1978): 78–79.

Hutt, C. *Males and Females*. Baltimore, Maryland: Penguin Education, 1972.

Inazu, J. K. and Fox, G. L. "Maternal Influence on the Sexual Behavior of Teen-Age Daughters." *Journal of Family Issues* 1 (March 1980): 81–102.

Inman, W. H. W., et al. "Thromboembolic Disease and the Steroidal Content of Oral Contraceptives: A Report to the Committee on the Safety of Drugs." *British Medical Journal* 2 (April 25, 1970): 203–209.

Jackson, D. D. "Family Roles: Marital Quid Pro Quo." In *Family Therapy: An Introduction to Theory and Technique*. Edited by G. D. Erickson and T. P. Hagan. Monterey, California: Brooks/Cole, 1972, pp. 76–85.

Jackson, J. J. "Marital Life Among Aging Blacks." *The Family Coordinator* 21 (1972): 21–27.

Jackson, R., and Jackson, J. *Living Together: A Guide for Unmarried Couples*. Unpublished manuscript. 1973.

Jaco, D. E., and Shepard, J. M. "Demographic Homogeneity and Spousal Consensus: A Methodological Perspective." *Journal of Marriage and the Family* 37 (February 1975): 161–169.

Jacobs, L.; Walster, E.; and Berscheld, E. "Self-esteem and Attraction." *Journal of Personality and Social Psychology* 17 (1971): 84–91.

Jacobson, C. B., and Stubbs, M. V. L. "Clinical and Reproductive Dangers Inherent in Use of Hallucinogenic Agents." *Proceedings of the American Association of Clinical Scientists,* Washington, D.C., 1968.

Jacobson, G., and Ryder, R. G. "Parental Loss and Some Characteristics of the Early Marriage Relationships." *American Journal of Orthopsychiatry* 39 (1969): 779–787.

Jacoby, A. P. "Transition to Parenthood: A Reassessment." *Journal of Marriage and the Family* 31 (November 1969): 720–727.

Jacques, J. M. and Chason, K. J. "Cohabitation: A Test of Reference Group Theory among Black and White College Students." *Journal of Comparative Family Studies* 9 (Summer 1978): 147–165.

Jacques, J. M. and Chason, K. J. "Cohabitation: Its Impact on Marital Success." *The Family Coordinator* 28 (January 1979): 35–39.

Jaffee, B., and Fanshel, D. *How They Fared in Adoption: A Follow-up Study.* New York: Columbia University Press, 1970.

Jakobovits, T. "The Treatment of Impotence with Methyltestosterone Thyroid." *Fertility and Sterility* 21 (January 1970): 32–35.

Jedlicka, D. "Sequential Analysis of Perceived Commitment of Partners in Premarital Coitus." *Journal of Marriage and the Family* 37 (May 1975): 385–390.

Jerome, J. *Families of Eden: Communes and the New Anarchism.* New York: Seabury, 1974.

Jensen, M. S. "Role Differentiation in Female Homosexual Quasi-marital Unions." *Journal of Marriage and the Family* 36 (May 1974): 360–367.

Jessor, S. L. and Jessor, R. "Transition from Virginity to Nonvirginity among Youth: A Social-Psychological Study Over Time." *Developmental Psychology* 11 (July 1975): 473–484.

Joffee, C. "Sex Role Socialization and the Nursery School: As the Twig is Bent." *Journal of Marriage and the Family* 33 (August 1971): 467–475.

Johnson, M. P. "Commitment: A Conceptual Structure and Empirical Application." *The Sociological Quarterly* 14 (Summer 1973): 395–406.

Johnson, R. E. Personal communication to L. G. Smith and J. R. Smith, January 5, 1971.

Johnson, R. E. "Some Correlates of Extramarital Coitus." *Journal of Marriage and the Family* 32 (August 1970): 449–456.

Jones, J. G. "Career Patterns of Women Physicians." Unpublished Ph.D. dissertation. Waltham, Massachusetts,: Brandeis University, 1971.

Jones, K. L.; Shainberg, L. W.; and Byer, C. O. *Marriage and Reproduction.* San Francisco: Canfield, 1970.

Jones, W. M. and Jones, R. A. *"Two Careers—One Marriage."* New York: AMACOM, 1980.

Jorgensen, S. R. "Social Class Heterogamy, Status Striving, and Perceptions of Marital Conflict: A Partial Replication and Revision of Pearlin's Contingency Hypothesis." *Journal of Marriage and the Family* 39 (November 1977): 653–661.

Jorgensen, S. R. "Socioeconomic Rewards and Perceived Marital Quality: A Re-examination." *Journal of Marriage and the Family* 41 (November 1979): 825–835.

Joregensen, S. R. and Gaudy, J. C. "Self-Disclosure and Satisfaction in Marriage: The Relation Examined." *Family Relations* 29 (July 1980): 281–287.

Jorgensen, S. R., King, S. L., and Torrey, B. A. "Dyadic and Social Network Influences on Adolescent Exposure to Pregnancy Risk." *Journal of Marriage and the Family* 42 (February 1980): 141–155.

Josephson, E. "The Matriarchy: Myth and Reality." *The Family Coordinator* 18 (1969): 268–276.

Jourard, S. M. *The Transparent Self: Self-Disclosure and Well-Being.* Rev. ed. Princeton, New Jersey: D. Van Nostrand, 1971.

Juhasz, A. M. "A Chain of Sexual Decision-Making." *The Family Coordinator* 24 (January 1975): 43–49.

Kaats, G. R., and Davis, K. E. "The Dynamics of Sexual Behavior of College Students." *Journal of Marriage and the Family* 32 (August 1970): 390–399.

Kacerguis, M. A. and Adams, G. R. "Implications of Sex Typed Child Rearing Practices, Toys, and Mass Media Materials in Restricting Occupational Choices of Women." *The Family Coordinator* 28 (July 1979): 269–375.

Kadushin, A. *Adopting Older Children.* New York: Columbia University Press, 1970.

Kahn, L.; Rocklin, N.; and Berman, A. L. "Cohabitation: Marriage without License?" Unpublished manuscript. Washington, D.C.: American University, 1972.

Kahn, M. "Non-Verbal Communication and Marital Satisfaction." *Family Process* 9 (1970): 449–456.

Kandel, D. B., and Lesser, G. S. "Marital Decision Making in American and Danish Urban Families: A Research Note." *Journal of Marriage and the Family* 34 (February 1972): 134–138.

Kanin, E.; Davidson, K.; and Scheck, S. "A Research Note on Male-Female Differentials in the Experience of Heterosexual Love." *The Journal of Sex Research* (February 1970): 64–72.

Kanter, R. M. *Commitment and Community: Communes and Utopias in Sociological Perspective.* Cambridge, Massachusetts: Harvard University Press, 1972.

Kanter, R. M.; Jaffe, D.; and Weisberg, D. K. "Coupling, Parenting, and the Presence of Others: Intimate Relationships in Communal Households." *The Family Coordinator* 24 (October 1975): 433–452.

Kaplan, H. S. *The New Sex Therapy.* London: Baillure Tindall, 1974.

Kaplan, H.S., and Sager, C. J. "Sexual Patterns at Different Ages." *Medical Aspects of Human Sexuality* (June 1971): 10–23.

Kargman, M. W. "The Revolution in Divorce Law." *The Family Coordinator* 22 (April 1973): 245–248.

Karp, E. S.; Jackson, J. H.; and Lester, D. "Idea-Self Fulfillment in Mate Selection: A corollary to the Complementary Need Theory of Mate Selection." *Journal of Marriage and the Family* 32 (May 1970): 269–272.

Katz, B. J. "Cooling Motherhood." *National Observer* (December 20, 1972).

Kay, A. W. *Moral Development.* New York: Schocken Books, 1969.

Kay, H. H. "A Family Court: the California Proposal." In *Divorce and After.* Edited by P. Bohannan. Garden City, New York.: Doubleday, 1970, pp. 243–281.

Kay, H. and Amyk, C. "Marvin v. Marvin: Preserving the Options." *California Law Review* 65 (1977): 937–977.

Keefe, S. E., Padilla, A. M. and Carlos, M. L. "The Mexican-American Extended Family as an Emotional Support System." *Human Organization* 38 (Summer 1979): 144–152.

Keely, R. K. *Courtship, Marriage, and the Family.* 2d ed. New York: Harcourt Brace Jovanovich, 1974.

Keidel, K. C. "Maternal Employment and Ninth Grade Achievement in Bismarck, North Dakota." *The Family Coordinator* 19 (January 1970): 95–97.

Keith, P. M. and Schafer, R. B. "Role Strain and Depression in Two-Job Families." *Family Relations* 29 (October 1980): 483–488.

Kelley, H. H. et al. "Sex Differences in Comments Made During Conflict Within Close Heterosexual Pairs." *Sex Roles* 4 (August 1978): 473–492.

Kelley, J. "Sexual Permissiveness: Evidence for a Theory." *Journal of Marriage and the Family* 40 (August 1978): 455–468.

Kelley W. J. *A Cost-Effectiveness Study of Clinical Methods of Birth Control: With Special Reference to Puerto Rico.* New York: Praeger, 1972.

Kennedy, E. C. *The New Sexuality: Myths, Fables, and Hang-Ups.* Garden City, New York: Doubleday. 1972.

Kennedy, W. A. *Child Psychology.* Englewood Cliffs, New Jersey: Prentice-Hall, 1971.

Kent, D. P., and Matson, M. B. "The Impact of Health on the Aged Family." *The Family Coordinator* 21 (January 1971): 29–36.

Kent, D. P., and Matson, M. B. "The 'Dysfunctional' Theory of Romantic Love: A Research Report." *Journal of Comparative Family Studies* (Autumn 1970).

Kephart, W. M. *The Family, Society, and the Individual.* 3d ed. Boston: Houghton Mifflin, 1972.

Kephart, W. M. "Some Correlates of Romantic Love." In *Love, Marriage, Family.* Edited by M. E. Lasswell and T. E. Lasswell. Glenview, Illinois: Scott, Foresman, 1973, pp. 177–181.

Kerchkoff, A. C. "Status-related Value Patterns among Married Couples." *Journal of Marriage and the Family* 34 (February 1972): 105–110.

Kerchkoff, A. C. and Parrow, A. A. "The Effect of Early Marriage on the Educational Attainment of Young Men." *Journal of Marriage and the Family* 41 (February 1979): 97–107.

Kieffer, C. "Consensual Cohabitation: A Descriptive Study of the Relationships and Sociocultural Characteristics of Eighty Couples in Two Florida Universities." Master's Thesis. Florida State University, School of Home Economics, August 1972.

Kieren, D.; Henton, J.; and Marotz, R. *Hers and His: A Problem Solving Approach to Marriage.* Hinsdale, Illinois: Dryden, 1975.

Kilpatrick, A. C. "Future Directions for the Black

Family." *The Family Coordinator* 28 (July 1979): 347–352.

Kimball, C. P. "Some Observations Regarding Unwanted Pregnancies and Therapeutic Abortions." *Obstetrics and Gynecology* 35 (1970): 293–296.

King, K., Balswick, J. O., and Robinson, I. E. "The Continuing Premarital Sexual Revolution among College Females." *Journal of Marriage and the Family* 39 (August 1977): 455–459.

Kinkade, K. *A Walden Two Experiment: The First Five Years of Twin Oaks Community.* New York: William Morrow, 1973.

Kinsey, A. C., et al. *Sexual Behavior in the Human Female.* Philadelphia: W. B. Saunders, 1953.

Kinsey, A. C., et al. *Sexual Behavior in the Human Male.* Philadelphia: W. B. Saunders, 1948.

Kirschner, B. F. and Walum, L. R. "Two-Location Families: Married Singles." *Alternative Lifestyles* 1 (November 1978): 513–525.

Kistner, R. W. *The Pill: Facts and Fallacies about Today's Oral Contraceptives.* New York: Delacourte, 1969.

Kitzinger, S. *The Experience of Childbirth.* London: Victor Gollancz, 1964.

Kivett, V. R. "Loneliness and the Rural Widow." *The Family Coordinator* 27 (October 1978): 389–394.

Klapper, Z. S. "The Impact of the Women's Libertaion Movement on Child Development Books." In *The Women's Movement.* Edited by W. Wortis and C. Rabinowitz. New York: John Wiley, 1972, pp. 21–31.

Klemer, R. H. *Marriage and Family Relationships.* New York: Harper, 1970.

Klemer, R. H. "Self-esteem and the College Dating Experience as Factors in Mate Selection and Marital Happiness: A Longitudinal Study." *Journal of Marriage and the Family* 33 (February 1971): 183–187.

Klimek, D. *Beneath Mate Selection and Marriage: The Unconscious Motives in Human Pairing.* New York: Van Nostrand Reinhold, 1979.

Knox, D. H., Jr. "Conceptions of Love at Three Developmental Levels." *The Family Coordinator* 19 (April 1970): 151–157.

Knox, D. Marriage: *Who? When? Why?* Englewood Cliffs, New Jersey: Prentice-Hall, 1975.

Kogan B. A. *Human Sexual Expression.* New York: Harcourt Brace Jovanovich, 1973, p. 115.

Kohl, R. N., and Kaplan, H. S., eds. *Cornell Symposium I—The Sexual Disorders: Current Concepts and Therapies.* New York: Brunner/Mazel, 1974.

Kohlberg, L. "A Cognitive-Developmental Analysis of Children's Sex Role Concepts and Attitudes." In *The Development of Sex Differences.* Edited by E. Maccoby. Palo Alto, California: Standord University Press, 1966, pp. 82–98.

Koller, M. *Families.* New York: McGraw-Hill, 1974a.

Koller, M. R. "WUMP Families." In *Families: A Multigenerational Approach.* New York: McGraw-Hill, 1974b, pp. 149–168.

Kolodny, R. C. "Androgens to Increase Female Libido." In *Medical Aspects of Human Sexuality.* Edited by H. I. Lief. New York: Williams and Wilkins, Co., 1975.

Komarovsky, M. "Patterns of Self-Disclosure of Male Undergraduates." *Journal of Marriage and the Family* 36 (November 1974): 667–686.

Komarovsky, M. *Blue Collar Marriage.* New York: Random House, 1964.

Komarovsky, M. "Cultural Contradictions and Sex Roles: The Masculine Case." *The American Journal of Sociology* (January 1973): 873–884.

Komisar, L. "The Image of Women in Advertising." In *Woman in Sexist Society.* Edited by V. Gornick and B. K. Moran. New York: Basic, 1971, pp. 207–217.

Kopell, B., et al. "Variations in Some Measures of Arousal during the Menstrual Cycle." *Journal of Nervous and Mental Diseases* 148 (1969): 180–187.

Kotelchuck, M. "The Nature of the Child's Tie to His Father." Unpublished doctoral dissertation. Cambridge, Massachusetts: Harvard University, 1972.

Krain, M., Cannon, D. and Bagford, J. "Rating-Dating or Simply Prestige Homogamy? Data on Dating in the Greek System on a Midwestern Campus." *Journal of Marriage and the Family* 39 (November 1977): 663–674.

Krantzler, M. *Creative Divorce.* New York: New American Library, 1974.

Kraus, R. *Recreation and Leisure in Modern Society.* New York: Appleton-Century-Crofts, 1971.

Krauskopf, J. M. *Marital and Non-Marital Contracts: Preventive Law for the Family.* Chicago: American Bar Association, 1979.

Kriesberg, L. *Mothers in Poverty.* Chicago: Aldine, 1970.

Krupenski, J.; Marshall, E.; and Yule, V. "Patterns

of Marital Problems in Marriage Guidance Clients." *Journal of Marriage and the Family* 32 (February 1970): 138–143.

Kurtz, I. "Make Love Not War." In *Life Styles: Diversity in American Society*. Edited by S. D. Feldman and G. W. Thielbar, Boston: Little, Brown, 1972, pp. 222–232.

Kutner, N. G., and Brogan, D. "An Investigation of Sex-related Slang Vocabulary and Sex-Role Orientation among Male and Female University Students." *Journal of Marriage and the Family* 36 (August 1974): 474–484.

LaBarre, M., and LaBarre, W. *The Triple Crises: Adolescence, Early Marriage and Parenthood*. New York: National Council on Illegitimacy, 1968.

Lake, A. "The Day-Care Business: 'Which Comes First—the Child or the Dollar?'" *McCall's* (November 1970): 96.

Lamaze, F. *Painless Childbirth*. London: Burke 1967.

Lamb, L. E. *Dear Doctor: It's About Sex*. New York: Dell Publishing Co., 1974.

Lamott, K. "Doing Their Thing at Morning Star." In *Communes: Creating and Managing the Collective Life*. Edited by R. M. Kanter. New York: Harper, 1973, pp. 133–141.

Landers A. *Portland (Maine) Press Herald* (May 24, 1975).

Landis, J. T. "A Comparison of Children from Divorced and Nondivorced Unhappy Marriages." *Family Life Coordinator* 11 (July 1962): 61–65.

Landis, J. T., and Landis, M. G. *Building a Successful Marriage*. 6th ed. Englewood Cliffs, New Jersey: Prentice-Hall, 1973.

Landis, P. H. *Making the Most of Marriage*. 5th ed. Englewood Cliffs, New Jersey: Prentice-Hall, 1975.

Landy, F., et al. "The Effect of Limited Father-Absence on Cognitive Development." *Child Development* 40 (1969): 941–944.

Laner, M. R. and Housker, S. L. "Sexual Permissiveness in Younger and Older Adults." *Journal of Family Issues* 1 (March 1980): 103–124.

Langley, R. and Levy, R. C. *Wife Beating: The Silent Crisis*. New York: E. P. Dutton, 1977.

Larzelere, R. E. and Huston, T. L. "The Dyadic Trust Scale: Toward Understanding Interpersonal Trust in Close Relationships." *Journal of Marriage and the Family* 42 (August 1980): 595–604.

Lasswell, M. E. "Is There a Best Age to Marry? An

Interpretation." *The Family Coordinator* 23 (July 1974): 237–242.

Lautenschlager, S. Y. "A Descriptive Study of Consensual Union among College Students." Unpublished Master's thesis. Northridge, California: California State University, 1972.

Laws, J. L. "A Feminist Review of Marital Adjustment Literature: The Rape of the Locke." *Journal of Marriage and the Family* 33 (Augus 1971). 483–516.

Lazarus, A. A. "Female Fear of Orgasm." In *Medical Aspects of Human Sexuality*. Edited by H. I. Lief. New York: Williams and Wilkins, 1975.

Lear, J. "Working Wives Busiest." *Seattle Post-Intelligencer* (November 12 1973).

Lebeaux, C. "Life on ADC: Budgets of Despair." In *Life Styles: Diversity in American Society*. Edited by S. D. Feldman and G. W. Thielbar. Boston: Little, Brown, 1972, pp. 166–174.

Leboyer, F. *Birth without Violence*. New York: Knopf, 1975.

Lehrman, N. *Masters and Johnson Explained*. Chicago: Playboy, 1970.

Leitsch, D. "Interview with a Homosexual Spokesman." *Sexual Behavior* 1 (1971): 15–23.

Lee, G. R. "Age at Marriage and Marital Satisfaction: A Multivariate Analysis with Implications for Marital Stability" *Journal of Marriage and the Family* 39 (August 1977): 493–504.

Lee, G. R. and Stone, L. H. "Mate-Selection Systems and Criteria: Variation According to Family Structure." *Journal of Marriage and the Family* 42 (May 1980): 319–326.

LeMasters, E. E. "Parents without Partners." In *Love, Marriage, Family*. Edited by M. E. Lasswell and T. E. Lasswell. Glenview, Illinois: Scott, Foresman, 1973, pp. 470–475.

LeMasters, E. E. "The Passing of the Dominant Husband-Father." In *Family, Marriage and the Struggle of the Sexes*. Edited by H. P. Dreitzel. New York: Macmillan, 1972, pp. 107–120.

Leslie, G. R. *The Family in Social Context*. 2d ed. New York: Oxford University Press, 1973.

Lester, G. "Reflection on Married Life." *Marriage and Family Living* 61 (October 1979): 6–9.

Levene, H. I., and Regney, F. J. "Law, Preventive Psychology, and Therapeutic Abortion." *Journal of Nervous and Mental Disease* 151 (July 1970): 51–59.

Levenson, R. A. *The Fallacy of Understanding: An In-*

quiry into the Changing Structure of Psychoanalysis. New York: Basic Books, 1972.

Levinger, G. "Husbands' and Wives' Estimates of Coital Frequency." *Medical Aspects of Human Sexuality* (September 1970): 42–57.

Levinger, G., and Senn, D. J. "Disclosure of Feelings in Marriage." In *Dating and Marriage.* Edited by A. F. Kline and M. L. Medley. Boston: Holbrook, 1973, pp. 264–278.

Levinger, G.; Senn, D. J.; and Jorgensen, B. W. "Progress toward Permanence In Courtship: A Test of the Kerchkoff-Davis Hypothesis." *Sociometry* 33 (1970): 427–443.

Lewis, H. "Child Rearing among Low-Income Families." In *Poverty in America.* Edited by L. A. Ferman et al. Ann Arbor: University of Michigan Press, 1965a, pp. 342–353.

Lewis, H. "The Child Rearing Unit Among Low Income Families." Paper presented at Merrill Palmer Institute, Detroit, 1965b.

Lewis, R. A. "The Marital Disenchantment-Disengagement Thesis Reconsidered: Dyadic Maintenance among Family Cohorts." Paper presented at the meeting of the International Gerontological Society, Jerusalem, Israel, June 24, 1975.

Lewis, R. A. "Satisfaction with Conjugal Power over the Family Life Cycle." Paper presented at the annual meeting of the National Council on Family Relations, 1973.

Lewis, R. A. Freneau, P. J., and Robert, C. L. "Fathers and the Postparental Transition." *The Family Coordinator* 28 (October 1979): 514–520.

Libby, R. W. "Extramarital and Comarital Sex: A Review of the Literature." In *Renovating Marriage.* Edited by R. W. Libby and R. N. Whitehurst. Danville, California: Consensus, 1973, pp. 116–145.

Libby, R. W., Gray, L., and White, M. "A Test and Reformulation of Reference Groups and Role Correlates of Premarital Sexual Permissiveness Theory." *Journal of Marriage and the Family* 40 (February 1978): 79–92.

Liddick, B. "Practicing Marriage without a License." *Los Angeles Times* (1971).

Lieberman, E. J. "Informed Consent for Parenthood." In *Abortion and the Unwanted Child,* The California Committee on Therapeutic Abortion. Edited by C. Reiterman. New York: Springer, 1971, pp. 77–83.

Lincoln, C. E. "The Absent Father Haunts the Negro Family." In *The Black Family.* Edited by R. Staples. Belmont, California: Wadsworth, 1971, pp. 343–348.

Lindsay, B. B. *The Companionate Marriage.* New York: Liveright, 1927.

Linn, E. L. "Women Dentists: Career and Family." *Social Problems* 18 (Winter 1971): 397.

Linton, S. "Primate Studies and Sex Differences." *Women: A Journal of Liberation* (Summer 1970): 43,44.

Lobsenz, N., and Blackburn, C. W. *How to Stay Married: A Modern Approach to Sex, Money, and Emotions in Marriage.* New York: Cowles, 1969.

Loiselle, R., and Mollenauer, S. "Galvanic Skin Response to Sexual Stimuli in a Female Population." *Journal of General Psychology* 73 (1965): 273–278.

Long, M. L. and Simon, R. J. "The Roles and Statuses of Women on Children and Family TV Programs." *Journalism Quarterly* 51 (Spring 1974): 107–110.

Lopata, H. Z. "The Absence of Community Resources in the Support Systems of Urban Widows." *The Family Coordinator* 27 (October 1978a): 383–388.

Lopata, H. Z. "Contributions of Extended Families to the Support Systems of Metropolitan Area Widows: Limitations of the Modified Kin Network." *Journal of Marriage and the Family* 40 (May 1978b): 355–365.

Lopata, H. Z. *Occupation: Housewife.* London: Oxford University Press, 1971.

Lopata, H. Z. *Widowhood in an American City.* Cambridge, Massachusetts: Sckenkman, 1973.

Loring, R. "Love and Women's Liberation." In *Love Today: A New Exploration.* Edited by H. A. Otto. New York: Association Press, 1972, pp. 73–85.

Louisell, D. W., and Noonan, J. T., Jr. *The Morality of Abortion.* Edited by J. Noonan. Cambridge: Harvard University Press, 1970, pp. 220–260.

Lowen, A. "The Spiral of Growth: Love, Sex and Pleasure." In *Love Today.* Edited by H. A. Otto. New York: Association Press, 1972, pp. 17–26.

Lowry, T. P. "First Coitus." *Medical Aspects of Human Sexuality* (May 1969): 91–97.

Lydon, S. "The Politics of Orgasm." In *Sisterhood Is Powerful.* Edited by R. Morgan. New York: Vintage, 1970, pp. 197–205.

Lydon, S. "Understanding Orgasm." In *Intimacy, Family and Society.* Edited by A. Skolnick and J.

H. Skolnick. Boston: Little, Brown, 1974, pp. 157–162.

Lueptow, L. B. "Social Structure, Social Change and Parental Influence in Adolescent Sex-Role Socialization: 1964–1975." *Journal of Marriage and the Family* 42 (February 1980): 93–103.

Lyle, J. R. *Affirmative Action Programs for Women: A Survey of Innovative Programs.* Equal Employment Opportunity Commission. Washington, D.C.: U.S. Government Printing Office, 1973.

Lyness, J. L. "Aspect of Long Term Effects of Nonmarital Cohabitation." Reports on two studies: no. 1—University of Colorado, NIMH Research Grant, 1969–1970; no. 2—Ft. Wayne, Indiana, 1973–1974. Unpublished manuscript, 1975.

Lyness, J. L.; Lipetz, M. E.; and Davis, K. E. "Living Together: An Alternative to Marriage." *Journal of Marriage and the Family* 34 (May 1972): 305–311.

Lynn, D. B., and Cross, A. D. "Parent Preference of Preschool Children." *Journal of Marriage and the Family* 36 (August 1974): 555–559.

"M." *The Sensuous Man.* New York: Lyle Stuart, 1971.

MacCorquodale, P. and DeLamater, J. "Self-Image and Premarital Sexuality." *Journal of Marriage and the Family* 41 (May 1979): 327–339.

Mace, D. R. *Abortion: The Agonizing Decision.* Nashville, Tennessee: Abingdon, 1972a.

Mace, D. R. "Contemporary Issues in Marriage." In *Encounter: Love, Marriage and Family.* Edited by R. E. Albrecht and E. W. Bock. Boston: Holbrook. 1972b, pp. 2–12.

Mace, D. R. "The Danger of Sex Innocence." *Sexology* (November 1970): 50–52.

Mace, D. R. *Getting Ready for Marriage.* Nashville, Tennessee: Abingdon, 1972c.

Mace, D. R. *Sexual Difficulties in Marriage.* Philadelphia: Fortress, 1972d.

Mace, D., and Mace, V. *We Can Have Better Marriages If We Really Want Them.* Nashville, Tennessee: Abingdon, 1974.

Mackey, B., and Milloy, M. "The Impact of Teenage Pregnancy on the Professional Educator." *The Family Coordinator* 23 (January 1974): 15–18.

Macklin, E. D. "Cohabitation in College: Going Very Steady." *Psychology Today* 8 (November 1974): 53–59.

Macklin, E. D. "Cohabitation Research Newsletter, Issue no. 1." Mimeographed. Ithaca, New York:

Cornell University, College of Human Ecology, September 1972a.

Macklin, E. D. "Cohabitation Research Newsletter, Issue no. 2." Mimeographed. Ithaca, New York: Cornell University, College of Human Ecology, April 1973a.

Macklin, E. D. "Cohabitation Research Newsletter, Issue no. 3." Mimeographed. Ithaca, New York: Cornell Unviersity, College of Human Ecology, October 1973b.

Macklin, E. D. "Heterosexual Cohabitation among Unmarried College Students." *The Family Coordinator* 21 (October 1972b): 463–472.

Macklin, E. D., "Nonmarital Heterosexual Cohabitation." *Marriage and Family Review* 1 (March/April 1978): 1–12.

Maddock, J. W. "Sex in Adolescence: Its Meaning and Its Future." *Adolescence* 8 (Fall 1973): 325–342.

Maeck, J. V. S., and Phillips, C. A. "Rubella Vaccine Program: Its Implications in Obstetric Practice." *American Journal of Obstetrics and Gynecology* 112 (February 15, 1972): 513–518.

Mahoney, E. R. "Gender and Social Class Differences in Changes in Attitudes toward Premarital Coitus." *Sociology and Social Research* 62 (January 1978): 279–286.

Mainardi, P. "The Politics of Housework." In *Intimate Life Styles: Marriage and Its Alternatives.* Edited by J. S. DeLora and J. R. DeLora. Pacific Palisades, California: Goodyear, 1972, pp. 283–287.

"Making a Marriage." In *Love, Marriage, Family.* Edited by M. E. Lasswell and T. E. Lasswell. Glenview, Illinois: Scott, Foresman, 1973, pp. 271–274.

Manosevitz, M. "The Development of Male Hormosexuality." *Journal of Sex Research* 8 (1972): 31–40.

Maranell, G. M.; Dodder, R. A.; and Mitchell, D. F. "Social Class and Premarital Sexual Permissiveness: A Subsequent Test." *Journal of Marriage and the Family* 32 (February 1970): 85–88.

Marcus, D. E. and Overton, W. F. "The Development of Cognitive Gender Constancy and Sex Role Preferences." *Child Development* 49 (June 1978): 434–444.

Marder, L. "Psychiatric Experience with a Liberalized Therapeutic Abortion Law." *American Journal of Psychiatry* 126 (March 1970): 1230–1236.

Margolis, A. J., et al. "Therapeutic Abortion Follow-Up Study." *American Journal of Obstetrics and Gynecology* 110 (1971): 243–249.

Margolius, S. "The Responsible Consumer." Public Affairs Pamphlet No. 453. New York: Public Affairs Committee, 1970.

Marini, M. M. "The Transition to Adulthood: Sex Differences in Educational Attainment and Age at Marriage." *American Sociological Review* 43 (August 1978): 483–507.

Marmor, J., et al. "Viewpoints: Why Are Some Orgasms Better than Others?" *Medical Aspects of Human Sexuality* (March, 1971): 12–23.

Martin, D., and Lyon, R. *Lesbian/Woman*. San Francisco: Glide, 1972.

Martin, D., and Mariah, P. "Homosexual Love: Woman to Woman, Man to Man." In *Love Today: A New Exploration*. Edited by H. A. Otto. New York: Association Press, 1972, pp. 120–134.

Martin, E. P. and Martin, J. M. *The Black Extended Family*. Chicago: The University of Chicago Press, 1978.

Martin, W. "Seduced and Abandoned in the New World: The Image of Woman in American Fiction." In *Woman in Sexist Society*. Edited by V. Gornick and B. K. Moran. New York: Basic, 1971, pp. 226–239.

Martinson, F. M. *Family in Society*. New York: Dodd, Mead, 1972.

"Marvin v. Marvin." *Family Law Reporter* 5 (1979): 3077.

Marx, J. H., and Spray, S. L. "Marital Status and Occupational Success among Mental Health Professionals." *Journal of Marriage and the Family* 32 (February 1970): 110–118.

Maslow, A. H. *Motivation and Personality*. 2d ed. New York: Harper, 1970.

Maslow, A. H. *Toward a Psychology of Being*. Princeton New Jersey: Van Nostrand, 1962.

Masters, W. H., and Johnson, V. E. *Human Sexual Inadequacy*. Boston: Little, Brown, 1970, p. 342.

Masters, W. H., and Johnson, V. E. *Human Sexual Response*. Boston: Little, Brown, 1966.

May, R. *Love and Will*. New York: W. W. Norton, 1970.

Mayer, M. F. *Divorce and Annulment in the 50 States*, New York: ARC Books, 1971.

Maynard, F. "Understanding the Crises in Men's Lives." In *Choice and Challenge*. Edited by C. E. Williams and J. F. Crosby. Dubuque, Iowa: Wm. C. Brown, 1974, pp. 135–144.

Mazur, R. *The New Intimacy*. Boston: Beacon, 1973.

McCary, J. L. *Freedom and Growth in Marriage*. Santa Barbara, California: Hamilton, 1975.

McCary, J. L. *Human Sexuality*. 2d ed. New York: Van Nostrand, 1973.

McCary, J. L., and Flake, M. H. "The Role of Bibliotherapy and Sex Education in Counseling for Sexual Problems." *Professional Psychologist* 2 (1971): 353–357.

McCormick, N. B. "Come-Ons and Put-Offs: Unmarried Students' Strategies for Having and Avoiding Sexual Intercourse." *Psychology of Women Quarterly* 4 (Winter 1979): 194–211.

McCoy, R. W. Statement at Minnesota State Hearings on a Resolution for a Constitutional Amendment, March 1973. In *National Association for Repeal of Abortion Laws, Newsletter* (June 15, 1973).

McCubbin, H. I. "Coping Behavior in Family Stress Theory." *Journal of Marriage and the Family* 41 (May 1979): 237–244.

McCubbin, H. I., Joy, C. B., Cauble, A. E., Comeau, J. K., Patterson, J. M., and Needle, R. H. "Family Stress and Coping: A Decade Review." *Journal of Marriage and the Family* 42 (November 1980): 855–871.

McDonald, G. W. "Determinants of Adolescent Perceptions of Maternal and Paternal Power in the Family." *Journal of Marriage and the Family* 41 (November 1979): 757–770.

McDonald, G. W. "Family Power: The Assessment of a Decade of Theory and Research, 1970–1979." *Journal of Marriage and the Family* 42 (November 1980): 841–854.

McDonald, G. W. "Parental Identification by the Adolescent: A Social Power Approach." *Journal of Marriage and the Family* 29 (November 1977): 705–719.

McDonald, R. L. "The Role of Emotional Factors in Obstetric Complication: A Review." *Psychosomatic Medicine* 30 (1968): 222–237.

McDowell, S. F. "Black-White Intermarriage in the United States." *International Journal of Sociology of the Family* 1 (May 1971): 49–58.

McGee, T. F., and Kostrubala, T. "The Neurotic Equilibrium in Married Couples Applying for Group Psychotherapy." In *Journal of Marriage and the Family* 26 (February 1964): 77–82.

McGuire, T. F., and Steinhilber, R. M. "Frigidity, the Primary Female Sexual Dysfunction." *Medical Aspects of Human Sexuality* (October 1970): 108–123.

McIntire, W. G.; Nass, G. D.; and Dreyer, A. S. "A Cross-Cultural Comparison of Adolescent Perception of Parental Roles." *Journal of Marriage and the Family* 34 (November 1972): 735–740.

McMillan, E. L. "Problem Buildup: A Description of Couples in Marriage Counseling." *The Family Coordinator* 18 (July 1969): 260–267.

McMurtry, J. "Monogamy: A Critique." In *Renovating Marriage.* Edited by R. W. Libby and R. N. Whitehurst. Danville, California: Consensus, 1973, pp. 48–58.

McNamara, M. L. L. and Bahr, H. M. "The Dimensionality of Marital Role Satisfaction." *Journal of Marriage and the Family* 42 (February 1980): 45–55.

McWhirter, W. A. "'The Arrangement' at College: Part I." In *Love, Marriage, Family* Edited by M. E. Lasswell and T. E. Lasswell. Glenview, Illinois: Scott, Foresman. 1973, pp. 203–207.

Mead, M. "Anomalies in American Post-Divorce Relationships." In *Divorce and After.* Edited by P. Bohannan. Garden City, New York: Doubleday, 1970, pp. 107–125.

Mead, M. "Marriage in Two Steps." *Redbook* 127 (1966): 48–49.

Mead, M. *Sex and Temperament in Three Primitive Societies.* New York: Merton, 1950, pp. 279–288a.

Mears, E., et al. "Preliminary Evaluation of Four Oral Contraceptives Containing Only Progestogens." *British Medical Journal* 2 (June 1969): 730–734.

Melody, G. F. "Role of the Clitoris." *Medical Aspects of Human Sexuality* (June 1970): 116.

Melville, K. *Communes in the Counter Culture: Origins, Theories, Styles of Life.* New York: William Morrow, 1972.

Menken, J. "The Health and Social Consequences of Teenage Childbearing." *Family Planning Perspectives* 4 (1972): 45–53.

Meryman, R. "A Marriage in Trouble." In *Love, Marriage, Family.* Edited by M. E. Lasswell and T. E. Lasswell. Glenview, Illinois: Scott, Foresman, 1973, pp. 415–423.

Meyerowitz, J. H. "Satisfaction during Pregnancy." *Journal of Marriage and the Family* 32 (February 1970): 38–42.

Michels, L. "Why We Don't Want Children." *Redbook* (January 1970).

Middendorp, C. P.; Brinkman, W.; and Koomen, W. "Determinants of Premarital Sexual Permissiveness: A Secondary Analysis." *Journal of Marriage and the Family* 32 (August 1970): 369–379.

Miller, A. A. "Reactions of Friends to Divorce." In *Divorce and After.* Edited by P. Bohannan. Garden City, New York: Doubleday, 1970, pp. 63–86.

Miller, B. C. "Gay Fathers and Their Children." *The Family Coordinator* 28 (October 1979): 544–552.

Miller, B. C. "A Multivariate Developmental Model of Marital Satisfaction." *Journal of Marriage and the Family* 38 (November 1976): 643–657.

Miller, B. C. and Sollie, D. L. "Normal Stress During the Transition to Parenthood." *Family Relations* 29 (October 1980): 459–465.

Miller, H., and Rivenback, W. H. "Sexual Differences in Physical Attractiveness as a Determinant of Heterosexual Liking." *Psychological Reports* 27 (1970): 701–702.

Miller, H. L., and Siegel, P. S. *Loving: A Psychological Approach.* New York: John Wiley, 1972.

Miller, M. M. and Reeves, B. "Dramatic TV Content and Children's Sex-Role Stereotypes." *Journal of Broadcasting* 20 (Winter 1976): 35–50.

Miller, S.; Corrales, R.; and Wackman, D. B. "Recent Progress in Understanding and Facilitating Marital Communication." *The Family Coordinator* 24 (April 1975a): 143–152.

Miller, S.; Nunnally, E. W.; and Wackman, D. B. *Alive and Aware: Improving Communication in Relationships.* Minneapolis: Interpersonal Communications Program, 1975b.

Miller, S., and Peterson, G. *Verbal Communication Styles Framework: A Method for Studying Dyadic Interaction.* A Technical Report. Minneapolis: University of Minnesota, Family Studies Center, 1974.

Miller, S. M. "On Men: The Making of a Confused Middle-Class Husband." *Social Policy* 2 (July/August 1971): 33–39.

Miller, W. B. "Psychological Vulnerability to Unwanted Pregnancy." *Family Planning Perspectives* 5 (Fall 1973): 199–201.

Miller, W. W., Jr. "Afrodex in the Treatment of Male Impotence: A Double Blind Crossover Study." *Current Therapeutic Research* 10 (July 1968): 354–359.

Millet, K. *Sexual Politics.* New York: Doubleday, 1970.

Mirande, A. M., and Hammer, E. L. "Premarital Sexual Permissiveness: A Research Note." *Journal of Marriage and the Family* 36 (May 1974): 356–358.

Mischel, W. "Sex-Typing and Socialization." In *Carmichael's Manual of Child Psychology.* Vol. 2. Edited by P. Mussen. New York: John Wiley, 1970.

Mitchell, J. "Women: The Longest Revolution." In *Family in Transition.* Edited by A. S. Skolnick and J. H. Skolnick. Boston: Little, Brown, 1971, pp. 271–278.

Moen, P. "Developing Family Indicators. Financial Hardship, a Case in Point." *Journal of Family Issues* 1 (March 1980): 5–30.

Moen, P. "Family Impacts of the 1975 Recession: Duration of Unemployment." *Journal of Marriage and the Family* 41 (August 1979): 561–572.

Moerk, E., and Becker, P. "Attitudes of High School Students toward Future Marriage and College Education." *The Family Coordinator* 20 (January 1971): 67–73.

Monahan, T. P. "Are Interracial Marriages Really Less Stable?" *Social Forces* 48 (June 1970): 469.

Monahan, T. P. "National Divorce Legislation: The Problem and Some Suggestions." *The Family Coordinator* 22 (July 1973): 353–357.

Money, J. "Psychologic Findings Associated with the XO, XXY, and XYY Anomalies." *Southern Medical Journal,* Supplement 1, 64 (1971): 59–64.

Money, J. *Sex Errors of the Body.* Baltimore: Johns Hopkins Press, 1968.

Money, J., and Ehrhardt, A. A. *Man and Woman, Boy and Girl.* Baltimore: Johns Hopkins Press, 1972.

Money, J., and Russo, A. J. "Homosexual Outcome of Discordant Gender Identity/Role in Childhood: Longitudinal Follow-Up." *Journal of Pediatric Psychology* 4 (March 1979): 29–41.

Montgomery, J. "Commitment and Cohabitation Cohesion." Unpublished manuscript. Edmonton, Alberta, Canada: University of Alberta, 1975.

Montgomery, J. E. "The Housing Patterns of Older Families." *The Family Coordinator* 21 (January 1972): 37–46.

Moos, R. H., et al. "Fluctuations in Symptoms and Moods during the Menstrual Cycle." *Journal of Psychosomatic Research* 13 (1969): 37–44.

Morgan, R. *Sisterhood Is Powerful.* New York: Random, 1970.

Mornell, P. *Passive Men, Wild Women.* New York: Simon and Schuster, 1979.

Morrison, J. R. "Parental Divorce as a Factor in Childhood Psychiatric Illness." *Comprehensive Psychiatry* 15 (1974): 95–102.

Mosher, D. L., and Greenberg, I. "Females Affective Responses to Reading Erotic Literature." *Journal of Counseling and Clinical Psychology* 33 (1969): 472–477.

Moss, J.J.; Apolonio, F.; and Jensen, M. "The Premarital Dyad during the Sixites." *Journal of Marriage and the Family* 33 (February 1971): 50–69.

Movius, M. "Voluntary Childlessness—The Ultimate Liberation." *The Family Coordinator* 25 (January 1976): 57–63.

Moyer, D. L., and Mishell, D. R. "Reactions of Human Endometrium to the Intrauterine Foreign Body." *American Journal of Obstetrics and Gynecology* 111 (September 1971): 66–80.

Mueller, B. J. "Reconciliation or Resignation: A Case Study." *The Family Coordinator* 19 (October 1970): 345–352.

Mukhopadhyay, C. C. "The Function of Romantic Love: A Re-appraisal of the Coppinger and Rosenblatt Study." *Behavior Science Research* 14 (1979): 57–63.

Mullen, P., et al. "A Vasectomy Education Program: Implications from Survey Data." *The Family Coordinator* 22 (July 1973): 331–338.

Murphy, D. C., and Mendelson, L. A. "Use of the Observational Method in the Study of Live Marital Communication." *Journal of Marriage and the Family* 35 (May 1973): 256–263.

Murstein, B. I. "Interview Behavior, Projective Techniques, and Questionnaires in the Clinical Assessment of Marital Choice." *Journal of Personality Assessment* 36 (1972a): 462–467.

Murstein, B. I. "Person Perception and Courtship Progress among Premarital Couples." *Journal of Marriage and the Family* 34 (November 1972b): 621–626.

Murstein, B. I. "Physical Attractiveness and Marital Choice." *Journal of Personality and Social Psychology* 32 (1972c): 8–12.

Murstein, B. I. "Self Ideal-Self Discrepancy and the Choice of Marital Partner." *Journal of Consulting and Clinical Psychology* 37 (1971b): 47–52.

Murstein, B. I. "Sex-drive and Courtship Progress

in a College Sample." Unpublished paper. Connecticut College, 1970.

Murstein, B. I. "A Theory of Marital Choice and Its Applicability to Marriage Adjustment." In *Theories of Attraction and Love.* Edited by B. I. Murstein. New York: Springer, 1971a, pp. 100–151.

Myers, L. "Marriage, Honesty, and Personal Growth." In *Renovating Marriage.* Edited by R. W. Libby and R. N. Whitehurst. Danville, California: Consensus, 1973, pp. 345–359.

Myricks, N. "Palimony: The Impact of Marvin v. Marvin." *Family Relations* 29 (April 1980): 210–215.

Naffziger, C. C. and Naffziger, K. "Development of Sex Role Stereotypes." *The Family Coordinatior* 23 (July 1974): 251–258.

Nash, J. "The Father in Contemporary Culture and Current Psychological Literature." In *Love, Marriage, Family.* Edited by M. E. Lasswell and T. E. Lasswell. Glenview, Illinois: Scott, Foresman, 1973, pp. 352–364.

National Council on Family Relations. Task Force on Divorce and Divorce Reform. *Task Force Report on Divorce and Divorce Reform.* Minneapolis: National Council on Family Relations, October 1973.

National Foundation—March of Dimes. "Birth Defects: Tragedy and Hope." 1977.

National Opinion Research Center. *General Social Survey.* 1973.

Neisser, E. G. "Emotional and Social Values Attached to Money." In *Encounter: Love, Marriage and Family,* edited by R. E. Albrecht and E. W. Bock. Boston: Holbrook Press, Inc., 1972, pp. 272–287.

Neisser, E. G. "How to Be a Good Mother-in-law and Grandmother." Public Affairs Pamphlet No. 174. New York: Public Affairs Committee, Inc.

Neubeck, G. "In Praise of Marriage." *The Family Coordinator* 28 (January 1979): 115–117.

Neumann, F.; Steinbeck, H.; and Hahn, J. D. "Hormones and Brain Differentiation." In *The Hypothalamus.* Edited by L. Martini, M. Motta, and F. Fraschini. New York: Academic, 1970.

Newcomb, P. R. "Cohabitation in America: An Assessment of Consequences." *Journal of Marriage and the Family* 41 (August 1979): 597–602.

New York Times (January 23, 1973): 1.

Nock, S. L. "The Family Life Cycle: Empirical or Conceptual Tool?" *Journal of Marriage and Family* 41 (February 1979): 15–26.

Norcross, C. "Today's Housing Solution: The Compact House." *Parade Magazine* (January 4, 1976): 14–16.

Norland, S.; James, J.; and Shover, N. "Gender Role Expectations of Juveniles." *The Sociological Quarterly* 19 (Autumn 1978): 545–554.

Norton, A. J. "The Influence of Divorce on Traditional Life-Cycle Measures." *Journal of Marriage and the Family* 42 (February 1980): 63–69.

Notman, M. T. "Pregnancy and Abortion: Implications for Career Development of Professional Women." *Annuals of the New York Academy of Sciences* 208 (1973): 205–210.

Novak, E. R.; Jones, G. S.; and Jones, H. W., Jr. *Novak's Textbook of Gynecology.* 8th ed. Baltimore: Williams and Wilkins, 1970.

Novak, F. "Experience with Suction Curettage." Edited by R. Hall. In *Abortion in the Changing World* 1 (1970): 74–79.

Nye, F. I., and Berardo, F. M. *The Family: Its Structure and Interaction.* New York: Macmillan, 1973.

Nye, F. I.; Carlson, J.; and Garrett, G. "Family Size, Interaction, Affect and Stress." *Journal of Marriage and the Family* 32 (May 1970): 216–226.

O'Connor, J. F., et al. "Behavioral Rhythms Related to the Menstrual Cycle." *Biorhythms and Human Reproduction.* New York: John Wiley, 1974.

O'Connor, J. F., and Stern, L. O. "Results of Treatment in Functional Sexual Disorders." *New York State Journal of Medicine* 72 (1972): 1927–1934.

Oldham, J. C. "Questions of Exclusions and Exceptions under Title VIII—'Sex Plus' and the BFOQ." *The Hasting Law Journal* 23 (November 1971): 55–94.

Olim, E. G. "The Self-Actualizing Person in the Fully Functioning Family: A Humanistic Viewpoint." In *American Marriage: A Changing Scene.* Edited by F. D. Cox. Dubuque, Iowa: Wm. C. Brown, 1972, pp. 182–193.

Olson, D. H. "Behavior Modification Research with Couples and Families: A System Analysis, Review, and Critique." Paper presented at the annual meeting of the Association for the Advancement of Behavior Therapy, New York, October 1972a.

Olson, D. H. "Marriage of the Future: Revolutionary or Evolutionary Change?" *The Family Coordinator* 21 (October 1972b) 383–393.

O'Neill, N., and O'Neill, G. *Open Marriage.* New York: Avon, 1972.

O'Neill, W. L. "Introduction." In *Women at Work.* Edited by W. L. O'Neill. New York: Quadrangle/New York Times, 1972, pp. v–xix.

Orthner, D. K. "Leisure Activity Patterns and Marital Satisfaction over the Marital Career." *Journal of Marriage and the Family* 37 (February 1975): 91–102.

Osmond, M. W. "Reciprocity: A Dynamic Model and a Method to Study Family Power." *Journal of Marriage and the Family* 40 (February 1978): 49–61.

Osmond, M. W. and Martin, P. Y. "A Contingency Model of Marital Organization in Low Income Families." *Journal of Marriage and the Family* 40 (May 1978): 315–329.

Osofsky, J. D., et al. "Psychological Effects of Legal Abortion." *Clinical Obstetrics and Gynecology* 14 (1971): 1.

Osofsky, J. D. and Osofsky, H. J. "Androgyny as a Life Style." In *Non-traditional Family Forms in the 1970's.* Edited by M. B. Sussman. Minneapolis: National Council on Family Relations, 1972, pp. 43–50.

Otto, H. "Has Monogamy Failed?" In *Choice and Challenge.* Edited by C. E. Williams and J. F. Crosby. Dubuque, Iowa: Wm. C. Brown, 1974, pp. 22–30,

Otto, H. "Today's Marriage or the New Marriage—Which Way for You?" In *Marriage Means Encounter.* Edited by G. Roleder. Dubuque, Iowa: Wm. C. Brown, 1973, pp. 158–159.

Otto, H. A. "Communes: The Alternative Life-Style." *Saturday Review* 54 (April 24, 1971): 16–21.

Otto, H. A. "Communication in Love." In *Love Today: A New Exploration.* Edited by H. A. Otto. New York: Association Press, 1972, pp. 66–72.

Ovesey, L., and Meyers, H. "Retarded Ejaculation." *Medical Aspects of Human Sexuality* (November 1970): 98–119.

Packard, V. *The Sexual Wilderness.* New York: David McKay, 1968, pp. 466–468.

Painter, B. "The Effect of a Structural Tutorial Program on the Cognitive and Language Development of Culturally Disadvantaged Infants." *Merrill-Palmer Quarterly* 15 (1969): 279–294.

Palme, O. "The Emancipation of Man. *Journal of Social Issues* 28 (1972): 237–246.

Pannor, R.; Massarik, F.; and Evans, B. *The Unmarried Father.* New York: Springer, 1971.

Papousek, H. "Group Rearing in Day Care Centers and Mental Health: Potential Advantages and Risks." *Research Publication Series, Association for Research in Nervous and Mental Diseases* 51 (1973): 398–411.

Pare, C. M. B., and Raven, H. "Follow-up of Patients Referred for Termination of Pregnancy." *Lancet* 1 (March 28, 1970): 635–638.

Parkes, C. M. *Bereavement.* New York: International Universities Press, 1972.

Parlee, M. B. "The Sexes Under Scrutiny: From Old Biases to New Theories." *Psychology Today* (November 1978): 62 ff.

Patterson, G. R., and Hops, H. "Coercion, A Game for Two: Intervention Techniques for Marital Conflict." In *The Experimental Analysis of Social Behavior.* Edited by R. E. Ulrich and P. Mountjoy. New York: Appleton-Century-Crofts, 1972, pp. 424–440.

Patterson, G. R.; Hops, H.; and Weiss, R. L. "Interpersonal Skills Training for Couples in Early Stages of Conflict." *Journal of Marriage and the Family* 37 (May 1975): 295–303.

Pearlman, C. K. "Frequency of Intercourse in Males at Different Ages." *Medical Aspects of Human Sexuality* (November 1972): 92–113.

Peck, E. *The Baby Trap.* New York: Geis, 1971.

Peel, J., and Potts, M. *A Textbook of Contraceptive Practice.* London: Cambridge University Press, 1969.

Peevers, B. N. "Androgyny on the TV Screen? An Analysis of Sex-Role Portrayal." *Sex Roles* 5 (December 1979): 797–809.

Pendleton, B. F.; Poloma, M. M.; and Garland, T. N. "Scales for Investigation of the Dual-Career Family." *Journal of Marriage and the Family* 42 (May 1980): 269–276.

Peplau, L. A., Rubin, Z., and Hill, C. T. "Sexual Intimacy in Dating Relationships." *Journal of Social Issues* 33 (1977): 86–109.

Perlman, D. "Self-esteem and Sexual Permissiveness." *Journal of Marriage and the Family* 36 (August 1974): 470–473.

Perlman, D. "The Sexual Standard of Canadian University Students." In *Readings in Canadian Social Psychology.* Edited by D. Koulack and D. Perlman. Rexdale, Ontario: Wiley of Canada, 1973.

Peterman, D. J.; Ridley, C. A.; and Anderson, S. M. "A Comparison of Cohabiting and Noncohabiting College Students." *Journal of Marriage and the Family* 36 (May 1974): 344–354.

Perlman, S. B. "Pregnancy and Parenting among Runaway Girls." *Journal of Family Issues* 2 (June 1980): 262–273.

Perrucci, C. C. "Minority Status and the Pursuit of Professional Careers: Women in Science and Engineering." In *Marriage and the Family*. Edited by C. C. Perrucci and D. B. Targ. New York: David McKay, 1974, pp. 376–397.

Perrucci, C. C. "Mobility, Marriage and Childspacing among College Graduates." *Journal of Marriage and the Family* 30 (May 1968): 273–282.

Perry, H. S. *The Human Be-In*. New York: Basic, 1970.

Pershing, B. "Family Policies: A Component of Management in the Home and Family Setting." *Journal of Marriage and the Family* 41 (August 1979): 573–581.

Persky, H.; Smith, K. D.; and Basu, G. K. "Relation of Psychologic Measures of Aggression and Hostility to Testosterone Production in Man." *Psychosomatic Medicine* 33 (1971): 265–277.

Peters, J. J. "Emotional Recovery from Rape." In *Medical Aspects of Human Sexuality*. Edited by H. I. Lief. New York: Williams and Wilkins Co., 1975.

Peterson, G. B., and Peterson, L. R. "Sexism in the Treatment of Sexual Dysfunction." *The Family Coordinator* 22 (October 1973): 397–404.

Peterson, J. A. "Marriage and Love in the Middle Years." Public Affairs Pamphlet no. 456. New York: Public Affairs Committee, 1970.

Pfeiffer, E., et al. "Sexual Behavior in Aged Men and Women." *Archives of General Psychiatry* 19 (1968): 753–758.

Pfeiffer, E.; Verwoerat, A.; and Davis, G. C. "Sexual Behavior in Middle Life." In *Sexual Development and Behavior*. Edited by A. M. Juhasz. Homewood, Illinois: Dorsey, 1973, pp. 69–79.

Piaget, J., and Inhelder, J. *The Psychology of the Child*. New York: Basic, 1969.

Pickford, J. H.; Signoria, E. I.; and Rempel, H. "Similar or Related Personality Traits as a Factor in Marital Happiness." *Journal of Marriage and the Family* 28 (May 1966): 190–192.

Pierson, E. C. *Sex Is Never an Emergency*. Philadelphia: Lippincott, 1971.

Pierson, E. C., and D'Antonio, W. V. *Female and Male: Dimensions of Human Sexuality*. Philadelphia: Lippincott, 1974.

Pingree, S. et al. "Anti-Nepotism's Ghost: Attitudes of Administrators toward Hiring Professional Couples." *Psychology of Women Quarterly* 3 (Fall 1978): 22–29.

Poffenberger, T. "Three Papers on Going Steady." *The Family Life Coordinator* 13 (January 1964): 7–13.

Pohlman, E. "Childlessness: Intentional and Unintentional." *Journal of Nervous and Mental Disease* 151 (1970): 2–12.

Polani, P. "Chromosome Phenotypes—Sex Chromosomes." In *Congenital Malformations, Excerpta Medica*. edited by F. C. Fraser and V. A. McKuisick, 1970.

Pollock, M. J. "Changing the Role of Women." In *The Women's Movement*. Edited by H. Wortis and C. Rabinowitz. New York: John Wiley, 1972, pp. 10–20.

Poloma, M. M., and Garland, T. N. "The Married Professional Woman: A Study in the Tolerance of Domestication." *Journal of Marriage and the Family* 33 (August 1971): 531–540.

Pope Pius XII. "Woman's Role: The Catholic View." Excerpts from address. *Marriage and Family Living* 8 (1946): 6–8.

Porter, S. *Sylvia Porter's Money Book*, Garden City, New York: Doubleday, 1975.

"Portrait of America—Latest Official Survey" *U. S. News and World Report* (May 21, 1979): 80, 81.

Potts, D. M. "Which is the Weaker Sex? *Journal of Biosocial Science*, Supplement 2 (1970): 147–157.

Power, P. W. "The Chronically Ill Husband and Father: His Role in the Family." *The Family Coordinator* 28 (October 1979): 616–621.

Powers, W. G. and Hutchinson, K. "The Measurement of Communication Apprehension in the Marriage Relationship." *Journal of Marriage and the Family* 41 (February 1979): 89–95.

Presser, H. "The Timing of the First Birth, Female Roles, and Black Fertility." Part 1. *Milbank Memorial Fund Quarterly* 49 (July 1971): 329–361.

Presser, H. B., and Bumpass, H. L. "The Acceptability of Contraceptive Sterilization among U.S. Couples, 1970." *Family Perspectives* 4 (October 1972): 18–26.

Propper, A. M. "The Relationship of Maternal Employment to Adolescent Roles, Activities, and Parental Relationships." *Journal of Marriage and the Family* 34 (August 1972): 417–421.

Rabkin, L. Y., and Rabkin, K. "Children of the Kibbutz." *Psychology Today* 3 (September 1969): 46.

Rainwater, L. "Marital Sexuality in Four Cultures of Poverty." *Journal of Marriage and the Family* 26 (November 1964): 457–466.

Ramey, J. W. "Communes, Group Marriage, and the Upper-Middle Class." *Journal of Marriage and the Family* 34 (November 1972a): 647–655.

Ramey, J. W. "Emerging Patterns of Innovative Behavior in Marriage." *The Family Coordinator* 21 (October 1972b): 435–456.

Ramey, J. W. "Intimate Groups and Networks: Frequent Consequence of Sexually Open Marriage." *The Family Coordinator* 24 (October 1975): 515–530.

Randall, G. C. "Living Together Can Be Very Taxing." *Family Advocate* 1 (Winter 1979): 2–5, 34,35.

Rao, S. L. N. "A Comparative Study of Childlessness and Never Pregnant Status." *Journal of Marriage and the Family* 36 (February 1974): 149–157.

Rappoport, A. F., and Harrell, J. "A Behavioral Exchange Model for Marital Counseling." *The Family Coordinator* 21 (April 1972): 203–212.

Rapoport, R. and Rapoport, R. N. *Dual-Career Families.* Baltimore: Penguin, 1971.

Rapoport, R. N. and Rapoport, R. "Dual-Career Families: Progress and Prospects." *Marriage and Family Review* 1 (September/October 1978): 1–12.

Rapoport, R.; Rapoport, R. N.; and Fogarty, M. *Sex, Career, and Family.* Beverly Hills: Sage, 1971.

Raschke, H. J. and Raschke, V. J. "Family Conflict and Children's Self-Concepts: A Comparison of Intact and Single-Parent Families." *Journal of Marriage and the Family* 41 (May 1979): 367–374.

Raush, H.L., et al. *Communication, Conflict and Marriage.* San Francisco: Jossey-Bass, 1974.

Rawlings, S. "Perspectives on American Husbands and Wives." *Current Population Reports.* Series P-23, no. 77. Washington, D.C.: U.S. Bureau of the Census, Department of Commerce, December 1978.

Rebelsky, F. G., and Hanks, C. "Fathers' Verbal Interaction with Infants in the First Three Months of Life." *Child Development* 42 (1971): 63–68.

Rebelsky, F. G.; Starr, R. H.; and Luria, Z. "Language Development: The First Four Years." In *Infancy and Early Childhood.* Edited by Brackill. New York: Free Press, 1967.

Reed, J. P. "The Current Legal Status of Abortion." In *Current Issues in Marriage and the Family.* Edited by J. G. Wells. New York: Macmillan, 1975, pp. 200–208.

Reik. T. *A Psychologist Looks at Love.* New York: Farrar and Rinehart, 1944.

Reik, T. *Of Love and Lust.* New York: Straus and Cudahy, 1957.

Reiner, B. S., and Edwards, R. L. "Adolescent Marriage: Social or Therapeutic Problem?" *The Family Coordinator* 23 (October 1974): 383–390.

Reiss, D, and Oliveri, M. E. "Family Paradigm and Family Coping: A Proposal for Linking the Family's Intrinsic Adaptive Capacities to Its Responses to Stress." *Family Relations* 29 (October 1980): 431–444.

Reiss, I. L. *The Family System in America.* New York: Henry Holt, 1971.

Reiss, I. L. "The Influence of Contraceptive Knowledge on Premarital Sexuality." *Medical Aspects of Human Sexuality* (February 1970): 71–86.

Reiss, I., Anderson, R. E., and Sponaugle, G. C. "A Multivariate Model of the Determinants of Extramarital Sexual Permissiveness." *Journal of Marriage and the Family* 42 (May 1980): 395–411.

"The Relentless Ordeal of Political Wives." *Time* (October 7, 1974).

"Renewable Marriage." *Time* (March 15, 1971): 3.

Renne, K. S. "Correlates of Dissatisfaction in Marriage." *Journal of Marriage and the Family* (February 1970): 54–67.

Reuben, D. *Everything You Always Wanted to Know about Sex—But Were Afraid to Ask.* New York: Bantam, 1969.

Reynolds, E. "Variations of Mood and Recall in the Menstrual Cycle." *Journal of Psychosomatic Research* 13 (1969): 163–166.

Rice, D. G. *Dual-Career Marriage: Conflict and Treatment.* New York: Free Press, 1978.

Rice, F. P. *The Adolescent: Development, Relationships, and Culture.* 3rd ed. Boston: Allyn and Bacon, 1981.

Rice, F. P. *Morality and Youth.* Philadelphia: Westminster Press, 1980.

Rice, F. P. *Parents, In-Laws and Grandparents in the Family.* Bulletin 521. Orono, Maine: University of Maine, Cooperative Extension Service, 1966.

Rice, F. P. *Sexual Problems in Marriage.* Philadelphia: Westminister, 1978a.

Rice, F. P. *Stepparenting.* New York: Condor, 1978b.

Rice, F. P. *The Working Mother's Guide to Child Development.* Englewood Cliffs, New Jersey: Prentice-Hall, 1979.

Ridley, C. A. "Exploring the Impact of Work Satisfaction and Involvement on Marital Interaction When Both Partners are Employed." *Journal of Marriage and the Family* 35 (May 1973): 229–237.

Ridley, C. A., Peterman, D. J., and Avery, A. W. "Cohabitation: Does It Make for a Better Marriage?" *The Family Coordinator* 27 (April 1978): 129–136.

Ridley, J. C. "Introduction—Women's Changing Status." In *The Family in Transition.* Fogarty International Center Proceedings No. 3. A round table conference sponsored by the John E. Fogarty International Center for Advanced Study in the Health Sciences, National Institutes of Health, Nov. 3–6, 1969, Bethesda, Maryland, Washington, D.C.: U.S. Government Printing Office, 1971, pp. 189–197.

Riley, L. E., and Spreitzer, E. A. "A Model for the Analysis of Lifetime Marriage Patterns." *Journal of Marriage and the Family* 36 (February 1974): 64–70.

Riley, M. W., and Foner, A. *Aging and Society.* Vol. 1, New York: Russell Sage Foundation, 1968.

Robbins, N. N. "End of Divorce—Beginning of Legal Problems." *The Family Coordinator* 23 (April 1974): 185–188.

Robbins, N. N. "Have We Found Fault in No Fault Divorce?" *The Family Coordinator* 22 (July 1973): 359–362.

Roberto, D. A., et al. "Marital and Family Planning Expectancies of Men Regarding Vasectomy." *Journal of Marriage and the Family* 36 (November 1974): 698–706.

Roberts, F. B., and Miller, B. C. "Infant Behavior Effects on the Transition to Parenthood: A Minitheory." Paper presented at a workshop of the National Council on Family Relations, October 1978.

Roberts, R. E. *The New Communes: Coming Together in America.* Englewood Cliffs, New Jersey: Prentice-Hall, 1971.

Robertson, J. F. "Grandmotherhood: A Study of Role Conceptions." *Journal of Marriage and the Family* 39 (February 1977): 165–174.

Robertson, J. F. "Women in Midlife: Crises, Reverberations, and Support Networks." *The Family Coordinator* 27 (October 1978): 375–382.

Rock, J. "Calendar Rhythm: General Considerations." In *Manual of Family Planning and Contraceptive Practice.* Edited by M. S. Calderone. 2d ed. Baltimore: Williams and Wilkins, 1970, pp. 376–381.

Rockefeller, J. D., III. *Population and the American Futre.* Washington, D.C.: U.S. Government Printing Office, 1972.

Roe v. Wade, 410 U.S. 113 (1973).

Rogers, C. R. *Becoming Partners: Marriage and Its Alternatives.* New York: Dell, 1972a.

Rogers, C. R. "A Humanistic Conception of Man." In *Marriage and Family in a Decade of Change.* Edited by G. B. Carr. Reading, Massachusetts: Addison-Wesley, 1972b, pp. 8–24.

Rogers, R. H. *Family Interaction and Transaction.* Englewood Cliffs, New Jersey: Prentice-Hall, 1973.

Roistacher, E. A. and Young, J. S. "Two-Earner Families in the Housing Market." *Policy Studies Journal* 8 (1979): 227–240.

Roleder, G. *Marriage Means Encounter.* Second Edition. Dubuque, Iowa: Wm. C. Brown, 1979.

Rollin, B. "The American Way of Marriage: Remarriage." In *Love, Marriage, Family.* Edited by M. E. Lasswell and T. E. Lasswell. Glenview, Illinois: Scott, Foresman, 1973, pp. 489–495.

Rollin, B. "Motherhood: Who Needs It" *Look* (September 22, 1970).

Rollin, S. A. and Dowd, E. T. "Conflict Resolution: A Model for Effective Marital and Family Relations." *The American Journal of Family Therapy* 7 (Spring 1979): 61–67.

Rollins, B. C., and Cannon, K. L. "Marital Satisfaction over the Family Life Cycle: A Reevaluation." *Journal of Marriage and the Family* 36 (May 1974): 271–282.

Rollins, B. C., and Feldman, H. "Marital Satisfaction over the Family Life Cycle." *Journal of Marriage and the Family* 32 (February 1970): 20–28.

Roper Organization. "Sex . . . Marriage . . . Divorce—What Women Think Today." *U.S. News and World Report* 77 (October 21, 1974): 107.

Rose, R. H.; Holaday, J. W.; and Bernstein, I. S. "Plasma Testosterone Dominance Rank and Aggressive Behaviour in Male Rhesus Monkeys." *Nature* 231 (1971): 366–368.

Rose, V. L., and Price-Bonham, S. "Divorce Adjustment: A Woman's Problem?" *The Family Coordinator* 22 (July 1973): 291–297.

Rose, W. M., and Burdette, W. J. "Some Sociological Aspects Inherent in Genetic Counseling." *Journal of Marriage and the Family* 28 (May 1966): 204–205.

Rosen, B. C. and Aneshensel, C. C. "Sex Differences in the Educational-Occupational Expectation Process." *Social Forces* 57 (September 1978): 164–186.

Rosen, L. "The Broken Home and Male Delinquency." In *Sociology of Crime and Delinquency.* Edited by M. Wolfgang, N. Johnson, and L. Savitz. New York: John Wiley, 1970, pp. 489–495.

Rosenbaum, V. "Friendship in Marriage." *Marriage and Family Living* 61 (September 1979): 6–7.

Rosenberg, M. *Society and the Adolescent Self-Image.* Princeton, New Jersey: Princeton University Press, 1965.

Rosenblatt, P. C. "Behavior in Public Places: Comparison of Couples Accompanied and Unaccompanied by Children." *Journal of Marriage and the Family* 36 (November 1974): 750–755.

Rosenblatt, P. C. et al. "Marital System Differences and Summer-Long Vacations: Togetherness-Apartness and Tension." *The American Journal of Family Therapy* 7 (Spring 1979): 77–84.

Rosenblatt, P. C., and Budd, L. G. "Territoriality and Privacy in Married and Unmarried Cohabiting Couples: An Exploratory Study." Unpublished manuscript. St. Paul, Minnesota: University of Minnesota. Department of Family Social Science, 1975.

Rosenfeld, A. "'The Arrangement' at College: Part II." In *Love, Marriage, Family.* Edited by M. E. Lasswell and T. E. Lasswell. Glenview, Illinois: Scott, Foresman, 1973, pp. 208–210.

Rosenthal, E. "Divorce and Religious Intermarriage: The Effect of Previous Marital Status upon Subsequent Marital Behavior." *Journal of Marriage and the Family* 32 (August 1970): 435–440.

Rossi, A. S. "Transition to Parenthood." *Journal of Marriage and the Family* 30 (February 1968): 26–39.

Rossi, A. S. "Why Seek Equality between the Sexes? An Immodest Proposal." In *Confronting the Issues: Sex Roles, Marriage, and the Family.* Edited by Kenneth C. W. Kammeyer. Boston: Allyn and Bacon, 1975, pp. 267–276.

Rubin, L. B. *Women of a Certain Age: The Midlife Search for Self.* New York: Harper & Row, 1979.

Rubin, Z. *Liking and Loving.* New York: Holt, Rinehart and Winston, 1973.

Rubin, Z. "Measurement of Romantic Love." *Journal of Personality and Social Psychology* 16 (1970): 265–273.

Rubin, Z. et al. "Self-Disclosure in Dating Couples: Sex Roles and the Ethic of Openness." *Journal of Marriage and the Family* 42 (May 1980): 305–317.

Rudikoff, S. "Communes and the Whole-Earth People." In *Marriage and Family in the Modern World: Readings.* Edited by R. S. Cavan. 4th ed. New York: Crowell, 1974, pp. 355–366.

Rushing, W. A. "Marital Status and Mental Disorder: Evidence in Favor of a Behavioral Model." *Social Forces* 58 (December 1979): 540–556.

Rusk, H. A.; Swinyard, C. A.; and Swift, M. R. "Solving the Mystery of Birth Defects." *Parents' Magazine* (November 1969): 61ff.

Russell, B. *Marriage and Morals.* New York: Bantam, 1961, pp. 106–113. Originally published in 1929 by Liveright Publishers of New York.

Russell, C. S. "Transition to Parenthood: Problems and Gratifications." *Journal of Marriage and the Family* 36 (May 1974): 294–302.

Rutter, M. *Maternal Deprivation Reassessed.* Baltimore: Penguin, 1972.

Ryan, W. *Blaming the Victim.* New York: Pantheon, 1971.

Rytina, J. H.; Form, W. H.; and Pease, J. "Income and Stratification Ideology: Beliefs about the American Opportunity Structure." *American Journal of Sociology* (1970): 703–716.

Safilios-Rothschild, C. "Answer to Stephen J. Bahr's 'Comment on the Study of Family Power Structure. A Review, 1960–1969.'" *Journal of Marriage and the Family* 34 (May 1972): 245–246.

Safilios-Rothschild, C. "Family Sociology or Wives' Family Sociology? A Cross-Cultural Examination of Decision-Making." *Journal of Marriage and the Family* 31 (May 1969): 290–301.

Safilios-Rothschild, C. "Patterns of Family Power and Influence." In *Dating and Marriage.* Edited by A. F. Kline and M. L. Medley. Boston: Holbrook, 1973, pp. 292–304.

Safilios-Rothschild, C. "The Influence of the Wife's Degree of Work Commitment upon Some Aspects of Family Organization and Dynamics." *Journal of Marriage and the Family* 32 (November 1970): 681–691.

Safilios-Rothschild, C. "The Study of Family Power

Structure: A Review of 1960–1969." *Journal of Marriage and the Family* 32 (November 1970): 539–552.

St. John-Parsons, D. "Continuous Dual-Career Families: A Case Study." *Psychology of Women* 3 (Fall 1978): 30–42.

Salamon, S. and Keim, A. M. "Land Ownership and Women's Power in a Midwestern Farming Community." *Journal of Marriage and the Family* 41 (February 1979): 109–119.

Salk, L. *Preparing for Parenthood.* New York: Bantam, 1974.

Santrock, J. W. Influence of Onset and Type of Paternal Absence on the First Four Eriksonian Developmental Crises." *Developmental Psychology* 3 (1970): 273–274.

Santrock, J. W. "Paternal Absence, Sex-Typing and Identification." *Developmental Psychology* 2 (1970): 264–272.

Santrock, J. W., and Wohlford, P. "Effects of Father Absence: Influences of Reason for, and Onset of, Absence." *Proceedings of the 78th Annual Convention of the American Psychological Assoiation* 5 (1970): 265–266.

Sarrel, P. M. "Teenage Pregnancy: Prevention and Treatment." Siecus Study Guide No. 14. New York: Sex Information and Education Council of the United States, January 1974.

Sarrel, P. M., and Davis, C. D. "The Young Unwed Primipara." *American Journal of Obstetrics and Gynecology* 95 (1966): 722.

Sarvis, B., and Rodman, H. *The Abortion Controversy.* New York: Columbia University Press, 1974.

Sass, T. "Demographic and Economic Characteristics of Nonbeneficiary Widows: An Overview" *Social Security Bulletin* 42 (November 1979): 3–14.

Satir, V. "Marriage as a Statutory Five Year Renewable Contract." Mimeographed. Paper presented at the American Psychological Association, 75th Annual Convention, Washington, D.C., September 1, 1967.

Saxton, L. *The Individual, Marriage, and the Family.* 3d ed. Belmont, California: Wadsworth, 1977.

Scanzoni, J. H. *The Black Family in Modern Society.* Boston: Allyn and Bacon, 1971.

Scanzoni, J. "Contemporary Marriage Types." *Journal of Family Issues* 1 (March 1980): 125–140.

Scanzoni, J. "A Social System Analysis of Dissolved and Existing Marriages." *Journal of Marriage and the Family* 30 (August 1968): 452–461.

Scanzoni, J. and Polonko, K. "A Conceptual Approach to Explicity Marital Negotiation." *Journal of Marriage and the Family* 42 (February 1980): 31–44.

Scarf, M. "The Promiscuous Woman." *Psychology Today* 14 (July 1980): 78ff.

Scarlett, J. A. "Undergraduate Attitudes towards Birth Control: New Perspectives." *Journal of Marriage and the Family* 34 (May 1972): 312–314.

Scarr, A., and Salapatik, P. "Patterns of Fear Development during Infancy." *Merrill-Palmer Quarterly* 16 (1970): 53–90.

Schachter, S. "The Interaction of Cognitive and Physiological Determinants of Emotional State." In *Advances in Experimental Social Psychology.* Vol. 1. Edited by L. Berkowitz. New York: Academic, 1964, pp. 49–80.

Schaffer, H. R., and Emerson, P. E. "The Development of Social Attachments in Infancy." *Monographs of The Society for Research in Child Development* 29 (1964): 3.

Schardt, A. "Saving Abortion." *Civil Liberties* 298 (September 1973): 1–2.

Scheff, E. and Koopman, E. J. "The Relationship of Women's Sex-Role Identity to Self-Esteem and Ego Development." *The Journal of Psychology* 98 (March 1978): 299–305.

Schlesinger, B. "The One-Parent Family, An Overview." In *Encounter: Love, Marriage, and Family,* edited by R. E. Albrecht and E. W. Bock. Boston: Holbrook, 1972, pp. 361–373.

Schlesinger, B. "The One-Parent Family in Canada: Some Recent Findings and Recommendations." *The Family Coordinator* 22 (July 1973): 305–309.

Schmitt, R. C. "Recent Trends in Hawaiian Interracial Marriage Rates by Occupation." *Journal of Marriage and the Family* 33 (May 1971): 373–374.

Schneider, D. M., and Smith, R. T. *Class Differences and Sex Roles in American Kinship and Family Structure.* Englewood Cliffs, New Jersey: Prentice-Hall, 1973.

Schram, R. W. "Marital Satisfaction over the Family Life Cycle: A Critique and Proposal." *Journal of Marriage and the Family* 41 (February 1979): 7–12.

Schulhofer, E. "Short Term Preparations of Children for Separation, Divorce, and Remarriage of Parents." *American Journal of Orthopsychiatry* 43 (1973): 248–249.

Schulman, M. L. "Idealization in Engaged Couples." *Journal of Marriage and the Family* 36 (February 1974): 139–147.

Schulz D. A. *The Changing Family.* Englewood Cliffs, New Jersey: Prentice-Hall, 1972.

Schulz, D. *Coming Up Black.* Englewood Cliffs, New Jersey: Prentice-Hall, 1969.

Schulz, D. A., and Wilson, R. A. *Readings on the Changing Family.* Englewood Cliffs, New Jersey Prentice-Hall, 1973.

Schwarz, J. C. "Infant Day Care: Behavioral Effects at Preschool Age." *Developmental Psychology* 10 (1974): 502–506.

Scott, J. F. "Sororities and the Husband Game." In *Modern Sociological Issues.* Edited by B. J. Wishart and L. C. Reichman. New York: Macmillan, 1979, pp. 274–283.

Scott, J. P. and Kivett, V. R. "The Widowed, Black, Older Adult in the Rural South: Implications for Policy." *Family Relations* 29 (January 1980): 83–90.

Scully, D., and Bart, P. "A Funny Thing Happened on the Way to the Orifice: Women in Gynecology Textbooks." In *Changing Women in a Changing Society.* Edited by J. Huber. Chicago: University of Chicago Press, 1973, pp. 283–288.

Seaman, B. *Free and Female.* New York: Coward, McCann and Geoghegan, 1972.

Seelbach, W. W. "Correlates of Aged Parents: Filial Responsibility Expectations and Realizations." *The Family Coordinator* 27 (October 1978): 341–350.

Segal, S., and Tietze, C. "Contraceptive Technology: Current and Prospective Methods." *Reports on Population/Family Planning.* No. 1. New York: The Population Council, July 1971, p. 2.

Semans, J. "Premature Ejaculation, A New Approach." *Southern Medical Journal* 49 (April 1956): 353–358.

Sena-Rivera, J. "Extended Kinship in the United States: Competing Models and the Case of La-Familia Chicana." *Journal of Marriage and the Family* 41 (February 1979): 121–129.

Sennett, R. "The Brutality of Modern Families." In *Marriage and Families,* Edited by H. Z. Lopata. New York: D. Van Nostrand Reinhold, 1973, pp. 81–90.

Shader, R. I., and Othey, J. I. "Premenstrual Tension, Femininity and Sexual Drive." *Medical Aspects of Human Sexuality* (April 1970): 42–49.

Shanas, E. "Family Help Patterns and Social Class in Three Countries." *Journal of Marriage and the Family* 29 (May 1967); 257–266.

Shanas, E., et al. "The Psychology of Health." In *Middle Age and Aging.* Edited by B. L. Neugarten. Chicago: University of Chicago Press, 1968, pp. 212–219.

Shaver, P. and Freedman, J. "Your Pursuit of Happiness." *Psychology Today* (August 1976): 26ff.

Shearman, R. P. *Induction of Ovulation.* Springfield, Illinois: Charles C. Thomas, 1969.

Sheresky, N., and Mannes, M. "A Radical Guide to Wedlock." In *Love, Marriage, Family.* Edited by M. E. Lasswell and T. E. Lasswell. Glenview, Illinois: Scott, Foresman, 1973, pp. 424–432.

Sherfey, M. J. *The Nature and Evolution of Female Sexuality.* New York: Vintage Books, 1973.

Sherman, J. A. *On The Psychology of Women.* Springfield, Illinois: Charles C. Thomas, 1971.

Shey, T. H. "Why Communes Fail: A Comparative Analysis of the Viability of Danish and American Communes." *Journal of Marriage and the Family* 39 (August 1977): 605–613.

Shideler, M. M. "An Amicable Divorce." *Christian Century* (May 5, 1971).

Shope, D. F. "The Orgastic Responsiveness of Selected College Females." *Journal of Sex Research* 4 (1968): 206–219.

Shortell, J. R., and and Biller, H. B. "Aggression in Children as a Function of Sex of Subject and Sex of Opponent." *Developmental Psychology* 3 (1970): 143–144.

Shulman, A. "A Marriage Agreement." *Out From Under* 1 (August/September 1970): 2, 5–8.

Shuttlesworth, G., and Thorman, G. "Living Together Unmarried Relationships." Unpublished manuscript. Austin, Texas: University of Texas, 1975.

Sigusch, V., et al. "Psychosexual Stimulation: Sex Differences." *Journal of Sex Research* 6 (February 1970): 10–24.

Silverman, A., and Silverman. A. *The Case against Having Children.* New York: David McKay, 1971.

Simmons, J. L., and Winograd, B. "Sex and the 'Hang-Loose' Ethic." *American Marriage: A Changing Scene.* Edited by F. D. Cox. Dubuque, Iowa: Wm. C. Brown, 1972, pp. 194–204.

Simon, W., and Gagnon, J. H. "Psychosexual Development." In *The Sexual Scene.* Edited by W. Simon and J. H. Gagnon. New Brunswick, New Jersey: Transaction, 1970, pp. 23–41.

Sindberg, R. M.; Roberts, A. F.; and McClain, D. "Mate Selection Factors in Computer Matched Marriages." *Journal of Marriage and the Family* 34 (November 1972): 611–614.

Singh, B. K. "Trends in Attitudes toward Premarital Sexual Relations." *Journal of Marriage and the Family* 42 (May 1980): 387–393.

Sjovall, E. "Coitus Interruptus." In *Manual of Family Planning and Contraceptive Practice*. Edited by M. S. Calderone. 2d ed. Baltimore: Williams and Wilkins, 1970, pp. 433–437.

Skard, A. G. "Maternal Deprivation: The Research and Its Implications." *Journal of Marriage and the Family* 27 (August 1965): 333–343.

Skinner, D. A. "Dual-Career Family Stress and Coping: A Literature Review." *Family Relations* 29 (October 1980): 473–481.

Skolnick, A. *The Intimate Environment*. Boston: Little, Brown, 1973.

Slater, P. E., "Must Marriage Cheat Today's Young Women?" In *Choice and Challenge*. Edited by C. E. Williams and J. F. Crosby. Dubuque, Iowa: Wm. C. Brown, 1974, pp. 112–120.

Slater, P. E. *The Pursuit of Loneliness: American Culture at the Breaking Point*. Boston: Beacon, 1970.

Smart, M. S., and Smart, R. C. *Children: Development and Relationships*. 2d ed. New York: Macmillan, 1972.

Smart, R. G., and Bateman, K. "The Chromosomal and Teratogenic Effects of Lysergic Acid Dimethylamide." *Canadian Medical Association Journal* 99 (1968): 805.

Smith, D. E., and Luce. J. *Love Needs Care: A History of San Francisco's Haight-Asbury Free Medical Clinic and Its Pioneer Role in Treating Drug Abuse Problems*. Boston: Little, Brown, 1971.

Smith, E. D.; Veolitze, M.; and Merkatz, R. "Social Aspects of Abortion Counseling for Patients Undergoing Elective Abortion." *Clinical Obstetrics and Gynecology* 14 (1971): 1.

Smith, E. M. "Counseling for Women Who Seek Abortion." *Social Work* 17 (1972): 2.

Smith, J. R.; and Smith, L. G. "Co-Marital Sex and the Sexual Freedom Movement." *Journal of Sex Research* 6 (1970): 131–142.

Smith, L. G., and Smith, J. R. "Co-Marital Sex: The Incorporation of Extramarital Sex into the Marriage Relationship." In *Critical Issues in Contemporary Sexual Behavior*. Edited by J. Money and J. Zuben. Baltimore: Johns Hopkins. 1973.

Smith, M. D. and Self, G. D. "The Congruence Between Mother's and Daughter's Sex-Role Attitudes: A Research Note." *Journal of Marriage and the Family* 42 (February 1980): 105–109.

Smith, R. A., and Symmonds, R. E. "Vaginal Salpingectomy (Fimbrectomy) for Sterilization." *Obstetrics and Gynecology* 38 (September 1971): 400–402.

Smith, R. H.; Downer, D. B.; and Lynch, M. T. "The Man in the House." *The Family Coordinator* 18 (April 1969): 107–111.

Smith, T. "Foundations of Parental Influence upon Adolescents: An Application of Social Power Theory." *American Sociological Review* 35 (October 1970): 860–873.

Smithells, R. W. "The Prevention and Prediction of Congenital Abnormalities." In *Scientific Basis of Obstetrics and Gynecology*. Edited by R. R. MacDonald. London: J. and A. Churchill, 1971, Chapter 10.

Snow, J. H. *On Pilgrimage: Marriage in the '70s*. New York: Seabury, 1971.

Snyder, D. K. "Multidimensional Assessment of Marital Satisfaction." *Journal of Marriage and the Family* 41 (November 1979): 813–823.

Soely, Sally, ed. *Women's Liberation and the Church*. New York: Association Press, 1970.

Soltz, D. F. "On Sex and the Psychology of 'Playing Dumb': A Reevaluation." *Psychological Reports* 43 (August 1978): 111–114.

Somerville, R. M. "The Future of Family Relationships in the Middle and Older Years: Clues in Fiction." *The Family Coordinator* 21 (October 1972): 487–498.

Sorensen, R. C. *Adolescent Sexuality in Contemporary America: Personal Values and Sexual Behavior, Ages 13–19*. New York: World, 1973.

Spanier, G. B. "Romanticism and Marital Adjustment." *Journal of Marriage and the Family* 34 (August 1972): 481–487.

Spanier, G. B. "Sexualization and Premarital Sexual Behavior." *The Family Coordinator* 24 (January 1975): 33–41.

Spanier, G. B.; and Cole, C. L. "Mate Swapping: Participation, Knowledge and Values in a Midwestern Community." Paper presented at the annual meeting of the Midwest Sociological Society, 1972.

Spanier, G. B. and Glick, P. C. "The Life Cycle of American Families: An Expanded Analysis."

Journal of Family History 8 (Spring 1980): 97–111.

Spanier, G. B.; Lewis, R. A.; and Cole, C. L. "Marital Adjustment over the Family Life Cycle: The Issue of Curvilinearity." *Journal of Marriage and the Family* 37 (May 1975): 263–275.

Spanier, G. B. and Sauer, W. "An Empirical Evaluation of the Family Life Cycle." *Journal of Marriage and the Family* 41 (February 1979): 27–38.

Speidel, J. J., and Ravenholt, R. T. "Present Status of Prostaglandins." *IPPF Medical Bulletin* 5 (August 1971): 3–4.

Spence, J. T. and Helmreich, R. L. *Masculinity and Feminity: Their Psychological Dimensions, Correlates, and Antecedents.* Austin: Univ. of Texas Press, 1978.

Spicer, J. W., and Hampe, G. D. "Kinship Interaction After Divorce." *Journal of Marriage and the Family* 37 (February 1975): 113–119.

Spock, B. "Pleasure in Parenthood." In *Confronting the Issues: Sex Roles, Marriage, and the Family.* Edited by C. W. Kammeyer. Boston: Allyn and Bacon, 1975, pp. 195–199.

"Spread in Borrowing Costs." *U.S. News and World Report* (March 15, 1976).

Sprey, J. "On the Management of Conflict in Families." *Journal of Marriage and the Family* 33 (November 1971): 722–731.

Spuhler, J. N. "Assortative Mating with Respect to Physical Characteristics." *Eugenic Quarterly* 15 (1968): 128–140.

Stafford, R., Backman, E. and Dibona, P. "The Division of Labor among Cohabiting and Married Couples." *Journal of Marriage and the Family* 39 (February 1977): 43–57.

Stannard, U. "The Male Maternal Instinct." In *Marriages and Families.* Edited by H. Z. Lopata. New York: Van Nostrand Reinhold, 1973, pp. 183–193.

Staples, R., ed. *The Black Family: Essays and Studies.* Belmont, California: Wadsworth, 1971.

Staples, R. *The Black Woman in America.* Chicago: Nelson-Hall, 1973.

Staples, R. "The Myth of the Black Matriarchy." *The Black Scholar* 1 (January–February 1970): 8–16.

Staples, R. "Race, Liberalism—Conservatism and Premarital Sexual Permissiveness: A Bi-Racial Comparison." *Journal of Marriage and the Family* 40 (November 1978): 733–742.

Staples, R. "Towards a Sociology of the Black Family: A Theoretical and Methodological Assess-

ment." *Journal of Marriage and the Family* 33 (February 1971): 119–138.

Stehouwer, J. "The Household and Family Relations of Old People." In *Old People in Three Industrial Societies.* Edited by E. Shanas et al. New York: Atherton, 1968, pp. 177–226.

Stein, J., ed. *The Random House Dictionary of the English Language.* Unabridged. New York: Random House, 1973.

Stein, R. L. "The Economic Status of Families Headed by Women." *Monthly Labor Review* 93 (December 1970).

Steinem, G. "What It Would Be Like If Women Win." In *American Marriage: A Changing Scene.* Edited by F. D. Cox. Dubuque, Iowa: William C. Brown, 1972, pp. 214–219.

Steiner, G. Y. "Day Care Centers: Hype or Hope?" In *Marriages and Families.* Edited by H. Z. Lopata, New York: D. Van Nostrand, 1973, pp. 316–324.

Steinhoff, P. G. "Background Characteristics of Abortion Patients." In *The Abortion Experience, Psychological and Medical Impact.* Edited by H. J. Osofsky and J. D. Osofsky. New York: Harper, 1973, pp. 206–231.

Steinhoff, P. G.; Smith, R. G.; and Diamond, M. "The Characteristics and Motivations of Women Receiving Abortions." *Sociological Symposium* 8 (Spring 1972): 83–90.

Steinmann, A., and Jurich, A. P. "The Effects of a Sex Education Course on the Sex Role Perceptions of Junior High School Students." *The Family Coordinator* 24 (January 1975): 27–31.

Steinmetz, S. K. "Violence Between Family Members." *Marriage and Family Review* 1 (May/June 1978): 1–16.

Steinmetz, S. K., and Straus. M. A. "The Family as a Cradle of Violence." *Society* 10 (September–October 1973): 50.

Steinmetz, S. K., and Straus, M. A. *Violence in the Family.* New York: Dodd, Mead, 1974.

Stekel, W. *Bisexual Love: The Homosexual Neurosis.* English translation by J. S. Van Teslaar, Boston, 1922.

Stewart, P. L. "Female Promiscuity: A Factor in Providing Abortion Service." Paper presented to the annual meeting of the American Sociological Association, August 1971.

Storm, V. "Contemporary Cohabitation and the Dating-Marital Continuum." Unpublished Master's Thesis. Athens, Georgia: University of Georgia, June 1973.

Straus, M. A. "Leveling, Civility, and Violence in the Family." *Journal of Marriage and the Family* 36 (February 1974): 13–29.

Straus, M. A. "Measuring Intrafamily Conflict and Violence: The Conflict Tactics (CT) Scales." *Journal of Marriage and the Family* 41 (February 1979): 75–88.

Straus, M. A. "Social Class and Farm-City Differences in Interaction with Kin in Relation to Societal Modernization." *Rural Sociology* 34 (December 1969): 476–495.

Strean, H. S. *The Extramarital Affair.* New York: The Free Press, 1980.

Streib, G. F. *The Changing Family: Adaptation and Diversity.* Reading, Massachusetts: Addison-Wesley, 1973.

Strong, E.; Wallace, W.; and Wilson, W. "Three-Filter Data Selection by Computer." *The Family Coordinator* 18 (April 1969): 166–171.

Strong, L. D. "Alternative Marital and Family Forms: Their Relative Attractiveness to College Students and Correlates of Willingness to Participate in Nontraditional Forms." *Journal of Marriage and the Family* 40 (August 1978): 493–502.

Stuart, R. B. "Behavioral Remedies for Marital Ills: A Guide to the Use of Operant-Interpersonal Techniques." In *International Symposium on Behavior Modification.* Edited by T. Thompson and W. Dorkin. New York: Appleton-Century-Crofts, 1973.

Suelzle, M. "Women in Labor." in *Marriages and Familes.* Edited by H. Z. Lopata. New York: D. Van Nostrand, 1973, pp. 325–334.

Sussman, M. B. "Family Systems in the 1970's: Analysis, Policies, and Programs." *Annals* 396 (July 1971): 40–56.

Sussman, M. B. "Personal Contracts Study: General and Specific Research Issues and Questions." Cleveland, Ohio: Case Western University, Institute on Family and Bureaucratic Study, April 1974a. Mimeographed.

Sussman, M. B. "Personal Marriage Contracts: Old Wine in New Bottles." Cleveland, Ohio: Case Western University, Institute on Family and Bureaucratic Society, March 1974b. Mimeographed.

Suter, L. E., and Miller, H. P. "Income Differences between Men and Career Women." In *Changing Women in a Changing Society.* Edited by J. Huber. Chicago: University of Chicago Press, 1973, pp. 200–212.

Swartz, D. P. "The Harlem Hospital Center Experience." In *The Abortion Experience, Psychological and Medical Impact.* Edited by H. J. Osofsky and J. D. Osofsky, New York: Harper, 1973, pp. 94–121.

Swensen, C. H. "The Behavior of Love." In *Love Today: A New Exploration.* Edited by H. A. Otto. New York: Association Press, 1972, pp. 86–101.

Tallman, I. "The Family as a Small Problem Solving Group." *Journal of Marraige and the Family* 38 (February 1970): 94–104.

Tamashiro, R. T. "Developmental Stages in the Conceptualization of Marriage." *The Family Coordinator* 27 (July 1978): 237–244.

Targ, D. B. "Toward a Reassessment of Women's Experience at Middle Age." *The Family Coordinator* 28 (July 1979): 377–382.

Tarr, L. H. "Developmental Sex-Role Theory and Sex-Role Attitudes in Late Adolescents." *Psychological Reports* 42 (June 1978): 807–814.

Tatum, H. J. "Intrauterine Contraception." *American Journal of Obstetrics and Gynecology* 112 (April 1972): 1000–1023.

Tavris, C., and Toby, J. "What 120,000 Young Women Can Tell You about Sex, Motherhood, Menstruation, Housework—and Men." *Redbook* 140 (1973): 3, 67–69, 127–129.

Taylor, D. A. "Some Aspects of the Development of Interpersonal Relationships: Social Penetration Process." *Journal of Social Psychology* 75 (1968): 79–90.

Teevan, J. J., Jr. "Reference Groups and Premarital Sexual Behavior." *Journal of Marriage and the Family* 34 (May 1972): 283–291.

TenHouten, W. D. "The Black Family: Myth and Reality." *Psychiatry* 33 (1970): 145–173.

Thal, H. M. and Holcombe, M. *Your Family and Its Money.* Rev. ed. Boston: Houghton Mifflin, 1973.

Thomas, L. E.; McCabe, E.; and Berry, J. E. "Unemployment and Family Stress: A Reassessment." *Family Relations* 29 (October 1980): 517–524.

Thompson, K. S. "A Comparison of Black and White Adolescents' Beliefs about Having Children." *Journal of Marriage and the Family* 42 (February 1980): 133–139.

Thompson, L. and Spanier, G. B. "Influence of Parents, Peers, and Partners on the Contraceptive

Use of College Men and Women." *Journal of Marriage and the Family* 40 (August 1978): 481–492.

Tickamyer, B. R. "Women's Roles and Family Intentions." *Pacific Sociological Review* 22 (April 1979): 167–184.

Tietze, C. "The Condom." In *Manual of Family Planning and Contraceptive Practice.* Edited by M. S. Calderone. 2d. ed. Baltimore: Williams and Wilkins, 1970, pp. 424–428.

Tindall, V. R. "Aetiology and Pathology of Pulmonary Embolism." In *Scientific Basis of Obstetrics and Gynaecology.* Edited by R. R. MacDonald. London: J. and A. Churchill, 1971.

Tissue, T. "Low-Income Widows and Other Aged Singles." *Social Security Bulletin* 42 (December 1979): 3–10.

Tognoli, J. "Male Friendships and Intimacy Across the Life Span." *Family Relations* 29 (July 1980): 273–279.

Tomeh, A. K. "Sex-Role Orientation: An Analysis of Structural and Attitudinal Predictors." *Journal of Marriage and the Family* 40 (May 1978): 341–354.

Torres, A. "Does Your Mother Know . . . ?" *Family Planning Perspectives* 10 (September/October 1978): 280–282.

Trainer, J. B. *Physiologic Foundations for Marriage Counseling.* St. Louis: Mosby, 1965.

Troiden, R. R. "Becoming Homosexual: A Model of Gay Identity Acquisition." *Psychiatry* 42 (November 1979): 362–373.

Tropman, J. E. "Social Mobility and Marital Stability." *Applied Social Studies* 3 (1971): 165–173.

Trost, J. "Married and Unmarried Cohabitation: The Case of Sweden with Some Comparisons." Paper presented at the Eighth World Congress of Sociology, Committee on Family Research, Toronto, Canada, August 18–24, 1974.

Trost, J. "Married and Unmarried Cohabitation in Sweden." Unpublished manuscript. Uppsala University, 1975b.

Trost, J. "Married and Unmarried Cohabiting Couples: Attitudes on their Degree of Integration." Unpublished Manuscript. Sweden: Uppsala University, 1975a.

Trost, J. "A Renewed Social Institution: Non-Marital Cohabitation." *Acta Sociologica* 21 (1978): 303–315.

Trost, J. "Various Forms of Cohabitation and Their Relation to Psychical and Social Criteria of Ad-

aptation." Unpublished manuscript. Sweden: Uppsala University, 1975c.

Turk, J. L., and Bell, N. W. "Measuring Power in Families." *Journal of Marriage and the Family* 34 (May 1972): 215–222.

Turner, R. H. *Family Interaction.* New York: John Wiley, 1970.

Udry, J. A. "Sex and Family Life." *Medical Aspects of Human Sexuality* (November 1968): 66–82.

Udry, J. R. *The Social Context of Marriage.* 3d ed. New York: J. B. Lippincott, 1974.

Uhlenberg, P. "Cohort Variations in Family Life Cycle Experiences of U.S. Females." *Journal of Marraige and the Family* 36 (May 1974): 284–292.

U.S. Consumer. Washington, D.C.: Consumer News. Inc., 601 National Press Building, 20004.

U.S. Department of Commerce. Bureau of the Census. "American Families and Living Arrangements." *Current Population Reports.* Series P-23, no. 104, May 1980.

U.S. Department of Commerce. Bureau of the Census. *Current Population Reports,* Series P-20, no. 212, February 1, 1971.

U.S. Department of Commerce. Bureau of the Census. *Current Population Reports.* Series P-20, no. 223, October 7, 1971.

U.S. Department of Commerce. Bureau of the Census. *Current Population Reports.* Series P-20, no. 257, November 1973.

U.S. Department of Commerce. Bureau of the Census. *Current Population Reports.* Series P-23, no. 32, July 1970.

U.S. Department of Commerce, Bureau of the Census "Divorce, Child Custody, and Child Support." *Current Population Reports.* Series P-23, no. 84, June 1979.

U.S. Department of Commerce. Bureau of the Census. "Household and Family Characteristics: March 1979." *Current Population Reports.* Series P-20, no. 352, July 1980.

U.S. Department of Commerce. Bureau of the Census. "Illustrative Projections of Money Income Size Distribution, for Households: 1980–1995." *Current Population Reports.* Series P-60, no. 122, March 1980.

U.S. Department of Commerce. Bureau of the Census. "Living Arrangements of College Students: October 1976." *Current Population Reports.* Series P-20, no. 248, November 1979.

U.S. Department of Commerce. Bureau of the Census. "Marital Status and Living Arrangements: March 1975." *Population Characteristics*. Series P-20, no 287. Washington, D.C.: U.S. Government Printing Office, 1975a.

U.S. Department of Commerce. Bureau of the Census. "Marital Status and Living Arrangements: March 1979." *Current Population Reports*. Series P-20, no. 249, February 1980a.

U.S. Department of Commerce. Bureau of the Census. "Marriage, Divorce, Widowhood and Remarriage by Family Characteristics: June 1975." *Current Population Reports*. Series P-20, no. 312, 1977.

U.S. Department of Commerce. Bureau of the Census. *1970 Census of Population, Marital Status*. Final Report PC (2)-4C, 1972, Table 12, p. 262.

U.S. Department of Commerce. Bureau of the Census. "Number, Timing, and Duration of Marriages and Divorces in the United States: June 1975." *Current Population Reports*. Series P-20, no. 297, 1976.

U.S. Department of Commerce. Bureau of the Census. "Perspectives on American Fertility." *Current Population Reports*. Series P-23, no. 70, July 1978a.

U.S. Department of Commerce. Bureau of the Census. "Population Profile of the United States: 1978." *Population Characteristics*. Series P-20, no. 336, April 1979.

U.S. Department of Commerce. Bureau of the Census. "School Enrollment—Social and Economic Characteristics of Students: October 1978." *Current Population Reports*. Series P-20, no. 346, October 1979.

U.S. Department of Commerce. Bureau of the Census. "Social and Economic Characteristics of the Older Population: 1978." *Current Population Reports*. Series P-23, no. 85, 1978b.

U.S. Department of Commerce. Bureau of the Census. *Statistical Abstract of the United States: 1979*. Washington, D.C.: U.S. Government Printing Office, 1979.

U.S. Department of Commerce. Bureau of the Census. *Statistical Abstract of the United States, 1980*. Washington, D.C.: U.S. Government Printing Office, 1980.

U.S. Department of Commerce. Bureau of the Census. "A Statistical Portrait of Women in the United States: 1978." *Current Population Reports*. Series P-23, no. 100, February 1980b.

U.S. Department of Health, Education and Welfare. *The Effect of Changes in State Abortion Laws*. Washington, D.C.: U.S. Government Printing Office, 1971a.

U.S. Department of Health, Education and Welfare. Bureau of Community Health Services. *Family Planning Digest* 1 (May 1972): 6.

U.S. Department of Health, Education and Welfare. Bureau of Community Health Services. *Family Planning Digest* 3 (March 1974a): 15.

U.S. Department of Health, Education and Welfare. *Fourth Annual Report on Marijuana, 1974*. Washington, D.C.: U.S. Government Printing Office, 1974b.

U.S. Department of Health, Education and Welfare. "Natality Statistics, Analysis United States, 1965–1967." Public Health Service Publication No. 1000, Series 21, No. 19, 1970. p. 26.

U.S. Department of Health, Education and Welfare. *Public Assistance Statistics, January 1973*. Number SRS 73-03100, NCSS Report A-2. Washington, D.C.: U.S. Government Printing Office. 1973a.

U.S. Department of Health, Education, and Welfare. *Remarriages: United States*. Publication no. (HRA) 74–1903. Washington, D.C.: U.S. Government Printing Office, 1973b.

U.S. Department of Health, Education and Welfare. "Smoking and Pregnancy." In *The Health Consequences of Smoking: A Report of the Surgeon General*. Washington, D.C.: U.S. Government Printing Office, 1971b.

U.S. Department of Health and Human Services, National Center for Health Statistics. "Births, Marriages, Divorces, and Deaths for May 1980." *Monthly Vital Statistics Report*. DHHS Publication no. (PHS) 80-1120, Vol. 29, no. 5, August 7, 1980.

U.S. Department of Health and Human Services, National Center for Health Statistics. "Final Divorce Statistics, 1978." *Monthly Vital Statistics Report*. DHHS Publication no. (PHS) 80-1120, Vol. 29, no. 4, July 31, 1980.

U.S. Women's Bureau. U.S. Department of Labor. *Day Care Facts*. Pamphlet 161. Rev. Washington, D.C.: U.S. Government Printing Office, 1973.

U'Ren, M. B. "The Image of Woman in Textbooks." In *Women in Sexist Society*, Edited by V. Gornick and B. K. Moran. New York: Basic, 1971, pp. 218–225.

Uzoka, A. F. "The Myth of the Nuclear Family: Historical Background and Clinical Implications." *American Psychologist* 34 (November 1979): 1095–1106.

Valeris, S. "Cognitive Effects of False Heart-rate Feedback." *Journal of Personality and Social Psychology* 4 (1966): 400–408.

Vanfossen, B. E. "Sexual Stratification and Sex-Role Socialization." *Journal of Marriage and the Family* 39 (August 1977): 563–574.

Varni, C. "Contexts of Conversion: The Case of Swinging." In *Renovating Marriage.* Edited by R. W. Libby and R. N. Whitehurst. Danville, California: Consensus, 1973, pp. 166–181.

Vatsyayana. *The Kama Sutra.* New York: Dutton, 1962.

Veevers, J. E. "The Life Style of Voluntarily Childless Couples." In *The Canadian Family in Comparative Perspective.* Edited by L. Larson. Toronto: Prentice-Hall, 1974a.

Veevers, J. E. "Voluntary Childlessness and Social Policy: An Alternative View." *The Family Coordinator* 23 (October 1974b) 397–406.

Veevers, J. E. "Voluntary Childlessness: A Neglected Area of Family Study." *The Family Coordinator* 22 (April 1973a) 199–205.

Veevers, J. E. "Voluntary Childless Wives." *Sociology and Social Research* 57 (1973b): 356–366.

Vener, A. M., and Stewart, C. S. "Adolescent Sexual Behavior in Middle America Revisited: 1970–1973." *Journal of Marriage and the Family* 36 (November 1974): 728–735.

Verna, M. E. "The Female Image in Children's TV Commercials." *Journal of Broadcasting* 19 (Summer 1975): 301–309.

Verwoerdt, A., et al. "Sexual Behavior in Senescence." *Geriatrics* (February 1969).

Vessey, M. P.; Doll, R.; ad Sutton, P. M. "Oral Contraceptives and Breast Neoplasia: A Retrospective Study." *British Medical Journal* 3 (September 1972): 719–724.

Veysey, L. *The Communal Experience: Anarchist and Mystical Counter-Cultures in America.* New York: Harper, 1973.

Vilar, Esther. *The Manipulated Man.* New York: Farrar, Straus and Giroux, 1972.

Vincent, C. E. "Sex and the Young Married." *Medical Aspects of Human Sexuality* (March 1969): 13–23.

Vincent, C. "When Married Love is Disappointing." In *Choice and Challenge.* Edited by C. E. Williams and J. F. Crosby. Dubuque, Iowa: Wm. C. Brown, 1974, pp. 47–63.

Vincent, C. E. ; Haney, C. A.: and Cochrane, C. M. "Familial and Generational Patterns of Illegitimacy." *Journal of Marriage and the Family* 31 (November 1969): 659–667.

Viorst, J. "Just Because I'm Married, Does it Mean I'm Going Steady?" In *Modern Sociological Issues.* Edited by B. J. Wishart and L. C. Reichman. New York: Macmillan, 1979, pp. 283–289.

Vitousek, B. M. "Mixed Marriages are a Mixed Bag." *Family Advocate* 1 (Winter 1979): 16–19, 37, 38.

Voeller, B. and Walters, J. "Gay Fathers." *The Family Coordinator* 27 (April 1978): 149–157.

Voydanoff, P. "Work Roles as Stressors in Corporate Families." *Family Relations* 29 (October 1980): 489–494.

Vreeland, R. S. "Is It True What They Say about Harvard Boys?" *Psychology Today* 5 (January 1972): 65–68.

Wachowiak, D. and Bragg, H. "Open Marriage and Marital Adjustment." *Journal of Marriage and the Family* 42 (February 1980): 57–62.

Waister, E. "Passionate Love." In *Theories of Attraction and Love.* Edited by B. I. Murstein. New York: Springer, 1971, pp. 85–97.

Waister, E., et al. "Importance of Physical Attractiveness in Dating Behavior." *Journal of Personality and Social Psychology* 4 (November 1966): 508–516.

Waite, L. J. and Moore, K. A. "The Impact of an Early First Birth on Young Women's Educational Attainment." *Social Forces* 56 (March 1978): 845–865.

Walker, C. "Some Variations in Marital Satisfaction." In *Equalities and Inequalities in Family Life.* Edited by R. Chester and J. Peel. New York: Academic Press, 1977, pp. 127–139.

Wallston, B. S., Foster, M. A., and Berger, M. "I Will Follow Him: Myth, Reality, or Forced Choice—Job-Seeking Experiences of Dual-Career Couples." *Psychology of Women Quarterly* 3 (Fall 1978): 9–21.

Walster, E., Walster, G. W., and Traupmann, J. "Equity and Premarital Sex." *Journal of Personality and Social Psychology* 36 (January 1978): 82–92.

Walters, J., and Stinnett, N. "Parent-Child Relationships: A Decade Review of Research." *Journal of Marriage and the Family* 33 (1971): 81–82.

Walters, J. and Walters, L. H. "Trends Affecting Adolescent Views of Sexuality, Employment, Marriage, and Child Rearing." *Family Relations* 29 (April 1980): 191–198.

Wampler, K. S. and Sprenkls, D. H. "The Minnesota Couple Communication Program: A Follow-Up Study." *Journal of Marriage and the Family* 42 (August 1980): 577–584.

Ward, T. J. "Cohabitation and Drift: A Conceptual Model." Unpublished paper presented at the Midwest Sociological Society, Chicago, April 1975.

Warner, J. "A House Divided: Arriving at a Property Settlement." *Marriage and Divroce* (March/April 1974): 86–91.

Watley, D. J. "Black and Nonblack Youth: Does Marriage Hinder College Attendance?" *NMSC Research Reports*. Vol 7, no. 5. Evanston, Illinois: National Merit Scholarship Corporation, 1971.

Watley, D. J., and Kaplan, R. "Career or Marriage? Aspirations and Achievements of Able Young Women." *Journal of Vocational Behavior* 1 (January 1971): 29–43.

Wegner, E. L., and Sewell, W. H. "Selection and Context as Factors Affecting the Probability of Graduation from College." *American Journal of Sociology* 75 (January 1970): 665–679.

Weichmann, G. H., and Ellis, A. L. "A Study of the Effect of 'Sex Education' on Premarital Petting and Coital Behavior." *The Family Coordinator* 18 (July 1969): 231–234.

Weil, A. *The Natural Mind: A New Way of Looking at Drugs and the Higher Consciousness.* Boston: Houghton Mifflin, 1972.

Weil, M. W. *Marriage, the Family, and Society.* Danville, Illinois: Interstate, 1971.

Weinberg, J. "Sexuality in Later Life." *Medical Aspects of Human Sexuality* (April 1971): 216–227.

Weinberg, M. S., and Bell, A. P. *Homosexuality: An Annotated Bibliography.* New York: Harper, 1972.

Weinberg, M. S, and Williams, C. J. *Male Homosexuals.* New York: Oxford University Press, 1974.

Weisman, M., and Psykel, E. "Moving and Depression in Women." *Society* 9 (July–August 1972): 24–28.

Weisner, T. S. and Martin, J. C. "Learning Environments for Infants: Communes and Conventionally Married Families in California." *Alternative Lifestyles* 2 (May 1979): 201–242.

Weiss, H. D. "Mechanism of Erection." *Medical Aspects of Human Sexuality* (February 1973).

Weiss, R. L.; Birchler, G. R.; and Vincent, J. P. "Contractual Models for Negotiation Training in Marital Dyads." *Journal of Marriage and the Family* 36 (May 1974): 321–330.

Weiss, R. L.; Hops, H.; and Patterson, G. R. "A Framework for Conceptualizing Marital Conflict, a Technology for Altering It, Some Data for Evaluating It." In *Critical Issues in Research and Practice: Proceedings of the Fourth Banff International Conference on Behavior Modification.* Edited by F. W. Clark and L. A. Hamerlynck. Champaign, Illinois: Research Press, 1973.

Weitzman, L. J. et al. "Contracts for Intimate Relationships: A Study of Contracts Before, Within and in Lieu of Legal Marriage." *Alternative Lifesytles* 1 (August 1978): 303–378.

Weitzman, L. J.; Kay, H. H.; and Dixon, R. B. "No-Fault Divorce in California: The View of the Legal Community." Paper presented at the annual meeting of the American Sociological Association in Montreal, Canada, August 25–29, 1974.

Wells, J. G. *Current Issues in Marriage and the Family.* New York: Macmillan, 1975.

Wells, T., and Christie, L. S. "Living Together: An Alternative to Marriage." *Futurist* 4 (April 1970): 50–51.

West, P., and Merriam, L. C., Jr. "Outdoor Recreation and Family Cohesiveness: A Research Appraoch." *Journal of Lesiure Research* 2 (1970): 251–259.

Westhues, K. "Hippiedom 1970: Some Tentative Hypotheses." *The Sociological Quarterly* 13 (1972): 81–89.

Westman, J. C., and Cline, D. W. "Divorce Is a Family Affair." In *Love, Marriage, Family.* Edited by M. E. Lasswell and T. E. Lasswell. Glenview, Illinois: Scott, Foresman. 1973, pp. 465–470.

Westoff, C. F."The Modernization of U.S. Contraceptive Practice." *Family Planning Perspectives* 4 (July 1972): 9–13.

Westoff, C. F.; Bumpass, L.; and Ryder, N. B. "The Pill and Coital Frequency." *Medical Aspects of Human Sexuality* (March 1971): 72–79.

Westoff, L. A. "Kids with Kids." *New York Times Magazine* (February 22, 1976): 24.

Westoff, L. A., and Westoff, C. F. *From New To Zero.* Boston: Little, Brown, 1971.

White, M., and Wells, C. "Student Attitudes toward Alternate Marriage Forms." In *Renovating Marriage.* Edited by R. W. Libby and R. N. Whitehurst. Danville, California: Consensus, 1973, pp. 280–295.

White, M. S. "Psychological and Social Barriers to Women in Science." *Science* 170 (October 23, 1970): 143.

Whitehurst. R. N. "Extramarital Sex: Alienation or Extension or Normal Behavior." In *Sex and Society.* Edited by J. N. Edwards. Chicago: Rand McNally, 1972a, pp. 236–248.

Whitehurst, R. N. "Living Together Unmarried: Some Trends and Speculations." Unpublished manuscript. Windsor, Ontario: University of Windsor, 1974a.

Whitehurst, R. N. "Sex-Role Equality and Changing Meanings in Cohabitation." Unpublished manuscript. Windsor, Ontario: University of Windsor, 1974b.

Whitehurst, R. N. "Some Comparisons of Conventional and Counterculture Families." *The Family Coordinator* 21 (October 1972b): 395–401.

Whitehurst, R. N. "Youth Views Marriage: Some Comparisons of Two Generation Attitudes of University Students." In *Renovating Marriage.* Edited by R. W. Libby, and R. N. Whitehurst. Danville, California: Consensus, 1973, pp. 269–279.

Wikler, A. "Drug Dependence." In *Clinical Neurology,* edited by A. B. Baker and L. H. Baker, 2 (1971): 1–53.

Wilkening, E. A., and Bharadwaj, L. K. "Dimensions of Aspirations, Work Roles, and Decision-Making of Farm Husbands and Wives in Wisconsin." *Journal of Marriage and the Family* 29 (November 1967): 703–711.

Wilkinson, M. L. "Romantic Love, and Sexual Expression." *The Family Coordinator* 27 (April 1978): 141–148.

Willett, R. S. "Working in 'A Man's World': The Woman Executive." In *Woman in Sexist Society: Studies in Power and Powerlessness.* Edited by V. Gornick and B. K. Moran. New York: Basic, 1971, pp. 367–383.

Williams, C. E. "Conflict: Modeling or Taking Flight." In *Choice and Challenge.* Edited by C. E. Williams and J. F. Crosby. Dubuque, Iowa: Wm. C. Brown, 1974, pp. 218–223.

Williams, C. J., and Weinberg, M. S. *Homosexuals and the Military: A Study of Less Than Honorable Discharge.* New York: Harper, 1971.

Willie, C. V. and Greenblatt, S. L. "Four 'Classic' Studies of Power Relationships in Black Families: A Review and Look to the Future." *Journal of Marriage and the Family* 40 (November 1978): 691–694.

Willamson, R. C. *Marriage and Family Relations.* 2d ed. New York: John Wiley, 1972.

Wilson, G. S.; Desmond, M. M.; and Verniaud, W. M. "Early Development of Infants of Heroin Addicted Mothers." *American Journal of Diseases of Children* 126 (1973): 457–462.

Wilson, G. T. and Lawson, D. M. "Expectancies, Alcohol, and Sexual Arousal in Women." *Journal of Abnormal Psychology* 87 (June 1978): 358–367.

Winch, R. F. "Another Look at the Theory of Complementary Needs in Mate Selection." *Journal of Marriage and the Family* 29 (November 1967): 756–762.

Winch, R. F., and Greer, S. A. "Urbanism, Ethnicity, and Extended Families." *Journal of Marriage and the Family* 30 (February 1968): 40–45.

Winick, C., and Kinsie, P. M. "Prostitution." *Sexual Behavior* (January 1973): 33–43.

Winthrop, H. "Love and Companionship." In *Love Today.* Edited by H. H. Otto. New York: Association Press, 1972, pp. 102–119.

Wood, V. and Robertson, J. F. "Friendship and Kinship Interaction: Differential Effect on the Moral of the Elderly." *Journal of Marriage and the Family* 40 (May 1978): 367–375.

Woodrow, K.; Hastings, D. W.; and Tu, E. J. "Rural-Urban Patterns of Marriage, Divorce, and Mortality: Tennessee, 1970." *Rural Sociology* 43 (Spring 1978): 70–86.

Wortis, R. P. "The Acceptance of the Concept of the Maternal Role by Behavioral Scientists: Its Effects on Women." *American Journal of Orthopsychiatry* 41 (October 1971): 733–746.

Wright, M. R., and McCary, J. L. "Postive Effects of Sex Education on Emotional Patterns of Behavior." *Journal of Sex Research* 5 (1969): 162–169.

Wylie, E. M. "The Disgrace of Our Divorce Laws." In *Current Issues in Marriage and the Family.* Edited by J. G. Wells. New York: Macmillan, 1975.

Wylie, E. M. *A Guide to Voluntary Sterilization: The New Birth Control.* New York: Grosset and Dunlap, 1972.

Wyly, M. V., and Hulicka, I. M. "Problems and Compensations of Widowhood." In *Empirical*

Studies in the Psychology and Sociology of Aging. Abstracted by I. M. Hulicka. New York: Crowell, 1977.

Wynn, M., and Wynn, A. *Some Consequences of Induced Abortion to Children Born Subsequently.* London: Foundation for Education and Research in Child-Bearing, 1972.

Yancey, W. L. "Going Down Home: Family Structure and the Urban Trap." *Social Science Quarterly* 53 (1972): 893–906.

Yankelovich. D. *The New Morality. A Profile of American Youth in the 70's.* New York: McGraw-Hill, 1974.

Yarber, W. L. "New Directions in Venereal Disease Education." *The Family Coordinator* 27 (August 1978): 121–127.

Yarburg, B. *The Changing Family.* New York: Columbia University Press, 1973.

Yarrow, M., et al. "Child-Rearing in Families of Working and Nonworking Mothers." In *Love, Marriage, Family: A Developmental Approach.* Edited by M. E. Lasswell and T. E. Lasswell. Glenview, Illinois: Scott, Foresman, 1973, pp. 365–373.

Yorburg, B. *The Changing Family: A Sociological Perspective.* New York: Columbia University Press, 1973.

Yost, E. D. and Adamek, R. J. "Parent-Child Interaction and Changing Family Values: A Multivariate Analysis." *Journal of Marriage and the Family* 36 (February 1974): 115–121.

"Young Brides, Unhappily Married, Most Prone to Unplanned Pregnancies." *Family Planning Perspectives* 11 (May/June 1979): 199.

Zabin, L. S., Kantner, J. F., and Zelnick, M. "The Risk of Adolescent Pregnancy in the First Months of Intercourse." *Family Planning Perspectives* 11 (1979): 215–222.

Zablocki, B. "The Joyful Community." Paper presented to the American Sociological Association, New Orleans, August 28–31, 1972.

Zablocki, B. *The Joyful Community: An Account of Bruderhof, a Communal Movement Now in Its Third Generation.* Baltimore: Penguin, 1971.

Zehv, W. "Trying New Positions in Intercourse." *Sexology* (January 1969): 364–367.

Zelnik, M. "Sex Education and Knowledge of Pregnancy Risk among U.S. Teenage Women." *Family Planning Perspectives* 11 (November/December 1979): 355–357.

Zelnik, M. and Kantner, J. F. "Contraceptive Patterns and Premarital Pregnancy among Women Aged 15–19 in 1976." *Family Planning Perspectives* 10 (May/June 1978a): 135–142.

Zelnik, M., and Kantner, J. F. "First Pregnancies to Women Aged 15–19: 1976 and 1971." *Family Planning Perspectives* 10 (January/February 1978b): 11–20.

Zelnik, M., and Kantner, J. F. "The Probability of Premarital Intercourse." *Social Science Research* 1 (September 1972): 335–341.

Zelnik, M. and Kantner, J. F. "Reasons for Nonuse of Contraception by Sexually Active Women Aged 15–19." *Family Planning Perspectives* 11 (September/October 1979): 289–298.

Zelnik, M., Kim, Y. J., and Kantner, J. F. "Probabilities of Intercourse and Conception among U.S. Teenage Women, 1971 and 1976." *Family Planning Perspectives.* 11 (May/June 1979): 177–183.

Zelson C. "Current Concepts: Infants of the Addicted Mother." *New England Journal of Medicine* 288 (1973): 1393–1395.

Zelson, C., et al. "Neonatal Narcotic Addiction: 10-Year Observation." *Pediatrics* 48 (August 1971): 178–179.

Zigler, E. *New York Times.* (June 14, 1971).

Zipper, J. A., et al. "Contraception through the Use of Intrauterine Metals, I: Copper as an Adjunct to the 'T' Device." *American Journal of Obstetrics and Gynecology* 109 (March 1971): 771–774.

Glossary

Altruistic love: unselfish concern care for the well-being of another.

Ambiguous adultery: an extramarital sexual relationship about which a spouse knows but does not fully approve.

Androgen: hormone with a masculinizing influence.

Androgynous: being both male and female.

Artificial insemination: injection of semen into the vagina or uterus with a syringe rather than by coitus.

Autocratic: exercising absolute power; domineering.

Autosexual: a preschool stage of psychosexual development where one's chief source of pleasure is one's self.

Bigamy: marriage to two persons at the same time.

Birth control pill: a form of contraception containing the female hormones estrogen and progestin.

Castration: removal of the testicles.

Catharsis: the discharge or relief of pent-up feelings or emotions.

Chauvinism: overzealousness or blind enthusiasm for a cause; male chauvinism is a blind belief in male supremacy.

Clandestine adultery: extramarital sexual relationships which the adulterer strives to keep secret from the spouse.

Coitus: sexual intercourse.

Coitus interruptus: an attempt at birth control by withdrawal of the penis prior to a ejaculation.

Collusion: a secret agreement between a husband and wife for fraudulent purposes of obtaining a divorce.

Comarital sex: sexual intimacy with an extramarital partner, to which a monogamous heterosexually married couple openly agree prior to involvement.

Commune: an organization of people who seek to live together out of common need or interests.

Compatibility: the capability of living together in harmony.

Complementarity: the ability of two people each to supply what is needed or lacking in the other to make a complete whole.

Condom: a thin sheath worn over the penis during sexual intercourse to prevent conception or venereal disease.

Condonation: the act of pardoning or of implying forgiveness for a wrong suffered.

Conjugal love: married love, which in this text is comprised of five types of love: altruistic, dependent, erotic, friendship and erotic love.

Connivance: One person gives encouragement or assent to the wrongdoing of another.

Consanguinity: descent from a common ancestor.

Consensual adultery: extramarital sexual relationships about which a spouse knows and approves.

445

Contraceptive: a device or means of preventing conception.

Cunnilingus: oral stimulation of the female genitalia.

D and C (dilation and curettage): a surgical method for removal of tissue from the inner lining of the uterus by means of scraping.

Dating: a social appointment or occasion arranged ahead of time with a person of the opposite sex.

Dependent love: that which develops toward another person who fills one's needs.

Diaphragm: a thin, dome-shaped device, usually of rubber, for fitting over the uterine cervix to prevent conception.

Douche: a jet or current of water squirted into the vagina.

Dual-career marriage: a marriage in which both the husband and wife pursue a career which requires a fairly continuous period of involvement.

Duress: compulsion by threat or coercion.

Dyspareunia: painful coitus.

Egalitarian marriage: the husband and wife are equals in a democratic relationship.

Ejaculatory incompetence: the inability of the male to ejaculate while his penis is in the women's vagina.

Embryo: a developing life within the womb up until the end of the eighth week after conception.

Empathy: identification with or experiencing the feelings, thoughts, or attitudes of another.

Empty nest period: that period in life after the last child is gone from the home.

Endogamy: the practice of marrying within one's own group: religion, race, ethnicity, or social class.

Erogenous zones: areas of the body that are sexually sensitive to stimulation.

Erotic love: sexual love.

Estrogen: hormone with a feminizing influence.

Evolutionary commune: a commune usually organized in urban areas whose members are successful, middle-class people older than thirty with straight jobs who pool their resources for financial or familial benefits.

Exogamy: marrying across social lines, outside one's group.

Extended family: a family group consisting of a nucleus of husband, wife, and their children plus various relatives.

Extramarital sex: sexual intercourse with someone else other than one's own spouse.

Fault divorce: divorce in which one spouse has to prove the other is at fault or responsible.

Fellatio: oral stimulation of the penis.

Feminity: the quality of being female or womanlike.

Feminism: the doctrine advocating political and social rights for woman equal to those of men.

Fetus: a life growing in the womb after the end of the eight weeks after conception in humans.

Foam: a frothy chemical contraceptive.

Fraud: deceit or trickery.

Friendship love: love between those with common bonds of concern, with common interests, and who are good companions.

Genetic counseling: examination to determine possible hereditary defects which might be passed on to a baby and guidance of the couple in making proper decisions.

Genitals: the external organs of reproduction.

Group marriage: marriage of at least four people, two female and two male, in which each partner is married to all partners of the opposite sex.

Hermaphrodite: an individual having both external and internal male and female organs.

Heterogamy: the tendency to be attracted to and to marry someone different than oneself.

Heterosexual: a stage of psychosexual development in which one's source of pleasure and satisfaction is with those of the opposite sex.

Homogamy: the tendency to be attracted to and marry someone similar to oneself.

Homosexual: a psychosexual stage of development where one's chief of pleasure and satisfaction is with members of one's own sex.

Hormones: biochemical substances secreted directly into the blood stream by the endocrine glands.

Hymen: mucuous membrane partially closing the external opening to the vagina in virginal females.

Hysterectomy: the surgical removal of the uterus.

Hysterotomy: the surgical cutting into the uterus as in a Caesarean section.

Identification: the process by which one person adopts and internalizes the characteristics, attitudes, values, and traits of another or of members of a group.

Illegitimacy: being born to parents who are not married.

Impotence: the inability to sustain an erection long enough to satisfactorily complete sexual intercourse.

Infertility: involuntary childlessness due to difficulties in conceiving.

Interfaith marriage: marriage between those of different religions.

Interlocutory period: the period of time between the decree of dissolution of marriage and the final granting of it.

Interpsychic sources of conflict: those which originate in relationships between people, because of tensions between them.

Interracial marriage: marriage between those of different races.

Intimate friendships: an otherwise traditional friendship in which sexual intimacy is considered appropriate behavior.

Intrapsychic sources of conflict: those which originate within the individual because of inner tensions.

Intrasomatic sources of conflict: inner tensions having a physical cause or origin.

Intrauterine device (IUD): a mechanical device inserted into the uterus as a contraceptive.

Intrinsic: belonging to a thing because of its own merit. Thus, intrinsic marriage has worth in and of itself.

Kibbutzim: a collective community or commune in Israel.

Kinsfolk: relatives.

Lamaze method: a method of prepared childbirth developed by Lamaze, a French obstetrician.

Laparoscopy: the surgical incision of the abdominal wall, often through the navel, and the insertion of a tubular instrument and scope to use in surgery.

Leboyer method: a method of care and loving treatment of the newborn established by the French obstetrician Leboyer.

Lesbian: female homosexuality.

Marital integration: the process by which a couple form a harmonious whole.

Masculinity: the qualities of maleness or manliness.

Masturbation: sexual stimulation or manipula-

tion of one's own genitals for purposes of pleasure and gratification.

Menopause: the permanent cessation of menstruation during midlife.

Menstruation: periodically discharging blood and mucus from the uterus through the vaginal opening.

Minipill: a contraceptive pill containing only progestin.

Miscarriage: a spontaneous abortion or expulsion of the fetus before it is viable.

Modeling: identifying with and imitating another person.

Morning sickness: nausea occuring in the early part of the day as a characteristic symptom of pregnancy.

Multilateral marriage: three or more partners living together each of whom considers himself/herself to be married to more than one of the other persons.

Nepotism: hiring two people from the same family

No-fault divorce: divorce granted without having to prove the other person at fault, usually on the basis of irreconcilable differences.

Nonmarital cohabitation: unrelated persons of the opposite sex living together without being married.

Nonverbal communication: communication between persons without audible speech.

Nuclear family: a social unit composed of father, mother, and children.

Oral: pertaining to the mouth. Thus, an oral contraceptive is a pill which is put in the mouth and swallowed.

Oral-genital sex: sexual stimulation by use of the mouth.

Orgasm: the sudden release of psychophysical neurological tension at the height of sexual stimulation, usually accompanied by ejaculation in the male.

Orgasmic dysfunction: the inability to reach a sexual climax.

Ovulation: the maturation and discharge of a mature ovum from the ovary of the female.

Planned parenthood: having children by choice and not by chance.

Postparental years: years of life after the last child leaves home.

Premature birth: the birth of a child before full-term, but sometimes defined as birth of a baby below a certain weight.

Premature ejaculation: the inability to delay ejaculation long enough for the woman to have orgasm 50 percent of the coital connections.

Prenatal care: care of the mother during pregnancy and before the birth of the baby.

Progesterone: a female hormone that prepares the uterus for a fertilized ovum and maintains pregnancy.

Progestin: the chemical equivalent of the natural hormone progesterone.

Prostaglandins: drugs used to induce labor.

Religious commune: community living groups organized around religious philosophies or goals.

Rh factor: an inheritable antigen in the red blood cell, classified as either positive or negative.

Rhythm method: a method of birth control which seeks to avoid conception by permitting sexual intercourse only during so-called "safe periods" of the month (when ovulation is not as likely to take place).

Role induction: trying to get a spouse to change his or her sex role while remaining the same oneself.

Role modification: a change in role expectations and a willingness to modify one's own role.

Role reversal: the male or female adopting the typical role of the other.

Romantic love: love characterized by strong emotions and passionate fervor, sometimes, but not always, dominated by idealism.

Rooming in: a method of childcare following birth where the baby sleeps and is cared for by the mother in her own hospital room.

Salpingectomy: the surgical incision of the Fallopian tube.

Self-disclosure: to disclose one's own feelings, ideas, and attitudes.

Sexism: discrimination against women and the naive, unconscious, unexamined institutionalizing of patriarchal attitudes and behavior.

Sex ratio: the ratio of male to female, or female to male.

Sexual dysfunction: a malfunctioning of the sexual response system.

"Show":   the discharge of pinkish fluid and mucus from the vagina due to the dislogement of the mucus plug that seals the neck of the uterus. Usually a sign that labor has begun.

Sperm count: the number of sperm in the ejaculatory fluid.

Spermicide: a chemical used to kill sperm.

Sterility: a condition in which the individual has zero capacity to produce egg cells or sperm cells.

Sterilization: to render one sterile through surgical procedure.

Succorant: wanting to be assisted, helped, or taken care of.

Suction curettage: a method of therapeutic abortion where the fetal material is removed from the uterus by vacuum suction.

Swinging: mate swapping without emotional involvement for sexual purposes.

Syncratic: an equal or democratic relationship and sharing of power between the husband and wife.

Testosterone: the male sex hormone secreted by the testes which stimulates the development of masculine characteristics.

Toxemia: a major illness and complication of pregnancy characterized by poisons in the bloodstream.

Trial marriage: a nonconjugal relationship in which a man and woman agree to live together for a specified period of time as a test of whether or not they want to become legally married.

Tubal ligation: surgical cutting of the Fallopian tubes.

Tubal pregnancy: the fertilized ovum implants itself in the wall of the Fallopian tube and starts to develop there.

Unisex: both male and female in one.

Utilitarian marriage: marriage that is entered into for motives outside the marriage itself, for practical, useful functions.

Utopian commune: a community of persons, usually with little organization or structure, with a drop-out, "do-your-own-thing," or revolutionary philosophy of a highly impractical and idealistic nature.

Vacuum aspiration: a method of therapeautic abortion where the fetal material is removed from the uterus by suction.

Vaginal cream: a special preparation, with or without spermicidal action, to insert into the vaginal canal. Creams are used to fight infections, for lubrication, or for contraception.

Vaginal jelly: a special preparation, having a jelly-like consistency, which is inserted into the vaginal canal for lubrication or for contraception.

Vaginismus: a powerful and painful involuntary contraction of the muscles surrounding the vaginal tract.

Vasectomy: the surgical incision and closure of the vas deferens to render the male sterile.

Venereal disease: any disease transmitted by sexual intercourse.

Withdrawal: voluntary removal of the penis from the vagina before ejaculation as a means of birth control.

Author Index

Abrahams, B., 109
Acock, A. C., 106
Adamek, R. J., 38, 127, 341, 394
Adams, B. N., 176, 251, 252
Adams, G. R., 104
Adams, V., 278
Ahern, L., 197
Ainsworth, M. D. S., 354, 355, 356
Albrecht, R. E., 369
Albrecht, S. L., 106
Aldous, J., 251
Aldridge, D. P., 334
Alexander, J. F., 205
Allen, G., 7
Allen, V., 146, 147
Almquist, E. M., 227
Altman, D., 111
Altman, I., 193, 203, 209, 218
Ambrose, L., 28
Ammons, P., 80
Amyk, C., 48
Anderson, R. E., 431
Anderson, R. N., 402
Anderson, S. M., 36
Aneshensel, C. C., 104, 105
Angrist, S. S., 127
Apolonio, F., 427
Arafat, I. S., 38
Araji, S. K., 90
Ard, Fr. B. N., 260
Arling, G., 180, 185
Arnstein, H. S., 306, 339
Astin, H. S., 391
Atchley, R. C., 184
Athanasiou, R., 110, 378, 397
Atkinson, R., 128
Avertt, C. P., 108
Avery, A. W., 20
Avery, C. E., 267

Bach, G. R., 7, 214, 215
Backman, E., 437
Bagarozzi, D. A., 402
Bagarozzi, J. I., 402
Bagford, J., 421

Bahm, R. M., 105, 144, 362
Bahr, H. M., 172
Bahr, S. J., 196, 197, 200, 305
Bailyn, L., 154
Bain, K., 335
Balkwell, C., 108, 177
Balkwell, J. W., 403
Ballard, W. M., 343
Balswick, J. O., 107, 108, 142
Bandura, A., 103
Barbara, J., 23
Bardwick, J. M., 123, 127, 210, 268, 269
Barnett, J. K., 360
Barrett, C., 223
Barry, W. A., 53
Bart, P., 122, 130, 265, 403
Bartell, G., 378
Barton, J. J., 313
Barton, K., 368
Bartz, K. W., 17, 57, 67
Basu, G. K., 102
Bateman, K., 319
Bateson, G., 201
Battle-Sister, A., 121
Bauder, W. W., 196
Baum, M., 59
Bayer, A. E., 25, 70, 126
Beacham, D. W., 306
Beachman, W. D., 306
Bean, C. A., 324, 325, 326
Bean, F. D., 172
Beck, D. F., 45
Becker, I., 67, 124
Becker, P., 427
Beggington, A. C., 151, 153
Bell, A. P., 110
Bell, C. S., 176
Bell, N. W., 195
Bell, P. L., 260
Bell, R. R., 8, 23, 59, 60, 65, 137, 145, 146, 180, 248, 260, 266, 268, 269, 323, 357, 369, 375, 376, 377
Bell, S. M., 353, 354, 355, 356
Belliveau, F., 260, 270, 404

Bem, D. J., 158
Bem, S. L., 158
Bender, S. J., 28
Bengtson, V. L., 106
Benson, L., 200
Berardo, F. M., 53, 131, 137, 156, 186, 252, 291, 360
Berelson, B., 349
Bergen, G. R., 70, 71
Bergen, M. B., 70, 71
Berger, B. M., 387, 390
Berger, C., 415
Berger, D. G. 24
Berger, M., 200
Berger, M. E., 43, 375
Bergstrom, S., 341
Berkove, G. F., 72
Berkowitz, L., 214, 215
Berman, A. L., 419
Bermant, G., 105
Bern, D. J., 295
Bern, S. L., 295
Bernard, J., 124, 128, 129, 201, 206, 296, 375, 397, 398
Bernard, S., 405
Berne, I., 201
Bernstein, I. S., 432
Bernstein, R., 339
Berry, J. E., 232
Berscheld, E., 419
Bharadwaj, L. K., 195
Bieber, I., 110
Bienvenu, M. J., 200
Biller, H. B., 103, 105, 106, 144, 361, 362, 363
Billings, A., 201
Billingsley, A., 363
Birchler, G. R., 221, 222
Bird, C., 120
Bischof, L. J., 184, 186
Black, J. D., 108
Blackburn, C. W., 230
Blanchard, R. W., 362
Blanton, J., 390
Blau, Z., 405

Blazer, J., 276
Blood, R. O., Jr., 194, 195, 196, 250, 361
Bluestone, B., 359
Blumberg, P. M., 83
Bock, E. W., 369
Bohannan, P., 286, 288, 291, 293, 294
Bokenmeier, J. L., 22
Bonham, G. S., 334, 335
Booth, A., 252, 375
Boss, P., 176
Bouvier, L. F., 313
Bowen, M., 38
Bower, D. W., 34
Bowerman, C. E., 298
Bowlby, J., 354
Bowman, H. A., 67, 68, 89, 137, 175, 248, 320, 369
Boxer, L., 81, 86
Boyd, P. R., 319
Bradford, D. L., 389
Braen, B. B., 339
Bragg, H., 172, 201
Brandwein, R. A., 294, 359, 360, 363
Brannon, R., 107, 108, 139
Brashear, D. B., 344
Braun, J., 327
Brayer, F. T., 315
Brehm, J. W., 60
Brenton, M., 138, 180
Brindley, C., 103
Brinkerhoff, D. B., 172
Brinkman, W., 426
Brissett, D., 269
Brogan, D., 108
Bronfenbrenner, U., 159, 357, 358
Bronzaft, A. I., 127, 153
Broschart, K. R., 407
Brown, B. B., 339
Brown, C. A., 294
Browning, R., 58
Broverman, D. M. B., 108
Broverman, I. K., 106, 108
Brownmiller, S., 120, 124
Bryson, B., 153
Bryson, J. B., 417
Bryson, R., 153
Budd, L. G., 47
Bukstel, L. H., 377
Bullock, R. C., 210, 268
Bultena, G., 182, 251
Bumpass, H. L., 311
Bumpass, L. L., 53, 55, 308
Burchinal, L. G., 196, 292
Burdette, W. J., 317
Burgess, E. W., 7, 56, 57, 79, 80
Burgess, J. K., 360
Burgess, R. L., 223
Burr, W. R., 132, 171, 197, 391
Bush, E. S., 108
Byer, C. O., 318, 319
Byrne, D., 30
Bytheway, B., 250

Calderone, M. S., 23, 276
Call, V. R. A., 57
Callahan, S. C., 120, 159
Cannon, D., 421
Cannon, K. L., 38, 171, 391

Cant, G., 407
Cantor, D. J., 288, 291
Caplow, T., 385
Carlos, M. L., 252
Carlson, E., 67
Carlson, J., 209, 211
Carlton, E., 271
Carter, H., 67, 85, 181, 183, 294, 297
Cattell, R. B., 81, 268
Cavan, J. T., 79
Cavan, R. S., 79
Cavan, S., 385
Cavanaugh, J. R., 268
Centers, R., 193, 194, 196
Chadwick, B. A., 305
Chafetz, J. S., 220
Chantiny, J., 160
Charny, I. W., 215, 276, 371
Chartham, R., 267
Chason, K. J., 35, 47
Cherlin, A., 47, 67
Chernick, A. B., 261
Chernick, B. A., 261
Chernovetz, M. E., 416
Chiazze, L., Jr., 315
Chilman, C. S., 70, 71, 147, 277, 349
Chilton, R. J., 292
Chodorow, N., 105
Christensen, H. T., 25, 79, 204, 350
Christie, L. S., 45
Christopherson, V. A., 34
Clark, J. H., 314
Clark, Joanna, 349
Clark, L., 262, 265
Clatworthy, N. M., 331
Clavan, S., 250, 252
Clayton, G., 376
Clayton, P. N., 361
Clayton, R. R., 22, 25, 34, 173, 193, 352
Cline, D. W., 292, 296
Cloyd, J. S., 70, 141
Cochrane, C. M., 441
Cofield, E., 127
Cole, A. L., 172
Cole, C. L., 171, 172, 377
Colten, N., 410
Comeau, J. K., 425
Comfort, A., 259
Conger, R. D., 223
Conklin, G. H., 198
Connell, D. M., 144
Connolly, J., 269
Conover, P. W., 385, 387
Constantine, J. M., 381, 382, 383, 384
Constantine, L., 381, 382, 383, 384
Coombs, R. H., 21
Cooper, A. J., 275
Corman, L., 28, 305
Corrales, R., 200
Coughey, K., 23
Coults, R. L., 6, 63, 80, 204
Cox, F., 287
Crawford, S. H., 418
Critelli, J. W., 58
Croak, J. W., 23
Croake, J., 44
Cromwell, R. E., 176, 198, 339
Cromwell, V. L., 198

Croog, S. H., 253
Crosby, J. F., 12, 63, 172, 209, 381
Cross, A. D., 105
Crowell, D., 408
Cuber, J. F., 140, 141
Culbert, S. A., 200
Currant, E. F., 105
Curtis, R. L., 172
Cutright, P., 229, 305

D'Antonio, W. V., 306, 333, 369
Danziger, C., 33
Darnley, F., 176
Dass, B. R., 382, 385
David, D. S., 107, 108, 139
Davidson, J. K., Sr., 25
Davidson, K., 420
Davies, R. C., 113
Davis, C. D., 338
Davis, G. C., 183
Davis, H. J., 310
Davis, J. D., 19
Davis, K. E., 25, 26
Davis, P., 25
Davis, S. A., 81
Dean, D. G., 60, 172
Dean, G., 79
DeBeauvior, S., 181
DeFrain, J., 109
DeLamater, J. D., 23, 26, 27
DeLissovoy, V., 65, 66
DeMartino, F., 267
Denfeld, D., 378, 379
Desmond, M. M., 443
Deur, J. L., 359
Deutsch, M., 221
Deutsch, R. M., 7
Deutscher, I., 180
Diamond, M., 343
Dibattista, B., 173
Dibble, U., 224
Dick-Read, G. D., 324
Dill, D., 229
Dishatsky, N. I., 319
Dixon, P. L., 287, 311, 313
Dixon, R. B., 442
Dodder, R. A., 424
Doherty, W. J., 198
Doll, R., 307
Doran, L., 418
Douglas, S. P., 194
Dowd, E. R., 432
Downer, D. B., 436
Dressel, P. L., 79
Dreyer, A. S., 426
Driscoll, R., 38, 60, 63
Duberman, L., 298
Duffy, B. J., 315
Dullea, G., 291
Duvall, E. M., 66, 67, 170, 218, 245, 246, 249, 356
Dweck, C. S., 108

Eckland, B. K., 79, 83
Ecstein, P., 307
Edmonds, V. H., 173
Edward, M. P., 38, 47
Edwards, J. N., 375, 376

Edwards, R. L., 47, 65, 66
Ehrhardt, A. A., 103
Ehrlich, R. M., 275
Einzig, J. E., 179
Elkind, D., 359
Ellis, A. L., 27, 384
Ellison, C., 274
Emerson, P. E., 353, 354
England, J. L., 284
Epstein, G. F., 125, 127, 153, 157
Erikson, E., 7, 352, 355
Eshleman, J. R., 12, 35, 87, 196, 372, 381
Estallachild, V., 387, 389
Etzkowitz, H., 139
Evans, B., 429
Evans, R. B., 105

Fairfield, R., 387
Fanshel, D., 336
Farley, F. H., 81
Fasteau, M. F., 144
Feinmann, S., 20
Feldman, H., 132, 169, 229, 230
Feldman, M., 169, 229, 230
Feldman, S. D., 67, 127, 171
Feldman, S. F., 401
Fenelon, B., 285
Ferrell, M. Z., 24
Ferris, A., 159, 295
Feshbach, S., 27
Figley, C. R., 305
Finch, S., 130
Fineberg, B. L., 172
Fink, P. J., 338
Firestone, S., 120, 296
Fischer, A., 277
Fisher, C. C., 334
Fisher, S., 265
Fithian, M. A., 278
Flake, M. H., 261
Flake-Hobson, C., 103, 105
Fleck, S., 344
Fleishman, W., 311, 313
Flora, C. B., 108
Flowers, C. E., 275
Fogarty, M., 162
Folkman, J. D., 331
Foner, A., 171
Ford, R., 377
Form, W. H., 229
Forrest, J. D., 30
Foster, H. H., 285, 287, 288
Foster, M. A., 441
Foster, M. E., 23
Fox, C. A., 278
Fox, E. M., 294
Fox, G. L., 25, 26
Frankl, V., 25
Freed, D. J., 285, 289
Freedman, M., 6, 105, 110
Freeman, J., 16, 119, 120
Freneau, P. J., 180
Freud, S. A., 62, 110
Friedan, B., 120
Fromm, E., 62, 63, 64
Fromme, A., 267
Frosch, W. A., 275
Fullerton, G. P., 7, 142, 287

Furth, H. G., 356

Gadpaille, W. J., 276
Gagnon, J. H., 144
Galdston, R., 223
Gallup, G. H., 86, 375
Gangel, J. L., 339
Gannon, M. J., 156
Garcia, C., 306
Gardner, J., 388, 389
Garland, T. N., 129, 161, 352
Garrett, G., 209, 211
Gaudy, J. C., 200
Gebhard, P. H., 260, 266, 267, 268, 274, 275
Gecas, V., 147, 349
Geismar, L. L., 172, 229, 338, 352
Gelles, R. J., 223, 224
Gendzel, I. B., 175
George, V., 295
Gerber, I., 184
Gerstel, N. R., 157
Gianturco, D. T., 184
Gibbs, J. R., 205
Gibson, B., 254
Gill, G. W., 20
Gillespie, D. L., 123, 197
Gilliland, N. C., 156
Gilman, A., 278
Gilmartin, B. G., 378
Ginsberg, G. L., 275
Giovannoni, J. M., 363
Glass, S. P., 377
Glasser, P., 360, 361
Glen, M. L., 9
Glenn, N. D., 7, 169, 171
Glick, I. O., 184
Glick, P. C., 3, 5, 6, 34, 67, 85, 170, 181, 183, 250, 283, 284, 286, 294, 296, 297
Goddard, H. L., 185
Goffman, E., 105
Gold, D., 415
Gold, E. M., 343
Goldman, D. R., 138
Goleman, D., 99
Good, H. G., 15
Goode, W. J., 287, 294, 295, 298
Goodenough, F. L., 355, 356
Goodman, L. S., 278
Goodrich, W., 248
Goodwin, M. S., 417
Gordon, F. E., 155
Gordon, M., 124, 129, 378
Gottman, J., 218
Gough, A. R., 288
Gough, K., 122
Gould, R., 139
Graham, P. A., 163
Granbois, D. H., 195
Grant, C. W., 151
Gray, L., 423
Greeley, A. M., 79
Greenberg, I., 266
Greenblatt, R. B., 278
Greenblatt, S. L., 197
Greene, B. A., 230, 276
Greene, R., 101
Greenwald, H., 43

Greer, G., 128
Greer, S. A., 251
Greiff, B., 275
Gross, H. W., 157, 158
Gunderson, M. P., 25, 27, 28
Gurak, D. T., 79
Guttmacher, A. F., 260, 306, 307, 309, 310, 311, 313, 318, 319, 321, 331, 341, 342

Hahn, J. D., 428
Hall, D. T., 416
Hall, J. R., 108
Halverson, C. F., Jr., 177
Hamilton, E., 259
Hammer, E. L., 19, 25
Hampe, G. D., 23, 296
Handel, G., 391
Haney, C. A., 338
Hanks, C., 352, 363
Hansson, R. O., 27
Hardy, J. B., 318
Harkins, E. B., 179
Harlow, H. F., 328
Harrel, J., 221
Harris, A. S., 163
Harris, T. A., 216
Harrof, P. B., 140, 141
Harry, J., 112
Harting, D., 341
Hartman, W. E., 278
Haskins, L., 313
Hassett, J., 47
Hastings, D. W., 272
Haughey, J. C., 385
Hawkins, J. L., 203
Hays, W. C., 252
Heckman, J., 389
Heckman, J. J., 154
Heckman, N. A., 156
Hedges, J. N., 360
Heegepath, W., 386
Heer, D. M., 81, 83
Heise, D. R., 358
Helmreich, R. L., 109
Hendrickson, D. H., 156
Hennig, M., 152
Henton, J., 92, 174, 230, 235
Henze, L. F., 34, 35, 37, 44
Hepker, W., 70, 141
Herbert, A., 334
Hern, W. M., 321
Herold, E. S., 23, 26
Herrigan, J., 155, 201, 230, 269
Herzog, E., 334, 363
Hess, B. B., 250, 253
Hetherington, E. M., 362
Heymann, D. K., 184
Hicks, M. W., 55, 140, 172, 229, 284
Hill, C. T., 429
Hill, R., 141, 194, 195, 218, 237, 250, 251, 253, 254
Hiller, D. V., 197
Hills, S. L., 417
Hiltz, S. R., 184
Hitchens, D., 113
Hite, S., 274
Hobbs, D. F., 177
Hochschild, A. R., 102, 185

Hogan, D. P., 67
Hokanson, J. E., 215
Holaday, J. W., 432
Hole, J., 120
Hollender, M. H., 259, 260
Holcombe, M., 227
Hollingshead, A. B., 16
Holmstrom, L. L., 121, 130, 151, 152, 153, 154, 155, 157, 158, 162
Honig, M., 294
Hooper, J. O., 72
Hops, H., 221
Hornick, J. P., 25, 28
Houriet, R., 388
Housker, S. L., 25
Howard, M., 339
Howe, V., 106
Huang, L. J., 35, 37, 41, 42
Hudson, J. W., 34, 35, 37, 44
Hulicka, I. M., 185, 186
Humphrey, F. G., 12
Humphreys, L., 418
Hungerford, M. J., 418
Hunt, M. M., 7, 128, 295, 383
Hunter, H. J., 341
Husbands, C. T., 18
Huser, W. R., 151
Huston, T. L., 63, 204
Hutchinson, K., 201
Hutt, C., 100, 101

Inazu, J. K., 25, 26
Inhelder, J., 356
Inman, W. H. W., 307
Irish, D. P., 298

Jackson, D. D., 418
Jackson, J., 48
Jackson, J. H., 420
Jackson, J. J., 197
Jackson, R., 48
Jaco, D. E., 80, 88, 317
Jacobs, L., 60, 61
Jacobson, C. B., 319
Jacobson, G., 362
Jacoby, A. P., 177
Jacques, J. M., 35, 47
Jaffee, B., 336
Jaffee, D., 420
Jakobovits, R., 278
James, J., 428
Jedlicka, D., 43, 44
Jensen, M., 427
Jensen, M. S., 113
Jerome, J., 385
Jessor, R., 23
Joffee, C., 103, 104
Johannis, T. B., 402
Johnsen, K. P., 408
Johnson, J. E., 144
Johnson, L. B., 25, 350
Johnson, M. F., 407
Johnson, M. P., 35
Johnson, R. E., 375, 377
Johnson, V. E., 124, 137, 183, 259, 264, 266, 270, 271, 278, 296, 308, 311, 315, 322
Jones, G. S., 428
Jones, H. W., Jr., 428

Jones, J. G., 419
Jones, K. L., 317, 318, 319
Jones, R. A., 151
Jones, W. H., 416
Jones, W. M., 151
Jorgensen, B. W., 423
Jorgensen, S. R., 25, 83, 172, 200, 230
Josephson, E., 363
Jourard, S. M., 201
Joy, C. B., 425
Juhasz, A. M., 30
Jurich, A. P., 105

Kaats, G. R., 25
Kacerguis, M. A., 104
Kadushin, A., 336
Kahn, L., 34, 36, 40, 41, 42
Kahn, M., 201
Kandel, D. B., 194, 195, 197
Kanin, E., 59
Kanter, R. M., 386, 390
Kantner, J. F., 21, 22, 28, 29
Kaplan, H. S., 267, 268, 272, 273, 275, 278
Kaplan, R., 67, 121
Kargman, M. W., 286
Karp, E. S., 79, 80
Katz, B. J., 26, 391
Kawash, G., 268
Kay, A. W., 358
Kay, H. H., 48, 287, 294
Keefe, S. E., 252
Keidel, K. C., 159
Keim, A. M., 197
Keith, P. M., 161
Kelley, H. H., 420
Kelley, J. F., 26
Kelley, R. K., 70, 136, 233, 253, 373
Kelley, W. J., 316
Kennedy, E. C., 7
Kennedy, W. A., 320, 323
Kent, D. P., 185
Kephart, W. M., 59, 60, 249, 349
Kerckhoff, A. C., 67, 79
Kieffer, C., 35, 38, 42
Kieren, D., 43, 89, 230, 235
Kilpatrick, A. C., 252
Kim, Y. J., 22
Kimball, C. P., 344
King, K., 23
King, S. L., 419
Kinkade, K., 388
Kinsey, A. C., 265, 266
Kinsie, P. M., 259
Kirschner, B. F., 157
Kistner, R. W., 308, 309
Kitzinger, S., 325
Kivett, V. R., 185, 186
Klapper, Z. S., 130
Klemer, R. H., 19, 249
Klevansky, S., 389
Klimek, D., 80
Knowles, E. M., 197
Knox, D. H., Jr., 46, 200, 202
Kogan, B. A., 309
Kohl, R. N., 273
Kohlberg, L., 103
Koller, M. R., 61, 65
Kolodny, R. C., 278

Komarovsky, M., 135, 140, 145, 197, 198, 204, 228, 229, 250
Komisar, L., 123, 124
Koomen, W., 426
Koopman, E. J., 109
Kopell, B., 102
Kostrubala, T., 212
Kotelchuck, M., 352, 363
Krain, M., 19
Krantzler, M., 293, 294, 295
Kraus, R., 172
Krauskopf, J. M., 370
Krauss, R. M., 221
Kriesberg, L., 295, 360
Krupensky, J., 212
Kuntz, R. P., 284
Kurtz, I., 131
Kusisto, D. V., 378
Kutner, N. G., 108

LaBarre, M., 65
LaBarre, W., 65
Lake, A., 130
Lamaze, F., 325
Lamb, L. E., 268
Lamott, K., 386, 389
Landers, A., 91
Landis, J. T., 6, 56, 69, 70, 143, 193, 194, 198, 234, 245, 246, 248, 267, 291, 336, 349
Landis, M. G., 6, 56, 69, 70, 143, 193, 194, 198, 234, 245, 246, 248, 267, 336, 349
Landis, P. H., 11, 56, 228, 320
Landy, F., 363
Laner, M. R., 25
Langley, R., 224
Larzelere, R. E., 63, 204
Lasswell, M. E., 53
Lautenschlager, S. Y., 38
Laws, J. L., 171, 193, 194, 266
Lawson, D. M., 277
Lazarus, A. A., 275
Lear, J., 391
Lebeaux, C., 228
Leboyer, F., 327
Lee, G. R., 53, 60
Lehrman, N., 259, 274
Leitsch, D., 113
LeMasters, E. E., 16, 17, 121, 136, 294, 349, 352, 359, 361
Lenski, J., 310
Lero, D. S., 417
Leslie, G. R., 25, 80, 245
Lesser, G. S., 194, 195, 197
Lester, D., 420
Lester, G., 64
Levene, H. I., 344
Levenson, R. A., 201
Levin, E., 120
Levine, S., 253
Levinger, G., 89, 205, 268
Leviton, D., 185
Levy, R. C., 224
Lewis, H., 229
Lewis, L. S., 269
Lewis, R. A., 171, 172, 180, 199
Libby, R. W., 25, 26, 377
Liddick, B., 46

Lieberman, E. J., 338, 342
Lincoln, C. E., 359
Lindsay, B. B., 374
Linn, E. L., 154
Linton, S., 423
Lipetz, M. E., 411
Lipson, A., 253
Lobsenz, N., 230
Locke, H. J., 407
Loiselle, R., 266
Long, M. L., 105
Long, R., 38
Lopata, H. Z., 129, 136, 184, 185, 186,
    230, 234, 352
Loring, R., 127, 128
Louisell, D. W., 342
Lowen, A., 59, 62, 260
Lowman, J., 172
Lowry, T. P., 269
Luce, J., 385
Lueptow, L. B., 106
Luria, Z., 431
Lydon, S., 265
Lyle, J. R., 125
Lynch, M. T., 436
Lyness, J. L., 35, 37, 44, 47
Lynn, D. B., 105
Lyon, R., 110

"M," 259
McCabe, E., 231
McCary, J. L., 25, 27, 28, 100, 209,
    234, 260, 261, 267, 269, 309,
    313, 315, 320, 331, 332, 333, 338
McClain, D., 436
McCormick, N. B., 24
MacCorquodale, P., 23, 26, 27
McCoy, R. W., 340
McCubbin, H. I., 172, 212
McDermott, R., 130
McDonald, G. W., 106, 197, 199
McDonald, R. L., 323
McDowell, S. F., 79
Mace, D. R., 8, 10, 89, 176, 201, 209,
    234, 259, 267, 269, 274, 341, 342
Mace, V., 8, 176, 201, 209
McGee, T. F., 212
McGuire, T. F., 272
McIntire, W. G., 105
Mackey, B., 339
Macklin, E. D., 33, 34, 36, 38
McMillan, E. L., 212
McMurtry, J., 375
McNamara, M. L. L., 90, 172
McWhirter, W. A., 33, 39, 44
Maddock, J. W., 25
Maeck, J. V. S., 318
Mahoney, E. R., 25
Mainardi, P., 128
Malamuth, N., 27
Mannes, M., 370, 371
Manosevitz, M., 113
Maranell, G. M., 25
Marcum, J. P., 172
Marcus, D. E., 103
Marder, L., 344
Margolis, A. J., 344
Margolius, S., 239

Mariah, P., 110
Marini, M. M., 67
Markle, G. E., 292
Markman, H., 218
Marotz, R., 230, 235
Marshall, D. G., 182
Marshall, E., 212
Martin, C., 7
Martin, D., 110
Martin, E. P., 252
Martin, J. C., 442
Martin, J. M., 425
Martin, P. Y., 91, 194
Martin, W., 104
Martinson, F. M., 6, 9
Marx, J. H., 142
Maslow, A. H., 61, 359
Massarik, F., 429
Masters, W. H., 124, 137, 183, 259,
    262, 266, 270, 271, 278, 296,
    308, 311, 315, 322
Matson, M. B., 185
May, R., 425
Mayer, M. F., 286
Maynard, F., 175, 176, 178
Mazur, R., 387
Mead, M., 106, 296, 374
Mears, E., 307
Mellenauer, S., 266
Melody, G. F., 261
Melville, K., 386
Mendelson, L. A., 205
Menken, J., 338
Merkatz, R., 436
Merriam, L. C., Jr., 172
Meryman, R., 205
Meyer, D. L., 70, 71
Meyerowitz, J. H., 178
Meyers, H., 272
Michels, L., 391
Middendorp, C. P., 25
Miller, A. A., 294
Miller, B. C., 112, 172, 176, 177
Miller, H. L., 20, 53, 63, 211
Miller, H. P., 125
Miller, M. M., 105
Miller, S., 200
Miller, S. M., 143, 200, 352
Miller, W. B., 317
Miller, W. W., Jr., 278
Millet, K., 427
Milloy, M., 339
Mindel, C. H., 252
Mirande, A. M., 19, 25
Mischel, W., 103
Mishell, D. R., 310
Mitchell, D. F., 424
Mitchell, J., 125, 131
Moen, P., 231
Moerk, E., 67
Monahan, T. P., 80, 84, 286
Money, J., 100, 103, 110
Montgomery, J., 39, 42
Montgomery, J. E., 182
Moore, K. A., 67
Moos, R. H., 427
Morgan, R., 128
Mornell, P., 201
Morrison, J. R., 291, 292

Mosher, D. L., 266
Moss, J. J., 16, 18, 102
Movius, M., 391
Moyer, D. L., 310
Mueller, B. J., 212
Mukhopadhyay, C. C., 60
Mullen, P., 313
Murphy, D. C., 205
Murphy, W., 405
Murstein, B. I., 19, 80, 81, 89
Myers, L., 7, 428
Myricks, N., 47, 48

Naffziger, C. C., 105, 106
Naffziger, K., 105, 106
Nash, J., 144
Nash, S. C., 401
Nass, G. D., 426
Navarre, E., 360, 361
Needle, R. H., 425
Neisser, E. G., 227, 248
Nesselroad, J. R., 81
Neubeck, G., 6
Neumann, F., 102
Newcomb, P. R., 43, 45, 47
Nock, S. L., 170
Noonan, J. T., Jr., 342
Norcross, C., 238
Norland, S., 112
Norton, A. J., 170, 284, 296, 297
Notarius, C., 218
Notman, M. T., 153
Novak, E. R., 333
Novak, F., 341
Nunnally, E. W., 200
Nye, F. I., 17, 53, 57, 67, 131, 137,
    147, 156, 209, 211, 291, 349, 360

O'Connor, J. F., 268, 278
Oldham, J. C., 360
Olim, E. G., 9
Oliveri, M. E., 431
Olson, D. H., 39, 221
O'Neill, G., 35, 62, 155, 175, 203, 372
O'Neill, N., 35, 62, 155, 175, 203, 372
O'Neill, W. W., 126
Orthner, D. K., 172
Osmond, M. W., 91, 194, 197
Osofsky, H. J., 109, 123
Osofsky, J. D., 109, 123, 344
Othey, J. I., 268
Otto, H. A., 7, 202, 385
Otto, L. B., 57
Overton, W. F., 103
Ovesey, L., 272

Packard, V., 375
Padilla, A. M., 252
Painter, B., 357
Palme, O., 138
Pannor, R., 339
Papousek, H., 160
Pare, C. M. B., 344
Parke, R. D., 359
Parkes, C. M., 184
Parlee, M. B., 101
Parrow, A. A., 67

Patterson, G. R., 221
Patterson, J. M., 425
Paul, P. W., 83
Pearlman, C. K., 183, 267
Pease, J., 229
Peck, E., 391, 392
Peek, C. W., 107
Peel, J., 307, 308
Peevers, B. N., 105
Pendleton, B. F., 156
Peplau, L. A., 23, 24, 26
Perlman, D., 28, 34
Perlman, S. B., 26
Perrucci, C. C., 67, 163
Perry, H. S., 385
Pershing, B., 234
Persky, H., 102
Peterman, D. J., 34, 35, 36, 37, 38
Peters, J. J., 275
Peterson, G., 200
Peterson, G. B., 272
Peterson, J. A., 179
Peterson, L. R., 272
Pfeiffer, E., 183, 268
Philliber, W. W., 197
Phillips, C. A., 318
Piaget, J., 356
Pickford, J. H., 79, 81
Pierson, E. C., 306, 310, 333, 369
Pingree, S., 157
Platt, M., 140, 172, 229, 284
Poffenberger, T., 16
Pohlman, E., 392
Polani, P., 100
Pollock, M. J., 120
Poloma, M. M., 129, 161, 352
Polonko, K., 198
Pope Pius, XII, 129
Porter, S., 290, 316
Potts, D. M., 100
Potts, M., 307, 308
Power, P. W., 200
Powers, W. G., 201
Presser, H. B., 311, 338
Price-Bonham, S., 291, 292
Propper, A. M., 156
Psykel, E., 295

Rabkin, K., 131
Rabkin, L. Y., 129, 131
Rainwater, L., 276
Ramey, J. W., 377, 380, 381, 382, 384, 386, 387
Randall, G. C., 33, 47
Rao, S. L. N., 331
Rapoport, A. F., 221
Rapoport, R., 151, 153, 154, 162
Rapoport, R. N., 151, 153, 154, 162
Raschke, H. J., 217
Raschke, V. J., 217
Raush, H. L., 200, 201, 203, 209, 220, 248
Raven, B. W., 193, 196
Raven, H., 344
Ravenholt, R. T., 341
Rawlings, S., 83, 87, 88, 151, 235
Ray, D. W., 203
Rebelsky, F. G., 352, 357, 363
Reed, J. P., 340

Reeves, B., 105
Regney, F. J., 344
Reik, T., 59, 62
Reiner, B. S., 47, 65, 66
Reiss, D., 431
Reiss, I. L., 16, 23, 338, 376
Remple, H., 430
Renne, K. S., 57, 140, 172, 229, 230, 305
Reuben, D., 273
Reynolds, E., 102
Rice, D. G., 151
Rice, F. P., 15, 17, 30, 46, 63, 65, 82, 101, 110, 159, 160, 249, 250, 272, 278, 292, 293, 298, 338, 359
Richter, L., 260, 270
Ridley, C. A., 36, 42, 47, 159
Ridley, J. C., 124
Riley, L. E., 285, 297
Riley, M. W., 171
Rivenback, W. H., 20
Robbins, N. N., 288
Robert, C. L., 180
Roberto, D. A., 313
Roberts, A. F., 436
Roberts, F. B., 177
Roberts, R. E., 387
Robertson, J. F., 179, 250, 253
Robinson, B. E., 413
Robinson, I. E., 421
Rock, J., 314
Rockefeller, J. D., III, 432
Rocklin, N., 419
Rodman, H., 340, 342, 343
Rodrigues, A., 193, 196
Rogers, C. R., 7, 9, 376, 385
Rogers, R. H., 161, 199, 209
Roistacher, E. A., 432
Roleder, G., 3
Rollin, B., 298, 391
Rollin, S. A., 432
Rollins, B. C., 132, 171, 196, 200, 391
Rose, R. H., 101
Rose, V. L., 291, 292
Rose, W. M., 317
Rosen, B. C., 104, 105
Rosen, L., 292, 376
Rosenbaum, V., 63, 202
Rosenberg, M., 292
Rosenblatt, P. C., 47, 178, 212
Rosenfeld, A., 35
Rosenthal, E., 86
Rossi, A. S., 161, 177
Rubin, L. B., 179
Rubin, Z., 19, 60, 63
Rudikoff, S., 388
Ruppel, H. J., Jr., 23
Rushing, W. A., 210
Rusk, H. A., 317
Russell, B., 374
Russell, C. S., 177, 178, 349
Russo, A. J., 110
Rutter, M., 159
Ryan, W., 338
Ryder, N. B., 442
Ryder, R. G., 198, 248, 308, 362
Rytina, J. H., 229

Safilios-Rothschild, C., 195, 197, 199

Sager, C. J., 267, 268
St. John-Parsons, D., 151
Salamon, S., 197
Salapatik, P., 434
Salk, L., 323, 328, 349, 355
Santrock, J. W., 362
Sarrel, P. M., 337, 338
Sarvis, B., 340, 342, 343
Sass, T., 186
Satir, V., 373
Sauer, W., 169
Saxton, L., 8, 20, 21, 56, 63, 79, 90, 238, 355
Scanzoni, J. H., 90, 140, 145, 156, 197, 198, 252
Scarf, M., 377
Scarlett, J. A., 28, 316
Scarr, A., 434
Schachter, S., 60
Schaefer, J. B., 28, 305
Schafer, R. B., 161
Schaffer, H. R., 353, 354
Schardt, A., 340
Scheck, S., 420
Scheff, E., 109
Schlesinger, B., 360, 361
Schmitt, R. C., 84
Schneider, D. M., 140
Schram, R. W., 171
Schulhofer, E., 292
Schulman, M. L., 56
Schulz, D. A., 130, 229
Schwarz, J. C., 159
Scott, J. F., 19
Scott, J. P., 186
Scriven, M., 375
Scully, D., 265
Seaman, B., 124, 160, 259
Seelbach, W. W., 253
Segal, S., 315
Self, G. D., 106
Semans, J., 270
Sena-Rivera, J., 252
Senn, D. J., 205
Sennett, R., 216
Sewell, W. H., 67, 126
Shader, R. I., 268
Shainberg, L. W., 318, 319
Shanas, E., 181, 182
Shankweiler, P. J., 124
Shapiro, T., 275
Shaver, P., 6, 110
Shearman, R. P., 333
Shepard, J. M., 80, 88, 317
Sheresky, N., 370, 371
Sherfey, M. J., 274
Sherman, J. A., 267, 321, 323, 328
Shey, T. H., 390
Shideler, M. M., 291
Shope, D. F., 260
Shortell, J. R., 103
Shover, N., 428
Shulman, A., 370, 371, 372
Shuttlesworth, G., 35, 36, 39, 40, 45
Siegel, P. S., 53, 63, 211
Signoria, E. I., 430
Sigusch, V., 265
Silvan, 377
Silverman, A., 391

Simmons, J. L., 42
Simon, R. J., 105, 144
Simon, W., 435
Sindberg, R. M., 81
Singh, B. K., 23
Sjovall, E., 315
Skard, A. G., 159, 160
Skeen, P., 413
Skinner, D. A., 153
Skolnick, A., 103, 120, 123, 138, 173, 370, 385
Slater, P. E., 129, 158, 385
Smart, M. S., 353, 355, 356, 357
Smart, R. C., 353, 355, 356, 357
Smart, R. G., 319
Smith, D. E., 385
Smith, E. D., 344
Smith, E. M., 344
Smith, J. R., 377, 378
Smith, K. D., 102
Smith, L. G., 377, 378
Smith, M. D., 106
Smith, R. A., 313
Smith, R. G., 343
Smith, R. H., 143, 145
Smith, R. T., 140
Smith, T., 436
Smithells, R. W., 318
Snow, J. H., 156
Snyder, D. K., 172
Soely, S., 122
Sollie, D. L., 176
Soltz, D. F., 108
Somerville, R. M., 179
Sorensen, R. C., 19
Spanier, G. B., 27, 29, 34, 59, 60, 169, 170, 171, 377, 391
Speidel, J. J., 341
Spence, J. T., 109
Spicer, J. W., 296
Spock, B., 349
Sponaugle, G. C., 431
Spray, S. L., 142
Spreitzer, E. A., 285, 297
Sprenkls, D. H., 442
Sprey, J., 213
Spuhler, J. N., 79, 81
Stafford, R., 40
Stannard, U., 131, 352, 355
Staples, R., 25, 124, 197, 252, 294, 359
Starr, R. H., 431
Stauss, J. H., 305
Stehouwer, J., 182
Stein, J., 58
Stein, R. L., 295, 360
Steinbeck, H., 428
Steinem, G., 122
Steiner, G. Y., 130
Steinhilber, R. M., 272
Steinhoff, P. G., 342, 343
Steinmann, A., 105
Steinmetz, S. K., 215, 223, 224
Stekel, W., 110
Stern, L. D., 278
Stevenson, M. H., 405
Stewart, C. S., 441
Stewart, P. L., 19, 22, 342
Stinnet, V., 38, 80, 105
Stone, L. H., 60

Storm, V., 42, 43
Straus, M. A., 215, 216, 217, 224, 251
Strean, H. S., 377
Streib, G. F., 131
Strong, E., 21
Strong, L. D., 393, 394
Stuart, R. B., 221
Stubbs, M. V. L., 319
Sudia, C. E., 363, 364
Suelzle, M., 124, 126
Suomi, S. J., 328
Sussman, M. B., 360, 369, 370, 373
Suter, L. E., 125
Sutton, P. M., 307
Swartz, D. P., 342
Sweet, J. A., 53, 55
Swensen, C. H., 63, 65
Swift, M. R., 317
Swinyard, C. A., 317
Symmonds, R. E., 313

Tallman, I., 212
Tamashiro, R. T., 169
Targ, D. B., 179
Tarr, L. H., 106
Tatum, H. J., 310
Tavris, C., 121
Taylor, D. A., 193, 203, 205, 209, 218
Teevan, J. J., 25, 26
TenHouten, W. D., 197
Thal, H. M., 227
Thomas, L. E., 231
Thomas, M. M., 407
Thompson, K. S., 171
Thompson, R., 29
Thorman, G., 35, 36, 39, 40, 45
Tickamyer, B. R., 153
Tietze, C., 311, 315
Tindall, V. R., 307
Tissue, T., 186
Toby, J., 121
Tognoli, J., 107
Tolone, W. L., 413
Tomeh, A. K., 439
Torres, A., 29
Torrey, B. A., 419
Trainer, J. B., 278
Traupmann, J., 441
Troiden, R. R., 110
Tropman, J. E., 142
Trost, J., 38, 39, 43, 47
Tu, E. J., 443
Turk, J. L., 195
Turner, R. H., 213
Turner, S., 376

Udry, J. A., 9, 261
Udry, J. R., 89, 197, 251
Uhlenberg, P., 171
U'Ren, M. B., 104
Uzoka, A. F., 251

Valeris, S., 61
Vanfossen, B. E., 106
Varni, C., 378
Vatsyayana, 259
Veevers, J. E., 392, 393
Vener, A. M., 19, 22
Veolitze, M., 436

Verna, M. E., 105
Verniaud, W., 443
Verwoerdt, A., 183, 268
Vessey, M. P., 307
Veysey, L., 386
Vilar, E., 138, 139
Vincent, C. E., 267, 338
Vincent, J. P., 221, 222
Viorst, J., 61, 441
Vitousek, B. M., 84, 85
Voeller, B., 112
Voss, H. L., 34
Voydanoff, P., 156, 158
Vreeland, R. S., 20

Wachowiak, D., 172, 201
Wackman, D. B., 200
Waite, L. J., 67
Walker, C., 170
Wallace, W., 438
Wallston, B. S., 156
Walsh, R. H., 413
Walster, E., 20, 24, 60, 61
Walster, G. W., 24
Walters, J., 15, 105, 112
Walters, L. H., 15
Walum, L. R., 157
Wampler, K. S., 442
Ward, T. J., 39
Waring, J. M., 250, 253
Warner, J., 289
Watley, D. J., 67, 68, 126
Weaver, C. N., 7, 169
Wegner, E. L., 24, 67, 126
Weichmann, G. H., 27
Weil, A., 385
Weil, M. W., 199
Weinberg, J., 268
Weinberg, M. S., 110, 111, 112
Weisberg, C., 203
Weisman, M., 295
Weisner, T. S., 390
Weiss, H. D., 275
Weiss, R. L., 221, 222, 370
Weiss, R. S., 184
Weitzman, L. J., 287, 369
Welch, S., 89
Welding, P., 295
Wells, C., 12, 373, 377, 393, 394
Wells, J. G., 288
Wells, T., 45
Wenger, M. G., 404
West, P., 172
Westhues, K., 386
Westman, J. C., 292
Westoff, C. F., 260, 306, 307, 308, 309, 310, 311, 315, 331
Westoff, L. A., 260, 306, 307, 308, 309, 310, 311, 315, 331, 337, 338, 339
Wheeler, L., 203
White, L. K., 406
White, M., 12, 373, 377, 393, 394
White, M. S., 443
Whitehurst, R. N., 10, 11, 41, 46, 129, 376, 383
Wikler, A., 319
Wilkening, E. A., 195
Wilkinson, M. L., 62

Willett, R. P., 195
Willett, R. S., 163
Williams, C. E., 211
Williams, C. J., 111, 112
Williamson, R. C., 59, 249
Willie, C. V., 197
Wilson, G. S., 319
Wilson, G. T., 277
Wilson, R. A., 435
Wilson, W., 438
Wimbish, J. M., 417
Winch, R. F., 80, 251
Wind, Y., 194
Winick, C., 259
Winograd, B., 42
Winthrop, H., 63

Withers, G., 173
Wohlford, P., 362
Wood, V., 253
Woodrow, K., 67
Wortis, R. P., 160
Wright, M. R., 267
Wright, T. L., 397
Wyden, P., 214, 215
Wylie, E. M., 289, 290, 291, 313
Wyly, M. V., 185, 186
Wynn, A., 343
Wynn, M., 343

Yancey, W. L., 197
Yankelovich, D., 12, 386

Yarber, W. L., 30
Yarrow, M., 159, 160
Yorburg, B., 38, 145, 160
Yost, E. D., 38, 394
Young, J. S., 432
Yule, V., 212

Zabin, L. S., 29
Zablocki, B., 385, 386, 388
Zarrow, M. X., 314
Zehv, W., 269
Zelnik, M., 21, 22, 27, 28, 29
Zelson, C., 319
Zigler, E., 130
Zipper, J. A., 309

Subject Index

Abortion
  legal considerations, 340
  moral aspects of, 341
  need for understanding, 340
  physical and medical aspects of, 340, 341
  psychological and personal aspects of, 343, 344
  reasons for, 343
  social and realistic aspects of, 342, 343
  and the women's movement, 131
Abstinence, premarital sexual, 23
Acceptance, 63
Adaptability. See Flexibility
Adjustment. See Marriage adjustment
Adolescents, premarital sexual behavior of, 21–23
Adoption
  changing philosophies of, 333
  numbers and children involved, 334
  private or independent, 335
  questions couples face, 334
  through a licensed agency, 335
Adultery. See also Comarital sex and Extramarital sex
  ambiguous, 376
  clandestine, 376
  consensual, 376
  as grounds for divorce, 286
Affection
  expression of, and marital satisfaction, 172
  fulfillment of, through dating, 19
Age
  of children, and working mothers, 159
  differentials in marriage, 54, 55
  as a factor in decision-making power, 198
  as a factor in divorce, 283
  as a factor in leaving child with sitter, 353–355
  as a factor in remarriage, 297
  of husband, as a factor in fertility, 331

and marital readiness, 53–56
  median, for marriage, 54, 55
  of mother, and birth defects, 318
Aged, care of in the future, 400
Aggression
  negative effects of, 214–216
  relationship of verbal and physical, 214–216
  and sex, 27
  and testosterone level, 102
  therapeutic, 214, 215
  and ventilation, 214
Agreement. See Consensus
Alcoholism
  and birth defects, 319
  as grounds for divorce, 286
Alimony, 290
Alternate life styles, 12
  attitudes of college students toward, 393, 394
  comarital sex, 377
  communes, 384–390
  group marriage, 381–384
  intimate friendships, 379–381
  marriage by stages, 373–375
  nonmarital cohabitation, 32–51
  one-parent families, 359–364
  renewable marriage, 373
  trial marriage, 374
  unwed parenthood, 337–338
  voluntary childlessness, 390–394
Androgens. See Hormones
Annulment, grounds, 286
Anxiety and worry as barriers to communication, 204, 205
Appearance, compatibility of, 81. See also Physical attraction
Artificial insemination, 333
Attachments
  emotional, of children to parents, 352–354
  and separation from attachment figure, 353, 354
Attitudes
  of college students toward sexual permissiveness, 23–27

compatibility of, 89, 90
  toward divorce, 294
  of husbands in dual-career marriage, 154, 155
  of students toward collegiate marriage, 69
  toward marriage, 3
Authority. See also Power in decision making
  definition, 193
  marital power patterns, 193
Automobile, buying an, 238
Autonomy
  in decision making, 193, 194
  development of, in children, 355
  in relation to parents, as factor in marital readiness, 66
Autosexual, 110

Baby
  development of emotional attachments in, 352–354
  effects of separation from attachment figure, 353
  organizing home for, 325
  sitter, choice of, 353, 354
Bigamy, 286
Birth control. See also Contraceptives and Planned parenthood
  methods, 306–316
  need for, 305
  and sexual satisfaction, 275, 317
  succeeding with, 317
Birth control pill
  advantages of, 306
  and birth defects, 308
  costs of, 316
  effectiveness of, 306
  and fertility, 308
  minipill, 307
  morning after pill, 307
  risks of, 307–309, 316
  and risk of cancer, 307
  other side effects of, 308
  and sexual drive and frequency of intercourse, 308

459

Birth control pill (*continued*)
  and thromboembolism, 307
  types and administration of, 306
  use and action of, 306
Birth defects
  and age of mother, 318
  and birth control pill, 308
  birth injuries and, 317, 320
  causes of, 317
  common defects, 317, 319
  environmental causes of, 318–320
  and fetal position, 318, 319
  genetic counseling and, 317, 318
  hereditary causes of, 317, 318
  and illness of mother, 318
  and nutritional deficiencies, 318, 319
  and use of drugs, 318, 319
  and X-rays, 318, 319
Birth rates
  and family planning, 305
  and overpopulation, 391
Bottle versus breast feeding, 328
Broken homes. *See* Divorce,
      Separation, Widows and
      widowers
Brother-in-law, 247. *See also* In-laws
Budgeting and record keeping, 234,
      235

Canada, sexual attitudes and behavior
      in, 26
Career
  and husbands in dual-career
      marriage, 153, 155
  versus marriage, 5, 6
  pursuit, and geographical mobility,
      156, 157
  women, 151–154
Castration, 311
Catharsis, 214
Catholic. *See also* Church and Religion
  church and abortion, 341
  -Jewish marriages, 85–87
  -Protestant marriages, 85–87
Chauvinism, 121, 122
Childbirth. *See also* Natural childbirth
  after, 327, 337
  father's role in, 324–326
  in the future, 398
  going to hospital, 326
  labor in, 326, 327
  mother-infant contact after, 327
  natural, 323–325
  prepared, 323–325
  and rooming in, 328
Child Care. *See also* Day care
  and dual-career marriage, 158–160
  in groups, 355
  individual solutions to, 158, 159
  institutional, 159
  in nuclear family, 158
  responsibility for, 130, 131
  by sitter, 353, 354
  type of substitute care, 160
Child custody, 290, 291
Child rearing
  in the future family, 398
  in group marriage, 383
  and husbands, 143, 144

and the low socioeconomic status
      husband, 145–149
  philosophies of, 349
  in rural communes, 387, 388
  in urban communes, 396
  and the women's movement, 129–
      131
Child support, 289, 290
Children
  adoptable and unadoptable, 334
  adopted, and relations with parents,
      335, 336
  benefits to, in dual-career marriage,
      156
  cognitive and intellectual growth of,
      356, 357
  desire for, as motive of marriage, 6
  development of autonomy in, 355
  and divorce, 286, 287, 290–293
  emotional needs of, 352–356
  fears of spoiling, 355
  group care of, 355
  in group marriage, 383
  influence on decision making, 199
  intellectual needs of, 350, 351
  and marriage contracts, 373
  moral needs of, 351
  needs of, 350, 351
  number involved in divorce, 286
  in one-parent families, 359–363
  physical needs of, 350
  separation and rejection of, 353–355
  sharing responsibilities in care of,
      352
  socialization and discipline of, 357–
      359
  social needs of, 350
Chromosomes, anomalies of, 100
Church. *See* Catholic, Jewish,
      Protestant, and Religion
Class. *See also* Social class
  homogamy of, 82, 83
  and marital power patterns, 194,
      197
  standing of students, and
      cohabitation, 36
Clergy, family life of, 142
Coitus. *See* Sexual intercourse
Coitus interruptus, 315
College
  costs of, 228
  degree recipients in, 126, 127
  students, attitudes toward
      alternative marital forms, 393,
      394
  students, attitudes toward sexual
      permissiveness, 23–25, 28
  students, marriage of, 68–73
Collusion, 289
Comarital sex, 377. *See also* Adultery
      and Extramarital sex
Commitment
  different levels of, in cohabitation,
      42–44
  premature, 25
Communes
  history of, 384, 385
  motivations and philosophies of,
      385, 386

rural, 387, 388
  urban, 389, 390
Communication
  barriers to, 203, 204
  clarity and accuracy in, 205, 206
  empathy in, 205
  feedback and reciprocity in, 206
  importance in marriage, 201
  improving skills of, 204–206
  listening as a factor in, 206
  and marital satisfaction, 172
  in new marriage, 10
  nonverbal, 202, 203
  self-disclosure in, 205
  verbal, 201
  what it involves, 200
Companionship
  through dating, 18, 19
  and marital satisfaction, 172
  need for, as motive for marriage, 6
  role of male in, 144–146
Companionship marriage versus
      traditional, 7–12
Compatibility, 79–95
  of attitudes and values, 89, 90
  of backgrounds, 82–89
  in dating, 20
  definition, 79
  of habit systems, 91, 92
  of interests and activities, 90, 91
  and mate selection, 92
  of needs, 80
  of personalities, 81, 82
  of role concepts, 90
Complementarity
  in dating, 21
  of needs, 80
Conception
  difficulties of, and infertility, 331,
      332
  and the rhythm methods, 313–315
Condom, 310
Condonation, 289
Conflict, 208–225
  as acceptance, 214
  avoidance of, 217
  as catharsis, 214
  causes and effects of, 212, 213
  constructive, 218
  destructive, 219
  family violence, 222–225
  focuses of, 212
  with in-laws, 246–249
  interpsychic, 210
  intrapsychic, 209
  intrasomatic, 210
  methods of dealing with, 217–222
  positive and negative values of,
      213–216
  as reality testing, 213
  solving through negotiation and
      contracting, 221
  solving through role induction,
      modification, and reversal, 221
  sources of, 209–212
Connivance, 289
Consanguinity, 80
Consensus and compatibility, 89, 90
Consumer economics

budgeting, 234
buying a car, 238
credit, 231, 238
getting the most for your money, 239, 240
housing, 235–238
investments, 239
money management, 233–235
Contraception, need for, 305. *See also* Planned parenthood
Contraceptives
chemical and spermicides, 309
condom, 310
costs of, 316
diaphragm, 311, 312
douching, 309
IUD, 309
making choice of, 315, 316
noncoital stimulation, 315
pill, 306–309
responsible use of, 30
rhythm methods, 313–315
salpingectomy, 313
use among adolescents, 27, 28
use among college students, 28
vasectomy, 311, 313
Contractual marriage, 369–373. *See also* Marriage contract
Corporations, and marriage, 142, 156, 157
Counseling
abortion, 344
genetic, 317, 318
of unwed fathers, 339
of unwed mothers, 338
Courtship
adjustment during, 20, 173
conflict with parents and in-laws during, 68
stages in, 16
Cream, vaginal, 269, 309
Credit. *See* Money
Crisis. *See also* Divorce, Death
as a source of marital conflict, 211, 212
spending and indebtedness, 231
Cruelty, as grounds for divorce, 286
Cunnilingus, 42

D and C, 341. *See also* Abortion
Dating, 15–21
experience and marital readiness, 57
in the 1940s to 1960s, 16, 17
partners versus marriage partners, 20, 21
reasons for, 18–20
as a sociological phenomenon, 15–18
steady, 16
today as contrasted with dating in previous generations, 17–18
Day care, 130, 355. *See also* Child care
Death
and bereavement, 183, 184
risk from birth control pill, 307–309, 316
Decision making. *See also* Power in decision making
early in marriage, 175

in group marriage, 383, 384
who does it, 194–196
Delinquency, and divorce, 292
Democratic sharing of power in decision making, 193, 194
Denmark, attitudes toward homosexuality in, 111
Dependent love, 61
Desertion
as grounds for divorce, 286
and motherhood, 361
Developmental tasks in marriage, 173–176
Diabetes, and sexual dysfunction, 278
Diaphragm, 311
Diet, 318
Discipline
meaning and goals of, 358
principles of, 358, 359
Discrimination, against women, 120–126
Disillusionment with marriage, 3, 35, 171, 173–175, 385
Divorce
adult adjustments after, 293–296
adversary approach to, 288
age factors in, 283
and alimony, 290, 295
attitudes of society toward, 294
and child custody, 291
children as pawns in, 290
children involved in, 286
and child support, 290, 295
costs of, 289, 290
duration of marriage before, 285
effects on children, 291, 292
emotional trauma of, 293
and family background, 284
finances after, 295
in the future, 399
geographic factors in, 285
grounds for, 286
kinship interaction after, 296
lawyers in, 290
no-fault, 286–289
number of, 4
property settlements in, 289
rates, 3
reactions of children to, 292, 293
realignment of responsibilities and work roles after, 295
sexual readjustments after, 295
socioeconomic factors in, 284
statistics, 283–286
visitation rights granted in, 291
Dominance-submission, 80
Double standard of sexual behavior, 23, 24
Douche, 309
Drug use
and cohabitation, 37
in communes, 385, 387, 389
as factor in birth defects, 319
and sexual dysfunction, 277, 278
Dual-career marriage
benefits of, 155, 156
child care and, 158, 159
effects on children, 159, 160
husbands and wives in, 151–155

job establishment and, 151, 156–158
strains, 161, 162
Duress and fraud, 286
Dyspareunia, 273

Early marriage
in college, 68–73
common problems and adjustments in, 71–73
and grade point averages, 70
incidence while in college, 68
satisfactions of, 70
student attitudes toward, 69, 70
while both in school, 71
Education. *See also* School
aspirations for, and marital readiness, 67
for childbirth, 323–325
differences of, and marital communication, 204
and divorce rates, 284
as a factor in compatibility, 87–89
for family life, need for, 37, 345
homogamy versus heterogamy with respect to, 87–89
level of, and decision-making power, 197
and marital satisfaction, 172
of women versus men, 126–128
Ejaculatory incompetence, description of, 272
Embryo, 318, 341
Emotional deprivation, 351–354
Emotional involvement and love, 52–65
Emotional maturity. *See also* Immaturity
of husbands in dual-career marriage, 155
parents' tasks in development of, in children, 352, 356
Emotions
as factors in sexual response, 260
during pregnancy and baby's health, 319
Empathy and rapport in communication, 205
Employment. *See also* Work
discrimination against women in, 121, 124–126
establishment and dual-career marriage, 156
influence on decision-making power, 197, 200
of male, 135–142
effect of marriage on, 142
that involves family, 141, 142
and marriage, 139–142
requiring special talent, 142
and self-image, 138, 139
that separates couples, 140, 141
and wife's satisfaction with, 140
satisfaction and marital satisfaction, 172
strains from, in dual-career marriage, 161
Empty nest period, 178–180
Endogamy, 79

Engagement, length of before
     marriage, 55, 56
Equalitarian
     marriage, 8, 9, 193
     power in decision making, 193, 194
Erogenous zones, 261
Erotic love, 61–63
Estrogen. *See also* Hormones
     and birth control pill, 306, 307
     in sexual development, 101, 102
Evolutionary communes, 386
Exogamy, 79
Extended family
     aid patterns of, 182, 253, 254
     attitudes toward, 250
     versus nuclear, 8, 11
     variables affect contacts with, 250–
        252
     visiting, 250–252
Extramarital sex, 375, 376. *See also*
     Adultery and Comarital sex

Family
     background, and divorce, 284, 285
     both-parent, need for, 359–365
     extended, 250–254
     and the future, 394, 397
     nuclear versus extended, 8, 11
     nuclear, future of, 394, 397
     of widow, 185–187
Family life cycle
     changes in marital satisfaction
        during, 169–172
     and decision-making power, 199
     and housing, 235
     stages of, 169, 170
Family planning. *See* Planned
     parenthood
Family violence, 222–225
     cycle of, 223
     definitions of, 222
     factors related to, 223, 224
     prevention and intervention in, 224,
        225
Father
     absence, effect on daughters, 362,
        363
     absence, effect on mother, 363
     absence, effects on sons, 362
     conflict of, between job and family,
        135
     as inappropriate model, 363
     low socioeconomic status, 144–146
     responsibilities of, 143, 144
     solo, and taking care of children,
        361
     unwed, help for, 339
Father-in-law, 247
Fault divorce. *See* Divorce
Fellatio, 42
Felony, as grounds for divorce, 286
Females
     general sexual dysfunction of
        description, 272
        physical causes of, 274, 277
        psychological causes of, 275–277
     and marriage in the future, 397, 398
Femininity, concepts of, 106–108
Feminism. *See* Women's movement

Fertility, and birth control, 340–342.
     See also Infertility
Fertilization. *See* Conception
Fetus, 318–322, 340–342
Fidelity, readiness for as factor in
     marital readiness, 66
Flexibility
     in decision making, 194–197
     in job pursuit, 156, 157
     of sex role concepts, 8, 10, 40, 108,
        109, 128, 129, 154, 155
     in time scheduling, 162
Foam, contraceptive, 309
Food, costs of, 228
France, and infant care centers, 130
Fraternities and sororities, 19
Fraud, 286
Friends
     adjustments to, early in marriage,
        174, 176
     through dating, 20
     of dual-career couples, 162
     friendship as love, 63
     and marital readiness, 56, 57
     of widows, 185
Frigidity. *See* Females, general sexual
     dysfunction of

Gender
     assignment at birth, 103
     genetic basis for, 99
General sexual dysfunction, 272, 273
Genetic counseling to prevent birth
     defects, 317, 318
Genitals
     female, 263
     and hermaphrodites, 103
     male, 262
Geographic considerations
     and divorce rate, 285
     and nonmarital cohabitation, 38
Glands, sex, 101–103
Grade school children
     and paternal absence, 362
     socialization of, 357, 358
Grandparents
     and aid patterns, 250, 253, 254
     intergenerational relationships of,
        250, 254
     relationships with grown children
        and grandchildren, 181, 182
Group marriage
     children in, 383
     definition and description of, 381
     integration and tenure in, 384
     jealousy in, 383
     money in, 382
     organization, decision making in,
        383, 384
     sex in, 383

Habits, compatibility of, 91
Hawaii, interracial marriage in, 84, 85
Health. *See also* Illness
     considerations in abortion, 340, 341
     and decision-making power, 206
     and infertility, 332, 333
     after retirement, 181

and use of birth control pill, 307–
     309
Heredity, and birth defects, 317, 318
Hermaphrodite, 103
Heterogamy, 79
Heterosexual adjustments, and father
     absence, 362
Heterosexual stage of development,
     110
Holland, attitudes toward
     homosexuality in, 111
Homemaking
     hiring help with, 128, 161
     male's role in, 128, 143, 144
     tasks, adjustments to, 175
     and women's movement, 128, 129
Homogamy, 79, 81
Homosexual
     concepts of, 109–112
     and marriage, 113
     problems of, 112
Honeymoon, adjustments during,
     173–176
Hormones
     influence on behavior, 101, 102
     influence on physical development,
        101, 102
     and sexual identity, 101
     use of, in infertility, 333
Housewife, and women's movement,
     120, 128, 129
Housing
     and cohabitation, 39
     costs of, 235–238
     of elderly, 182, 183
     and the family life cycle, 235, 237
     future trends, 399
     home ownership versus renting,
        335, 336
     newer trends in, 237, 238
     problems in college and
        cohabitation, 34
     shortage, and doubling up, 250
Husbands
     changing roles of, 135–138
     and child care, 131, 143
     companionship role, 144, 145
     conflict of, 135
     decision-making powers of, 194–196
     in dual-career marriage, 154, 155
     effect of role on himself, 138, 139
     housekeeping and parental roles,
        143, 144
     and housework, 128, 129, 143
     low socioeconomic status, 145, 146
     occupational roles and marriage,
        139–142
     relationship with wife after
        retirement, 180
Hygiene and cleanliness, 91, 92, 276
Hymen, initial defloration of, 269
Hysterectomy, 341
Hysterotomy, 341

Identification and modeling
     in sex role development, 103–106
     in socialization of children, 357, 358,
        362, 363
Illegitimacy

causes of, 337, 338
rates of, 337
tragic results of, 338
Illness. *See also* Health
and marital conflict, 210
of mother as cause of birth defects, 318
Immaturity. *See also* Emotional maturity
and conflict with in-laws, 248, 249
Impotence, 270, 271
as grounds for divorce, 286
physiological causes of, 277, 278
psychological causes of, 275–277
Income. *See also* Money
and divorce rates, 284
male-female differentials of, 124–126
and marital satisfaction, 171, 172
after retirement, 180
of widows, 186
Infants
and adoption, 334–336
and breast versus bottle feeding, 328
and day care, 130, 131, 353–355
early contact with mothers, 327
emotional needs of, 352–354
intellectual development of, 356, 357
and maternal separation, 353, 354
and need for fathers, 131
and rooming-in care of, 328
Infertility. *See also* Fertility
and artificial insemination, 333
causes of, 331–333
definition of, 331
and frequency of sexual intercourse, 331
help for, 332
incidence of, 331
In-laws. *See also* Kinsfolk
adjustment with, and marital happiness, 245
and the extended family network, 250–254
people dislike, 246, 247
people like, 245, 246
relationships with, when living with them, 250
roots of conflict with, 247–249
Insanity, as divorce grounds, 286
Insurance loans, 238
Intelligence
growth of, in children, 356, 357
homogamy of, 87
Interests
compatibility of, 90
and decision-making power, 198
Interfaith marriage, 85–87
Interlocutory period, 288
Interracial adoptions, 334
Interracial marriage, 83, 84
Intimacy
as goal of future marriage, 399
need for, as motive for marriage, 6
Intimate friendships
description of, 379, 380
effects of, 380
motivations for, 380
Intrauterine device (IUD), 309, 310

Intrinsic marriage, 7, 8
Investments, 239

Japanese-American marriages, 84, 85
Jealousy
in comarital sex, 376
in group marriage, 383
in swinging, 379
Jelly, vaginal, 309
Jewish. *See also* Religion
-Catholic marriages, 85–87
-Protestant marriages, 85–87
Judeo-Christian ethics, and sexual exclusiveness, 375

Kibbutzim, in Israel, 130, 131
Kinsfolk. *See also* In-laws
and extended family network, 250
relations with, after divorce, 296
Kissing, 262. *See also* Affection

Labor, in childbirth, 326, 327
Lamaze method, 324, 325
Laparoscopy, 313
Laws
of adoption, 335, 336
and cohabitation, 47
of divorce, grounds for, 286–289
marriage, 369
relating to abortions, 340
Lawyers
and divorce, 288
fees, 290
Leboyer method, 327
Legal equality for women, 122
Leisure
dating as recreation, 18
lack of, in early marriage, 72
Lesbian. *See* Homosexual
Life expectancy, 170, 183
Loneliness
after divorce, 294
of widows, 185
Love
altruistic, 63
conjugal, 57, 64, 65
dependent, 61
as end in itself, 8
erotic, 61
friendship, 63
as motive for marriage, 6, 7
romantic, 57–61
and sex, 61–63
Low sex drive
of husbands, 268, 272
of wives, 272, 273
Low socioeconomic status
and family living, 228, 229
husbands, 145–147
father roles, 146, 147
marital roles, 145, 146

Male-female differences
in contacts with families, 252
in dating aspirations, 20
and similarities in sexual stimulation and response, 265, 266
in use of money, 230, 231

in viewing cohabiting relationship, 43, 44
Marriage
adjustment
after retirement, 180–183
during courtship, 173
during parenthood, 176–178
during postparental years, 178–180
early in marriage, 173–176
meaning, 169, 172
tasks, 173
of widows and widowers, 183–187
attitudes toward, 3, 6, 397
careers and children, 6
communication in, 200–206
conflict in, 209–225
contracts
civil, 369
personal, 369–372
renewable, 373
by stages, 373–375
dual-career, 151–163
duration before divorce, 285
early, and personal mobility, 68
early, while in college, 68–73
expectations, 11
and the future, 397
happiness, 169
and adjustment to in-laws, 245
in remarriage, 297, 298
and sex, 260, 261
as institution, 9
integration, 11
intrinsic, 8
and male's occupation, 139–142
and money, 227–242
motives for, 6
negative motives for, 65, 66
to avoid stigma of being single, 65
as escape, 65
out of pity, gratitude, 65
to prove something, 65
to spite another, 65
new versus traditional, 7–12
power patterns, 193–200
problems, as cause and effect of conflict, 212
rates, 5
readiness, 53–68
readiness, evaluation of, 73
roles, and women's movement, 119–132
satisfaction, 12, 169–172
changes in, 170–172
and communication, 201
over the family life cycle, 169–172
and money, 229–230
personal correlates with, 172
and power patterns, 193, 194
and relationship factors, 172
and self-disclosure, 205
social correlates with, 172
sex adjustment in, 267–269
stability, 169
stability and age, 53
success, 3

Marriage (*continued*)
  utilitarian, 8
  variant forms of, 368–394
    attitudes of college students
      toward, 394
    and communal living, 384–390
    and extramarital or comarital sex,
      375–377
    group marriage, 381–384
    and intimate friendships, 379–381
    and swinging, 377–379
    and voluntary childlessness, 390–
      394
Masculine-feminine concepts, 106–109
Masculinity, concepts of, 107, 108
Masturbation, of elderly, 183
Mate selection
  and altruistic love, 63, 64
  and cohabitation, 46, 47
  and compatibility, 92
  through dating, 20, 21
  and dependent love, 61
  and erotic love, 61–63
  and friendship love, 63
  and romantic love, 57–61
Mate swapping. *See* Swinging
Menopause, 179
Menstruation
  and fertility, 313–315
  and sexual appetite, 268
Mental health
  and marital conflict, 210
  during pregnancy, 323
Minipill, 307
Miscarriage, 319, 321
Miscegenation, 83, 84
Mobility
  and early marriage, 68
  geographical, and dual-career
    marriage, 156
Modeling, 103, 105, 106, 362
Modesty, 267, 275
Money
  and aid given to other family
    members, 253, 254
  arrangements in cohabitation, 40
  careless use of, 232
  compulsive spending of, 233
  consumer economics and, 238–240
  cost of adoption, 335
  cost of housing, 235–238
  credit privileges for women, 122,
    123
  for crisis, 231, 232
  and debt, 231
  and early marriage, 71
  factors in birth control, 316
  in group marriage, 382
  lack of, and family life, 228
  management, 233–235
  and marital satisfaction, 229
  masculine-feminine differences in
    use of, 230, 231
  matters after divorce, 295
  and poverty, 228
  as a reflection of values, 227
  rewards in dual-career marriage, 155
  savings and investments, 239
  use of credit, 231, 238

Monogamy, 397
Morals
  and abortion, 341
  growth of, in children, 351
  and sexual standards, 25, 28, 36,
    379, 393
  sexual, of college students, 25, 27,
    28
Morning-after pill, 307
Morning sickness, 320, 321
Mortality and birth control methods,
  316
Motherhood, negative views of, 129,
  130, 171
Mother-infant contact after childbirth,
  327
Mother-in-law, 246–248. *See also* In-
  laws
Motivation
  for adoption, 234
  to marry, 65
Multilateral marriage, 381

Natural childbirth, 323–325. *See also*
  Childbirth
Need
  for children, 6
  for companionship, 6, 7, 18, 144
  complementary needs, 80
  dependency, as factor in mate
    selection, 61
  emotional, as motive for marriage,
    7, 8
  for emotional security, 35, 352, 353
  frustration as source of marital
    conflict, 210, 214
  fulfillment and compatibility, 80
  fulfillment as motive for marriage,
    6, 8
  for love, 6, 7, 19
  parallel needs, 80
  for physical help, labor, and
    services, 7, 8
  for sexual satisfaction and
    fulfillment, 10, 19, 259
  for status, esteem, recognition, and
    acceptance, 19
New marriage, 7–12
No-fault divorce. *See* Divorce
Nonmarital cohabitation, 32–51
  adjustments in, 39–42, 44, 45
  beneficial effects of, 45
  decision making regarding, 48
  definition of, 33
  description of, 39–42
  effects and implications of, 45–48
  effects on marriage, 46, 47
  incidences of, 34
  increase of, 34, 35
  legal implications of, 47
  nature of the relationships, 42–44
  negative effects of, 45, 46
  persons involved, 36–39
  problems with, 44, 45
  reasons why some students aren't
    involved, 35, 36
  students attitudes toward, 35
  tenure of, 36
Nonverbal communication, 202, 203

Nuclear family. *See* Family
Nursery school. *See* Child care and
  Day care
Nurturance-succorance, 80
Nutrition and diet as factor in birth
  defects, 318, 319

Occupations. *See* Employment and
  Work
One-parent family
  occurrence of, 359
  problems of female-headed, 359–361
  problems of male-headed, 361
Oral contraceptives. *See*
  Contraceptives
Oral sex, 42
  cunnilingus, 42
  fellatio, 42
Orgasm
  and happy marriage, 260
  male-female differences in, 266, 267
  multiple, 266
  phase of sexual response, 264
  vaginal versus clitoral, 265
Orgasm dysfunction, causes of, 274–
  278
Orientals in interracial marriage, 84,
  85
Ovulation, 313–315, 333

Parallel needs, 80
Parent-child relationships
  with adopted children, 336
  after parents retire, 181, 182
  with working parents, 160
Parenthood
  adjustments of the husband to, 178
  adjustments of the wife to, 177, 178
  fostering cognitive and intellectual
    growth, 356, 357
  meeting emotional needs of
    children, 350, 352–356
  one-parent families, 359–364
  philosophies of child rearing, 347
  preparation for, 323–325
  pressures to be parents, 392
  roles of parents, 392
  socialization and discipline, 357–359
  as stress, 176, 177
Parents
  and cohabitation, 44
  importance of having two, 364, 365
  influence of, in children's
    socialization, 357
  marriages of, and cohabitation, 37,
    38
  readiness of, for child to marry, 68
  resentment of mate, 249
  roles of, 350–352
  sharing responsibilities as, 352
  versus peers in influencing
    premarital sexual standards, 25
Parents without Partners, 361
Personality
  compatibility, 81
  in dating problems, 20, 21
  factors in decision-making power,
    198

factors and premarital sexual
permissiveness, 26
Phobias, sexual, 275, 276
Physical attractiveness in date
selection, 20
Pill. *See* Birth control pill
Pinned, 17
Planned parenthood
and early marriage, 72, 73
goal of, 305
and marital conflict, 212
need for, 305
and women's movement, 131
Postparental period
adjustments during, 171, 178–180
myths about, 179
time span, 170, 178
Postpartum
contacts with infant, 327
rooming in, 328
Poverty. *See* Low socioeconomic status
Power in decision making, 193–200.
See also Decision making
influence of children on, 199
influence of cultural and racial
factors on, 197, 198
influence of employment on, 197
influence of interest and
competence on, 198
influence of level of education on,
197
influence of personality and age on,
198
in relation to circumstances, 200
relationship to marital satisfaction,
194
relationship to stage of family life
cycle, 199
sex differences in, 195
sources of, 196–200
types of power patterns, 193
who makes the decisions, 194, 195
Pregnancy
and career, 158
and drinking, 319
duration of, 321
major complications of, 321
and marital communication, 203
minor side effects of, 321
and mother's mental health, 323
and prenatal care, 321–323
sex relations during, 322, 323
signs and symptoms of, 32
and smoking, 319
tests for, 320
and use of drugs, 319
Premarital pregnancy as motive for
marriage, 65. *See also*
Unmarried pregnancy
Premarital sexual behavior
of college students, 23–27
correlations with, 25–27
of young adolescents, 21–23
Premarital sexual intercourse
among adolescents, 21–23
among college students, 23–27
Premature birth, 319, 321
Premature ejaculation, 270
Prenatal care, 321–323

Preschool children
and autonomy, 355
and child care, 158, 160, 355
and discipline, 358, 359
and divorce, 286, 290–293
and family life cycle, 170–171
and fathers, 137, 143, 144
and intellectual growth, 356, 357
and parental separation, 159, 160,
353, 354
and remarriage, 298
and socialization, 357, 358
and working mothers, 128–131, 354
Progesterone and progestin
in birth control pill, 306
in minipill, 307
in morning-after pill, 307
Propinquity as a factor in
communication, 203
Prostaglandins, 341
Protestant. *See also* Religion
-Catholic marriages, 85–87
interdenominational marriages, 86
-Jewish marriages, 85–87
Psychosexual development, 110

Quarreling. *See* Conflict

Race
and education, 127
homogamy of, 83, 84
and marital power in decision
making, 197
Rapport, 205
Read method, 324
Reason in solving conflict, 215, 216
Relatives. *See* In-laws and Kinsfolk
Religion. *See also* Catholic, Jewish,
Protestant
and cohabitation, 38
and premarital sexual
permissiveness, 25
Religious communes, 386
Remarriage
age as factor in, 297
partners, 297
and stepchildren, 298
success and quality of, 297
who marries and when, 296, 297
Reproduction
systems of, 261–263
voluntary control over, 131
Responsibility, readiness for, as a
factor in marital readiness, 66
Retirement
adjustments after, 180–183
health and medical problems after,
181
housing and living conditions after,
182
husband-wife relationships after,
180
and identity, 180
and income, 180
relations with grown children after,
181, 182
sexual adjustments after, 183
Rh factor, 322
Rhythm method, 313–315

Roles. *See* Sex roles
Romanticism, 57–61
description of, 57–59
research on, 60, 61
Romantic love, 57–61
Rooming in, 328
Rural communes, 387, 388

Salpingectomy, 313
Savings, 239
School. *See also* Education
achievement and early marriage, 67,
68, 70
attainment of women versus men,
126–128
dropout and marriage, 67
grades and cohabitation, 38
Security
emotional, need for as motive for
marriage, 6, 7
financial, desire for as motive for
marriage, 8
Self
actualization, 7, 9
concept, of male, 138, 139
concept, and premarital sexual
permissiveness, 26
disclosure in communication, 200,
205
fulfillment, 6
identity, after retirement, 180
identity, in dual-career marriage,
162
Separation
anxiety in children, 353, 354
marital, 360–362
Sex education
and moral behavior, 27
in preventing abortions, 345
Sex and aggression, 27
Sexism, 122
Sex and love, 61–63
Sex ratios
at birth, 100
at conception, 100
of widows to widowers, 183, 184
Sex roles
cognitive development theory of
development of, 103
and cohabitation, 40, 41
concepts of, and compatibility, 90
in dating, 19
and decision-making power, 195,
196
development, theories of, 102
differentiation and discrimination
of, 123
in early marriage, 72
expectations, conformity to, and
marital satisfaction, 172
flexible versus rigid, 8, 10
in the future, 398
of husbands
companionship role, 144
effects on himself, 138
housekeeping roles, 143
and marriage, 139–142
new concepts, 136
parental roles, 143, 144

Sex roles (*continued*)
  traditional, 135
  induction, modification, and
    reversal of, 221
  of low socioeconomic status
    husband, 145–147
  parental identification theory of
    development of, 105, 106
  social learning theory of
    development of, 103–105
  of widows, 186
Sexual adjustments, 267–269
  and cohabitation, 45
  after divorce, 295
  of elderly, 183
Sexual attitudes toward women, 124
Sexual barriers to communication, 204
Sexual behavior, standards, and
    norms in the future, 399, 400.
    See also Premarital sexual
    behavior
Sexual decisions, 25–27
Sexual difficulties. *See also* Sexual
    dysfunction
  because of anxiety, 275
  differences over frequency, 268, 269
Sexual drive
  and birth control pill, 308
  during pregnancy, 322
Sexual dysfunction
  causes of, 274–278
  dyspareunia, 273
  ejaculatory incompetence, 272
  female, general, 222–273
  impotence, 270, 271
  orgasmic dysfunction, female, 273,
    274
  premature ejaculation, 270
  vaginismus, 274
Sexual intercourse
  and cohabitation, 41, 42
  frequency of, 268, 269
  frequency of, and fertility, 332
  functions of, 259, 260
  in group marriage, 383
  motives for, 10, 11
  during pregnancy, 322
Sexual organs, 261–264
Sexual response
  and anxiety, 275
  and emotional feelings, 260
  four stages of, 262, 264
  male-female differences in, 264–267
  patterns of, 264–267
  physical manifestations of, 264, 265
  and time factors, 267–269
Sexual revolution, 15, 21, 23
Sexual satisfaction
  through dating, 19
  and marital happiness, 260
Sexual stimulation, 27, 261–267
"Show," 326
Single persons
  and adoption, 434
  as parents, 361
  stigma against, 65
Sister-in-law, 246
Smoking and pregnancy, 319

Social class. *See* Socioeconomic class
Socialization
  through dating, 19
  family's role in relation to children,
    357
Social life
  adjustments to, early in marriage,
    176
  experience, and marital readiness,
    56, 57
Social pressure to marry, 11, 65
Socioeconomic class
  and cohabitation, 38
  homogamy of, 82
Sororities and fraternities, 19
Sperm count, and infertility, 332
Spermicide, 309, 310
Stability. *See* Marriage stability
Status
  through dating, 19
  marriage as desire to gain, 65
Stepchildren, 298
Stepparents, 298
Stepsiblings, 298
Sterility, 331
Sterilization
  salpingectomy, 313
  vasectomy, 311
Succorance, 80
Suction curetage, 341
Suicide, among elderly, 181
Sweden, 47
Swinging
  become involved in, 377, 378
  characteristics of participants in, 378
  dropouts from, and reasons for,
    378, 379
  effects on marriage, 378
  incidence of, 377

Testosterone, 101, 102
Theories of child rearing. *See* Child
    rearing philosophies
Time
  of acquaintance before engagement,
    marriage, 55, 56
  as a factor in sexual response, 267,
    268
  scheduling in dual-career marriage,
    162
  for sexual adjustment, 267
Toxemia, 321
Trial marriage, 43, 374
Trust, 63, 377
Tubal ligation, 313
Tubal pregnancy, 322

Understanding in parent-couple
    relationships, 250
Unisex (androgynous), 114, 123
Unmarried pregnancy
  rates, 337
  reasons for, 337, 338
  tragic results of, 338
Unwed mothers
  help for, 338
  tragedy of, 338
Urban communes, 389, 390

Urbanization, influence on dating, 15
Utilitarian marriage, 8
Utopian communes, 386

Vacuum aspiration, 341
Vaginismus, 274
Values
  and cohabitation, 38
  compatibility of, 89
  in making sexual decisions, 23, 25
  and premarital sexual behavior, 25
  in use of money, 227
Vasectomy, 311. *See also* Sterilization
Venereal disease, 311, 318
Violence
  and coercion in decision making,
    198
  family, 222–225
  physical, and verbal aggression,
    214–216
Voluntary childlessness
  arguments for, 390–392
  decision concerning, 392
  motives for parenthood, 349
  who decides, 392

Widows and widowers, 183–187
  adjustments of widowers, 186, 187
  ages, 183
  bereavement of, 184
  problems of widows, 185
  relationships with friends and
    family, 185
  role changes of, 186
  socioeconomic status differences in
    adjustment, 185, 186
  widowed mother, 361
Wife
  decision-making powers of, 194–200
  in dual-career marriage, 152
Wife working
  and absence from children, 159
  and age of children, 159, 160
  effects on children, 158–160, 353–
    355
  reaction of mothers, 159
Withdrawal (coitus interruptus), 315
Women's movement
  and chauvinism and sexism, 121
  and child rearing, 129–131
  and female education, 126–128
  and female employment and
    income, 124–126
  and female sexuality, 124
  history of, 119–121
  and housework, 128
  influence on dating, 16
  and legal equality for women, 122
  and marriage contracts, 369
  and reproduction, 131, 132
  and sex differentiation and
    discrimination, 123
Work, vocational aspirations, and
    marital readiness, 67. *See also*
    Employment

X-rays, and birth defects, 319